PENSIONS: LAW, POLICY AND PRACTICE

State pensions are the largest item in the UK social security budget, costing £93.8 billion in 2017/18. In 2018, 45.6 million people were members of UK occupational pension schemes (out of a total population of 66.4 million) and the total amount saved into workplace schemes was £90.4 billion. A consequence of the pensions sector's large size has been that pensions law and social security law have become increasingly specialised areas of practice. Yet despite the social and economic importance of pensions and the fascinating issues that they generate, pensions law and policy have not been the subject of sustained academic attention. This book starts to fill this gap by initiating a dialogue between practitioners and scholars working in this area.

Pensions

Law, Policy and Practice

Edited by
Sinéad Agnew
Paul S Davies
and
Charles Mitchell

•HART•
OXFORD • LONDON • NEW YORK • NEW DELHI • SYDNEY

HART PUBLISHING

Bloomsbury Publishing Plc

Kemp House, Chawley Park, Cumnor Hill, Oxford, OX2 9PH, UK

1385 Broadway, New York, NY 10018, USA

First published in Great Britain 2020

A catalogue record for this book is available from the British Library.

Library of Congress Cataloging-in-Publication data

Names: W.G. Hart Workshop (2019 : University College, London) | Agnew, Sinéad, editor. | Davies, Paul S. (Law teacher), editor. | Mitchell, Charles (Charles Christopher James), editor.

Title: Pensions : law, policy and practice / edited by Sinéad Agnew, Paul S Davies and Charles Mitchell.

Description: Oxford ; New York : Hart, 2020. | "The essays in this book were originally presented at the WG Hart Legal Workshop 2019, held at UCL on 20 and 21 June 2019"—ECIP acknowledgements. | Includes bibliographical references and index.

Identifiers: LCCN 2020011772 (print) | LCCN 2020011773 (ebook) | ISBN 9781509922703 (hardcover) | ISBN 9781509922710 (Epub)

Subjects: LCSH: Pensions—Law and legislation—Great Britain—Congresses.

Classification: LCC KD3249.A2 . W4 2020 (print) | LCC KD3249.A2 (ebook) | DDC 344.4101/252—dc23

LC record available at https://lccn.loc.gov/2020011772

LC ebook record available at https://lccn.loc.gov/2020011773

ISBN: HB: 978-1-50992-270-3
ePDF: 978-1-50992-272-7
ePub: 978-1-50992-271-0

Typeset by Compuscript Ltd, Shannon

Preface

GREAT WEALTH IS held and managed by the trustees of occupational pension schemes on behalf of the members to whom distributions are made in due course as a form of deferred remuneration for their work. In 2018, about 45.6 million people were members of occupational pension schemes in the UK, out of a total population of about 66.4 million (Office for National Statistics, *Occupational Pension Schemes Survey, UK: 2018*). The annual total amount saved by eligible savers into workplace schemes in 2018 was £90.4 billion (Department for Work & Pensions, *Workplace Pension Participation and Savings Trends of Eligible Employees Official Statistics: 2008 to 2018*). Meanwhile, state pensions are the largest item in the UK social security budget, costing some £93.8 billion in 2017/18 (Office for Budget Responsibility, Economic and Fiscal Outlook (Cm 9572, 2018), Table 4.23).

The social, economic and political significance of the law affecting the management and administration of occupational and state pension schemes law is therefore very large, and the development of this area of law is relevant to every citizen. One consequence of the pensions sector's size has been that pensions law and social security law have become increasingly specialised areas of legal practice. At the same time, the rules in both areas have become increasingly complex and technical, and possibly as a result of this, there are very few non-specialist legal academics who pay them any attention, and few scholars who have made them their particular field of study. This book of essays was conceived with the purpose of reversing these trends, and, in this spirit, we have chosen to define 'pensions' broadly, taking this to include both occupational pension schemes and state pension schemes, in the UK and elsewhere; we have also welcomed contributions from a diverse group of legal practitioners, legal scholars and academics from other disciplines, who have addressed themselves to a wide range of issues concerned with pensions law, policy and practice.

The scene is set in the opening chapter by Sinéad Agnew, entitled 'Trusts as Pension Pots: A Legal-Historical Perspective, c 1800–1925'. She draws on doctrinal and historical sources to give an account of how the trust became the legal mechanism of choice for holding and administering occupational pension schemes in the early twentieth century. The discussion then shifts to the challenges currently facing those who wish to establish occupational pension schemes. Sandeep Maudgil and Hans Van Meerten, in 'UK Collective DC: Is it "Dutch-style" CDC?', consider the topical issue of collective money purchase schemes, which may soon become permissible in the UK. They reflect on the Dutch experience of collective defined contribution schemes, compare the schemes that are available in the Netherlands with the UK proposals, and discuss what lessons may be drawn for the development of CDC in this jurisdiction. In 'The Employer Covenant: Status in Law and Operation in Practice', Paul Brice then analyses the legal status of the employer covenant and evaluates its impact on the funding and governance of defined benefit schemes in practice. He argues that it is likely that it will remain a central element of defined benefit scheme funding in the future.

To create occupational pension schemes, extensive documentation is typically required, and questions can then arise as to what these mean and whether their meaning accurately captures what the parties intended. In 'Interpretation of Pension Trusts: Applying the General Rules?', David Pollard analyses the recent decision of the Supreme Court in *Barnardo's v Buckinghamshire* [2019] ICR 495 and asks what principles underpin the interpretation of pension scheme documents. He argues that particular principles have been developed in the pension context, such that less weight is given to 'background factors' than one would expect to find when comparable questions arise in the world of commercial contracting. Paul Davies then considers the role of rectification in 'Rectification and Pensions'. Given the increasing complexity of many pension schemes it is unsurprising that mistakes are sometimes made, and this is reflected in the growing number of claims for rectification. Davies argues that where a document fails to record the parties' actual intentions, rectification should, in principle, be available, subject to any defences and the discretion of the court to grant rectification on terms.

The following chapters concern the relationships between the parties to occupational pension schemes and the agents to whom they typically delegate some of their functions; these chapters also look at the control of discretionary power-holders in schemes and the influences which bear on their decision-making. In 'The Pension Fund as a "Virtual" Institution', Scott Donald investigates the relations between 'internal' actors within schemes who are charged with a variety of roles and responsibilities, and between such 'internal' actors and 'external' parties to whom tasks are commonly assigned. He also considers the difficulties created for those who seek to use regulation to protect members' interests by the complex character of this web of relationships. In 'Legal Consequences of the Flawed Exercise of Scheme Powers', Jessica Hudson and Charles Mitchell identify the scheme powers which are typically invested in trustees and employers, the rules which govern their exercise of these powers, and the consequences of non-compliance with these rules. They argue that these have often been misunderstood because insufficient attention has been paid to differences between the substantive content of various rules and differences between the effects which non-compliance with the rules can have on the exercise of various powers.

In 'Expertise in Pension Trusteeship', Deborah Mabbett discusses the tensions created when the power to take decisions about the running of schemes is vested in a group of trustees some of whom can invoke a representative mandate as their source of authority (employee and employer representatives) and some of whom can invoke professional expertise (independents with a background in investment or actuarial science). This can result in power battles over contentious issues such as investment policy which are intensified when the Pensions Regulator applies pressure for one group's favoured option to be preferred to that of another group. Charles Cameron then offers a view from practice in 'Pension Scheme Decision-Making Influencers', offering a glimpse behind the curtain that is usually drawn over trustee and employer negotiations respecting these and other issues. He explains the thought processes which typically lead trustees to decide what initial negotiating position to take and where they hope they will end up, and he identifies the 'influencers' to whose opinions trustees must pay regard when forming positions that are not only legal but also likely to satisfy stakeholders and regulatory bodies. In 'The Social Role of Occupational Pension Schemes', James Kolaczkowski then approaches similar issues from a very different perspective, observing that pension disputes are typically characterised as having the rights and duties of private actors as their sole concern, explaining the historical reasons for this, and arguing that the narrow focus of this characterisation ignores the social role played by schemes. He argues that this is too important a feature of schemes to be ignored.

This leads us into a debate regarding the extent to which an employer's exercise of powers in the employment contract and the pension scheme trust deed are constrained by the duty of 'mutual trust and confidence' owed under the contract and by the *Imperial* duty of good faith (named after *Imperial Group Pension Trust Ltd v Imperial Tobacco Ltd* [1991] 1 WLR 589). These questions were recently considered by the Court of Appeal in *IBM United Kingdom Holdings Ltd v Dalgleish* [2018] ICR 1681. In 'Public Law Perspectives on the *IBM* Case', Lord Sales cautions against the use of public law ideas in the pensions context, as he believes there are important differences between the *Imperial* duty and the doctrine of legitimate expectation in public law. Alan Bogg and Mark Freedland challenge this stance in 'Pensions Law, *IBM v Dalgleish*, and the Public/Private Divide', and support a doctrine of legitimate expectations in the context of both labour law and pensions law, arguing that the contract of employment is a distinctive type of contract with public law dimensions. Daniel Schaffer in 'The Improper Purpose Rule: An Employer's Tool to Control Pension Trustees in Need of Reappraisal', then analyses the Court of Appeal's decision in *British Airways plc v Airways Pension Scheme Trustee Limited* [2018] Pens LR 19 and criticises the use of the improper purpose rule in the pensions context. He argues that courts should either not intervene on the basis of 'proper purpose' or only do so on much narrower grounds.

A global phenomenon of recent decades has been the effect on both public and private pension schemes of the instability of financial markets, resulting in the capital value of scheme funds decreasing just as their costs have significantly grown with increases in the longevity of members' lives. This has placed huge pressure on scheme managers to increase contributions and reduce benefits in an effort to balance their books, and these measures have created resentment among members who often resort to litigation to challenge such attacks on their rights and/or expectations. Their claims have been grounded on various arguments in different jurisdictions and have resulted in varying degrees of success. In 'Pensions and the Modern Workforce', Alysia Blackham examines different ways of conceiving of old age pensions from a theoretical perspective, and considers how traditional views of this are challenged by the changing nature of work, including factors such as growing job and international mobility, work precarity, women's workforce participation, and demographic ageing. She argues that existing pension systems are not yet able to accommodate the changing nature of work, and she suggests normative criteria for evaluating and developing more appropriate pension systems for the modern workforce.

The financial challenges of supplying satisfactory pensions to retired workers have also led to disputes in the public sphere. In 'The Courts, Non-Discrimination and Systemic Change in UK Public Sector Pension Schemes', Lydia Seymour considers age discrimination in public sector pension schemes in the UK, focusing on the recent litigation brought by groups of judges and firefighters. She considers the policy implications of the Court of Appeal's decision in *Lord Chancellor v McCloud* [2019] ICR 1489, and the extent to which the courts should defer to the government when considering whether welfare policy decisions which result in less favourable treatment for particular groups of workers are justified. In 'Cutting Pension Rights for Public Workers in the United States: Don't Look to the Courts for Help', Ronald Rosenberg then examines the mostly unsuccessful efforts which have been made to challenge the alterations made in recent years to pensions schemes established by state governments in the US for the benefit of their employees – teachers, police officers, firefighters and other local government workers. He describes the different arguments which workers have made, explains the bases on which these have been rejected, and concludes that if workers are to get anywhere they will have to pursue their grievances in the political rather than the legal sphere.

Finally, two chapters consider the roles played by pension entitlements in other contexts – family proceedings and social care. In 'Till Pensions Do Us Part: The Pension Advisory Group and the Search for Consensus on Divorce', Hilary Woodward and Rhys Taylor, both of whom were involved in the creation and execution of the Pensions Advisory Group project, explain how the project evolved and offer insights into some of the themes which emerged from the Group's work, such as the characterisation and valuation of pensions on divorce and the psychology of pensions in financial remedy proceedings. In '"Pension Freedoms", Social Care and Inheritance', Brian Sloan analyses the implications of 'pension freedoms' for liability to fund social care, a hugely important issue given the increasing numbers of people requiring social care. He concludes that pension freedoms may well complicate care funding assessments and create difficulties in relation to inheritance. For this reason, he emphasises the need to take proper advice so that the interaction between a person's pension arrangements and their social care funding needs can be addressed and any unintended consequences that might otherwise ensue can be avoided.

The essays in this book were originally presented at the WG Hart Legal Workshop 2019, held at UCL on 20 and 21 June 2019. We are very grateful for the lively participation and comments of all those who attended the event, and for generous financial support from the University of London Institute of Advanced Legal Studies and from Slaughter and May. We greatly benefited from the enthusiasm and expertise of Daniel Schaffer, Charles Cameron and Sandeep Maudgil from our first conception of the project through to its final completion. We thank Abe Chauhan, Joyman Lee, Helena Ratcliff and Daniel Thorpe for their research assistance. We also thank Sinead Moloney and the team at Hart Publishing for their early support for this volume and their help in bringing it to fruition, and Anne Bevan for her expert copy-editing skills.

Sinéad Agnew,
Paul S Davies and
Charles Mitchell
December 2019

Contents

Contributors

Sinéad Agnew is the Catherine Seville Lecturer in Law and a Fellow of Newnham College at the University of Cambridge.

Alysia Blackham is an Associate Professor in Law and Discovery Early Career Researcher at the University of Melbourne.

Alan Bogg is Professor of Labour Law at the University of Bristol.

Paul Brice is the Head of Pensions Advisory at Grant Thornton UK LLP.

Charles Cameron is the Head of Pensions and Employment Practice at Slaughter and May.

Paul S Davies is Professor of Commercial Law at University College London.

M Scott Donald is Director of the Centre for Law, Markets and Regulation at the University of New South Wales.

Mark Freedland FBA is Emeritus Professor of Employment Law at the University of Oxford and an Emeritus Research Fellow in Law at St John's College, Oxford.

Jessica Hudson is a Senior Lecturer in Law at the University of New South Wales.

James Kolaczkowski is a Lecturer in Law at the University of the West of England.

Deborah Mabbett is Professor of Public Policy in the Department of Politics at Birkbeck, University of London.

Sandeep Maudgil is a partner in the Pensions and Employment department of Slaughter and May.

Charles Mitchell QC (Hon) FBA is a Professor of Law at University College London.

David Pollard is a barrister practising from Wilberforce Chambers, London.

Ronald H Rosenberg is Chancellor Professor of Law at William and Mary Law School.

Philip Sales is a Justice of the United Kingdom Supreme Court.

Daniel Schaffer is a partner in the Pensions and Employment department of Slaughter and May.

Lydia Seymour is a barrister practising from Outer Temple Chambers, London.

Brian Sloan is a Fellow in Law at Robinson College, Cambridge.

Rhys Taylor is a barrister practising from The 36 Group (London) and 30 Park Place (Cardiff).

Hans Van Meerten is Professor of International Pensions Law at Utrecht University.

Hilary Woodward is an Honorary Senior Research Fellow at the Cambridge University Faculty of Law.

Table of Cases

EU and International

United Kingdom and Commonwealth

United States

Table of Legislation

Australia

New Zealand

EU and International

Netherlands

United Kingdom

United States

1

Trusts as Pension Pots: A Legal-Historical Perspective, c 1800–1925

SINÉAD AGNEW*

I. INTRODUCTION

TODAY, OCCUPATIONAL PENSION trusts are ubiquitous: membership of an employer-sponsored scheme, coupled with reliance on the state pension, is the way in which most of us provide for our old age. Yet both occupational pension trusts and the state pension are relatively recent phenomena. Before the late nineteenth century few organised pension schemes existed, and some of those which did – such as the civil service scheme – operated largely on a discretionary, ex gratia basis.[1] Large-scale occupational schemes run by private employers developed slowly in the nineteenth century, and became common only in the early years of the twentieth, while the state pension was not introduced until 1908.[2]

This chapter explores the historical development of the trust as the default legal mechanism for holding and administering pension schemes. It has been suggested that a novel feature of the early-twentieth-century occupational schemes was their 'use of the private trust as a legal vehicle for pensioning', and that '[T]rust law had been developed for quite other purposes but, from being virtually unknown in large pension schemes in the nineteenth century, it became the most favoured vehicle in the twentieth'.[3] Here it is argued that in fact the trust relationship underpinned various methods of pension provision during the nineteenth century. This is unsurprising, given the trust's obvious utility in holding funds and facilitating the provision of concurrent benefits to groups of people. From a legal perspective, therefore, the widespread adoption of the trust in early-twentieth-century pension schemes was neither

* I am grateful to Paul Brice, Professor Charles Mitchell, David Pollard QC and Kathryn Purkis for their comments on this chapter.

[1] See M Raphael, *Pensions and Public Servants, A Study of the Origins of the British System* (Paris, Mouton & Co, 1964) 135, 148.

[2] L Hannah, *Inventing Retirement: The Development of Occupational Pensions in Britain* (Cambridge, Cambridge University Press, 1986) 15–16.

[3] ibid 18–19.

novel nor surprising. Rather, it was an obvious incremental step in pensions law and practice.

The chapter also discusses how the courts conceptualised pensions during the nineteenth century. Ultimately, this seems to have been an exercise in interpretation, which depended on the terms of the instrument creating the relevant pension arrangements. If the terms suggested that pension payments were a discretionary matter for the employer, the courts treated them as ex gratia; if the terms gave employees an entitlement to pension payments, the courts would give effect to that entitlement. Thus, the law tracked and accommodated employers' decisions as to whether and how to help their employees in old age.

II. METHODS OF PENSION PROVISION IN THE NINETEENTH CENTURY

Historically, provision for old age was neither as systematic nor as comprehensive as it is now. During the nineteenth century, it was largely regarded as a matter of individual responsibility,[4] and a variety of methods were adopted: some were individual, others were collective, and the type of provision depended on one's class and occupation. Despite the patchwork of different types of assistance and provision, inevitably there were many who could not save for their old age at all, and so there was a close correlation between old age and poverty.[5] The development and proliferation of occupational pension schemes towards the end of the nineteenth century was therefore of profound social significance.

The most obvious methods of individual provision were private savings and investment. These took different forms. An active share market did not develop until the late nineteenth century but in the meantime government bonds were perennially popular as they offered security of capital and interest rates of 4–5 per cent.[6] During the eighteenth century, landowners and middle-class investors had started to engage in the practice of lending against the security of mortgages over land,[7] and commercial life insurance houses had developed in both England and Holland.[8] The Victorian values of self-help and thrift led to a dramatic expansion in the life insurance business during the first half of the nineteenth century.[9] Although the industry was unregulated and unstable for most of the century, it was nevertheless popular. From 1853 income tax relief was available on premiums for life insurance and deferred annuities,[10]

[4] A Russell, *The Growth of Occupational Welfare in Britain* (Aldershot, Avebury, 1991) 24–25.

[5] R Blackburn, *Banking on Death Or, Investing in Life: The History and Future of Pensions* (London, Verso, 2002) 47.

[6] E Hutson, 'The Early Managed Fund Industry: Investment Trusts in 19th Century Britain' (2005) 14 *International Review of Financial Analysis* 439, 441–42; W Cornish et al, *Law and Society in England, 1750–1950*, 2nd edn (Oxford, Hart Publishing, 2019) 251.

[7] Cornish et al (n 6) 130.

[8] Blackburn (n 5) 39. See also Russell (n 4) 24–25.

[9] Hannah, *Inventing Retirement* (n 2) 5; M Zimmeck, 'Gladstone Holds His Own: The origins of Income Tax Relief for Life Insurance Policies' (1985) 58 *Bulletin of the Institute of Historical Research* 167, 176.

[10] Income Tax Act 1853, s 54; Zimmeck (n 9).

which made them an attractive form of saving for old age, and after legislative reform in 1870 the market became safer for investors.[11]

As far as collective provision was concerned, the livery companies had a strong philanthropic tradition, which sometimes involved the payment of pensions. By 1880 approximately one-third of their extensive income came from gifts and wills constituting trusts for benevolent or charitable purposes.[12] It seems likely that by 1884, the companies had approximately 10,000 members. Membership entitled an individual to be received into the company's almshouses, to pensions and relief out of the trust funds which had been left to the company for that purpose, and to apply for general relief out of the company's corporate income.[13] Workers also tended to contribute to friendly societies and, later, trade unions.[14] By the end of the nineteenth century approximately 50 per cent of adult males in the UK were members of friendly societies,[15] but the contribution rates were higher than many unskilled workers could afford, and so – much like livery companies – the societies tended to operate for 'an artisanal elite'.[16] Some societies operated superannuation schemes towards the end of the century but there was a low take-up among members, perhaps because there were more immediate demands on working-class saving, such as food, education and shelter, and because friendly societies supported their older members through the provision of sickness benefit anyway.[17] Widows' and orphans' funds, which effectively facilitated the private provision of widows' pensions, were also popular during this period.

Before the 1680s, it had been conventional for officers in the civil service, the armed forces[18] and the professions who wished to retire to sell their office to their successors for a lump sum or an annuity.[19] In the late seventeenth century, pension schemes were put in place for former members of the armed forces and private entities whose fortunes were closely associated with those of the British state, such as the Bank of England and the East India Company.[20] In the early eighteenth century, customs and excise officers benefited from the first civil service superannuation

[11] T Alborn, *Regulated Lives: Life Assurance and British Society, 1800–1914* (Toronto, University of Toronto Press, 2009) 53–75; L Hannah, 'Why Employer-based Pension Plans? The Case of Britain' (1985) 45 *Journal of Economic History* 347, 349.

[12] *City of London Livery Companies Commission Report* (C (2nd series) 4073, 1884) 13, 26–28.

[13] ibid 22–24.

[14] Hannah, *Inventing Retirement* (n 2) 6.

[15] J Macnicol, *The Politics of Retirement in Britain, 1878–1948* (Cambridge, Cambridge University Press, 1998) 115.

[16] P Johnson, *Saving and Spending, The Working-Class Economy in Britain 1870–1939* (Oxford, Clarendon Press, 1985) 57–58; Macnicol (n 15) 115.

[17] Macnicol (n 15) 117, 118; Johnson (n 16) 49, 83; D Weinbren, 'The Good Samaritan, Friendly Societies and the Gift Economy' (2006) 31 *Social History* 319, 328.

[18] Anyone who left the armed forces with a disabling injury, as an invalid or having completed an agreed term of service, was entitled to a pension from the Royal Hospital Chelsea in London (established in 1678) or the Royal Hospital Kilmainham in Dublin (established in 1681). Officers could provide for their retirement by selling their commission, a practice which was eventually abolished by the Cardwell reforms in 1870–71. I am grateful to Charles Mitchell for drawing these examples to my attention.

[19] P Thane, *Old Age in English History: Past Experiences, Present Issues* (Oxford, Oxford University Press, 2000) 237; see also Raphael (n 1) 34–05.

[20] Thane (n 19) 244.

scheme.[21] These early schemes were not always comprehensive,[22] and payments were usually discretionary. In the private sector, paternalistic employers would often look after their ageing employees by giving them easier jobs to do.[23] Sometimes they would make contributions to friendly societies on behalf of workers who were members.[24] Others exercised their discretion to reward long-serving employees with an ex gratia pension.[25]

There was little in the way of formal, organised pension provision in the private sector until much later in the nineteenth century. Utility companies were some of the first private sector employers to instigate formal pension schemes: for example, the Imperial Gas Light and Coke Company paid discretionary pensions during the 1830s[26] and introduced a superannuation scheme for its employees in 1842.[27] By the 1860s many railway companies had also established superannuation schemes.[28] Large-scale manufacturers, such as Colman's, Lever Bros, Cadbury and Rowntree followed suit at the turn of the twentieth century.[29] In 1900 there were approximately one million employees in formally constituted schemes across the public and private sectors, and by 1936 this number had more than doubled.[30]

The impetus for the proliferation of occupational pension schemes appears to have come from employers, particularly large ones.[31] There were at least four reasons for this. The first was rooted in the quest for greater productivity and efficiency. There were hidden costs in *not* providing pensions and keeping on older employees as they became less productive.[32] Employers wished 'to be able without hardship, to get rid of employees when they are past efficiency and vigorous work',[33] and an employer-led pension scheme facilitated this goal. Pension schemes that operated on the basis of deferred remuneration which could be withheld (for example, whereby employers' contributions were not returned to leavers) also helped them to extract loyalty and longevity from younger workers who had specialist skills, or were in positions of financial responsibility, such as clerks in banks and railways.[34]

The second reason was the need for employers to improve industrial relations. The Trade Union Act 1871 relaxed some of the constraints which had hitherto been imposed on trade unions[35] and the union movement grew in size and strength.[36] Some

[21] Raphael (n 1) 34–48.
[22] eg, the first comprehensive civil service scheme was only established a century later: Raphael (n 1) 132.
[23] Macnicol (n 15) 52.
[24] Hannah, *Inventing Retirement* (n 2) 11.
[25] ibid 9.
[26] Thane (n 19) 244.
[27] Hannah, *Inventing Retirement* (n 2) 12. This was extended to manual workers in 1870.
[28] Board of Trade, *Report of the Departmental Committee on Railway Superannuation Funds* (Cd 5349, 1910).
[29] Hannah, *Inventing Retirement* (n 2) 18.
[30] ibid 13; Hannah, 'Why Employer-based Pension Plans?' (n 11) 350; Thane (n 19) 247.
[31] Hannah, 'Why Employer-based Pension Plans?' (n 11) 350–51; Thane (n 19) 244.
[32] A point made by Seebohm Rowntree: Russell (n 4) 28–29.
[33] Document entitled 'Statement of the Points we have Arrived at in Connection with the Proposed Pension Scheme', 6 May 1905, 2, Rowntree & Co Ltd Archive (RCA), R/DH/SR/10.
[34] Hannah, *Inventing Retirement* (n 2) 24–25; Hannah, 'Why Employer-based Pension Plans? (n 11) 351–52.
[35] Cornish et al (n 6) 306; J Armour, 'Companies and Other Associations' in A Burrows (ed), *English Private Law* (Oxford, Oxford University Press, 2013) [3.99].
[36] Cornish et al (n 6) 309–10.

trade unions provided superannuation and other benefits to their members, albeit on a small scale and at a reasonably high cost.[37] Preventing the growth of trade unionism and encouraging employees to identify with corporate goals appears to have been a major factor in the development of some railway superannuation schemes in the 1890s.[38] Third, a new commitment to 'fair dealing in employment contracts' was apparent in the conduct of some of the large manufacturers,[39] such as Rowntree and Cadbury which were run by socially minded Quaker families. Finally, in 1921 the government extended income tax relief to employer contributions to pension funds and pension fund investment income for pension schemes established on irrevocable trusts,[40] which made occupational schemes much cheaper to run.

It is true to say that the idea of a 'pension trust' as we know it – in the form of an occupational pension scheme sponsored by the employer, embedded in the employment contract, governed by an express private trust instrument and rules, and overlaid by statutory regulation – only became common in the twentieth century. However, as the next section demonstrates, the trust relationship was far from absent in the pensions landscape before then.

III. THE TRUST AND PENSION PROVISION IN THE NINETEENTH CENTURY

A. Collective Provision by or on Behalf of Workers

i. Livery Companies: Charitable Trusts

During the eighteenth and nineteenth centuries, the livery companies offered financial support in old age to their members and the poor more generally. They did this either by acting as trustees of assets settled on them by donors for philanthropic purposes or by establishing pension trusts for their poorer members. In this way, their practices reflected those of their predecessors, the early modern craft guilds and differed from those of friendly societies, which operated a system of mutual insurance.[41]

In some cases, livery companies acted as trustees of assets settled on them by donors for the benefit of their older members who had fallen on hard times. For example, in 1794 Samuel Whitbread (the brewer) gave to the Brewers Company land in Bedfordshire on trust 'as a perpetual Charitable provision for or towards the support and relief of decayed Master Brewers and their Widows',[42] who were aged 50 and above and who as a result of losses in the brewing trade had 'come to decay or been reduced in circumstances' so as to require relief.[43] By a second indenture of

[37] Macnicol (n 15) 117.

[38] J Melling, 'Welfare Capitalism and the Origins of Welfare States: British Industry, Workplace Welfare and Social Reform, c 1870–1914' (1992) 17 *Social History* 453, 462–64.

[39] Hannah, *Inventing Retirement* (n 2) 22.

[40] Finance Act 1921, s 32(1).

[41] P Wallis, 'Guilds and Mutual Protection in England' (2018) LSE Economic History Working Papers no 287.

[42] Indenture of trust dated 26 March 1794, Samuel Whitbread's Charity Trust Deed and Minute Book (Whitbread Indenture), City of London Livery Company Archives (CLLCA), LCL/L/BF/G/129/MS05488, 1.

[43] ibid 7.

the same date, he gave three houses in Whitecross Street to the Company upon trust to invest the rents after his death and apply them to make payments in support of poor freemen and their widows, 'particularly preferring such objects as shall be blind, lame, or afflicted with palsy, or very aged'.[44] The trustees had the power to collect the rents and profits from the land and houses, and after payment of tax and charges and payments to the livery company and its clerk, to invest the residue in public funds or government securities. The Fund was to accumulate during Mr Whitbread's life but after his death the trustees held the residue for the purpose of making two half-yearly payments to one or two members of the class of objects, who were of good character and whom the Master and Court of Assistants (the Company's governing body) thought to be fit objects of support.

In other cases, livery companies would act as trustees of assets settled on them by donors for the benefit of poor and elderly members of the public. In 1813 John Baker transferred a number of annuities and government bonds to the Master and Wardens of the Company of Brewers upon trust to sell a sufficient part of them to purchase or build six cottages 'as an asylum for the dwelling and support of six poor widows or unmarried women of the age of fifty years or upwards' in Spitalfields.[45] The investment powers were similar: the trustees were to sell the stock and purchase the cottages or the land on which they were to be built, and to hold any surplus as an accumulating fund for the further support of the women. As trustee, the Company had a wide discretion as to who would benefit: to qualify, the women needed to have resided in the parish for five years, and be 'of good life and conversation', and they were to be 'chosen elected and continued by and at the sole discretion of' the Master, Wardens and Court of Assistants.

Occasionally, livery companies established their own trusts for the explicit purpose of providing pension benefits for their members: the trust established by the Master and Wardens of the Merchant Tailors Company on 6 July 1830 is an example.[46] The indenture of trust records the resolution of the Master and Wardens to create a pension fund for 'the benefit of such poor persons who are Members of the said Company or related to the Members thereof as the Court of Assistants of the said Company for the time being shall from time to time think proper to select'. To this end it paid £100 to four members of the Court of Assistants, who were to act as trustees. As in the case of the Whitbread and Baker trusts, the trustees were empowered to invest the Fund in public stocks or at interest on government securities. The indenture records the expectation that some members of the Company and others who were 'willing to repose perfect confidence in the discretion of' the Court of Assistants with respect to the disposition of the Fund and its income and profits would contribute to the Fund by way of donations and bequests. The Fund was to be 'under the absolute control' of the Court of Assistants and the payment of pensions was entirely at their discretion.

As the clear primary intention of Messrs Whitbread and Baker appears to have been to relieve poverty, these are likely to have been valid charitable trusts, and they

[44] ibid 16.

[45] Indenture of trust dated 18 December 1813, John Baker's Charity, CLLCA, LCL/L/BF/G/018/MS18362.

[46] Deed of the Pension Fund of the Merchant Tailors Company, 6 July 1830, CLLCA, LCL/L/MD/G/043/MS34165.

appear to have been treated as such.[47] And although not explicitly described as pension trusts, they are clearly directed at providing financial support to the aged poor. The way in which the Merchant Tailors indenture was drafted – with its emphasis on poor employees and their relations, and the inclusion of a 21-year limit on accumulations[48] – suggests that it was also intended to be a valid charitable purpose trust. There was, and is, no difficulty with the charitable status of employee poverty trusts per se.[49] However, exceptionally wide powers were reserved to the Company, as settlor, to direct how the trustees were to administer the Fund, and to apply the Fund for any other purposes they thought fit, other than expenditure on its own property, expenses or entertainment. Therefore, it is doubtful whether – by today's standards, at least – its purposes could be said to have been exclusively charitable; if not, it would be void as a non-charitable purpose trust.[50]

None of the three trusts required contributions from the objects in exchange for the provision of benefits, and there was no sense in which the objects had any right to support: in all three cases the trustees had a broad discretion as to who would benefit, when and how. It is also notable that the investment powers of the trustees in all three trusts were narrowly drawn and extended only to investment in public funds or securities. This is consistent with the fact that at the beginning of the nineteenth century the investment powers of private trustees were tightly circumscribed by the Court of Chancery. The rule of thumb was not to put the trust property in jeopardy. For this reason, unless the trust instrument contained a clause expressly providing for wider investment powers, the only unequivocally accepted trust investments were government securities.[51] It is unsurprising that self-styled charitable trustees adopted a similarly conservative investment policy.

ii. Unincorporated Associations and Friendly Societies: Mutual Insurance and Private Trusts

An additional method by which workers could provide collectively for a pension for themselves and, in case of their death, their dependants, was to establish funds through the legal mechanisms of unincorporated associations and friendly societies. These funds effectively operated as mutual insurance systems: in exchange for contributions members would receive sickness and funeral benefits and, occasionally, pension payments.

Originally, workers' funds were administered through unincorporated associations, which were managed by a committee of members, and whose assets were held by trustees. Subsequently, they were permitted to register themselves as friendly societies under a series of nineteenth-century statutes, culminating in the Friendly Societies Act 1896. This made it a legal requirement that the assets be vested in

47 See *City of London Livery Companies Commission Report* (n 12) Vol V, 54, 55.

48 Presumably in an effort to comply with the Accumulations Act 1800.

49 *Dingle v Turner* [1972] AC 601 (HL); *cf AG v Charity Commission* [2012] WTLR 977 [57]–[59].

50 *Chichester Diocesan Fund v Simpson* [1944] AC 341 (HL).

51 C Stebbings, *The Private Trustee in Victorian England* (Cambridge, Cambridge University Press, 2001) 129–33.

trustees, in whose name any proceedings relating to those assets had to be brought. However, the Act also permitted them to sue and be sued in their own names, and at the turn of the twentieth century the courts appear to have treated friendly societies as having quasi-corporate status.[52] Friendly societies enjoyed state support in the form of tax exemptions,[53] and their membership was significantly larger than that of livery companies.

Although friendly societies mainly assisted their infirm elderly members through the provision of sickness benefit,[54] some also ran widows' and orphans' funds.[55] Members would contribute on the basis that after their death, the fund would pay out a lump sum and/or an annuity (effectively a widow's pension) to their wife and children. The extent to which employers were involved in these schemes varied: some had nothing to do with the scheme,[56] others made an initial capital contribution,[57] and some made regular contributions and were involved on an ongoing basis in matters to do with the fund.[58] Few friendly societies ran separate superannuation schemes,[59] but some better paid workers, such as railway employees, established friendly societies that did so.[60] For example, the Great Western Railway Enginemen and Firemen's Mutual Assurance, Sick, and Superannuation Society was established in 1901[61] to provide, inter alia, the payment of sick benefit to members, the payment of superannuation allowances to retired members, and the payment of allowances to widows and orphans of deceased members.[62] The objects were to be funded by members' contributions and donations, including contributions from the employer.[63]

For present purposes, the important point is that the business of an unincorporated association or friendly society was carried out by a committee of its members, while its assets vested in trustees nominated under the institution's constitution to be held on behalf of the society and its members.[64] As a matter of law, the rights of the members, inter se, were governed by the constitution and the express or implied

[52] Armour (n 35) [3.105].

[53] Johnson (n 16) 49.

[54] Macnicol (n 15) 116–19.

[55] eg, The Trinity House Widows' and Orphans' Fund (established 1843), the rules of which appear at London Metropolitan Archive (LMA) CLC/526/MS30234 and MS30235; the Railway Unity Benevolent Fund for Widows and Orphans, the rules of which may be found at Public Records Office (PRO) RAIL 1166/87; the Coal Meters' Benefit Society and Widows Aid Fund (established 1863), the rules of which are at LMA CLC/B/052/MS10176; and the London Fire Brigade Widows' And Orphans' Friendly Society, the rules of which appear at LMA ACC/1730-1.

[56] eg, the London Fire Brigade Fund (n 55).

[57] eg, the Trinity House Fund (n 55).

[58] eg, the Coal Meters' Benefit Society (n 55).

[59] Two notable exceptions were the Manchester Unity and the Ancient Order of Foresters, but the uptake by members in each case was under 1 per cent: J Treble, 'The Attitudes of Friendly Societies Towards the Movement in Great Britain for State Pensions, 1878–1908' (1970) 15 *International Review of Social History* 266, 278–79.

[60] Hannah, *Inventing Retirement* (n 2) 14.

[61] Rules of the Great Western Railway Enginemen and Firemen's Mutual Assurance Sick & Superannuation Society (1901) clause i, PRO RAIL 1174/7.

[62] ibid clause ii. The detailed provisions relating to the different benefits are set out in clauses ix–xiii.

[63] ibid clause ii. There was also a separate superannuation fund for non-salaried servants of the company.

[64] See, eg, clauses 17–18 of the Rules of the Trinity House Fund (n 55); clauses viii, ix and xiii of the rules of the Coal Meters' Fund (n 55); clauses 5 and 19 of the London Fire Brigade Fund (n 55); and clauses xiv, xv and xxv of the Rules of the Great Western Railway Enginemen and Firemen's Society (n 61).

contractual arrangements between them.[65] Thus, the private trust facilitated the creation of a fund into which members' contributions were paid, and from which sickness and funeral benefit, widows' pensions and, occasionally, superannuation allowances could be paid.

B. Collective Provision Involving Employers

i. British Public Sector Schemes

The civil service superannuation scheme was one of the earliest and biggest employer-sponsored pension schemes in Britain: for most of its life, the scheme was non-contributory, and trusts law did not feature in its operation. In 1810 an Act conferred a power on the Treasury to pay superannuation allowances to civil servants generally.[66] To reduce public expenditure,[67] deductions were made from civil servants' salaries during a brief period between 1822[68] and 1824.[69] Thereafter, the scheme was non-contributory and funded entirely by the Treasury.

To make cost savings, the Superannuation Act 1834[70] reduced the scales of superannuation allowances.[71] It also reintroduced contributions by providing that the salaries of new officers entering the civil service after 1829 would be subject to an 'abatement' in respect of superannuations, the amount to be decided by the Treasury.[72] However, it made no provision for the establishment of a superannuation fund into which deductions from salaries were to be paid. Thus, the system implied that a percentage of civil servants' salaries was being held back by the government and paid into a separate superannuation fund, when this was not the case.

In 1857 a Royal Commission reported on the operation of the system established by the 1834 Act.[73] The Commissioners rejected the suggestion that a superannuation fund should be established to which civil servants would have to contribute and for the administration of which the Treasury would have been directly responsible. Its reasons for this view included, inter alia, the fact that were the fund to run a surplus, difficult questions would arise as to 'the equitable appropriation of that surplus'.[74] The Commissioners recommended that the system of abatement be abolished, as it gave the misleading impression that a fund existed 'to which each Civil Servant has contributed, and in which he, therefore, may be supposed to possess a certain right of property'.[75] This was thought likely to produce a sense of hardship, and it also raised

[65] *Re Bucks Constabulary Widows and Orphans Fund Friendly Society (No 2)* [1979] 1 WLR 936 (Ch).
[66] 50 Geo 3 c 117, 21 June 1810; Thane (n 19) 239; Raphael (n 1) 132–35.
[67] Treasury Minute, dated 10 August 1821, Royal Mail Archive (RMA) Post 66/2.
[68] Contributions were introduced by 3 Geo 4 c 113, 5 August 1822; Raphael (n 1) 139.
[69] Contributions were abolished by 5 Geo 4 c 104, 24 June 1824; Raphael (n 1) 141–42.
[70] 4 & 5 W 4 c 4, 24, 25 July 1834.
[71] ibid s 9.
[72] ibid s 27.
[73] Board of Trade, *Report of Commissioners Appointed to Inquire into the Operation of the Superannuation Act* (1857) (*Report into the Superannuation Act*) RMA, Post 66/12.
[74] ibid xii.
[75] ibid xiv.

questions as to the sufficiency of the superannuation allowances paid by the Treasury as an equivalent for the deductions paid. The Commissioners' comments implicitly suggest that in their view a true contributory scheme would require the payment of employees' contributions into a separate fund, in which the employees would have some sort of property right, and which presumably would be held by the Treasury as trustee. However, following the Commissioners' recommendation that *no* such fund be established, the abatement system was abolished in 1857.[76]

Two years later the Superannuation Act 1859 introduced a revamped non-contributory scheme and repealed some (but not all)[77] of the 1834 Act. For the rest of the nineteenth century, the civil service scheme provided pensions to civil servants (but not their dependants) on a non-contributory and wholly discretionary basis. Under the 1859 Act it was unlawful for the Treasury to grant a superannuation allowance unless satisfied that the individual civil servant had served with diligence and fidelity.[78] Section 30 of the 1834 Act survived and expressly stipulated that nothing in the Act 'shall extend or be construed to extend to give any Person an absolute Right to Compensation for past Services, or to any Superannuation or Retiring Allowance'. The courts held that although civil servants could rely on the expectation of an allowance with reasonable certainty, they did not have any contractual *right* to a pension: allowances under the scheme were discretionary gratuities, paid out of the bounty of the Crown.[79] They interpreted section 30 of the 1834 Act very strictly and refused to correct mistakes made by the Treasury in calculating superannuation allowances.[80] As civil service pensions were discretionary and, if granted, wholly funded by the Treasury out of its own coffers, the scheme could function effectively without recourse to the legal mechanism of the trust.

When superannuation was extended to other public sector employees towards the end of the nineteenth century, some of the schemes were contributory, involved the establishment of a fund, and implicitly recognised the trust as the legal mechanism which underpinned the administration of that fund. Moreover, the state (as employer) and the courts were prepared to treat these schemes as generating pension entitlements for employees rather than operating on an ex gratia basis. For example, as part of the professionalisation and centralisation of the county police forces, the Police Act 1890 introduced a nationwide contributory superannuation scheme for police officers.[81] For the first time,[82] every police constable had a right to a pension (a maximum of two-thirds of the weekly wage) on the completion of 25 years' approved service.[83] Provision was also made for their widows and children in case of their death.[84]

[76] Superannuation Act 1857.

[77] Superannuation Act 1859, s 19.

[78] ibid ss 9–10.

[79] *Considine v McInerney* [1916] 2 AC 162 (HL) 170 (Lord Buckmaster), 171 (Lord Loreburn), 174 (Lord Atkinson); *Nixon v Attorney General* [1931] AC 184 (HL).

[80] *Cooper v The Queen* (1880) 14 Ch D 311 (Ch); *Yorke v The King* [1915] 1 KB 852 (KB).

[81] Cornish et al (n 6) 594–95.

[82] *Garbutt v Durham Joint Committee* [1904] 2 KB 514 (CA) 523 (Collins MR).

[83] Police Act 1890, s 1.

[84] ibid s 2.

These generous terms encouraged police officers to remain in service.[85] Contributions were to be deducted from salary and carried to a pension fund,[86] which was to be established by every police force.[87] The Act provided that the pension funds of police forces should be kept separately, and that the treasurer of each force would act as the treasurer of its fund.[88] These funds were guaranteed by the police force, with any deficiencies to be met out of the general police fund.[89] The Act directed that at the end of each financial year the surplus of the annual income of each pension fund should be invested 'in such name as the police authority direct, and in any manner authorised by law for investments by trustees'.[90]

The contributory pension scheme established by the Poor Law Officers' Superannuation Act 1896 did not provide for the establishment of a separate superannuation fund: instead contributions were to be made to and pensions paid from the common fund of the union (out of which salaries were paid).[91] Nevertheless, the courts appeared to take the view that the scheme conferred pension rights on Poor Law officers. In *Guardians of the Poor of Salford Union v Dewhurst*[92] the House of Lords had to consider whether it was possible for the employer to contract out of the Act in respect of certain officers. They concluded that the language of the Act precluded this. Section 2 provided that every officer and servant, on reaching the relevant retirement age or being no longer capable of performing his duties, 'shall be entitled … to receive during life out of the common fund of the union, a superannuation allowance according to the scale laid down in this Act'. Viscount Cave LC interpreted this as a command to the public authority to provide pensions. Section 12 imposed an obligation on employees to contribute to the scheme, while section 10 stated that every superannuation allowance granted under the Act would be 'payable to or in trust for the officer or servant' and would not be assignable or chargeable with his debts or other liabilities. Both Lord Shaw and Lord Parmoor[93] set great store by section 10 as militating against the conclusion that the employer could contract out of the grant of the pension in the first place. Lord Shaw held that the obligation to contribute under section 12 had its 'practical correlative in the ticketing or earmarking of the funds so contributed in the common fund of the guardians', and that section 10 provided a clear declaration that pensions would be paid to or in trust for the officers.[94] This view is consistent with the idea that the earmarked contributions in the common fund were held on trust by the employer to provide pensions to officers.

Subsequently, the House of Lords confirmed that the Poor Law scheme generated an inalienable vested right to a pension.[95] This right was obviously subject to the

[85] H Shpayer-Makov, 'The Making of a Police Labour Force' (1990) 24 *Journal of Social History* 109, 112–13.
[86] Police Act 1890, s 15.
[87] ibid s 16.
[88] ibid s 18(1) and (2).
[89] ibid s 19.
[90] ibid s 18(3).
[91] Poor Law Officers' Superannuation Act 1896, ss 2, 12 and 19.
[92] *Guardians of the Poor of Salford Union v Dewhurst* [1926] AC 619 (HL).
[93] ibid 635–36.
[94] ibid 627–28.
[95] *Gissing v Liverpool Corporation* [1935] Ch 1 (HL) 24 (Lord Hanworth MR).

satisfaction of conditions precedent set by the employment contract and/or the relevant statute or instrument establishing the scheme. Members were entitled to draw down a pension on retirement only if they had completed the requisite number of years of service and contributed as required. Furthermore, both the police and Poor Law pensions could be forfeited in cases of fraud or grave misconduct,[96] and leavers were not automatically entitled to a refund of their own contributions if they left the scheme.[97] Thus, although by the end of the nineteenth century the idea of pension 'rights' was taking hold in relation to contributory schemes in the public sector,[98] such rights were not unqualified, nor were they universal.[99]

ii. The Bengal, Madras and Bombay Annuity Funds

By the late eighteenth century, the East India Company had become a significant land power in India, which exercised civil and military governmental functions in different regions, such as Bengal, Madras and Bombay,[100] and by the early nineteenth century the Company had the power to grant pensions to its civil servants in England,[101] as well as those servants overseas.[102] However, such pensions were discretionary,[103] and the Company's civil servants in India were not, and had not been previously, entitled to any allowances on retirement.[104]

In the early 1800s some enterprising civil servants in Madras and Bombay organised collective benefit schemes for themselves, to which they persuaded the Company to contribute.[105] The Madras Civil Fund was established by deed poll in 1787 to provide subsistence to the widows and children of members who might die 'in circumstances of indigence and distress' and members who had fallen on hard times and were not provided for by the Company.[106] The civil servants contributed to the Fund, and the Company also made an annual donation.[107] By deed poll dated 1 September 1800, the Fund was augmented and its objects enlarged to include the purpose of providing annuities to civil servants who wished to retire. The Company

[96] Police Act 1890, s 8; Poor Law Officers' Superannuation Act 1896, s 7.

[97] See: Police Act 1890, s 20; and Poor Law Officers' Superannuation Act 1896, s 8.

[98] eg, *Watts v Manchester Corporation* [1917] 1 KB 791 (CA) 793 (Lord Cozens-Hardy MR), 797 (AT Lawrence J) (Fire Brigade pension scheme).

[99] Other schemes still stipulated that pensions did not form part of the employment contract and were construed accordingly: eg, *Admiralty Commissioners v SS Amerika* [1917] AC 38 (HL); *Baker v Dalgleish Steam Shipping Co Ltd* [1922] 1 KB 351 (CA).

[100] M Moir, *A General Guide to the India Office Records* (London, The British Library, 1988) 15–18.

[101] 53 Geo 3 c 153, 1813.

[102] *Gibson v East India Co* [1839] 5 Bing (NC) 262, 132 ER 1105 (military pensions).

[103] ibid.

[104] Despatch from the Court of Directors to the Governor of Madras, dated 31 December 1824, p 859, India Office Records (IOR) E/4/930.

[105] Little in the way of fund documentation appears to have survived. What follows is taken largely from the Madras Civil Fund Deeds dated 1 July 1814 and 1 May 1818 and the Rules of the Civil Service Annuity Fund dated 1 May 1825, published 1838 (Madras Civil Fund Deeds) IOR/Tr.31.d, 1838, and the detailed description of the organisation of the Madras and Bengal funds which appears in *East India Co v Robertson* (1859) 12 Moo PC 400, 14 ER 963. The operation of the Bombay scheme is described in *Edwards v Warden* (1876) 1 App Cas 281 (HL).

[106] Preamble to the 1814 Deed, Madras Civil Fund Deeds (n 105) 1.

[107] ibid 2.

also increased its contribution to the Fund.[108] The Bombay Civil Service Fund developed in a similar way. In 1804 some Bombay civil servants set up an association to assist those who had to resign on the ground of ill health or whose dependants might be left unprovided for after their death in service. The committee of managers of the association acted as trustees of the Fund, the Company made donations to it and eventually the original scheme expanded its objects to provide annuities for those who wanted to retire.

Subsequently, the Madras civil servants wished to separate out the charity and annuity branches of the Madras Civil Fund, and to increase the number of annuitants, and this was achieved by two further deed polls in 1814 and 1818.[109] The 1814 deed[110] assigned the joint capital stock of the Fund to trustees, five-eighths of which was to be held on trust for the charitable objects (ie, provision for widows and children, etc) and three-eighths of which was to be held on trust to provide annuities for members. There were to be seven trustees, five of whom were to be elected annually from the body of civil servants, and two were to hold office ex officio. A treasurer was appointed. Consistently with the narrow investment powers of trustees in the early nineteenth century, all monies belonging to the Fund were to be invested in government securities or kept in the public Treasury.[111] It was envisaged that 23 annuities of £400 would be provided each year, and a capital sum was to be raised for this purpose through a combination of the three-eighths of capital from the previous funds, interest and contributions from the members and the Company. Initially, membership of the Fund was not compulsory for civil servants, although it became so in 1823.[112] Those who were dismissed from the Company's service were entitled to a refund of their contributions, but those who voluntarily ceased to subscribe forfeited their subscriptions and all future rights and benefits to which they would otherwise have been entitled.

The early incarnations of the Madras and Bombay Funds look like pension funds run by unincorporated associations of civil servants for themselves, to which the Company donated on a regular basis. The Company was not a party to deeds establishing the Madras Fund, its contributions were gratuitous and it was not represented on the board of trustees,[113] and there is no suggestion in the authorities[114] that it was a party to the Bombay Fund deed either. However, this changed in 1824, when the Company received a request from its civil servants in Bengal to establish an annuity fund for them. The Company acceded to the proposal, and it took the opportunity to standardise the provision of retirement allowances across its civil service in all three regions.

[108] ibid 4.

[109] *East India Co v Robertson* (n 105) 403.

[110] The general provisions of the 1814 Deed are set out in Madras Civil Fund Deeds (n 105) 9–34, and the provisions of the Annuity Branch, 70–85. The 1818 Deed provided for an increase in the number and value of the annuities and the contribution rate.

[111] Paras 56 and 57 of the 1814 and 1818 Deeds, Madras Civil Fund Deeds (n 105).

[112] See para 31 of the 1814 Deed, Madras Civil Fund Deeds (n 105) 21.

[113] *Secretary of State for India v Underwood* (1869–70) LR 4 HL 580 (HL) 584 (Lord Hatherley).

[114] *Boldero v East India Co* (1865) 11 HL Cas (Clark's) 405, 11 ER 1390.

In a Despatch to the Government of India[115] (the Despatch) the Company stated that it had resolved that an annuity fund be formed in Bengal to 'afford a reasonable expectation that at the end of twenty-five years from the date of appointment to the service, a civil servant … would obtain the offer of an annuity'.[116] The Despatch set out the proposed terms of the Bengal scheme. Membership was to be compulsory. The aim was to build up a capital sum which after 25 years would generate an income sufficient to pay up to nine annuities of £1,000 per year to be offered to civil servants on the basis of seniority.

The Fund was to be constituted out of contributions from the civil servants at a rate of 4 per cent on their salaries during their whole period of service, which were to be matched by an annual contribution from the Company. If by the time a subscriber was offered an annuity, his contributions had not amounted to half the capital value of the annuity, he was obliged to pay the difference.[117] The calculations suggested that, together with accumulated interest, the contributions from members and the Company would produce a balance every year beyond what was necessary for securing the annuities. Quinquennial adjustments were to be made to the balance of the Fund, whereby the Company would make good any shortfall and its contributions would be reduced by the value of any surplus. After 25 years a final adjustment was to be made, which would leave the Company contributing only the difference between the sum of the civil servants' contributions and the income of the Fund, on the one hand, and the sum necessary to secure the regular payment of the annuities on the other.[118] In this way, the Company was virtually guaranteeing the number of annuities per year, but its contribution was limited to the accomplishment of that object.[119]

The Fund was to be managed by a committee of nine civil servants, of whom four were ex officio, and a treasurer was to be appointed. The rules stated that 'all money and securities for money, belonging to the fund in India' were to be kept in the public treasury, 'subject to the direction and control of the trustees and managers of the fund'.[120] The direction as to investment in public securities, which had featured in the earlier Madras Fund rules, was absent.

The Company sent the rules of the Bengal scheme to the Madras government[121] and invited the Madras civil servants to change the rules of their funds to bring them into line with the Bengal scheme, so that they could benefit from the more generous terms that the Bengal scheme offered. The Madras civil servants agreed and the Madras Civil Service Annuity Fund was established on 1 May 1825. The rules were derived from the Bengal scheme, modified only to the extent necessary to deal with the existence of the earlier Madras funds and any extant obligations.[122] In the same

[115] The terms of the Despatch dated 8 December 1824 and the Bengal scheme rules attached to it are discussed in detail in *East India Co v Robertson* (n 105) 408 et seq, and discussed in *Boldero v East India Co* (n 114).

[116] *East India Co v Robertson* (n 105) 410.

[117] *Boldero v East India Co* (n 114) 410 (Lord Westbury LC).

[118] ibid 421 (Lord Westbury LC).

[119] *East India Co v Robertson* (n 105) 415 (Turner LJ).

[120] ibid 419 (Turner LJ), quoting rule 21 of the Bengal Fund.

[121] Despatch dated 31 December 1824 to the Governor of Madras (n 104) p 859.

[122] *East India Co v Robertson* (n 105) 452–53 (Turner LJ). The Rules of the 1825 Madras Fund appear at Madras Civil Fund Deeds (n 105) 95–103.

year the Bombay Fund was also remodelled along similar lines. The provision for widows and children was to be given only to those who were not adequately provided for: every widow was to be entitled to a pension of £300 per year, but if she had other property her pension was to be reduced proportionately so that the income should not exceed £500 per year.

A series of mid-nineteenth century cases gives some insight into the courts' interpretation of the three Funds after 1825. First, they regarded them as creating trusts for persons, of which both the members of the scheme and anyone else intended to benefit were *cestuis que trustent*. In *Edwards v Warden*[123] the daughter of a Bombay civil servant sought an order for an account on the basis that she and her late mother had been entitled to annuities from the date of her late father's death. The managers of the Fund argued, inter alia, that they were not trustees for the widow and daughter but only for the association of civil servants which had been established when the Fund was created. On this basis, they alleged that the daughter's claim was time-barred. The Court of Appeal accepted this argument. James LJ held that the case was indistinguishable from that of a mutual assurance society, and that there was no fiduciary relationship between such a body or its trustees and the grantee of an annuity.[124] Instead, under the contract among the members of the Fund, provision could be made for widows and children, but they were not themselves *cestuis que trustent*.[125] The House of Lords reversed the Court of Appeal's decision on this point. In reaching this conclusion, they referred to the regulations of the Fund, which provided that the Fund 'shall be applicable to the payment of all demands arising from' the first objects of the institution, which included provision for widows and children, and that every widow 'shall be entitled' to receive a pension not exceeding £300. The Court was satisfied that the whole property of the Fund was vested in the committee of managers as trustees, not just for the association, but for widows and daughters as objects of the Fund.[126] As the relevant limitation period did not apply to a claim by a beneficiary against a trustee, the daughter's claim was not time-barred, although her late mother's delay in applying for an annuity counted against her, and the daughter's entitlement was reduced accordingly.

Second, the Company was also regarded as a beneficiary of the trusts on which the Funds were held. In *East India Co v Robertson*[127] Mr Robertson, a subscriber to the 1825 Madras Fund, claimed a refund of his contributions to the extent that they exceeded half the value of his annuity. The Privy Council rejected his claim that the rules of the Madras Fund or the rules of the Bengal Fund on which they were based provided for a refund of excess contributions. Nevertheless, it accepted the argument that he had become entitled to a refund through a course of dealing. The trustees had been granting refunds to new annuitants in Madras and Bombay since 1834, and in 1838 they amended the Madras Fund rules to make this explicit. Initially, the Company received the accounts showing these refunds and learned

[123] *Edwards v Warden* (HL) (n 105).
[124] *Edwards v Warden* (1873–74) LR 9 Ch App 495 (CA) 505.
[125] *Edwards v Warden* (HL) (n 105) 292 (Lord Cairns LC).
[126] ibid 293 (Lord Cairns LC), 297 (Lord Chelmsford), 391 (Lord Hatherley).
[127] *East India Co v Robertson* (n 105).

about the publication of the 1838 rules without objection.[128] Subsequently, in 1850, it recommended that the Madras and Bombay Fund rules should be amended to abolish the practice of granting refunds. In 1853 the subscribers of the 1825 Madras Fund adopted new rules abolishing the grant of refunds.[129] Mr Robertson made his claim to an annuity in 1852, before the new rules had been adopted.

Turner LJ held that because the Company was responsible for making good any shortfall between contributions and annuities, it had 'a direct and immediate interest in the application of the funds by the trustees. The trustees were responsible, not merely to the subscribers, but to the Company, for the due application of the fund'.[130] It had a right to call for the accounts and check them. Therefore, there was no doubt that the Company had sanctioned the refunds which had been made. In his view, the Company stood 'in the position of the ultimate beneficiaries of the fund with which we have, in this case, to deal, subject to prior trusts for the benefit of the subscribers'.[131] The practice of granting refunds was a breach of trust in which the Company concurred, and thus it was precluded by its conduct from disputing Mr Robertson's claim.[132] The modern view of the position of the employer is slightly different. The employer may benefit indirectly from the fund, such as where a surplus is held on resulting trust for it and the scheme members;[133] and although scheme trustees do not owe fiduciary duties to the employer, provided they have regard to the primary purpose of the scheme they may also have regard to the employer's interests.[134]

Although the Funds had now begun to look more like modern occupational pension trusts, there were still some differences. The Company was closely involved but it was not represented on the committee of trustees, nor was it involved in scheme administration or management. Furthermore, the extent to which the courts regarded the Funds as giving the civil servants enforceable rights against the Company is unclear. The Fund documents and regulations do not appear to have contained any stipulation that the payment of pensions was discretionary or dependent on good conduct.[135] The Despatch clearly indicates the Company's view that civil servants should have the reasonable expectation of a pension after 25 years' service. Yet judicial opinion differed as to whether the Company was contractually bound by the terms of the Bengal and 1825 Madras Funds. For example, in *Boldero v East India Co*[136] Mr Boldero sought to recover from the Company a refund of his excess

[128] ibid 458, 463.
[129] ibid 439–44.
[130] ibid 434–35, 458.
[131] ibid 462.
[132] *East India Co v Robertson* (n 105) 464–66.
[133] *Air Jamaica Ltd v Charlton* [1999] 1 WLR 1399 (HL).
[134] *Keymed (Medical and Industrial Equipment) Ltd v Hillman* [2019] EWHC 485 (Ch) [119] (Marcus Smith J). See also *Re Merchant Navy Ratings Pension Fund* [2015] EWHC 488 (Ch); and C Nugee, 'The Duties of Pension Scheme Trustees to the Employer – Revisited' (2015) 29 *Trust Law International* 59. I am very grateful to David Pollard QC for drawing these points to my attention.
[135] The Madras Fund documentation does not contain any stipulation. The Bengal and Bombay Fund Rules were not available in the East India Company archives, but nothing in the authorities discussing those funds suggests that they contained such restrictions.
[136] *Boldero v East India Co* (n 114).

contributions to the Bengal Fund. Unlike in Madras and Bombay, the trustees of the Bengal Fund had not engaged in the practice of granting refunds to subscribers. The Privy Council rejected Mr Boldero's claim. Lord Westbury, Lord Hanbury and Lord Cranworth seemed to regard the Despatch as creating a contract between the directors of the Company and the subscribers,[137] although they rejected the argument that the Fund documentation gave the subscribers any enforceable right to a refund. Lord Chelmsford took a different view. He noted that if the Company had declined to donate to the Fund, the subscribers would have had to have provided the entire cost of the annuities themselves. For this reason, the Despatch 'merely signified the directors' approval of the scheme' and 'their willingness to promote it by a donation from their own funds'.[138]

iii. Railway Superannuation Funds

Railway superannuation schemes proliferated during the second half of the nineteenth century. Their emergence marked a more generous approach on the part of employers towards pension provision. Furthermore although the typical railway scheme had a statutory basis in a private Act of Parliament promulgated by the company,[139] it appears that at least in some cases the trust relationship was relevant to their operation.

In 1853 the London and Northwestern Railway Company (LNWR) Superannuation Fund Association was established by deed poll,[140] and the following year the scheme was put on a statutory footing.[141] The London Brighton and South Coast Railway Company (LBSCR) Fund was established in 1872 and put on a statutory footing in 1874.[142] Having obtained prior statutory authorisation, the North Eastern Railway Company (NER) Superannuation Fund and Metropolitan Railway Company (Metropolitan) Railway Fund were established in 1882 and 1907 respectively.[143]

All four schemes were contributory, and their purpose was to provide contributing members with, inter alia, a superannuation allowance, which could be drawn down upon retirement at a certain age: usually 60[144] or 65.[145] The employees contributed

[137] ibid 409, 411, 419 and 422. For a similar view, *Secretary of State for India v Underwood* (n 113) 584, 586 (Lord Hatherley, who dissented on the merits).

[138] ibid 434.

[139] See Hannah, *Inventing Retirement* (n 2) 10. Railway companies and other companies which engaged in activities of a quasi-public nature were incorporated by statute. See Armour (n 35) [3.36].

[140] Extract from the Deed Poll Declaring the Constitution and Regulation of the Superannuation Fund Association of the London and Northwestern Railway Company, *Report into the Superannuation Act* (n 73) App IV, 33–34.

[141] The London and North Western Railway Act 1854 (LNWR Act 1854) ss 26–28, PA, 17 & 18 Vic, *Cap* cci. The LNWR Scheme Rules appear in the Schedule to the Act.

[142] The London Brighton and South Coast Railway Act 1874 (LBSCR Act 1874) s 18, PA, 37 & 38 Vict, Ch Liv. The Fund Regulations (LBSCR Fund Regulations 1872) appear in the Schedule to the Act.

[143] See the North Eastern Railway Company Act 1878 (NER Act), Parliamentary Archives (PA) 41 & V2 Vict, Ch ccv; The North Eastern Railway Superannuation Fund (NER Fund Rules) (York, 1881) RCA, R/B6/21; Metropolitan Railway (Pension Fund) Act 1907 (the Metropolitan Act) and Scheme for the Management of the Pension Fund and Rules (Metropolitan Fund Rules), Transport For London Archive (TFLA) LT 443/184.

[144] NER Fund Rules (n 143) clause 19; LBSCR Fund Regulations 1872 (n 142) clause 9.

[145] LNWR Scheme Rules (n 141) clause 8; Metropolitan Fund Rules (143) clause 5.

2.5 per cent of their annual salary[146] or a fixed weekly contribution[147] to the scheme by way of salary deduction, which the Company bound itself to match with an equivalent sum. To begin with, these schemes were open only to salaried staff, but in 1899 the original LBSCR fund was merged into a new Pension Fund for all classes of employees.[148] As Metropolitan's salaried staff were contributors to the Railway Clearing System Superannuation Fund, its scheme was for waged staff only.

Each scheme was managed by a committee, on which both the Company itself and the members of the scheme were represented, but the extent of employee representation varied. The Company and members were equally represented on the LNWR and NER managing committees.[149] When the LBSCR scheme was first established, the directors had sole management of the Fund. This changed on revision of the scheme rules in 1899:[150] thenceforth, the Fund was to 'be administered by and be under the management control and regulation of' a new managing committee, of whom only two were elected by the members.[151] The Company also had majority representation on the managing committee of the Metropolitan scheme.[152]

As regards the security of employee benefits, these schemes represented a step forward from the earlier nineteenth-century schemes, and they shared some of the features of the more sophisticated occupational pension schemes adopted by large employers in the early twentieth century. The employer was not simply a discretionary donor: it was a party to the scheme and was statutorily bound to match the employees' contributions. It also took an active role in the management of the scheme through its presence on the committee. The schemes were generous to early leavers, and they also made provision for the grant of benefits to those retiring early through ill health and for the refund of contributions and/or one-off payments to the dependants of a member who died in service. What is more, LNWR and LBSCR undertook to make good out of their revenues the payment of superannuation allowances to the extent to which the funds of the LNWR Association and the income of the LBSCR Fund, respectively, were insufficient for this purpose.[153] In this way, they effectively gave their employees a guaranteed right to a pension contingent upon payment of their contributions.

The language of trusteeship appears in the Fund documentation of all four schemes, but its precise significance in the earlier schemes is opaque. For example, the committee responsible for the establishment of the LNWR scheme requested the chairman and deputy chairman of the Company for the time being and two other

[146] LNWR Scheme Rules (n 141) clauses 1 and 2; NER Fund Rules (n 143) clauses 6 and 10; LBSCR Fund Regulations 1872 (n 142) clauses 14–15.

[147] Metropolitan Fund Rules (n 143) clause 6.

[148] The London Brighton and South Coast Railway (Pensions) Act 1899 (LBSCR Act 1899) recitals and ss 1–4.

[149] LNWR Scheme Rules (n 141) clause 17; NER Fund Rules (n 143) clause 23.

[150] LBSCR Fund Regulations 1872 (n 142) clause 16.

[151] LBSCR Act 1899, s 11.

[152] Metropolitan Fund Rules (n 143) clause 26.

[153] London and North Western Railway (Pension Fund) Act 1907 (LNWR Act 1907) ss 4 and 7; LBSCR Act 1899, s 6.

individuals to act as trustees for the Fund.[154] The deed poll establishing the scheme stipulated that all monies constituting the fund of the association were to be 'accumulated at interest in the hands and under the trust of the Company' at the average rate of interest paid on the Company's bond, which was to be 'carried to the credit of the fund' on a half-yearly basis.[155] When the LNWR scheme was revised in 1907, the wording changed slightly: from then on the Fund monies were to be 'accumulated and invested in the hands and under the trust of the company'.[156]

The statute authorising the establishment of the NER Fund gave the committee responsible for preparing the scheme (comprising five directors and four officers of the Company) the power to decide 'the securities upon which the moneys received on account of the fund shall from time to time be invested'.[157] The scheme rules drawn up by them provided that 'the fund shall be invested on loan to the Company as trustees thereof, bearing interest at the rate of 4 per cent per annum' and '[T]he interest ... shall be carried to the credit of the fund on a half-yearly basis'.[158]

Under the original LBSCR Fund Regulations, '[T]sole management and direction of the fund' was vested in the directors,[159] and the Fund was to be invested 'on loan to the Company as trustees thereof, interest being allowed thereon at the rate of 4 per cent per annum'.[160] When the scheme was revised in 1899, the enabling statute envisaged that 'a limit should be fixed beyond which any amount standing to the credit of the Pension Fund on loan to the Company should not carry interest';[161] this was fixed at £1 million.[162] It also provided that when the new Pension Fund came into operation

> all moneys property and assets then belonging to or standing to the credit of the old fund shall be transferred to and thenceforth remain and be in the hands of the Company upon trust for the purposes of the Pension Fund.[163]

Pensions were to be paid out of the income of the Fund; and the Company undertook both to make good any deficiency in that income[164] and to hold any surplus income 'upon trust as part of the capital of the Pension Fund and such surplus ... shall carry interest as aforesaid'.[165]

A question arises as to the nature of the 'trust' arrangements described above. Was the Company really a trustee of the Fund in each case, or did the committee invest the Fund monies by lending them to the Company so that the 'trust' was in fact a security device, such as a charge over the Company's profits or assets? A loan secured

[154] Minutes of Meeting, 8 April 1853, LNWR Superannuation Fund, Minutes of General Committee (No 1), PRO, RAIL 1174/84, 1.
[155] LNWR Scheme Rules (n 141) clause 16.
[156] Schedule to the LNWR Act 1907, 6.
[157] NER Act 1878, s 14(14).
[158] NER Fund Rules (n 143) clause 74. This wording was carried forward into clause 71 of the NER Fund Rules (n 143).
[159] LBSCR Fund Regulations 1872 (n 142) clause 16.
[160] ibid clause 18.
[161] LBSCR Act 1899, recitals.
[162] ibid s 5.
[163] LBSCR Act 1899, s 4.
[164] ibid s 6(1).
[165] ibid s 6(2).

by a charge (for example, by investment in the Company's debenture stock) would have given the Company freedom to use the Fund monies in the ordinary course of its business, whereas as a trustee the Company would have owed custodial duties in respect of the Fund. Both arrangements would have conferred priority on the Fund members over the Company's unsecured creditors in insolvency. However, the protection offered by the charge would have been limited by the value of the Company's assets, whereas a trust would have offered the additional advantage of a claim for breach of trust if the Company dissipated the Fund, with the possibility of personal and proprietary relief against the Company and/or third parties.

The historical evidence on this point is patchy but it seems plausible that both types of arrangement were in use by railway companies. The report of a committee appointed by the Board of Trade to inquire into the position of the railway superannuation funds (the Superannuation Report)[166] confirmed that generally speaking under salaried schemes the fund assets were 'held in the hands of the company, who allow interest on the accumulated amount at a guaranteed rate of 4 per cent. per annum'.[167] This tends to suggest that the Company acted as custodian of the Fund. The report added that in certain cases 'the money is, however, invested in debenture or other stock of the companies or in various trustee stocks'.[168] In response to a suggestion by a witness that the system of leaving the money in the hands of the companies was unsatisfactory,[169] the committee remarked that from the members' perspective, 'it has to be considered that their money is invested on a security which has priority to the company's debenture stock',[170] but it did not identify the nature of the security. This fits with Hannah's suggestion that in a typical railway scheme the funds were either left on deposit with the company to accumulate at interest or invested in fixed interest securities.[171] He adds that the railway schemes provided 'a segregated fund safe from creditors in the event of bankruptcy'.[172]

The early minutes of the LNWR and LER Funds are ambiguous as to the precise nature of the arrangements. They contain references to: 'the Balance due from the Company to the Society',[173] which is consistent with the idea of a loan. However, there are also references to 'the Balance in the hands of the Company',[174] and 'the Balance belonging to the Association in the hands of the London and North Western Railway Company at interest',[175] both of which are suggestive of a trust. There is no obvious evidence of loan documentation.

[166] *Report on the Railway Superannuation Funds* (n 28).
[167] ibid [125].
[168] ibid [37]; see also Hannah, *Inventing Retirement* (n 2) 11.
[169] *Report on the Railway Superannuation Funds* (n 28) [126].
[170] ibid [127].
[171] Hannah, *Inventing Retirement* (n 2) 11.
[172] ibid 12.
[173] See, eg, minutes dated 7 February 1856, LNWR Superannuation Fund, Minutes of General Committee (No 1) PRO, RAIL 1174/84.
[174] eg, LNWR minutes dated 9 April 1857 and 13 May 1859, PRO, RAIL 1174/84. Similar wording appears in the NER Fund's own statements of account. See eg, North Eastern Railway Superannuation Fund, Statement of Account and Balance Sheet, 31 December 1884, PRO, RAIL 526/1193.
[175] eg, LNWR minutes dated 11 May 1860, 17 May 1861 and 16 May 1862, PRO, RAIL 1174/84.

The three Companies' accounts are also inconclusive. The Company's contribution to the Fund was usually recorded under general charges in the revenue account.[176] The value of the superannuation fund itself appeared as a liability in the general balance sheet, under the heading '[T]o Superannuation Fund',[177] or '[T]o Benevolent and Superannuation Funds'.[178] It increased year on year and there is no evidence of any debits from the Fund. The capital accounts contained sections for capital raised by loans and debentures but the figures were broken down by interest rate rather than debtor, and so it is unclear whether they included the Fund monies as a capital asset of the Company (which would be consistent with the idea of a loan or investment in debenture stock). Thus, the accounts tend to suggest that the Fund was treated as a liability of the Company but they do not reveal whether the Company's obligation to discharge it arose under a loan or a trust. It is also not obvious whether the Fund was segregated from the Company's own assets, but this does not conclusively rule out a trust, as the rules on segregation of trust assets from trustees' own assets were quite lax until the late nineteenth century.[179]

In the Superannuation Report's[180] summaries of the administration of the three schemes, under the heading 'Officers and Trustees' it noted that: the LNWR scheme had a secretary and '[T]he Company are the Trustees';[181] the NER scheme had a secretary but no trustee;[182] and the LBSCR scheme had a secretary and auditors but no trustee.[183] Its summary of the financial position of the LBSCR scheme records that the Company 'holds the assets of the fund upon trust to satisfy its purposes and is liable by statute to credit it interest at 4 per cent on monthly balances, with a limit of £40,000 per year'.[184]

In light of the above, the use of the language of accumulation rather than loan in the LNWR Fund documentation and the Superannuation Report's confirmation that the Company administered the Fund as trustee suggests that the trust explanation is plausible in that case. The use of the phrase 'on loan to the Company as trustees' in the NER and original LBSCR schemes might be thought to be more consistent with a loan or investment in debenture stock or other securities. However, the prevalence of the explicit language of trusteeship in the statute revising the LBSCR scheme and the

[176] See the LNWR accounts for the half-year ending 30 June 1867 and subsequent years, London and North Western Railway Company Accounts 1862–1888, PRO, RAIL, 1110/270; the NER accounts for the half-year ending 30 June 1882 and subsequent years: North Eastern Railway Company Accounts 1873–1882 and 1883–1893, PRO, RAIL, 1110/361. The LBSCR accounts do not contain a separate entry for the Company's contribution.

[177] ibid.

[178] See the LBSCR accounts for the half-year ending 30 June 1872 and thereafter: LBSCR Accounts 1867–1876 and 1897–1906, PRO, RAIL 1110/287–88 and RAIL 1110/290. the LBSCR accounts for the half-year ending 30 June 1872 and thereafter: LBSCR Accounts 1867–1876 and 1897–1906, PRO, RAIL 1110/287–88 and RAIL 1110/290.

[179] Before then, for example, solicitors could mix client funds with their own money with impunity: G Virgo, '*Re Hallett's Estate*' in C Mitchell and P Mitchell (eds), *Landmark Cases in Equity* (Oxford, Hart Publishing, 2014) 361.

[180] *Report on the Railway Superannuation Funds* (n 28).

[181] ibid 43.

[182] ibid 46.

[183] ibid 44.

[184] ibid 60.

Superannuation Report's summary of its financial position clearly suggests that the Company held the Fund on trust for the purposes of the scheme.

If a trust relationship *did* arise under any of these schemes, a question arises as to whether it was for persons or purposes. In view of the wording of the revised LBSCR scheme the latter may be more likely. It is not inconceivable that the phrase 'on loan to the Company as trustee' was meant to describe an arrangement which exhibited some of the features now associated with an intentional *Quistclose* trust,[185] whereby the Fund was a liability of the Company, the money was to be used for the exclusive purpose of paying superannuation allowances, and to the extent that purpose could not be achieved – for example, because of the Company's insolvency – it was to be held on trust for the purposes of the scheme or its members. However, such an observation is necessarily speculative. Questions also arise as to the nature of any duties that the Company would have owed. At the very least, they are likely to have been custodial, but where the scheme was run by a managing committee (as was the case in all but the original LBSCR scheme) it seems unlikely that the Company would also have been subject to administrative duties. As to the enforcement of any custodial duties owed by the Company, it is possible that in view of their approach to the East India schemes[186] the courts might have treated the objects of the scheme as having standing on the basis that they indirectly benefited from the trust.[187]

The Metropolitan Fund rules operated quite differently from the earlier schemes. The Act establishing the scheme empowered the management committee to place the fund monies on deposit with the Company at an interest rate of 4 per cent. There is no suggestion that if the committee chose to do this, the Company was to hold the monies as trustee. Rather, the sums deposited were explicitly secured by a charge 'on the net profits of the company's undertaking next after any debt or money which the company owe or are liable to pay at the passing of the Act and any money for the time being borrowed by them'.[188] Alternatively, the management committee could invest the monies in their own names as investment trustees in the Metropolitan Railway Provident Savings Bank or

> in such investments authorised by law as investments of money in the hands of trustees as they shall think fit or as the scheme may provide with power for the managing committee from time to time to vary or transpose such investments.[189]

Thus, the intention seems to have been that the management committee, rather than the Company, would act as trustees of the Fund and have wider investment powers than were possible under the three earlier schemes.

The foregoing discussion demonstrates that the development of the railway schemes heralded a new willingness on the part of employers to shore up the security of employee benefits and to take the lead in establishing and managing schemes. It also seems likely that the trust relationship was present in some schemes.

[185] *Barclays Bank Ltd v Quistclose Investments Ltd* [1970] AC 567 (HL).
[186] See eg, *Edwards v Warden* (HL) (n 105).
[187] This is the modern view: see *Re Merchant Navy Ratings Pension Fund* (n 134) [214].
[188] Metropolitan Act 1907, s 7.
[189] ibid.

IV. OCCUPATIONAL PENSION TRUSTS AT THE TURN OF THE TWENTIETH CENTURY

The trust became the preferred legal mechanism for establishing large occupational pension schemes in the first few years of the twentieth century, even though tax relief on employer contributions and investment income for pension trusts was only introduced in 1921.[190] Several reasons for this have been suggested: such trusts could be administered by representatives from both the employer and the employees and this was appealing to those trying to improve industrial relations; trusts were cheaper to establish than statutory funds; and trusts offered employers flexibility as to the terms of the scheme.[191] The occupational pension trusts adopted by Lever Bros Ltd in 1905, and Rowntree & Co Ltd and Cadbury Bros Ltd in 1906, suggest that the choice of trust as legal form was driven by both practical and legal considerations, and that employers were still cautious about the idea of granting pension rights to employees.

The Lever Bros scheme demonstrates the attraction of the trust as a legal mechanism to employers who wished to retain discretion over benefits and significant control over the operation of the scheme. It was a very generous non-contributory scheme.[192] Members who had completed at least 15 years of service and had reached retirement age[193] would receive a pension in the sum of one-sixtieth of their salary multiplied by their years of employment at retirement age, up to a maximum of £300 per year.[194] After 45 years' service, this would have amounted to 75 per cent of an employee's salary. Benefits to those who had to retire early because of ill health or injury, and to widows and children, were also provided.

Although the scheme was to be managed by trustees drawn from representatives of both the Company and its employees,[195] extensive powers were reserved by the Company. It stated its intention to make such voluntary contributions as from time to time required to place the fund on a sound financial basis, but also expressly stipulated that it was under no obligation to continue contributions and reserved the freedom to terminate or alter them.[196] All benefits were gratuitous and did not vest any right or cause of action in any employee. They too could be altered, withheld or terminated by the Company as it saw fit.[197] The language was quite moralistic in tone: the establishment of the scheme was not to be regarded as relieving employees of their duty to provide for their own old age[198] and 'intemperance or improper conduct' would disqualify them from benefiting from it.[199]

[190] Finance Act 1921, s 32(3)(a)–(d).

[191] Hannah, *Inventing Retirement* (n 2) 19; see also E Shilton, *Empty Promises: Why Workplace Pension Law Doesn't Deliver Pensions* (Quebec, McGill-Queen's University Press, 2016) 31–34.

[192] Trust Deed of the Employees' Benefit Fund of Lever Brothers Limited, Port Sunlight RCA, R/B6/19, clauses 3 and 6.

[193] ibid clause 9.

[194] ibid clause 28.

[195] ibid clause 22.

[196] ibid clause 5.

[197] ibid clause 7.

[198] ibid clause 4.

[199] ibid clause 12.

Lever Bros controlled the investment of the Fund monies quite tightly. The first £1,000 was to be placed on deposit with the Company at interest. All other monies were to be invested in the names of trustees

> in such shares, securities or investments, and generally in such manner as the Company may from time to time direct in writing, but in the absence of such direction and so far as the same shall not extend, in Preference Shares of the Company.[200]

If the trustees wished to alter the benefits under the scheme or make payments to employees or their dependants who otherwise would not be entitled to benefit, they needed the consent of the Company in writing.[201] The Company also reserved the power to amend the Fund regulations with the trustees' consent in writing, and to make new regulations.[202]

The trust was also attractive to the Rowntree and Cadbury families, who were Quakers and collaborated closely in establishing their pension schemes.[203] They were paternalistic employers who were concerned to deal fairly with their employees at a time when good industrial relations were important because the unions were strong and modern management techniques were evolving.[204] The Rowntree family's generosity is notable. When the Rowntree Pension Fund was first established, Joseph Rowntree made an initial personal donation of £10,000 to the Fund and the Company contributed a lump sum of £9,000 to ensure that existing older employees could draw pensions immediately.[205] The Rowntrees also felt that as the Company would largely be responsible for the fortunes of the Fund, it should guarantee the Fund's solvency to ensure that the fixed pensions subscribed for by members could be paid.[206] Later, in 1917 the Company introduced and bore the entire cost of a widows' benefit scheme, which was the first of its kind.[207] However, the Rowntrees also had an eye to commercial concerns: 'The *commercial* reason for the scheme is to facilitate the shelving of men who have ceased to be effective'.[208] They thought they could achieve this by introducing a compulsory retirement age but ensuring that pension payments were high enough (about 66 per cent of the average wage on retirement after 45 years' service) to prevent a serious loss of income for employees.

In planning the Rowntree scheme, cost, control and flexibility were relevant factors. It was always intended that the scheme would be contributory but that membership would not be compulsory, and the Company wished to retain some flexibility to withhold its contributions if for any reason it needed to, something that would not be possible if the Company's contributions were fixed at a proportion of the employees'

[200] ibid clause 20.
[201] ibid clause 28.
[202] ibid clause 29.
[203] eg, Notes of Interview with Mr Joseph Rowntree and Mr BS Rowntree, 3 July 1905, RCA, R/DH/SR/10.
[204] Hannah, *Inventing Retirement* (n 2) 21; Thane (n 19) 243–44, 246.
[205] Draft speech for the Rowntree Pension Fund Golden Jubilee in 1956, RCA, R/B6/22.
[206] Note read by Joseph Rowntree at Meeting of Trustees, 1 December 1911, RCA, R/B6/15.
[207] Letter to employees setting out details of the widows' benefit scheme, RCA, R/DL/LP/4.
[208] Notes of Interview with Mr BS Rowntree, Mr C Appleton and Mr WJ Fox at the Homestead, 17 July 1905, RCA, R/DH/SR/10 (emphasis in original).

salaries.[209] Four options were under consideration: (i) the whole responsibility for the scheme could be handed over to an insurance company; (ii) the contributions could be transferred to a life insurance company that would guarantee a fixed rate of compound interest during the scheme but would not undertake any further responsibility; (iii) trustees could be appointed – partly by the directors and partly by the employees – who would be responsible for the management and investment of the fund; or (iv) a special limited company limited either by guarantee or shares could be incorporated.[210]

By the time Counsel was instructed to draft the Rowntree scheme in August 1905, the Company seemed to have settled on a proposal to establish the scheme by trust.[211] The positive reasons for this are not entirely clear, but there were good reasons for not adopting the insurance company options. It seems that the cost of handing over responsibility for the scheme to an insurance company would have been very high.[212] Placing the Fund with an insurance company at a fixed rate of interest would have enabled the trustees to withdraw money at any time on notice but the insurance company could have determined the arrangement as to future contributions,[213] which would have resulted in a loss of control and flexibility.

Rowntree also had three main legal concerns about the establishment of the scheme, on which it sought legal advice.[214] There was a question as to whether the scheme might require registration under the Shop Clubs Act 1902, which made it an offence for employers to require their workmen to join a shop club or thrift fund, unless it was registered as a friendly society.[215] The difficulty was that if the scheme had to be registered in this way, the pensions payable would have been limited to a maximum of £50,[216] and Rowntree intended its pensions to be more generous. It also wished to know whether a trust would breach the rule against perpetuities and if testamentary gifts to the trust would be charitable gifts or otherwise legally valid. Counsel's advice[217] on these two points was that as the employees' contributions to the scheme were voluntary, there was no reason to think the scheme would require registration under the Shop Clubs Act, and there was no difficulty with the rule against perpetuities or the validity of testamentary gifts to the fund.[218]

The third legal concern related to the application of the Truck Acts to the scheme. The truck system involved the payment of wages in kind rather than in cash.[219] This allowed unscrupulous employers to exploit employees by paying them partly in overvalued goods, such as groceries, or to grant wage advances in the form of tokens

[209] Statement dated 6 May 1905 (n 33) 4–5.

[210] Undated draft instructions to Counsel, RCA, R/DH/SR/10, 3.

[211] Letter from Wragge & Co (solicitors to Cadbury) to Birdsall & Cross (solicitors to Rowntree), 11 July 1905, RCA, R/DH/SR/11.

[212] Case for the Opinion of Counsel, 24 August 1905, RCA, R/B6/19. See also the letter from George King (actuary to the fund) to Rowntree's solicitors, 19 July 1905, RCA, R/DH/SR/11.

[213] Case for the Opinion of Counsel (n 212).

[214] ibid.

[215] Shop Clubs Act 1902, ss 1 and 2.

[216] Friendly Societies Act 1896, s 8(1)(b).

[217] Opinion of Mr Howard Wright, 5 September 1905, RCA, R/B6/19.

[218] See also the letter from Howard Wright, 11 December 1905, RCA, R/DH/SR/11.

[219] Cornish et al (n 6) 296.

which could only be exchanged for items supplied by the Company.[220] These practices were outlawed by the Truck Act 1831,[221] which rendered illegal and void any contract between a workman and his employer that imposed conditions regarding the place where, the manner in which, or the persons with whom any of the workman's wages should be spent.[222]

Rowntree sought advice as to whether the fact that employee contributions would be effected through wage deductions would bring the scheme within the scope of section 2 of the Act. There was previous authority to the effect that where an employer deducted money from its workmen's monthly wages for a fund that was supposed to benefit them, but in fact retained the money itself, the arrangement offended the Truck Acts.[223] Although dicta suggested that contributions to a sick or accident club or a pension fund were unlikely to fall within the scope of the legislation,[224] counsel for Rowntree did not feel that the Company could safely assume that its scheme would fall outside it, as the point was not directly covered by authority.[225] Cadbury's solicitors took a more robust approach. In their view, although the scheme might come within the letter of the legislation, there were only two risks: (i) that the workmen might seek to recover their contributions, which was unproblematic as the fact that they had consented to the deductions would preclude this, and in any event, it was proposed to allow employees to withdraw from the Rowntree and Cadbury schemes and receive a refund of their contributions; and (ii) that the employers would be prosecuted for penalties under the Truck Acts, but this seemed very unlikely.[226]

At a meeting between Rowntree, Cadbury and their respective counsel in October 1905,[227] Cadbury's counsel endorsed the robust view taken by their solicitors on the basis that no attempt had ever been made to invalidate a pension fund under the Truck Acts. Rowntree's counsel remained unconvinced on the legal point but thought the courts might take a pragmatic view. Both counsel concluded that the use of a trust as the legal mechanism for the scheme would not improve the position, as the deductions would remain an arrangement between employer and employee. Nevertheless, in view of the advice from Cadbury's legal team Rowntree concluded that it was prepared to run the slight risk involved.[228]

The Rowntree and Cadbury schemes were launched in 1906.[229] Both took the form of trusts and were to be managed by committees of trustees drawn from representatives of both the Company and its employees.[230] They were contributory schemes,

[220] GW Hilton, 'The Truck Act of 1831' (1958) 10 *The Economic History Review* 470.

[221] ibid; see also the Truck Acts of 1887 and 1896.

[222] Truck Act 1831, ss 2 and 9.

[223] *Ex parte Cooper, In re Morris* (1884) 26 Ch D 693 (CA). Deductions applied by an employer at the direction of the workmen or to which they had tacitly assented were acceptable: ibid 699 (Cotton LJ); *Hewlett v Allen* [1894] AC 383 (HL) 390, 392 (Lord Herschell LC), 394 (Lord Watson).

[224] *Hewlett v Allen* (n 223) 396 (Lord Watson), 396–98 (Lord Shand).

[225] Opinion of Mr Howard Wright (n 217); Letter from Howard Wright to Rowntree, 20 September 1905, RCA, R/DH/SR/10.

[226] Letter from Wragge & Co to Birdsall & Co, 12 October 1905, RCA, R/DH/SR/11.

[227] Notes of Conference with Counsel at Mr Neison's Chambers, 18 October 1905, RCA, R/DH/SR/10.

[228] Letter from Rowntree to Birdsall & Co, 18 October 1905, RCA, R/DH/SR/11.

[229] Rowntree & Co Ltd Pension Fund, Trust Deed & Rules, 30 October 1906 (Rowntree Deed) RCA, R/B6/1; draft Trust Deed and Rules of Cadbury Bros Ltd's Scheme (Cadbury Deed) RCA, R/B6/19.

[230] Schedule to Rowntree Deed (n 229) rule 22; Cadbury Deed (n 229) clause 19.

which provided that subject to the conditions set out in the rules, subscribers who had paid their contributions and continued in the employment of the Company until they reached pension age would receive a pension.[231] Pensions were also available for those who retired early due to incapacity (subject to a minimum period of service). In both cases membership of the scheme was optional,[232] and the contributions of those who were dismissed from the Company's employment, ceased to subscribe or died in service were to be refunded with interest.[233] Pensions were forfeited if the subscriber became bankrupt,[234] disclosed company secrets or entered into a competing business without its consent.[235] Both schemes also offered flexibility to the employers and the trustees: the Rowntree trustees had the power to enter into contracts with British insurance offices for the provision of pension benefits if they wished to do so, and both sets of trustees had the power to vary or amend the trusts with the consent of the Company.[236]

It is striking that the investment powers of the Rowntree and Cadbury trustees were much wider than those held by the managers of any of the other pension schemes discussed in the previous parts of this chapter. Due to company law reform in the mid-nineteenth century which introduced limited liability and made incorporation easier,[237] opportunities for private equity investment had increased. Investment in private securities had grown in popularity and by the late 1880s the yield from government bonds had dropped below 3 per cent.[238] In response to pressure from settlors and trustees, a series of statutes culminating in the Trust Investment Act 1889 gradually expanded the list of permitted 'safe' trust investments to include, for example, mortgages, real securities, government securities, stocks in railway and water companies with established minimum dividend rates, stocks in Indian railway companies and stock issued by municipal boroughs or water Commissioners.[239] However, the list was not unlimited, and investments which the law still regarded as too risky were only possible if the trust contained an express investment clause permitting them.[240]

Both trust deeds included express investment clauses, but Rowntree seems to have taken a more cautious approach to investment than Cadbury. At least 75 per cent of the money available for investment by the Rowntree trustees was either to be invested in 'securities in which trustees are for the time being by law authorised to invest trust funds, or deposited with one or more British Insurance Offices certified by the actuary as solvent and proper for such deposit'.[241] The other 25 per cent could be invested in the investments listed in the investment clause, which went beyond the list

[231] Schedule to Rowntree Deed (n 229) rule 2; Schedule to Cadbury Deed (n 229) rule 4.
[232] Schedule to Rowntree Deed (n 229) rule 1; Cadbury Deed (n 229) clause 1.
[233] Schedule to Rowntree Deed (n 229) rule 6; Schedule to Cadbury Deed (n 229) rule 7.
[234] Schedule to Rowntree Deed (n 229) rule 11; Schedule to Cadbury Deed (n 229) rule 16.
[235] Schedule to Rowntree Deed (n 229) rule 17; Schedule to Cadbury Deed (n 229) rule 19, which has the same effect but also stipulates for the refund of the subscriber's contributions plus interest in that scenario.
[236] Rowntree Deed (n 229) clauses 9 and 16; Cadbury Deed (n 229) clause16.
[237] Limited Liability Act 1855 (18 & 19 Vict c 133); Companies Acts 1862 and 1867.
[238] Hutson (n 6) 444; Stebbings (n 51) 140.
[239] See Stebbings (n 51) 136–44.
[240] ibid 145 et seq.
[241] Rowntree Deed (n 229) clause 7.

of permitted investments in the Trustee Act 1893. The Cadbury express investment clause[242] permitted a more extensive range of investments; the only caveat was that the proportion of the pension fund available for investment in *some* of the vehicles listed in the clause was to be capped at one-third.

The main difference between the two schemes related to the Company's contributions. Rowntree set its employee subscription level at a minimum percentage of wages which would produce a weekly pension of 15s for men at the age of 65 and 7/6 for women at the age of 55,[243] and undertook to make such contributions as were necessary to keep the fund solvent.[244] The subscriptions for Cadbury's employees ranged between 2.5 per cent and 5.4 per cent of wages, depending on age at the date of entry to the scheme,[245] and the Company undertook to match them. From the age of 60, each employee was to receive a pension equal to 1 per cent of the total wages in respect of which he had made contributions to the fund.[246] In neither scheme did subscribers have any claim or right in respect of the Fund save under the trust deed and rules,[247] Cadbury reserved the right to reduce its contributions if a system of old age pensions was introduced,[248] and both schemes stipulated that the Company's contributions were voluntary and could be suspended or withdrawn on six months' notice to the trustees.[249]

The Rowntree scheme expressly provided that if the Company gave six months' notice of its intention to terminate its contributions, the actuary should thereafter make such reductions in 'the pensions … to be paid to persons not in receipt of pensions at the termination of such notice as shall be necessary', and

> on the termination of such notice the Company shall carry to the credit of the Trustees such sum (if any), as shall be certified by the actuary to be necessary to render the Pension Fund a solvent Fund at the date of the termination of such notice.[250]

Thus, Rowntree appears to have effectively guaranteed a pension to anyone who had reached retirement age within six months of it deciding to terminate its contributions. This suggests that although Rowntree reserved the power to terminate the scheme, it came much closer to embracing the idea of pension 'rights' than Cadbury, which at best gave its subscribers a reasonable expectation of a pension.

V. CONCLUSION

Given the prevalence of the trust relationship in earlier pension arrangements, the adoption of the trust by early-twentieth-century employers as their instrument of

[242] Cadbury Deed (n 229) clause 9.
[243] Schedule to Rowntree Deed (n 229) rules 3–5.
[244] Rowntree Deed (n 229) clause 4.
[245] Schedule to Cadbury Deed (n 229) rule 2.
[246] ibid rule 4.
[247] Schedule to Rowntree Deed (n 229) rule 20; Schedule to Cadbury Deed (n 229) rule 22.
[248] Cadbury Deed (n 229) clause 6.
[249] Rowntree Deed (n 229) clause 4; Cadbury Deed (n 229) clause 4.
[250] Rowntree Deed (n 229) clause 4.

choice for administering occupational pension schemes is best regarded as a small but logical step in pensions practice. Nevertheless, in combination, the drafting of sophisticated and detailed trust instruments, the transfer of pension funds to a separate board of trustees, and the expansion of trustees' investment powers were significant, as they offered flexibility, facilitated the balancing of employers' and employees' interests within the scheme, and allowed for the diversification of investments for the benefit of scheme members.

It is also notable that the increased popularity of the trust per se did not signify a paradigm shift in the legal conceptualisation of pensions. As a legal mechanism, the trust was just as useful to employers like Lever Bros, who wished to offer non-contributory, discretionary, ex gratia pensions, as it was to employers like Rowntree, who were moving closer to the idea of pension rights.[251] Ultimately, as the authorities relating to the East India funds and the British public sector schemes demonstrate, the extent of members' rights under any schemes depended on the courts' interpretation of the legal instruments by which they were created.

[251] See also Hannah, *Inventing Retirement* (n 2) 19.

2

UK Collective Defined Contribution: Is it 'Dutch-Style' Collective Defined Contribution?

SANDEEP MAUDGIL AND HANS VAN MEERTEN

I. INTRODUCTION

Parts 1 and 2 of the UK's Pension Schemes Bill 2020 make provision for collective schemes to be permissible in Great Britain and Northern Ireland. The Bill calls them 'collective money purchase schemes' to ensure consistency with existing UK pensions statutory terminology. Although the Original Pension Schemes Bill fell when Parliament dissolved on in advance of the December 2019 general election, the Conservative Party reintroduced the legislation in January 2020 following their return to government and the collective money purchase parts of it have broad cross-party support.

Collective DC (Defined Contribution) pensions are seen in the UK as a potential means of navigating through the unwillingness of employers to shoulder the financial risks associated with defined benefit pension plans on the one hand, and the inefficiencies associated with the traditional UK 'individual retirement account' approach to defined contribution retirement savings provision on the other. The key novelty of the collective DC concept from a UK pensions perspective is that it will allow employers to sponsor a pension scheme which expresses and pays its benefits in pension form, but on terms which would respond to a scheme's experience being worse than anticipated by reducing members' benefits rather than by requiring employers to put in extra money.

Collective DC has its supporters in the UK as well as its sceptics. Both sides of the argument point to the Netherlands as a country whose experience of 'collective DC' shows (for the supporters) the benefits and (for the sceptics) the potential pitfalls of such a system. This chapter considers the differences between collective DC as seen in the Netherlands and how the equivalent schemes might work in the UK, and how far the (still to be enacted) UK legislation seems to have learned from the Dutch experience.

II. COLLECTIVE DEFINED CONTRIBUTION IN THE DUTCH PENSIONS LANDSCAPE[1]

In the simplest archetypes, Dutch pension schemes can be divided into Defined Benefit (DB) and Defined Contribution (DC) schemes.[2] They can be most easily differentiated from each other by remembering who – in principle – bears the risk: in a DC scheme, the scheme members themselves bear the risk; the employer commits merely to paying a fixed sum as a contribution. Pension benefits are determined by what has been paid into the scheme and the investment yield, minus costs. A pure DC scheme in the Netherlands features no risk sharing, apart from elements of solidarity which are required by Netherlands statute,[3] and the sharing of investment risks that appears inherent to the collective management of the investments.[4] In a DB scheme, the risk bearer is typically the employer or a pension provider. The employer commits to a certain level of benefits to be received by the employee upon retirement.

In reality, few Dutch pension schemes conform to the description of either archetype. Most can thus be placed on the spectrum that exists between them. On that spectrum, Collective Defined Contribution (CDC) can be found. From the Netherlands perspective, the main features of a CDC scheme are as follows. First, the employer contributions are expressed as a fixed percentage or a fixed amount, so the employer has no legal or constructive obligation to make good any shortfall between the amount of the target benefits in the CDC scheme and the value of the assets of the CDC scheme whenever a valuation of the CDC scheme is done. The CDC scheme benefits are expressed as a target retirement income (or target pension) payable for the life of the member (with associated conditional target revaluation in the pre-payment period and conditional target indexation in the post-payment starting period to protect the purchasing power of the benefit). Members of a CDC scheme pool (either intragenerationally or intergenerationally, or both) longevity, inflation and investment risks and rewards in accordance with the rules for doing that in the CDC scheme (and subject, where applicable, to overriding legislation). If, as at a valuation date, the value of the CDC scheme assets is below the capital value of the scheme benefits, then future target revaluation and future target indexation does

[1] This section is a revised version of three working papers: P Bennett and H Van Meerten, 'How do CDC Schemes Qualify Under the IORP II Directive?' (2019) VUZF Review, University of Sofia 2/2019, available at: www.papers.ssrn.com/sol3/papers.cfm?abstract_id=3354549; P Bennett and H Van Meerten, 'Apples and Oranges: A Comparison of the Key Features of the Legislative and Regulatory Framework for UK and Dutch Defined Benefit Pension Schemes (Including Dutch CDC Schemes)' (2018), available at: www.papers.ssrn.com/sol3/papers.cfm?abstract_id=3163137; E Schmidt and H Van Meerten, 'The Legal Differences between CIDC and CDC' (2019) The Pensions Institute Discussion Paper PI-1801, available at: www.papers.ssrn.com/sol3/papers.cfm?abstract id=3121141. Any errors in the revised version should be attributed to Hans van Meerten.

[2] P Borsjé and H van Meerten, 'Pension Rights and Entitlement Conversion ("Invaren"): Lessons from a Dutch Perspective with Regard to the Implications of the EU Charter' (2016) 18 *European Journal of Social Security* 46.

[3] E Schols-Van Oppen, 'De Collectieve Beschikbarepremieregeling' in *De CDC-Regeling: Stand van Zaken Anno 2008* (Amersfoort, Sdu Fiscale & Financiële Uitgevers, 2008) 8.

[4] D Blake, 'We Need a National Narrative: Building a Consensus Around Retirement Income' (Report, Independent Review of Retirement Income, 2016) 492.

not occur (or is reduced). And if that control mechanism is not sufficient, ultimately the accrued target benefits (both in payment and not yet in payment) are reduced to 'balance the books'.

III. THE HISTORY OF COLLECTIVE DEFINED CONTRIBUTION IN THE NETHERLANDS IN PRACTICE

A. General

The first CDC schemes started in the Netherlands at the beginning of 2000.[5] The benefit structure is, in general, an average salary benefit structure with conditional revaluation[6] before the pension comes into payment and conditional indexation once the pension is in payment. CDC schemes were introduced in the Netherlands by way of a response to changes in accounting standards which had the effect of bringing the deficits in Dutch DB schemes on to the balance sheet of Dutch companies. So the CDC scheme offered a similar benefit structure to a traditional Dutch DB pension scheme: it provided average salary benefits, with the employer contribution rate being fixed as a percentage of pensionable pay (but for a period of no more than five years).[7] The key point is that, even if the employer contribution rate is renegotiated after the end of that period of up to five years, there would be no legal requirement to pay any contributions to make up a deficit.

In the Netherlands, CDC schemes of two types exist. In the first, an assessment is made annually of the annuity that can be purchased on the basis of the contributions paid. Most CDC schemes in the Netherlands, however, are based on a career average salary like traditional DB schemes, but with the clear message that no guarantee as to the level of benefits is given. The employer seems not to be burdened by any legal or economic risk regarding the level of pension benefits achieved. In the Netherlands, CDC plans *can* also qualify as DB schemes if there is a sufficient amount of certainty that the agreed upon level of pensions will be attained.[8] Members of CDC schemes should be clearly informed of the manner in which the amount of the contributions have been determined and how likely it is that these premiums will achieve the indicated level of benefits.[9]

It is important to note that although the boundary between a Dutch DB pension scheme and a Dutch CDC scheme is not a 'hard' boundary, a Dutch CDC scheme is

[5] See Schols-Van Oppen (n 3).

[6] In this chapter a distinction is drawn between the increase of the accrued but not in payment pension (referred to as revaluation) and the increase to the pension in payment referred to as indexation. The rates of revaluation and indexation may be identical or they may differ depending on the benefit design.

[7] For more detail, see the explanation of the Dutch Central Bank of this five-year requirement, De Nederlandsche Bank, 'Q&As Pensioenfondsen – Collective Defined Contribution (CDC) Regelingen' (8 May 2015), available at: www.toezicht.dnb.nl/3/50-228388.jsp.

[8] M Heemskerk, *Pensioenrecht* (The Hague, Boom Juridische Uitgevers, 2015) 59.

[9] 'Juridische Aspecten Van Een CDC-Regeling', available at: www.vvpensioenrecht.nl/download/werkgroepmemo_juridische_aspectien_cdc.pdf.

not per se a DB scheme. Article 10 of the Dutch Pensions Act says that there are three types of pension schemes:

a. *een uitkeringsovereenkomst* (a DB scheme);
b. *een kapitaalovereenkomst* (a hybrid scheme);
c. *een premieovereenkomst* (a DC scheme).

A Dutch CDC scheme is not defined in law as falling within category (a), (b) or (c). However, the Explanatory Memorandum relating to Article 10 of the Dutch Pensions Act states that:

> In a CDC scheme too, therefore, one of these three forms of (declining) risks will always be present for the members of a pension scheme, based on the content of the pension scheme (and not on the basis of the name) and the communication about this with the participants, it will be necessary to assess the type of pension scheme.

In other words, if the pension agreement qualifies for the CDC scheme as an *uitkeringsovereenkomst*, it is a DB scheme.

In Dutch CDC schemes without sponsor guarantees, surpluses or deficits are not transferred back to the sponsoring undertaking or made up by it, but are rather shared by the scheme members collectively between young, old and future generations 'by adjusting either contributions, or benefit levels or both, which leads to inter-generational transfers'.[10] *Ex ante*, the contributions are set in such a manner that a newly entering generation funds its own retirement, but *ex post*, it may turn out that a given generation is a net payer or a net receiver.[11] It is clear, then, that in comparison to a DB scheme, any risks are transferred to the scheme members. This need not be a problem in itself, although the scheme members should be duly informed of their new economic and legal position.

In addition, for a CDC scheme, the premiums are not determined individually but collectively.[12] In the Netherlands, a system of so-called average premiums is used for DB and most CDC schemes, whereby all pension participants – regardless of their age – contribute the same percentage of their salary and receive a set percentage of accrual in return. This system of average accrual has been under discussion recently in the context of talks on pension reform,[13] as it is said to be unfair to young employees whose contributions still have years of investment returns ahead of them, while those of older employees do not – yet under the current system, they are valued the same.[14] This system finds its origins in the post-war era, when it was necessary

[10] J Cui, F de Jong and E Ponds, 'Intergenerational Risk Sharing Within Funded Pension Schemes' (2011) 10 *Journal of Pension Economics & Finance* 4.

[11] ibid.

[12] Schols-Van Oppen (n 3) 50.

[13] 'Advies Raad van State met betrekking tot de afschaffing van de doorsneesystematiek bij pensioenopbouw' (14 June 2017), available at: www.rijksoverheid.nl/documenten/kamerstukken/2017/07/14/advies-raad-van-state.

[14] AJ van de Griend and H van Meerten, 'Hervorming pensioenstelsel: degressieve opbouw in uitkeringsovereenkomsten en vlakke premies in premieovereenkomsten' (2017) 5 *Sociaal Economische Wetgeving* 189.

to enable older employees to build up a decent pension in a relatively short period of time.[15] The Netherlands Bureau for Economic Policy Analysis (CPB) notes that this system is 'not ideal and even problematic', as it leads to a structural redistribution from younger to older scheme members, and from scheme members with low life expectancy to those with a high life expectancy.[16] This system hinders portability and labour mobility.[17]

B. Legal Form of Dutch Pension Funds

The most common arrangement for establishing a pension scheme in the Netherlands is to establish a *Stichting*. Under Dutch law, a '*Stichting*'[18] is a body corporate which has its own separate legal personality just like any other company. But a *Stichting* set up to provide pension benefits has a limited purpose under its constitutional documents, to use the assets of the *Stichting* to provide those benefits to the members of the *Stichting*, ie, the employer's employees and the former employees and their respective survivors. The members derive their rights as against the *Stichting* from the memorandum and articles of association (or the Pension Regulations) of the *Stichting* which confer legally enforceable rights to the pension benefits on the member against the *Stichting*.[19]

The relationships between the interested parties in relation to the *Stichting* are triangular as follows:

- First, there is the relationship between the employer and employee, which is formed under the contract of employment. It includes any terms incorporated via the collective bargaining agreement between the employer or the employer's association and the recognised trade union which provides for the terms on which the employer will make available, via the *Stichting*, pension benefits to its employees as members of the scheme and their surviving dependants. This is known as the '*pensioenovereenkomst*' or Pension Agreement.[20]

[15] Netherlands Bureau for Economic Policy Analysis, 'Eindrapportage Voor- en nadelen van de doorsneesystematiek: Uitgevoerd op verzoek van het Ministerie van Sociale Zaken en Werkgelegenheid' (28 October 2013) 8.

[16] ibid 99.

[17] L Bovenberg and R Gradus, 'Reforming Occupational Pension Schemes: The Case of the Netherlands' (2015) 18 *Journal of Economic Policy Reform* 244, 248.

[18] All Dutch pension funds established after 2015 are required to have the legal form of a *Stichting*. However, prior to 2016 it was possible for a Dutch pension fund to have a separate legal personality (eg, a BV) although not established as a *Stichting*. That said, pension funds in the Netherlands are typically established as *Stichtings*. This article looks at the position on the basis that the legal form of the pension fund is a *Stichting* (although, as a practical matter, little turns on this point).

[19] See for more details, E Lutjens, *Mr C Assers Handleiding tot de beoefening van het Nederlands Burgerlijk Recht. 7. Bijzondere overeenkomsten. Deel XI. Pensioen* (Deventer, Wolters Kluwer, 2016); and Heemskerk (n 8).

[20] E Lutjens (ed), *Pensioenwet: Analyse en commentaar*, 4th edn (Deventer, Wolters Kluwer, 2013) 103–65.

- Second, there is a funding agreement between the employer and the *Stichting*, under which the employer has agreed with the *Stichting* the premiums it will contribute to the *Stichting* to fund the retirement benefits to be provided by the *Stichting*. These benefits are more particularly described in the memorandum and articles of association (or Pension Regulations) of the *Stichting*. This is known as the '*uitvoeringsovereenkomst*' or Administration Agreement.
- Third, there is a relationship between each member (including his or her surviving eligible dependants) and the *Stichting*. The *Stichting* is required by its memorandum and articles of association (or Pension Regulations) to make payments to the member (and his or her eligible surviving dependants) of the benefits as determined in accordance with the terms of the memorandum and articles of association (or Pension Regulations) of the *Stichting*. These arrangements are referred to as the '*pensioenreglement*' or Pension Regulations.

It is worth noting that because the Dutch pension fund takes the legal form of a *Stichting*, its balance sheet will show both the assets and the liabilities (including pensions obligations) within it. By way of contrast, a UK private sector occupational pension scheme, established almost invariably by way of irrevocable trust, will not show in its balance sheet its obligations to provide pensions. Instead the balance sheet will be limited to the assets of the scheme and its liabilities to external third parties (such as accrued but unpaid fees to service providers).[21]

In the Netherlands, it is possible, as an alternative to using a *Stichting*, for the retirement benefits to be provided either by an insurance company (ie, premiums are paid to the insurance company by the employer to purchase retirement benefits for the employee under an insurance contract), or by a premium pension institution.[22] However, these practices are less common.

As set out in previous research,[23] there must be a distinction between two archetypes of pension frameworks. In the first archetype, the Institution for Occupational Retirement Provision is an independent legal entity, at some distance from the employer, with full recourse to its own funds. The IORP has upfront provisions on its balance sheet to bear biometric risks or to guarantee a certain investment performance or level of benefits. This IORP is the most common in the Netherlands.[24]

In the second archetype, the sponsor and the IORP are closely related and the IORP may have been set up by the sponsor. The sponsor provides the ultimate pension security to its employees and stands ready to supply financing in the event of

[21] See, eg, the Occupational Pension Schemes (Requirement to obtain Audited Accounts and a Statement from the Auditor) Regulations 1996 (SI 1996/1975) reg 3(b)(iii), which says that the accounts are to show a true and fair view of 'the liabilities of the scheme, other than the liabilities to pay pensions and benefits after the end of the scheme year'.

[22] A description of some elements of these vehicles can be found here: P Borsjé and H van Meerten, 'A EU Pensions Union' in F Pennings et al (eds), *Research Handbook on European Social Security Law* (Cheltenham, Edward Elgar Publishing, 2015); H van Meerten and ART IJlzinga Veenstra, 'De Premiepensioeninstelling: Internationaal Aantrekkelijk vehikel' (2009) 4 *Pensioenmagazine* 6.

[23] Borsjé and van Meerten, 'Pension Rights and Entitlement Conversion' (n 2).

[24] AJ van de Griend and H van Meerten, 'Hervorming Pensioenstelsel: Degressieve Opbouw in Uitkeringsovereenkomsten en Vlakke Premies in Rremieovereenkomsten' (2017) 65(5) *Sociaal-Economische Wetgeving* 189.

an adverse shock to the IORP. Most Member States have a combination of the two archetypes. As will be shown below, the legal framework of the pension provider will determine to a large extent the legal character of a CDC pension scheme.

C. Protection of Accrued Rights under a Dutch Pension Scheme

Article 20 of the Dutch Pensions Act confers protection for accrued rights but does not prevent those accrued rights being amended in accordance with the terms of any reserved rights to do so (or in accordance with any mandatory obligation on the pension fund to do so).[25] Thus, there is no equivalent restriction, under Dutch law, to section 67 of the UK Pensions Act 1995 which prevents a reserved power to amend benefits to 'balance the books' from adversely affecting accrued rights.[26]

The *Stichting* has a mechanism for 'balancing its books' which means that prima facie it cannot become insolvent for its pension liabilities.[27] Under its memorandum and articles of association (or Pensions Regulations),[28] provision will be made for benefits to be reduced if the scheme is underfunded and cannot recover its Minimum Required Funding Level over a recovery period (currently five years on average, depending on the facts). The articles of association (or Pensions Regulations) of the *Stichting* must contain information about the possibility of benefit reductions in accordance with Article 134. In the context of good governance, it is important to adequately inform the (former) participants that accrued entitlements and rights can possibly be reduced. Where benefits are cut, this is a uniform reduction applied to all pensions in payment, all deferred pensions, and all accrued pensions. There is an initial permitted five-year recovery period before any cuts to accrued pension benefits (including those in payment) have to be made. Thereafter, cuts to accrued benefits in payment (including those in payment) must be made on a uniform basis over a 10-year period to bring the value of the scheme's liabilities back into line with the value of the scheme's assets to at least the Minimum Required Funding Level.

If there is a reduction in benefits in the Dutch DB or CDC scheme as a result of underfunding, whether the employee has a claim against the employer will primarily depend on the applicable terms of the contract of employment (including any collective bargaining agreement) applicable to the employee in question, ie, the Pension

[25] See Arts 76, 78, 83 and 134 of the Pensioenwet (Dutch Pensions Act) which allow for pension rights of beneficiaries to be restricted or reduced (ie, they are not fixed).

[26] See, eg, *Aon Trust Corporation Ltd v KPMG (A Firm) & Ors* [2005] EWCA Civ 1004, [2005] 1 WLR 97, which decided that s 67 of the UK Pensions Act 1995 prevented a power in the scheme's governing documentation to reduce benefits for a deficit in the scheme to balance the books from being used. The UK Court of Appeal held that the exercise of such a power would adversely affect accrued rights which was prohibited by s 67 of the UK Pensions Act 1995.

[27] The *Stichting* can, of course, become insolvent for its 'normal' (ie, non-pension) liabilities. For further analysis as to whether the duty, under Dutch law, for a pension fund to reduce its pension liabilities to 'balance its books' is compatible with the correct transposition of Directive 2008/94/EC, see H van Meerten, 'European Ruling on Pensions: Second Warning for The Netherlands' in FANJ Goudappel and EMH Hirsch Ballin (eds), *Democracy and Rule of Law in the European Union: Essays in Honour of Jaap W de Zwaan* (The Hague, Asser Press, 2016) 146–54.

[28] And Art 134 of the Dutch Pensions Act.

Agreement). It is possible that the terms of the Administration Agreement between the employer and the *Stichting* may make provision for additional payments in this situation. Alternatively, the Funding Agreement may just be limited to an agreement to pay contributions for a specified period and to agree, thereafter, separately, the contributions to be paid for another specified period. In other words, even Dutch DB or CDC pension rights can be reduced.

D. Conclusion on Dutch CDC

CDC schemes aim to fix the afflictions of the current pension system in the Netherlands. From the perspective of the employer and/or the pension fund (the scheme sponsor(s)), an appealing feature is the absence of a guarantee of a certain level of pension benefits, and the contributions are fixed for a number of years. The risks in CDC schemes are transferred unambiguously to the scheme members, and they should be clearly informed of that.

The Dutch Central Bank requires those CDC schemes which are based on an average career salary to comply with the same funding requirements as a 'conventional' average salary DB scheme, which – in principle – guarantees a level of pension benefits.[29] The Dutch Central Bank's guidelines state that the maximum premium for CDC schemes should not be fixed for a period longer than five years. This is in contrast to a DC scheme, for which a fixed premium is permitted for an indefinite period.[30]

In the Netherlands, the discussion on the revision of the pension system to a certain extent revolves around creating a system that allocates 'clear and individual property rights' to pension scheme members, and CDC schemes are favoured by some because they are said to be able to provide such rights.[31] However, such terminology is confusing as the assets in the scheme do not *belong* to the scheme member as such. In a DC and CDC scheme, it is possible to *value* an individual's pension pot, but that is not the same as saying that the participant *owns* that sum.

It is therefore best to avoid the term 'ownership' in the context of pensions,[32] as that term is of no consequence in relation to pensions either in the Netherlands[33] or the UK, where occupational pensions are typically operated by trusts.[34] It is therefore not a *legal* property right – not even in EU law terms – but an *economic* right to the

[29] Schols-Van Oppen (n 3) 12.

[30] See: www.toezicht.dnb.nl/3/50-228388.jsp.

[31] Social and Economic Council of the Netherlands, Advice 2015/01, 40–42; A van den Brink et al, 'Collectieve Solidariteit, Individuele Zekerheid: Naar een Toekomstbestendig Pensioencontract voor Nederland' (Position paper by Rabobank Pensioenfonds, Syntrus Achmea and Cardano, 2015).

[32] M Heemskerk and J Tangelder, 'Pensioen Wijzigen: Klem Tussen Eigendomsrechten en Vetorecht?' (2016) 21 *Pensioenmagazine* 1.

[33] ibid; M Heemskerk, R Maatman and B Werker, 'Heldere en Harde Pensioenrechten Onder een PPR' (2016) 46 *Netspar Design Paper*.

[34] HM Revenue & Customs, 'Responsibilities of a Pension Trustee' (Guidance, 16 September 2016), available at: www.gov.uk/guidance/pension-trustees-appointment-and-role.

sum defined in the individual account: it is typically the pension provider or trust fund that owns the pension capital.[35]

IV. COLLECTIVE DEFINED CONTRIBUTION: THE UK PROJECT

A. History: The UK's Binary Occupational Pension System

The UK is arguably approaching the Collective DC project from a different place when compared with the Netherlands. In the Netherlands, Collective DC as a concept arose largely as a way of avoiding pension deficits appearing as an accounting liability on sponsoring employer balance sheets. However, the obligation assumed by an employer in the Netherlands is, in the ultimate resort, a 'soft' liability in both DB and CDC contexts other than to the extent the employer has, by separate agreement (most often collective agreement with union or works council) contracted to make good the deficit in a DB scheme.

In contrast, there is a much stricter dividing line in the UK between occupational pension schemes which are 'money purchase' schemes (also referred to as 'defined contribution' (or DC) schemes) and those which are not, both in terms of definition and in terms of the legal obligation assumed by the sponsoring employer. In summary, it is only if the pension scheme it sponsors satisfies the statutory definition of a 'money purchase scheme' in the UK that the employer can be sure of limiting its cash funding obligation to the amount initially contracted for; otherwise employers are at risk of changes in pension benefit cost leading to unexpected cash calls which can take the form of statutory debts, waivable only in certain tightly prescribed circumstances.

A 'money purchase scheme'[36] under UK law is a scheme under which all the benefits that may be provided are 'money purchase benefits' as defined in section 181 and section 181B of the Pension Schemes Act 1993. For these purposes, a benefit will only be a 'money purchase' if during the pre-pension period its rate or amount is calculated solely by reference to assets which (because of the nature of the calculation) must necessarily suffice for the purposes of its provision to or in respect of the member. As a practical matter, therefore, the benefit will usually be defined and expressed as the value from time to time of a 'pot' (or 'retirement account') earmarked for the provision of benefits exclusively to or in respect of the member, and the benefit which the member is said to have will fluctuate, typically on a daily basis, in line with that value from time to time. On reaching retirement, the member can draw down on their DC 'pot' as they would draw down on any other savings account; but assuming the DC retirement account is the member's primary source of income in retirement, this gives members the challenge that they do not know what a 'safe' rate of drawdown will be,

[35] T Hulshoff, H van Meerten, GCM Siegelaer and FR Valkenburg, "Individueel Eigendomsrecht in een Beschikbarepremieregeling" (2016) 7 *Pensioen Magazine*, available at: www.ssrn.com/abstract=2781207.

[36] See Pension Schemes Act 1993, s 181(1).

as no member knows how long he or she will live. The 'prudent' member risks being too cautious, and so enjoying a less comfortable retirement than, with hindsight, they could have afforded. The less prudent member risks outliving their DC 'pot', and so running out of money and becoming wholly dependent on the state at a time when they are elderly and potentially at their most vulnerable. A member who does not wish to risk either of these outcomes can convert their 'pot' into a pension for life, but only if the value of the pension is secured through an annuity contract taken out with an authorised insurer. Any scheme which provides benefits which do not fall precisely within these definitions as regards both the pre-pension and pensioner period will not qualify as 'money purchase schemes'.

If an occupational scheme in the UK is *not* a money purchase scheme, then the consequences for the sponsoring employer are significant. All the economic and demographic risks associated with the changing costs of pension provision will be borne by the sponsoring employer, as a result of the operation of a number of statutory mechanisms. First, the scheme will be subject to the statutory funding objective contained in section 222 of the Pensions Act 2004, which requires that the scheme have sufficient and appropriate assets to cover its 'technical provisions', and to the other provisions of Part 3 of the Pensions Act 2004 which provide, inter alia, that the employer contribution obligations must be set by trustees and employer in agreement and that, if no such agreement can be reached within 15 months of the date of the valuation, they can be imposed by the Pensions Regulator. Separately, on scheme termination,[37] the employers in a non-money purchase scheme are liable to pay into the scheme such amount as is required to secure all scheme benefits by the purchase of insurance company annuities (the so called 'Section 75 debt').[38]

In the UK, these funding and employer debt obligations apply to what we think of as DB schemes, even if the original rules of the scheme gave the employer a veto over the rate at which it was required to contribute to the scheme. However, it is important to note that there is no definition of a 'defined benefit' scheme under UK legislation. Rather, the statutory funding and employer debt obligations[39] apply to all schemes, subject to a disapplication for 'money purchase' (or DC) schemes.

It is perhaps worth noting that this was not always the case. Before the 1980s, what UK employees may have thought of as their 'guaranteed defined benefit' scheme might well not have been as 'guaranteed' as they thought – the question would turn on the specific provisions of their trust deed. What happened from the 1980s onwards in the UK was that schemes had their trust deeds overridden through various pieces of supervening legislation. At first this was through the introduction of compulsory

[37] Or earlier, on an employer insolvency or employer cessation of participation – in which case the liability is on the employer which has become insolvent or ceased to participate, for its pro rata share of the relevant s 75 deficit.

[38] See Pensions Act 1995, s 75 and the Occupational Pension Schemes (Employer Debt) Regulations 2005 (SI 2005/678).

[39] And various other obligations, such as compulsory revaluation in deferment according to Part IV of the Pension Schemes Act 1993, compulsory indexation of pensions in payment under s 51 of the Pensions Act 1995, and the corporate veil-piercing upstream liability provisions of ss 38 and 43 of the Pensions Act 2004.

benefit features such as revaluation in deferment,[40] then indexation in payment,[41] followed by 'Section 67' prohibitions on reducing accrued rights.[42] This was then backed up by the compulsory funding legislation referred to above. All this led to a position in relation to UK DB pension plans – which, subject to their contractual and collective bargaining position, employers are free to offer or not to employees as they choose – which has been described as being one where 'you do not have to provide a company car, but if you do it has to be a Rolls Royce'.[43]

The binary position above has left the UK in a difficult place as regards occupational retirement benefit provision. As the House of Commons Work and Pensions Committee explained in 2018:

> DB pensions have been in steady decline. Sponsoring employers have found meeting their pension obligations difficult in the context of increased life expectancy, low interest rates and the decline of some traditional industries. In 2016, 1.3 million employees were actively contributing to a private sector DB scheme, compared to 3 million a decade previously. Many companies have sought to reduce financial risk by closing schemes to the accrual of further pension benefits. Alan Rubenstein, former chief executive the Pension Protection Fund (PPF), which pays reduced pensions in the event sponsoring employers became insolvent, said 'we now all recognise that we are moving towards an endgame for defined benefit pensions'.[44]

However, money purchase (or DC) plans are not seen as necessarily the best way to plug the gap left by the decline of DB schemes. In particular, they are not seen as properly answering the question of the decumulation phase, viz, how to move from the accumulation 'savings pot' phase to the phase of actually providing members with an income in retirement. To quote the Work and Pensions Committee once more:

> When an individual [in a DC plan] decides to start drawing a retirement income they must identify a suitable retirement income product from a range of options. Those include:
>
> - Annuity – an insurance product that offers the individual a guaranteed income, usually for the rest of their life.
> - Drawdown – a product that enables the consumer to withdraw some income as cash while leaving the remainder invested in funds.[45]
>
> Individuals, many of whom will have been saving passively,[46] can find making an appropriate choice of retirement income product difficult. Drawdown options are currently twice as popular as annuities. Annuities have offered poor value in recent years given low

[40] Part IV of the Pension Schemes Act 1993.

[41] Pensions Act 1995, s 51.

[42] ibid, s 67.

[43] The authors note that other brands of luxury car are also available.

[44] See introduction to House of Commons Work and Pensions Committee, *Collective Defined Contribution Pensions*, Sixteenth Report of Session 2017–19, HC 58, published 16 July 2018, 5, available at: www.parliament.uk/business/committees/committees-a-z/commons-select/work-and-pensions-committee/publications.

[45] ibid, 5–6.

[46] "Passively" here is not being used to refer to "index-tracking" funds, but rather to individuals making no investment choice and therefore being placed into the provider "default" investment option rather than an option which they have positively chosen.

> interest rates. The regular income generated is also dependent on the value of the pot at the point of purchase, which can leave it at the whim of market conditions. Drawdown may provide higher total returns and the pot remains invested, meaning it is less dependent on market conditions at a single point in time. But the individual bears ongoing investment risk and could exhaust their pot, particularly if they live longer than they expect (this is known as longevity risk). Research suggests that a high proportion of DC savers aspire to a predictable, regular income in retirement – one survey found that over two-thirds of DC savers counted themselves as either 'certainty seekers' or 'steady spenders' – without having to manage risk on an individual basis.

Or, putting the statement that 'a high proportion of DC savers aspire to a predictable, regular income in retirement' another way: most people just want a pension.

B. Enter 'Collective Money Purchase'?

The question, therefore, was whether UK legislation could be amended to permit a pension plan to express and pay its benefits in the form of what most people want when they retire (viz, a pension) without requiring:

a. The employer to be fully responsible for ensuring that the scheme has sufficient assets to pay all pensions in full. This is the open-ended risk which led many employers to close down their defined benefit schemes; or
b. the scheme/member to secure that pension through the purchase of an insurance company annuity. This is what puts members off converting their DC retirement pot into pension form because annuities are perceived to be poor value. From the insurers' perspective, this is an inevitable result of their prudential regulatory obligation to 'back' their liability to provide pensions with appropriately low-risk assets and to reserve prudently contingencies (without which UK regulators in turn would be concerned by the potential for further Equitable Life-style insurer failures).

In other words, could UK legislation be amended to as to permit the members of the scheme collectively to 'self-insure' such that the scheme becomes, in effect, a mutually owned provider of pensions in payment?

The Department for Work and Pensions had considered enabling new forms of pension provision in the past, and in the Pension Schemes Act 2015 had legislated for new occupational pensions definitions to facilitate this. But there were significant difficulties with the legislation. It would have required all existing UK pension schemes to test themselves against new definitions, with the result (among other things) that current 'defined benefit' schemes[47] might have found that they were not in fact DB schemes (which would have meant that their members would no longer have been protected by the employer funding requirements applying to such schemes). For these reasons, relevant parts of the Pension Schemes Act 2015 were never brought into force.

[47] eg, the scheme referred to in *Aon Trust Corporation v KPMG* (n 26).

A new Pension Schemes Bill was introduced into Parliament on 15 October 2019. The purpose of Parts 1 and 2 of the Bill was to achieve the reform objective referred to above, ie, to allow pension schemes to become mutually owned providers of pensions in payment.[48] The Bill sought to achieve this by adding a new limb to the definition of money purchase benefits under section 181B of the Pension Schemes Act 1993, namely 'collective money purchase benefits'. In order to be a collective money purchase benefit, the benefit must be a 'qualifying benefit' established under a 'qualifying scheme'.

Under the Bill, the key requirement that must be satisfied for a benefit to be a 'qualifying benefit' is that the rate or amount of the benefit is subject to periodic adjustments designed to achieve a balance between the value of the available assets of the scheme and the amount expected to be required, applying appropriate actuarial assumptions, for the purpose of providing benefits under the scheme to or in respect of its membership collectively.[49] Importantly, given the intention to address the aspiration of 'DC savers … to a predictable, regular income in retirement', the qualifying benefits provided under a qualifying scheme must consist of or include the payment of a pension.

The Pension Schemes Bill received its first reading in the House of Lords on 15 October 2019. Like other legislation it fell when Parliament was dissolved on 6 November in advance of the December 2019 general election. However, a replacement Bill was introduced on 7 January 2020 and assuming relevant parts of that are ultimately enacted in their current form, we would be in a position where once again in the UK it will possible for an employer to sponsor an occupational pension plan which expresses and pays its benefits in the form of a pension for life but where: (i) members are not required to incur the cost of backing their pension for life by the purchase of an insurance company annuity at the moment of retirement; *and* (ii) employers are not required to underwrite the risk of investment underperformance in the scheme relative to assumptions, or increased benefit cost (for example, because of rising longevity).

C. How would this Work in Practice?

To think about how such a 'collective money purchase' scheme might work in practice in the UK, the detailed proposal for such a scheme which Royal Mail developed with the Communication Workers Union and published in November 2018 is potentially helpful.[50] Leaving aside the traditional defined benefit lump sum element of the

[48] As to 'mutual ownership', the legal form of such schemes is still expected to be a trust, as is customary for funded UK occupational pension plans. The legal ownership of scheme assets will reside in the plan's trustees, who will be subject to the same fiduciary obligations as other pension scheme trustees. But beneficial ownership of the plan's assets will reside entirely in the plan's members collectively; because the scheme can by definition never have a surplus, the reversionary interest of the plan sponsor, which is often preserved in a defined benefit plan, will never be relevant,

[49] It should be noted that this could still in theory lead to a risk of existing DB schemes being recharacterised as collective money purchase. However, that risk is expected to be covered off by appropriate secondary legislation.

[50] Royal Mail Group (RMG) and Communication Workers Union (CWU), 'Anticipated Collective Defined Contribution (CDC) Pension Design' (November 2018), available at: www.royalmailgroup.com/media/10542/scheme-design-summary-booklet.pdf.

Royal Mail proposal, the collective money purchase part of the scheme would, in summary, operate as follows:

a. Each year the employer and employees would make contributions to the collective money purchase part of the scheme. These would total 15.2 per cent of salary.
b. An active member in each year of service would be credited with a pension block of 1/80th of his pensionable pay in that year (subject always to adjustment as explained in sub-paragraphs (c), (d) and (e) below). This would be payable for life from the age of 67.
c. Each year, the scheme actuary would value the assets of the scheme as against the blocks of pensions so far credited (as adjusted to date under the increase/cut process described below) on a 'best estimate' basis. The actuary would then determine the percentage rate of increase which would, if assumed to apply to those accrued adjusted pension blocks over the expected future lives (working and non-working) of the members so far, render the value of those blocks equal to the market value of the assets in the scheme as at the effective date of the valuation. These would be the 'periodic adjustments' required by clause 2(1)(b) of the Pension Schemes Bill.
d. If the rate of increase determined under sub-paragraph (c) above were a positive number, that rate would be applied that year to all the adjusted accrued pension blocks and form part of them.
e. If, because of, for example, a significant fall in asset values or anticipated asset returns, or an increase in longevity expectations, at the effective date of the valuation the value of the accrued pension blocks were to exceed the market value of the assets even without granting any further increases, then a cut to all pension blocks would be required. The actuary would calculate the percentage cut, which if applied to all adjusted pension blocks so far accrued, would bring the value of the pension blocks in the scheme in line with the value of the assets in the scheme. That cut would then be immediately applied (with no discretion to 'hold over').
f. Regardless of what happened with the rebasing of existing blocks, active members would continue to be credited with new blocks of pension at the rate of 1/80th of their pensionable pay in the relevant year.
g. The rebasing process would be repeated each year, with active members continuing to be credited with a flat 1/80th of pensionable pay in each year of service. All increases and cuts would apply in the same way to active members in respect of their accrued blocks, pre-retiree leavers and pensioners.

Under the proposal, members would be free to 'opt out' of the fund at any time. A member who wishes to take a transfer out, would have their usual cash equivalent transfer value right under Part 4ZA of the Pension Schemes Act 1993. Transfer values would be calculated on a 'share of fund' basis, ie, they would be $\frac{L}{TL} \times A$, where:

- L is the value of the member's accrued pension blocks at the time of the transfer valuation calculation (allowing for all adjustments to date).

- TL is the value of all accrued blocks in the scheme at the time of the transfer value calculation (allowing for all adjustments to date).
- A is the value of the assets of the scheme at the time of the transfer value calculation.

Assets would be valued at market value, and pension blocks would be valued using the same 'best estimate' assumptions as used in the annual adjustment process.

D. Is this a 'Dutch-Style' CDC Scheme?

The question arises: how similar is Royal Mail's proposed 'collective money purchase' scheme to the Dutch CDC schemes described in section III above? As explained above, the starting context is different in that Dutch DB schemes permit benefits to be reduced if costs increase, even if the employer could afford to fund the increased cost. But even beyond that, there are some potentially important differences between Dutch CDC and UK 'collective money purchase' schemes of the type proposed by Royal Mail and its union and legislated for in the Pensions Schemes Bill 2019.

First, the Dutch CDC model overtly starts from a 'target' benefit, albeit expressed in conditional terms and subject to reduction where minimum required funding levels are not met. In contrast, while the Royal Mail CDC proposal may 'model' projected outturns, it does not make any presumption that in any one year that outturn will be delivered. On the contrary, it would be surprising if in any particular year the modelled long-term average outcome (revaluation and increases of 1 per cent per annum over the CPI on initial credits of 1/80th of pensionable pay) were precisely achieved. The 'fixed points' in the UK collective DC model are the rate of initial credit granted to members (1/80th of pensionable pay in that year), the rate of contributions paid by employer and employee, and the investment strategy of the scheme. Once these matters are set, the benefit outcomes for members will simply be what emerges from the annual valuation process described in the proposal, ie, as would be expected from a DC scheme, but arguably not quite what would be expected in the Netherlands. Importantly, and again unlike in the Netherlands, this outcome can lead to a greater increase than expected in one year as well as a lower increase (or a cut). This is consistent with the fact that, unlike the Dutch CDC model, the UK plan is not targeting a particular benefit. Instead, it proceeds on the basis that members get what they will, as they would do in a traditional UK individual DC plan, but determined collectively and expressed and paid in pension form, rather than as an individual DC savings 'pot' which is then drawn down on or converted into pension form through an annuity purchase.

Another point of contrast with the Netherlands is also linked to this 'non-target' nature of the UK plan, namely that the UK collective DC plan is expected to have, at least in high-level terms, an asset allocation strategy set out in its plan rules which the plan trustees are obliged to follow. In a collective money purchase scheme, member benefit outcomes will depend to a large degree on the investment performance of the scheme, and the strategic allocation of the scheme's investments as between reward-seeking assets and lower-risk investments could have intergenerational implications. However, section 33 of the UK Pensions Act 1995 expressly voids any form of exoneration provision in relation to trustee breach of any obligation to take care or exercise skill in the performance of any investment functions. Trustees of a collective money purchase scheme could therefore be placed in a difficult position if scheme rules do not circumscribe their investment powers by requiring them clearly to follow a set asset allocation approach. This should be an investment strategy that is consistent with the strategy assumed when the scheme's projected benefit outcomes were modelled. Having such a strategy that is clearly stated from the outset (albeit it will presumably prescribe whether the scheme's investments will de-risk as the scheme matures and if so how) may also be an important aspect of the scheme's transparency, which many commentators regard as critical to public confidence in such schemes in the UK.

We understand that the modelling which Royal Mail has commissioned shows that on average the scheme and contribution rates proposed would provide their 140,000-strong workforce with pensions equivalent to a career average pension of 1/80th of pensionable pay for each year of service revalued in deferment/indexed in payment at 1 per cent pa above the CPI. However, as stated above, this is not a 'target'. In a 'target' benefit scheme, if and to the extent there was more than required to meet the 'target', it would be logical to build up a reserve or to de-risk investments so as to reduce the future risk of undershooting that 'target'. This would have intergenerational implications. Instead, this scheme provides for automaticity of valuation outcomes; for good or bad, the rate of increase applied to all benefits in the year immediately following the relevant valuation will be whatever the valuation showed to be the long-term sustainable rate which, assumed to apply over the whole expected lives of the membership, would raise the value of scheme benefits so as to equal the value of the scheme's assets. This is also the reason for another expected point of difference between UK and Dutch CDC schemes; the UK schemes will conduct their valuations on a 'best estimate' basis rather than a 'prudent' basis. This means that liabilities will be valued using assumptions which the actuary considers to be 50:50, in other words as likely to turn out overly conservative as to turn out overly optimistic. By definition, a 'prudent' approach to valuation (such as DB plans are required to use) would mean that the actuary considered that the assumptions were more likely than not to be over-reserving for pension payments. Thus, a 'prudent' approach to valuation necessarily involves holding back something from one generation in case it is needed for a future generation.

Clearly, as a matter of luck it could be that one generation ends up doing better than another because of how investment markets or longevity expectations operate at one particular time. That is accepted as an unavoidable feature of any long-term arrangement. What the scheme design is intended to minimise so far as possible is not these questions of luck, but rather issues of inherent bias. Similarly, the intention is to minimise trustee discretion so far as possible: hence the requirement for clear rules at the outset for determining the initial rate at which blocks are credited and when and how those blocks would then increase or be cut if necessary. There will always be areas of actuarial judgement, but the intention is that by stipulating 'best estimate' as the valuation basis the number of variables is reduced.

As well as automaticity, one further area of difference is that UK collective DC schemes will have annual valuations feeding immediately through into benefit increases or cuts, rather than potentially permitting up to five years of 'wait and see' before adverse experience feeds through into benefit reductions. This, coupled with the fact that unlike Dutch CDC schemes, UK collective money purchase schemes are absolutely intended to have employer (and employee) contribution rates which are fixed for the long term (rather than just the five years recommended by the Dutch Central Bank), serves to demonstrate the 'DC' rather than 'DB' roots of the UK collective DC project. The hope of UK employers and policy-makers is that this will also help to make the 'no-guarantees' nature of the scheme clear to employees, so that if benefits have to be cut in the future, any arguments that the scheme was mis-sold to them can be avoided.

E. Has the UK Approach Learned from the Dutch Experience?

It appears that some difficulties have arisen with Dutch CDC plans, which the UK proposals for collective money purchase schemes should be able to avoid. The first seems to have arisen because of a misperception on the part of members, who believed that their pensions were 'guaranteed', when the legal reality of the schemes was that they afforded no such guarantee.[51] In contrast, in the UK, the Department for Work and Pensions has always been clear that transparent member communications will be extremely important. The Pension Schemes Bill addresses this concern by providing that it will be an offence to operate a collective money purchase scheme without due authorisation from the Pensions Regulator. It also stipulates as one of the criteria for determining authorisation that the Pensions Regulator be satisfied that the scheme has adequate systems and processes for communicating with members and others, including adequate systems and processes for securing the information provided is correct and not misleading. It is expected that the matters which will need to be covered in such communications will be of the non-guaranteed nature of benefits, and that this is something which the Pensions Regulator will expect schemes to make explicit to members when they first join and to remind them of that each year as part of the annual exercise of communicating to members what level of increase (or cut) is to be applied for their accrued benefits for that year.

It is also relevant to note that in the Netherlands, membership of a particular occupational pension scheme can be made a compulsory term of employment. Where that scheme requires member contributions, this can lead to a position where members are forced to pay into schemes which they do not feel are right for them. This appears to have led to particular concerns from younger members, who feel that by pensioning older and younger members in the same amount the scheme is inter-generationally unfair because it does not take into account the fact that, allowing

[51] In the Netherlands the *AKZO Nobel* case is quite famous. See, eg: www. ipe.com/countries/netherlands/unions-to-strike-at-akzonobel-over-400m-pension-payment-demand/www.ipe.com/countries/netherlands/unions-to-strike-at-akzonobel-over-400m-pension-payment-demand/10025667.fullarticle.

for assumed investment returns, the younger member's benefit may be significantly cheaper than that of the older member. The UK CDC scheme – at least on the Royal Mail model – seems to share this element of cross-generational subsidy. However, the broader UK context is, of course, critically different in that if employees do not wish to join their employer's collective money purchase plan, they can choose not to. Instead they can pay their contributions to their own individual DC plans and avoid this element of (potential) cross-subsidy. They will then benefit from statutory transfer value rights, with transfer values calculated as described above.

V. CONCLUSION

There are of course similarities between UK collective money purchase schemes and Dutch CDC schemes. However, the authors would argue that there are also significant differences between them. These may derive from the fact that the two arrangements were devised in answer to different questions.

In the Netherlands, CDC developed in response to the impact of international accounting standards. There was a need to clarify to auditors that the post-retirement benefits being provided by large Dutch multinationals could properly be accounted for as DC schemes on the corporate balance sheet rather than scheme deficits that would need to appear as a company liability. However, legally Dutch CDC involves the provision of what in the Netherlands would be seen as defined benefits. This is confusing, and such confusion should be avoided in this jurisdiction.

In the UK, by contrast, the defined benefits ship is seen as largely having already sailed. UK employers are now unlikely to establish a new DB scheme, whatever name it is given. But it seems clear that individual DC plans in the UK are at significant risk of not providing adequate member retirement outcomes. This in turn could cause issues for employers from a workforce planning perspective (the need to give employees sufficient post-employment financial security to enable them to feel confident to retire), as well as potential industrial relations issues. For these reasons, the UK collective DC project has developed in an effort to 'fix' the potential issues with individual DC.

The differential roots of CDC are, we would argue, clear in several elements of difference between the UK collective DC project and its Dutch equivalent. If these differences are properly communicated, it may mean that the non-guaranteed nature of CDC in the UK can be more readily understood by employees in the UK than it has been in the Netherlands.

3

The Employer Covenant: Status in Law and Operation in Practice

PAUL BRICE*

I. INTRODUCTION

FOLLOWING THE INTRODUCTION of the scheme-specific funding regime for UK defined benefit pension schemes in the Pensions Act 2004 (the Act), in its guidance to scheme trustees and advisers the then recently established UK Pensions Regulator (TPR) placed considerable emphasis on understanding and taking account of the 'Employer Covenant' in scheme funding decisions and corporate transactions. That emphasis on the importance of the Employer Covenant remains.[1] Early regulatory guidance around the Employer Covenant required trustees and advisers to assess the 'willingness and ability' of sponsoring employers to meet their funding obligations to defined benefit pension schemes. The initial emphasis on 'willingness and ability' changed to 'legal obligation and financial ability' in subsequent guidance.[2] This regulatory emphasis on the Employer Covenant acted as a catalyst for the development of a new discipline of specialist financial and legal advice to scheme trustees and sponsoring employers, which is now provided by a broad range of firms including accountancy firms, specialist advisory firms, actuarial firms and

* I am grateful to Sinéad Agnew, Daniel Schaffer, Paul Burnett, Phil Green and Tim Birkett for their comments on this chapter. This chapter is designed to provide a high level, non-exhaustive overview of the legal and regulatory provisions surrounding the 'Employer Covenant' (as defined in this chapter); and to describe a number of practical issues connected to the evaluation and use of the Employer Covenant in practice. This chapter does not purport to be a comprehensive analysis of, or advice in relation to, the legal and regulatory provisions surrounding, or connected with, the Employer Covenant, nor of its operation in practice. Readers of this chapter should seek independent legal and financial advice in relation to Employer Covenant matters of relevance to them or organisations which they represent. The author expressly disclaims all responsibility to third parties reading this chapter who read it entirely at their own risk.

[1] See, eg, the emphasis on Employer Covenant: The Pensions Regulator, 'Annual Funding Statement 2019 for Defined Benefit Pension Schemes' (March 2019), available at: www.thepensionsregulator.gov.uk/-/media/thepensionsregulator/files/import/pdf/db-annual-funding-statement-2019.ashx.

[2] See The Pensions Regulator, 'Assessing and Monitoring the Employer Covenant' (August 2015), available at: www.thepensionsregulator.gov.uk/en/document-library/regulatory-guidance/assessing-and-monitoring-the-employer-covenant.

pensions lawyers. During the period following the Act, the emphasis on the Employer Covenant in scheme funding regulatory guidance, and in the political debate around defined benefit pension scheme funding and employer support, has grown, particularly in the light of a series of corporate failures which have left substantial scheme funding shortfalls.

Against this backcloth, this chapter seeks to provide a synopsis of the legal status of the Employer Covenant and its operation in practice, and is structured as follows: first, it explores definitions of the Employer Covenant. Second, it considers – in outline – the legal relationship between sponsoring employers and pension schemes both in general terms and in terms of the nature of the creditor relationship between employers and schemes. Third, it considers the role of the Employer Covenant in practice in scheme funding decisions, including its integration with other elements of scheme funding. Fourth, it considers the role of the Employer Covenant in corporate transactions and structuring, including the application of statutory 'moral hazard' regimes. Fifth, it considers issues connected with the Pension Protection Fund (PPF). Finally, before drawing its conclusions, it looks at two key current developments where the Employer Covenant is likely to be relevant: pension consolidation vehicles (colloquially known as 'superfunds'); and the impact on schemes of climate change.

II. WHAT IS THE EMPLOYER COVENANT?

The concept of the Employer Covenant is principally relevant to UK defined benefit pension schemes. In its regulatory guidance on the Employer Covenant, TPR states that '[T]he covenant is the extent of the employer's legal obligation and financial ability to support the scheme now and in the future.'[3] According to the Employer Covenant Practitioners Association (ECPA),[4] the 'ability to support the scheme' can be distilled further into 'an employer's ability to put cash (or other assets that can be converted to cash) into a pension scheme when needed'.[5] The legal framework surrounding the Employer Covenant, and its operation in practice, is discussed below.

III. THE EMPLOYER COVENANT: BASIC LEGAL FRAMEWORK

To understand the application of the Employer Covenant in practice, it is necessary first to consider the key elements of the relevant legal framework in which it operates.[6] These include: the core legal relationship between a single employer and a scheme; the funding obligations of employers to schemes, including the involvement of employers in scheme funding decisions, and how the 'Employer Covenant'

[3] ibid.

[4] For details of the Association, see: www.ecpa.org.uk.

[5] See: Employer Covenant Practitioners Association, 'Principles of Covenant Assessment for Scheme Valuations: A Practical Guide for Advisors, Trustees and Sponsors' (March 2016) 4, available at: ecpa.org.uk/publications.html.

[6] The author emphasises that this synopsis is non-exhaustive and simply designed to provide a high-level overview of relevant provisions.

is relevant to determining those obligations; the Employer Covenant in the context of multi-employer schemes; and the nature of the creditor relationship between employers and schemes. Each of these is discussed in turn below.

A. The Core Legal Relationship between a Single Employer and a Scheme

In the first instance, a legal relationship between a single employer and a defined benefit pension scheme (and, as a consequence, the employer's statutory and contractual obligations to the scheme) arises consequent to the employer's execution of an appropriate Deed of Participation in the scheme, and the provisions of the scheme's trust deed and rules.

In the context of the Employer Covenant, this relationship imposes obligations upon the employer to make contributions to the scheme[7] subject to various statutory provisions and the terms of the Trust Deed and Rules. It creates a creditor relationship between the employer and the scheme for sums due and payable, for example, under a Schedule of Contributions. And it gives rise to a requirement to comply with various statutory obligations, including – amongst other matters – prescribed bases for calculating deficits upon the insolvency of the employer[8] which need to be met by the employer (to the extent the employer is able to do so).

As a separate matter, employer insolvency, and whether there is a 'qualifying insolvency event' in relation to an employer sponsoring an 'eligible scheme', are relevant factors for the purposes of determining entry into the PPF under Chapter 3 of Part 2 of the Act.

B. Funding Obligations of Employers to Schemes: Overview

The present funding regime applicable to UK defined benefit pension schemes is the 'scheme-specific' regime reflected in the EU Directive known as 'IORP 1'[9] and enacted in UK domestic legislation through the Act.

Part 3 of the Act incorporates a statutory funding objective for schemes,[10] and provides, amongst other matters, for the basis upon which 'technical provisions' (scheme-specific actuarial liabilities) are to be calculated,[11] together with the basis upon which actuarial valuations are to be conducted,[12] and how any recovery plan to make good a deficit arising is to be determined and agreed.[13] In relation to the

[7] Noting that some schemes operate on a 'shared cost' basis with contributions shared between sponsoring employers and scheme members.

[8] eg, a debt arising under s 75 of the Pensions Act 1995 (a 'section 75 debt') upon 'an insolvency event in relation to the employer'.

[9] Directive 2003/41/EC of the European Parliament and of the Council of 3 June 2003 on the activities and supervision of institutions for occupational retirement provision [2003] OJ L235/10.

[10] Pensions Act 2004, s 222.

[11] ibid s 222(2)–(4).

[12] ibid ss 224–25.

[13] ibid s 226.

statutory funding objective, section 222(1) of the Act stipulates that: 'Every scheme is subject to a requirement ("the statutory funding objective") that it must have sufficient and appropriate assets to cover its technical provisions'.[14]

It follows that to meet the statutory funding objective, employers are required[15] to make contributions to schemes that they sponsor on an ongoing basis, either to provide for the ongoing accrual of benefits or to make good any actuarial deficit under a recovery plan. Section 229(1) and (2) of the Act provide for the involvement of the employer in various aspects of scheme funding decisions.

Although the Employer Covenant is the subject of numerous guidance publications by TPR – including, for example, its code of practice on funding defined benefits[16] (Code of Practice No 3) and certain secondary legislation,[17] it is not referred to at all in the Act. In terms of ongoing scheme funding, the concept and application of the Employer Covenant seems to derive its legal basis from a combination of other sources. Regulation 15 of The Occupational Pension Schemes (Scheme Funding) Regulations 2005, SI 2005/3377 (Regulation 15) provides a link between the scheme funding requirements in Part 3 of the Act (in particular, the basis upon which technical provisions are to be set) and Code of Practice No 3. It specifies that a scheme actuary (a statutory appointment under the Act) shall have regard to guidance issued by the Financial Reporting Council (FRC). The FRC's guidance states that: '[I]n giving relevant advice the actuary must have regard to [Code of Practice 3] and any other relevant guidance on funding defined benefits issued by the Regulator'.[18] The Employer Covenant also derives its legal status from: the obligations of an employer to fund a scheme consequent to participation under a scheme's trust deed and rules; the general obligations of the employer as creditor of a scheme for specific debts, such as payments due under a schedule of contributions; and the specific obligations of employers to schemes on events such as insolvency where a debt arising under section 75 of the Pensions Act 1995 (a 'section 75 debt') becomes due.

Besides ongoing scheme funding, there are specific legislative provisions which involve changes to the strength of the Employer Covenant as a consequence of certain transactions or where schemes are sponsored by 'service companies' or are 'insufficiently resourced'. These are discussed in part V below.

[14] s 222(2) provides that 'A scheme's "technical provisions" means the amount required, on an actuarial calculation, to make provision for the scheme's liabilities'.

[15] Noting again that some schemes operate on a 'shared cost' basis with contributions shared between sponsoring employers and scheme members.

[16] The Pensions Regulator, 'Code of Practice No 3: Funding Defined Benefits' (July 2014), available at: www.thepensionsregulator.gov.uk/-/media/thepensionsregulator/files/import/pdf/code-03-funding-defined-benefits.

[17] The term does appear in secondary legislation including, eg, in subsection 6(h)(ii) of Regulation 6F in the deferred debt provisions introduced by The Occupational Pension Schemes (Employer Debt and Miscellaneous Amendments) Regulations 2018, SI 2018/237. These Regulations amend The Occupational Pension Schemes (Employer Debt) Regulations 2005, SI 2005/678.

[18] Financial Reporting Council, 'Guidance Note GN49: Occupational Pension Schemes – Scheme Funding Matters on which Advice of Actuary Must be Obtained', para 2.2, available at: www.frc.org.uk/getattachment/1e1f0f6c-404b-4873-b413-07e43efe59d9/GN49-Occupational-Pension-Schemes-—-Scheme-funding-matters-cease-to-apply.pdf.

C. The Employer Covenant in the Context of Multi-Employer Schemes

Where more than one employer sponsors a scheme, a number of complexities arise in considering the strength of the Employer Covenant. These relate to: how to form a view of Employer Covenant strength for schemes sponsored by a diverse range of associated or non-associated employers; how to assess the strength of the Employer Covenant when there is a risk that one or more employers depart the scheme; and how to assess the implications for the Employer Covenant of various scheme restructuring options in line with statutory requirements.

Multi-employer schemes broadly fall into two categories: associated multi-employer schemes (where all employers are members of the same ownership group); and non-associated multi-employer schemes (where the employers are not connected with each other in any common ownership sense). Non-associated multi-employer schemes are typically industry-wide, non-sectionalised schemes formed to provide pensions for a wide cohort of people working in that industry. In this way, they differ from industry-wide sectionalised, or segregated, schemes where employers sponsoring each 'section' typically have full funding responsibility for that section but no others. A full analysis of the statutory provisions governing multi-employer schemes and the respective obligations of historic, current and departing employers, together with the comprehensive body of case law[19] in this area, is beyond the scope of this chapter.[20] However, it comments on the three complexities identified above.

When attempting to form a view of Employer Covenant strength for schemes sponsored by a diverse range of non-associated employers, complexities arise due to the diverse nature and scale of the employer population and the 'last man standing' basis of many multi-employer schemes. In the latter case, the ultimate obligation to fund the scheme rests on the last sponsoring employer supporting the scheme (where the others have either become insolvent or ceased participation). One option for assessing Employer Covenant strength can be to consider a 'weighted average' assessment of the covenant strength of the relevant employers – although the actual approach adopted will be scheme-specific.

In terms of considering Employer Covenant strength when there is a risk that one or more employers might leave the scheme, the precise provisions governing an employer's ability to leave will be governed by the trust deed and rules and relevant statutory provisions. Judgement is required in assessing the strength of the Employer Covenant supporting such schemes. Account must be taken of a diverse range of employer support and the possibility of different employers departing the scheme at different times.

Specific problems can arise in associated multi-employer schemes where there are 'Employer Cessation Events':[21] very broadly, in multi-employer schemes, an employer

[19] eg, *PNPF Trust Co Ltd v Taylor* [2010] EWHC 1573 (Ch), [2010] Pens LR 261.

[20] Summary guidance around departures from multi-employer schemes, including references to decided cases, is provided by TPR: see The Pensions Regulator, 'Multi-Employer Schemes and Scheme Departures' (July 2012), available at: www.thepensionsregulator.gov.uk/en/document-library/regulatory-guidance/multi-employer-schemes-and-employer-departures.

[21] Set out in reg 6ZA of The Occupational Pension Schemes (Employer Debt) Regulations 2005, SI 2005/678.

may settle its obligations to a scheme upon the occurrence of an Employer Cessation Event whereby they cease to employ any active members of the scheme when at least one other employer employs active members.[22] In this case, they will generally be obliged to pay their attributable share of any section 75 debt, subject to deferral arrangements introduced in 2018.[23]

In Employer Covenant evaluation terms, understanding the likelihood and impact of employer departures is crucial. Consider a scheme which has two associated employers, A and B. A is financially strong but employs a single active member and has 20 deferred members and pensioners. B is financially weak, but employs 500 active members and has 2,000 deferred members and pensioners. The financial strength of A and B together on a combined basis may seem strong. However, subject to any counter-provisions in the scheme's trust deed and rules and to any relevant statutory provisions, A may be able to discharge itself from its obligations to the scheme upon its sole active member ceasing to be active by settling its (in this example, comparatively modest) cessation debt. If A chooses to do this, it would leave B, the financially weaker employer, to support the balance of the scheme in its entirety going forward. Extreme care is therefore needed before attributing material employer covenant strength to an employer which might leave the scheme in the short to medium term for modest cost.

Finally, the legal nature of the relationship between employer and scheme, together with an understanding of Employer Covenant strength, is also relevant when considering the impact of both corporate transactions and scheme restructuring options[24] such as Flexible Apportionment Arrangements (FAAs)[25] whereby an employer's obligations to support a scheme are apportioned to another employer. FAAs are subject to a 'funding test', including the requirement that the remaining employers will be 'reasonably likely to fund the scheme'.[26] This means that an evaluation of the covenant of the remaining employers will be required before a decision to proceed with the FAA can be taken.

D. The Nature of the Creditor Relationship between Employers and Schemes

On the basis that the relationship between the employer and the scheme is one which gives rise to either an ongoing funding obligation to meet the scheme's statutory funding objective or, where relevant, a section 75 debt, then wherever there are debts due from the employer to the scheme these debts are usually unsecured.

[22] Conditions stipulated in reg 6ZA(1)(c)(i) and (ii) of The Occupational Pension Schemes (Employer Debt) Regulations 2005, SI 2005/678.

[23] See reg 6F of The Occupational Pension Schemes (Employer Debt and Miscellaneous Amendments) Regulations 2018, SI 2018/237, amending the Occupational Pension Schemes (Scheme Debt) Regulations 2005, SI 2005/678.

[24] The full range of scheme restructuring options is not considered in this chapter. For a summary, see TPR, 'Multi-Employer Schemes and Scheme Departures' (n 20).

[25] The legislation for FAAs is set out in reg 6E of The Occupational Pension Schemes (Employer Debt) Regulations 2005, SI 2005/678.

[26] For details of the funding test, see reg 2 4A of The Occupational Pension Schemes (Employer Debt) Regulations 2005, SI 2005/678.

Debts due and payable under the relationship need to reflect specific contractual or statutory obligations: for example, contributions due under an agreed schedule of contributions, or a debt arising under section 75. Absent the scheme being wound up, trustees cannot usually seek to 'create' a creditor position by calculating an arbitrary deficit between triennial valuations by reflecting movements in investment values or changing actuarial and economic assumptions. That said, a valuation between scheduled triennial valuation dates can be called in some circumstances.

Given the actuarial basis of funding used to determine section 75 liabilities, it can often be the case in an insolvency that a section 75 scheme claim represents by far the largest unsecured creditor in an insolvent estate, and this may substantially dilute the claims of other unsecured creditors.

An exception to the unsecured creditor relationship arises where, as part of Employer Covenant enhancement discussions, the employer or a member of the employer's group grants security over one or more assets so as to provide support for the Employer Covenant. In this case, the scheme will rank as a secured creditor on any insolvency up to the level of the security provided, and in accordance with the relevant statutory 'waterfall' of creditor priorities under the insolvency and any agreed inter-creditor arrangements.

Although disclosed as liabilities, deficits disclosed for accounting purposes under applicable accounting standards such as IAS19 have no legal enforceability as creditor relationships as they do not reflect amounts actually due and payable under a schedule of contributions. The calculation of funding positions under international accounting standards is undertaken in a manner which seeks to provide consistency and comparability between enterprises so as to assist users of financial statements. To this end, liabilities are broadly discounted using the yield on a High Quality Corporate Bond[27] as at the accounting reference date.

IV. THE EMPLOYER COVENANT IN PRACTICE: ONGOING SCHEME FUNDING

Building on the high-level legal commentary above, this section considers aspects of the assessment and application of the Employer Covenant in practice.

A. The Basis for Assessing the Employer Covenant

In its guidance on the Employer Covenant,[28] TPR suggests that covenant assessments should focus on the following three key areas:

1. **The employer's legal obligations to the scheme** – the strength of the covenant depends on the nature and enforceability of the legal agreements in place to support the scheme.

[27] The yield on a High Quality Corporate Bond is commonly interpreted to be that on a corporate bond rated 'AA' or higher.

[28] See 'Assessing and Monitoring the Employer Covenant' (n 2) s 2, 16 (emphasis in original).

2. **The funding needs and investment risk of the scheme** – the strength of the employer and its ability to meet its obligations should be viewed in the context of the scheme's size, funding position, exposure to investment risk and maturity.
3. **The financial support from the employer and any other entities which materially affect the covenant by virtue of their relationship to the employer** – the strength of the covenant depends on the likelihood of these legal obligations being met now and in the future.

Trustees commonly – but not always – commission an external assessment of the Employer Covenant by a specialist firm. The scope of that assessment may vary depending on the nature of the employer's business, the complexity of the group structure, and the nature and scale of pension obligations supported by the employer and its group. Employers may sponsor more than one scheme, which means that the assessment will need to consider the risks attached to multiple schemes. Any assessment of the Employer Covenant should be proportionate to the scale and risks of the scheme sponsored by the employer(s).

As the ECPA observes,[29] '[f]unding pensions is ultimately a "cashflow business" where the inflows come from contributions, investment returns and investment realisations and the outflows are payments of benefits to members and scheme expenses'. The ability of an employer to generate cash available for a scheme is what truly underpins the 'financial ability' element of the Employer Covenant, and an assessment of this ability underpins much of the analysis undertaken in forming a view of Employer Covenant strength.

An employer might generate cash to be injected into a pension scheme from a variety of sources. First, cash generated from trading might be assumed to be available for pension scheme funding. In practice, however, employers may have other obligations to be financed from the cash generated from trading, including the need to invest in capital expenditure to sustain and grow their businesses, payments due by way of interest or principal to third-party lenders, tax payments, or dividend expectations to sustain the support of equity investors. The tension between financing pension obligations and paying dividends presents a complex moral hazard which is discussed further in part V below.

Second, employers may have surplus cash or other assets, or assets which can be financed in other ways compared with outright ownership (for example, the sale and leaseback of freehold properties). Subject to any tax consequences and other associated expenses, these assets could be realised with a view to generating cash which might be injected into a pension scheme. Third, an employer may be able to borrow money, perhaps on an intra-group basis, to generate cash to inject into a scheme. Finally, in addition to intra-group borrowings, group companies may facilitate the injection of cash into pension schemes through structures such as Asset-Backed Lending (ABL) structures. They might also provide contingent support in the form of guarantees for example.

Whilst the past may be a useful point of reference when considering trading results, future cash generation will support ongoing scheme funding. Looking forward to the

[29] See 'Principles of Covenant Assessment for Scheme Valuations' (n 5).

future will involve some evaluation of likely corporate longevity and market positioning, whilst recognising that predictions in either area can be extremely challenging. In an environment of rapid technological and other disruption, 'today's winners can be gone tomorrow'. Therefore, it is vital for trustees and their advisers, when forming views over long-term future trading cash generation, to understand the market in which a sponsoring employer operates and the likely future position of the employer in that market. There is a range of tools for understanding possible corporate longevity and strategic positioning.

One piece of analysis often undertaken, particularly where there is a risk of employer insolvency, is an Estimated Outcome Statement (EOS) which seeks to form a view of the extent to which a section 75 debt arising on insolvency might be covered by net assets in an insolvency process. Considerable care is needed to ensure that EOSs are realistic and take into account the fact that employers can often absorb cash and other assets in their fight for survival prior to insolvency, and may increase their liabilities through additional borrowings. It is also important to note that asset realisation values can be disappointing when markets are depressed or where speed of realisation is of the essence. Other contingent liabilities – such as other guarantees, bonds, and lease obligations – might also crystallise on insolvency, and these need to be considered in any analysis.

B. Metrics of Employer Covenant Strength

Various professional firms and TPR have each developed 'rating scales' which attribute an assessment of strength of an employer's covenant. By way of example, TPR classifies Employer Covenant strength in accordance with the following 'four-grade' scale:[30]

Covenant Grade 1 (CG1) – Strong

Very strong trading, cash generation and asset position relative to the size of the scheme and the scheme's deficit. The employer has a strong market presence (or is a market leader) with good growth prospects for the employer and the market. The scheme has good access to trading and value if the employer is part of a wider group. Overall low risk of the employer not being able to support the scheme to the extent required in the short/medium term.

Covenant Grade 2 (CG2) – Tending to Strong

Good trading, cash generation and asset position relative to the size of the scheme and deficits. Operates in a market with a reasonably positive outlook and the employer

[30] The Pensions Regulator, 'Defined Benefit Regulatory and Enforcement Policy' (June 2014) App B, available at: www.thepensionsregulator.gov.uk/-/media/thepensionsregulator/files/import/pdf/db-funding-regulatory-enforcement-policy.ashx.

has a stable market share. Outlook is generally positive but medium-term risk of employer not being able to support the scheme and manage its risks.

Covenant Grade 3 (CG3) – Tending to Weak

Concerns over employer strength relative to the size of the scheme and deficit and/or signs of significant decline, weak profitability or balance sheet concerns and/or high vulnerability to economic cycle. No immediate concerns over insolvency but potential risk of decline.

Covenant Grade 4 (CG4) – Weak

Employer is weak, to the degree that there are concerns over potential insolvency, or where the scheme is so large that, without fundamental change to the strength of the employer, it is unlikely ever to be in a position to adequately support the scheme.

C. Scheme Funding Needs, Investment Risks and Gearing Effects

In evaluating the strength of the Employer Covenant, it is important to consider the employer's cash-generating ability relative to the size of the scheme it supports ('the gearing effect'), and the investment risk that the scheme carries in its investment strategy.

In the context of scheme funding decisions, the Employer Covenant evaluation plays a crucial role in determining the likely level of available contributions to a scheme. For the purposes of an actuarial valuation, the trustees, working with the scheme actuary and the sponsoring employer(s), need to agree a schedule of contributions which takes account of the projected scheme liabilities, anticipated investment returns and realisations, and scheme costs (unless met directly by the employer). As a general rule, higher expected returns from investments are usually accompanied by higher risk. For example, equities may offer superior returns to gilts over the long term but – depending on time horizons – may also be accompanied by higher degrees of price and return volatility. At actuarial valuations, a scheme's assets are valued on a 'mark-to-market' basis. Absent a compensatory movement in scheme liabilities, any major investment market downturn as at the valuation date can result in a substantial funding deficit which needs to be addressed by additional cash contributions through a recovery plan. Against this background, trustees need to be satisfied that the strength of the Employer Covenant is adequate to support the prospective funding requirements of the scheme should the performance of the investment portfolio move off-plan or other actuarial assumptions change.

Scheme gearing effects are best illustrated by two examples of different schemes which might be sponsored by Company A, an employer with a stable and predictable annual free cash-generating ability available to fund the pension scheme of £10 million. Scheme 1 has assets of £10 million, is well funded with no deficit on a technical provisions (ie, ongoing) basis of scheme liability calculation, and is invested in moderately low-risk assets which are likely to display low to moderate levels of price and return volatility. In these circumstances, the likely funding requirements of the scheme under a downturn, net of any compensatory liability movements, are likely to be comfortably met by the company's available annual free cash flow to fund the pension scheme of £10 million. Put simply, all other things being equal, the Employer Covenant is strong. Scheme 2 has assets of £500 million, is well funded with no deficit on a technical provisions basis, and is invested in similar low-to-moderate risk assets. However, in these circumstances, any asset price volatility, net of any compensatory liability movements, is likely to have a much greater negative effect given the scale of the scheme. The position compared with Scheme 1 is more geared to modest movements in a large pool of assets. All other things being equal, therefore, Company A's Employer Covenant strength will be greater in respect of Scheme 1 than Scheme 2.

D. Integrated Funding and Integrated Risk Management

Building on the comments above, it follows that reconciling an analysis of the strength of the Employer Covenant with different risk and return profiles of possible investment strategies and potential funding requirements requires careful scenario analysis and the collaborative work of experienced professionals from all disciplines (known as 'integrated funding'). The process of evaluating and managing the tripartite risks of the Employer Covenant, investment strategies and funding requirements underpins Integrated Risk Management (IRM) by trustees and their advisers. TPR has placed significant emphasis on IRM in its guidance:[31] this guidance stresses that one of the key risks in IRM discussions is an evaluation of the strength of, and risks associated with, the Employer Covenant.[32]

E. Financial Support from Other Entities

As discussed above, absent enforceable security, a scheme is an unsecured creditor of a sponsoring employer. Further, notwithstanding its membership of a wider group of companies, without legally binding support, the scheme can legally only look to the employer's cash generation ability and asset strength to support the scheme.

There may be circumstances where sponsoring employers wish to enhance their covenant to a scheme, perhaps to facilitate a more 'on risk' investment strategy by the scheme than the trustees would otherwise be comfortable with. This may require less cash to be injected directly into the scheme by the sponsoring employer itself in the first instance but would be clearly subject to financing any future investment downturns.

[31] See, eg, The Pensions Regulator, 'Regulatory Guidance: Integrated Risk Management' (December 2015), available at: www.thepensionsregulator.gov.uk/en/document-library/regulatory-guidance/integrated-risk-management.

[32] ibid para 26.

The covenant position of the sponsoring employer can be enhanced through legally binding support in various ways. For example, guarantees can be obtained from financially strong guarantors such as substantial parent companies. Trustees and their advisers need to take care when deciding on the nature and level of guarantees. For example, a short-dated guarantee with a financial cap (perhaps limited to payments due under a recovery plan) is likely to be of considerably less support to the Employer Covenant than an uncapped, 'evergreen' guarantee covering all liabilities up to and including a section 75 debt. Indeed, short-dated guarantees risk creating 'cliff edge' effects if there is a risk that they can expire whilst still leaving a substantially underfunded position. Furthermore, asset security in favour of a scheme can improve realisations available to a scheme on the insolvency of an employer, but care needs to be taken when evaluating the extent to which the security enhances the Employer Covenant. It is important to be realistic about the likely net disposal proceeds from the secured asset, the circumstances in which the security can be called, and the time taken to realise those proceeds in a market which the insolvency of the employer might signal is depressed. Loan subordination arrangements (whereby liabilities such as inter-company debts are made subordinate to the claims of the scheme in insolvency) and negative pledges (prohibiting, for example, security being granted to third parties or the payment of dividends) may also be possible. And of course, it is always possible to seek external support such as bank letters of credit, which may be drawable on payment default or insolvency. But here again, care needs to be taken with instruments such as these to avoid 'cliff edge' effects from the expiry of short-dated support. More complex support structures such as asset-backed arrangements might seek to generate cash for the scheme from an income stream from another company within the sponsoring employer's group.

The extent to which such enhancement options might strengthen an employer's covenant will clearly be circumstance-specific. It is important that trustees have directly enforceable rights over any enhancements when giving credit for them. By way of example, an inter-company debt due from a parent to an employer may seem to provide a degree of enhanced balance sheet strength for the employer, but if the debt is long-dated (rather than being 'on demand') it may prove challenging for the directors of the sponsoring employer to draw down on it, and impossible for trustees to force the drawdown themselves.

F. Monitoring the Employer Covenant

The nature of the Employer Covenant is dynamic: markets and businesses change, there is often a high turnover of personnel, and strategic transactions by competitors – such as major mergers – can leave hitherto strong companies trailing from a once dominant market position. TPR emphasises that monitoring developments in the strength of the Employer Covenant is often a vital action for trustees and their advisers.[33] However, the nature and scale of this monitoring needs to be proportionate given the relative scale of the employer and scheme.

[33] See 'Assessing and Monitoring the Employer Covenant' (n 2) s 3.

V. CORPORATE TRANSACTIONS AND MORAL HAZARD ISSUES

A. Introduction

In as much as the Employer Covenant can be enhanced through the provision of additional support of the types described above, it can also be weakened by a range of corporate actions. For example, the sponsoring employer may dispose of a major part of its business and 'upstream' cash within its corporate group out of reach of the pension scheme. Alternatively, it may grant security over assets to third parties in a way which reduces likely recoveries by a scheme on the employer's insolvency, perhaps in conjunction with increased financial leverage; or it may pay material dividends which weaken its balance sheet and cash position, particularly where a scheme is underfunded. The Employer Covenant can also be weakened where an employer makes a substantial but risky acquisition, particularly one which is financially leveraged and where security is granted to lenders ranking ahead of the scheme, which reduces available cash flow to a scheme for a period of time, and relies upon a series of assumptions (for example, business synergies) to deliver longer-term value.

TPR has provided guidance for scheme trustees and employers in relation to evaluating the impact on an employer's covenant of undertaking corporate transactions.[34] The guidance essentially requires them to form a view as to whether a transaction has resulted in 'detriment' to the strength of the Employer Covenant. Very broadly, if such 'material detriment' arises and the scheme has a 'relevant deficit', then trustees should seek 'mitigation' to compensate for the detriment.

The Act contains a number of 'moral hazard' provisions. Two sets of provisions are of particular importance: those which may allow TPR to issue a Contribution Notice to restore a scheme's financial strength in circumstances of 'material detriment'; and those which may allow TPR to issue a Financial Support Direction.[35] Details of examples where TPR has exercised its powers and imposed Contribution Notices or Financial Support Directions have been provided on their website in response to a 2017 Freedom Of Information request.[36]

B. Contribution Notices

Under the provisions of sections 38–42 of the Act, and subject to a statutory defence in section 38B,[37] TPR can issue a Contribution Notice to an employer, or a person connected with, or an associate of the employer, requiring them to contribute to the scheme (trustees) or, where relevant, the PPF. The potential amount of the

[34] Eg, The Pensions Regulator, 'Corporate Transactions' (June 2009), available at: www.thepensionsregulator.gov.uk/en/document-library/regulatory-guidance/corporate-transactions.

[35] ss 52–56 Pensions Act 2004 deal with transactions between an employer and a scheme at an undervalue, and the ability of TPR to issue, eg, a Restoration Order. These are not considered in detail here.

[36] See The Pensions Regulator, 'Details of TPR's Anti-Avoidance Investigations' (FOI 2017-01-25, 25 January 2017), available at: www.thepensionsregulator.gov.uk/en/about-us/freedom-of-information-(foi)/recently-released-information/details-of-tprs-anti-avoidance-investigations.

[37] Introduced in the Pensions Act 2008.

Contribution Notice is described in section 39: under section 39(1), the amount 'may be either the whole or a specified part of the shortfall sum in relation to the Scheme'.

Under section 38(3), TPR may issue a Contribution Notice to a person provided a number of tests are met, including amongst other things, that the person was 'party to an act or a deliberate failure to act' which falls within section 38(5), and it is of the view that it is reasonable to impose a penalty, having regard to whether it was reasonable for the person to act or fail to act in the way they did and any other matters which the Regulator considers relevant. An act falls within section 38(5) if the Regulator is of the opinion that either: (i) the 'material detriment test' is met under section 38A; or (ii) the main purpose, or one of the main purposes, of the act was to prevent the recovery of the whole or part of a section 75 debt or to prevent such a debt falling due, to compromise it or to reduce it in amount.

Section 38(A)(1) of the Act defines the 'material detriment test' as follows:

> 38A—(1) For the purposes of section 38 the material detriment test is met in relation to an act or failure if the Regulator is of the opinion that the act or failure has detrimentally affected in a material way the likelihood of accrued scheme benefits being received (whether the benefits are to be received as benefits under the scheme or otherwise).

The material detriment test does not specifically refer to the term 'Employer Covenant', but in section 38(A)(4) two of the factors to which TPR must have regard in deciding whether the test is met are identified as:

> (e) the extent to which any person is likely to be able to discharge any scheme obligation in any circumstances (including in the event of insolvency or bankruptcy),
>
> (f) the extent to which the act or failure has affected, or might affect, the extent to which any person is likely to be able to do as mentioned in paragraph (e).

It follows that actions which weaken the 'employer's legal obligation and financial ability to support the scheme now and in the future' (the Pension Regulator's definition of Employer Covenant),[38] and, in turn, detrimentally affect in a material way the likelihood of scheme benefits being received, are likely to constitute 'material detriment'. Such changes to the strength of the Employer Covenant may therefore justify the issuance of a Contribution Notice.[39]

C. Financial Support Directions

Sections 43–51 of the Act provide for TPR to issue a Financial Support Direction in support of a pension scheme. These arrangements are complex. A Financial Support Direction requires the persons to whom it is issued 'to secure that financial support for the scheme is put in place within the period specified in the direction', to maintain financial support for the duration of the scheme, and to notify the Regulator in

[38] 'Assessing and Monitoring the Employer Covenant' (n 2).

[39] s 103 of the Pensions Schemes Bill 2019 includes further grounds for issuing Contribution Notices and associated defences. For the full text of the Bill as introduced and further versions as amended, see: services.parliament.uk/Bills/2019-19/pensionschemes/documents.html.

writing 'of prescribed events in respect of the financial support as soon as reasonably practicable after the event occurs'.[40]

The apparent intent behind the legislation is to ensure appropriate financial support for schemes being sponsored by financially weak entities or entities whose principal purpose is to provide employment services elsewhere in a corporate group. Thus, section 43(2) provides that TPR can issue a Financial Support Direction where

> the Regulator is of the opinion that the employer in relation to the scheme – (a) is a service company, or (b) is insufficiently resourced, at a time determined by the Regulator which falls within subsection (9) ('the relevant time').

An employer is a service company if, broadly, it is a member of a group and its historic turnover is 'solely or principally derived from amounts charged for the provision of the services of employees of E to other members of that group'.[41] An employer is 'insufficiently resourced' if 'at that time the value of the resources of the employer is less than the amount which is a prescribed percentage of the estimated section 75 debt in relation to the scheme – set out in the Regulations'.[42] Further provisions are set out in The Pensions Regulator (Financial Support Directions etc.) Regulations 2005, SI 2005/2188.

TPR may issue a Financial Support Direction if it is reasonable to do so. The test of reasonableness is set out in sections 43(5)(b) and 43(7) of the Act. Subject to the test being satisfied, Financial Support Directions can be issued to a number of parties including the employer and persons connected or associated with the employer.[43]

D. Dividend Payments

Whilst accepting that shareholders will typically seek dividends as a return on their investment, TPR has signalled strong concerns over excess dividend payments. In its 2019 Annual Funding Statement, it stated as follows:

> As the pension scheme is a key financial stakeholder, we expect to see it treated equitably with other stakeholders. In last year's annual funding statement we highlighted our concerns about inequitable treatment of schemes relative to that of shareholders. We remain concerned about the disparity between dividend growth and stable DRCs [Deficit Repair Contributions]. Recent corporate failures have highlighted the risk of long recovery plans while payments to shareholders are excessive relative to DRCs. We are also concerned about other forms of covenant leakage which may be occurring in preference of higher DRCs and shorter recovery plans for schemes.[44]

An argument that publicly quoted companies 'need' to pay substantial dividends to support their share price can appear less robust where the company sponsors a materially underfunded pension scheme whose funding is being materially compromised by

[40] Pensions Act 2004, s 43(3).
[41] ibid s 44(2)(a)–(c).
[42] ibid s 44(3)(a).
[43] ibid s 43(6).
[44] The Pensions Regulator, 'Annual Funding Statement 2019' (n 1) 19.

the dividends. The scheme involves a debtor/creditor relationship. The scheme claims rank ahead of any shareholder claims on the company's insolvency, and it is necessary to address any scheme deficit within an appropriate period. A dividend profile might in some circumstances support either a rights issue or an injection of fresh capital into the company, which may in turn increase corporate longevity and help support the pension scheme. Nonetheless, shareholders are likely to be extremely wary of injecting fresh capital into a business simply for the money to be paid to the scheme.

E. Clearance Applications

Employers concerned as to whether TPR might seek to use their enforcement powers against them following a corporate transaction can, in conjunction with input from scheme trustees, request clearance under sections 42 and 46 of the Act. Clearance is a process led by the employer rather than the trustee. Professional Pensions reported that in 2015/16, only nine clearance applications had been received by TPR.[45] This amounted to a mere 3 per cent of the number when the arrangements were originally introduced in 2004.

F. TPR's Enforcement Powers

Under the Act, TPR has a range of enforcement powers in connection with scheme valuation and funding-related matters. Certain of these may involve the Employer Covenant. In addition to the ability to issue Contribution Notices and Financial Support Directions, TPR has a range of other powers. For example, section 231 enables it to act in circumstances where trustees and scheme managers have failed to comply with various provisions of the Act relating to scheme funding and valuation requirements and the payment of contributions under an agreed schedule of contributions. These circumstances may arise where there has been a failure to agree the nature and strength of the Employer Covenant for the purposes of settling the actuarial valuation in time. In that scenario, TPR may, for example, prescribe how technical provisions are to be calculated, stipulate the length of a recovery plan and/or impose a schedule of contributions.[46]

G. Problems in Practice – And Prospective Legislative and Regulatory Responses

The voluntary nature of the employer-led clearance regime may have led to situations where employers have undertaken corporate transactions, or paid substantial

[45] J Phillips and S Baxter, 'Clearance applications to TPR just 3% of when regime was introduced' *Professional Pensions* (London, 26 October 2016), available at: www.professionalpensions.com/professional-pensions/news/2475322/clearance-applications-to-tpr-just-3-of-when-regime-was-introduced.

[46] Pensions Act 2004, s 231(2).

dividends, with minimal or no trustee involvement, leaving trustees to seek mitigation and (if appropriate) TPR to exercise its powers, 'after the event'.

During 2018, the Department for Work and Pensions (DWP) consulted on options to broaden the powers available to TPR to protect defined benefit pension schemes following several high-profile corporate events which had left schemes underfunded. The outcome of the consultation was published in February 2019.[47] The Ministerial Foreword stated that:

> These changes will enable the Pensions Regulator to intervene where employers might evade their obligations, and help to meet their ambition to be 'clearer, quicker, and tougher'. They will also further protect individuals' pensions and ensure greater clarity for employers.[48]

The outcome of the consultation was that a number of key proposals were made in relation to matters connected with the Employer Covenant.[49] First, it was recommended that a number of new 'notifiable events' relating to matters that may have a bearing on the Employer Covenant be recognised. These include certain business sales, the granting of security to third-party lenders which give priority over a pension scheme, significant employer board restructuring, and circumstances where a sponsoring employer takes pre-insolvency or restructuring advice. It was also proposed to introduce:

> [A] Declaration of Intent made [to the Trustees and TPR] by the corporate transaction planner, which will include an explanation of the transaction, confirmation that the trustee board has been consulted and how any detriment to the scheme is to be mitigated.[50]

Notwithstanding the potential benefits to schemes from the proposed Declaration of Intent regime, the consultation outcome also highlighted a number of concerns raised by stakeholders, including confidentiality and possible negative impacts on transactions.

The recently published Pensions Schemes Bill 2019[51] contains a number of additional anti-avoidance powers for TPR, including additional notification requirements, although of course the final form of any legislation remains to be seen as and when enacted. It is also anticipated that TPR will publish a revised code of practice relating to the funding of defined benefit schemes in 2020, and it will be interesting to see how the role of the Employer Covenant is dealt with in that. Meanwhile, it may be observed that as a matter of practice TPR appears to engage closely with employers and scheme trustees in relation to a variety of aspects of scheme funding, including covenant assessment and the role of covenant strength in funding decisions and corporate transactions.

[47] Department for Work & Pensions, 'Protecting Defined Benefit Pension Schemes – A Stronger Pensions Regulator' (Consultation, 26 June 2018), available at: assets.publishing.service.gov.uk/government/uploads/system/uploads/attachment_data/file/777758/response-protecting-defined-benefit-pension-schemes.pdf.

[48] ibid 3.

[49] ibid 8–37.

[50] ibid 14–15.

[51] Pensions Scheme Bill 2019 (n 39) ss 108 and 109.

VI. EMPLOYER COVENANT ISSUES CONNECTED WITH THE PENSION PROTECTION FUND (PPF): OVERVIEW

There are two key areas where Employer Covenant assessments are of particular relevance to matters connected with the PPF. First, trustees may seek to improve an employer's banding for risk-based levy purposes through contingent support such as 'Type A' guarantees or other mechanisms set out by the PPF.[52] If the improvement in the levy is £100,000 or more, the PPF require an independent professional valuation report to support the additional likely recovery assumed from a guarantee. Second, Regulated Apportionment Arrangements (RAAs) are a form of restructuring,[53] where – very broadly – TPR with approval from the PPF may allow a financially troubled employer to separate itself from the scheme in exchange for appropriate mitigation, including a stake by the PPF in the employer following the restructuring. The PPF and TPR will only allow the Arrangement to proceed provided a number of tests are met: the Arrangement must be likely to lead to a better outcome than insolvency; and the employer is either in a PPF assessment period or likely to be within one within a year (absent an agreement for a consensual scheme restructuring being reached). These arrangements typically require extensive input from Employer Covenant and insolvency practitioners. A Freedom of Information response[54] on TPR's website shows that between 2009 and 2017, the maximum number of RAAs in any one year was seven (in 2013), whilst in other years the number was as low as zero or one.

VII. OTHER RECENT DEVELOPMENTS RELEVANT TO THE EMPLOYER COVENANT

A. Pension Consolidation Vehicles: 'Superfunds'

Statistics from TPR suggest that there are some 5,700 defined benefit schemes in the UK.[55] The statistics stratify the schemes by, amongst other metrics, reference to both status of benefit accrual[56] (for example, open to new members, closed to new members but still open to accrual, or closed to new members and future accrual) and scale of assets.[57]

Various potential business models have emerged which seek to offer potentially improved outcomes to members of schemes and more certainty to schemes and

[52] For details, see Pension Protection Fund, 'What are Contingent Assets?', available at: www.ppf.co.uk/what-are-contingent-assets.

[53] See s 7A of The Occupational Pension Schemes (Employer Debt) Regulations 2005, SI 2005/678.

[54] The Pensions Regulator 'Number of RAA Applications and Approvals' (FOI 2017-07-06, 6 July 2017), available at: www.tpr.gov.uk/en/about-us/freedom-of-information-(foi)/recently-released-information/number-of-raa-applications-and-approvals.

[55] The Pensions Regulator, 'The DB Landscape: Defined Benefit Pensions 2018' (November 2018) 6, available at: www.thepensionsregulator.gov.uk/-/media/thepensionsregulator/files/import/pdf/db-pensions-landscape-2018.ashx.

[56] ibid 8.

[57] ibid 16.

sponsoring employers. Such models involve the consolidation of schemes with particular characteristics in ways which seek to achieve economies of scale in governance and administration and investment benefits through the use of pooled investment funds, with a view to targeting superior risk-adjusted returns and, possibly, an ultimate 'buy-out' with an insurance company. Businesses seeking to operate in this way have become referred to as 'consolidation vehicles' or, colloquially, 'superfunds'.

The models by which consolidation vehicles operate are many and varied. The DWP has taken a keen interest in the possibility of the 'superfunds' market developing so as to offer better outcomes for schemes and members. However, the decision as to whether to transfer a scheme to a consolidation vehicle is not straightforward. The DWP has consulted on a range of matters connected with, amongst other things, the governance and decision-making around possible scheme transfers. In its December 2018 Consultation Document,[58] the DWP placed considerable emphasis on understanding the Employer Covenant dynamics of any transaction involving the transfer of a scheme to a superfund as part of a proposed 'gateway' approach. Under the heading 'Covenant Advice', the document states that '[a]n important part of any assessment will be the trustees' ability to form an objective view on the likelihood of the employer (or its parent group if legally liable) to be able to fund the scheme now and in the future'.[59] The DWP also remarks: '[W]e think professional covenant advice should be the norm, and we would expect trustees to take such advice, on a comply or explain basis'.[60] It will be interesting to observe the outcome of the consultation and the detail of any legislation which follows.

B. Climate Change

There is growing evidence that climate change effects are having an impact on the financial strength and outlook of a number of businesses. In a 2015 speech,[61] Mark Carney, the Governor of the Bank of England, identified three key categories of business risk arising from climate change which threaten financial stability: physical risks, liability risks and transition risks.[62] The financial results of a number of businesses have been negatively affected by, for example, not keeping pace with transitional developments in technology given the shift towards a lower carbon economy. Others, such as retailers or insurance companies, have been affected by physical developments, such as unusually hot or cold weather or material 'weather events'. There is still ongoing debate around the scale and impact of climate change. However, the

[58] Department for Work & Pensions, *Consolidation of Defined Benefit Pension Schemes* (Consultation issued by the DWP, 7 December 2018).

[59] ibid para 212.

[60] ibid para 215.

[61] M Carney, 'Breaking the tragedy of the horizon – climate change and financial stability' (Speech given at Lloyd's of London, 29 September 2015), available at: www.bankofengland.co.uk/-/media/boe/files/speech/2015/breaking-the-tragedy-of-the-horizon-climate-change-and-financial stability.pdf?la=en&hash=7C67E785651862457D99511147C7424FF5EA0C1A.

[62] ibid 5–6.

Institute and Faculty of Actuaries has recommended that scenario analysis for scheme funding considers climate risk, including the impact on covenant strength.[63] Whilst the prospective impacts of climate change may be difficult to evaluate in relation to specific businesses, it will be increasingly important for scheme trustees and advisers to consider them in forming their views of the long-term strength of covenant of sponsoring employers.

VIII. CONCLUSION

Whilst the concept of the Employer Covenant and its importance in defined benefit pension scheme decisions is comparatively recent, its impact on scheme funding and governance has been very substantial. Trustees are obliged to consider the strength of, and any changes to, the Employer Covenant in a broad range of circumstances: for example, for triennial valuations, in respect of corporate transactions, or on other occasions where legal and financial support for schemes by sponsors might be weakened. The emphasis on the Employer Covenant continues to influence policy-making and prospective legislative provisions. In turn, the Employer Covenant advisory industry has grown, and continues to grow, to meet the highly specialist needs of this market. In line with investment and actuarial professionals, Employer Covenant advisers need to provide collaborative, integrated advice around aspects of scheme funding and how the strength of the Employer Covenant sits alongside different investment strategies and scheme funding options. Thus, it seems likely that the Employer Covenant will remain a central element of a range of aspects of defined benefit scheme funding for many years to come.

[63] Resource and Environment Issues for Pensions Actuaries Working Party, 'Resource and Environment Issues for Pensions Actuaries: Considerations for Setting Financial Assumptions: A Working Paper Outlining Climate Change Considerations for Financial Assumptions and Practical Examples of the Role of Scenario Analysis to Support Them' (Institute and Faculty of Actuaries, 15 October 2018) 19, available at: www.actuaries.org.uk/system/files/field/document/Considerations%20for%20Setting%20Financial%20Assumptions%20-%20Final_CJ_2.pdf.

4

Interpretation of Pension Trusts: Applying the General Rules?

DAVID POLLARD

I. INTRODUCTION

INTERPRETATION OF PENSION trust instruments is a big issue. Occupational pension schemes are long-term structures, needing to adapt to changing situations. Unforeseen external changes (for example, to taxation, retirement age or indexation) can result in major impacts, including large differences in projected funding liabilities. Large amounts can depend on the meaning of provisions in trusts drafted many years before. Commonly the necessary flexibility would be achieved by using a widely drafted amendment power in the scheme. But there are limits on the width of the changes that can be made using the amendment power, both under statute and commonly under the terms of the scheme itself. This can force the parties back onto considering the interpretation of the scheme before any formal amendment. Can a relevant change be made within the existing terms of the pension scheme?

The Supreme Court has tried, in a series of well-known judgments over the last few years, to set out high-level principles on how courts should interpret all written documents, including contracts, wills and trusts. Despite statements that the same rules should apply to all three categories, pension trusts are developing their own sub-group of interpretation principles, partly based on their context and the nature of pension trusts as having many individual beneficiaries.

This chapter looks at the application of the general principles to pension trusts and how helpful high-level principles are on day-to-day interpretation issues. Principles of construction, particularly of formal written documents, have caused a number of difficulties in the last few years, at least if the number of decisions in the Supreme Court and public speeches by senior judges is any guide.[1] Occupational

[1] See, in particular, Lord Sumption, 'A Question of Taste: The Supreme Court and the Interpretation of Contracts' (Harris Society Annual Lecture, Keble College, Oxford, 8 May 2017); Sir Geoffrey Vos 'Contractual Interpretation: Do judges Sometimes Say One Thing and Do Another?' (2017) 23 *Canterbury Law Review* 1; Lady Justice Asplin, 'It's all a matter of interpretation' (Association of Pension Lawyers Prestige Lecture, London, 23 October 2017); Lord Hoffmann, 'Language and Lawyers' (2018) 134 *LQR* 553.

pension schemes have been no exception to this. Indeed, one of the most recent decisions of the Supreme Court on interpretation, in *Barnardo's v Buckinghamshire*,[2] is one dealing with interpretation of an occupational pension scheme trust instrument.

Interpretation rules look to be broadly very similar in Australia as they are in the UK (indeed some of the Australian cases cite the UK cases). But there are some differences – in particular as to the admissibility of background documents and the need to show there is an ambiguity before the court looks at the surrounding circumstances.[3]

II. WHY DO PENSION SCHEMES NEED TO LOOK AT INTERPRETATION ISSUES?

There are various reasons for this in a pensions context:

a. Occupational pension schemes are long-term institutions – they can last for decades, even hundreds of years (the usual rules about perpetuities generally do not apply).[4]
b. The legislation governing them tends to change, both as a matter of regulation through legislation (Parliament is constantly changing tax laws and mandatory laws relating to private sector pensions, but giving less opportunity compared with public sector pensions for the terms to be changed)[5] and through changes in practice of the Pensions Regulator.
c. The commercial needs of the employer and the members in relation to retirement provision may change over time. An example is the shift in recent years away from defined benefit (DB) accrual, towards defined contribution (DC) arrangements.
d. Tax rules are constantly changing. Pension schemes need to adapt to these changes.
e. The anticipated future cost (actuarial liability) of pension provision is changing, particularly as projected longevity of members increases and with a reduction in expected investment returns in recent years. This leads to employers

[2] *Barnardo's v Buckinghamshire* [2018] UKSC 55, [2019] 2 All ER 175. Dismissing an appeal from the Court of Appeal [2016] EWCA Civ 1064, [2017] Pens LR 2.

[3] *Cherry Tree Investments Ltd v Landmain Ltd* [2012] EWCA Civ 736, [2013] Ch 305 [22] (Arden LJ). See also, on the Australian approach, Sir Kim Lewison, *The Interpretation of Contracts*, 6th edn (London, Sweet & Maxwell 2017) [1.02] and Supplement [1.04].

[4] The rules against perpetuities and accumulations do not, in general, apply to occupational pension schemes; from 6 April 2010, the Perpetuities and Accumulations Act 2009, s 2(4) exempts 'relevant pension schemes' (defined in s 15 to include an occupational pension scheme as defined under the Pension Schemes Act 1993, s 1). Before 6 April 2010, contracted-out schemes and those with tax registration were excluded under the Pension Schemes Act 1993, s 163 and the Personal and Occupational Pension Schemes (Perpetuities) Regulations 1990 (SI 1990/1143).

[5] Sometimes overriding amendment powers are included in the legislation, in particular under the Pensions Act 1995, s 68. But in other cases such a power is not given (eg, on the changes to the indexation provisions from 2010, the changes in retirement ages, where public sector schemes were changed, even for accrued benefits, by legislation, but private sector schemes were prohibited from making such changes without individual member consent (Pensions Act 1995, s 67).

(and employees) seeking changes in pension provision (employers seeking to switch to defined contribution instead of defined benefit, or to reduce commitments to indexation (for example, to switch from Retail Price Index (RPI) to Consumer Price Index (CPI), the government's current preferred index for public sector schemes).

f. The climate for regulation is also changing. This is demonstrated by the introduction of the Pensions Ombudsman and the Pensions Regulator. Regulators, governments and parliaments see a public interest in pension provision (particularly since the setting up under the Pensions Act 2004 of the Pension Protection Fund, funded by levies payable by all eligible DB pension schemes).

Pension schemes tend to include an amendment provision – this is essential for schemes to be able to keep up with change.[6] But too much flexibility can be given – amendment provisions themselves give rise to interpretation issues:

a. Parliament has intervened by the Pensions Act 1995, section 67[7] to prohibit scheme amendments (under a power in the scheme) for tax registered occupational pension schemes where an 'accrued right' or 'subsisting right' would be adversely affected (unless the individual member gives his or her individual written consent, following a consultation process). The ambit and limits in section 67 themselves cause difficulties in interpretation.[8] For example, the meaning of various fundamental concepts (such as, what is 'pensionable service'[9] and who is an 'employer')[10] can themselves cause difficulties.
b. The scheme amendment power itself can be difficult to interpret.[11]
c. Pensions legislation is also often unclear – for example, the application of sex equality laws to the complex provisions dealing with guaranteed minimum pensions (GMPs) – see the two decisions in 2018 in *Lloyds Bank*.[12] Parliament can be reluctant to clarify the law, either because of worries about the political reaction or because it feels constrained by relevant EU laws (particularly in the discrimination area) or by human rights legislation (if accrued rights are potentially affected). These factors can all throw the interested parties (employers, trustees, members etc) back on to looking at interpretation of existing trust instruments.

[6] See D Pollard, *The Law of Pension Trusts* (Oxford, Oxford University Press, 2013) [17.2].

[7] Re-enacted in a revised form by the Pensions Act 2004.

[8] Compare the decisions of the Court of Appeal in *KPMG v Aon* [2005] EWCA Civ 1004, [2005] Pens LR 301 and *Barnardo's* (n 2) (the s 67 issue was not dealt with in the Supreme Court). Section 67 is discussed in D Pollard et al (eds), *Freshfields on Corporate Pensions Law 2015* (London, Bloomsbury Professional, 2015) [4.2].

[9] See *Re G4S Pension Scheme, G4S Plc v G4S Trustees Ltd* [2018] EWHC 1749 (Ch), [2019] ICR 141 (Nugee J).

[10] See *Hearn v Dobson* [2008] EWHC 1620 (Ch) (Morgan J); *Cemex UK Marine Ltd v MNOPF Trustees Ltd* [2009] EWHC 3258 (Ch), [2010] ICR 732 (Peter Smith J); and *PNPF Trust Co Ltd v Taylor* [2010] EWHC 1573 (Ch) (Warren J), discussed in Pollard et al (n 8) [14.7].

[11] See Pollard, *The Law of Pension Trusts* (n 6) ch 17.

[12] *Lloyds Banking Group Pensions Trustees Ltd v Lloyds Bank Plc* [2018] EWHC 2839 (Ch), [2019] Pens LR 5 and [2018] EWHC 3343 (Ch), [2019] Pens LR 6. A further hearing is due to be held in 2020.

III. ARE PENSION SCHEMES INTERPRETED IN THE SAME WAY AS CONTRACTS?

Much of the case law on interpretation of written instruments has focused on the position of contracts.[13] In *Barnardo's*,[14] Lord Hodge (giving the only judgment) commented that recent case law has applied the same 'general approach' to all written instruments, but that in looking at the various interpretive tools, the court 'must have regard to the nature and circumstances of the particular instrument'.

A. The Structure of Occupational Pension Schemes

Benefits for members under private sector occupational pension schemes are derived from the employment relationship, but they are, in general, not contractual obligations on either the trustees or the employer.[15] Instead the schemes are set up under trust, with a trustee[16] holding relevant funds and paying benefits in due course to the relevant beneficiaries.[17]

The beneficiaries taking benefits under the scheme include the members of the scheme (employees or ex-employees of the relevant employers), but the schemes also usually envisage that others may take monetary benefits. Schemes commonly provide for benefits to be paid following the death of the member to the member's spouse or dependants[18] (pensions) or to those within a scheme defined (fairly wide) class at the discretion of the trustee board (death benefit lump sum). Beneficiaries of an occupational pension scheme also usually include the employer, either expressly (lien rules[19] or surplus reversion on winding-up or before)[20] or (arguably) in a DB scheme impliedly by reason of the employer's funding obligation.[21]

B. Pensions: Parties and Process

The governing instrument in relation to an occupational pension scheme is usually an express declaration of trust, with the parties executing the instrument being the 'Principal Employer' and the initial trustee.

[13] eg, the modern 'trilogy' in the Supreme Court: *Rainy Sky SA v Kookmin Bank* [2011] UKSC 50, [2011] 1 WLR 2900; *Arnold v Britton* [2015] UKSC 36, [2015] AC 1619; and *Wood v Capita Insurance Services Ltd* [2017] UKSC 24, [2017] AC 1173.

[14] *Barnardo's* (n 2) [13] (Lord Hodge).

[15] *Air Jamaica Ltd v Charlton* [1999] 1 WLR 1399 (PC).

[16] This can either be a trustee company (more common in recent times) or individuals acting as trustees.

[17] See Pollard, *The Law of Pension Trusts* (n 6) ch 1.

[18] ibid ch 8.

[19] See D Pollard, *Employment Law and Pensions* (London, Bloomsbury Professional, 2016) ch 32.

[20] See Pollard, *The Law of Pension Trusts* (n 6) ch 20.

[21] ibid ch 10. This is not a new concept – see, eg, the references to the employer's interest by the Privy Council in 1859 in *East India Co v Robertson* (1859) 12 Moo PC 400, 458, 14 ER 963, 985, a new case to me, until cited in Sinéad Agnew's contribution in this volume.

The process is for a Principal Employer[22] to execute the initial trust instrument (usually a deed) with the initial trustee being a party (to indicate acceptance of its role as trustee). Later amendments (or new consolidating deeds) will need to comply with the terms of the relevant amendment power, but commonly this requires agreement by both the trustee and the Principal Employer.

The modern cases on pension trusts have also been consistent in stating that the trust deed and rules of a pension scheme are to be interpreted in the same way as any other written instrument. An early example was the decision of Millett J, in one of the first cases on pensions in the modern era, *Re Courage Group's Pension Schemes*:

> I should make some general observations on the approach which I conceive ought to be adopted by the court to the construction of the trust deed and rules of a pension scheme. First, there are no special rules of construction applicable to a pension scheme; nevertheless, its provisions should wherever possible be construed to give reasonable and practical effect to the scheme, bearing in mind that it has to be operated against a constantly changing commercial background. It is important to avoid unduly fettering the power to amend the provisions of the scheme, thereby preventing the parties from making those changes which may be required by the exigencies of commercial life.[23]

In 2002 in the British Airways case, *Stevens v Bell*,[24] Arden LJ (with whom Waller and Auld LJJ agreed) set out a number of interpretation principles for pension schemes, starting with:

> There have been several reported cases about the interpretation of provisions of pension schemes in recent years. There are no special rules of construction but pension schemes have certain characteristics which tend to differentiate them from other analogous instruments. I mention some of those characteristics in the following paragraphs.[25]

This approach has been followed in a number of cases.

This chapter focuses on the construction principles for pension schemes focusing on the overall statement that 'there are no special rules of construction' for the interpretation of pension schemes. At first reading, this is not an obvious approach to take. Written instruments, whether contracts, trusts or wills take many forms and can have many parties. Should the same general rules of interpretation apply to all of them?

The case law is clearly answering this with a broad 'yes' but going on to make it clear that the relevant general interpretation principles must be applied having

[22] ie, main sponsor. Sometimes called a 'Principal Company' or 'Sponsor'.

[23] *Re Courage Group's Pension Schemes* [1987] 1 WLR 495 (Ch) 505 (Millett J). When I started practising pensions law in the late 1980s, there were thought to be only three major reported cases in the field: *Courage*, *Cowan v Scargill* [1985] Ch 270 (Ch); and *Re Imperial Foods Ltd Pension Scheme* [1986] 2 All ER 802 (Ch). A lawyer could read the pension case law canon in an afternoon. We were mistaken – there are earlier cases – eg, *Tibbals v Port of London Authority* [1937] 2 All ER 415 (HL) (pointed out by M Tennet, 'Pension Cases that Time Forgot' (2007) 21 *Trust Law International* 125) and *East India Co* (n 21).

[24] *Stevens v Bell* [2002] EWCA Civ 672, [2002] OPLR 207 (CA) [26] (Arden LJ), also called *British Airways Pension Trustees Ltd v British Airways plc* [2002] Pens LR 247 and sometimes cited as such (eg, in *Barnardo's* (n 2) [17]).

[25] *Stevens* (n 24) [26] (Arden LJ).

'regard to the nature and circumstances of the particular instrument' (Lord Hodge in *Barnardo's*); or noting that 'pension schemes have certain characteristics which tend to differentiate them from other analogous instruments' (Arden LJ in *Stevens v Bell*).[26]

IV. INTERPRETATION PRINCIPLES FOR OTHER WRITTEN DOCUMENTS

English and Welsh law applies its general interpretation principles to written documents generally. This includes such instruments as wills, loan notes, articles of association, mortgages and bills of lading. In some cases the decisions make the point that nature of the document and how it is used mean that the relevant background or matrix of fact may need to be more limited than usual.

A. Wills and Unilateral Documents

In 2014, in *Marley v Rawlings*,[27] Lord Neuberger (with whom the remainder of the Supreme Court agreed)[28] held that the approach to interpreting wills should be the same as that adopted in relation to contracts, the aim being 'to identify the intention of the party or parties to the document by interpreting the words used in their documentary, factual and commercial context'. He stated that, subject to any statutory provision to the contrary, the approach to the interpretation of contracts which he had set out is just as appropriate for wills as other unilateral documents. He held:

> When interpreting a contract, the court is concerned to find the intention of the party or parties, and it does this by identifying the meaning of the relevant words, (a) in the light of (i) the natural and ordinary meaning of those words, (ii) the overall purpose of the document, (iii) any other provisions of the document, (iv) the facts known or assumed by the parties at the time that the document was executed, and (v) common sense, but (b) ignoring subjective evidence of any party's intentions.[29]

B. Notices and Unilateral Documents

Lord Neuberger also commented in *Marley v Rawlings*[30] on the same approach being adopted for unilateral documents (for example, notices) as for bilateral

[26] ibid.
[27] *Marley v Rawlings* [2014] UKSC 2, [2015] AC 129 [19]–[23] (Lord Neuberger). See also *Sammut v Manzi* [2008] UKPC 58, [2009] 2 All ER 234 [4]–[6]; and the discussion in *Reading v Reading* [2015] EWHC 946 (Ch), [2015] WTLR 1245 (Asplin J).
[28] Lord Hodge confining himself to some observations as to how Scots law might have dealt with the issues had it been the governing law.
[29] *Marley* (n 27) [19] (Lord Neuberger).
[30] ibid.

(or multilateral) contracts, citing the notice case, *Mannai Investment*[31] and a patent case, *Catnic Components*.[32] Lord Neuberger noted that:

> Of course, a contract is agreed between a number of parties, whereas a will is made by a single party. However, that distinction is an unconvincing reason for adopting a different approach in principle to interpretation of wills: it is merely one of the contextual circumstances which has to be borne in mind when interpreting the document concerned. Thus, the court takes the same approach to interpretation of unilateral notices as it takes to interpretation of contracts: see *Mannai Investment Co Ltd v Eagle Star Life Assurance Co Ltd* [1997] AC 749 at 770–771, 779–780 per Lord Steyn and Lord Hoffmann respectively.[33]

In *Public Trustee v Harrison*,[34] Marcus Smith J considered the construction of a unilateral instrument and held that the same approach as to commercial contracts should apply. A similar position on construction of notices is taken in Australia – see *JPA Finance Pty Ltd v Gordon Nominees Pty Ltd*,[35] a case on the meaning of a notice of termination.

C. Loan Notes and Debt Securities

In *Re Sigma Finance Corp*,[36] the Supreme Court considered a trust deed relating to 'debt securities' issued to 'a variety of creditors, who hold different instruments, issued at different times, and in different circumstances'. Lord Collins held '[c]onsequently this is not the type of case where the background or matrix of fact is or ought to be relevant, except in the most generalised way'.[37] More generally, he held:

> Where a security document secures a number of creditors who have advanced funds over a long period it would be quite wrong to take account of circumstances which are not known to all of them. In this type of case it is the wording of the instrument which is paramount. The instrument must be interpreted as a whole in the light of the commercial intention which may be inferred from the face of the instrument and from the nature of the debtor's business.[38]

In *BNY Mellon*[39] the Supreme Court considered whether a redemption trigger had occurred in relation to contingent convertible loan notes issued by Lloyds Bank Group. The majority held that when construing a contract or trust deed which governed the

[31] *Mannai Investment Co Ltd v Eagle Star Life Assurance Co* Ltd [1997] AC 749 (HL).
[32] *Catnic Components Ltd v Hill and Smith Ltd* [1982] RPC 183 (HL).
[33] *Marley* (n 27) [21] (Lord Neuberger).
[34] *Public Trustee v Harrison* [2018] EWHC 166 (Ch), [2018] WTLR 299 [18] (Marcus Smith J).
[35] *JPA Finance Pty Ltd v Gordon Nominees Pty Ltd* [2019] VSCA 159 [67] (McLeish JA, Beach and Niall JJA agreeing) referring to 'Lord Steyn's articulation of the principles in *Mannai Investment*'. McLeish JA also cited *MLW Technology Pty Ltd v May* [2005] VSCA 29 [78]–[82], which was endorsed in *Salta Constructions Pty Ltd v St George Bank* (2014) 45 VR 245 [28]; and also *Yan v Zhang* [2018] VSC 694 [111] (Kennedy J).
[36] *Re Sigma Finance Corp (in administrative receivership)* [2009] UKSC 2, [2010] 1 All ER 571. Cited by Lord Neuberger in *BNY Mellon Corporate Trustee Services Ltd v LBG Capital No 1 plc* [2016] UKSC 29, [2017] 1 All ER 497 [31].
[37] *Re Sigma Finance Corp* (n 36) [37] (Lord Collins).
[38] ibid [37] (Lord Collins).
[39] *BNY Mellon* (n 36).

terms on which a negotiable instrument was held, very considerable circumspection was appropriate before the contents of another document were taken into account. In this case, the trust deed could not be understood without some appreciation of the regulatory policy of the Financial Services Authority (FSA) at and before the time that the notes were issued. Accordingly, the general thrust and effect of the FSA regulatory material published in 2008 and 2009 could be taken into account when interpreting the terms and conditions of the notes. Lord Neuberger held:

> Over the past 20 years or so, the House of Lords and Supreme Court have given considerable (some may think too much) general guidance as to the proper approach to interpreting contracts and indeed other commercial documents, such as the Trust Deed in this case. What, if any, weight is to be given to what was said in other documents, which were available at the time when the contract concerned was made or when the Trust Deed in question took effect, must be highly dependent on the facts of the particular case. However, when construing a contract or Trust Deed which governs the terms upon which a negotiable instrument is held, as in the present case, very considerable circumspection is appropriate before the contents of such other documents are taken into account.[40]

Lord Neuberger went on to refer with approval to the judgment of Lord Collins (above) in *Re Sigma Finance*[41] and, presumably to show that this is not a new concept, then to quote a Privy Council decision (from 1931) to the same effect, *Egyptian Salt and Soda Co Ltd v Port Said Salt Association Ltd*.[42]

D. Deeds

Deeds are interpreted in the same way as written contracts – for an example of this, see the Supreme Court decision in *Re Sigma Finance*.[43] To the same effect in Australia, see *Mercanti v Mercanti*[44] and *Royal Botanic Gardens*.[45]

E. Bills of Lading

The usual principles apply. In *The Starsin*,[46] the House of Lords construed words identifying the carrier on the front of a bill of lading identifying the carrier without reference to what it said on the back. This was on the grounds that 'the bankers to whom the bill would be tendered could not be expected to read the small print'.[47] An alternative could be that a bill of lading is addressed to third parties.[48]

[40] ibid [30] (Lord Neuberger).
[41] *Re Sigma Finance* (n 36).
[42] *Egyptian Salt and Soda Co Ltd v Port Said Salt Association* Ltd [1931] AC 677 (PC) 682.
[43] *Re Sigma Finance* (n 36). See also *Lloyds TSB Foundation v Lloyds Banking Group* [2013] UKSC 3, [2013] 1 WLR 366 (a Scottish decision, but applying the English case law).
[44] *Mercanti v Mercanti* [2016] WASCA 206, (2016) 50 WAR 495 [72] (Buss P).
[45] *Royal Botanic Gardens and Domain Trust v South Sydney City Council* [2002] HCA 5, (2002) 240 CLR 45 [9]–[10] (Gleeson CJ, Gaudron, McHugh, Gummow and Hayne JJ).
[46] *Homburg Houtimport BV v Agrosin Private Ltd (The Starsin)* [2003] UKHL 12, [2004] 1 AC 715.
[47] *Chartbrook Ltd v Persimmon Homes Ltd* [2009] UKHL 38, [2009] 1 AC 1101 [40] (Lord Hoffmann).
[48] A point made by Arden LJ in *Cherry Tree Investments* (n 3) [43].

F. Mortgages

Mortgages are interpreted in the same way as written contracts: *Re Sigma Finance*[49] and *Cherry Tree Investments*.[50]

G. Consent Orders

A consent order is to be construed in accordance with the same principles that apply to the construction of contracts: *Weston v Dayman*[51] following *Sirius International*.[52]

H. Interpretation Principles: Third Parties or Public Documents?

The courts have also considered whether these general interpretation principles should still apply in relation to instruments that could be considered by third parties.

I. Assignees

An obvious example here is whether background knowledge held by the parties to the instrument can be used for interpretation even if the benefit of the instrument was held by an assignee (who did not necessarily have the background knowledge). However such an approach, limiting the use of background material because there may be an assignment, was roundly rejected by Lord Hoffmann in *Chartbrook*.[53] He noted that:

> Ordinarily … a contract is treated as addressed to the parties alone' and held that 'an assignee must either enquire as to any relevant background or take his chance on how that might affect the meaning a court will give to the document.

J. Leases

Before the decision in *Chartbrook*, in *KPMG v Network Rail*[54] it was argued that a lease is an interest in land and so background material, including the original contract that gave rise to the lease, should not be used unless available to later parties. This argument was rejected by the Court of Appeal, Carnwath LJ holding that this

[49] *Re Sigma Finance* (n 36).

[50] *Cherry Tree Investments* (n 3).

[51] *Weston v Dayman* [2006] EWCA Civ 1165, [2008] 1 BCLC 250 [3], [5] (Arden LJ). Followed in *Viagogo AG v Competition and Markets Authority* [2019] EWHC 1706 (Ch) [10].

[52] *Sirius International Insurance Co v FAI General Insurance Ltd* [2005] 1 All ER 191, [2004] 1 WLR 3251 [18] (Lord Steyn).

[53] *Chartbrook* (n 47).

[54] *KPMG LLP v Network Rail Infrastructure Ltd* [2007] EWCA Civ 363, [2007] Bus LR 1336 [41] (Carnwath LJ).

was an issue of proof rather than principle and holding that the original agreement for lease was admissible in evidence.

This approach was followed by Lewison LJ in *Cherry Tree Investments*,[55] a decision after *Chartbook*, but dealing with a registered charge. Lewison LJ commented that admitting a background document in evidence was not decisive as to the question of what weight was given to the background.[56]

K. Articles of Association

Lord Hoffmann in *Chartbrook*[57] held that where a document was addressed to third parties it could be unfair if extrinsic evidence was taken into account in the interpretation of a document. He gave the examples of a company's articles of association. Lord Hoffmann followed the decision of the Court of Appeal in in *Bratton Seymour Service Co Ltd v Oxborough*

> that in construing the articles of association of the management company of a building divided into flats, background facts which would have been known to all the signatories were inadmissible because the articles should be regarded as addressed to anyone who read the register of companies, including persons who would have known nothing of the facts in question.[58]

This was followed by the Court of Appeal in *Cherry Tree Investments*.[59] Arden LJ commented:

> The test for the exclusion of extrinsic material is thus whether the document is to be treated as addressed to third parties. Lord Hoffmann did not, for instance, suggest that the fact that the document had to be registered at a public registry was sufficient to exclude extrinsic evidence about the background. The test was satisfied in the case of a company's articles of association, a point also made by Lord Hoffmann in his speech in *Attorney General of Belize v Belize Telecom Ltd* [2009] 1 WLR 1988. In determining persons to whom a document is to be treated as addressed the court has to consider whether account has to be taken of their interests. Lord Hoffmann does not exclude the possibility of dealing with the problem of fairness to third parties in ways other than excluding extrinsic evidence altogether.[60]
>
> Articles of association have special characteristics that justify the conclusion that they are to be regarded as addressed to third parties as well as to the shareholders at the time of their adoption. There is often a substantial number of other persons who have to rely on them and they may be in force for many years. Registration gives constructive notice of their contents to the entire world: *Ernest v Nicholls*.[61] Third parties frequently have to rely on a company's articles of association to determine the powers of its directors.

[55] *Cherry Tree Investments* (n 3) [101]–[103] (Lewison LJ).
[56] ibid [104] (Lewison LJ), citing Lord Steyn in *Mannai Investment* (n 31) 768.
[57] *Chartbrook* (n 47).
[58] *Bratton Seymour Service Co Ltd v Oxborough* [1992] BCLC 693 (CA).
[59] *Cherry Tree Investments* (n 3) [22] (Arden LJ), [124] (Lewison LJ).
[60] ibid [41] and [44]–[45] (Arden LJ).
[61] *Ernest v Nicholls* (1857) 6 HL Cas 401.

> In addition, it is well established that articles of association cannot be rectified by the court: see the *Bratton Seymour* case.[62] As I shall show, this is not the case with documents creating interests in land.
>
> In the case of articles of association, therefore, the balance to be struck between the shareholders at the date of their adoption and third parties comes down in favour of protecting the third parties. Protection is achieved by the total exclusion of extrinsic evidence. The position was the same in *The Starsin*, although the document in that case was a bill of lading. It is necessary to consider how far these points apply to a registered charge, which brings me to my third reason.

L. Public Documents

A limited approach to background matrix of fact can also be seen in cases considering the interpretation of public documents or documents on a public register.[63] See *Opua Ferries Ltd v Fullers Bay of Islands Ltd*[64] and *Trump International Golf Club Scotland Ltd v Scottish Ministers*.[65]

In *Cherry Tree Investments*[66] the Court of Appeal was considering whether a registered charge should be read to include a power of sale included in the underlying facility agreement (not a registered document), but not included in the registered charge. Lewison and Longmore LJJ held[67] that the facility agreement should be admitted as part of the background matrix, but even with this the fact that the charge was in a public document meant that the power of sale should not be changed. Arden LJ dissented.[68] She would have construed the registered charge as including the modified power of sale in the facility agreement.

Lewison LJ explained the position on registered documents, considering[69] that the case law indicates that 'the role of background is limited' for documents which are public documents, citing the position of planning permission[70] a company's memorandum and articles of association,[71] and the interpretation of an injunction or receivership order.[72]

[62] *Bratton Seymour* (n 58).

[63] R Thomas 'The Interpretation of Documents on the Register' (2016) 1 *Conveyancer and Property Lawyer* 1; M Barber and R Thomas 'Contractual Interpretation, Registered Documents and Third Party Effects' (2014) 77 *MLR* 597; and P Davies, 'The Meaning of Commercial Contracts' in P Davies and J Pila (eds), *The Jurisprudence of Lord Hoffmann* (Oxford, Hart Publishing, 2015) ch 12, D.

[64] *Opua Ferries Ltd v Fullers Bay of Islands Ltd* [2003] UKPC 19, [2003] 3 NZLR 740.

[65] *Trump International Golf Club Scotland Ltd v Scottish Ministers* [2015] UKSC 74, [2016] 1 WLR 85. See also *Lambeth LBC v Secretary of State for Communities and Local Government* [2018] EWCA Civ 844, [2018] 2 P&CR 17.

[66] *Cherry Tree Investments* (n 3).

[67] ibid [132] (Lewison LJ) and [150] (Longmore LJ).

[68] ibid [59] (Arden LJ).

[69] ibid [124] (Lewison LJ).

[70] *Slough Estates Ltd v Slough Borough Council (No 2)* [1971] AC 958 (HL); and *Secretary of State for Communities v Bleaklow Industries Ltd* [2009] EWCA Civ 206, [2009] 2 P&CR 385.

[71] *Egyptian Salt and Soda Co* (n 42).

[72] *Masri v Consolidated Contractors (Oil and Gas) Co SAL* [2009] EWCA Civ 36, [2009] 1 CLC 82.

Similarly in the Australian decision on registered documents under the Australian Torrens system in *Westfield Management Ltd v Perpetual Trustee Co Ltd*:

> The third party who inspects the register cannot be expected, consistently with the scheme of the Torrens system, to look further for extrinsic material which might establish facts or circumstances existing at the time of the creation of the registered dealing and placing the third party (or any court later seized of a dispute) in the situation of the grantee.[73]

Opua Ferries[74] was a case where the Privy Council considered the scope of a licence to operate a ferry service. Opua argued for the admission of extrinsic evidence to explain the terms of the registered certificate. The Privy Council rejected that argument. Lord Hope held that a different approach should apply to public documents held on a register:

> There would much to be said in favour of this argument if the relevant documents were contained in a contract between the parties which the court was being asked to construe. If that were so the court would wish to put itself into the same position as the contracting parties were when they entered into their contract. As Lord Hoffmann said in *Investors Compensation Scheme Ltd v West Bromwich Building Society* [1998] 1 WLR 896, 912H, when one is interpreting a document of that kind one is seeking to ascertain the meaning which it would convey to a reasonable person having all the background knowledge which would reasonably have been available to the parties in the situation in which they were at the time of the contract. The parties' knowledge of how the ferry service was in fact being operated from day to day at the time when such a contract was entered into would be part of the background.[75]
>
> But it does not follow that the same approach is to be taken when one is construing a public document. The documents included in the register maintained by a regional council under section 52(1) of the Act have that character. This is, and is intended to be, a public register of passenger transport services. Members of the public who consult the register may come from far and near. They may have some background knowledge, but they may have none at all. In *Slough Estates Ltd* … Lord Reid said that extrinsic evidence may be used to identify a thing or place referred to in a public document.[76] But he went on to say that this was a very different thing from using evidence of facts known to the maker of the document but which are not common knowledge to alter or qualify the apparent meaning of words or phrases used in it. As he put it, members of the public, entitled to rely on a public document, ought not to be subject to the risk of its apparent meaning being altered by the introduction of extrinsic evidence. Moreover, the only information which a regional council is obliged by section 53 to ensure is reasonably readily available to the public is that which gives details of the service which the council has registered. The statute makes the position clear. The register is expected to speak for itself.

[73] *Westfield Management Ltd v Perpetual Trustee Co Ltd* (2007) 81 ALJR 1887 [39] (Gleeson CJ, Gummow, Kirby, Hayne And Heydon JJ), cited by Lewison LJ in *Cherry Tree Investments* (n 3) [126]. Discussed in New Zealand by the Court of Appeal in *Big River Paradise Ltd v Congreve* [2008] NZCA 78, [2008] 2 NZLR 402. Considered but the point not decided, by the Supreme Court in *Escrow Holdings Forty-One Ltd v District Court at Auckland* [2016] NZSC 167, [2017] 1 NZLR 374 [41]–[43] (Arnold J).

[74] *Opua Ferries Ltd* (n 64). As explained in *Cherry Tree Investments* (n 3) [124] (Lewison LJ).

[75] *Opua Ferries Ltd* (n 64) [19]–[20] (Lord Hope).

[76] *Slough Estates Ltd* (n 70) 962 (Lord Reid).

In *Trump International*,[77] the Supreme Court was considering the disputed terms of a planning consent. Lord Hodge held that other documents could be considered if incorporated by reference or if there was an ambiguity in the consent:

> When the court is concerned with the interpretation of words in a condition in a public document such as a section 36 consent, it asks itself what a reasonable reader would understand the words to mean when reading the condition in the context of the other conditions and of the consent as a whole. This is an objective exercise in which the court will have regard to the natural and ordinary meaning of the relevant words, the overall purpose of the consent, any other conditions which cast light on the purpose of the relevant words, and common sense. Whether the court may also look at other documents that are connected with the application for the consent or are referred to in the consent will depend on the circumstances of the case, in particular the wording of the document that it is interpreting. Other documents may be relevant if they are incorporated into the consent by reference (as in condition 7 set out in para 38 below) or there is an ambiguity in the consent, which can be resolved, for example, by considering the application for consent.[78]

In a concurring judgment, Lord Carnwath commented to the same effect:

> I see dangers in an approach which may lead to the impression that there is a special set of rules applying to planning conditions, as compared to other legal documents, or that the process is one of great complexity.[79]

And later in the same judgment, Lord Carnwath added:

> Any such document of course must be interpreted in its particular legal and factual context. One aspect of that context is that a planning permission is a public document which may be relied on by parties unrelated to those originally involved … It must also be borne in mind that planning conditions may be used to support criminal proceedings. Those are good reasons for a relatively cautious approach, for example in the well established rules limiting the categories of documents which may be used in interpreting a planning permission … But such considerations arise from the legal framework within which planning permissions are granted. They do not require the adoption of a completely different approach to their interpretation.[80]

More recently, in *London Borough of Lambeth v Secretary of State for Housing*,[81] another case on planning consent, Lord Carnwath referred to these statements in *Trump International* and held:

> In summary, whatever the legal character of the document in question, the starting-point – and usually the end-point – is to find 'the natural and ordinary meaning' of the words there used, viewed in their particular context (statutory or otherwise) and in the light of common sense.[82]

[77] *Trump International* (n 65).
[78] ibid [34] (Lord Hodge).
[79] ibid [53] (Lord Carnwath).
[80] ibid [66] (Lord Carnwath).
[81] *London Borough of Lambeth v Secretary of State for Housing* [2019] UKSC 33, [2019] 1 WLR 4317.
[82] ibid [19] (Lord Carnwath).

V. INTERPRETATION PRINCIPLES AND TRUSTS

As already mentioned, in *Barnardo's*,[83] a case concerning the interpretation of the trust instrument governing an occupational pension scheme, Lord Hodge commented that recent case law has applied the same 'general approach' to all written instruments.

Older cases on the construction of trusts state that this should be the same as for other documents – see, for example, *Vestey's Executors v IRC*[84] and *Re Gulbenkian's Settlements*.[85] There are also decisions on pension trusts to the same effect: see *Re Courage Group's Pension Schemes*[86] and *Stevens v Bell*[87] (cited above) and *Breakspear v Ackland*.[88] Two of the recent Supreme Court decisions mentioned above, *Re Sigma Finance*[89] and *BNY Mellon*[90] both apply contractual interpretation principles to commercial trusts.

In Australia, the High Court has held that the usual interpretation principles should apply to trusts. In *Byrnes v Kendle*[91] the High Court held that the interpretation principles should apply to the issue of whether a trust had been created. The fullest treatment of this issue was in the judgment of Heydon[92] and Crennan JJ. They held that the rules for the construction of contracts apply also to trusts, noting that 'is not surprising',[93] even though trusts and contracts are distinct as institutions. They held that this approach should apply both because the 'contractual relationship provides one of the most common bases for the establishment or implication and for the definition of a trust',[94] and because 'the same considerations which limit recourse to surrounding circumstances and oral testimony in relation to contracts applies in relation to trusts'.[95]

Heydon and Crennan JJ also commented[96] on some of the UK pension trust cases,[97] referring to their use of the matrix of fact, the fiscal background and tax

[83] *Barnardo's* (n 2) [13] (Lord Hodge).

[84] *Vestey's Executors v IRC* [1949] 1 All ER 1108 (HL) 1131 (Lord Simonds): 'applying to these words the ordinary principles of construction'.

[85] *Re Gulbenkian's Settlements* [1970] AC 508 (HL) 522 (Lord Upjohn): 'applying the usual canons of construction'.

[86] *Re Courage* (n 23) 505 (Millett J).

[87] *Stevens* (n 24) [26] (Arden LJ).

[88] *Breakspear v Ackland* [2008] EWHC 220 (Ch), [2009] Ch 32 [6] (Briggs J). See the comments by M Conaglen and E Weaver, 'Protectors as Fiduciaries: Theory and Practice' (2012) 18 *Trusts & Trustees* 17, 25.

[89] *Re Sigma Finance* (n 36).

[90] *BNY Mellon* (n 36).

[91] *Byrnes v Kendle* [2011] HCA 26, (2011) 243 CLR 253.

[92] Note the (extra-judicial) comments by Heydon J some five and a half months before in JD Heydon, 'Implications of Chartbrook Ltd v Persimmon Homes Ltd for the Law of Trusts' (The Law Society of South Australia Trusts Symposium, Adelaide, 18 February 2011).

[93] *Byrnes* (n 91) [102]–[104] (Heydon and Crennan JJ).

[94] ibid [103], citing Mason and Deane JJ in *Gosper v Sawyer* [1985] HCA 19, (1985) 160 CLR 548, 568–69.

[95] ibid [104], citing old case law on interpretation of written instruments: Lord Gifford in *Buttery & Co v Inglis* (1877) 5 R 58 (CS); and Popham CJ in *Countess of Rutland's Case* [1572] EngR 423, (1604) 5 Co Rep 25b.

[96] *Byrnes* (n 91) [111] (Heydon and Crennan JJ).

[97] *Mettoy Pension Trustees Ltd v Evans* [1990] 1 WLR 1587 (Ch); *National Grid Co plc v Mayes* [2001] UKHL 20, [2001] 1 WLR 864; *Stevens* (n 24); and *Imperial Group Pension Trust Ltd v Imperial Tobacco Ltd* [1991] 1 WLR 589 (Ch).

practices. More recently, in *Mercanti v Mercanti*[98] the Court of Appeal in Western Australia held that general contract interpretation principles apply to trusts and deeds.

VI. *BARNARDO'S* AND PENSION SCHEMES: BACKGROUND MATRIX OF FACT?

Although the general interpretation principles apply to pension schemes, the case law is indicating that the nature of a pension scheme, in particular that its beneficiaries will usually not have been a party to the signing or execution of the relevant trust deed (or later deed of amendment) may mean that the background 'matrix of fact' that may otherwise be relevant in interpretation (at least to a degree) is given lesser weight or ignored altogether.

A. *Barnardo's*

In *Barnardo's* Lord Hodge raised five 'distinctive characteristics' relevant for a court when considering interpretation of a pension scheme. He held that:

> A pension scheme … has several distinctive characteristics which are relevant to the court's selection of the appropriate interpretative tools.
>
> First, it is a formal legal document which has been prepared by skilled and specialist legal draftsmen.
>
> Secondly, unlike many commercial contracts, it is not the product of commercial negotiation between parties who may have conflicting interests and who may conclude their agreement under considerable pressure of time, leaving loose ends to be sorted out in future.
>
> Thirdly, it is an instrument which is designed to operate in the long term, defining people's rights long after the economic and other circumstances, which existed at the time when it was signed, may have ceased to exist.
>
> Fourthly, the scheme confers important rights on parties, the members of the pension scheme, who were not parties to the instrument and who may have joined the scheme many years after it was initiated.
>
> Fifthly, members of a pension scheme may not have easy access to expert legal advice or be able readily to ascertain the circumstances which existed when the scheme was established.[99]

So this means for a pension scheme that there will be more of a focus on textual analysis than use of background materials. Even for contracts generally, background materials must usually be limited to those 'reasonably available to the parties',[100]

[98] *Mercanti* (n 44). Buss P cited at [72] and [73]: *Royal Botanic Gardens* (n 45) [9]–[10]; *Byrnes* (n 91) [53] (Gummow and Hayne JJ), [102]–[107] (Heydon and Crennan JJ); and also *Smith v Lucas* (1881) 18 Ch D 531, 542 (Sir George Jessel MR); and *Commissioners of Inland Revenue v Raphael* [1935] AC 96 (HL) 142–43 (Lord Wright).

[99] *Barnardo's* (n 2) [14] (Lord Hodge). I have divided Lord Hodge's points into separate paragraphs for ease of reading.

[100] *Investors Compensation Scheme v West Bromwich Building Society* [1998] 1 WLR 896 (HL) 912 (Lord Hoffmann).

which is usually envisaged as referring to the parties (ie, signatories) to the contract itself – and hence probably not to third parties such as assignees or holders of third-party rights (for example, beneficiaries under a trust or under the Contracts (Rights of Third Parties) Act 1999).

Lord Hodge stated:

> Judges have recognised that these characteristics make it appropriate for the court to give weight to textual analysis, by concentrating on the words which the draftsman has chosen to use and by attaching less weight to the background factual matrix than might be appropriate in certain commercial contracts.[101]

This approach has its merits. A court is not assisted by assertions as to whether or not the pensions industry in 1991 could have foreseen or did foresee the criticisms of the suitability of the RPI, which later emerged in the public domain, or then thought that it was or was not likely that the RPI would be superseded.[102]

In *Barnardo's* Lord Hodge went on to comment that there was still a need to 'avoid undue technicality' and to 'have regard to the practical consequences of any construction'.[103] 'Such an analysis does not involve literalism but includes a purposive construction when that is appropriate'. Lord Hodge approved Millett J's comments in *In Re Courage Group's Pension Schemes*[104] that there are no special rules of construction applicable to a pension scheme but 'its provisions should wherever possible be construed to give reasonable and practical effect to the scheme'.

Lord Hodge continued:

> [T]he focus on textual analysis operates as a constraint on the contribution which background factual circumstances, which existed at the time when the scheme was entered into but which would not readily be accessible to its members as time passed, can make to the construction of the scheme.[105]

However, Lord Hodge held that it was still necessary to consider tax rules:[106] the pension scheme should be construed against fiscal background, citing *National Grid v Mayes*[107] and *Stevens v Bell.*[108] Lord Hodge commented that a focus on textual analysis should not prevent a court from

> being alive to the possibility that the draftsman has made a mistake in the use of language or grammar which can be corrected by construction, as occurred *in Chartbrook Ltd v Persimmon Homes Ltd* [2009] AC 1101, where the court can clearly identify both the mistake and the nature of the correction.[109]

[101] *Barnardo's* (n 2) [15] (Lord Hodge).
[102] See, eg, *Atos IT Services UK Ltd v Atos Pension Schemes Ltd* [2020] EWHC 145 (Ch) (Nugee J) in particular at [51]–[55] distinguishing the Supreme Court decision in *Lloyds TSB Foundation* (n 43).
[103] ibid [16] (Lord Hodge).
[104] *Re Courage* (n 23) 505.
[105] *Barnardo's* (n 2) [16] (Lord Hodge).
[106] ibid [17] (Lord Hodge).
[107] *Mayes* (n 97) [18] (Lord Hoffmann).
[108] *Stevens* (n 24) [30] (Arden LJ).
[109] *Barnardo's* (n 2) [18] (Lord Hodge).

He further said:

> It is trite both that a provision in a pension scheme or other formal document should be considered in the context of the document as a whole and that one would in principle expect words and phrases to be used consistently in a carefully drafted document, absent a reason for giving them different meanings.[110]

There are echoes here of Lord Collins in *Re Sigma Finance*,[111] where he said that in complex documents such as the Exchange Offer Memorandum: 'there are bound to be ambiguities, infelicities and inconsistencies' and had gone on to warn against an 'over-literal interpretation of one provision without regard to the whole', which may 'distort or frustrate the commercial purpose'.

In *Barnardo's*, Lord Hodge commented that he gained no real assistance from considering previous rules.[112] This was because the 1988 rules involved 'wholesale re-drafting'; and 'members who have no knowledge of the prior rules, makes it unprofitable to delve into the archaeology of the rules'. He also agreed with the *Stevens v Bell*[113] analysis, for 'the court must construe the scheme without any preconceptions as to whether a construction should favour the sponsoring employer or the members: [*Stevens v Bell*]. The sponsoring employer's gain may be the members' loss and vice versa'.[114]

B. Cases Cited by Lord Hodge

i. Spooner v British Telecommunications plc

In a case decided in 2000, *Spooner v British Telecommunications plc*,[115] Jonathan Parker J had held that the background 'matrix' for a pension scheme should be restricted, compared with a commercial contract. He considered that 'it cannot be right that, in order to understand what the scheme means, a new member is obliged to undertake a process of historical research, the requisite materials for which may well not be readily available to him' and that in relation to such an approach, 'the practical consequences would be well nigh unworkable'.[116]

Jonathan Parker J however went on (in a paragraph not cited by Lord Hodge in *Barnardo's*) to confirm that the express terms of a trust instrument could refer to an external document.

[110] ibid [23] (Lord Hodge).
[111] *Re Sigma Finance* (n 36) [35].
[112] *Barnardo's* (n 2) [18] (Lord Hodge).
[113] *Stevens* (n 24).
[114] *Barnardo's* (n 2) [28] (Lord Hodge).
[115] *Spooner v British Telecommunications plc* [2000] Pens LR 65 (Ch) (Jonathan Parker J).
[116] Echoes here of the later decision of the Court of Appeal in *Stevens* (n 24) [28] (Arden LJ) 'reasonable and practical effect'.

ii. BESTrustees v Stuart

In 2001, in *BESTrustees v Stuart*,[117] Neuberger J referred to the likelihood that the scheme would last for a considerable time, members are entitled to protection from the trustee and the employer 'and indeed the court'. The members 'will be people who are comparatively poor, who will not have easy access to expert legal advice, and who will not know what has been going on in relation to the management of the Scheme'. He held that this meant that the court has to be very careful before it permits a departure from the plain wording and plain requirements of the trust deed. Neuberger J held:

> In this connection, I bear in mind that a pension scheme is likely to continue for a substantial period of time and that those most affected by them and entitled to protection from the trustee, the employer and indeed the court, will be people who are comparatively poor, who will not have easy access to expert legal advice, and who will not know what has been going on in relation to the management of the Scheme. In those circumstances, it seems to me that protection of the beneficiaries requires the court to be very careful before it permits a departure from the plain wording and plain requirements of the trust deed. Further, it is not as if this was a case where at the date of the trust deed there was a difference of identity between the trustee and the employer: they were the same person even then. Accordingly, I think the court should be particularly careful before effectively overriding the requirement that there is some sort of written record which can be said to amount to an authority within the meaning of clause 16 of the definitive deed.[118]

iii. Safeway v Newton

In 2017, in *Safeway Ltd v Newton*,[119] Lord Briggs, giving the judgment of the Court of Appeal, stated (in a passage repeated by Lord Hodge in *Barnardo's*) that the fact that a pension deed 'exists primarily for the benefit of non-parties' is a context which is

> antipathetic to the recognition, by way of departure from plain language, of some common understanding between the principal employer and the trustee, or common dictionary which they may have employed, or even some widespread practice within the pension industry which might illuminate, or give some strained meaning to, the words used.

Lord Briggs held, in the three paragraphs cited by Lord Hodge:

> The judge rejected substantially similar submissions from Mr Green to those summarised above. In our view he was clearly right to do so. The starting point is that the Clause 19 power of amendment forms part of a sophisticated, professionally drafted code for the administration of a valuable and complex business trust, a context in which those having recourse to the terms of the written instruments which regulate it are in principle entitled to assume that clear language means what it says.

[117] *BESTrustees v Stuart* [2001] EWHC 549 (Ch), [2001] OPLR 341, [2001] Pens LR 283. See also Warren J in *IBM UK Holdings Ltd v Dalgleish* [2014] EWHC 980 (Ch), [2015] Pens LR 425 [155].

[118] *BESTrustees* (n 117) [33] (Neuberger J).

[119] *Safeway Ltd v Newton* [2017] EWCA Civ 1482, [2018] Pens LR 2.

> The parties to the 1984 Deed are the principal employer, upon which the Deed imposes substantial financial obligations, and the corporate Trustee, upon which the Deed imposes fiduciary duties. But the Deed exists primarily for the benefit of non-parties, that is the employees upon whom pension rights are conferred whether as members or potential members of the Scheme, and upon members of their families (for example in the event of their death). It is therefore a context which is inherently antipathetic to the recognition, by way of departure from plain language, of some common understanding between the principal employer and the Trustee, or common dictionary which they may have employed, or even some widespread practice within the pension industry which might illuminate, or give some strained meaning to, the words used.[120]

C. Looking at Old Deeds?

Lord Hodge in *Barnardo's*[121] agreed with Lewison LJ[122] at the Court of Appeal stage that the nature of a pension scheme, which may have members who have no knowledge of the prior rules, makes it unprofitable to delve into the archaeology of the rules in this case. Similarly, Asplin LJ in *British Telecommunications*:

> Before considering the terms of the 1993 Rule, it is important to bear in mind that both Robert Walker J (as he then was) in *National Grid v Laws*[123] and more recently, Lewison LJ in the *Barnardo's case*, made clear that pension scheme archaeology is unlikely to be of much assistance. This is as a result of the fourth distinctive characteristic to which Lord Hodge referred at [14] of his judgment in the *Barnardo's* case, namely that members of a scheme are not parties to the instrument which confers significant rights upon them and may have joined the scheme many years after it was initiated. In such circumstances, background facts have a very limited role to play in the task of interpretation.[124]

This runs slightly contrary to the comments by Robert Walker J (as he then was) at a High Court stage in *National Grid v Laws*. He would allow such an examination of previous deeds where the validity of a power of amendment or its scope were at stake, but not otherwise. Robert Walker J stated:

> [I]n a case where the scope of a power of amendment and the validity of a particular amendment are in issue, examination of the history of the matter is plainly permissible and indeed indispensable. In other cases my instinct would be … to stick to the current text as a general rule, while bearing in mind that the text of any long established pension scheme is likely to be a patchwork. There is a serious policy issue here: it is often hard enough for trustees and their advisers (and even harder for members or pensioners who may not have easy access to advice) to interpret a pension scheme as it stands, without also having to delve into the archaeology of the scheme.[125]

[120] ibid [21]–[22] (Lord Briggs).
[121] *Barnardo's* (n 2) [26] (Lord Hodge).
[122] ibid [23] (Lewison LJ).
[123] *National Grid Co plc v Laws* [1997] Pens LR 157 [73].
[124] *British Telecommunications Plc v BT Pension Scheme Trustees* Ltd [2018] EWCA Civ 2694 [32].
[125] *National Grid Co plc v Laws* [70] (Walker J).

i. Stevens v Bell

In 2002, in *Stevens v Bell*[126] Arden LJ held (in a passage cited by Lord Hodge in *Barnardo's*):

> Fourth, as with any other instrument, a provision of a trust deed must be interpreted in the light of the factual situation at the time it was created. This includes the practice and requirements of the Inland Revenue at that time, and may include common practice among practitioners in the field as evidenced by the works of practitioners at that time. It has been submitted to us that the factual background is only relevant if the document is ambiguous. I do not accept this submission, which is inconsistent with the approach laid down by Lord Hoffmann in *Investors Compensation Scheme v West Bromwich Building Society* [1998] 1 WLR 896. In Lord Hoffmann's words '[i]nterpretation is the ascertainment of the meaning which the document would convey to a reasonable person having all the background that would reasonably have been available to the parties in the situation in which they were at the time of the contract' (912H). Lord Hoffmann also distinguished the meaning of the words to be found in dictionaries from the meaning of documents:
>
> '(4) The meaning which a document (or any other utterance) would convey to a reasonable man is not the same thing as the meaning of its words. The meaning of words is a matter of dictionaries and grammars; the meaning of the document is what the parties using those words against the relevant background would reasonably have been understood to mean. The background may not merely enable the reasonable man to choose between the possible meanings of words which are ambiguous but even (as occasionally happens in ordinary life) to conclude that the parties must, for whatever reason, have used the wrong words or syntax: see *Mannai Investments Co Ltd v Eagle Star Life Assurance Co Ltd* [1997] AC 749'.[127]

D. Cases After *Barnardo's*

In *University Superannuation Scheme v Scragg*,[128] Rose J was considering the interpretation of an ill-health rule. She held that the rule meant that the trustee needed to be satisfied of fact of incapacity (as well as the employer). Counsel sought to rely on the fact that rule had not been changed in the 2015 Rules, despite a Pensions Ombudsman decision (two months earlier) about the meaning of the rule. Rose J held this was 'the kind of interpretive tool which the Supreme Court has disapproved in *Barnardo's*'.[129]

In *Coats UK Pension Scheme Trustees Ltd v Styles*[130] Morgan J cited *Barnardo's* and explained the principles outlined by Lord Hodge. Morgan J then construed the Notes to the Appendix to the 1996 Rules of a pension scheme 'in the context of a number of other provisions in the 1996 Rules and against the background of the [tax legislation]'.

British Telecommunications PLC v BT Pension Scheme Trustees Ltd[131] was another case on the meaning of an indexation rule. The Court of Appeal held that the

[126] *Stevens* (n 24).
[127] ibid [30] (Arden LJ).
[128] *University Superannuation Scheme v Scragg* [2019] EWHC 51, [2019] ICR 738.
[129] ibid [27] (Rose J).
[130] *Coats UK Pension Scheme Trustees Ltd v Styles* [2019] EWHC 35 (Ch) [62]–[63] (Morgan J).
[131] *BT Pension Scheme Trustees* (n 124).

power to change the index would only apply if a relevant factual gateway had been satisfied (either that RPI ceased to be published or that RPI 'becomes inappropriate'). The Court of Appeal held that both of these gateways were objective matters of fact and not matters for either the trustee or the employer's opinion to be conclusive. If necessary the issue could be determined by a court.

Asplin LJ[132] (who gave the main judgment) referred to *Barnardo's* and stated (at [19]) that 'I approach the construction of Rule 10.2 with all of Lord Hodge's guidance in the *Barnardo's* case in mind and give due weight to textual analysis by concentrating on the words that the draftsman chose to use'. The use here by Asplin LJ of the term 'concentrating', does not seem to rule out giving some weight to background facts, but in practice later these were ignored.

Asplin LJ also dealt with an argument about whether previous rules or background notes could be used to construe the relevant provision,[133] holding that they did not assist in that case, because it was clear that a rewrite and substantive amendments had been made by the new rules and because the previous background notes (exchanged between the employer and the trustee) were not allowed by *Barnardo's*. This latter point seems to have been obiter as Asplin LJ went on to say that in any event the notes did not help interpretation of the new rules.

VII. IMPACT OF *BARNARDO'S*

Following *Barnardo's*, the approach for construction of pension schemes seems to be similar to that for other types of instrument, in particular those relied on by third parties or on a public register (where there may not be reasonable access to background documents). This means potentially less reliance on the background matrix of fact. But pension beneficiaries can require some background information to be given to them: *Re Londonderry*[134] and *Schmidt v Rosewood*.[135] This is not a point mentioned in *Barnardo's*.

It is relevant that Lord Hodge in *Barnardo's* did not prohibit all use of background material. Lord Hodge did not say that a court *cannot* ever rely on background facts:

> [T]hese characteristics make it appropriate for the court to give weight to textual analysis, by concentrating on the words which the draftsman has chosen to use and by attaching *less weight* to the background factual matrix than might be appropriate in certain commercial contracts.[136]

Lord Hodge expressly allowed reference to the fiscal background (this may be more generally available, but it cannot be said that most individuals can understand pensions tax legislation without specialist advice). Rose J in *University Superannuation Scheme v Scragg*[137] seems to be a bit terse in ruling out a previous Pensions Ombudsman decision altogether, although seemingly understandable in that particular case.

[132] With whom Patten and David Richards LJJ agreed.
[133] *BT Pension Scheme Trustees* (n 124) [35] and [36].
[134] *Re Londonderry's Settlement* [1965] 1 Ch 918 (CA).
[135] *Schmidt v Rosewood Trust Ltd* [2003] UKPC 26, [2003] 2 AC 76 (PC).
[136] *Barnado's* (n 2) [15] (Lord Hodge) (emphasis added).
[137] *Scragg* (n 128).

Notwithstanding *Barnardo's* and the comments of Asplin LJ in *British Telecommunications*[138] quoted above, there seems to be no reason why parties to a pension trust deed or a deed of amendment cannot mandate the use by the courts of background documents if these are expressly referred to in the document (for example, in a recital). An example, would be a reference to a briefing note given to both the trustees and the employer.

It also may be arguable that the decision in *Barnardo's* may have less impact on interpretation of non-benefit provisions, ie, provisions that do not affect members directly (for example, investment powers). Here it may be more reasonable to expect the trustees to stand in for members. For example, the comments by Newey J in *Arcadia*[139] holding that a power to select a new index should be exercised by the company and the trustee jointly.

A. Commentary on *Barnardo's*

The Supreme Court's decision in *Barnardo's* is a clear suggestion that background information may have a more limited role in a trust than it may do in a commercial contract. This is not because the trust is a public document on a register, but more because of the third-party interests in the trust instrument on the part of the beneficiaries, in the case of a pension scheme, the members (and other beneficiaries).

But the judgment in *Barnardo's* does not preclude background information being used to help interpretation.[140] Such background information may be used:

a. If the background information is readily available to third parties, for example, the tax and statutory backgrounds.
b. Arguably may still be used where the background information is specifically referred to in the trust instrument (for example, if a new deed expressly refers to a background paper, such as briefing note)[141] and so is available to third parties.
c. Arguably also should allow a special position for information available to both the executing parties (ie, the Principal Employer and the trustee board) for a particular instrument. Amendments to an occupational pension scheme tend in practice to require the consent of the Principal Employer and the trustee and not require individual consent from members (or their dependants). It seems clear that rectification will look only to the knowledge of the Principal Employer and the trustee board (and not the members). It seems to be more arguable that this approach should apply to interpretation as well[142] – but this is not discussed in *Barnardo's*.

[138] *BT Pension Scheme Trustees* (n 124).

[139] *Arcadia Group Ltd v Arcadia Group Pension Trust Ltd* [2014] EWHC 2683 (Ch), [2014] ICR D35 (Newey J).

[140] See *Britvic Plc v Britvic Pensions Ltd* [2020] EWHC 118 (Ch) (HHJ Hodge) [79].

[141] See, eg, *Trump International* (n 65).

[142] See the points made by one of the counsel for the company in *Barnardo's* (n 2): E Campbell, 'Barnardo's v Buckinghamshire and the Interpretation of Pension Schemes' (*Wilberforce Chambers Recent Cases*, 21 November 2018), available at: www.wilberforce.co.uk/barnardos-v-buckinghamshire-and-the-interpretation-of-pension-schemes/.

5

Rectification and Pensions

PAUL S DAVIES

PENSION SCHEMES CAN be very complicated. They can be governed by different documents which are detailed, intricate and subject to change over a long period of time. Inadvertent errors are inevitable. As a result, rectification is a potentially important remedy. In *Lansing Linde Ltd v Alber*, Rimer J observed that '[t]he need for the remedy is because it is a fact of life that sometimes mistakes arise in the drafting of documents which the signatories do not spot before they sign'.[1]

However, it is only relatively recently that attention has been given to rectification in the context of pensions. The first reported case was *Lansing Linde*, a decision of 1999, but there have since been a large number of claims for rectification – even on summary judgment.[2] It is not entirely clear why cases on rectification do not seem to have arisen earlier.[3] Perhaps the recent growth coincides with an increased awareness or vigilance of those administering or advising pension schemes, and a more difficult economic climate (such that most benefits amendments from the early 1990s onwards were no longer benefit improvements). Or maybe the replacement of final salary schemes with defined contributions schemes has required a greater number of general reviews of scheme documentation, and consequently the revelation of previous mistakes. Both factors are probably significant, but it is suggested that the major reason why claims for rectification were not often brought before the late 1990s is because employers and trustees used to be able to agree an amendment between themselves that would have retrospective effect and achieve the same goal as rectification. This is no longer straightforwardly available as a result of section 67 of the Pensions Act 1995, which provides that any power to modify an occupational pension scheme 'cannot be exercised on any occasion in a manner which would or might affect any entitlement, or accrued right, of any member of the scheme acquired before the power is exercised' unless certain stringent requirements are satisfied. As a result, parties are more likely to seek relief from a court.

[1] *Lansing Linde Ltd v Alber* [2000] Pens LR 15 (Ch) [123].
[2] See part VIII below.
[3] P Newman, 'Rectification and Pension Schemes' (2002) 16 *Trust Law International* 21.

Huge sums of money can turn upon whether a mistake in the documentation can be rectified. Yet in important respects the law is not clear, and should be examined more closely. As Sir Terence Etherton has observed, extra-judicially, rectification in occupational pension schemes

> raises particular difficulties because in many instances (most obviously, where the exercise of a power of amendment is in issue) the legal and factual context is not a bilateral contractual one but nor are the members of the scheme mere volunteers or donees.[4]

Moreover, difficult issues of policy may arise. Whilst not granting rectification as a result of a mistake of an employer may give certain employees a windfall, large payouts could have a damaging impact on the employer's covenant and the security of other members' benefits. The law in this area has not been subjected to much analysis,[5] and the aim of this chapter is to cast further light on this subject and some particularly difficult issues that arise.

I. RECTIFICATION WILL NOT BE ORDERED WHERE AN ALTERNATIVE REMEDY IS POSSIBLE

As Lord Walker recognised in *Pitt v Holt*, '[r]ectification is a closely guarded remedy, strictly limited to some clearly-established disparity between the words of a legal document, and the intentions of the parties to it'.[6] It is, rightly, difficult to convince a court that a formal, written document should be altered as a result of a mistake. Whilst mistakes do happen, parties should be encouraged to check the documents they sign carefully and the strong presumption must be that the parties intended to be bound by the plain meaning[7] of a legal instrument. 'Strong irrefragable evidence' is required to support a claim for rectification.[8]

Rectification will not be granted if an alternative remedy is available to the parties at common law. After all, if the common law can provide satisfactory relief to the parties then there is no reason for equity to intervene. A hard example of this point is provided by *Whiteside v Whiteside*.[9] A husband executed a deed in favour of his

[4] T Etherton, 'The Role of Equity in Mistaken Transactions' (2013) 27 *Trust Law International* 159, 163.

[5] Although, for an overview of the cases, see D Hodge, *Rectification: The Modern Law and Practice Governing Claims for Rectification for Mistake*, 2nd edn (London, Sweet & Maxwell, 2015) [9–39] ff.

[6] *Pitt v Holt* [2013] UKSC 26, [2013] 2 AC 108 [131].

[7] It has been suggested that this term is problematic: see, eg, L Solan, *The Language of Judges* (Chicago, IL, University of Chicago Press, 1993) especially ch 4; A Corbin, *Corbin on Contracts* (St Paul, MN, West Publishing, 1960) vol 3, especially §535 and §542. But compare R Lord, *Williston on Contracts*, 4th edn (Rochester, NY, Lawyers Co-operative Publishing Company, 1999) §602; E Farnsworth, *Contracts*, 4th edn (New York, Aspen Publishers, 2004) §7.7. The term also continues to be invoked judicially: eg, *Charter Reinsurance Co Ltd v Fagan* [1997] AC 313 (HL) 384; *Lloyds TSB Foundation for Scotland v Lloyds Banking Group plc* [2013] UKSC 3, [2013] 1 WLR 366; *Lehman Brothers International (Europe) v Lehman Brothers Finance SA* [2013] EWCA Civ 188, [2014] 2 BCLC 451 [71]. See too *Arnold v Britton* [2015] UKSC 36, [2015] AC 1619 [15]; *Royal Devon and Exeter NHS Foundation Trust v Atos IT Services UK Ltd* [2017] EWCA Civ 2196, [2018] 2 All ER (Comm) 535 [45]. However, where a document is ambiguous, the court may have recourse to a wider range of background factors in order to establish the proper meaning of the document; for further analysis, see David Pollard's contribution to this volume.

[8] *Countess of Shelburne v Earl of Inchiquin* (1784) 1 Bro CC 338, 341 (Lord Thurlow LC); see too *James Hay Pension Trustees Ltd v Kean Hird et al* [2005] EWHC (Ch) 1093 [81] (Lawrence Collins J).

[9] *Whiteside v Whiteside* [1950] 1 Ch 65.

former wife upon dissolution of their marriage. There was a mistake in the formulation of the amount to be paid. The husband brought proceedings for rectification, but also executed a supplemental deed amending the error. The Court of Appeal refused to grant rectification because the supplemental deed resolved the issue between the parties. This was harsh on the husband since the supplemental deed only had prospective effect against the Revenue, whereas rectification would have had retrospective effect. But the Court insisted that rectification is a narrow remedy which is 'cautiously watched and jealously exercised'.[10]

Voluntary amendments are not, generally, an effective substitute for rectification, especially in the context of pensions. This is partly because amendments which have retrospective effect and prejudice the position of scheme members may well fall foul of section 67 of the Pensions Act 1995.[11] Moreover, parties which proceed on the basis that a court would grant rectification and so the scheme can be administered as if rectification were inevitable run a very substantial risk of being wrong. At one point there appeared to be a view that an 'equity of rectification' may arise in situations where rectification would be granted, and trustees should operate on the basis of a rectified instrument even where no application to court had been made.[12] But the better view is that 'unless and until a document is rectified by an order of the Court, the document takes effect as it stands'.[13] Trustees should obey the terms of the trust instrument,[14] and seek rectification if the terms, by mistake, do not accurately reflect the relevant party's (or parties') intentions.

Some mistakes may be corrected by interpretation at common law. Indeed, some cases even refer to 'common law rectification'.[15] But such language is dangerous and prone to mislead. There are important differences between interpretation and rectification. As Lord Neuberger said in *Marley v Rawlings*:

> At first sight, it might seem to be a rather dry question whether a particular approach is one of interpretation or rectification. However, it is by no means simply an academic issue of categorisation. If it is a question of interpretation, then the document in question has, and has always had, the meaning and effect as determined by the court, and that is the end of the matter. On the other hand, if it is a question of rectification, then the document, as rectified, has a different meaning from that which it appears to have on its face, and the court would have jurisdiction to refuse rectification or to grant it on terms (eg, if there had been delay, change of position, or third party reliance).[16]

[10] ibid 71 (Sir Raymond Evershed MR).

[11] ibid.

[12] *cf South West Trains Ltd v Wightman* [1997] OPLR 249, [1998] Pens LR 113, [77] and [120] (Neuberger J). See, eg, Newman (n 3) 21, 21–22.

[13] *Singla v Brown* [2007] EWHC 405 (Ch), [2008] 2 WLR 283 [23] (Thomas Ivory QC); see too Briggs LJ in *Safeway Ltd v Newton* [2017] EWCA Civ 1482, [2018] Pens LR 2 [26].

[14] In *Perrins v Bellamy* [1899] Ch 797, 798 Lindley MR famously said that 'My old Master, the late Selwyn LJ, used to say: "The main duty of a trustee is to commit judicious breaches of trust"', but it is suggested that trustees should not follow this flippant remark.

[15] See *Westway Homes Ltd v Moore* (1992) 63 P&CR 480, 489; *Holding & Barnes Plc v Hill House Hammond Limited* [2001] EWCA Civ 1334, [2002] 2 P&CR 11 [47]; *KPMG v Network Rail Infrastructure Ltd* [2007] EWCA Civ 363, [2008] 1 P&CR 11 [48]; *Chartbrook Ltd v Persimmon Homes Ltd* [2009] UKHL 38, [2009] 1 AC 1101 [22]–[24].

[16] *Marley v Rawlings* [2014] UKSC 2, [2014] 2 WLR 213 [40].

It is important that interpretation does not expand beyond its proper limits and engulf the equitable remedy of rectification.[17] There has recently been something of a 'check' upon the liberal approach favoured by Lord Hoffmann[18] to interpretation of contracts,[19] and a focus upon the 'plain meaning' of written instruments helps to limit the scope of interpretation and allow room for rectification to operate. This has recently been mirrored in the context of pensions. For example, in *Barnardo's v Buckinghamshire*,[20] Lord Hodge confirmed that a 'textual interpretation' was appropriate (rather than departing from the meaning of the text due to 'contextual' considerations).[21] Lord Hodge pointed to a number of factors to support this conclusion: pension schemes are formal legal documents prepared by skilled and specialist legal draftsmen; they are not generally concluded under considerable pressures of time; they are designed to operate in the long term; they confer important rights upon members who were not party to the instrument; and members of a pension scheme may not easily be able to access legal advice or ascertain the circumstances that exist when the scheme was created.[22] However, it appears that there is still scope to correct obvious 'typos' through interpretation, even in the context of pensions.[23]

Other avenues to correcting mistakes appear less promising. For example, the possibility of estoppel by convention was previously flirted with[24] but sensibly rejected in *Lansing Linde* and has not arisen in the pensions context since.[25] Similarly, a claim to the Pensions Ombudsman is unlikely to be effective since the Ombudsman cannot entertain class actions,[26] and a non-complainant cannot be bound by a decision in the complainant's favour even where the complainant and non-complainant have the same interests.[27] The intervention of a court through rectification remains desirable.

Of course, one reason why a mistake may have been made could be a breach of duty by professionals – such as lawyers – involved in the drafting and execution of the legal instrument. Such professionals may be exposed to professional negligence claims if a claim for rectification is unsuccessful or not pursued. As a result, those who made the mistake may well fund rectification proceedings in order to ensure that any losses are minimised or eradicated. Many rectification claims are therefore brought in order to mitigate losses that may arise from professional negligence claims,[28]

[17] P Davies, 'Rectification Versus Interpretation: The Nature and Scope of the Equitable Jurisdiction' (2016) 75 *CLJ* 62.

[18] For an overview, see P Davies, 'The Meaning of Commercial Contracts' in P Davies and J Pila (eds), *The Jurisprudence of Lord Hoffmann* (Oxford, Hart Publishing, 2015).

[19] See especially *Rainy Sky SA v Kookmin Bank* [2011] UKSC 50, [2011] 1 WLR 2900; *Arnold v Britton* (n 7). See too Lord Sumption, 'A Question of Taste: The Supreme Court and the Interpretation of Contracts' (2017) 17 *Oxford University Commonwealth Law Journal* 301. *cf* Lord Hoffmann, 'Language and Lawyers' (2018) 134 *LQR* 553.

[20] *Barnardo's v Buckinghamshire and Ors* [2018] UKSC 55, [2019] 2 All ER 175.

[21] See too *Safeway Ltd v Newton* (n 13) [23], citing *BESTrustees v Stuart* [2001] Pens LR 283 [33] (Neuberger J).

[22] *Barnardo's* (n 20) [14]. See further David Pollard's contribution to this volume.

[23] *Barnardo's* (n 20) [18]. See too *ICM Computer Group Ltd v Stribley* [2013] EWHC 2995 (Ch), [2013] Pens LR 409 (Asplin J).

[24] *Icarus (Hertford) Ltd v Driscoll* [1990] Pens LR 1; *ITN v Ward* [1997] Pens LR 131.

[25] *Lansing Linde* (n 1) [197]–[201].

[26] *Edge v Pensions Ombudsman* [2000] Ch 602.

[27] *Marsh Mercer Pension Scheme v Pensions Ombudsman* [2001] 16 PBLR (Ch).

[28] *Walker v Medlicott* [1999] 1 All ER 685(CA).

which may be especially efficient where the claims are unopposed. However, it should be remembered that the duty to mitigate loss does not go so far as to require a party to embark on a difficult piece of litigation.[29]

II. IDENTIFYING THE DOCUMENT TO BE RECTIFIED

The nature of the document to be rectified must be clearly identified. In the pensions context, rectification claims tend to concern either the original deed setting up the trust, or a deed of amendment. The most problematic cases considered in this chapter concern the latter, but it is important to appreciate that the original trust deed may also be rectified, and this possibility will be analysed first.

Rectification requires some disparity between the terms contained in a trust deed and the intention of the party that executed it. The clearest examples are those cases where there has been a drafting error in the preparation of the final trust deed, such that it does not reflect earlier drafts.[30] In such cases the mistake relates to the terms of the trust deed, as the document does not say what the settlor intended. The following passage of Brightman J in *Re Butlin's Settlement Trust* has been influential when considering the rectification of trusts:

> [I]n the absence of an actual bargain between the settlor and the trustees, (i) a settlor may seek rectification by proving that the settlement does not express his true intention, or the true intention of himself and any party with whom he has bargained, such as a spouse in the case of an ante-nuptial settlement; (ii) it is not essential for him to prove that the settlement fails to express the true intention of the trustees if they have not bargained; but (iii) the court may in its discretion decline to rectify a settlement against a protesting trustee who objects to rectification.[31]

This passage has been cited with approval on many occasions.[32] In a voluntary settlement, it is generally appropriate to focus upon whether the settlor was actually mistaken.[33] However, where the trust was only set up pursuant to a contract, the contractual test for rectification should be applied[34] and the intentions of both parties will usually be relevant. This will often be important in the pensions context: the trust deed is rarely entered into by the employer as a uniquely voluntary act, but after reaching agreement with the employees, generally through their representatives.

Determining the appropriate test for rectification of a contract for common mistake has provoked much controversy recently. In *Chartbrook*, Lord Hoffmann expressed the view that a contract could be rectified for common mistake even where

[29] *Pilkington v Wood* [1953] Ch 770; *Moda International Brands Limited v Gateley LLP* [2019] EWHC 1326 (QB), [2019] PNLR 27 [113] (Freedman J).

[30] eg, *Re Farepak Food and Gifts Ltd* [2006] EWHC 3272, [2008] BCC 22.

[31] *Re Butlin's Settlement Trust* [1976] Ch 251, 262.

[32] See, eg, *Day v Day* [2013] EWCA Civ 280, [2014] Ch 114 [21]. See too *Giles v The Royal National Institute for the Blind* [2014] EWHC 1373 (Ch), [2014] STC 1631 [25].

[33] *Day* (n 32).

[34] *Konica Minolta Business Solutions (UK) Ltd v Applegate* [2013] EWHC 2536 (Ch) (Edward Bartley Jones QC).

one party was not actually mistaken: it was sufficient that a reasonable observer would conclude, objectively, that both parties had made a common mistake.[35] The other members of the House of Lords agreed with Lord Hoffmann's speech, but his Lordship's views on rectification were, strictly, obiter. This left the law in a troublesome position: should judges follow Lord Hoffmann's lead, or continue to apply the orthodox test that required both parties actually (or 'subjectively') to have made a mistake? In *Daventry District Council v Daventry & District Housing Ltd*[36] the parties assumed, without further argument, that the objective approach to rectification favoured in *Chartbrook* should be applied, and the Supreme Court frustratingly refused permission to appeal. However, in *FSHC Group Holdings Ltd v Glas Trust Corporation Ltd* the Court of Appeal has very recently had a chance to examine common mistake rectification thoroughly, and restored traditional orthodoxy in setting out the following test:

> [W]e are unable to accept that the objective test of rectification for common mistake articulated in Lord Hoffmann's *obiter* remarks in the *Chartbrook* case correctly states the law. We consider that we are bound by authority, which also accords with sound legal principle and policy, to hold that, before a written contract may be rectified on the basis of a common mistake, it is necessary to show either (1) that the document fails to give effect to a prior concluded contract or (2) that, when they executed the document, the parties had a common intention in respect of a particular matter which, by mistake, the document did not accurately record. In the latter case it is necessary to show not only that each party to the contract had the same actual intention with regard to the relevant matter, but also that there was an 'outward expression of accord' – meaning that, as a result of communication between them, the parties understood each other to share that intention.[37]

Although *FSHC* did not concern pensions, the decision is likely to be very important in the pensions context and will be discussed further below.

The majority of claims for rectification in the pensions context concern deeds of amendment. Such deeds may be executed unilaterally, in which case the focus will generally be upon the intentions of the party executing the deed when deciding whether a mistake has been made that should be rectified.[38] But often the power to amend will be given to either the employer or the trustee, and the consent of the other party will be required. Moreover, sometimes the consent of the members may also be necessary, or the power to amend can only be exercised jointly. In those situations, it is more appropriate to consider the intentions of all the relevant parties, rather than to focus exclusively upon the intention of the party with the formal power to execute the deed. Rectification is necessarily fact-sensitive, and courts will consider carefully the particular circumstances in which a deed was executed. For example, a power to amend might be exercised by one party taking the sole initiative, and another party

[35] *Chartbrook* (n 15).

[36] *Daventry District Council v Daventry & District Housing Ltd* [2011] EWCA Civ 1153, [2012] 1 WLR 1333.

[37] *FSHC Group Holdings Ltd v Glas Trust Corporation Ltd* [2019] EWCA Civ 1361 [176]. This decision was handed down after this chapter had been written, and at the time of writing it is understood that the respondent is likely to seek permission to appeal to the Supreme Court.

[38] eg, *Merchant Navy Officers Pension Fund Trustees v Watkins* [2013] EWHC 4741 (Ch) [12] (John Martin QC).

giving its consent but being rather passive in the matter. Or the parties may negotiate in detail about the most appropriate way to exercise a power to amend. Some form of 'common intention' may be much more important in the second scenario than the first.

Regardless of the precise document at issue, it is important to remember that rectification is an equitable remedy. Parties cannot demand rectification as of right, and the court retains a discretion whether or not to order rectification. For example, a court may be unwilling to grant rectification if the trustee reasonably opposes the application and had accepted the office of trustee on the basis of the settlement as executed.

It should also be noted that in most claims for rectification of pension schemes, it is the employer who takes the lead. This is because it will usually be up to the employer to fund the additional liability if the mistake is not corrected. Trustees will usually be neutral or 'support' the application, without serving any substantive defence.[39] The parties who may be prejudiced by rectification are the scheme members: a representative order is generally made to allow the court to take into account a considered position of the beneficiaries under the pension trust.[40]

However, in principle there is no reason why, if the benefits documented are less generous than what had been agreed and were intended to be implemented, the trustees could not seek rectification to the apparent detriment of the employer if the latter refuses to correct the mistake.[41] Indeed, the beneficiaries may also be able seek rectification. Even volunteers may claim rectification,[42] and pension scheme members are more than just mere volunteers.[43]

III. OUTWARD EXPRESSION OF ACCORD

The cases on rectification of amendments to pension schemes have vacillated on a supposed requirement that the claimant establish an outward expression of accord. The better view is probably that it is not necessary to do so. Where a power to amend can be exercised unilaterally, there is no reason to demand an accord with any other party.[44] But a power to amend often requires the consent of the employer or trustee (depending on which of the two exercises the power) and it is controversial whether an outward expression of accord must be shown.

The first reported case on rectification of a pension scheme – *Lansing Linde v Alber* – did favour a requirement of an outward expression of accord. That case concerned an attempt to rectify a deed which represented a poor attempt at

[39] See, eg, *Gallaher Ltd v Gallaher Pensions Ltd* [2005] EWHC 42 (Ch), [2005] Pens LR 103.

[40] See part VIII below.

[41] If the trustee and employer agreed to correct the mistake in such a scenario that should not fall foul of s 67 of the Pensions Act 1995 because it would be to the advantage, rather than the detriment, of the scheme members.

[42] *Thompson v Whitmore* [1860] 1 J&H 268.

[43] *LRT Pension Fund Trustee Co Ltd v Hatt* [1993] Pens LR 227 (Ch).

[44] *Watkins* (n 38) [12].

equalisation. All nine trustees admitted to not having read the definitive deed (which was 160 pages long) before executing it, and Rimer J held that the employer had failed to show that the relevant deeds did not give effect to the intentions of the principal employer and trustees. As a result, his comments on the requirement of an outward expression of accord were strictly obiter. Nevertheless, his views were clearly expressed:

> This case is all about an amendment of the 1977 deed pursuant to clause 20(A). That provides that '[Lansing] may … with the consent of the Trustees by Deed amend the … [1977] Deed or by Deed or Board Resolution amend … the rules'. Any amendment has, therefore, to be proposed, or made, by Lansing with the accord of the trustees. What is required is a bilateral, consensual transaction whose substance is equivalent, or at least very close, to that of a contract save only for the absence of consideration. I cannot see how an amendment pursuant to clause 20 could ever be validly effected except in circumstances in which there is objective evidence of the accord between Lansing and the trustees: if there is not, how can it be shown that the trustees have consented to what Lansing has proposed? Moreover, since any such amendments are potentially of great importance to the scheme members generally (to whom Lansing owes a duty of good faith – see *Imperial Group Pension Trust Ltd & ors v Imperial Tobacco Ltd & ors* [1991] 1 WLR 589, at 597 – and for whom the trustees act as such) it is in my view essential that there should be objective evidence showing that the amendment proposed by Lansing has been consented to by the trustees; and I cannot see that the need for such evidence is any less compelling than it is in the case of a contract. The fact that an amendment pursuant to clause 20 does not involve the moving of consideration between the parties appears to me to be irrelevant. The relevant feature of a clause 20 amendment is that, just like a contract, it is a bilateral transaction, involving the need for an accord.[45]

This approach takes the requirement of consent very seriously, treating it as tantamount to contract.

However, the approach of Rimer J was not followed by Lawrence Collins J in *AMP v Barker*. In that case, a deed of amendment inadvertently extended the right to take generous early retirement pensions to all classes of members, rather than to members suffering from incapacity only. There was cogent evidence of a continuing common intention of both the trustees and principal employer to improve only incapacity benefits, and not to benefit early leavers generally. The judge generously recognised that he 'had the benefit of a more elaborate argument on the requirement of common accord in a case like the present one'[46] than Rimer J had in *Lansing Linde* and continued:

> No agreement between the Principal Employer and the trustees is envisaged by the rules. The Principal Employer simply has to consent to the exercise of the power of amendment by the trustees. But the consent is not to the exercise of the power of amendment in general. The Principal Employer must consent to the actual amendments
>
> …
>
> Consequently, the intentions of the trustees and the Principal Employer must converge. But they do not have to agree inter se. The resolution, however cannot be rectified to reflect

[45] *Lansing Linde* (n 1) [156].
[46] *AMP (UK) Ltd v Barker* [2000] EWHC (Ch) 42, [2001] Pens LR 77 [64].

> the intentions of the trustees when that is not also the intention of the Principal Employer, for otherwise the resolution could take a form to which the Principal Employer had not consented, and the consent of the Principal Employer is an essential part of the machinery of amendment.[47]

This decision minimises the importance of an outward expression of accord, and simply requires that the intentions of the trustee and employer 'converge'.

Such convergence is the least that should be required. To demand anything less would strip the requirement of consent of any content. But the extent to which there will be agreement may depend on whether there have been any serious negotiations between the parties prior to exercising the amending deed. If there has not been much discussion, then it seems overly stringent to demand an outward expression of accord. And even if there has been, the fact that 'consent' is not the same as 'bargained-for agreement' should provide a sufficient basis for distinguishing the pensions context from the contractual sphere, and require only convergence rather than accord.

The majority of pensions cases have followed *AMP v Barker* rather than *Lansing Linde*.[48] However, some judges continue to treat the issue as unsettled where they do not need to decide the point,[49] and the Court of Appeal has not been required to consider the issue.[50] In *IBM United Kingdom Pensions Trust Limited v IBM United Kingdom Holdings Limited*,[51] Warren J gave what is now taken to be the leading guidance,[52] even if some equivocation can still be seen.[53] That case concerned the rectification of a deed of amendment made 30 years previously. Warren J held that there was 'a significant difference of approach in the contractual cases and a case such as the present'[54] and said:

> There needs to be cogent evidence of the intentions of both the trustee and the employer where the power of amendment requires the consent of both … This is not a surprising result. In a case such as *Chartbrook* or *Daventry*, what is sought to be rectified is a contract; it makes sense that, in order to displace the contract actually made by rectifying it, there should be found a consensus, albeit not one giving rise to a legally binding agreement. In contrast, in a case such as the present, no sort of agreement is required for there to be a

[47] ibid [64]–[65].

[48] eg, *Gallaher* (n 39) [115]; *Drake Insurance Plc v MacDonald* [2005] EWHC 3287 (Ch), [2005] Pens LR 401 [34] (Warren J); *ZF Lemforder UK Ltd v Lemforder UK Pension Trustee Ltd* [2005] EWHC 2882 (Ch), [2006] Pens LR 85 [41] (Warren J); *IBM United Kingdom Pensions Trust Limited v IBM United Kingdom Holdings Limited* [2012] EWHC 2766 (Ch), [2012] Pens LR 469 (Warren J); *Sovereign Trustees Ltd v Lewis* [2016] EWHC 2593 (Ch), [2016] Pens LR 345 (CM Marsh); *Hogg Robinson Plc v Harvey* [2016] EWHC 129 (Ch), [2016] Pens LR 61 (Timothy Fancourt QC). See too *Irish Pensions Trust Ltd v Central Remedial Clinic* [2005] IEHC 87, [2006] 2 IR 126 [130] (Kelly J); *Boliden Tara Mines Ltd v Cosgrove* [2007] IEHC 60 [56]–[60] (Finlay Geoghegan J).

[49] *XChanging Global Insurance Systems Ltd v Clark* [2005] EWHC 3389 (Ch) [15] (Hart J); *Scania Ltd v Wager* [2007] EWHC 711 (Ch), [2007] 50 PBLR [17] (Sir Andrew Morritt C); *Colorcon Ltd v Huckell* [2009] EWHC 979 (Ch), [2009] Pens LR 201 [36] (HHJ Toulmin QC), *Konica Minolta Business Solutions* (n 34).

[50] The comments of Lewison LJ in *Day* were obiter: (n 32) [46]–[48]. See, eg, *Saga Group Ltd v Paul* [2016] EWHC 2344 (Ch), [2016] Pens LR 329 [36]–[42] (HHJ Hodge QC).

[51] *IBM* (n 48).

[52] *Harvey* (n 48); *Lewis* (n 48) [15].

[53] *Konica Minolta Business Solutions* (n 34) [35]–[36].

[54] *IBM* (n 48) [23].

> valid deed of amendment. What is needed is an exercise of the power of amendment by the trustee and the consent of the employer to the exercise of that power. If that is to be called a consensus, so be it, but it is a different animal from the agreement or consensus which is relevant in a contractual case.

This stands in stark contrast to the approach adopted by Rimer J in *Lansing Linde*. Rather than draw a close analogy with contract, Warren J held that the relevant 'consensus' is markedly different in nature.

The above passage from *IBM* was cited with approval by the Court of Appeal in *FSHC*.[55] Leggatt LJ distinguished between the pension cases and contract cases since the former do not require mutual agreement, but only approval by one party of what the other has done. As a result, an 'outward expression of accord' is only a substantive requirement in the contractual context; in the pensions context, it is sufficient that the trustees and employer independently had the same intention regarding the effect of the amendment. This is likely to prove controversial. The requirement of an outward expression of accord for rectification of a contract for common mistake stems from the decision of the Court of Appeal in *Joscelyne v Nissen*,[56] and was previously considered to be merely an evidential requirement in order to satisfy the Court that a claim for rectification should be granted.[57] Its elevation to a substantive requirement in a rectification claim may have hard results: if it can be proved that both *A* and *B* intended *X*, but the contract states *Y*, it might appear fair to rectify the contract to say *Y* even if *A* and *B* did not communicate their intentions to one another.

Given the fact that a substantive requirement for an outward expression of accord may operate in a harsh manner even in the contractual context, it appears sensible for the pensions cases not to adopt a similar requirement. Nevertheless, distinguishing the pension cases on the basis that mutual agreement is not necessary may lead to very fine distinctions being drawn. After all, it has been held that it does not matter whether the power to amend is properly regarded as a joint power held jointly by the trustee and employer, or whether it is a power to be exercised by one with the consent of the other.[58] Yet a distinction could be drawn between the two: whereas consent may be given without the sort of 'consensus' required for a contract, as Warren J pointed out in *IBM*, joint powers often will require agreement in a strong sense. If the power must be exercised jointly, should that mean that the 'outward expression of accord' *does* need to be established?

It is suggested that even in such circumstances an 'outward expression of accord' should not be required. A substantive requirement for an outward expression of accord may operate in a harsh manner even in the contractual context, so it appears sensible for the pensions cases not to adopt a similar requirement. Even in the context of a joint power, the agreement between trustee and employer is not contractual in nature, so it is probably preferable not to employ the requirement of an outward expression of accord at all. But none of the cases so far have concerned an actual

[55] *FSHC* (n 37) [79].

[56] *Joscelyne v Nissen* [1970] 2 QB 86.

[57] eg, *Munt v Beasley* [2006] EWCA Civ 370 [36] (Mummery LJ), relying on, inter alia, *Gallaher* (n 39) considered below.

[58] *MacDonald* (n 48) [33]. See too *AMP* (n 46) [64].

negotiation or bargain between the trustee and principal employer. Such a case may shift a court back towards the approach of Rimer J in *Lansing Linde* and a closer analogy to contract. That should be resisted. The focus should really be upon whether there is a mistake in the recording of the document, such that it does not align with the relevant parties' actual intentions. The importance of an outward expression of accord should not be exaggerated. There is much force behind the suggestion that the pension cases may be useful more generally as the 'thin end of the wedge' in ridding contract law of the element of an 'outward expression of accord' more generally,[59] although that prospect is unlikely in the short term in this jurisdiction as a result of the decision in *FSHC*.

IV. DO COMMUNICATIONS BETWEEN THE PARTIES NEED TO 'CROSS THE LINE'?

Consistently with a tendency to reject a requirement for an outward expression of accord, most pensions cases which consider the point do not require reliance on communications between the parties which cross the line from one side to another. This is sensible. After all, in some situations there may be no negotiations between the parties, and no communications from one side to the other. A good example may be *IBM United Kingdom Pensions Trust Limited v IBM United Kingdom Holdings Limited*.[60] The employer wanted to introduce changes which were optional for existing members, although compulsory for new recruits. The trustee took the reasonable view that the provision of benefits for new recruits was a matter for the employer's discretion, and that the changes did not prejudice any existing members, so was happy to take an essentially passive role. As Warren J observed, '[w]ithout being a rubber stamp, [the Trustee] would always, or almost always, accept [the Employer's] proposals so far as benefits were concerned'.[61] The lack of communications 'crossing the line' was especially understandable since there was a significant overlap between membership of the employer and trustee boards. Yet such lack of communications did not, rightly, prevent rectification.

It is helpful to remember that rectification may be granted even if there is no positive evidence that the parties did not intend to make a relevant change. As HHJ Hodge QC put it in *Saga Group Ltd v Paul*, '[t]hat is because an intention not to make the change can be sufficiently proved by the absence of any evidence that the change was intended'.[62] Courts will still require 'formidable evidence'[63] that rectification should be granted, but this approach shows that the parties do not need to have explicitly discussed their intentions with each other for rectification to be appropriate. In *FSHC*

[59] D Maclean SC, 'Recent Developments in the Law of Rectification' (2006) 80 *Australian Law Journal* 427, 431.

[60] *IBM* (n 48).

[61] ibid [110].

[62] *Saga Group* (n 50) [42]. See too *Industrial Acoustics Company Limited v Crowhurst* [2012] EWHC 1614 (Ch), [2012] Pens LR 371 [44]–[46] (Vos J); *Konica Minolta Business Solutions* (n 34) [31].

[63] See above (n 8).

the Court of Appeal insisted that shared understandings could be tacit and include understandings that were so obvious as to go without saying.[64] Furthermore, the court may rely upon the parties' conduct after the deed has been executed to support a claim for rectification.[65] Such evidence may help to bolster a court's conclusions about the parties' intentions at the time of the execution of the legal instrument.

It will very often be possible to rely upon evidence of communications which have crossed the line. For instance, a practice now seems to have developed where employers and trustees prepare a 'briefing note' to explain the purpose of an amendment. That briefing note may be relied upon as strong objective evidence to show what the parties intended, and whether a mistake was made in the formal written document. Nevertheless, in some situations such helpful evidence will not be available, and it is important that the court be able to consider all useful evidence, regardless of whether it 'crossed the line'.

V. 'OBJECTIVE' OR 'SUBJECTIVE' INTENTIONS?

Even if it is accepted that a claim for rectification in the pensions context can be established without evidence of an outward expression of accord, or communications between parties which 'cross the line', it is still important to consider whether the focus should be upon establishing the 'objective' or 'subjective' intentions of the relevant parties. These are loaded terms which are not always helpful. But the essential difference seems to be whether a court needs to be satisfied about the appearance given by the trustees (objective intention) or what they actually thought (subjective intention).

Before the troublesome decision of the House of Lords in *Chartbrook*, the focus of rectification was invariably upon the subjective intentions of the parties in pensions claims.[66] But *Chartbrook* and *Daventry* applied an objective approach in contract law, and this has been accepted by a number of cases in the pensions context.[67] Courts have generally been able to swerve the debate by pointing out that the same result would be reached regardless of whether a subjective or objective approach is favoured, and have not expressed a firm conclusion either way.[68] It is unsurprising that the subjective and objective intentions of the parties will often be the same. After all, the intentions parties actually have will generally be the intentions they reasonably convey to an objective observer or reasonable addressee. But in some circumstances the subjective and objective intentions may diverge. This was seen in both *Chartbrook* and *Daventry* in the contractual context, where the courts found that rectification for common mistake should be granted, despite it being found as a matter of fact that one party was not mistaken. This has harsh results: it imposes a contract upon a party

[64] *FSHC* (n 37) [80]–[87].

[65] eg, *Gallaher* (n 39); *Saga Group* (n 50); *Watkins* (n 38).

[66] eg, *Gallaher* (n 39); *MacDonald* (n 48); *Lemforder* (n 48); and *Scania* (n 49).

[67] eg, *Crowhurst* (n 62); *IBM* (n 48) [15]–[17]; *Unipart Group Ltd v UGC Pension Trustees Ltd* [2018] EWHC 2124 (Ch), [2018] Pens LR 18 [5] (CM Marsh); *St Modwen Properties Plc v Herbert* [2016] EWHC 428 (Ch), [2016] Pens LR 113 (Rose J).

[68] See, eg, *Pioneer GB Ltd v Webb* [2011] EWHC 2683 (Ch), [2011] Pens LR 425 [23] (Sales J).

when that party did not consent to such an agreement. Indeed, this was one reason why the Court of Appeal in *FSHC* sought to depart from the objective approach to common mistake rectification adopted in *Chartbrook*, and instead insisted that both parties must actually be mistaken.

It is suggested that the decision in *FSHC* should be followed in the pensions context.[69] Where a subjective intention can be established, that should trump any objective appearance of an intention for a rectification claim.[70] Since an intention can be established even where an issue has not been discussed at all,[71] it does not seem problematic to take into account evidence of the parties' actual intentions.

Indeed, this appears to have been recognised by Warren J in *IBM*. Although the judge accepted that *Chartbrook* and *Daventry* stated the relevant law, he went on to note that there may be 'a tension, however, between what the internal documents show and what is in fact communicated to the other party'.[72] He discussed the example of the employer actually holding one intention, but innocently communicating a different intention to the trustee. If the trustee acted upon the apparent intention, but the actual intention is what was contained in the document, should the trustee be able to obtain rectification? Warren J thought the answer should be no. If the employer's actual intention could be established – even on the basis of internal documents alone which did not cross the line to the trustee (such as, perhaps, board minutes) – then there is no mistake actually shared by the parties and rectification should not be granted. This approach should be welcomed. Unless there is sharp practice, rectification should not be granted where the employer's actual intentions correspond to the contents of the written instrument. The equitable remedy of rectification operates as a 'safety valve' to the strict approach taken by the common law to interpretation, and courts should be prepared to rely upon evidence of what the parties actually thought.

VI. DETERMINING RELEVANT INTENTIONS IN THE CORPORATE CONTEXT

It is often important to determine whose intentions are relevant for a claim of rectification. This is because both the employer and trustee may be legal persons but not natural persons. But a company, for example, cannot itself act or intend something; it acts and intends through the agency of natural persons. Acts and intentions of natural persons can be attributed to a company. Attribution raises a host of difficulties,[73] which have often been overlooked in the context of rectification.[74]

[69] Indeed, Leggatt LJ thought rectification should operate in a similar manner as regards both bilateral and unilateral instruments: *FSHC* (n 37) [164]–[166].

[70] Unless sharp practice is involved: in the context of a claim for unilateral mistake rectification: *A Roberts & Co Ltd v Leicestershire County Council* [1961] 2 All ER 545 (Ch); *Thomas Bates and Sons Ltd v Wyndham's Lingerie Ltd* [1981] 1 All ER 1077; *Commission for New Towns v Cooper (Great Britain) Ltd* [1995] Ch 259.

[71] See above (n 64).

[72] *IBM* (n 48) [25].

[73] See, eg, S Worthington, 'Corporate Attribution and Agency: Back to Basics' (2017) 133 *LQR* 118 (and a response by P Watts, 'Actual Authority: The Requirement for an Agent Honestly to Believe that an Exercise of Power is in the Principal's Interests' (2017) 4 *Journal of Business Law* 269).

[74] For an initial attempt to deal with some of the difficulties in the contractual sphere, see P Davies, 'Agency and Rectification' (2020) 133 *LQR* 77.

In the well-known decision of the Privy Council in *Meridian Global Funds Management Asia Ltd v Securities Commission*,[75] Lord Hoffmann broke away from the strictures of requiring an individual to be identified as the 'directing mind and will' of a company for his or her acts or intentions to be attributed to the company.[76] Actors who cannot be identified as such may still have their acts and intentions attributed to the company.

In *Meridian*, Lord Hoffmann influentially said that there are primary, general and special rules of attribution.[77] Primary rules of attribution will generally be found in a company's constitution. They need to be supplemented by general rules of attribution which are equally applicable to natural persons. These may be found in the general principles of agency. The primary and general rules will often suffice, but in some circumstances there may be a rule of law which excludes attribution on the basis of general principles of agency, in which case the court must fashion a special rule of attribution. Such special rules require close attention to the context and purpose of the rule at issue, often regarding statutory liability.

Identifying which individual's intention should represent the intention of the company for the purposes of rectification might involve recourse to the primary, general or special rules of attribution, depending on the context.[78] It is important to appreciate that principles of agency law are therefore not necessarily conclusive when determining whose intention should count. Particularly acute problems can arise where the mistake is made by a person with no apparent or actual authority to bind their principal to a contract.[79]

Where an agent is authorised to bind the company and does so the position is generally straightforward. For example, if the board is authorised by the company's constitution to enter into a contract, and does so under a mistake – perhaps reflected in the minutes of a board meeting – then it is clear why a rectification claim may succeed.[80] However, in some unusual circumstances the correct approach may not be so straightforward. As Sir Terence Etherton C observed in *Day v Day*,[81] 'the doctrine of rectification is concerned with intention, or rather the mistaken implementation of intention, rather than the power and authority to effect a particular transaction'.[82] That case concerned a voluntary disposition rather than a bilateral contract. Mrs Day granted a general power of attorney to her solicitor. The solicitor then conveyed property from Mrs Day to Mrs Day and one of her sons, Terence, as beneficial joint tenants. Upon Mrs Day's death, her other children sought rectification of the conveyance since Mrs Day did not intend Terence to acquire any beneficial interest

[75] *Meridian Global Funds Management Asia Ltd v Securities Commission* [1995] AC 500.

[76] cf *Lennard's Carrying Co Ltd v Asiatic Petroleum Co Ltd* [1915] AC 705, 713 (Viscount Haldane LC).

[77] *Meridian* (n 75) 506–07.

[78] See, eg, *Bilta (UK) Ltd (In Liquidation) v Nazir* [2015] UKSC 23, [2016] AC 1.

[79] See Davies, 'Agency and Rectification' (n 74).

[80] eg, *George Cohen, Sons & Co Ltd v Docks & Inland Waterways Executive* (1950) 84 Lloyd's Rep 97. Of course, the other party to the contract must share or at least know of the mistake; if unaware of the mistake made by the board, as a general rule the counterparty to the contract will be protected by the 'indoor management rule': *Royal British Bank v Turquand* (1856) 6 E&B 327; Companies Act 2006, s 40.

[81] *Day* (n 32).

[82] ibid [25]. See too Lewison LJ at [38]: 'equity intervenes not on the ground of lack of authority but on the ground of a failure of intention'.

in the property. The trial judge held that what the solicitor did was within the scope of his authority, and since he was not mistaken, rectification should not be ordered. But the Court of Appeal allowed the appeal, and insisted that the relevant intention for rectification was that of the principal, Mrs Day. That was because she was the true 'decision maker',[83] rather than the solicitor. On the basis that Mrs Day was the person who truly decided to enter into the conveyance of the property, the decision is sensible.[84] It highlights that even if an agent is authorised, a contrary 'superior' intention of the principal may trump that of the agent.[85]

Day v Day was perhaps unusual in that the intentions of the principal and agent were different. Often, where the agent is authorised to enter into a contract and does so, the principal will not have any relevant intention as to the particular terms of the contract, and will not be considered to be the true 'decision-maker'. In such circumstances, the relevant intention for the purposes of rectification will be that of the agent. It is important to ascertain who the true decision-maker is.[86]

This was one issue that Warren J had to decide in *IBM*.[87] Both the principal employer and scheme trustee were corporate bodies. As discussed above,[88] the employer wanted to rectify a deed of amendment and the trustee played a passive role in allowing the employer to take what it considered to be appropriate action. Decisions regarding pensions were delegated by the employer's board of directors to a management committee, which played the active role in taking decisions. However, changes to the pension scheme were 'powers reserved' to the ultimate parent company of the employer. Warren J considered whose intentions should be relevant for the rectification claim: the board of the parent company, or of the management committee? The judge adopted a robust approach in favouring the latter. On the facts, Warren J found that the 'powers reserved' did not deprive the employer or its management committee of the power or authority to make its own corporate decisions. The relevant 'decision-maker' as regards the pension scheme was the management committee, so the intentions of its board were crucial for any claim for rectification. Interestingly, the judge said that the position may be different if the management committee knew, or ought to have known, of non-compliance with the 'powers reserved' and consequent power of the parent company to make decisions. That perhaps highlights that the relevant decision-maker whose intentions should be attributed to a company can be fact-specific.

A further problem which does not yet appear to have been considered is what approach should be taken if the members of the board are not unanimous, or act with different intentions. It is common to find reference to the 'collective intention

[83] ibid [37] (Lewison LJ).

[84] Although whether Mrs Day's intentions were sufficiently clear has been questioned: F Dawson, 'Rectification of Voluntary Settlements' (2014) 130 *LQR* 356.

[85] *cf Daventry* (n 36).

[86] eg, *Thomas Bates & Sons Ltd v Wyndham's (Lingerie) Ltd* [1981] 1 WLR 505. See too *Hawksford Trustees Jersey Limited as Trustee of the Bald Eagle Trust v Stella Global UK Limited* [2012] EWCA Civ 55, [2012] 2 All ER (Comm) 748, which has been cited with approval in claims for rectification involving pension schemes: see, eg, *Girls Day School Trust v GDST Pension Trustees Ltd* [2016] EWHC 1254 (Ch), [2016] Pens LR 181; *Saga Group* (n 50) [44].

[87] *IBM* (n 48) [94]–[110].

[88] See part V above.

of the board'[89] but it may be possible to establish that some members of the board were mistaken and some were not. This can produce tricky situations, especially if different individuals have made different mistakes with different effects in the context of a majority decision. In principle, it is suggested that rectification should only be granted if strong evidence is produced to show that a mistake has been made in recording the intention of the majority of the board, and rectification would align the written instrument with the intention of the majority of the board.

One final aspect of *IBM* is worth noting. Having decided that the deed executed in 1983 should be amended, Warren J then needed to determine whether subsequent deeds and rules should be rectified as well.[90] The most important of these occurred in 1990, when the decision-makers were significantly different from those of 1983. The judge thought that it is not necessarily the case that earlier intentions continue unchanged; the relevant intentions need to be determined as a question of fact. On the facts, Warren J found that neither the employer nor the trustee had intended to make any material change to the early retirement provisions, and simply intended to continue what was already in place. He concluded that 'a serial error contained in successive deeds is capable of elimination by serial rectification'.[91]

VII. DEFENCES

There are various defences generally available to claims for rectification. Most importantly, rectification will not be granted to the prejudice of a bona fide purchaser for value without notice who takes an interest conferred by the instrument;[92] and laches or acquiescence will bar the claim.[93] Where rectification is sought of a voluntary settlement and one of the trustees objects, the court may in its discretion refuse rectification.[94]

In the context of pensions, a very long time may elapse between the execution of the relevant documents and the claim for rectification. For example, in *Gallaher Ltd v Gallaher Pensions Ltd* 17 years had passed.[95] But that did not bar rectification. The cases have consistently held that mere delay without any prejudice to the members is unlikely to bar rectification.[96] And if the scheme has been administered as was intended, rather than in accordance with an instrument drafted in error, it is unlikely that any prejudice would be suffered.

[89] eg, *Watkins* (n 38) [12].

[90] *IBM* (n 48) [399]–[459].

[91] ibid [414]. See too *CIT Group (UK) Ltd v Gazzard* [2014] EWHC 2557 (Ch) (Barling J).

[92] *Bell v Cundall* (1750) Amb 101; *Garrard v Frankel* (1862) 30 Beav 445; *Coates v Kenna* (1873) 7 IR Eq 113; and see *Smith v Jones* [1954] 1 WLR 1089 (Ch); *Thames Guaranty Ltd v Campbell* [1985] QB 210, 240, citing this passage.

[93] *Beale v Kyte* [1907] 1 Ch 564 (holding that time runs from discovery of the mistake); *McCausland v Young* [1949] NI 49; *cf Dormer v Sherman* (1966) 110 SJ 171, 172. See also *Milton Keynes Borough Council v Viridor (Community Recycling MK) Ltd* [2017] EWHC 239 (TCC), [2017] BLR 216 [100]–[111].

[94] *Re Butlin's* (n 31) 262.

[95] *Gallaher* (n 39) [146].

[96] *Lemforder* (n 48) [94]; *Unipart v UGC* (n 67).

More tricky is the potential defence of a bona fide purchaser. After all, members have given value in return for their pensions, and are not mere volunteers. Nevertheless, when this defence has been run on behalf of members it has not been successful. For example, in *AMP v Barker* Lawrence Collins J held that the beneficiaries gave no value for any *additional* benefits erroneously conferred upon them,[97] and this was supported by Etherton J in *Gallaher*.[98] Admittedly, in *Citifinancial Europe PLC v Davidson*[99] David Halpern QC, sitting as a Deputy High Court Judge, found this 'slightly surprising', but on balance the approach in *AMP v Barker* should be supported. If there is truly no value given for the extra benefits that would be conferred under the mistakenly drafted instrument, then the fact that scheme members have given value for some 'lesser' entitlements should not prevent rectification absolutely.

VIII. SUMMARY JUDGMENT

It has become common for parties to apply for summary judgment for the rectification of pension documents.[100] This is understandable: applications are often unopposed, and this procedure is cheaper and quicker than proceeding to a full trial. Indeed, members may not oppose the application on the grounds that rectification best serves the interests of the members as a whole, and dealing with the claim through summary judgment reduces the drain on the scheme's resources.

However, one interesting and controversial issue which has arisen through dealing with matters at the stage of summary judgment concerns the court's approach to advice given to the members. For claims to be resolved by summary judgment, the employer, trustee and representative of the members invariably agree that the application should not be opposed. If the application is opposed, the summary judgment procedure is unlikely to be appropriate. As part of this procedure, courts have developed a tendency to have the position of the representative beneficiaries of the scheme explained to the court by means of a confidential opinion from counsel of at least 10 years' standing.[101] This is permitted under the Chancery Practice Guide[102] and allows the judge to have a confidential discussion with counsel. As Chief Master Marsh explained in *Unipart Group Ltd v UGC Pension Trustees Ltd*:

> [T]he representative party provides the court with a confidential opinion about the merits of the application. It is to my mind a useful procedure in a case that is undefended because it brings to the hearing a degree of stringency which might not otherwise be there if the hearing is dealt with on the basis of submissions in open court. It is helpful for the court to be able to explore possible gaps in the approach adopted by the claimants or the evidence which they have brought to bear.

[97] *AMP* (n 46) [72]–[77].

[98] *Gallaher* (n 39).

[99] *Citifinancial Europe PLC v Davidson* [2014] Pens LR 625 (Ch) [11].

[100] eg, *Davidson* (n 99); *Lewis* (n 48); *Saga Group* (n 50); *Herbert* (n 68); *Webb* (n 69); *Scania* (n 49); *Colorcon* (n 49); *Crowhurst* (n 62); *Girls Day School Trust* (n 86); *Unipart v UGC* (n 67).

[101] See, eg, *Scania* (n 49); *Re Mysis Ltd* [2012] EWHC 4250 (Ch) (Briggs J); *Crowhurst* (n 62) (Vos J); *Konica Minolta Business Solutions* (n 34).

[102] HM Courts and Tribunals Service, *Chancery Guide* (2016) [29.96].

> The provision of a confidential opinion is allied with the opportunity to have a private conversation with counsel who appears for the representative party, at which, in the absence of the other parties, a candid discussion with the court can take place. If the court has any concerns, they can be explored but, more importantly, it gives the representative party the opportunity to raise points of concern given that it is rare (particularly in a claim for rectification) for the application of the principles to the evidence to lead to an entirely black or white outcome; always bearing in mind that the remedy is a discretionary one.[103]

This approach has recently been challenged. In *Girls' Day School Trust v GDST Pension Trustees Ltd*, Norris J insisted that the mere fact that the parties wanted to keep the advice privileged 'does not preclude the Court from taking the view that after judgment the evidence ought to be "open" and in particular available for inspection by scheme members on the Court file'.[104] Ultimately, however, the judge did not order disclosure of the opinion in that particular case.[105] That is because the evidence presented in the case, even without the opinion, was full, scrutinised and tested in open court. Moreover, all the relevant facts were set out in the full judgment of the court, and it was a straightforward case.

Importantly, Norris J also said that he was influenced by the fact that when writing the opinion, counsel would not have been contemplating the disclosure of the opinion outside a very small circle. The judge put future parties on warning that disclosure may well be ordered in subsequent cases. The principle of open justice is important. He said:

> For the future any party seeking to rectify a mistake in the expression of a pension scheme by obtaining an order for summary judgment *without a hearing* must understand that it is likely that the Court will insist that after judgment *all* evidence be open to inspection: and that if this is not acceptable then the application for summary judgment must be listed for a public hearing.[106]

The judgment of Norris J has prompted very different responses. In *Saga Group Ltd v Paul* HHJ Hodge QC offered robust support for the important principles of transparency and open justice,[107] whereas in *Sovereign Trustees Ltd v Lewis* CM Marsh thought the confidential procedure useful and acceptable.[108] *Saga Group* was heard after *Sovereign Trustees Ltd*, although judgment in the former case was handed down first. In *Saga Group*, the judge said that hearing the evidence in public had three significant advantages:

> (1) it complies with the presumption that matters should be heard in public and avoids the fact that any departure therefrom is anomalous; (2) it avoids the practical difficulties of retaining a copy of the confidential opinion on the electronic court file; and (3) it avoids the issues concerning the inspection of the confidential opinion by an affected member or person claiming through them that so affected the views of Norris J in The Girls' Day School Trust case.[109]

[103] *Unipart v UGC* (n 67) [8]–[9].
[104] *Girls' Day School Trust* (n 86) [17].
[105] ibid [49]–[51].
[106] ibid [50] (emphasis in the original).
[107] *Saga Group* (n 50).
[108] *Lewis* (n 48).
[109] *Saga Group* (n 50) [18].

These are powerful considerations, although they did not persuade CM Marsh to abandon the approach he adopted in *Sovereign Trustees Ltd* in *Unipart v UGC*.[110] But given that, where the summary judgment procedure is used, the members will have already accepted that there is no reason for them to oppose the application, it does not seem prejudicial for them to reveal their advice. As the judge said in *Saga Group*, '[o]ne's hand has already been revealed by acknowledging that an application for summary judgment will not be opposed'.[111] If summary judgment is refused that is most likely to be because the judge has identified a new point not previously considered, and not in the opinion given to the members anyway. Disclosing the opinion allows justice to be seen to be done transparently, which is particularly important where there has been no public hearing, and should be encouraged.

IX. CONCLUSION

The rectification of pension schemes raises important questions. It is to be hoped that they will soon be addressed by an appellate court to provide a greater degree of certainty. Interestingly, pensions cases have been relied upon in leading decisions on rectification of contracts[112] and voluntary settlements,[113] but with controversial results. The context of pension schemes are important to consider, although ultimately the law concerning the rectification of legal instruments should largely be aligned. Where a document fails to record the parties' actual intentions, rectification should, in principle, be available, subject to any defences and the discretion of the court to grant rectification on terms.

[110] *Unipart v UGC* (n 67).
[111] *Saga Group* (n 50) [20].
[112] eg, *Munt v Beasley* (n 57).
[113] eg, *Day* (n 32).

6

The Pension Fund as a 'Virtual' Institution

M SCOTT DONALD

I. INTRODUCTION

IT WOULD BE trite to observe that a trust is not a separate legal entity were it not for the frequency with which legislative and regulatory measures appear to regard the trusts that underlie many occupational pension funds as precisely that. The law is however clear: a trust is incorporeal, the nexus and product of a set of obligations imposed in equity on an identified individual (or individuals) in respect of identifiable property.[1] That individual, the trustee, is the fulcrum of the institution, personally responsible and ultimately accountable for its prudent and proper administration. However, the need for a wide range of specialist skills inspires most trustees to retain third parties to assist them. Unlike the agents performing ministerial duties in the traditional trust paradigm, these third parties often perform tasks integral to the efficient operation of the fund, interacting directly with members and making investment decisions of great consequence. Although these third parties are individually replaceable, in combination with the trustee they constitute the 'virtual' institution we know as a pension fund.

This chapter assesses the way that familiar trust law principles and bespoke regulatory regimes engage with this 'virtual' institutional structure. It identifies the way in which departures from the familiar trust paradigm redistribute accountabilities across the institution, most especially as a result of the interaction between the limited liability of the trustee, its right of indemnity and the presence of exclusion of liability clauses, and the way in which the legislature and regulators in Australia have attempted to regulate aspects of this redistribution. It also identifies the additional set of issues posed by decentralised operating models for regulators, including the efficacy of licensing and regulatory regimes which cover some, but not all, of the parties involved in the administration of the fund and the potential for risk contagion

[1] JD Heydon and MJ Leeming, *Jacobs' Law of Trusts in Australia*, 8th edn (Chatswood, NSW, LexisNexis Butterworths, 2016) [1-01].

propagating through the network of these third parties, many of whom serve multiple funds. Although the analysis references the Australian position most commonly, the basic insights and issues are common to many common law jurisdictions to a greater or lesser extent.

The chapter, then, does not argue for or against the decentralised 'virtual' operational model of pension (superannuation) fund administration. It does however strongly encourage caution against relying on traditional assumptions about where accountability for failures of administration may lie in such an institution. Expectations that accountability will match that seen in the simple trust paradigm in which the trustee is personally accountable to the beneficiary for losses caused by its maladministration are likely to be disappointed in the face of the complex interplay of rules and organisational structures considered in this chapter.

II. THE RISE OF THE 'VIRTUAL' INSTITUTION

The rapid development of the internet since the turn of the millennium could easily obscure the fact that the concept of a 'virtual' organisation is not new. It grew to prominence in the late 1980s in recognition of the way that advances in information technology were revolutionising the speed and quality of price discovery in supply chains and markets.[2] The new technologies had the effect of redrawing the Coasian boundary between tasks it was more efficient to conduct within a firm, and those where the economics inherent in the activity recommended what came to be known as 'outsourcing'.[3]

Although the concept of a virtual organisation has always been a contested one,[4] the proposition that a modern pension fund is a virtual institution *par excellence* has some attractions. At one level it rehearses the familiar refrain that a trust is incorporeal.[5] However, more importantly, it captures fundamental characteristics of an institution comprising not one but a multiplicity of organisations that integrate functionally to deliver the 'product' (superannuation fund membership) to members. These include the decision of which tasks the trustee ought to outsource, the importance of communication across the institution and the location of accountability within it. The concept therefore offers insights relevant to the governance and regulation of the institution that do not arise in the simple trust paradigm in which all the activity in administering the trust is undertaken by the trustee personally.

This perspective is important in the context of pension funds because the trustee of a modern pension fund will typically employ a wide variety of third parties to

[2] See, for instance, WH Davidow and MS Malone, *The Virtual Corporation: Structuring and Revitalizing the Corporation for the 21st Century* (New York, HarperBusiness Publishers, 1992).

[3] The seminal article was R Coase, 'The Nature of the Firm' (1937) 4 *Economica* 386. See also DC North, 'Institutions' (1991) 5 *Journal of Economic Perspectives* 97.

[4] See U Schultze and WJ Orlikowski, 'Metaphors of Virtuality: Shaping An Emergent Reality' (2001) 11 *Information and Organization* 45.

[5] *Kelly v Mina* [2014] NSWCA 9 [103] (Leeming JA); *Agricultural Land Management Ltd v Jackson (No 2)* [2014] WASC 102, (2014) 48 WAR 1 [302] (Edelman J); *Lane v Deputy Commissioner of Taxation* [2017] FCA 953, (2017) 253 FCR 46 [2] (Derrington J).

assist it in the administration of the trust.[6] The details vary between funds, but in any particular fund the third parties may include some or all of the following: investment managers, asset custodians, property valuers, asset consultants, member benefit administrators, actuaries and auditors.[7] The trustee may also purchase interests in financial products, such as managed investment schemes, pooled superannuation trusts and insurance policies, which create legal obligations in the parties offering the financial product in favour of the trustee. The decision whether to outsource specific tasks will in many cases be impelled by commercial considerations of a type analogous to those described by Coase.[8] In some cases these third parties offer specialist skills or capabilities; in others the opportunity to exploit economies of scale not available to the superannuation fund acting alone. In other circumstances the involvement of an independent third party is required by law.[9] To understand fully the complex matrix of accountabilities within and surrounding the pension fund, it is crucial to recognise and have regard to this pattern of distributed responsibility and to the impact of the legal relationships by which it is constituted.

III. LEGAL RELATIONSHIPS AND ACCOUNTABILITY WITHIN THE INSTITUTION

A number of reasons can be posited for the pervasiveness of the trust amongst the legal devices deployed for the administration of the trust assets supporting occupational pension schemes. Prominent amongst these is the way in which the law of trusts focuses accountability on the office of trustee. In the paradigm case, the beneficiaries of the trust have a right to approach a court to request that the court order that the trust be performed by the trustee or that remedial measures be taken to address losses incurred (or indeed for the trustee to disgorge any profits it has derived without authority). The trustee will be accountable to the beneficiaries for losses resulting from failures to perform duties required under the trust, however seemingly trivial.[10] The trustee will also be accountable to the beneficiaries for losses resulting from breaches of duties of a more qualitative nature, such as a failure to exercise due care, a failure to act honestly or in good faith, a failure to eschew conflicting interests and duties or a failure to act impartially. The trustee may employ agents to perform ministerial (ie, non-discretionary) acts on its behalf, but will be liable to beneficiaries for losses caused by those agents where such appointments were ultra vires or tainted by

[6] See K Liu and B Arnold, 'Australian Superannuation Outsourcing: Fees, Related Parties and Concentrated Markets' (2010) 4 *Journal of the Securities Institute of Australia* 6; MS Donald et al, 'Too Connected to Fail: The Regulation of Systemic Risk Within Australia's Superannuation System' (2016) 2 *Journal of Financial Regulation* 56.

[7] Donald et al (n 6).

[8] See for instance, D Gallagher, T Gapes and G Warren, 'In-House Asset Management in the Australian Superannuation Industry' (2017) 59 *Accounting and Finance* 615.

[9] eg, the requirement that the accounts of a superannuation be audited (Superannuation Industry (Supervision) Act 1993 (Cth) (SIS Act 1993) s 35A) and that a qualified actuary be appointed to certify the funding and solvency status of a defined benefit fund (Superannuation Industry (Supervision) Regulations 1994 (Cth) reg 9.09).

[10] *Youyang Pty Ltd v Minter Ellison Morris Fletcher* [2003] HCA 15, (2003) 212 CLR 484 [33].

an improper purpose or some other qualitative deficiency, most commonly an absence of care or the presence of a conflicting interest or duty.[11] The trustee will also be liable to third parties with which it or its agents contract in the course of administering the trust, and it will have a right of indemnity against the assets of the trust, or in limited cases against the beneficiaries themselves, in respect of such liabilities provided they are properly incurred.[12] Only in limited circumstances will the beneficiaries have rights against those contractual counterparties.[13]

The complexity of modern commercial trusts, including those so often employed as the legal foundation for occupational pension funds in common law countries, has inspired a variety of departures from this simple paradigm. Three in particular stand out as relevant in the current context: the use of incorporated trustees; the use of agents in roles that involve a measure of discretion; and constitutional measures to limit liability. These departures each have important implications for the matrix of accountabilities within and around the pension fund.

A. The Use of Incorporated Trustees

The use of incorporated entities to serve as the trustees of occupational pension funds is prevalent in some jurisdictions, such as Australia, and increasingly common in others, such as the United Kingdom. There are some obvious practical advantages to this practice. Incorporation provides perpetual succession, which is important in an institution as potentially long-lived as a pension fund. It also simplifies the administration of asset ownership and the process of contracting with external parties. Crucially it also permits more sophisticated governance structures and practices, because those structures and practices occur behind the corporate veil and do not, ordinarily, impinge on the 'governance' of the trust. Trust governance, formally at least, is simplified by the existence of a unitary, incorporated trustee; all the messy, complicated decision-making can occur within the more permissive milieu of the corporate environment. Human actors can be replaced, or change roles, and decisions can be delegated to a wider range of individuals or groups, much more easily in a corporate setting than would be the case if the human actors were trustees themselves of the assets in the fund.

One obvious consequence of incorporation, at least in the form it is most commonly found in common law countries, is that it means the trustee also provides the protection of limited liability to key stakeholders such as the shareholders of the trustee company. Large financial organisations use this as a means to quarantine the liability arising from trusteeship activities from other commercial activities, and vice versa. Corporate and government employers, though increasingly seeking to offload their occupational pension responsibilities entirely, have historically also used specially designated subsidiaries as a way to quarantine risk and also, in Australia at least, regulatory oversight. A challenge does, however, arise for funds emanating

[11] *Speight v Gaunt* (1883) 22 Ch D 727 (CA), (1883) 9 App Cas 1 (HL).
[12] *Re Beddoe* [1893] 1 Ch 547 (CA) 562; *Nolan v Collie* [2003] VSCA 39, (2003) 7 VR 287.
[13] *Alexander v Perpetual Trustees WA Ltd* [2004] HCA 7, (2004) 216 CLR 109 [55].

from a more mutual-style heritage, such as so-called 'industry funds' in Australia: who owns the shares in the trustee company? In Australia the usual solution is that the shares are held by the directors of the company acting as trustee, on behalf of the members of the fund, although there are funds in which the shares are held by other parties, such as the entities possessing a right to nominate those directors. That peculiarity aside, as in other areas of corporate law, the main implications of limited liability fall on third parties providing services to the trust. Although on the one hand the reporting requirements and other creditor protection measures afforded by corporate law give such parties more protection than they might have in the paradigm case where they deal with natural persons serving as trustees, the limited liability attaching to the corporate entity means that creditors will typically have limited recourse against the shareholders of the trustee in the event of commercial failure by the trustee. This risk is exacerbated by the fact that the creditors' right to be subrogated to the trustee's right of indemnity for expenses properly incurred in the administration of the trust may also be less effective than they might hope, for reasons that are explored more fully below.

The second important consequence of incorporation is that many of the important decisions made by the corporate trustee in relation to the fund and its members will be made within the governance structures and processes of the corporate body when acting in that role. However as is common across many companies, the complexity and volume of issues arising continuously in the administration of the fund will almost inevitably exceed the capacity and combined personal skill set of the directors of that company. As Parker J noted in *Re Barings*:

> [S]ome degree of delegation is almost always essential if the company's business is to be carried on efficiently: to that extent there is a clear public interest in delegation by those charged with the responsibility for the management of a business.[14]

Delegations to 'management' and to sub-committees are likely to be required That is also a way in which shortcomings in the expertise of individual directors can be overcome. That said, it is important that such parsing of the trustee's decision-making responsibilities does not facilitate a small subset of parties (such as the chair, or the CEO) dominating deliberations.[15] One of the motivations for the representative structure of many superannuation and pension fund boards is access to the diverse experiences, preoccupations and priorities of board members drawn from diverse backgrounds, and the political legitimacy that this can engender.[16]

Moreover, and this applies both to delegations by the company to external parties and to delegations by the directors to individuals and groups within the company, there is a crucial need for all delegations to be carefully and precisely framed, documented

[14] *Re Barings plc (No 5)* [1999] 1 BCLC 433, 487.

[15] In an analogous setting, see Australian Prudential Regulation Authority, *Prudential Inquiry into the Commonwealth Bank of Australia* (April 2018) 17, 18, available at: www.apra.gov.au/sites/default/files/CBA-Prudential-Inquiry_Final-Report_30042018.pdf.

[16] MS Donald and S LeMire, 'Independence in Practice: Superannuation Fund Governance Through the Eyes of Fund Directors' (2019) 42 *University of New South Wales Law Journal* 300. See also Deborah Mabbett's chapter in the present volume.

and monitored.[17] The notion of an institution as the nexus and product of a myriad of informational transactions is very apposite in this respect. Indeed, perhaps the greatest challenge for the individuals serving as directors of a corporate trustee in an institution as complex and interdependent as a modern pension fund may be to ensure that information flows across the institution are timely, accurate and relevant.

It is also the case that the nature of the delegations to sub-committees may vary, from decision-making authority at one end of a spectrum to recommendations and advice, and ultimately fact-finding, at the other end. Identifying the precise nature of the delegation, and its implications for accountability for different types of possible deficiencies in execution or for resulting losses, will be required in order to complete a comprehensive map of the matrix of accountabilities across the institution. Finally, it should be noted that the delegations which occur in this respect have to be carefully distinguished from those made by the corporate trustee to third parties because the powers granted to boards of directors to delegate are typically far greater in scope than those granted to the company *qua* trustee.[18]

B. The Use of Agents

It is commonly asserted that, subject to statute and the relevant trust instrument, trustees cannot delegate their duties, and that they can only employ agents to perform tasks of a ministerial nature.[19] Against that, it is an empirical fact that the trustees of occupational pension plans do commonly appoint agents to perform tasks which are both materially consequential to the administration of the trust and in which an element of discretion is present. As Lehane noted nearly 25 years ago,[20] how they do so is not entirely clear, because the nature of which decisions are 'discretionary' has never been comprehensively determined by the courts.

In Australia, at least, the answer to that question has moved forward since the time of Lehane's writing. The Australian High Court in *Finch v Telstra Super Pty Ltd*[21] distinguished between decisions of a trustee for which there were objectively verifiable correct answers, and those decisions in which no such objectively correct answer was possible. In so doing, they implicitly adopted an approach mapped out and justified by Campbell in a masterly 2009 article.[22] Although there may be uncertainty with regard to the first type of decision, that uncertainty could be resolved by appropriate

[17] *Daniels v Anderson* (1995) 37 NSWLR 438.

[18] For a useful discussion of the modern approach to delegation within a corporate law environment, see A Gibbs and J Webster, 'Delegation and Reliance by Australian Company Directors' (2015) 33 *Company and Securities Law Journal* 297.

[19] *Speight* (n 11). In both Australia and the UK, clauses expressly permitting delegation are common in pension fund instruments. However, in Australia that mechanism is complicated by provisions in the SIS Act 1993, Pt 6, discussed immediately below.

[20] J Lehane, 'Delegation of Trustees' Powers and Current Developments in Investment Funds Management' (1995) 7 *Bond Law Review* 36, 45.

[21] *Finch v Telstra Super Pty Ltd* [2010] HCA 36, (2010) 242 CLR 254.

[22] J Campbell, 'Exercise by Superannuation Trustees of Discretionary Powers' (2009) 83 *Australian Law Journal* 159.

enquiry. The trustee may be required to form an 'opinion', but that is an opinion whether certain facts have been established or criteria satisfied, a common enough decision that is qualitatively different from a decision in respect of which there is no objectively correct answer. The High Court found that only decisions of the latter type are truly discretionary. Taking that lead, it is suggested that this distinction should be applied to the question of which types of decision ought to be delegable, and which therefore should be regarded as the province only of the trustee.

The appointment of investment managers to make decisions with respect to the trust assets is a prime example of a situation where this issue arises, and the manner in which it is addressed in different jurisdictions is instructive. In the United Kingdom, the Pensions Act 1995, section 34(2) expressly permits delegation of the investment function to an investment manager. In Australia, in contrast, although the appointment of investment managers is anticipated by the SIS Act 1993, section 124, which prohibits 'non-written appointments of an investment manager', section 59 of the same Act prohibits the exercise of discretion by someone other than the trustee, unless the governing rules of the fund require the consent of the trustee to the exercise of that discretion. That is to say, trustees must formally consent to the decisions of their delegates, which in practice they do generically in advance as part of the appointment process. However, the question whether a court would regard such a process as fulfilling the requirement that the trustee must give its consent has never been tested.

Another important example is the appointment of member benefit administrators. Historically this task was delegated to the human resources function of the employer company, or was undertaken by the staff of the corporate trustee. Increasingly, however, the task has been outsourced to commercial service providers. It is easy to see that much of what a member benefit administrator does is purely ministerial. There is no discretion involved in the processing and recording of member contributions and benefit payments. However, there are other aspects of the role which are not so clear. The first example is the decision required of a superannuation fund trustee upon the death of a member as to how to allocate the death benefit between potential recipients. In the absence of a valid and current binding death benefit nomination by the deceased member, the trustee has a discretion to determine which family members and other parties should receive benefits, and in what proportion. Although the courts have established factors that the trustee should take into account in exercising that discretion,[23] there is no mathematical equation or other objective means of ascertaining what is appropriate. Could such a decision be taken by a member benefit administrator? Following the logic outlined above, the better answer would seem to be 'no', even though a decision as to whether an individual member was entitled to receive an insurance payout in respect of a disability claim (which superficially looks similar and would also involve interactions with the fund's insurance provider) was held not to be discretionary in *Finch v Telstra*.

[23] See, eg, *Edwards v Postsuper Pty Ltd* [2007] FCAFC 83 [93]. See more generally, D Browne, 'Inheritance Issues with Superannuation Death Benefits: Can a Legal Personal Representative Ignore the Deceased's Death Benefit?' (2018) 46 *Australian Bar Review* 1.

Why does this matter? It matters from a trust law perspective because the identity of the party expected by the settlor to exercise the discretion is fundamental to the nature of a trust. As Chadwick LJ observed in *Edge v Pension Ombudsman*:

> It is clear that the trustees are entrusted with the powers which they have under the scheme for just the reason that they are likely to be persons with the knowledge and experience relevant to the questions with which (with the benefit of advice from the actuary) they will, from time to time, be faced.[24]

It also matters because the member will not enjoy contractual privity with the agent and absent some statutory ground will not therefore usually have an action against the service provider and must rely on the trustee to take action. Further, as is discussed below, it matters from a regulatory perspective, because licensing regimes and the like need to identify clearly which parties are involved and responsible for different tasks if they are to be effective. Finally, it matters because it underscores the important role played by the monitoring processes employed by the trustee. Having delegated authority, whether by statutory power or some other means, they retain responsibility for monitoring the delegate's conduct.[25] A trustee whose delegate's conduct causes loss to the trust may be able to argue that it ought not be accountable to members for the loss because the 'fault' lay with the agent, but if its own monitoring processes were inadequate, or were not implemented appropriately, it may find itself accountable on that ground.

C. Constitutional Measures to Limit Liability

The primacy of the trust instrument in defining each party's responsibilities and accountabilities makes it possible for those drafting the instruments to craft provisions that relocate accountability across the institution, most commonly away from the trustee and its service providers. There are a variety of ways in which this is commonly done, some of which have attracted legislative or regulative responses. The result, as Campbell compellingly demonstrates, can be complex.[26]

i. Exemption Clauses

The most obvious way in which a trustee can evade liability for losses arising in the administration of a trust is to rely on clauses in the deed that seek to limit or exclude that liability.[27] Indeed, as the authors of the seventh edition of *Jacobs' Law of Trusts* memorably opined:

> The essential freedom to mould the terms of a trust has been employed on many occasions to excuse trustees from the consequences of their own breaches of trust. It is a melancholy

[24] *Edge v Pensions Ombudsman* [2000] Ch 602 (CA) 630.

[25] In the UK, expressly by the Pensions Act 1995, s 34(4).

[26] J Campbell, 'Some Aspects of the Civil Liability Arising from Breach of Duty by a Superannuation Trustee' (2017) 44 *Australian Bar Review* 24.

[27] In practice these clauses can take a number of forms. One crucial distinction is between those that excuse trustees from liability in some way and those that negative the original duty in some way so that no

> fact that such clauses are usually insisted on by highly paid professional trustees (like trustee companies) who hope to gain immunity from the consequences of departing from their own advertised standards of expertise. It should also go without saying that any ambiguities in such clauses should be construed against the trustee relying on them.[28]

Despite the melancholy of the learned authors of *Jacobs*, such clauses are enforceable so long as they do not purport to limit liability for dishonesty, as the English Court of Appeal held in *Armitage v Nurse*.[29]

The trust instruments governing pension funds today inevitably include such clauses. Their scope is limited in the Australian context by section 56 of the SIS Act in much the same way as that described in *Armitage*. Section 56(2) states that:

> A provision in the governing rules of a superannuation entity is void in so far as it would have the effect of exempting a trustee of the entity from, or indemnifying a trustee of the entity against:
>
> (a) liability for breach of trust if the trustee:
>
> (i) *fails to act honestly* in a matter concerning the entity; or
>
> (ii) *intentionally or recklessly fails to exercise*, in relation to a matter affecting the entity, *the degree of care and diligence that the trustee was required to exercise*; or
>
> (b) liability for a monetary penalty under a civil penalty order; or
>
> (c) the payment of any amount payable under an infringement notice; or
>
> (d) liability for the costs of undertaking a course of education in compliance with an education direction; or
>
> (e) liability for an administrative penalty imposed by section 166.[30]

That is to say, the trust instrument may excuse all breaches of trust by the trustee that are not dishonest or intentionally or recklessly careless. There are however two important wrinkles.

First, section 56(2)(b) has achieved new significance with the transformation of the trustee conduct covenants imposed by section 52 of the SIS Act into civil penalty provisions.[31] This would mean that breaches of a covenant that were covered by a clause consistent with section 56(2)(a) might nevertheless sound in a regulatory sanction by virtue of section 56(2)(b).

Less obvious, perhaps, is the way that the SIS Act extends liability to others 'involved' in the breach of one of the covenants. Section 55(3) of the SIS Act provides that:

> Subject to subsection (4A), a person who suffers loss or damage as a result of conduct of another person that was engaged in in contravention of subsection 54B(1), 54B(2) or 54C(1)

'breach' ever arises. An example of this possibility is discussed more fully below in the text accompanying nn 38 and 39. It is arguable that the latter form of clause reduces the incidence of 'breaches' reportable to be a relevant regulator.

[28] JD Heydon and MJ Leeming, *Jacobs' Law of Trusts*, 7th edn (Chatsworth, NSW, LexisNexis Butterworths, 2006) [1619]. This opinion has not been repeated in the current, eighth edition.

[29] *Armitage v Nurse* [1998] Ch 241 (CA).

[30] Emphasis added.

[31] SIS Act 1993, s 54B(1) was inserted by the Treasury Laws Amendment (Improving Accountability and Member Outcomes in Superannuation Measures No 1) Act 2019 (Cth) sch 3. The director covenants in SIS Act 1993, s 52A were likewise transformed into civil penalty provisions and similar arguments would apply.

> may recover the amount of the loss or damage by action against that other person *or against any person involved in the contravention*.[32]

Subsection (4A) provides that actions taken against the directors of the trustee can only proceed with the leave of the court. There is now no definition of 'involved' in the SIS Act.[33] The issue for service providers to the trustee is that accessorial liability of the type accommodated within the phrase 'person involved in the contravention' would rarely be addressed in the trust instrument of a superannuation fund, and so service providers may well be liable to members for breaches by the trustee in which they were involved and for which the trustee has been exempted. The service provider may of course seek indemnification from the trustee if its contract with the trustee contains such a provision,[34] but it is exposed to the risk that the trustee will not have the resources personally to satisfy that indemnity, and may be barred from exercising its right of indemnity against trust assets because the expense was not properly incurred. It is to that possibility that regard should be had next.

ii. Limits on Rights of Indemnity

The right of a trustee to indemnity for any expenses properly incurred is commonly regarded as inherent to the office of trustee.[35] Although primarily designed to assist trustees to administer the trust efficiently, its role in protecting the interests of contractual counterparties to the trustee is also now well recognised.[36] Moreover, although it is sometimes said that in recognising the trustee's right the court must be vigilant to ensure that beneficiaries' rights are not harmed by rapacious claims by the trustee,[37] it is also the case that it is in those same beneficiaries' interests that the trustee have the assistance of professional assistance in the administration of the trust. To that end, section 56(1) of the SIS Act provides that:

> Subject to subsections (2) and (2A), a provision in the governing rules of a superannuation entity is void if:
>
> (a) it purports to preclude a trustee of the entity from being indemnified out of the assets of the entity in respect of any liability incurred while acting as trustee of the entity; or
>
> (b) it limits the amount of such an indemnity.

[32] Emphasis added.

[33] SIS Act 1993, s 10 provides that 'involved' is defined in s 17 of the Act. However, SIS Act 1993, s 17 was repealed in 2001.

[34] Australian Prudential Regulation Authority (APRA), *Superannuation Prudential Standard SPS 231: Outsourcing* (November 2012) (SPS 231), requires (at [21]) that all agreements to outsource a 'material business activity' must be in writing and address, amongst other things, 'liability and indemnity'. It does not specify what liability and indemnity settings the APRA regards as appropriate, but the relevant guidance from APRA notes: 'It would typically specify the extent of liability for each party and, in particular, whether liability for negligence is limited. It would also specify any indemnities and provide details of any insurance arrangements. Also, consideration would usually be given to the extent of liability to both the RSE licensee and service provider in relation to subcontracting arrangements': APRA, *SPG 231: Outsourcing* (July 2013) [22].

[35] *Worrall v Harford* (1802) 8 Ves Jun 4, 32 ER 250.

[36] *Carter Holt Harvey Woodproducts Australia Pty Ltd v Commonwealth* [2019] HCA 20 [34] (Kiefel CJ, Keane and Edelman JJ). See also K Lindgren, 'A Superannuation Fund Trustee's Right of Indemnity' (2010) 4 *Journal of Equity* 85.

[37] For instance, see *Re Beddoe* (n 12) 561.

The legislature, then, has intervened to stop those drafting superannuation fund deeds from undermining the value of the right of a creditor of the trustee to be subrogated to the trustee's right of indemnity in appropriate circumstances. This is crucial in the context of trustees who administer funds the assets of which often total many billions of Australian dollars. As Campbell has noted, however, there is a wrinkle in this provision also. Subsection (1) makes reference to the 'governing rules'. Although on first blush this may appear merely to be what *Fowler's Modern English Usage* describes as an 'elegant variation' on the trust instrument, in fact the phrase is a defined term in the SIS Act. Section 10 specifies that:

> **governing rules**, in relation to a fund, scheme or trust, means:
>
> (a) any rules contained in a trust instrument, other document or legislation, or combination of them; or
>
> (b) any unwritten rules;
>
> governing the establishment or operation of the fund, scheme or trust.

Read strictly, the provision is tautological. However, even taken at its best, the definition is surprisingly expansive. It would, for instance, override provisions in the Trustee Acts of the Australian States related to indemnities, as well as the relevant principles of equity. The result of that interpretation would be that the trustee's right to indemnity could be completely untrammelled, even to the extent of permitting the trustee to indemnify itself for breaches that would hitherto have offended against the condition that the expense be 'properly incurred'. That interpretation, which is not far-fetched given the wording of the definition, would completely dissolve the accountability matrix in and around the superannuation fund. Perhaps the only effective brakes, then, on the trustee's right of indemnity are the trustee's duty under the Corporations Act 2001 (Cth), section 912A, to administer the fund 'efficiently, honestly and fairly' in situations where the trustee is an Australian Financial Services Licence holder[38] or licence conditions imposed by APRA as part of its Registrable Superannuation Entity licensing regime. It remains to be seen whether a court faced with a trustee having indemnified itself for a loss that it itself caused would regard such an action,[39] though arguably lawful, as 'unfair'.

iii. Prescriptive Drafting

Another way to take advantage of the primacy of the trust instrument to adjust the accountability matrix is to craft the instrumental duties in such a way as to sidestep the familiar qualitative duties owed by the trustee. One common example of this has recently been addressed by legislation, but others remain.

[38] Campbell, 'Some Aspects of the Civil Liability' (n 26) 49 opines that the requirement of a trustee to comply with the impartiality covenants articulated in SIS Act 1993, s 52(2)(e)–(f) might be a brake, but that works only in circumstances where members are differentially affected by the breach of the trustee.

[39] As it happens, APRA has recently announced proceedings against a trustee which APRA alleges has done precisely that: see www.apra.gov.au/media-centre/media-releases/apra-takes-action-against-ioof-failing-act-best-interests-superannuation.

It was common before the passage of the Stronger Super reforms in 2012 that the trust instruments governing superannuation funds would nominate specific third parties to perform certain functions. Almost inevitably these third parties would be associates of the trustee, either subsidiaries, parents or siblings in the same corporate group. Although in theory the corporate group could have consolidated all the functions within one corporate entity, this arrangement enabled the corporate group to manage risk and, very often, to offer these services to competitors of the trustee. Having disaggregated the overall service, however, questions might have arisen about whether the trustee could properly appoint an associate, given the obvious conflicts of interest involved. Entrenching the appointment of that associate in the trust instrument as a non-discretionary duty of the trustee bypassed those concerns. It also obviated the need for the trustee to exercise care in the selection (though not necessarily the monitoring) of the associated service provider. The Stronger Super reforms inserted into the SIS Act sections 58A–58B, address this point directly.[40] Specifically, they render void provisions of a trust deed that purport to require the trustee to make such appointments. Those provisions do not prohibit the appointment of associates, but by removing the protection from scrutiny afforded by the trust instrument, they expose the decision-making of the trustee to the rules regulating trustees in relation to conflicts of interest and duty and also due diligence.

Another example of prescriptive drafting that has yet to be entirely resolved is the practice in Australian defined contribution superannuation funds of providing for 'member investment choice'. This facility enables the trustee to sidestep its usual duty to ensure that the investment strategy is appropriate for its members by permitting the trustee to act in accordance with appropriately delivered instructions from the member.[41] Although there continues to be some difference of opinion between APRA and some parts of the superannuation fund industry about the extent of the roll-back of responsibility effected by section 58(2)(d) of the SIS Act,[42] market practice has seen most APRA-regulated funds offer a menu of investment options to defined contribution members. The result is that except in the most egregious cases in which the trustee ought clearly to have recognised the inappropriateness of a strategy for a member,[43] the member bears the risk that the investment option into which their contribution is placed may be inappropriate to his or her needs.

[40] The Stronger Super reforms were a suite of legislative and regulatory measures responding to the recommendations of the Review into the Governance, Efficiency, Operation and Structure of the Superannuation System, available at: www.supersystemreview.gov.au. The recommendations spanned system architecture (including the design of a new type of default product, MySuper), fund governance (including new directors' duties and rules applying to related party appointments) and the powers of the prudential regulator. For description see P Heng, SJ Niblock and JL Harrison, 'Retirement Policy: A Review of the Role, Characteristics, and Contribution of the Australian Superannuation System' (2015) 29 *Asia Pacific Economic Literature* 1.

[41] SIS Act 1993, s 58(2)(d).

[42] APRA's views on member investment choice were articulated in Superannuation Circular No II.D.1: Managing Investments and Investment Choice (March 2006) 10–13 and more recently, Superannuation Prudential Standard SPS 530: Investment Governance (November 2013) (SPS 530) 7.

[43] See, for instance, the circumstances in *Perpetual Trustees Australia Ltd v Wallace* [2007] FCA 527. The case ultimately turned on jurisdictional issues related to the Superannuation Complaints Tribunal (SCT) but in the trustee conduct impugned by the SCT its decision involved permitting an aged member to direct 98% of his superannuation balance into a high-risk fund available on the fund's menu of investment options.

IV. THE REGULATORY PERSPECTIVE

Occupational pension schemes play an increasingly important role in many modern capitalist economies. They serve a very large number of working age and retired individuals: over 60 million in the UK and Australia alone.[44] They house over US$41 trillion of what is sometimes termed 'patient' capital: financial accumulations that are a vital source of capital and liquidity in world financial markets.[45] In countries such as Australia and the United Kingdom they are a pillar on which key social policies rely increasingly heavily.

With that importance comes a strong regulatory imperative. Responsible governance, competence and efficiency are required. The law of trusts can only do so much. It embodies norms which promote good governance and, to a lesser extent, competence. Its open textured nature also arguably accommodates the dynamics of competition and innovation that promote local and systemic efficiency. However, it has shortcomings. The same open texture that accommodates competition and innovation leaves it vulnerable to self-interested product design that might, if unchecked, sidestep the protective norms of the law of trusts. The enforcement apparatus of the courts is also arguably ill-equipped to ensure accountability in a context in which the collective action problem and information asymmetries are almost inevitable. Targeted legislative support, and processes of supervision and enforcement, are therefore vital to buttress the law of trusts in this context.

The 'virtual' nature of pension funds in many countries adds a further level of complexity to the challenge. Most obviously, it complicates the process of identifying where responsibility for decisions actually resides. In countries such as Australia, where the trustees of pension funds are subject to licensing regimes, there is a challenge to ensure that key decisions occur within parts of the virtual institution that are within the scope of that licensing regime. In Australia, member benefits administrators, asset custodians and investment managers lie outside that regime and beyond the direct reach of the prudential regulator primarily responsible for the pensions (superannuation) system. Those three functions, member benefit administration, asset custody and investment management, are undoubtedly core elements of the administration of the trust that is the superannuation fund, but APRA's only current means of regulating the entities responsible for those functions is indirectly, through regulating the form of the contractual relations a licensed trustee can enter with a third-party provider of such functions.[46] In countries without a formal licensing

[44] There are approximately 45.6 million in the United Kingdom: Office for National Statistics, Occupational Pension Schemes Survey, UK: 2018, 2, available at: www.ons.gov.uk/peoplepopulationandcommunity/personalandhouseholdfinances/pensionssavingsandinvestments/bulletins/occupationalpensionschemes-survey/2018. There are approximately 15.6 million in Australia: Australian Taxation Office data, available at: www.ato.gov.au/About-ATO/Research-and-statistics/In-detail/Super-statistics/Super-accounts-data/Multiple-super-accounts-data/.

[45] Willis Towers Watson, Global Pension Assets Study 2018, available at: www.willistowerswatson.com/en-AU/Insights/2019/02/global-pension-assets-study-2019. Note this figure is inflated by the inclusion of assets in private pensions vehicles in some jurisdictions where such vehicles are to give effect to occupational arrangements.

[46] APRA, SPS 231 (n 34).

regime, formal jurisdiction may not be the problem but there is still a problem of identifying where across a network of actors responsibility lies.

The problem of identifying the location of responsibility is not unusual in the law. However, the regulatory perspective introduces a new dimension. Regulatory measures such as 'fit and proper' tests, capital requirements and reporting protocols only make sense if they are directed to the parties actually responsible for the functions intended to be regulated. Supervisory activity, likewise, needs to be directed at key decision nodes, communication channels and information repositories. Indeed, Donald Duval, actuary and government architect of the SIS Act, noted in a presentation in 1994, in respect of the trustee covenants imposed to deem certain qualitative trustee duties as inalienably part of the trust's governing rules, that

> the main reason for these provisions ... is to ensure that trustees are in fact in control of their funds and can be held accountable. At the ISC we had observed that a number of trust deeds gave effective power to a party other than the trustee.[47]

As history has shown, that attempt to locate accountability in the office of trustee has only been partly successful. The entity acting as trustee may have nominal responsibility and accountability for all non-ministerial decision-making undertaken in the administration of the trust, but if the trustee has little substance, having distributed practical responsibility across a network of external service providers, that nominal accountability may have little value either in a prophylactic or remedial sense.

The other risk that the virtual organisational structure poses in practice is that it creates a pathway for risk propagation that would not exist were each pension fund functionally independent.[48] This in turn gives rise to a genuine risk that a local failure in one fund, or service provider, could have systemic implications in much the same way as has been identified in the banking system.[49] Little analysis of this possibility has been conducted outside Australia, but the basic insight has global application. With a few notable exceptions, occupational pension funds in most jurisdictions are sufficiently numerous that 'too big to fail' problems do not appear to exist in respect of them. However, the market for other services on which fund trustees rely, particularly asset custody and (in Australia at least) member benefit administration, are typically very concentrated, by virtue of the natural economies of scale that exist in those domains. These service providers typically serve multiple funds, and sometimes significant parts of the fund industry as a whole. A failure in one of these underlying service providers, or a failure by a fund that then affected the viability of one of the service providers, could quickly affect many other funds. The paradigm case is the failure of an asset custodian owned by a bank (think Lehman Brothers or Barings) which fails.[50] In theory, the commercial failure of the bank ought not to affect the

[47] D Duval, 'The Objectives of the Superannuation Supervisory Legislation' in MS Donald and LB Beatty (eds), *The Evolving Role of Trust in Superannuation* (Alexandria, NSW, Federation Press, 2017) 15. The Insurance and Superannuation Commissioner ('ISC' was the precursor to APRA.

[48] Donald et al (n 6).

[49] See for instance M Dungey et al, *Transmission of Financial Crises and Contagion: A Latent Factor Approach* (New York, Oxford University Press, 2011).

[50] MS Donald and R Nicholls, 'Bank Custodians and Systemic Risk in the Australian Superannuation System' (2015) 26 *Journal of Banking and Finance Law and Practice* 25.

assets held by the custodian arm of the bank, being segregated as a trust asset from the non-trust liabilities owed by the banking group. However, in practice, the failure of the bank does affect the custody activities, whether through complicated co-mingling of accounts (as in Lehman) or simply the drying up of the capital needed by the custodian subsidiary to maintain systems and processes. These challenges can be resolved given time, but in the meantime the administration of all funds employing the failing bank as a custodian or sub-custodian will be hamstrung, to the detriment of the members.

Of course, the linkages between fund trustees and their service providers is more variegated than that between commercial banks. Some are contractual, some equitable and, as observed above, there are limitation of liability clauses and insurance arrangements to consider as well. There are also sociological links to consider, such as shared world views and herding behaviour, given the emulative and often insular culture of the industry.[51] The aetiology of potential contagion in occupational pension systems is therefore altogether more nuanced and conditional than in the simple models of banking crises popular in the aftermath of the credit crisis of 2007–08.

V. CONCLUDING COMMENTS

Modern pension (superannuation) funds are complex and dynamic institutions. The trustee at the core of the institution has commonly been regarded as bearing accountability for administration of the trust, notwithstanding the presence of a myriad of service providers on whom the trustee relies. As the analysis in this chapter demonstrates, that allocation of accountability underestimates the presence of a complex set of contractual arrangements, statutory interventions and regulatory rules that are typically in place in reality.

[51] In the Dutch context, see R Bauer, M Bonetti and D Broeders, 'Pension Fund Interconnections and Herd Behavior' (2018) DNB Working Paper No 612, available at: www.dnb.nl/en/binaries/Working%20Paper%20No.%20612_tcm47-379838.pdf.

7

Legal Consequences of the Flawed Exercise of Scheme Powers

JESSICA HUDSON AND CHARLES MITCHELL

I. INTRODUCTION

A. Overview

OCCUPATIONAL PENSION SCHEMES typically confer powers on employers and trustees which must be exercised in accordance with legal rules and scheme requirements. There is much to be said about the content and purpose of these rules and requirements, but we are primarily interested in another topic, namely, what happens when power-holders fail to comply with them. In part II, we state the main powers which are typically vested in employers and trustees under pension schemes, and in part III, we discuss the rules and requirements which most commonly govern their exercise, a failure to comply with which we describe here as a 'flawed exercise of power'. In part IV, we examine flawed exercises of power to amend pension schemes, and in part V, we consider flawed exercises of power to transfer scheme assets. These are not the only cases in which non-compliance might occur in the pensions context, but we have focused our attention on them because they often arise in practice, and because the consequences that flow from non-compliance in such cases are often misunderstood. Finally, in part VI, we discuss some of the ways in which the legal consequences of non-compliance might be negated. In practice, this can be a key question for parties who discover that something has gone awry, especially if this has had the result not only that an apparently valid transaction was ineffective, but also that a series of further transactions premised on the validity of the first transaction were ineffective as well.

B. Voidness and Voidability

When analysing the legal consequences of flawed exercises of power, courts and legal scholars often speak of transactions entered by the relevant power-holders being 'void' or 'voidable'.[1] As we discuss in parts IV and V, however, a number of distinct consequences can flow from non-compliance with the rules and requirements governing the exercise of scheme powers, and the terms 'void' and 'voidable' are insufficiently fine-grained to capture the differences between these. As a result, the use of this language can be ambiguous and confusing, and this has contributed to a widespread failure to understand this area of the law.[2]

Our preferred approach is therefore to ask whether a flawed exercise of power 'creates or varies [or extinguishes] … legal or equitable rights and obligations'.[3] Some flawed exercises of power have these effects and others do not. We describe a flawed exercise of power as *effective* if it succeeds in creating or varying or extinguishing rights and obligations, albeit that it may also produce other consequences, such as susceptibility to rescission or rectification and the creation of personal liabilities. We describe a flawed exercise of power as *ineffective* if it does not create, vary or extinguish rights and obligations. We believe that this language is more stable than the language of 'void' and 'voidable' transactions, and that it helps us to distinguish between different types of case more precisely and so produce a clearer account of our topic.

II. POWERS COMMONLY VESTED IN EMPLOYERS AND TRUSTEES

A. Powers Vested in Employers

'A decision to have a pension scheme and the consequential decisions about the structure and design of the scheme are … matters primarily for the employer' and not for the trustees, whose role is to administer and manage the scheme in line with the employer's purposes and the terms of the scheme as set out in the documentation.[4] Obviously, pension schemes are not all the same and the powers which are vested in employers and trustees vary from one scheme to the next. Nonetheless, some powers are frequently conferred on them.

To enable the employer to perform its ongoing functions as the designer and overseer of a pension scheme, it will commonly give itself the following powers: to

[1] eg, *Re Courage Group's Pension Schemes* [1987] 1 WLR 495 (Ch) 512; *Mettoy Pension Trustees Ltd v Evans* [1990] 1 WLR 1587 (Ch) 1624; *AMP (UK) Ltd v Barker* [2001] Pens LR 77 (Ch) [90]; *Hearn v Younger* [2002] EWHC 963 (Ch), [2005] Pens LR 49 [91]; *Abacus Trust Co (Isle of Man) Ltd v Barr* [2003] EWHC 114 (Ch), [2003] Ch 409 [28]–[33]; *Walker Morris Trustees Ltd v Masterson* [2009] EWHC 1955 (Ch), [2009] Pens LR 307 [46]; *Roadchef (Employee Benefits Trustees) Ltd v Ingram Hill* [2014] EWHC 109 (Ch) [5], [89], [105]–[110] and [123]; *IBM UK Holdings Ltd v Dalgleish* [2015] EWHC 389 (Ch), [2015] Pens LR 99 [55]; *Bradbury v BBC* [2015] EWHC 1368 (Ch), [2015] Pens LR 457 [38]. See too R Nolan 'Controlling Fiduciary Power' [2009] *CLJ* 293, esp 316 ff; G Thomas, *Thomas on Powers*, 2nd edn (Oxford, Oxford University Press, 2012) para [9.90]; L Tucker, N Le Poidevin and J Brightwell, *Lewin on Trusts*, 19th edn (London, Sweet & Maxwell, 2018) para [29.312]; M Ashdown, *Trustee Decision Making: The Rule in Re Hastings-Bass* (Oxford, Oxford University Press, 2015) paras [9.08]–[9.13] and [9.20]–[9.42].

[2] Outside the pensions context, similar problems were noted by Lord Walker in *Pitt v Holt* [2013] UKSC 26, [2013] 2 AC 108 [62], discussing *Cloutte v Storey* [1911] 1 Ch 18 (CA) 30–32.

[3] *IBM* (Ch) (n 1) [55] (Warren J).

[4] *Smithson v Hamilton* [2007] EWHC 2900 (Ch), [2008] Pens LR 41 [87]; *British Airways plc v Airways Pension Scheme Trustee Ltd* [2018] EWCA Civ 1533, [2018] Pens LR 19 [102].

appoint and remove the trustees; to amend the rules of the scheme, either on its own or jointly with the trustees, and/or to agree to or veto amendments proposed by the trustees; and to wind up the scheme.

Powers of amendment are discussed further in part IV.A and part VI.B. They are generally essential for the effective functioning of schemes, for reasons which have been well summarised by David Pollard:[5] (1) schemes often last for a long time; (2) the pensions legislation and tax position of schemes is constantly changing; (3) pensions legislation often imposes new mandatory requirements on trustees without overriding the existing terms of schemes or supplying the employers (or trustees) with amendment powers; (4) the needs of employers and members in relation to retirement provision often change; and (5) discrimination laws have now become directly applicable to pension schemes and this has created a need for amendments to the rules of many schemes. In the light of all this, as Arden LJ once observed, it would be 'crying for the moon' to expect the draftsman of a scheme to provide for every eventuality,[6] and a preferable approach is to give employers (and/or trustees) a broad power to amend the terms of schemes in response to changes in their operating environments which could not have been foreseen at the time when they were first created.

B. Powers Vested in Trustees

An employer which chooses to use a trust structure when creating a pension scheme thereby chooses to give the trustees certain powers relating to the scheme assets that necessarily follow from the fact that ownership of the assets is transferred to the trustees, with binding directions that they should hold the assets for the benefit of other people.

In their capacity as owners of the trust property, the trustees acquire a power to transfer ownership of this property to others. The scheme assets may consist of legal or equitable property rights (or a mixture of the two), but whatever types of property right the trustees acquire, their power to transfer these rights 'arises independently of, and irrespective of, the terms of the trust, as it depends simply on … [their status as owners]: it is the same power as that held by … an unencumbered owner of property'.[7]

Additionally, and as a consequence of the creation of the trust, trustees have a power to overreach the beneficiaries' equitable interests in the trust property. This overreaching power is essential to the operation of a pension scheme because it enables the trustees to exchange ownership of scheme assets for ownership of other assets when they need to do this for investment purposes, and to transfer ownership of the assets to the members, their dependants and/or the employer when the need arises to pay them income or capital in accordance with the purposes of the scheme. Exercise of these powers in relation to scheme assets is discussed further in part V.B.

[5] D Pollard, 'A "Two Steps" Tango: Amending Amendment Powers' (2015) 29 *Trust Law International* 16, 17–18.

[6] *Stevens v Bell* [2002] EWCA Civ 672, [2002] Pens LR 247 [28]. See also *Courage* (n 1) 505: schemes must be 'operated against a constantly changing commercial background'.

[7] S Agnew and B McFarlane, 'The Paradox of the Equitable Proprietary Claim' in S Agnew and B McFarlane (eds), *Modern Studies in Property Law, Volume 10* (Oxford, Hart Publishing, 2019) 307.

Trustees are also typically given other powers which they need to perform their roles: to agree the actuarial valuation of the scheme and set the contribution rate from employers and members;[8] to accept contributions from employers and members into the scheme; to decide the investment policy for the scheme assets;[9] to decide the rights of members and their dependants to benefits; to augment the members' benefits; to allocate actuarial surpluses to the members and/or employers; to amend the scheme rules, on their own or jointly with the employers, and/or to agree or veto amendments proposed by the employers; and to wind up the scheme.[10]

C. Dispositive and Administrative Powers

It is often said of all the foregoing powers, and indeed of trustee powers more generally, that some are 'dispositive' while others are 'administrative'; that sometimes it does not matter which category a power falls into, because some rules governing the exercise of powers apply to both (for example, the rule that a power must be exercised for a proper purpose);[11] but that sometimes this matters, because other rules affect the exercise of one type of power but not the other (for example, the rule that a power-holder must take all and only relevant matters into account when making decisions, which applies to dispositive but not administrative powers).[12]

There is little clarity, however, as to how dispositive and administrative powers should be distinguished. On one approach, this distinction turns on the effect of a power's exercise, and dispositive powers are those which create, vary or extinguish beneficial interests, while administrative powers are those which do not.[13] On this view, a power of appointment is clearly a dispositive power, for example, but so too is a power of amendment which results in changes being made to the members' benefits, and one might even say that a power of investment was dispositive, as its exercise affects the property in which the members have a beneficial interest.

[8] Note the statutory provisions on scheme funding in the Pensions Act 2004, pt 3.

[9] Note the Pensions Act 1995, ss 34–35, which empower trustees, subject to scheme restrictions, to make investments as if they were absolutely entitled to the assets of the scheme; to delegate investment decisions to fund managers; and to prepare and maintain written statements of their investment policies. Section 35(4) also states that 'Neither the trust scheme nor the statement may impose restrictions (however expressed) on any power to make investments by reference to the consent of the employer'.

[10] The exercise of which power will trigger a statutory debt on the employer based on buy-out funding: Pensions Act 1995, s 75.

[11] *Vestey's Executors v IRC* [1949] 1 All ER 1108 (HL) (powers to give investment directions); *Re Skeats' Settlement* (1889) 42 Ch D 522 (Ch) (powers to appoint or remove trustees); *Courage* (n 1) (powers of amendment); *Re Pauling's ST (No 1)* [1964] Ch 303 (CA) and *Wong v Burt* [2004] NZCA 174, [2005] WTLR 291 (powers of appointment); *Independent Trustee Services Ltd v Hope* [2009] EWHC 2810 (Ch), [2010] ICR 553 (power to buy out benefits conferred on scheme members).

[12] *Re Duxbury's ST* [1995] 1 WLR 425 (CA) 427–28 (rule does not apply to powers to appoint new trustees); *Donaldson v Smith* [2006] EWHC B9 (Ch), [2007] WTLR 421 (rule does not apply to power to enter contract of sale or lease with third parties). However, Cayman and Jersey courts have taken a broader view of the rule's application: *Barclays Private Bank and Trust (Cayman) Ltd v Chamberlain* (2005) 9 ITELR 302; *Re Howe Family No 1 Trust* [2007] JRC 248, [2009] WTLR 419.

[13] eg, Ashdown (n 1) paras [4.10]–[4.11].

Another approach, though, is to focus on a power's general purpose (as opposed to its effect),[14] and this leads to the different conclusions that an amendment power could belong to either category and that an investment power should always belong to the administrative category.

More work is needed to resolve this uncertainty, but we shall not undertake this task here. Our discussion presupposes that a power-holder has failed to comply with a requirement or rule governing her exercise of a scheme power, and our focus is on the consequences which can follow from such non-compliance.

III. REASONS WHY PURPORTED EXERCISES OF POWER MIGHT BE FLAWED

Purported exercises of power under pension schemes can go awry for various reasons. In this part we set out some of the rules, a failure to comply with which results in a purported exercise of power being flawed.[15] We have not tried to create an exhaustive list of these, and there are others which can affect the purported exercise of pension scheme powers.[16] In our summary we identify 10 rules. These are not always clearly distinguished in the cases, but we believe them to be distinct. This is not because the consequences of failing to comply with them are necessarily different – they may or may not be – but because they have different content and purposes.

In our summary, we avoid describing particular rules by saying either that they impose a duty on the power-holder not to exercise the power in certain ways, or that they disable her from doing so. Courts and legal scholars often use language of this kind,[17] but they do not always use it consistently and it begs the question in which we are interested, namely whether a flawed exercise of power results in particular consequences, such as a failure to create new legal or equitable property rights, or the imposition of a personal liability on the power-holder or another party to pay compensation for loss or to disgorge profits.

[14] eg, Tucker et al (n 1) para [29.009]: 'Broadly, the line of distinction lies between powers which enable the donee to create a beneficial interest in an object of the power or otherwise to change the beneficial entitlements under the trusts and powers which enable the donees to safeguard and enhance the trust property'. See too Thomas (n 1) paras [1-12]–[1-14].

[15] Mention should also be made of cases where power-holders are asked to exercise their powers and refuse to do so, either for bad reasons or because they correctly regard themselves as prevented from acting by a conflict of interest. In cases of the first sort, the court will not exercise the power itself but may order the power-holder to consider doing so: *Finch v Telstra Super Pty Ltd* [2010] HCA 36, (2010) 242 CLR 254; *Erzurumlu v Kellogg Superannuation Pty Ltd* [2013] NSWSC 1115. In cases of the second sort, the court may step in and exercise the power itself: *Mettoy* (n 1).

[16] eg, the rules established by the Equality Act 2010, ss 67–69, applied in *Lloyds Banking Group Pensions Trustees Ltd v Lloyds Bank plc* [2018] EWHC 2839 (Ch), [2019] Pens LR 5; subsequent proceedings [2018] EWHC 3343 (Ch), [2019] Pens LR 6.

[17] 'Duty' language is used in, eg, *Mettoy* (n 1) 1613 (power-holder 'owes a duty … not to misuse the power'); *Pitt* (SC) (n 2) [73] ('inadequate deliberation on the part of the trustees must be sufficiently serious as to amount to a breach of fiduciary duty'); *IBM United Kingdom Holdings Ltd v Dalgleish* [2017] EWCA Civ 1212, [2018] ICR 1681 [3] ('*Imperial* duty'); Thomas (n 1) ch 10. 'Disability' language is used in, eg, *Re Egerton Trust Retirement Benefit Scheme* (Ch D, 1995), quoted in *Public Trustee v Cooper* [2001] WTLR 901 (Ch) 922 (trustees 'disabled as a result of a conflict of interest'); for other examples see the sources cited in C Mitchell, 'Equitable Compensation for Breach of Fiduciary Duty' (2013) 66 *Current Legal Problems* 307, 312–16.

A. Exercise of Power without Complying with Applicable Formalities

As noted in part II.B, the assets of a pension scheme may consist of legal or equitable property rights (or a mixture of the two). The trustees have a power to transfer these rights to other people which follows from their status as owners. Just like any other property owner, however, the trustees are subject to rules which require some transfers to take particular forms. Examples are rules governing the transfer of choses in action[18] and land.[19]

Trustees and/or employers may alternatively wish to enter other types of transaction which must be done by deed, for example, because this is required by the terms of the scheme; in such cases the formality rules governing the execution of deeds will apply.[20]

B. Power does not Exist/Excessive Execution

A power cannot be validly exercised if the power does not exist because it was never conferred on the relevant employer or trustee,[21] or was conferred but was made subject to requirements which have not been satisfied.[22] Examples of the latter situation are where a scheme stipulates that an exercise of power by trustees is valid only if the employer consents to it, or vice versa; and where a scheme provides that an exercise of power is valid only if implemented by a deed signed by all the power-holders.[23] In cases of this general type, the motives of the relevant employer or trustee are irrelevant and the only question that matters is whether she had the power to act in the way that she purported to act.[24]

C. Improper Exercise of Power/Fraud on a Power

A power must be exercised in order to accomplish the purpose for which it was given and must not be exercised in order to accomplish some other purpose chosen by the

[18] eg, Law of Property Act 1925, ss 53(1)(c) and 136; *William Brandt's Sons & Co v Dunlop Rubber Co Ltd* [1905] AC 454 (HL) 462; *Corin v Patton* (1990) 169 CLR 525. See generally D Fox, 'Assignment of Choses in Action' in J McGhee (ed), *Snell's Equity*, 33rd edn (London, Sweet & Maxwell, 2015); YK Liew, *Guest on the Law of Assignment*, 3rd edn (London, Sweet & Maxwell, 2018).

[19] eg, Land Registration Act 2002.

[20] eg, Law of Property (Miscellaneous Provisions) Act 1989, s 1(3), applied in *Briggs v Gleeds (Head Office) (a firm)* [2014] EWHC 1178 (Ch), [2015] 1 Ch 212.

[21] *Re Reevie and Montreal Trust Co of Canada* (1986) 25 DLR (446) 312; *Schmidt v Air Products Canada Ltd* [1994] 2 SCR 611; *Air Jamaica Ltd v Charlton* [1999] 1 WLR 1399 (PC) 1411; *BHLSPF Pty Ltd v Brashs Pty Ltd* [2001] VSC 512, (2001) 8 VR 602; *British Airways* (CA) (n 4) [153]–[163]; *Re IMG Pension Plan* [2009] EWHC 2785 (Ch), [2010] Pens LR 23 [115]–[125] (reversed on a different point [2010] EWCA Civ 1349, [2011] Pens LR 11); *UC Rusal Alumina Jamaica Ltd v Miller* [2014] UKPC 39, [2015] Pens LR 15 [46].

[22] See *BESTrustees v Stuart* [2001] Pens LR 283 (Ch); *HR Trustees Ltd v Wembley plc* [2011] EWHC 2974 (Ch); *Gleeds* (n 20). See too the Pensions Act 1995, s 67: some powers to amend schemes cannot be exercised without the consent of scheme members.

[23] As in, eg, *BIC UK Ltd v Burgess* [2019] EWCA Civ 806, [2019] ICR 1386 [23]; *Gleeds* (n 20) [2]–[7].

[24] *Re UEB Industries Ltd Pension Plan* [1992] 1 NZLR 294, 301; *IMG* (n 21) [126].

power-holder. Whether this rule is distinct from the 'excessive execution' rule is a question to which the English courts have given inconsistent answers. Older cases say that there is no difference between them: for example, Lord Parker said in *Vatcher v Paull* that the 'fraud on a power' doctrine concerns the exercise of a power 'beyond the scope of or not justified by the instrument creating the power'.[25] More recent authorities hold the opposite: for example, Lord Sumption said in *Eclairs Group Ltd v JKX Oil & Gas plc* that the 'fraud on a power' doctrine is 'not concerned with excess of power by doing an act which is beyond the scope of the instrument creating it', but with 'abuse of power, by doing acts which are within its scope but done for an improper reason'.[26]

On either approach, the question whether a power-holder commits a fraud on the power must be answered by identifying her reasons for exercising the power and by deciding whether these were in line with the purposes for which the power was given. To identify these purposes in the pensions context it is usually necessary to construe the scheme documents.[27] Schemes are often drafted to include benefiting the employer as well as the members among their purposes, and since such arrangements are legally valid, it follows that power-holders under pension schemes, whether they are trustees or employers, are not subject to any mandatory stand-alone rule that they must always act in the best interests of the members.[28]

D. Power Exercised with Dishonest Motive

It has often been observed that the term 'fraud on a power' is misleading because the rule applies regardless of whether a power-holder has acted with a fraudulent or dishonest motive.[29] Where a power-holder does exercise a power with a dishonest motive, however, this constitutes a breach of the general duty of honesty identified

[25] *Vatcher v Paull* [1915] AC 372 (PC) 378. See too *Topham v Duke of Portland* (1869–70) LR 5 Ch App 40 (CA) 59; G Farwell, CJW Farwell and FK Archer, *A Concise Treatise on Powers*, 3rd edn (London, Stevens & Sons, 1916) 458: 'the essential notion is disposition beyond the scope of the power, not breach of trust by the donee'.

[26] *Eclairs Group Ltd v JKX Oil & Gas plc* [2015] UKSC 71, [2015] Bus LR 1395 [15].

[27] *Bank of New Zealand v Bank of New Zealand Officers Provident Association Management Board* [2003] UKPC 58, [2003] OPLR 281 [21]; *British Airways* (CA) (n 4); *Airways Pension Scheme Trustee Ltd v Fielder* [2019] EWHC 29 (Ch), [2019] 4 WLR 9. On the interpretation of scheme documentation, see also David Pollard's chapter in the present volume.

[28] *Re Merchant Navy Ratings Pension Fund* [2015] EWHC 448 (Ch), [2015] Pens LR 239 [212], [228], endorsing extra-judicial comments in Lord Nicholls, 'Trustees and Their Broader Community: Where Duty, Morality and Ethics Converge' (1995) 9 *Trust Law International* 71. According to Marcus Smith J in *Keymed (Medical and Industrial Equipment) Ltd v Hillman* [2019] EWHC 485 (Ch) [117]–[120], however, while pension trustees are entitled to have regard to the employer's interests where these do not conflict with the interests of the members, they must prioritise the members' interests in cases of conflict. On this topic, see also *Cowan v Scargill* [1985] Ch 270 (Ch); *Courage* (n 1) 511–12; *British Coal Corp v British Coal Staff Superannuation Scheme Trustees* [1995] 1 All ER 912 (Ch); *Hillsdown Holdings plc v Pensions Ombudsman* [1996] Pens LR 427 [73]–[76]; *Scully v Coley* [2009] UKPC 29 [47]–[49]; *Independent Trustee Services Ltd v Hope* (n 11) [71]–[104]; *Roadchef* (n 1). And see too E Nugee, 'The Duties of Pension Scheme Trustees to the Employer' (1998) 12 *Trust Law International* 216; C Nugee, 'The Duties of Pension Scheme Trustees to the Employer – Revisited' (2015) 29 *Trust Law International* 59; D Pollard, 'Application of the Proper Purpose Test to Pension Schemes' (2016) 30 *Trust Law International* 159.

[29] *Duke of Portland v Topham* (1864) 11 HL Cas 32, 54, 11 ER 1242, 1251; *Vatcher* (n 25) 378.

by Viscount Haldane LC in *Nocton v Lord Ashburton*, where he said that if 'a man intervenes in the affairs of another he must do so honestly, whatever be the character of that intervention'.[30] This rule was said to apply to the exercise of powers under pension schemes by Scott V-C in *Edge v Pensions Ombudsman*.[31] However, we have not identified any pension case where an exercise of power has been successfully challenged on this ground. Reasons for this may be that scheme members are often unwilling to risk the costs of litigation with the result that challenges are rare, that dishonesty is hard to prove, and that the other rules described here usually provide claimants with all the grounds of challenge that they need.[32]

E. Power Exercised in Bad Faith

'Good faith' is often used as a synonym for 'honesty'. So it is easy to understand why a rule that requires power-holders to act in 'good faith' might be confused with the foregoing rule that requires them to act honestly. However, the 'good faith' doctrine we have in mind requires something rather different of power-holders, viz, that they must make a sincere commitment to the purposes for which their powers have been given, pay proper regard to the interests of those whose position will be affected by exercise of these powers, make their decisions in a candid, rational and fair-minded way, and refrain from conduct that is secretive, capricious, perverse, or misleading. Lord Mance spoke in these terms in *UC Rusal Alumina Jamaica Ltd v Miller*, where he accepted that the rule requiring a power-holder to act 'bona fide' did not 'merely mean that it must act honestly', but additionally meant that 'it must avoid irrational or arbitrary behaviour and must not exercise its power to give or refuse consent for extraneous reasons'.[33] Similarly, in *Hayes v Willoughby*, Lord Sumption said that a rule requiring decisions to be taken rationally

> imports a requirement of good faith, a requirement that there should be some logical connection between the evidence and the ostensible reasons for the decision, and … an absence of arbitrariness, of capriciousness or of reasoning so outrageous in its defiance of logic as to be perverse.[34]

These dicta were followed in *IBM United Kingdom Holdings Ltd v Dalgleish*,[35] putting it beyond doubt that power-holders under pension schemes, just like every other power-holder, must act in good faith, using that term in the sense we have described.[36]

[30] *Nocton v Lord Ashburton* [1914] AC 932 (HL) 954.

[31] *Edge v Pensions Ombudsman* [1998] Ch 512 (Ch) 535: power-holders 'certainly had a duty to exercise their discretionary power honestly'.

[32] *cf Independent Trustee Services Ltd v GP Noble Trustees Ltd* [2010] EWHC 1653 (Ch) [42]: no need to decide whether defendant trustees liable for fraud as they were liable for negligence.

[33] *Rusal* (n 21) [51].

[34] *Hayes v Willoughby* [2013] UKSC 17, [2013] 1 WLR 935 [14].

[35] *IBM* (CA) (n 17) [227].

[36] See too *Harris v Lord Shuttleworth* [1994] ICR 991 (CA) 999; *cf Dundee General Hospitals Board of Management v Walker* [1952] 1 All ER 896 (HL) 900; *Re Manisty's ST* [1974] Ch 17 (Ch) 26.

F. Power Exercised in a Manner Inconsistent with the Relationship of Trust and Confidence between the Power-Holder in its Capacity as Employer and its Employees

In the *IBM* case, the Court of Appeal also approved the finding by Browne-Wilkinson V-C in *Imperial Group Pension Trust Ltd v Imperial Tobacco Ltd*,[37] that an employer with powers under a pension scheme fails to exercise these powers in good faith if it fails to exercise them in a manner which is consistent with the relationship of trust and confidence that exists between the employer and its employees. It may be, therefore, that the *Imperial* requirement is merely a subset of the good faith requirement described above, the exact content of which will vary according to the nature of the relevant employment relationship in each case. The two rules cannot exactly overlap, however, since the *Imperial* rule applies only to power-holders who are employers and does not apply to trustee power-holders who are not employers.

G. Power Exercised with Self-Interested Motive

It is sometimes said that a power-holder who is required to act in good faith can never exercise the power in a self-interested way if the power could alternatively be exercised for the benefit of other people, because 'good faith' always requires the power-holder to prioritise the interests of these others. However, this is to misunderstand the good faith requirement. As we have said, this requires power-holders to make a sincere commitment to the purposes for which the power has been given, but if these purposes include benefiting the power-holder, then exercising the power to produce such an outcome is not necessarily a bad faith action.[38] The consequences of this principle for pension schemes were noted by Scott V-C in *Edge*:[39] schemes may authorise trustees to exercise their powers in a self-serving way, provided that they act in good faith, and if schemes require employer and/or employee trustees to be appointed then they impliedly authorise these trustees to do the same thing.[40] However, if power-holders under pension schemes are not authorised to exercise their powers in a self-serving way, then any such purported exercise of power will be

[37] *Imperial Group Pension Trust Ltd v Imperial Tobacco Ltd* [1991] 1 WLR 589 (Ch). See too *National Grid Co plc v Laws* [1997] Pens LR 157 (Ch) 177; *Re Prudential Staff Pension Scheme* [2011] EWHC 960 (Ch), [2011] Pens LR 239 [118]–[153]. *cf Commonwealth Commercial Bank of Australia v Barker* [2014] HCA 32, (2014) 253 CLR 169, discussed in S Donald and C Hodkinson, 'Imperial Tobacco – Up in Smoke in Australia?' (2015) 29 *Trust Law International* 39.

[38] C Mitchell, 'Good Faith, Self-denial and Mandatory Trustee Duties' (2018) 32 *Trust Law International* 92.

[39] *Edge* (Ch) (n 31) 538–42; approved [2000] Ch 602 (CA). In this passage of his judgment, Scott-VC took due note of the Pensions Act 1995 s 39, which abrogated prior decisions to the contrary in *Re William Makin & Sons Ltd* [1992] Pens LR 177 (Ch) and *British Coal Corp v British Coal Staff Superannuation Fund Scheme Trustees* [1993] Pens LR 303 (Ch).

[40] See too *Rath v Association of Investment Trust Companies* Pensions Ombudsman Determination, 24 September 2009, 27884/2; and see RL Nobles, 'The Exercise of Trustees' Discretion under a Pension Scheme' [1992] *Journal of Business Law* 261, 276–79; M Fitzsimmons, 'Managing Pension Scheme Trustee Conflicts of Interest' (2006) 20 *Trust Law International* 211; and *cf Sun Indalex Finance LLC v United Steelworkers* [2013] SCC 6, [2013] 1 SCR 271.

flawed not only because it is unauthorised, but also because trustees and employers hold their powers in a fiduciary capacity and are therefore subject to the rules which require them to avoid conflicts of interest.[41]

H. Power Exercised without Taking All and Only Relevant Considerations into Account

Power-holders must take all and only relevant considerations into account when deciding whether and if so how to exercise their powers. The leading case is now *Pitt v Holt*,[42] not itself a pensions case, where Lord Walker stated that the rule would apply only where the power-holder's failure amounts to a 'breach of fiduciary duty'. By this, he cannot have meant a breach of the power-holder's duty to subordinate her personal interests to those of the power's objects, since the cases from which Lord Walker derived the principle did not concern self-interested action by power-holders. It seems likely that instead he meant the duty previously identified by Lightman J in *Abacus Trust Co (Isle of Man) v Barr*, namely a duty of 'proper care and diligence in obtaining the relevant information and advice'.[43]

In this connection, we note that in *Finch v Telstra Super Pty Ltd*,[44] the High Court of Australia held that superannuation trustees who are required to make decisions about factual matters must undertake a 'more intense' set of enquiries than other types of trustees. In Australia, then, even if not elsewhere, more is expected of pension trustees than of other types of trustee when it is asked whether they have successfully identified all the considerations relevant to their decision-making.

I. Power Exercised Carelessly

Power-holders under pension schemes must exercise their powers with reasonable care and skill. For example, they must not fall below a reasonable standard of care when exercising their investment powers,[45] or their powers to assess members' applications for benefits.[46]

[41] As in *Re Drexel Burnham Lambert UK Pension Plan* [1995] 1 WLR 32 (Ch). Note also that statutory limits are placed on the investment of pension scheme funds in the employer's business: Pensions Act 1995, s 40; Occupational Pension Schemes (Investment) Regulations 2005 (SI 2005/3378) reg 12.

[42] *Pitt* (SC) (n 2); followed in a pensions context in *British Airways plc v Airways Pension Scheme Trustee Ltd* [2017] EWHC 1191 (Ch), [2017] Pens LR 16 [482]–[493]. Pension cases applying this rule which were decided prior to the rule's formulation in *Pitt* include: *Kerr v British Leyland (Staff) Trustees Ltd* [2001] WTLR 1071 (CA); *Mettoy* (n 1); *Stannard v Fisons Pension Trusts Ltd* [1991] Pens LR 225 (CA); *Edge* (Ch) (n 31) 533–34, 536.

[43] *Abacus Trust Co* (n 1) [23]. Lightman J's ruling that an exercise of power would be flawed only if this duty was breached was endorsed by Lloyd LJ in *Pitt v Holt* [2011] EWCA Civ 197, [2012] Ch 132 [94], whose own judgment was approved by Lord Walker in the SC.

[44] *Finch* (n 15) [66].

[45] For the standard governing the exercise of investment powers, see the Pensions Act 1995, ss 35–36 and the Occupational Pension Schemes (Investment) Regulations 2005; the Pensions Act 1995, s 33 prohibits the exclusion of trustee liability for losses caused by the negligent investment of scheme funds.

[46] *Apostolovski v Total Risk Management Pty Ltd* [2010] NSWSC 1451, (2010) 79 NSWLR 432 (negligent failure to consider member's application in a timely fashion).

J. Power Exercised by Mistake

Whether or not a power-holder has acted carelessly, or indeed breached any of the other rules described here, legal consequences may flow from the fact that the power has been exercised by mistake. Common examples are mistaken amendments to schemes,[47] and mistaken transfers of scheme assets to recipients who are not entitled to them under the terms of the scheme.[48]

IV. FLAWED AMENDMENTS OF PENSION SCHEMES

A. Powers of Amendment

Employers and trustees are often granted powers to amend the terms of a pension scheme.[49] Examples are powers to increase the members' retirement age; to close the scheme to new members; to change or terminate the members' future accrual of benefits; to increase or remove the employers' liability to make contributions; to introduce, increase or remove the members' liability to make contributions; to convert a defined benefit scheme into a defined contribution scheme or vice versa; and to replace the trustee or other power-holder under the scheme.

Many of the rules summarised in part III can apply to the purported exercise of a power of amendment, and in the rest of this part we examine the consequences which can follow from non-compliance with these rules: we discuss the effectiveness of flawed exercises of amendment powers in part IV.B; the personal liability of power-holders in part IV.C; and the personal liability of other parties in part IV.D.

B. Effective and Ineffective Amendments

The scheme terms give content to a trustee's duty to use and hold her title over scheme assets in accordance with those terms, and to the members' correlative entitlements under the scheme. The exercise of an amendment power which has the effect of changing the scheme terms also changes the parties' rights and obligations that are defined by those terms. In other words, when an exercise of an amendment power is effective, the trustee will thereafter be required to use her ownership of the scheme assets in accordance with the terms as varied. This may have the effect of depriving

[47] As in *AMP* (n 1); *IBM* (Ch) (n 1); *Merchant Navy Officers Pension Fund Trustees v Watkins* [2013] EWHC 4741 (Ch); *Saga Group Ltd v Paul* [2016] EWHC 2344 (Ch), [2017] 4 WLR 12.

[48] Since 2014, many mistaken payments to pension scheme members have been discovered following a massive record-checking exercise initiated by HMRC. This has involved comparing HMRC records with those of employers whose employees participated in 'guaranteed minimum pension' schemes between 1978 and 1997. Under these schemes, many employees 'contracted out' of contributing to part of the state pension. However, HMRC's enquiry revealed that numerous errors were made in the way that their guaranteed minimum pensions were calculated, which resulted in many overpayments.

[49] The important but tricky question whether amendment powers can be drafted to operate with retrospective effect is considered in part VI.B.

beneficiaries of their rights under the trust as previously drafted, but if the power of amendment was validly exercised, they cannot complain about this since:

> The rights arising under a constitution or a trust deed or a set of rules which is susceptible to amendment are rights that exist subject always to the possibility that the governing instrument will be changed. It is an incident or aspect of every right arising from that instrument that the amendment power may alter or abolish the right.[50]

As noted in part I.B, we do not think it helpful to ask whether purported amendments are 'void' or 'voidable'. We believe it is more illuminating to ask whether there has been an exercise of power which is effective, meaning that it effects a variation of the terms of the scheme, and the rights and obligations defined by those terms. Depending on the requirement or rule with which the power-holder has failed to comply, a number of different consequences may follow: (i) the purported exercise of power might be ineffective to vary the terms of the scheme, so that the rights and obligations defined by those terms are unchanged; (ii) it might be effective to vary the terms of the scheme, but the variation might be rescinded with retrospective effect; (iii) it might be effective to vary the terms of the scheme but the new terms might be rectified with retrospective effect; or (iv) it might be effective to vary the terms of the scheme, but the power-holders and/or other parties might incur a personal liability.

i. Ineffective Exercise

When non-compliance with a scheme requirement or legal rule renders the purported exercise of an amendment power ineffective, this means that the terms of the scheme and the rights and obligations defined by those terms remain the same. This consequence follows, for example, when the purported exercise of an amendment power is flawed by reason of (a) excessive execution,[51] (b) fraud on a power,[52] or (c) failure to comply with the requirements for execution of a deed.[53] The exercise of an amendment power can be effective only to the extent that a court is willing to compel the trustees to act in accordance with the varied scheme terms. A power-holder's failure to act within the terms of the power, or for a proper purpose, each provide a reason for a court to refuse to recognise the purported variation as effective. So, for example, the Full Federal Court of Australia in *Australian Super Pty Ltd v Woodward* explained that a purported exercise of an amendment power for an improper purpose 'would not be cognisable by a court of equity'.[54] In addition to declaratory relief acknowledging the invalidity of the flawed exercise of power, further relief might also be awarded, such as an order requiring the delivery up of relevant documents.

[50] *ING Funds Management Ltd v ANZ Nominees Ltd* [2009] NSWSC 243, (2009) 228 FLR 444 [149] (Barrett J).

[51] *Air Jamaica* (n 21) 1411; *BESTrustees* (n 22) [48]–[50]; *BHLSPF* (n 21) [44]; *Courage* (n 1) 510–12; *Walker Morris* (n 1) [46]; *IMG* (n 21) [125], [148]–[149].

[52] *Courage* (n 1) 510–12; *Austec Wagga Wagga Pty Ltd v Rarebreed Wagga Pty Ltd* [2012] NSWSC 343 [71].

[53] *Gleeds* (n 20) [2]–[7].

[54] *Australian Super Pty Ltd v Woodward* [2009] FCAFC 168, (2009) 262 ALR 402 [38].

An ineffective exercise of an amendment power means that there is no change, and that *there never was a change*, to the scheme terms. This may have further cascading consequences for subsequent exercises of power made on the assumption that the terms of the scheme were validly amended. For example, in *British Airways plc v Airways Pension Scheme Trustee Ltd*,[55] the trustees purported to amend the scheme terms to give themselves a power to increase pension benefits. This was done for an improper purpose,[56] with the result that no valid amendment took place. It followed that when the trustees purported to exercise their supposed power to increase pension benefits this was also ineffective because the trustees had no such power. In this case, the trustees deferred payment of the increased pension benefits, and so no payments were made that needed to be repaid.[57] But if such payments had been made pursuant to a supposed but non-existent power to transfer the scheme assets, then this would have created further consequences of the kind which are considered below in part V.

ii. Effective Exercise Subject to Rescission

Non-compliance with a rule sometimes has the consequence that the exercise of an amendment power is effective but may be rescinded. In other words, the flawed exercise of power varies the scheme terms and the parties' rights and obligations, *unless and until* rescission is granted. In this case, although the exercise of the power is prima facie effective, members, employers and/or trustees may nevertheless be able to obtain a court order that the amendment should be set aside with retrospective effect, accompanied by consequential relief such as a declaration that the trust terms are those which previously existed.[58]

This consequence follows, for example, from the purported exercise of an amendment power by a power-holder who fails to take all and only relevant considerations into account – as Sir Andrew Park held in *Smithson v Hamilton*.[59] Rescission may also be awarded where an amendment power has been exercised by mistake,[60] and an effective exercise of an amendment power may be subject to being set aside by the Pensions Regulator if the amendment relates to members' accrued or subsisting rights and fails to comply with various statutory limitations.[61]

[55] *British Airways* (CA) (n 4).

[56] ibid [110], [126]–[127].

[57] As Morgan J found at first instance: *British Airways* (Ch) (n 42) [120].

[58] *cf Shalson v Russo* [2003] EWHC 1637 (Ch), [2005] Ch 281 [120]–[127]. For general discussion of rescission, see D O'Sullivan, S Elliott and R Zakrzewski, *The Law of Rescission*, 2nd edn (Oxford, Oxford University Press, 2014) esp para [16.17]; B Häcker, *Consequences of Impaired Consent Transfers: A Structural Comparison of English and German Law* (Oxford, Hart Publishing, 2013).

[59] *Smithson* (n 4) [79]–[80]. *cf Pitt* (SC) (n 2) [60], [70], [93], [99]–[101].

[60] A possibility contemplated in *AMP* (n 1) [80]–[82] and *Gallaher Ltd v Gallaher Pensions Ltd* [2005] EWHC 42 (Ch), [2005] Pens LR 103 [153], though Sir Andrew Park declined to follow these dicta in *Smithson* (n 4) [114], [119], [121]. See also N Stallworthy, 'Rationalising Mistake in the Law of Trusts: *Smithson v Hamilton*' (2009) 23 *Trust Law International* 51; *Pitt* (SC) (n 2) [114]; C Mitchell, 'Rescission of Voluntary Settlements and Dispositions of Trust Property on the Ground of Mistake' (2017) 2 *Private Client Business* 41.

[61] Pensions Act 1995, s 67. See also *Danks v Qinetiq Holdings Ltd* [2012] EWHC 570 (Ch), [2012] Pens LR 131 [39]; *Pensions Regulator Determination Notice: DCT Civil Engineering Staff Pension Fund* (Case Ref C26276259), available at: www.thepensionsregulator.gov.uk/-/media/thepensionsregulator/files/import/pdf/dn3610595.ashx.

The question can arise whether an order for rescission should take effect from the date of judgment or should be backdated to run from an earlier point in time. The answer to this question can have ramifications for any exercise of powers that has occurred in the period running from the date when the initial flawed exercise of power occurred and the date of judgment. Where an order is made with retrospective effect, to produce the result, for example, that an effective exercise of the amendment power is deemed never to have taken place, there may be cascading consequences of the kind already described in part IV.B.i.

However, it must be borne in mind that rescission is an equitable remedy, and that the court accordingly has a discretion whether or not to award it. Case law suggests that orders for rescission may not be made in cases where there are intervening factors, as for example where subsequent decisions have been taken on the (good faith) assumption that the amendment power was validly exercised and/or if there are intervening interests, such as accrued member entitlements. Such factors may operate as complete bars to rescission, or at least necessitate relief on terms, so that subsequent exercises of power are saved, and accrued rights preserved. Authorities include *Breadner v Granville-Grossman*,[62] where Sir Andrew Park stated that it would 'be astonishing, and … unacceptable' for a power-holder's non-compliance with an applicable rule to be used to 'upset some action by trustees which may have been taken decades ago … and on the basis of which many intervening decisions and actions have been taken'.

iii. Effective Exercise Subject to Rectification

Another possible consequence is that an exercise of an amendment power is effective, but there is an equity for rectification.[63] Pension scheme documents are amenable to rectification, just like 'any other documents with a legal effect'.[64] Where an amendment power has been exercised by mistake, an equity for rectification will arise if the instrument executed in exercise of the power of amendment fails to reflect the power-holder's intention owing to her mistake. In cases of this kind, the party seeking rectification (who might be a trustee, employer or member) must show: first, that the parties had a common continuing intention as to the exercise of a power of amendment;[65] second, that the intention continued at the time of the execution of

[62] *Breadner v Granville-Grossman* [2001] Ch 523 (Ch) [553]. See too *Smithson* (n 4) [79], where the same judge said that intervening factors may provide a 'good reason in the particular circumstances' of the case not to set aside the flawed exercise of a power.

[63] See, eg, *IBM* (Ch) (n 1) [394] and [397]; *Drake Insurance Plc v MacDonald* [2005] EWHC 3287 (Ch), [2005] Pens LR 401 [33]; *AMP* (n 1) [66]; *Watkins* (n 47) [24]; *Saga Group* (n 47); *Hogg Robinson Plc v Harvey* [2016] EWHC 129 (Ch), [2016] Pens LR 61.

[64] *Scania Ltd v Wager* [2007] EWHC 711 (Ch) [17]; D Hayton, P Matthews and C Mitchell, *Underhill & Hayton: The Law Relating to Trusts and Trustees*, 19th edn (London, LexisNexis, 2016) paras [15.21]–[15.25].

[65] Where a power is granted to a party unilaterally, and not subject to the consent of another, the relevant intention is that of the power-holder alone: *Watkins* (n 47) [12]. In the case of a corporate trustee, the relevant intention is the collective intention of the board: ibid [12].

the power of amendment; and third, that as a result of the mistake, the instrument did not reflect that common intention.[66]

Where rectification is ordered, the court will change the wording of the pension scheme so that it ceases to state what was mistakenly expressed and instead states what was intended from the outset.[67] The court substitutes a correct version for the incorrect version. Rectification is also an equitable remedy, awards of which are at the court's discretion. Hence, while orders can be made with retrospective effect so that the parties' rights under the pension scheme are ascertained on the basis that the scheme always contained the correct terms, orders can also be made on the different basis that rights and obligations which accrued prior to rectification should continue in existence.[68]

iv. Effective Exercise but Personal Liability Incurred

Sometimes a power-holder may fail to comply with a rule governing the exercise of an amendment power, non-compliance with which may or may not render the flawed exercise of power ineffective, but, in either case, exposes the power-holder to liability for compensation. This might occur, for example, in a case where the rule imposes a legal duty on the power-holder to act with reasonable care, and she breaches this duty with the result that the members suffer a loss. Situations of this kind are discussed in part V.C and part V.D.

v. Total or Partial Consequence

Finally, there is the question whether a consequence applies in whole or part.[69] In the pensions context, it appears that the determinative factor is whether a transaction involves a single exercise of power, or can be divided into multiple exercises of the one or multiple powers.[70] In the former class of case, the consequence will apply *in toto* to the flawed exercise. In the latter class of case, the consequence will apply *in toto* but only to exercises of powers that are flawed: any other, valid, exercises of power are unaffected. Those cases in which the effect of a rule appears to be partial can thus be understood as the total application of the rule to some but not all, exercises of power by a power-holder.[71]

[66] These requirements were applied in the pensions context in *IBM* (Ch) (n 1) [15]; *Drake* (n 63) [33]; *AMP* (n 1) [66]. However, the general law of rectification is now on the move as a result of *FSHC Group Holdings Ltd v GLAS Trust Corp Ltd* [2019] EWCA Civ 1361, [2020] 1 All ER 505, and it remains to be seen what the consequences of this will be for the rectification of pensions documents. This topic is addressed in Paul Davies's chapter in the present volume.

[67] See, eg, *Smithson* (n 4) [67]–[68]; S Douglas, 'Misuse of Rectification in the Law of Trusts' (2018) 134 *LQR* 138.

[68] *AMP* (n 1) [79]; *IBM* (Ch) (n 1) [492].

[69] Left open in *Pitt* (CA) (n 43) [72], referring to *Smithson* (n 4) [68]–[72].

[70] See also Stallworthy (n 60) 75.

[71] As in, eg, *Burrell v Burrell* [2005] EWHC 245 (Ch), [2005] Pens LR 289 [25]; *BESTrustees* (n 22) [48].

Having said that, however, we must finally add that special problems can arise where there are multiple and divisible exercises of power, some of which are valid in themselves and therefore prima facie effective, but which are connected with flawed exercises of power which are ineffective, or which may be rescinded or rectified. In this type of case, the ineffectiveness of the flawed exercises of power may render otherwise valid exercises of power ineffective.[72]

V. FLAWED TRANSFERS OF PENSION SCHEME ASSETS

A. Transfers of Scheme Assets

Transactions involving scheme assets may be facilitated by the exercise of multiple powers, such as: (i) the trustee's power to transfer ownership of trust property to another party; (ii) the trustee's power to vary or overreach the equitable interests under the trust on which the scheme assets are held; and (iii) in relation to certain transactions concerning scheme assets, the trustee's power to enter an agreement respecting these assets with a third party. A single transaction may involve the exercise of one or more of these powers, and these must be distinguished because different consequences may ensue with respect to flawed exercises of each type of power. Our discussion in this part focuses on flawed exercises of the first two types of power only.[73] In part V.B, we discuss whether such exercises of power are effective or ineffective to alter the parties' rights and obligations in connection with the scheme assets; in part V.C, we look at the imposition of personal liabilities on power-holders; and in part V.D, we examine the imposition of personal liabilities on members and third parties.

B. Effective and Ineffective Transfers of Scheme Assets

As stated in part I.B, we believe it is unhelpful to speak of 'void' and 'voidable' transfers when analysing the consequences of a flawed exercise of power to transfer scheme assets. Instead we ask whether the flawed exercise of power is, or is not, effective to change the parties' legal or equitable rights and obligations. In our discussion, we use this language to describe four consequences that might follow from a flawed exercise of power. These are: (i) an ineffective exercise of the trustee's power as owner of the scheme assets to transfer ownership to another person; (ii) an effective exercise of the trustee's power to transfer ownership of the assets but an ineffective exercise of her power to overreach the beneficiaries' equitable interest in the assets; (iii) an effective exercise of the trustee's powers as owner and an effective exercise of her power to overreach the beneficiaries' interests, but susceptibility to rescission; and (iv) an

[72] *cf Re Abrahams' WT* [1969] 1 Ch 463 (Ch) 478–85; and in the pensions context, see *BESTrustees* (n 22) [48]–[49]; Thomas (n 1) para [5.41].

[73] For general discussion of the third, see M Conaglen and R Nolan, 'Contracts and Knowing Receipt: Principles and Application' (2013) 129 *LQR* 359.

effective exercise of the trustee's powers as owner and an effective exercise of her power to overreach the beneficiaries' beneficial interests and no other impugnment of the transfer is possible.

The question may arise whether these various consequences apply *in toto* or *pro tanto*, and the discussion of this issue in connection with amendment powers in part IV.B.v also applies in this context. A further possibility to be considered is that personal liabilities may be incurred by members and/or third parties, as discussed in part V.C and part V.D below.

i. Ineffective Exercise of the Trustee's Power to Transfer Ownership

In her capacity as owner of the scheme assets, a trustee has the power to transfer her ownership to others.[74] The effectiveness of any exercise of this power is determined by the general law governing assignments of the relevant property, as mentioned in part III.A. If she complies with these, there will be an effective transfer of the assets; if she does not, the purported transfer will be ineffective. So, for example, if the scheme assets are choses in action, the general law governing assignment of choses in action will determine whether the trustee has effectively exercised her power to transfer ownership of the assets;[75] likewise, if the assets are real property, the law governing transfers of real property will be determinative.[76]

The exercise of a trustee's power to transfer her ownership of scheme assets is not affected by non-compliance with the rules set out in part III.B–J, and she can effectively exercise her power to do this despite a failure to comply with them.[77] For example, a trustee's failure to act in line with the scheme terms, or to act for a proper purpose, does not in itself make an exercise of her power to transfer ownership of the scheme assets ineffective. This is demonstrated by *Roadchef (Employee Benefits Trustees) Ltd v Ingram Hill*,[78] where the trustee's exercise of a power to transfer ownership of the scheme assets was effective although this power was exercised for an improper purpose. The same can be said about other cases concerning the misapplication of scheme assets, where ownership of the assets was effectively transferred despite the trustee's failure to comply with one or more of the rules described in part III.B–J.[79]

This is not to say that a trustee's non-compliance has no consequences at all. We have spoken here only of effective transfers of ownership, and the recipient's new property rights may still be impeachable by the beneficiaries in equity. In other words, the question whether the recipient can retain ownership may depend on whether the

[74] Preserved in the Pensions Act 1995, s 34, 'The trustees of a trust scheme have, subject to … any restriction imposed by the scheme, the same power to make an investment of any kind as if they were absolutely entitled to the assets of the scheme'.

[75] See above n 18.

[76] See above n 19.

[77] As acknowledged in *Rolled Steel Products (Holdings) Ltd v British Steel Corp* [1986] Ch 246 (CA) 303; *Independent Trustee Services Ltd v GP Noble Trustees Ltd* [2012] EWCA Civ 195, [2013] Ch 91 [106]; *Akers v Samba Financial Group* [2017] UKSC 6, [2017] AC 424 [51].

[78] *Roadchef* (n 1).

[79] See, eg, *Hillsdown* (n 28); *Allan v Rea Brothers Trustees Ltd* [2002] EWCA Civ 85, [2002] Pens LR 169; *Noble* (CA) (n 77) [101]; *Fouche v Superannuation Fund Board* [1952] HCA 1, (1952) 88 CLR 609.

trustee has succeeded in transferring this clear of any subsisting equitable interest in the property or equity to rescind on which the beneficiaries might rely to recover the property. These are distinct issues, which are discussed next in subsections ii and iii.

ii. Effective Exercise of the Power to Transfer Ownership of the Assets but Ineffective Exercise of the Power to Overreach the Beneficiaries' Equitable Interests

In addition to a trustee's power as owner of the scheme assets to transfer ownership she may also have a power to overreach and extinguish the beneficiaries' equitable interests in the assets, and with them, any possibility of an equitable proprietary claim against the recipient.[80] However, the power to overreach their interests will be ineffective if the trustee fails to comply with particular rules, such as the rules that she must act in accordance with the trust terms and that she must act for a proper purpose. An illustrative example is *Independent Trustee Services Ltd v GP Noble Trustees Ltd*,[81] where a trustee made unauthorised transfers of scheme funds to himself and third parties. His failure to comply with scheme rules meant that the exercise of his power to overreach the beneficiaries' equitable interests was ineffective.

If an exercise of the power to overreach a beneficiary's equitable interest is ineffective, this means that the equitable interest is not extinguished, and so the beneficiary can rely on this interest to seek relief against the recipient, including recovery of the assets.[82] The recipient's vulnerability to such an equitable proprietary claim is discussed in part V.D. The overall result is that the effective exercise of the trustee's power to transfer ownership does not result in unimpeachable ownership of the scheme assets for the recipient, because the ineffective exercise of the trustees' overreaching power leaves the beneficiary with equitable rights that can be relied on to recover the property.[83]

iii. Effective Exercise of the Power to Transfer Ownership of the Assets and Effective Exercise of the Power to Overreach but Susceptibility to Rescission

If ownership of the assets is effectively transferred and the beneficiaries' equitable interests are extinguished by overreaching, they cannot make an equitable proprietary claim against the assets.[84] In some cases, however, they have an alternative route to equitable relief, namely that they can ask the court to rescind the transfer and make

[80] See generally *Noble* (CA) (n 77) [76]–[77], [101]–[106]; *Akers* (n 77) [52]; C Harpum, 'Overreaching, Trustees' Powers and the Reform of the 1925 Legislation' (1990) 49 *CLJ* 27; D Fox, 'Overreaching' in P Birks and A Pretto (eds), *Breach of Trust* (Oxford, Hart Publishing, 2002); J Hudson, 'One Thicket in Fraud on a Power' (2019) 39 *OJLS* 577.

[81] *Noble* (CA) (n 77) esp [75]–[77], [101]–[106], [128].

[82] ibid [76]–[77], [101]–[106]. See also *Hillsdown* (n 28); *Allan* (n 79); *Roadchef* (n 1) [123], [127]–[131], [173]; *Fouche* (n 79) 640, 643. Outside the pension context, see *Foskett v McKeown* [2001] 1 AC 102 (HL) 127–32 (Lord Millett); *Akers* (n 77) [51]–[52].

[83] For pragmatic reasons, the beneficiary's proprietary claim might be asserted by a replacement trustee on behalf of the scheme members, as in *Noble* (CA) (n 77) [107].

[84] *Campbell v Walker* (1800) 5 Ves Jun 678, 680–82, 31 ER 801, 802–03; *Pitt* (CA) (n 43) [99]–[101], affirmed in *Pitt* (SC) (n 2) [93].

an order for reconveyance. An example is *M v St Anne's Trustees Ltd*,[85] where pension trustees failed to take all and only relevant matters into account when deciding to transfer the scheme assets.

Some cases of this kind result in the same overall outcome as that achieved in cases where the beneficiaries' equitable interests have not been effectively overreached, ie, that the recipient must return the scheme assets. However, in cases where the beneficiaries' equitable interests are overreached, they have no subsisting equitable interests to rely on, and instead there is a new equity to rescind the flawed exercise of power.[86] Unless and until a beneficiary invokes this equity to rescind, she has no equitable interest in the scheme assets, even though the trustee's exercise of her power to transfer the assets was flawed.[87] A beneficiary who wins an order that the transfer should be set aside will then acquire a new equitable interest in the assets, which can itself be relied on to win a consequential order that the assets or their traceable proceeds should be returned.[88]

The order bringing the beneficiary's new equitable interest into effect can be backdated, so that the recipient is treated as though the assets were subject to the equitable interest at the time of receipt.[89] And to this extent, the cases considered here can produce the same outcome as the cases discussed in subsection ii, where an exercise of the trustee's power to overreach is ineffective, and the beneficiary's subsisting equitable interest is given at least a default priority over a third party with a later equitable interest.[90] However, these two groups of cases are not identical. Unlike the beneficiary's subsisting equitable interest, the new equity to rescind the flawed exercise of power, and thereby acquire a newly created but backdated equitable interest, can be defeated by a good faith purchaser of a later legal or equitable interest in the property, and is subject to discretionary factors and bars.[91]

iv. Effective Exercise of the Power to Transfer Ownership of the Assets and Effective Exercise of the Power to Overreach and no other Impugnment of the Transfer is Possible

Finally, there may be an effective exercise of the trustee's powers to transfer ownership and overreach the beneficiaries' equitable interests, without any equity to rescind the transfer or any other means for the beneficiaries to impugn the transfer. Take, for

[85] *M v St Anne's Trustees Ltd* (Guernsey CA, 20 June 2018) [64], [81], [83]–[87]. See also *Pitt* (SC) (n 2) [129]–[130].

[86] On the power model of rescission see O'Sullivan et al (n 58) para [16.17]; B Häcker, 'Proprietary Restitution after Impaired Consent Transfers' (2009) 68 *CLJ* 324; Häcker, *Consequences of Impaired Consent Transfers* (n 58) 129–59.

[87] *Shalson* (n 58) [120]–[127]. See also Mitchell, 'Rescission of Voluntary Settlements' (n 60) 48.

[88] *Shalson* (n 58); *Pitt* (CA) (n 43) [99]; Mitchell, 'Rescission of Voluntary Settlements'(n 60) 48. The basis of the claim to traceable proceeds is controversial: Häcker, *Consequences of Impaired Consent Transfers* (n 58) 277–95; N McBride, 'Rescission' in G Virgo and S Worthington (eds), *Commercial Remedies: Resolving Controversies* (Cambridge, Cambridge University Press, 2017) para [7.4.2].

[89] *Re Pallen Trust* 2015 BCCA 222, (2015) 76 BCLR (5th) 256 [61].

[90] *Rice v Rice* (1853) 2 Drew 73, 78, 61 ER 646, 648; *Phillips v Phillips* (1861) 4 De GF & J 208, 45 ER 1164.

[91] As in *M* (n 85) [64]. See too *Campbell* (n 84) 680–82; O'Sullivan et al (n 58) paras [16.63]–[16.64].

example, an exercise of power that constitutes a breach of the trustee's duty of care. Although the exercise of power is flawed, owing to the breach of duty, this does not affect the recipient's rights as the new owner of the assets.[92] It may, however, result in the imposition of a personal liability.

C. Personal Liability of Power-Holders

Whether or not flawed exercises of a trustee's powers to transfer ownership of scheme assets and overreach the beneficiaries' equitable interests have been effective, they may result in the power-holder incurring a personal liability. Three forms of liability can arise, which we shall describe in a moment. First, though, we should note that some power-holders can escape such liability by invoking statutory exoneration and indemnity provisions,[93] and that many pension schemes include clauses designed to shield power-holders from liability, or at least to protect them from its consequences. Clauses may exempt a power-holder from liability for breach of certain duties, exclude certain duties from applying in the first place, and/or allow the power-holder to recover an indemnity from the employer and/or scheme assets.[94] Clauses of this kind are usually stated to be inapplicable in cases of fraud or wilful default. Irrespective of how they are drafted, however, they cannot disapply any mandatory trustee duties nor exempt trustees from liability for breaching these.[95] Nor can they exonerate trustees from liability for losses incurred through investing the trust assets, by operation of the Pensions Act 1995, section 33.[96]

i. Substitutive Compensatory Liability

A power-holder who is a trustee may be liable to pay a money sum as a means of substitutively performing her ongoing obligation as trustee to produce trust assets *in specie* when called upon to do so.[97] A scheme member might make a claim for the trustee to pay such a money sum where the trustee has failed to act in accordance

[92] *Re Salmon* (1889) 42 Ch D 351 (CA) 367–68, 370–71. See too R Nolan 'Powers – General' in J McGhee (ed), *Snell's Equity*, 33rd edn (London, Sweet & Maxwell, 2015) paras [10–38], [30-12], [30-50]; Ashdown (n 1) paras [4.03]–[4.30]; Nolan, 'Controlling Fiduciary Power' (n 1) 294; M Conaglen, 'Remedial Ramifications of Conflicts between a Fiduciary's Duties' (2010) 126 *LQR* 72, 73–79; Tucker et al (n 1) para [41-014].

[93] See, eg, Trustee Act 1925, s 61 (a court may relieve a trustee from liability for breach of trust where the trustee has acted honestly and reasonable, and ought fairly to be excused); Trustee Act 2000, s 31 (a statutory power of indemnity from scheme assets where costs have been properly incurred in connection with the execution of the trust); Pensions Act 1995, s 34 (exemption of liability for delegation to authorised funds manager).

[94] eg, *Minister of Cook Islands National Superannuation Fund v Arorangi Timberland Ltd* [2014] CKCA 4 [16].

[95] *Armitage v Nurse* [1998] Ch 241 (CA) 251–54. *cf* New Zealand Trusts Act 2019, ss 22–26, 37, 39; discussed in Mitchell, 'Good Faith, Self-denial and Mandatory Trustee Duties' (n 38) 100–05.

[96] Applied in *Dalriada Trustees Ltd v Mcauley* [2017] EWHC 202 (Ch), [2017] Pens LR 8.

[97] S Elliott and J Edelman, 'Money Remedies against Trustees' (2004) 18 *Trust Law International* 116; S Elliott, 'Personal Monetary Claims' in J McGhee (ed), *Snell's Equity*, 33rd edn (London, Sweet & Maxwell, 2015); *Agricultural Land Management Ltd v Jackson (No 2)* [2014] WASC 102, (2014) 285 FLR 121 [333]–[349]; Hayton et al (n 64) paras [87.2]–[87.30].

with the trust terms when transferring ownership to trust property.[98] Claims of this sort may be mediated through proceedings for an account in common form, and if successful they will lead to a falsification of the accounts and an order that the trustee must pay the current market value of the property into the trust fund.[99] There is a controversy regarding the nature of such claims under English law, following the decisions in *Target Holdings Ltd v Redferns (a firm)*,[100] *AIB Group (UK) Plc v Mark Redler & Co (a firm)*,[101] and *Main v Giambrone & Law (a firm)*.[102] It is beyond the scope of this chapter to enter into that debate, but we will make one observation. It has been argued that these cases exclude substitutive performance claims being made only where the trust is a bare trust created as part of a commercial transaction, and where the role of the trust in that transaction has been exhausted.[103] If that is the right interpretation of the authorities, then it means that substitutive performance claims can still be made in pension cases where there was no commercial transaction and where the pension trust is on foot.

ii. Reparative Compensatory Liability

A second form of personal liability is to pay money as a form of reparative compensation for loss caused by the trustee's or employer's breach of duty when exercising a power. Unlike the liability described in the previous paragraph, this liability responds to a breach of a primary duty,[104] such as the power-holder's duty of care,[105] or her duty of good faith (as conceived in *Imperial* and *IBM*).[106] The power-holder will be required to pay the value of the loss caused by the breach, either to the pension fund or to a member, depending on the circumstances. A claim for compensation for loss against a trustee may also be effected through the accounting process, on the basis of wilful default. If a scheme member can show that a loss in value to the trust fund was caused by the trustee's breach of duty,[107] the trust accounts will be surcharged, and the trustee will be required to pay the amount of this value into the fund.[108]

[98] *Youyang Pty Ltd v Minter Ellison Morris Fletcher* [2003] HCA 15, (2003) 212 CLR 484 [32]–[40].

[99] *Libertarian Investments Ltd v Hall* [2013] HKCFA 94, (2013) 16 HKCFAR 681 [168]–[170]; *Ultraframe (UK) Ltd v Fielding* [2005] EWHC 1638 (Ch), [2007] WTLR 835 [1513]; *Head v Gould* [1898] 2 Ch 250 (Ch) 266.

[100] *Target Holdings Ltd v Redferns (a firm)* [1996] AC 421 (HL).

[101] *AIB Group (UK) Ltd v Mark Redler & Co Solicitors (a firm)* [2014] UKSC 58, [2015] AC 1503.

[102] *Main v Giambrone & Law (a firm)* [2017] EWCA Civ 1193, [2018] PNLR 2.

[103] See further Hayton et al (n 64) paras [87.32]–[87.42].

[104] See, eg, *Betafence Ltd v Veys* [2006] EWHC 999 (Ch), [2006] Pens LR 137 [67]; *Houghton v Immer (No 155) Pty Ltd* [1997] NSWSC 608, (1997) 44 NSWLR 46.

[105] *Noble* (Ch) (n 32) [238]; *Fouche* (n 79) 640–45; *Apostolovski* (n 46) [28]–[39].

[106] *IBM* (Ch) (n 1) [380]–[399]: employer in breach of the *Imperial* duty may incur liability to pay equitable compensation to employees who suffer loss; not considered on appeal: *IBM* (CA) (n 17) [29].

[107] *Swindle v Harrison* [1997] 4 All ER 705 (CA) 733; *O'Halloran v RT Thomas & Family Pty Ltd* [1998] NSWSC 596, (1998) 45 NSWLR 262, 275; *AIB* (n 101) [64]; *Agricultural* (n 97) [392]–[396]. Other principles such as remoteness and contributory fault may apply depending on the nature of the duty breached. In *Day v Mead* [1987] NZCA 74, [1987] 2 NZLR 443, 450–51, equitable compensation for loss caused by breach of fiduciary duty was reduced in light of the plaintiff's conduct. The question is left open in Hayton et al (n 64) paras [87.61]–[87.64] regarding the position in England after *Nationwide Building Society v Balmer Radmore (a firm)* [1999] PNLR 606 (Ch). In Australia, the relevance of concepts such as remoteness and contributory negligence has been questioned: see, eg, *Pilmer v Duke Group Ltd (in liq)* [2001] HCA 31, (2001) 207 CLR 165 [85]–[86].

[108] *Meehan v Glazier Holdings Pty Ltd* [2002] NSWCA 22, (2002) 54 NSWLR 146, 149–50.

iii. Liability to Disgorge Profits

A third form of liability which might be incurred by power-holders is to account for profits earned by reason or use of their fiduciary position.[109] This liability will arise where the relevant power was held in a fiduciary capacity, a prerequisite that will be satisfied by all powers held by trustees and some powers held by an employer. Where the power-holder earns a profit by reason or use of her fiduciary power, she will be personally liable to pay the value of the profit to the trust estate, and a proprietary claim might also be available.[110]

D. Third-Party Liability

A flawed exercise of power may result in a range of different consequences for third parties. These include:[111] (i) proprietary or personal restitutionary liability; (ii) liability on the basis of knowing receipt of misapplied trust property; (iii) liability on the basis of dishonest assistance in a breach of duty by the powerholder; and (iv) liability under the Pensions Act 2004, section 16.

i. Restitutionary Liability

A third party may incur a proprietary or personal restitutionary liability where beneficiaries can bring an equitable proprietary claim to misapplied trust assets or their traceable proceeds. As discussed above in part V.B.i, if a trustee's power to overreach the beneficiaries' equitable interests is exercised ineffectively, a beneficiary can assert an equitable proprietary claim to recover the misapplied property or its traceable proceeds from a third-party recipient. The third party will be liable either to return the property *in specie*, or to pay the monetary value of that property.[112] An example is *Independent Trustee Services Ltd v GP Noble Trustees Ltd*,[113] where a pension trustee made unauthorised transfers of scheme funds to himself and third parties. There was no effective exercise of the power to overreach the equitable interest under the trust and the third-party recipients were liable to repay the funds that were the traceable substitute of the misapplied scheme assets.[114] Other flawed exercises of power can

[109] *Regal (Hastings) Ltd v Gulliver* [1967] 2 AC 46, 143; *Howard v Commissioner of Taxation* [2014] HCA 21, (2014) 253 CLR 83 [62].

[110] See generally *Chan v Zacharia* [1984] HCA 36, (1984) 154 CLR 178, 199; *Sinclair Investments (UK) Ltd v Versailles Trade Finance Ltd* [2011] EWCA Civ 347, [2012] Ch 453 [88]–[89]; *FHR European Ventures LLP v Cedar Capital Partners LLC* [2014] UKSC 45, [2015] AC 250; *Grimaldi v Chameleon Mining NL (No 2)* [2012] FCAFC 6, (2012) 200 FCR 296 [575].

[111] There are other bases on which a third party might incur liability in relation to a defective exercise of scheme powers, eg, as a trustee de son tort: *Mara v Browne* [1896] 1 Ch 199 (CA) 209; Hayton et al (n 64) paras [98.6]–[98.10].

[112] *Foskett* (n 82) 127–32; *Noble* (CA) (n 77) [76]–[77], [101]–[106].

[113] *Noble* (CA) (n 77). See also *Hillsdown* (n 28) [139], where the complainant member had not specifically pleaded the 'tracing claim', but Knox J, after distinguishing this claim from knowing receipt indicated 'a tracing claim would in principle lie against [the recipient]'; *Allan* (n 79): equitable proprietary claim acknowledged in principle but unavailable on the facts; *Roadchef* (n 1) [173]; *Fouche* (n 79).

[114] *Noble* (CA) (n 77) [75]–[77], [101], [104]–[106].

also lead to this result. For example, a third party might incur a liability to make restitution of payments made by a trustee by mistake.[115]

Where a recipient of misdirected funds is a member of the pension scheme, the trustees may exercise their right of equitable recoupment, which allows them to impound or reduce future benefits in satisfaction of the member's liability to make restitution. The trustees may sometimes have a duty to exercise this right,[116] although it is subject to statutory restrictions.[117] There may be strategic advantages for a trustee to recover via its right of recoupment rather than bringing a claim for restitution against the member. For example, the trustee's right of recoupment is not subject to the Limitation Act 1980, unlike other restitutionary claims.[118] Whether it is justified for these different routes to recovery to be governed by different limitation rules is a debateable question, but one that lies beyond the scope of this chapter.

ii. Liability for Knowing Receipt

A second possibility is that a third party may incur personal liability to account as a constructive trustee on the basis they are a knowing recipient of scheme assets.[119] This form of constructive trusteeship means that the recipient comes under primary obligations in relation to her handling of the assets,[120] including 'a duty not to part with the remaining funds ... otherwise than by restoring them to or for the benefit of the beneficiaries'.[121] This means that if the recipient deals with the subject property in a manner inconsistent with her constructive trusteeship, she may incur the same types of substitutive and reparative compensatory liability that are incurred by express trustees, as discussed in part V.C.[122] Similarly, she may also incur a personal liability to account for profits obtained from the property received.[123]

[115] *Burgess v BIC UK Ltd* [2018] EWHC 785 (Ch), [2018] Pens LR 13 [162]. See also *Wakelin v Read* [2000] Pens LR 319 (CA), where the parties accepted that the trustee could impound a member's future benefits to satisfy his liability as a dishonest assistant.

[116] *BIC* (Ch) (n 115) [162], [176].

[117] In *BIC* (Ch) (n 115), it was common ground that the trustee's right of recoupment was subject to the Pensions Act 1995, s 91, and that s 91 would prevent recoupment where the member disputed the amount, except under an order of 'a competent court'. Arnold J said that this did not include a determination by the Pensions Ombudsman, although it would include an order by the County Court pursuant to the Pensions Schemes Act 1993, s 150(5)(a): *BIC* (Ch) (n 115) [164]–[168]. See further P Newman, 'Owing Me, Owing You' (2020) 33 *Trusts Law International* 186.

[118] *BIC* (Ch) (n 115) [169]–[172]. Although laches may still apply. Other reasons for trustees to rely on equitable recoupment rather than unjust enrichment are discussed in Newman (n 117).

[119] *Hillsdown* (n 28) [121]–[140]; *Noble* (Ch) (n 32) [48]–[51]; *Roadchef* (n 1) [173]–[174]. On knowing receipt generally, see *El Ajou v Dollar Land Holdings Plc (No 1)* [1993] BCC 698, 715–16; *Bank of Credit and Commerce International (Overseas) Ltd v Akindele* [2001] Ch 437 (CA); *Fistar v Riverwood Legion and Community Club Ltd* [2016] NSWCA 81, (2016) 91 NSWLR 732 [45].

[120] C Mitchell and S Watterson, 'Remedies for Knowing Receipt' in C Mitchell (ed), *Constructive and Resulting Trusts* (Oxford, Hart Publishing, 2010) 128–31, endorsed in *Arthur v AG of the Turks and Caicos Islands* [2012] UKPC 30 [37]; Hayton et al (n 64) paras [98.2], [98.33].

[121] *Noble* (CA) (n 77) [81]; Mitchell and Watterson (n 120) 131–47.

[122] See further Mitchell and Watterson (n 120) 117–31; Hayton et al (n 64) para [98.33].

[123] *Ultraframe* (n 99) [1577]. See further, Mitchell and Watterson (n 120) 128–33; Lord Walker, 'Dishonesty and Unconscionable Conduct in Commercial Life – Some Reflections on Accessory Liability and Knowing Receipt' (2005) 27 *Sydney Law Review* 187, 202.

iii. Liability for Dishonest Assistance

A third possibility is that a third party may be liable for dishonest assistance.[124] Such liability is not conditional on receipt of misdirected trust property[125] and unlike a knowing recipient, a dishonest assistant is not liable to account to the beneficiaries as if she were an express trustee subject to duties in relation to her stewardship of property. Some dicta suggest that a dishonest assistant might still be described as a constructive trustee in the sense that her compensatory liability 'derives from and duplicates' that of the errant trustee.[126] But the tendency of recent English cases is to treat dishonest assistance as a stand-alone liability, with the result, for example, that a dishonest assistant is liable to disgorge the profits of her wrongdoing, regardless of whether these were shared with the trustee whose breach was assisted.[127]

iv. Liability Under the Pensions Act 2004, Section 16

A third party might be liable to a claim by the Pensions Regulator who can seek a court order against any person involved in a misuse or misappropriation of any of the assets of a pension scheme. Such a person can be required to reconstitute the trust fund if she is 'knowingly concerned' in a misapplication of scheme assets; this does not require proof of dishonesty.[128]

VI. NEGATING THE CONSEQUENCES OF NON-COMPLIANCE

The consequences which can flow from flawed exercises of power have the potential to create very serious difficulties for any or all of the members, employer, trustees or third parties.[129] However, there are various means which they might use to avoid or at least mitigate these problems. Space constraints prohibit a full survey, but we note the following possibilities:[130] ratification; exercise of an amendment power with

[124] *Wakelin* (n 115). See generally *Royal Brunei Airline Sdn Bhd v Tan* [1995] 2 AC 378 (PC) 382–85; *Twinsectra Ltd v Yardley* [2002] UKHL 12, [2002] 2 AC 164 [107].

[125] *Royal Brunei* (n 124) 382.

[126] ibid 385; *Ultraframe* (n 99) [1506]. See too S Elliott and C Mitchell, 'Remedies for Dishonest Assistance' (2004) 67 *MLR* 16; Mitchell and Watterson (n 120) 150–54.

[127] *Novoship (UK) Ltd v Mikhaylyuk* [2014] EWCA 908, [2015] QB 499; *Ancient Order of Foresters in Victoria Friendly Society Ltd v Lifeplan Australia Friendly Society Ltd* [2018] HCA 43, (2018) 92 ALJR 918 [5]–[7].

[128] Pensions Act 2004, s 16; *Pensions Regulator v Payae Ltd* [2018] EWHC 36 (Ch), [2018] Pens LR 8. See also Pensions Act 2004, ss 18–20 in relation to 'pension liberation' schemes.

[129] Consider, eg, *Gleeds* (n 20): 30 separate documents were created over a period of time to require members to make contributions, reduce the rate of accrual, cut the rate of pension increases and close the scheme to further accrual; none of these took effect as intended owing to non-compliance with the statutory rules governing the creation of deeds; the scheme's deficit on an ongoing basis was thereby increased by some £45 million.

[130] Cases where amendments have been made by mistake might also be cured by obtaining an order under the Administration of Justice Act 1985, s 48, which empowers the court to direct trustees to administer a scheme in line with a preferred interpretation of the amended scheme rules endorsed by senior counsel, as in *Re BCA Pension Trustees Ltd* [2015] EWHC 3492 (Ch), [2016] Pens LR 17. Recipients of misdirected funds might also escape liability by the invocation of defences, eg, bona fide purchase of misdirected assets: argued but unavailable on the facts of *Noble* (CA) (n 77); and limitation: *BIC* (Ch) (n 115) [169]–[172]: *Webber v Department for Education* [2016] EWHC 2519 (Ch), [2017] ICR 198.

retrospective effect; invocation of the maxim that equity treats as done that which ought to be done; and estoppels.

A. Ratification

It may be possible to cure some flawed exercises of power by ratification: for example, exercises of power which fail to comply with a formality rule such as obtaining members' consent.[131] However, ratification may not be possible in relation to other flawed exercises of power: for example, where an exercise of power is ineffective,[132] or where there is a flawed exercise that goes to 'the essence of the power'.[133] In cases where flawed exercises of power are curable by ratification, this might by achieved with the agreement of the scheme members or alternatively by court order.[134]

B. Exercise of Amendment Powers with Retrospective Effect

Can amendment powers be validly drafted to operate with retrospective effect so as to render a flawed exercise of power effective? The leading case is now *BIC UK Ltd v Burgess*,[135] where Henderson LJ held that the answer depends on why the relevant exercise of power is flawed.

The starting point for his analysis was *Bank of New Zealand v Bank of New Zealand Officers Provident Association Management Board*, where Lord Walker said that:

> In the amendment of pension scheme rules, back-dating (that is, deeming a change of the rules to have been made at a date earlier than the date of the actual change) cannot be used as a device so as to rewrite history or validate an amendment which would otherwise be beyond the scope of the power of amendment. But if the substance of what is proposed is within the power, back-dating will not by itself lead to invalidity.[136]

In *BIC*, Henderson LJ similarly held that parties can agree 'that their past relationship is to be treated as having departed from historical reality in specified respects', but added that 'the problem has to be confronted of possible conflict between the hypothetical state of affairs and the historical reality of what did or did not happen'.[137] He considered that a crucially important distinction exists 'between having the power

[131] YK Liew and C Mitchell, 'Beneficiaries' Consent to Trustee's Unauthorised Acts' in P Davies, S Douglas and J Goudkamp (eds), *Defences in Equity* (Oxford, Hart Publishing, 2018) 84–85.

[132] *Daubeny v Cockburn* (1816) 1 Mer 626, 35 ER 801; *Cloutte* (n 2) 32; Hayton et al (n 64) para [57.59]; P Matthews, 'The Doctrine of Fraud on a Power: Part 1' (2007) *Private Client Business* 131, 138–39, albeit that the same practical outcome as ratification might be achieved through retrospective amendments, as to which see part VI.B, or if all beneficiaries and the donee of the power together executed a deed assigning the equitable interest(s) to the appointee and releasing the power respectively: see, eg, *Preston v Preston* (1869) 21 LT 346.

[133] See further, Farwell et al (n 25) 380.

[134] See, eg, *In re Z Trust* [2016] JRC 048.

[135] *BIC* (CA) (n 23) [55].

[136] *Bank of New Zealand* (n 27) [26].

[137] *BIC* (CA) (n 23) [55].

to do something, and actually exercising the power';[138] that it is possible to use an appropriately drafted power of amendment to change a scheme with retrospective effect so as to deem a power-holder to have had a power at a moment in the past when she did not actually have this power; but that an amendment power cannot be used to deem a power-holder to have exercised a power at a moment in the past when she did not actually exercise it, or even purport to do so.

Thus, the judge drew a line between cases where a power-holder purports to exercise a power but fails to comply with a rule governing its exercise, and cases where a power-holder never purports to exercise a power. Cases of the first kind might be cured by the exercise of an appropriately drafted amendment power operating retrospectively to deem the flawed exercise of power to have been effective, by rewriting the terms on which it could have been validly exercised. But cases of the second kind cannot be cured by retrospectively deeming the power-holder to have possessed a power in the past, because this cannot alter the fact that the power-holder never purported to exercise the power.

C. Invocation of the Maxim that Equity Treats as Done that which should be Done

Invocation of this maxim has sometimes persuaded courts to treat flawed exercises of power as effective. An example is *HR Trustees Ltd v Wembley plc*[139] where the maxim was applied to cure an exercise of an amendment power that failed to comply with formalities. The court reasoned that the power-holder could have been compelled to comply with the formalities at the time of execution.[140] It seems, however, the position may be different where application of the maxim might override the rights of scheme members that have accrued in the meantime.[141]

D. Estoppels

An estoppel, sometimes by convention[142] or representation,[143] might be raised by a trustee or employer seeking to uphold the exercise of an amendment power against members who claim that the exercise of power was flawed.[144] Alternatively, an estoppel

[138] ibid [28].

[139] *HR Trustees* (n 22) [66]. See also *Davis v Richards & Wallington Industries Ltd* [1990] 1 WLR 1511 (Ch) 1535; *Harwood-Smart v Caws* [2000] Pens LR 101 (Ch) [48]. *cf Briggs* (n 20) [70]–[82]. On the maxim generally, see Farwell et al (n 25) ch 7.

[140] *HR Trustees* (n 22) [66].

[141] ibid [59].

[142] *Amalgamated Investment and Property Co Ltd v Texas Commerce International Bank Ltd* [1982] QB 84 (CA) 121; *Redrow plc v Pedley* [2002] EWHC 983 (Ch), [2002] Pens LR 339; *Icarus (Hertford) Ltd v Driscoll* [1990] Pens LR 1 (Ch); *ITN v Ward* [1997] Pens LR 131 (Ch); *Lansing Linde Ltd v Alber* [2000] Pens LR 15 (Ch); *IMG* (n 21) [185]–[191].

[143] *Steria Ltd v Hutchison* [2006] EWCA Civ 1551, [2007] ICR 445 [91]–[92], considered but not raised on the facts of *IMG* (n 21) [175]–[184]; *Hearn* (n 1) [95]–[127].

[144] As in *IMG* (n 21), although not made out in the facts of the case.

might be raised by a member, for example who seeks to uphold an increase to pension benefits.[145] There is some debate as to the differences between various estoppels and their effects,[146] which we will not discuss. Generally speaking, the outcome of an estoppel in this context is that the parties are treated as if the relevant exercise of power was not flawed.[147]

The elements to some estoppels have particular definition when applied to the pensions context, and which may make it difficult for an estoppel to be established.[148] For example, it is necessary to show that all necessary parties, including members and sometimes future members, trustees and employers, are party to an estoppel, and which requires 'clear evidence of intention or positive conduct'.[149] Further, the requirement for a clear and unequivocal representation will not be made out from members' passive acceptance[150] of a transaction presented by trustees and employers as a '*fait accompli*'.[151] Even if the elements are made out, an estoppel might not be enforced where to do so would place the trustee in breach of her trustee or fiduciary duties.[152]

VII. CONCLUSION

In this chapter, we have discussed some of the things which can go wrong when employers and trustees purport to exercise their powers under pension schemes but fail to comply with scheme requirements and legal rules. A notable feature of the cases is the complexity of their facts and of the legal rules which govern their outcome. The reasons for this are not hard to find. Many pension schemes are intricate legal structures designed to achieve a variety of purposes for the benefit of stakeholders whose interests are not all the same. The transactions entered by power-holders can be elaborate and can require the exercise of several interconnected powers. The rules which govern exercises of power serve multiple aims, and non-compliance with these rules

[145] As in *Hearn* (n 1), although not made out in the facts of the case.

[146] See, eg, B McFarlane, 'The Limits to Estoppels' (2013) 7 *Journal of Equity* 250; B McFarlane, 'Understanding Equitable Estoppel: From Metaphors to Better Laws' (2013) 66 *Current Legal Problems* 267; P Feltham et al, *Spencer Bower: Reliance-Based Estoppel*, 5th edn (London, Bloomsbury Professional, 2017) ch 1; K Handley, *Estoppel by Conduct and Election*, 2nd edn (London, Sweet & Maxwell, 2016); J Hudson, 'The True Purpose of Estoppel by Representation' (2015) 32 *Journal of Contract Law* 275.

[147] Had an estoppel been made out, this would have been the effect in *IMG* (n 21). See also *Briffa v Hay* (1997) 75 FCR 428, 445 (Merkel J): 'in substance the [scheme rules are] … treated as if [they were] … amended to accord with the assumption binding on all parties or Equity could require amendment of the [rules] … to accord with the assumption'; *Catchpole v Trustees of the Alitalia Airlines Pension Scheme* [2010] EWHC 1809 (Ch), [2010] ICR 1405 [51]–[55].

[148] See, eg, *ITN* (n 142); *Hearn* (n 1) [111]; *Redrow* (n 142) [60]–[65]; *Trustee Solutions Ltd v Dubery* [2006] EWHC 1426 (Ch), [2006] Pens LR 177, not questioned on appeal: [2007] EWCA Civ 771, [2007] Pens LR 237; *BIC* (Ch) (n 115) [150]–[155]; *Gleeds* (n 20) [43]–[52].

[149] *Redrow* (n 142) [61]–[64], applied in *IMG* (n 21) [185]; *BIC* (Ch) (n 115) [153].

[150] *Redrow* (n 142); *Hodgson v Toray Textiles Europe Ltd* [2006] EWHC 2612 (Ch), [2006] Pens LR 253 [98]–[99]; *Foster Wheeler Ltd v Hanley* [2008] EWHC 2926 (Ch), [2009] Pens LR 39 [90].

[151] *IMG* (n 21) [178] and [182].

[152] *BIC* (Ch) (n 115) [154].

can produce different outcomes, depending on the power which has been exercised. A single event may entail non-compliance with several different rules, producing several different outcomes. According to circumstances, the interests of affected parties may coincide or conflict, prompting some to seek relief in relation to non-compliance and others to oppose these claims.

Disentangling all of this potential complexity is a task that lies beyond the scope of a single chapter. Our less ambitious goal has been to discuss flawed exercises of amendment powers and flawed exercises of power to transfer scheme assets. The legal consequences of these are often misunderstood, and one reason for this has been that judges, practitioners and academics have tried to fit the cases into too few conceptual categories, and have used labels to describe these categories – 'void' and 'voidable' transactions – which cannot capture all the differences that exist between the cases. All legal problems have their own level of complexity and it leads to trouble when reductive attempts are made to solve them by treating them as though they were simpler than they actually are. We hope we have made a step towards a better understanding of the law in this area by distinguishing different cases, and explaining the principles governing their resolution and the ways in which these are connected.

8

Expertise in Pension Trusteeship

DEBORAH MABBETT*

I. INTRODUCTION

OCCUPATIONAL DEFINED BENEFIT (DB) pension schemes in the UK are generally constituted as trusts, placing control over pension fund assets in the hands of trustees who make or shape decisions about investment, contributions and benefits. Regulatory reforms since the turn of the century have fastened on trustees as crucial actors in pension scheme governance. Reforms have sought to strengthen their role, define their responsibilities and improve their qualifications. In this chapter, I examine the hopes and expectations of these reforms. More trustee expertise has been advocated as the solution to two quite different kinds of problem: first, increasing the security of pension promises and reducing the risk of calls on public funds; and second, improving schemes' investment strategies. These different problems are matched by different conceptions of what expertise really entails. I argue that there has been a tendency to promote expertise in the form of conventional and shared knowledge. This has created an illusion of greater security in pension promises, and has done nothing to improve schemes' investment strategies.

It is commonly said that trustees have wide discretion, but in the context of pension funds this claim is misleading. Trustees have to make decisions and find solutions that are acceptable to employers, members and the regulator. While only the regulator has a formal (if rarely exercised) veto power over trustee decisions, employer agreement is necessary for decisions on ongoing contributions to a pension scheme. Disaffected employers can respond to trustee demands by closing the scheme to new members or new accruals. Even members can respond if they are not satisfied with trustee decisions: they can sometimes choose not to join a scheme; they can negotiate a cash alternative; and via employer–union negotiations they can influence employers' decisions.

* I am grateful to the editors, particularly Charles Mitchell, for their comments and suggestions on earlier drafts of this chapter. I am also grateful to my fellow members of the Joint Expert Panel on the UK Universities Superannuation Scheme, from whom I have learned a lot about pension scheme valuation and governance. All remaining errors and contentious interpretations are my own responsibility.

These possibilities for exit may seem remote, but many occupational pension schemes have closed in recent years, and so it is clear that exit is happening. This may be for reasons unrelated to trustee decisions, or because trustees are powerless to make a difference given the pressures that schemes are under. However, closure may also indicate that trustees have exercised their discretion poorly, and have failed to steer a course sufficiently close to the interests of the parties to prevent exit. The following discussion explores this possibility. Specifically, it examines whether moves to enhance the financial expertise of trustees could have had the effect of propelling more schemes towards closure.

At first sight, this is a counterintuitive hypothesis. More financial expertise should mean that funds are better managed, increasing the size of the pension 'pie' and making it easier for trustees to settle on decisions which satisfy the conflicting interests of the parties. However, when one looks carefully at what financial expertise is meant to bring to pension management, few claims are made for 'pie', and the evidence reviewed below is inconclusive and even sometimes negative. The reason for this can be summarised briefly as follows. If financial markets are efficient, it is not possible systematically to 'beat the market'. Star managers cannot deliver 'alpha': sustained outperformance in a particular asset class. Instead, a pension fund's investment performance will depend on two things: the selection of asset classes, and the fees and commissions incurred. By investing in riskier classes of asset, a pension fund can achieve higher returns. For reasons discussed below, however, financial experts may advocate low-risk investment, which will mean less 'pie'.[1]

Thus, the appointment of more financial experts to be pension fund trustees is not generally advocated on the grounds that it will mean that the scheme will achieve investment outperformance. The following discussion takes a close look at exactly what advocates of more expertise have sought. It is shown that advocates have rested their arguments on two opposing conceptions of financial expertise. One, which I term 'pluralist', sees expertise in terms of capacity to challenge, contest and argue. This is the conception advanced in the 2001 Myners Review of institutional investment in the UK. This review is often seen as the inspiration for reforms of trusteeship in the Pensions Act 2004, and yet the promotion of trustee expertise subsequent to that Act has embraced a quite different conception, in which expertise means a common body of knowledge and understanding. It is argued below that the incentives of the regulator have contributed to the promotion of this conformist or conventional notion of expertise. Conformist experts may choose policies which are close to the preferences of the regulator but too distant from the interests of employers and members to ensure scheme survival.

The following discussion starts in part II by reviewing available studies on the difference that trustees make to outcomes. The lack of conclusive evidence of a

[1] One of the most reliable ways to increase the pie is to reduce costs. One way to do this is to adopt a passive (index-tracking) investment strategy, which should mean that the scheme matches benchmarks for the asset classes chosen, while incurring minimal costs. Another way is to create larger schemes which can take advantage of economies of scale to reduce costs. Insofar as such schemes could also support more expertise on their trustee boards, this can mean that expertise is correlated with lower costs, but this is not necessarily a causal connection.

relationship between trustee expertise and scheme performance presents a puzzle: why has there been such a drive to enhance expertise? Focusing on the UK case, part III takes up the arguments of the Myners Review in detail, and part IV describes how trustee expertise has been promoted post-Myners. Part V reviews theoretical accounts of the tension between representation and expertise, and examines why experts might not have the same preferences over outcomes as members and employers. Part VI concludes by drawing out some implications of the expertise-based distancing of trusteeship from member and employer engagement.

II. EXPERTISE AND THE SIZE OF THE PENSION PIE

Funded pension schemes gather contributions now and promise to pay pensions later. For schemes to thrive, the promise must be credible. The employer's backing is one source of credibility, but the thrust of regulatory change in UK occupational pensions has been to create another source of credibility, based on the pension fund itself. There is a focus on valuation: the promise is credible if the fund can be demonstrated to be adequate to meet the commitments that have accrued. But the process of valuation leaves margins of discretion, and members' confidence in the exercise of discretion depends on the governance of the fund. Members themselves are not in a position to take decisions about the investment strategy of the fund, nor to establish an appropriate discount rate for liabilities (accrued commitments). The task of making these decisions is delegated to trustees.

Trustees are a particular kind of agent. One of their distinguishing features is the suppression of their own pecuniary interests: the duty of loyalty requires them to act without regard to their personal gain. Traditionally, trustees have often executed their functions without payment, a practice which emphasised their lack of financial interest in the trust. Pension fund trustees are nowadays usually paid in compensation for the time they spend, but they do not have incentive contracts which reward them for achieving specified outcomes. Such a contract would be wrong in principle as it presumes that trustees are financially motivated; it could also be seen as fettering the discretion of trustees in the direction desired by the incentive designer.

In large UK pension funds, there are usually three groups of trustees: employer nominated trustees (ENTs); member nominees (MNTs); and 'independents', selected for their expertise, particularly in investment matters. In DB schemes, ENTs have a strong incentive to put effort into enhancing the performance of the scheme, as employers are the residual claimants against the fund: they have to make up deficits, and they benefit from surpluses through reduced contributions.[2] However, while ENTs have clear incentives to control administrative costs, their effectiveness in enhancing investment returns is more contentious. They have incentives to seek high returns; the difficulty is that they also have incentives to accept risk, perhaps excessively so. If corporate decision-makers contemplate insolvency with equanimity, they have a one-way bet. Either the strategy pays off, or the employer becomes insolvent and

[2] T Besley and A Prat, 'Credible Pensions' (2005) 26 *Fiscal Studies* 119, 128.

defaults on its obligations to the scheme. As discussed in part III, statutory efforts to strengthen the institution of trusteeship, and make trustees more independent of the employer, followed from employer failures.[3]

In the (presumably) more general case where insolvency is not in prospect, Exley et al drew on the insights of financial economics to argue that a pension scheme that uses a risky strategy to meet its liabilities imposes a hidden cost on the shareholders of the firm, who are bearing more risk than they (may) realise.[4] If shareholders are alert to the risks being taken with their equity, they should insist that the pension fund is de-risked, and place a discount on the market price of equity if this is not done. It follows that attention to shareholder value maximisation may raise the cost of pension schemes.[5] However, there is no conclusive evidence that shareholders 'punish' employers for pension scheme risks.[6]

If ENTs have incentives to favour a high-risk, high-return investment strategy, this might be countered by MNTs concerned to ensure that members' benefits are safe. But the choice of investment strategy for MNTs is complex.[7] If the employer's backing in case of deficits is secure, and at the same time any surplus accrues to the employer, MNTs have no reason to concern themselves with asset allocation. If there is a possibility of employer default, MNTs will tend to favour a lower-risk investment strategy than the employer, and instead press the employer to repair the scheme by increasing contributions. In this situation, MNTs might act as a counterweight to employer influence over the running of the scheme. But if a scheme is threatened with closure or if there is cost-sharing between employers and members, MNTs may tilt towards seeking higher investment returns. The assessment of the costs and benefits of risk-taking will be different for different cohorts of members, from pensioner members to recent joiners. For pensioners, a low-risk strategy may be most effective in protecting their benefits. For the workforce, a low-risk investment strategy means higher demands for contributions, which will mean lower take-home pay if there is cost-sharing.[8] If the employer sees the scheme as too costly and closes it, younger members are worst affected. It follows that MNTs who are oriented towards the current and future workforce may accept more risk than those who are oriented towards protecting the benefits of pensioner members.

[3] J Mesher, 'The Operation of Pension Funds' (1992) 21 *Industrial Law Journal* 232.

[4] CJ Exley, SJB Mehta and AD Smith, 'The Financial Theory of Defined Benefit Pension Schemes' (1997) 3 *British Actuarial Journal* 835.

[5] AHB Monk, 'The Financial Thesis: Reconceptualizing Globalisation's Effect on Firms and Institutions' (2009) 13 *Competition and Change* 51.

[6] JM Orszag and N Sand, 'Corporate Finance and Capital Markets' in GL Clark, AH Munnell and JM Orszag (eds), *The Oxford Handbook of Pensions and Retirement Income* (Oxford, Oxford University Press, 2006).

[7] Some sense of this complexity can be gained from an epic study by McCarthy and Miles which showed how trustees' preferred investment allocation will depend on the security of the employer covenant, the existence of insurance (eg, a Pension Protection Fund) and the current level of scheme funding: D McCarthy and D Miles, 'Optimal Portfolio Allocation for Corporate Pension Funds' (2013) 19 *European Financial Management* 599. They do not distinguish between trustee types, but their account fits the problem facing a trustee who seeks to maximise the welfare of scheme beneficiaries.

[8] Most economists would expect that higher employer pension contributions reduce take-home pay even in the absence of formal cost-sharing.

Some indirect evidence that MNTs do not always force employers to reduce risk and pay more contributions comes from experience in the UK in the decade after the Pensions Act 1995. This Act mandated that boards should have at least one-third MNTs, although there were loopholes. But MNTs apparently failed to force more conservative strategies on employers, leading to further statutory changes in 2004. These sought to change the weight of MNTs' concerns towards conservatism by, among other things, promoting more representation of pensioner interests.[9] Since the Pensions Act 2004 there has also been a sustained drive towards having more independent trustees. For reasons discussed below, independents may promote less risky investment strategies.

Turning to the available evidence, a much cited UK study found that, the more control the employer exercised over the pension fund (measured by the proportion of ENTs), the more likely it was to pursue a high-risk, high-return investment strategy.[10] The authors interpret this as an agency problem, with employer nominees more inclined to take risks with members' benefits. But this interpretation has been challenged. For example, Phan and Hegde argue that high-risk and return investment strategies are associated with sponsoring employers that are in a strong position to bear risk in their scheme because they are protected by anti-takeover provisions, and that this is to the benefit of members.[11] More generally, there is a fundamental disagreement in the literature between those who think that any employer-sponsored risk-taking is suspect[12] and those who argue that an employer might choose to use its risk-bearing capacity to offer an attractive contract to employees. On the latter interpretation, it can be in the employer's business interest to control contribution costs by taking investment risk.[13]

Andonov et al examined how trustee board composition affects the investment strategy of US public (state and municipal) pension funds, and found that boards containing more politicians engage in more risk-taking, which they interpret as arising from political incentives to maintain a high discount rate and thereby make the funding position look strong, postponing difficult decisions about contributions and benefits.[14] They also found that the presence of elected plan participants (MNTs) leads to riskier strategies. Accrued benefits are less well protected in the US than the UK, and so MNTs may be acting on a desire to delay reforms which could have negative effects for them. Andonov et al also argue that overall plan performance suffers from acting on these incentives, but their evidence for this is open to interpretation.

[9] V Cockerill, 'Does Size Matter – How Should Trustees Approach the New Member Trustee Requirement?' (2006) 12 *Pensions* 12.

[10] JF Cocco and PF Volpin, 'Corporate Governance of Pension Plans: The UK Evidence' (2007) 63 *Financial Analysts Journal* 70.

[11] HV Phan and S Hegde, 'Corporate Governance and Risk-Taking in Pension Plans: Evidence from Defined Benefit Asset Allocations' (2012) 48 *Journal of Financial and Quantitative Analysis* 919.

[12] See, eg, Exley et al (n 4).

[13] D Blake, 'UK Pension Fund Management After Myners: The Hunt for Correlation Begins' (2003) 4 *Journal of Asset Management* 32.

[14] A Andonov, R Bauer and M Cremers, 'Pension Fund Asset Allocation and Liability Discount Rates' (2016), available at: www.icpmnetwork.com/wp-content/uploads/2013/08/Andonov-Bauer-and-Cremers-Asset-Allocation-and-Liability-Disc_September-2016.pdf.

They find that public funds with politician trustees marginally underperform the benchmark for each asset class they invest in, but they do not find that risk-taking damages the overall performance of the fund. In other words, it is possible that risk-taking pays off, despite the suspect political incentives that induce it.

Harper also examined the asset allocation and investment performance of US public pension plans, and reached conclusions which are partly consistent with Andonov et al and partly contradictory.[15] Focusing on outsider trustees with expertise, he found that they had no effect on benchmarked investment performance, but they promoted a more conservative asset allocation (a lower share of investment in equities). This is the mirror image of Andonov et al's finding that politicians promote more risk-taking, but contrary to them Harper found that the presence of elected MNTs correlated with a higher funding level, giving more security to members' pensions.

The extensive literature review in Harper indicates that researchers have struggled to find robust relationships between trustee board characteristics and various performance outcomes. The findings of the wider finance literature that 'alpha' (outperformance in a specific asset class) is elusive are not refuted, but some relationships between board composition, risk-taking and funding levels are found. These findings cannot prove that outside experts make 'better' decisions without knowing what risk profile or funding level is optimal for the scheme. Clearly deep and sustained underfunding is undesirable, but the proportion of funds in this position is small and the causes of their difficulties multiple, preventing generalisations about their governance. Furthermore, Harper notes that there might be endogeneity: funds with certain attributes pick trustees who fit those attributes.

These issues have not deterred advocates of more expertise in pension fund governance, who have assembled other evidence to support their position. Clark claimed that 'there is a significant premium associated with the proper internal governance of pension funds'.[16] However, Clark's conception of that premium is very general; he does not attempt to test the quality of pension fund governance by measuring a premium in investment returns. A later study by Clark and Urwin did argue that 'good governance' generated higher long-term risk-adjusted rates of return, but they presented no evidence of this, and indeed noted that a high level of 'noise' around investment outturns prevents statistical inferences being drawn.[17] Instead, their method was to examine the governance arrangements of a number of funds which have performed well against their own benchmarks, and thereby identify what appeared to be the key elements of good governance. These key elements turn out to be primarily about clear understanding of goals and effective delegation, rather than trustee skills as such.

[15] JT Harper, 'Board of Trustee Composition and Investment Performance of US Public Pension Plans' (2008) Rotman ICPM Working Paper, available at: www.icpmnetwork.com/wp-content/uploads/2016/03/Joel_Harper_Board_of_Trustee_Composition_and_Investment_Performance_of_US_Public_Pension_Plans_February_2008.pdf.

[16] GL Clark, 'Pension Fund Governance: Expertise and Organizational Form' (2004) 3 *Journal of Pension Economics & Finance* 233, 237.

[17] GL Clark and R Urwin, 'Best-Practice Pension Fund Governance' (2008) 9 *Journal of Asset Management* 2.

Ambachtsheer et al claimed to present evidence of a 'positive correlation between governance quality and fund performance'.[18] Their measure of 'governance quality' was based on the judgements of senior executives in 81 pension funds. Fund performance was measured as 'Net Value Added' (NVA), which is excess returns relative to a passive investment strategy, net of investment expenses. As the authors acknowledged, the NVA metric has some limitations and the time period for the assessment was rather short. Furthermore, CEOs' subjective assessments of governance quality could be affected by fund performance, implying reverse causation.

Ambachtsheer et al found that assessments of governance quality are correlated with an indicator of 'oversight/management costs'. They argued that poorly managed funds underinvest in oversight and management, and they found the correlation of costs with governance quality 'an encouraging finding': 'the CEOs and boards of governors of the high-scoring funds are putting their money where their mouth is'.[19] Clearly other interpretations are possible. CEOs may simply see spending, notably on executive pay, as an indicator of quality. If the results on NVA are robust, it may be that executives in funds which achieve positive NVA capture these returns in management remuneration, raising management costs. There is little that is 'encouraging' for pension fund members in these findings; instead, they are a salutary reminder that expertise tends to come at a price.

Finally, Davis cited a study by the Australian Prudential Regulation Authority which found that investment returns in corporate funds with lay trustees outperformed returns on retail funds with expert trustees.[20] The findings, while clear, do not address the question of whether occupational pension funds with expert trustees outperform those with lay members, as retail funds have different characteristics from occupational funds. Their costs are higher, at least in part for justifiable reasons to do with scale and account administration. Critics also argued that the findings were not appropriately adjusted for risk. Retail funds had adopted lower-volatility investment strategies, which arguably they have to do because there is no corporate sponsor to bear risk. What the study really shows is that employers' willingness to bear risk in DB pensions is potentially a significant benefit to those workers who are covered, if it is reflected in the investment strategy.

Summing up, it is difficult to demonstrate that trustee expertise is correlated with superior performance by pension funds. There is some evidence that independent trustees steer funds towards lower-risk investment strategies, and authors writing from a conventional financial economics perspective tend to interpret this as a sign of good governance. Others are inclined to assume that expertise is inherently a good thing, especially given evidence that non-experts make elementary mistakes in interpreting financial risk and choose inconsistent strategies, but the benefits of expertise are not clearly revealed by statistical measures.

[18] K Ambachtsheer, R Capelle and H Lum, 'The State of Global Pension Fund Governance Today: Board Competency Still a Problem' (2007) ICPM Working Paper.

[19] ibid xi.

[20] RB Davis, 'The Survival of the Trustee Model of Governance in the Era of Financial Engineering' in MS Donald and L Butler Beatty (eds), *The Evolving Role of Trust in Superannuation* (Leichhardt, NSW, Federation Press, 2017) 112.

III. EXPERTISE IN THE MYNERS REVIEW

In the UK, the sustained drive to enhance trustee expertise can be traced back to the Myners Review of 2001.[21] Boeri et al applauded Myners for 'blowing the whistle' on the low level of financial literacy among pension fund trustees.[22] Surveys conducted for the Myners Review[23] and by a team led by Gordon Clark at Oxford University[24] confirmed that both ENTs and MNTs had deficient knowledge of financial markets and investment issues.

The primary focus of the Myners Review was the overall performance of institutional investors in the UK economy. Myners was asked by the Labour government to consider how investment practices could be made less oriented to achieving short-term gains on the stock market and more supportive of long-term 'patient' investment. Pension funds, with their high levels of funds under management and long-dated liabilities, were a natural focus for this enquiry. However, trustees were not a natural focus: it was Myners' decision to put them centre-stage. This section seeks to demonstrate that Myners adopted a pluralistic view of desirable trustee expertise, while the next section shows that this orientation has been lost in the subsequent drive to equip trustees with a received conventional understanding of finance and investment issues in pensions.

Myners' main concern was that the relevant segment of the financial services industry – the market for investment consultancy and management – was highly concentrated and had developed a structure of competition which did not serve the interests of ultimate beneficiaries well. Investment managers competed to hit performance benchmarks. Trustees, presented with a market organised around these benchmarks, could conduct fund manager 'beauty parades', assessing the performance of managers against their peers. But this was not good practice: it resulted in herding around stock market indices; where there was active investment management, it was short-term in its goals and costly in execution, with fees levied for transactions when a 'buy and hold' strategy would be a better fit with pension fund objectives.

Myners alighted on trustees as the actors in the system who could change these practices and had incentives to do so. However, he argued that they did not know and understand the industry well enough to challenge the advice of consultants. They lacked the resources and expertise to make investment decisions well. They spent insufficient time and effort on questions of asset allocation and did not develop investment strategies to match their prime objective of meeting pension obligations.[25]

Two themes recur throughout the Myners report: the need for advice to be contested and challenged; and the desirability of adopting an investment strategy that fitted the particular nature of pension fund liabilities. Myners emphasised that funds had different liability structures (some had more older and pensioner members,

[21] P Myners, *Institutional Investment in the UK: A Review* (HM Treasury 2001).

[22] T Boeri and others, 'Dealing with the New Giants: Rethinking the Role of Pension Funds' (2006) *Geneva Reports on the World Economy* 8, 26.

[23] Myners (n 21) Appendix A.

[24] Clark (n 16).

[25] Myners (n 21) 1.

others a more youthful profile)[26] as well as different 'risk appetites' on the part of the sponsoring employer. Taking these factors into account, trustees should adopt 'scheme-specific' investment strategies. This emphasis on 'scheme specificity' was central to Myners' critique of the impact of regulation on pension fund investment. The Pensions Act 1995 had established a regime for checking that the accumulated assets of pension funds were adequate to cover the benefit promises that had been made (the liabilities that had accrued). Central to this regime was a valuation procedure centred on the Minimum Funding Requirement (MFR). Myners argued that this procedure had driven funds to make investments which matched the reference assets used to calculate MFR discount rates. The valuation rules were distorting funds' investment decisions and doing nothing for the security of pension promises in the process.[27]

If trustees were to challenge investment consultants and insist on scheme-specific strategies, they needed to understand investment advice as well as knowing the nature of their own scheme. This implied that it was not sufficient that trustees seek expert advice; they should have some expertise themselves. Furthermore, the ideal trustee was not necessarily an industry 'insider', because trustees should be inclined to challenge the assumptions of advisers and the conventions of the industry. MNTs could fulfil this function: Myners did not see a conflict between his proposals for more trustee expertise and the statutory requirements for trustee boards to include a certain proportion of MNTs. Trustees should think of themselves as accountable to members, and embrace transparency in investment decision-making, for example, by providing an annual statement of investment principles to members. Wider public scrutiny would also be valuable in making trustees think about whether their investment strategy is sound. Bodies in the wider public which could undertake this scrutiny included trade unions, pensioner support groups and the media.[28]

Some of the tenor of Myners' views can be illustrated by the issue of shareholder activism. Generally, the investment industry has not embraced activism, preferring to signal discontent with company management through exit (selling shares) rather than voice. To the extent that pension funds were being pushed towards activism, a good deal of the push was coming from members. Myners strongly endorsed activism,[29] going so far as to report submissions which suggested that the investment industry's lack of activism might reflect conflicts of interest which placed fund managers in breach of their fiduciary duties.[30]

Myners' embrace of contestation over investment advice and support for pluralism in scrutinising investment allocation took a more concrete form when he discussed the need for investment strategies to match the particular long-term nature of pension fund liabilities. The desirability of 'asset-liability matching' or 'liability-driven' investment strategies is uniformly endorsed in the investment management

[26] ibid para 3.28 and fn 5.
[27] ibid Summary, para 64.
[28] ibid para 8.33.
[29] ibid Summary, para 79.
[30] ibid paras 5.86–5.87.

field, but the interpretation of exactly what these terms mean is contested. To give a succinct sense of the issues, we can focus on whether bonds are particularly suitable assets to match pension liabilities.

For Myners, they were not. Writing in the context of the MFR, he argued that pension fund investment was excessively oriented towards bonds because funds tried to reduce volatility in valuations by matching MFR reference assets. Regulation had created an artificial bias towards bonds, which scheme-specific funding should go some way to remove. But his argument also implied a more general criticism of the notion that bonds are the assets that best match pension liabilities. In brief, the claim that bonds are matching assets rests on their effectiveness as a hedge for interest rate risk affecting the valuation of pension liabilities. If the present value of liabilities is calculated using a discount rate based on current interest rates, it follows that liabilities will rise when interest rates fall. Since bond prices go up when interest rates go down, the rise in liabilities is matched by an increase in the value of the scheme's assets.

This 'asset-focused' view of risk can be contrasted with an 'income-focused' view. On an income-focused view, the liabilities of a pension fund are promises to pay benefits at specific times in the future. To match these promises, fund managers might seek assets which will provide a stream of income at corresponding future dates. It does not matter if the price of these assets is volatile, provided the income stream they deliver is secure.[31] This is why pension funds can be 'buy and hold' investors, tolerating volatility in asset prices because they could afford to take a long view.

Myners was sharply critical of the emerging trend for UK pension funds to shift into bonds, which he attributed to an asset-focused view of risk driven by the regulatory regime for pension fund valuation (the MFR). There is considerable academic support for his argument that bonds are not necessarily the best match for pension fund liabilities.[32] Blake showed that, while the conventional understanding is that pension liabilities are 'bond-like', a matched portfolio based on the empirical characteristics of UK DB pension fund liabilities and the available assets would contain only a modest proportion of bonds.[33] Surprisingly, property investments turned out to be well matched with pension liabilities. This result was not idiosyncratic to Blake's approach; a contemporaneous study by PWC found that most asset-liability matching (ALM) models produced a high weight on property, but this result was 'often suppressed by the programmer'.[34]

Summing up: for Myners, the small community of investment consultants had adopted conventional practices which should be challenged by informed trustees. They would need some expertise to make this challenge, as well as time and in-house support. The adoption of scheme-specific funding would advance the cause of less

[31] RC Merton, 'The Crisis in Retirement Planning' (2014) July–August *Harvard Business Review*, available at: hbr.org/2014/07/the-crisis-in-retirement-planning.

[32] R Bauer, RPMM Hoevenaars and T Steenkamp, 'Asset Liability Management' in GL Clark, AG Munnell and JM Orszag (eds), *The Oxford Handbook of Pensions and Retirement Income* (Oxford, Oxford University Press, 2006).

[33] Blake (n 13) Table 3.

[34] Quoted in Blake (n 13) 49.

herding and less investment in bonds, provided trustees were sufficiently equipped to develop a suitable investment strategy for their own scheme. Myners' approach was pluralistic, in that he saw public debate and challenge as fruitful for investment management.

IV. EXPERTISE IN THE REGULATORY REGIME

Myners' recommendations were, apparently, warmly embraced, but it should not be forgotten that they landed in an environment in which key policy actors had other concerns. In particular, the government was dealing with other emerging difficulties with the MFR. The MFR was widely understood as ensuring that pensions were secure, but it did not promise or achieve this, and in the early 2000s there were some high-profile scheme failures where members were left bearing losses. In 2004, the Parliamentary Ombudsman announced an enquiry into complaints made by about 100 members and trustees of pension schemes, which claimed that the government had ignored evidence in failing to warn members of the risks to their schemes, and also had provided members and trustees with inaccurate information.[35] Eventually, the government was forced to compensate those affected.

In this context, Myners' recommendation for a scheme-specific funding regime was very attractive, because it would place on trustees, rather than the government, the responsibility for assessing the adequacy of a scheme's funding. However, the regulator had a strong interest in ensuring that trustees produced the 'right' answer, because, if they made the wrong assessment, the newly created Pension Protection Fund (PPF) would have to step in. Compared with the public liability that the MFR had created, the PPF promised less: accrued rights were only partly protected. This 'co-payment' by members should mitigate any tendency for trustees to take excessive risks, but studies at the time suggested that there could be some gaming of the PPF.[36] It followed that it was necessary for the regulator to monitor the solvency of schemes in order to protect the PPF, and indeed this was one of the primary elements in the mandate bestowed on the newly created Pensions Regulator (TPR) in the 2004 Act. TPR monitored solvency in the only way it knew how: by focusing on the triennial valuation. In so doing, it took the opposite direction from Myners, upholding an asset-focused approach to risk and embracing the conventions that went with that. Compounded by changes in accounting standards that made companies more sensitive to valuation volatility, one effect was that UK funds continued their trend of moving out of equity and raising the share of bonds in their portfolios.[37]

The main reception of Myners' recommendations focused on the provision of training for trustees. TPR produced a Code of Practice for trustees which emphasised their duty to ensure that they had an adequate understanding of their functions, and a

[35] D Thurley, 'Minimum Funding Requirement' (2008) House of Commons Library Standard Note: SN/BT/ 1215, 13.

[36] D McCarthy and A Neuberger, 'The Pension Protection Fund' (2005) 26 *Fiscal Studies* 139.

[37] J Kay, *The Kay Review of UK Equity Markets and Long-Term Decision Making: Interim Report* (London, HM Government Department for Business, Innovation and Skills, 2012) paras 4.8–4.9.

modular training programme called the Trustee Toolkit was developed. These initiatives were widely welcomed: for example, Cockerill argued that the emphasis in the legislation on ensuring adequate trustee skills and training 'represent[ed] an opportunity for a step change in effective trustee governance'.[38]

However, there is very little match between the Myners report and the training material produced by TPR. The focus of the latter is on trustees' understanding of the analyses produced by actuaries and advisers: particularly, their understanding of how different assumptions affect the valuation. In the Toolkit, trustees are encouraged to think of how they can implement an investment strategy within an 'integrated risk-management' framework. This framework, as developed by TPR, instructs trustees to think of investment allocation in terms of the division of the fund between 'matching assets' and 'growth assets', where matching assets are deemed to be gilts and corporate bonds, and growth assets are equities, property and various kinds of alternative investment. The balance that trustees can strike between matching and growth assets depends primarily on the strength of the employer covenant.[39]

The Toolkit gives a fair summary of current mainstream thinking about pension valuation and investment strategy, but it deviates substantially from Myners' central arguments. First and foremost, it is highly oriented towards the triennial valuation. Myners was critical of investment strategies that were designed to minimise valuation volatility, yet that is effectively what the regulator advocates. The tolerable level of volatility depends on the strength of the employer covenant: if a scheme goes into deficit and the covenant is deemed insufficiently strong, it is compelled to change (specifically, 'de-risk') its investment allocation. Furthermore, the classification of investments into 'matching' and 'growth' categories is conventional and not empirically supported.[40]

In short, the Codes of Practice for trustees, the Toolkit and other regulatory efforts to educate trustees incorporate conventional knowledge rather than promoting expertise. This is not a reflection on specific failings of the regulator: it works in close concert with the industry, and the Toolkit has been developed with industry advice. Within the industry, the issues raised here about the nature of matching assets are reasonably well known, and yet no sense of disputation found its way into the Toolkit. Evidently, there is a strong drive to promote certain conventions. The following discussion seeks to illuminate the reasons why.

V. THE TENSION BETWEEN EXPERTISE AND REPRESENTIVITY

The discussion so far has shown that there is a significant and consequential gulf between the conventional application of financial expertise and the views advanced by critics. The conventional interpretation is asset-focused and biased towards investment in bonds, often described in financial sector shorthand as 'de-risking'. Myners envisaged that trustees with expertise might challenge the asset-focused view of risk.

[38] Cockerill (n 9) 17.

[39] The Trustee Toolkit, Investment in a DB scheme, Tutorial 1.

[40] See Blake (n 13).

They could be robust in accepting that triennial valuations would show volatility in scheme balances, and keep their eyes on the longer term, where so-called de-risking can substantially *increase* the risk that income from the pension fund will not be adequate to pay the pensions promised.[41]

Myners offered few clues about where these exemplary trustees would be found. Given the available evidence that ENTs and MNTs lacked financial knowledge, one possibility endorsed by Myners was that 'independents' might be recruited who would be able to test and challenge the advisers to pension schemes. However, as the first section showed, there is little evidence that independent trustees do improve the running of pension schemes. This part of the chapter considers the hypothesis that independent trustees are susceptible to a kind of agency drift because they are not primarily oriented towards serving the interests of employers or members. This can potentially produce a tension between expertise and representation, assuming that representatives do cleave faithfully to the interests of those they represent.

Besley and Prat set up their analysis of pension fund trustees by positing that there can be two types: professional experts and caring insiders.[42] Professional experts are assumed to be motivated by career concerns, and their performance is evaluated by their peers. Given the emphasis on financial expertise in pensions, it is safe to assume that these peers are found in the financial services sector. Caring insiders have intrinsic motivation stemming from their responsibility to their fellows: they lack a wider career interest in financial services. Using this simple distinction, it is possible to make some predictions about the level of effort that the two types of trustee will put in, and the direction of that effort. Caring insiders will always make a certain amount of effort, whereas the effort invested by experts will depend on the relationship between effort and the outcomes monitored by peers. Besley and Prat provide only a brief sketch of what those peer-monitored outcomes might be. One possibility is that peers monitor benchmarked investment returns, which implies that they would be susceptible to the herding behaviour that Myners criticised, or at least that they would fail to counter herding. More generally, there is no reason to suppose that professional experts drawn from the world of financial services will deviate from conventional practices if their performance is judged by their peers. Furthermore, there is a risk that professional experts will invest little effort compared with caring insiders: this will happen if the relationship between effort and outcome is very noisy: for example, if monitored investment returns are dominated by the effect of exogenous shocks.

Davis saw the incentives of experts somewhat differently, taking the lack of evidence for the benefits of expertise as a sign that experts can have interests that conflict with those of members.[43] His analysis implies that experts do know more than non-experts about the relationship between policy decisions and outcomes,

[41] S Jacka and E Hernandez, 'Monetary Risk and Prudence in Pension Fund Valuation', paper given at Royal Society Conference, 'How Should Pension Liabilities Be Valued? Risk Aversion and Demographic Uncertainty' (London, 2019).

[42] T Besley and A Prat, 'Pension Fund Governance and the Choice Between Defined Benefit and Defined Contribution Plans' (2003) No 03/09 IFS Working Papers, Institute for Fiscal Studies, available at: ideas.repec.org/p/ifs/ifsewp/03-09.html.

[43] Davis (n 20).

but they misuse this knowledge to pursue outcomes that are not in the interests of members. Specifically, they have a conflict of interest with members over administrative fees and charges, allowing these to become inflated. They might derive excessive fees directly from the trust, or the sharing-out of work can create a circuit of excessive remuneration. There are hints of similar issues among independent trustees in the UK, especially where corporate trustees have ties to large pension consultancies. For example, the Work and Pensions Select Committee hearings on the failure of the retailer BHS included exchanges with the professional chair of the trustees about the remuneration that his company derived from the scheme and its relationship to the scheme's adviser, Willis Towers Watson.[44]

If experts have interests which diverge from those of members and employers, this produces a tension between expertise and representation. The structure of the problem is often analysed in the political theory of delegation as follows.[45] Experts know more about the relationship between policy decisions and outcomes than representatives; indeed, this knowledge about the policy 'production function' defines their relevant expertise. Setting uncertainty and random events to one side, if experts desire outcome A, they know the policy that will achieve A. Suppose now that representatives desire outcome B, but they do not know the policy that will achieve B. If they make policy themselves, they may end up with C or D. If A is nearer to B than C or D, representatives will delegate to experts even though they know that experts do not share their preferences about the outcome, and will be able to use their knowledge to pursue their own preferences. Representatives will resent this 'drift' on the part of experts, but there is little they can do about it.

This analysis is straightforward to apply to the case discussed by Davis. Outcome A is good investment performance with high fees; B is good performance with low fees. If representatives take over investment management, they will not achieve good performance (but instead C or D), and so they resentfully pay the fees of financial experts. As it happens, advocates of passive investment strategies have offered a way out, demonstrating how B might be attainable by investing in tracker or index funds.

The analysis can also be applied to the case discussed here, where the nub of the issue is that different groups of actors have different preferences about risk. As discussed above, ENTs can be expected to accept a relatively high level of investment risk in order to contain contribution costs, subject to various caveats.[46] The standard expectation is that MNTs are more risk-averse, but this depends on the weight given to pensioner members compared with young members, as well as the degree of cost-sharing and the threat of scheme closure. The regulator has an incentive to contain risk, as it reaps no benefit from scheme risk-taking, while incurring reputational and PPF costs if schemes fail. Arguably, the incentives of independent trustees mirror those of the regulator: an independent trustee of a failed scheme incurs a reputational cost, but does not reap clear benefits from risk-taking.

[44] Work and Pensions Committee, Minutes of Evidence, Wednesday 25 May 2016, Questions 615–29.

[45] K Bawn, 'Political Control Versus Expertise: Congressional Choices About Administrative Procedures' (1995) 9 *American Political Science Review* 62.

[46] In a more fully specified analysis, such as that provided by Blake (n 13), employers also take into account that a risky investment strategy is likely to make contributions more volatile (although lov… overall).

In this setting, the conflict between expertise and representation can be described as follows. Suppose that the regulator prefers de-risked outcome A, while the ENTs and MNTs prefer to accept more risk at outcome B. The policy to produce outcome B is not known to the ENTs and MNTs: it involves a complex sequence of interrelated decisions about investment strategy and valuation. Independent trustees understand investment strategy and valuation, and can steer these processes towards their desired outcome, which, due to their career concerns, is nearer A than B.

An important objection to this type of argument is that it assumes that trustees make decisions in accordance with their own interests. The law is clear that trustees have a duty of loyalty, which means that they should not be unduly influenced by their personal interests, whether pecuniary or reputational. The political theory of delegation assumes that the interests of the relevant actors can readily be identified, and that actors pursue those interests. The theory is blind to the possibility that trustees are sincere in their insistence that they seek to do the right thing for the scheme as a whole.

This objection gains force when the interests in question concern attitudes to risk and uncertainty. Uncertainty leads actors to have recourse to patterns of behaviour that are not calculative and strategic. They may turn to rules of thumb or ethical principles in response. Furthermore, actors like trustees have to formulate responses to uncertainty in a collective setting, in cooperation with other actors (other trustees and the scheme executive, employers and the regulator). The adoption of common standards or principles facilitates agreement between the parties, reducing the transaction costs of uncertainty. In this setting, expertise in the form of conventional knowledge is valuable in bringing about cooperation and agreement. However, coordination around conventional knowledge can also produce bad outcomes. Arguably, the incentives to coordinate in finance are excessive, producing herding and instability.[47]

It is possible to accept that (all) trustees are acting sincerely to produce the best outcome for the scheme, and nonetheless defend a pluralistic conception of expertise in which the varied social backgrounds of trustees lead to disagreement about the best course of action. But here we find another tension between expertise and representation, in which experts are portrayed as impartial and without interests, while representatives are impugned for their assumed responsiveness to interests. Both ENTs and MNTs are vulnerable to the claim that they cannot comply with the duty of impartiality if they participate in decisions which benefit them personally as employers or scheme members. However, the courts have set aside this concern when there are 'substitute guarantees of fairness' such as the presence of a balance of interests on the board of trustees.[48] Moreover, issues regarding the impartiality of MNTs were addressed by the Pensions Act 1995, section 39, which explicitly provides that MNTs should not be prevented from exercising their powers as trustees merely because such exercise may benefit them as members of the scheme.[49]

[47] SC Nelson and PJ Katzenstein, 'Uncertainty, Risk, and the Financial Crisis of 2008' (2014) 68 *International Organization* 361.

[48] S Gardner, *An Introduction to the Law of Trusts*, 3rd edn (Oxford, Oxford University Press, 2011) 162 and fn 44.

[49] I am grateful to Charles Mitchell for bringing this statutory provision and the relevant case law to my attention.

However, TPR's guidance on conflicts of interest betrays a different understanding from that upheld by Parliament and the courts. It is highly attentive to conflicts of interest affecting ENTs, arguing, for example, that it is 'inappropriate' for a trustee who is also the finance director of the employer to be involved in funding negotiations. Furthermore, 'trustees who, for example, are scheme members or who hold trade union representative roles' are also seen as susceptible to conflicts of interest.[50] This conflates the representative role of ENTs and MNTs with a conflict of interest, and implies that representative trustees are less well-equipped for their role than independents.

This is a tendentious position for the regulator to take. A consistent account of trusteeship might be based on trustees' own interests or it might assume that trustees act sincerely in the interests of beneficiaries. If an own-interest analysis is adopted, it is possible to identify the interests of all trustees: independents as well as ENTs and MNTs. By the same token, if it is possible for some trustees – independents – sincerely to set aside their own interests and comply with the duty of loyalty, then it is possible for others (ENTs and MNTs). The regulator's promotion of independent trusteeship appears in this light to be based on a biased account of trustee interests that constrains the pluralistic exercise of judgement and entrenches conventional expertise. Trusteeship does not have to be rule-bound in this way. The pursuit of the common good means that each trustee sets to one side the interests of the faction that placed them on the board, but it also means that trustees bring to the table their own best judgement of the common good and how to achieve it.

VI. CONCLUSION

This chapter has sought to investigate how the expertise of trustees might be expected to affect the operation of pension schemes. It has examined both the nature of expertise – whether it is conventional or pluralistic – and the nature of the agents carrying that expertise. While it is not inevitable that independent trustees bring conventional expertise, there is much in the regulatory set-up that points in that direction. Conversely, representative trustees (ENTs and MNTs) may have little expertise or may be highly receptive to conventional views, but they could also be important sources of pluralism in expertise.

One interpretation of the decline of DB pensions in the UK is that regulation has driven schemes towards closure. The regulator has been an important promoter of conventional expertise. Independent trustees in particular might be seen as agents of the regulator, adopting similar views about the desirable level of risk in a scheme. Analysis of the interests of TPR and independent trustees, compared with the interests of ENTs and MNTs, supports this view.

However, a more subtle process may be at work to defeat the pluralistic conception of expertise advanced by Myners and replace it with a set of conventional practices.

[50] See: www.thepensionsregulator.gov.uk/en/trustees/managing-db-benefits/governance-and-administration/conflicts-of-interest.

The financial soundness of a pension scheme is profoundly uncertain. Practices around scheme valuation can be seen as attempts to manage this uncertainty by coordinating the beliefs of interested parties. In this process, expertise is important in lending authority to one set of beliefs over others, which facilitates coordination. We can see that experts themselves are affected by uncertainty, and seek reassurance in agreed positions. Despite the known limitations of an asset-focused approach to assessing risk, the approach offers a computable and replicable assessment of pension scheme soundness. It may be quite wrong or misleading in fundamental ways, but it provides a reassuring anchor for its users.

It follows that the tension between representation and expertise runs more deeply than that identified by Davis.[51] In Davis's account, experts have different interests from representatives, and yet representatives must still rely on them. In the account advanced here, all parties are affected by uncertainty. Only the experts appear to offer a way of converting uncertainty into calculable risk. Even though there is much that is spurious in that calculation, representatives can offer nothing comparable. This is, fundamentally, the reason why Myners' pluralistic vision has never come to pass. Representatives on trustee boards may have a strong sense that the investment strategy could be different and that the assessment of risk is flawed, but conventional financial models have a coordinating function and problem-solving capacity that is difficult to dispense with.

There are no simple prescriptions for resolving this problem, so long as risk management is essentially financial and financialised. Trustees can avoid the regulator's Toolkit and develop more pluralistic expertise, but this could just make it harder to reach agreements about the soundness of schemes. The best alternatives for MNTs and ENTs may lie in the promotion of non-financial ways of managing risk. Most notably, faced with unexpectedly good or bad outcomes, representatives might agree to manage the consequences by renegotiating the benefits provided by the scheme. Renegotiation is not part of the regulatory approach to risk management, and legislation has constrained the renegotiation of accrued rights. Furthermore, the trend in UK pension fund governance has been to detach trusteeship of the pension fund from negotiations between employers and scheme members. The autonomy of trustees from employers and members steers schemes towards financial risk management. The fact that closure is more common than reform is an indication of the rigidity of this structure, perpetuated by the dominance of conventional expertise.

[51] Davis (n 20).

9

Pension Scheme Decision-Making Influencers

CHARLES CAMERON

I. INTRODUCTION

A. Overview

THIS CHAPTER IS written from the perspective of a solicitor in private practice, whose thought processes, professional experience and modes of expression differ from those of a barrister or legal academic. I hope that it is nevertheless comprehensible and of interest for its exposition of the thought processes and analytical approaches that typify decision-making by trustees and employers, and for its account of the difference, and of the reasons for the difference, between the opening and end positions which are typically adopted in their negotiations about the operation of schemes. These features of pensions practice are not readily observable in the case law generated by pensions disputes, but they are central to the management, administration and evolution of schemes.

There are two groups of people whose decisions can significantly influence the running of occupational pension schemes and their future direction: the trustees and the employers. Their decision-making falls into three categories: (i) business-as-usual decisions; (ii) scheme events; and (iii) corporate events. This chapter aims to show that in all three categories of case, the decisions taken by trustees and employers can be affected by a number of 'influencers'. These obviously include any applicable legislation and the scheme trust deed and rules, but in practice less obvious influencers can be equally important: the Pensions Regulator (TPR) and the Pension Protection Fund (PPF), members of the Work and Pensions Select Committee (the Committee), scheme members, employee representatives, members of other schemes operated by the same employer, parent companies (whether based in the UK or overseas), other types of shareholder, and share market analysts.

The influence exerted by all these groups can make it more difficult for trustees and employers to reach an agreement. This chapter discusses how this can happen, with a view to affording readers a better understanding of the intricacies of trustee and employer decision-making. Some practical suggestions are also offered for the benefit of trustees and employers when they negotiate with one another.

B. Scope of the Discussion

Pensions trustees must act with 'prudence'. An entire chapter (or even a whole book) could focus on the legal meaning of 'prudence',[1] and discuss such questions as whether there is such a thing as a 'risk-free basis' for decision-making from which you could work back to formulate a range of possible outcomes measured according to the risks they pose; whether there is a minimum point on that range below which a decision-maker should not fall as the outcomes which would follow would not be prudent; and whether negotiations can only ever lead to one permissible, because prudent, outcome or can sometimes produce a number of different possible and permissible outcomes. Interesting though they are, however, questions of this kind are not discussed here.

Nor will this chapter investigate the legal rules which govern the question whether trustee decision-making is legally valid,[2] noting, for example, that trustees must act within the scope of their powers; that their powers must be exercised for a proper purpose; that when making decisions trustees must take all relevant and no irrelevant matters into account, albeit that the relative weight to be placed on different relevant factors is a matter for the trustee alone to determine; and that particular difficulties are created in circumstances where the employer's interests are a matter to which the trustees must pay regard along with other matters.[3]

Instead, this chapter will describe and categorise the situations in which trustee and employer decision-making is needed; identify the influencers on such decision-making and the aims of these influencers; and note how trustees' and employers' decision-making is typically affected by those influencers. I will finally offer some thoughts from my own experience.

II. SITUATIONS WHERE TRUSTEE AND/OR EMPLOYER DECISION-MAKING IS NEEDED

At this point, it may be helpful to describe the situations where trustee and/or employer decision-making is needed. These fall into three broad categories: business-as-usual decisions; scheme events; and corporate events.

[1] *cf* J Hilliard and L Bowman, 'A Focus on Funding 1: Prudence and Other Tricky Areas', Lecture to the Association of Pension Lawyers Annual Conference (14 November 2019).

[2] A survey of these rules is undertaken in the chapter by Jessica Hudson and Charles Mitchell in the present volume. *cf* B Friedman, D Pollard and T Taylor, 'Aspects of the *Braganza* Duties: Review of Employer and Trustee Decisions', Edward Nugee Memorial Lecture (Wilberforce Chambers, London, 12 June 2019).

[3] As in, eg, *Keymed (Medical and Industrial Equipment) Ltd v Hillman* [2019] EWHC 485 (Ch).

A. Business-as-Usual Decisions

Decisions of this kind occur as part of the ongoing operation of pension schemes, rather than being driven by an external event. Examples of situations in which such decisions are made include scheme funding and actuarial valuations, covenant changes, investment strategy and PPF levy mitigation measures.

Scheme funding involves setting or agreeing the technical provisions, schedule of contributions, and recovery plan of schemes. Covenant protection involves arrangements such as guarantees, security structures, performance bonds, letters of credit, comfort letters, and negative pledges. It also involves associated information-sharing agreements. Investment strategy involves the setting and implementation of a scheme's investment, including entry into de-risking transactions such as bulk purchase annuity contracts. PPF levy mitigation measures involve measures to reduce the amount of the PPF levy.

B. Scheme Events

Examples of scheme-related events are unexpected deficit increases (whatever the reason may be for these), benefit augmentation (ie, the exercise of a trustee power to increase the benefits payable under the scheme), and buy-out proposals (ie, proposals to transfer the assets and liabilities of a scheme to an external insurer).

C. Corporate Events

These are external events related to the business of the employer. For example, decisions made before, or in light of, the payment of dividends (or other distributions) to the shareholders of an employer company, a change of control of the employer, the sale of the employer's business or a subsidiary to an outside party, and situations where the employer's business is in jeopardy.

Dividends or other distributions can occur in accordance with existing dividend policy, or as part of a proposed change to dividend policy, or as a one-off special dividend (whether or not this is related to a corporate transaction). This includes intra-group dividends and dividends payable by the ultimate parent company within a corporate group to its shareholders. Business-in-jeopardy situations occur when the employer or its group is in, or may end up in, financial difficulties or has entered into insolvency arrangements. Change of control for listed companies can be hostile or recommended. There can also be private change of control for private companies. The sale of the employer's business or subsidiary can be with or without the pension scheme.

III. INFLUENCERS ON TRUSTEE AND/OR EMPLOYER DECISION-MAKING

A. Preliminary Points

The starting point for any trustee decision in relation to a particular situation must clearly be applicable legislation and the provisions of the scheme's trust deed and rules. Sometimes the former can only be determined by reference to the latter, but sometimes they can be independent. Once this has all been clarified, the further question arises whether the trustee's decision-making may be affected by any of the other influencers which have already been identified in part I.A. There is some overlap between these, for example, applicable legislation and TPR: some of TPR's actions are firmly grounded in its statutory powers, others are less obviously so. Finally, 'influencers' is a catch-all word here, and I acknowledge I am stretching its meaning somewhat by including 'minimum legal requirements', but that is the intention.

B. Statutory Provisions

Clearly it will depend on the matter in question which (if any) pensions legislation may bear on the decisions to be taken. Many areas of decision-making are affected by statutes, including the following:

i. Preservation of benefits on leaving service – Pension Schemes Act 1993.
ii. Guaranteed minimum pensions – Pension Schemes Act 1993.
iii. Amendment protection – Pensions Act 1995, section 67.
iv. Pension increase protection – Pensions Act 1995, section 51.
v. Scheme funding – Pensions Act 2004, Part 3.
vi. The Pension Protection Fund – Pensions Act 2004, Part 2.

C. Scheme Trust Deed and Rules

Many questions may arise to which the answer may be found in the pension scheme trust deed and rules. These include the following:

i. In all cases – what are the areas of doubt? (There is almost no such thing as a trust deed which has no areas of doubt within it.)
ii. Powers of amendment – who controls these, and are there any restrictions?
iii. Funding – who controls this? Does the Scheme actuary have a role?
iv. Winding up – who controls this? Is there a trustee power to defer?
v. Investment – are there any restrictions on what may be invested in?
vi. Trustee board – who appoints and removes them? What are the eligibility conditions?
vii. Change of control or sale of employer – are there any prewired consequences?
viii. Pension increases and indexation definition – what exactly is the promise?

D. The Pensions Regulator

TPR replaced the Occupational Pensions Regulatory Authority (OPRA) following enactment of the Pensions Act 2004 and inherited a number of OPRA staff. After an initial period during which some were concerned that it would prove to have too many teeth, many would say that there followed a period in which it had no teeth, or if it did, did not choose to display them.

The British Home Stores (BHS) case in particular resulted in a great deal of scrutiny of TPR, and PPF, by members of the Work and Pensions Select Committee among other interested parties.[4] Partly as a result of that, the government and TPR now have a renewed focus on pension scheme regulation. In September 2018, TPR set out its new 'TPR Future' regulatory model and stated that its new focus would be on being 'clearer, quicker, tougher'.[5] The key aims of this new regime are to identify risks to schemes earlier and to drive compliance through prioritisation, monitoring, supervision and early proactive intervention. The 2018 White Paper,[6] and subsequent consultation,[7] also set out proposed changes to TPR's powers and the Defined Benefit system to strengthen the regulatory framework. Even if the Pension Schemes Bill does not pass in 2020, TPR will still revamp their funding code[8] and begin a more directive-based approach to prudence in funding valuations.[9] TPR's renewed focus is reflected in recent increases in the total number of its staff, which rose from 319 to 675 employees between 2012[10] and 2019.[11]

TPR produces Codes of Practice, Regulatory Guidance and Statements which set out requirements intended to influence the way trustees and employers administer and fund pension schemes. The topics covered are numerous and extensive, ranging from corporate dividend policy, to the way in which trustees and employers approach negotiating funding valuations, to encouraging employers to seek clearance statements for proposed corporate transactions.

E. Pension Protection Fund

The creation of the PPF by the Pensions Act 2004, with corresponding changes to the law which require employers to pay exit debts on the winding-up of schemes, has taken a lot of heat out of the public protests that had previously faced the government, most notably those mounted by the employees of Allied Steel and Wire, which went insolvent in 2002 leaving a large deficit in its pension fund.[12] The operation of

[4] S Butler and G Ruddick, 'Philip Green Agrees to Pay £363m into BHS Pension Fund' *The Guardian* (28 February 2017).

[5] The Pensions Regulator, *Corporate Plan 2019–2022* (May 2019), available at: www.thepensionsregulator.gov.uk/en/document-library/corporate-information/corporate-plans/corporate-plan-2019-2022.

[6] Department for Work & Pensions, *Protecting Defined Benefit Pension Schemes* (Cm 9591, 2018).

[7] Department for Work & Pensions, *Government Response to the Consultation on Protecting Defined Benefit Pension Schemes – A Stronger Regulator* (February 2019).

[8] The Pensions Regulator, *TPR Code of Practice No 3: Funding Defined Benefits* (July 2014).

[9] The Pensions Regulator, *Annual Funding Statement 2019 for Defined Benefit Pension Schemes* (March 2019) 4.

[10] The Pensions Regulator, *Annual Report and Accounts 2011–2012* (HC 340, 2012).

[11] The Pensions Regulator, *Annual Report and Accounts 2018–2019* (HC 2176, 2019).

[12] eg, 'It's Robbery!' (*Wales Online*, 18 April 2004), available at: www.walesonline.co.uk/news/wales-news/its-robbery-2441245.

the PPF has been relatively uncontroversial,[13] in large part due to its limited remit of acting as a lifeboat to pension scheme members faced with an insolvent employer and an underfunded scheme.

For the most part, trustee decision-making in relation to the PPF has been influenced less by officials of the PPF than it has been by officials of TPR, which has been assigned the role of protecting the PPF as one of its statutory objectives.[14] However, there are two exceptions to this general rule.

First, the PPF itself is responsible for the methodology used to set the PPF levy, and for deciding which structures can be used to reduce the payment of levies in cash (guarantees, letters of credit, etc). Related to this is the Scheme Without a Substantial Sponsor (SWASS) regime,[15] which was introduced in response to the prospect of certain types of employer structure. This regime had the effect of discouraging such structures by causing the amount of the applicable levy to be uneconomic.

Second, the PPF takes the lead in approving 'Regulated Apportionment Arrangements',[16] which allow a financially troubled employer to detach itself from its liabilities in respect of a defined benefit pension scheme, with the usual result that the scheme enters into the PPF. A number of conditions must be met, including that insolvency is otherwise inevitable and the recovery by the scheme would be greater than if insolvency were to occur. The purpose is to make sure the scheme is no worse off, indeed slightly better off, but to avoid the damage to employees, suppliers and customers that would result were the insolvency to occur. A prominent recent example concerned the British Steel Pension Scheme.[17]

In 2016, the Committee questioned Alan Rubenstein, the CEO of the PPF at that time, in relation to the BHS case. There were two key lines of enquiry: what his views were on the regulatory powers and approach of TPR; and how companies were tending to abuse the levy system by using weak, unchecked guarantees to reduce their levy payments. A consequence of this enquiry was the introduction of a new, stricter levy regime in 2012 which provides that trustees must now sign off on such guarantees.

F. Work and Pensions Select Committee

The Committee,[18] which is chaired by Stephen Timms MP (who succeeded Frank Field MP),[19] has increasingly become a significant influence on trustee and employer

[13] Perhaps the biggest issue has been whether PPF compensation levels are or are not compliant with applicable law: Case C-17/17 *Hampshire v Board of the Pension Protection Fund* [2019] ICR 327. See also Case C-168/18 *Pensions-Sicherungs-Verein VVaG v Günther Bauer* [2020] Pens LR 9.

[14] Under s 5(1)(c), one of TPR's objectives is 'to reduce the risk of situations arising which may lead to compensation being payable from the Pension Protection Fund'.

[15] Pension Protection Fund, '2017/18 Consultation on a Levy Rule for Schemes Without a Substantive Sponsor' (PPF, February 2017).

[16] Occupational Pension Schemes (Employer Debt and Miscellaneous Amendments) Regs 2008, reg 8.

[17] The Pensions Regulator, *Regulatory Intervention Report issued under Section 89 of the Pensions Act 2004 in Relation to the British Steel Pension Scheme* (February 2018).

[18] On the Work and Pensions Committee, see: www.parliament.uk/business/committees/committees-a-z/commons-select/work-and-pensions-committee.

[19] On Stephen Timms MP, see: www.stephentimms.org.uk.

decision-making. Trustees, company board members, TPR and PPF executives and (even) professional advisers are asked to attend parliamentary hearings before the Committee. For example, during the Committee's inquiry into BHS, oral evidence was heard from a variety of people, including Sir Philip Green (the Chairman of Arcadia Group), Lesley Titcomb (the CEO of TPR), Alan Rubenstein (ex-CEO of the PPF), current and former BHS Pension Fund Trustees, and several financial and legal advisers to both Arcadia and Taveta Investments. Field also frequently wrote to trustee chairs and CEOs demanding action in various situations and published this correspondence on the Committee's website. It remains to be seen whether Stephen Timms adopts the same approach.

i. Influencer on Employers

The key area in which the Committee has sought to exert influence over employers is in making sure they are not avoiding, limiting, or removing their pension scheme liabilities and responsibilities. The letters sent by the Committee have served as pointed reminders to employers that they must consider the impact of corporate events on their pension schemes. There is also a focus by the Committee (and TPR) on employers to ensure that they do not pay excessive dividends at the expense of their pension schemes. In addition to TPR's comments in the 2019 Annual Funding Statement and various statements, Frank Field sent letters to CEOs, trustee boards and regulatory bodies, calling corporate dividend policies into question.

ii. Influencer on Trustees

Employer CEOs were not the only recipients of Mr Field's letters – trustee chairs also received them. A common technique employed by Mr Field was to identify a sizeable pension deficit or a recent increase in the size of a pension deficit before interrogating trustees about the following questions: what had caused the deficit; what had they done to prevent the deficit from growing; and what did they plan to do about it?

iii. Influence on TPR

TPR also comes under pressure from the Committee, which actively seeks to ensure that TPR takes a proactive role in specific cases. This clearly has a knock-on effect on the way in which TPR then deals with those cases.

iv. Commentary

Depending on when the matter becomes public, a letter from the Committee might arrive when a deal has been, or almost been, reached between trustee and employer, but it might also be written at the very outset of the process. The purist would probably say that the ideal would be to receive such a letter just before the deal is concluded. That way, it can be taken into account, but not given undue weight. The purist might, in the past, have attached little significance to the wider court of public opinion, ie, to the views of those other than the scheme members including employees, and their representatives. But times have clearly changed. Whether or not the Committee sends a letter, parties to transactions involving large pension schemes must accept that there is a legitimate public interest in those transactions, and that everyone involved in a scheme may receive an invitation to a select committee hearing, whether it be employer management, trustee board members, advisers, TPR or PPF. This is potentially highly problematic. It is impossible to predict what line the Committee may take, influenced as it is by changing political considerations. That will certainly be the case in cases where there is no pre-agreement letter from the Committee, but it will probably also be the case even where there is one. Furthermore, it is perfectly possible to have reached an agreement which is compliant with pensions law and regulation, but, having been scrutinised by the Committee, later becomes subject to fierce criticism, first by the Committee, and then in the press.

G. Scheme Members

The conventional view is that trustees consider the interests of the members in a rather conceptual fashion, and do not take steps to discover what the members actually think. There are no referenda in the world of pension trustees. From my own experience, this is still generally the case. It is true that there is more emphasis on communication of trustee decisions to members, but this is mainly a one-way street. In some situations, member action groups are formed, which may have particular agendas that they want the trustee to follow. However, this seems to have become less common since the creation of the PPF and the application of buy-out debts on employer exits and winding-up.[20]

H. Employee Representatives (Local and National)

It could be that member-nominated trustees are, in a different capacity, employee representatives; and/or it could be that employee representatives wish the trustee to take a particular line, for example, to object to a proposed closure or to future accrual.

I. Other Schemes of the Same Employer

Some employers will have more than one UK scheme. If one trustee considers that another trustee is getting a better 'deal', this may encourage the trustee to seek more.

[20] See Pensions Act 1995, s 75.

J. Shareholders and Analysts

Company management may come under pressure from shareholders to take action which trustees may not welcome. For example, the shareholders may wish them to accept a hostile takeover bid or to increase dividends. Analysts following a particular company may be thought to be more or less sensitive to its pension scheme risk; the more sensitive they are, the more positive a movement in the share price there might be from a material scheme de-risking, for example.

K. Overseas Parents

It is not safe to generalise, but overseas parent companies can be good and bad for trustees. In many cases, they provide a material source of funding to the UK scheme, and without the parent, the future of the scheme might have looked less certain. But often this is coupled with, perhaps, no formal guarantee and a lack of connection as between the trustee and senior management. This does depend on the covenant of the UK company. A takeover by an overseas company of a strong UK parent may be seen as less desirable than one by a UK company, due perhaps to a perception of a greater risk of restructuring devaluing the UK employer and a loss of connection with senior management; such risks can be mitigated by guarantees and information-sharing agreements.

IV. HOW DO INFLUENCERS AFFECT DECISION-MAKING IN PRACTICE?

When approaching this question, one must bear in mind that the type of decision is highly relevant. There are two possibilities. First, there may be a trustee decision with no employer agreement. This can occur as part of a scheme's normal operation, or in response to an event which itself is not conditional on the trustee's decision, or in response to an event which is conditional on the trustee's decision. Examples of this first category include: changing the investment strategy for the scheme; setting technical provisions and recovery plan (if scheme rules give the trustee sole responsibility for these decisions); and changing the scheme employer. Second, an agreement between the trustee and employer may be required before a decision can be taken. Particularly where the decision is made in response to an event (for example, a change of control of the employer) there will be uncertainty, there may be publicity, and the trustee decision-making process may have to contend with all of the influences which have been summarised above.

A. Information/Options/Pros and Cons of Each Option

It may go without saying that the trustee needs information to calibrate its decision correctly. The employer may or may not be willing to provide this information; or, even if it is willing to do so, this may depend on provision of the information by a third party, for example, a bidder which is seeking to buy the employer. A strong trustee board relationship with employer senior management is a good way to increase the likelihood of the right level of information being provided at the right time. Then if the trustee obtains advice on the facts of the event – for example, covenant advice as to the effect of a change of control – it is good practice to share a redacted version of that advice with the employer so that there is an opportunity to reach agreement as to the factual matrix. It is then sensible for the trustee board to be presented with the two extreme ends of the range of options which in principle would be open to them to require. These would run from 'risk-free' options (a phrase to be used with caution) through to options that are 'low enough risk to still be prudent'. There should then be a pros and cons analysis of illustrative options taken from within this range. From this, one option, or at any rate a small number of options should then present themselves as front runners.

B. Decision-Making First Cut: Ignore TPR, the Committee and Others

I think it is important that this initial thought process is undertaken without specific regard being paid to what TPR or the Committee, or other parties, are saying (or, if they are silent, to what they might say). This is important for governance purposes, and it is also important to help ensure that the trustee's decision-making is legally compliant – courts are interested in applying the law and acting as the Committee or TPR (or others) would have you act does not equate to compliance with the law.

C. Decision-Making Second Cut: Consider what TPR, the Committee and Others would Say or are Saying

Following completion of stage one, it is then certainly appropriate to consider the following questions: what would the TPR position be, were they to become involved; were TPR to become involved, are the options under consideration consistent with TPR's position; and if the Committee is involved, are the options being considered consistent with the position taken by the Committee?

D. Contact them Proactively?

Should TPR be contacted by the trustee or employer at the outset? Often this will be appropriate and it is better not to find out after the event that TPR is opposed to whatever has been agreed and now wishes to inflict a world of pain on the employer and the trustee. We have found that TPR now has the resources to send representatives in cases where this would never have happened in the past, even for example to attend trustee meetings in M&A situations.

E. Anticipate their Reaction?

Both TPR and the Committee are in the business of scrutinising trustee decisions. They each bring a different type of scrutiny to bear.

In most cases, the range of TPR reactions is relatively predictable. There is a bank of published Codes[21] and Guidance[22] to which reference can be made. Advisers know what TPR has said and done on previous matters. In many situations, there is, in effect, a negotiation with TPR, rather than TPR necessarily saying 'As a regulator, I direct you to do x'.

The Committee is a very different animal. You might be in direct correspondence with the chair, in which case it might be made public (when Frank Field was the chair, the Committee published its correspondence on its website). However, the prospect of being asked to appear before the Committee will need some thought – in that situation, you might well be judged with the benefit of hindsight, and the questioning environment would certainly not be a supportive one. The best test here is what people have always called the 'smell test' or the 'conversation in the pub test': is what you are doing sensible, fair and explainable in all the circumstances?

F. Consider the Actual Versus the Communicated Position

A relevant question in this connection is what communications at the time actually say. If the matter later goes before the court or TPR then everything except privileged information will be disclosable. This will include, for example, letters and emails (formal or informal) between trustee and employer, and to members; slides prepared for internal employer management and trustee governance purposes, including drafts; and advice from advisers which is not legally privileged.

One particular point to watch for is discrepancies between what is said externally and internally. The courts and TPR will feel natural antipathy towards any party who has said one thing while thinking another. The 'smell test' needs to be thought about not only in the context of what is being said publicly, but also by reference to any confidential information, since it should be assumed that, if scrutinised, that confidential information will get out.

G. Impact on the Employer?

Where does the impact on the employer fit into this? The following considerations are potentially relevant: whether the direct or indirect consequence on the employer could cause the employer to have to change its existing business plans or have an adverse

[21] On Codes of Practice, see: www.thepensionsregulator.gov.uk/en/document-library/codes-of-practice.

[22] On Regulatory Guidance, see: www.thepensionsregulator.gov.uk/en/document-library/regulatory-guidance.

impact on the employer share price; whether the decision would have an adverse impact on the relationship with the employer; and whether these potential effects might adversely affect members, for example, by prejudicing the covenant supporting the scheme. If any such matters might arise then they must be relevant factors for the trustee to take into account in its decision-making. This is so regardless of whether any legal duty is owed by the trustee to consider the employer's interests.

H. Conduct of Negotiations/Final Determination as to Valid Option

Finally, what about the effect on the way negotiations between employer and trustee are conducted? TPR, in its latest Funding Statement,[23] wants to have a line of sight into the conduct of negotiations. The Committee is very focused on what trustees have asked for and the extent to which they have pursued these asks. A legal question arises here, namely: if a trustee has concluded with advice that Options A, B and C are equally valid (A being the most beneficial to the scheme, and C the least), then if the trustee tables C at the outset, and the employer agrees to it, has the trustee discharged its duties? How will the trustee know that the employer would not have agreed to A or B? However, this is a legal question which rarely needs an answer. Conventional negotiating strategy suggests that you should start with A or B, and if you end up at C then so be it. This must be subject to A and B not being so extreme that they damage trustee credibility or cause the employer to walk away (depending on the matter in question).

A much more difficult question in practice, and one which is only becoming more difficult as time passes, is whether an adviser can safely sign off on B and C as being acceptable outcomes. If so, then the trustee is faced with an often equally difficult question which is why and when the trustee should move off A, even if the employer is not agreeing to it. Is it safer to keep to A until such time as TPR or a court points you in a different direction? This will continue to be a major issue facing trustees, and therefore employers, for so long, at least, as the memory of cases such as BHS is fresh.

V. HOW DOES TPR OPERATE IN PRACTICE?

A. Scheme Funding Valuations

TPR may well try to set the bar higher than the legal minimum. A good example is scheme funding. If the trustee agreed a funding valuation with the employer within the statutory time limit, TPR can only undo that valuation if it falls below the minimum statutory criteria as to prudence. This is difficult for TPR to show. If, however, no valuation is agreed within the time limit, then TPR can itself determine the valuation.

In practice, if TPR makes known its views to the trustee before it has agreed a valuation, then it can make the trustee nervous about agreeing a valuation which

[23] The Pensions Regulator, *Annual Funding Statement 2019* (n 9).

passes the test, if the valuation falls below what TPR wants. In this way, the effect is that valuation outcomes in excess of the legal minimum are achieved. Of course, the trustee could ignore TPR and agree a valuation with which the trustee is content, and afterwards seek to rely on TPR not being able to use any of its statutory powers in consequence. However, there is not much incentive for a trustee to take the risk of that going wrong. Also, if there is new pensions legislation and a new Funding Code, we may find that the legal minimum and TPR practice align, at least in relation to funding valuations.

B. 'Equitable Treatment' of Pension Schemes along with Other Employer Stakeholders

TPR expects a pension scheme to be 'treated equitably' with other stakeholders; and has expressed concern about 'inequitable treatment of schemes relative to that of shareholders', exemplified by the disparity between dividend growth and stable deficit repair contributions.[24] However, the term 'equitable treatment' has no objective meaning and it has become a convenient stick to beat employers and trustees with. For example, if a dividend is being paid or a business is being sold, and the scheme is 100 per cent funded on a technical provisions basis, does 'equitable share' mean zero? Or, if the technical provisions basis has to become more prudent in light of the action that has given rise to the value shift, does equitable share mean that the whole of the extra deficit thereby created must be paid to the scheme? There is no set formula. There is a sense in this of 'who blinks first'.

C. What is Required and what is Aspirational in TPR's Codes and Guidance?

Neither TPR's Codes of Practice nor its Guidance are statements of the law and there is no direct penalty for failing to comply with them. However, Codes of Practice are admissible in evidence in any legal proceedings and the court or tribunal must take into account any relevant code provisions when determining whether the legal requirements have been met.[25] Yet in its Codes of Practice and Guidance, TPR has consistently failed to draw a distinction between the minimum statutory requirements of trustees and what TPR itself requires of trustees.

This is shown most clearly in the Codes for Defined Benefit (DB) and Defined Contribution (DC) schemes. In the Department for Work and Pensions's (DWP) recent review of TPR,[26] it was generally complimentary of TPR's new, tougher approach, but it criticised this aspect of TPR's operational effectiveness. Particular criticism was made of the key requirements set out in TPR's DB Code[27] and DC Code.[28]

[24] ibid 19.
[25] Pensions Act 2004, s 90(5).
[26] Department for Work & Pensions, *Tailored Review of The Pensions Regulator* (April 2019).
[27] The Pensions Regulator, *Annual Funding Statement 2019* (n 9).
[28] The Pensions Regulator, *TPR Code of Practice No 13: Governance and Administration of Occupational Trust-based Schemes Providing Money Purchase Benefits* (July 2016).

DWP pointed to the DB[29] and DC[30] Surveys carried out by TPR, which measured the extent to which schemes were complying with these requirements. The DB Survey found that only 19 per cent of all DB schemes met TPR's expectations under each of the seven DB Code principles, while the DC Survey found that only 5 per cent of DC schemes met all the key governance requirements set out by the DC Code. Given that a significant number of schemes were not fully complying with the Codes, the DWP concluded that 'the key requirements (set out in the Codes) may not give an accurate picture of whether a scheme is well run and protecting its members'. The DWP then went further, calling for TPR to give clearer guidance on the distinction between the minimum standards of compliance and what was merely TPR guidance:

> We still recommend that the regulator assess whether the codes of practice they measure schemes against are the correct minimum standards of compliance they expect of all schemes. This would assist TPR in its mission to become 'clearer', clarifying to schemes what things the regulator asks of them are requirements and what are merely guidelines.

A second point is that TPR gives itself credit for movement in employer opening positions. This applies no matter how much gold-plating and/or logic supports the employer's opening position. This is bound to encourage employers to hold back initially and unfortunately it also causes trustees to push for more. When an employer and a trustee are well informed and both want to do the right thing – which in my own experience is most of the time, contrary to what you might believe from examples reported in the press – then if there is thought to be a need to choreograph positions for the file, for TPR, or for the Committee, then this can be an obstacle to getting the right deal done on time, and can also lead to unnecessary friction and lasting harm to the relationship.

Third, it is questionable whether TPR has an interest in encouraging trustees not to be excessively prudent. The main objectives of TPR in exercising its functions are set out in the Pensions Act 2004, section 5, where it is stated that TPR should minimise any adverse impact on the sustainable growth of the employer in the exercise of its powers under the scheme funding regime. Yet the other main statutory objectives of TPR – protection of member benefits and reduction of the risk of compensation being payable by the PPF – mean that it is not always a straightforward matter to persuade TPR that it should do this.

Fourth, the threat of the use of TPR power can often achieve agreement even in cases where its powers are not directly engaged. The threat, or possibility, of the exercise of any TPR power is often a strongly persuasive factor for a trustee or employer to follow a TPR suggestion. There need not be a direct connection with the event in question. For example, a dividend is paid just before a triennial valuation and so TPR's statutory funding powers are referred to in light of the dividend payment.

[29] IFF Research, *Defined Benefit Trust-based Pension Schemes Research: A Summary Report on the 2018 Research Survey* (September 2018), available at: www.thepensionsregulator.gov.uk/-/media/thepensionsregulator/files/import/pdf/db-research-summary-report-2018.ashx.

[30] OMB Research, *Defined Contribution Trust-based Pension Schemes Research: Summary Report on the 2018 Survey* (June 2018), available at: www.thepensionsregulator.gov.uk/-/media/thepensionsregulator/files/import/pdf/dc-research-summary-report-2018.ashx.

Finally, one may ask whether the Committee would be needed if we had a fully functioning TPR. This is a slightly unfair question. The Committee partly fulfils a function that Parliament did not give to TPR. On the other hand, the Committee clearly thinks that TPR has not been proactive enough in the use of the powers that it does have. It could be that this latter role of the Committee will diminish if TPR is given more powers by new legislation and if it uses its powers more vigorously.

VI. POINTERS FOR TRUSTEES AND EMPLOYERS

The Pension Schemes Act 2020, if, as seems likely, it makes it on to the statute book, and the new Funding Code, which seems a certainty, may make things clearer at least in relation to ongoing valuations. But there will continue to be many other reasons for trustees to feel the need to start as closely as they can to the selection of 'risk-free' options, and to be nervous of moving away from these. Meanwhile, TPR and the Committee will continue to be driven by strong memories of cases in which schemes and employers have gone wrong in a very public fashion, and this will continue to affect the governance and operation of schemes even in cases where the employer and the trustee want to do the right thing and are capable of reaching agreement. As a result, employers and trustees have difficult straits to navigate where decision-making is required. There is no magic solution to these problems, but I offer some pointers gleaned from practice.

A. Pointers for Trustees

i. Rationalise the ask – it is much easier for an employer to give proper consideration to a trustee's proposal if each element of it is rationalised by reference to the factual context, and the range of options available.
ii. Consider offering alternative proposals – this can make it much easier to get a dialogue going, and is more likely to encourage the employer to believe that the trustee and the employer can work together.
iii. Be aware of the employer governance process.

B. Pointers for Employers

i. Give early warning of events/timing of agreement – in most cases it is better to reach agreement before, rather than after, the event; apart from anything else, it fosters cooperation, rather than creating suspicion.
ii. Have a transparent factual matrix, including structure, timing (and drivers) and variables – the more information the trustee has, the easier it should be to work collaboratively to achieve a solution.
iii. Anticipate the reaction of trustee influencers.
iv. Be aware of trustee governance process.

C. Pointers for Both Trustees and Employers

i. Communicate both within and outside formal meetings.
ii. Create joint working adviser groups.
iii. Seek a common factual matrix – this can be very beneficial; even if it has been prepared by one party's advisers, it can be shared with the other party, redacted if necessary, for review and comment, in order to achieve an agreed form report.
iv. Aim for a common message to TPR where possible – it is not necessary for all communications to be separate and confidential; it is often highly beneficial for joint communications and meetings to take place.

VII. CONCLUSION

Before the Pensions Act 1995 and the Maxwell scandal,[31] the pensions sector was unregulated and in many cases relationships between trustees and employers were too cosy and the approach taken by trustees to discharging their duties was often insufficiently rigorous. A swing of the pendulum in the opposite direction has been given momentum not only by the Pensions Act 2004, but also by high-profile cases such as BHS.

A positive consequence of this is the emergence of an appropriate focus, in corporate activity, on the pension scheme as a corporate creditor. However, it is also causing trustees and TPR in many cases to be very anxious about the terms on which the trustee reaches agreement with employers, with the result that employers are often finding it hard to resist outcomes which, for no objective reason, are at the very prudent end of the prudent scale.

If you compare different schemes and employers, and take all factors into account – covenant, investment strategy, liability profile, scheme powers – the range of valuation outcomes and types of credit support is extremely wide. But there is often no calibration against other schemes in discussions with trustees and TPR.

The practical steps outlined above can help to reduce the risk of a stalemate in interactions between trustees and employers, but it would be a positive development if there were a greater general awareness of how different schemes compare. I would also suggest that TPR has a role to play in helping trustees with this, and in particular with helping to calibrate trustees' approach to risk and, potentially, with helping trustees to recognise whether a particular approach is insufficiently or excessively prudent.

[31] H Wheelan, 'Tales of Pension Fund Abuse' (*IPE*, May 2001), available at: www.ipe.com/analysis/analysis/tales-of-pension-fund-abuse/14159.article.

10

The Social Role of Occupational Pension Schemes

JAMES KOLACZKOWSKI

I. INTRODUCTION

THE LEGAL AND organisational structures of occupational pension schemes invite detailed technical analysis that is strongly focused on the relationships between the parties to such schemes, with consideration of such issues as the framework within which benefits are provided and the duties which are owed by trustees when they invest pension funds. It is argued in this chapter, however, that important insights into pensions law and policy can also be gained by looking outside the legal rights and duties of the parties to the wider social role of pension schemes. Some attention has been paid to this in the existing scholarly literature, but it is suggested that this social role could usefully be investigated further. Occupational pension provision involves many stakeholders with rights and obligations that interact in a complex manner. Drawing on scholarship that uses Social Contract theory to explain state pension provision, it is argued that a deeper understanding of the law and policies affecting occupational pension schemes could also be gained if more attention were paid to their public, 'social' role. It is also suggested that if there were statutory recognition of this social role, and if greater efforts were made to understand the interaction between this social role and the private, 'individualistic' role played by occupational pension schemes in supplying benefits to employees and their dependants, then this would lead to changes in the drafting of a scheme's constitutional documents and in decision-making by the courts when they adjudicate pensions litigation. And this would lead in turn to the development of rules that paid proper regard to the reasons why occupational pension schemes matter in contemporary society.

Occupational pension schemes often generate disputes between scheme members and sponsoring employers. These can lead to litigation, the outcome of which is usually determined by judicial analysis of the parties' rights and obligations as private individuals. When the courts decide such disputes, the wider context within which the employer provides pension benefits is treated as relevant, but it is not given the same amount of consideration. It is suggested here that it would also be desirable for the courts to have recourse to legislative and other sources of support such as through existing regulatory guidance and codes of practice, which explicitly authorise them to pay attention to the more general public interest role of a pension scheme. To explain this further, an account is given here of the historical development of occupational pension schemes in the UK, to explain why schemes have a wider social role. Examples of the extent to which current judicial reasoning takes account of this social role are then considered. Finally, it is discussed how the social role of occupational pension schemes can be understood, what a more formalised, statutory definition of this role might look like, and how the adoption of such a definition might benefit stakeholders.

II. THE PURPOSES OF OCCUPATIONAL PENSION SCHEMES

A trust-based occupational pension scheme generates rights and obligations for trustees, employers and employees by the application of well-established rules of contract and trust law. In addition to these important stakeholder groups, government also has a key interest in the operation of occupational pensions, in its capacity as a social policy-maker which must account to the general public. It is in the public interest for the financial savings of elderly people to be increased so that their living standards go up and the total costs of general healthcare go down. The function of occupational pension schemes therefore goes beyond the private provision of financial benefits in exchange for work as an incident of the employer–employee relationship. The wider social benefits that schemes provide may come directly in the form of pensions for the spouses and/or children of employees and lump sum benefits on their death. Benefits may also arise indirectly for family members who may enjoy a better quality of life, if employees are able to save for retirement in a cost-efficient way with support from employer contributions.

The policy issues surrounding occupational pension schemes are notoriously complex, owing both to the size and scope of schemes and to the number and range of their stakeholders. In their annual report of defined benefit liabilities, the Pensions Regulator and the Pension Protection Fund calculated UK defined benefit pension assets as at 31 March 2018 to be £1,573.3 million, with liabilities of £1,643.8 million.[1] The management of pension liabilities and risks forms an essential part of a sponsoring employer's financial planning, but it also occupies a key position in government policy-making. Legislation is needed to ensure that individual workers' savings towards retirement are adequately protected, but at the same time employers must be afforded the freedom to pursue commercial activity to generate sufficient profits to ensure that their pension liabilities are met.

[1] Pension Protection Fund, *The Purple Book DB Pensions Universe Risk Profile* (Pension Protection Fund and Pensions Regulator Joint Publication, Sequel Group, December 2018) 12. Figures calculated on a s 179 basis; data taken from 5,420 schemes with 10.4 million members.

A. Development of the Public and Private Functions of Occupational Pension Schemes

To understand the social role now played by occupational pension schemes, the circumstances in which state pension provision was first introduced into the UK are particularly relevant, since the structure of modern occupational pension provision rests on the legacy inherited from the Beveridge Plan for state welfare provision,[2] first implemented in 1946.[3] The original intention of the Plan's promoters was for the state to become the main provider of pension benefits, but post-war financial shortages forced some compromises.[4] As a result, as Pemberton has observed, occupational pension schemes grew rapidly in the 1950s and 1960s, when their 'niche' position developed into a 'central role in Britain's system of pension provision', with a 'minimalist state pension' creating 'the conditions for the development of a parallel and extensive system of private occupational pensions provision on a vastly greater scale than had been expected at the time of the Beveridge report'.[5]

In Pemberton's view, therefore, the growth of occupational pension schemes was a direct result of the inadequacy of the state pension provided by the Beveridge settlement in the social and political environment of post-war Britain. Workers expected pensions that were linked to their earnings rather than the small, flat-rate pensions provided by the state. Furthermore, increasing numbers of post-war government employees and a stronger post-war labour market led to a desire on the part of employers to incentivise their workers to remain in post by providing them with more generous pension benefits.[6] As a result, as Whiteside has written, occupational pension schemes came to play a number of diverse roles: they might

> represent deferred salary (on a socialized or individual basis), the means to secure long and better service from essential employees, a necessary investment in industrial re-structuring, [and] a source of venture capital, as well as protection against destitution in old age.[7]

In 1959, the Conservative government decided to retain the flat-rate state pension and introduce a low earnings-related element in the form of the state graduated pension. This was followed in the 1960s by unsuccessful moves for reform of the state pension system. Proposals by the Labour opposition at that time included a pension of 50 per cent final salary, to be funded by an increase in contributions and a more ambitious investment strategy.[8] Whiteside observes, though, that the Labour Party's proposals were resisted by trade unions as well as government, employers and the financial services sector, out of a fear that they would threaten 'monetary stability, private sector investment and the public finance'.[9]

[2] W Beveridge, 'Social Insurance and Allied Services' (National Archives PREM/4/9/82, November 1942).

[3] The National Insurance Act 1946 established universal social security, following the Old Age Pensions Act 1908, which had provided a limited amount of coverage.

[4] H Pemberton, 'Politics and Pensions in Post-war Britain' in H Pemberton, P Thane and N Whiteside (eds), *Britain's Pension Crisis* (Oxford, Oxford University Press, 2006).

[5] ibid 48.

[6] ibid 46–49.

[7] N Whiteside, 'Occupational Pensions and the Search for Security' in H Pemberton, P Thane and N Whiteside (eds), *Britain's Pension Crisis* (Oxford, Oxford University Press, 2006) 126.

[8] ibid 133–34.

[9] ibid 134.

Trade unions therefore played an important role in the development of occupational pensions. The improvement of occupational pension schemes was seen by the unions as a way of avoiding state policies on wage restraints, and they fought hard for increases in occupational pension benefits, which were characterised as deferred pay.[10] However, their policy of fighting for increases in occupational pension benefits as part of wage negotiations, rather than pushing for increases in state pension provision as a matter of public policy, contributed to a tendency for all sides to conceptualise disputes about occupational pension provision as falling within the private rather than the public sphere. Despite the social role played by occupational pension schemes, this tendency was also exacerbated by the hands-off attitude taken by government, which chose not to intervene in industrial disputes about occupational pensions, viewing this as a private matter to be determined by trade union and employer negotiation.

To understand how occupational pension schemes came to be seen as private arrangements, it is also helpful to consider the incentives which led employers to establish such schemes and the goals which employees hoped to achieve through scheme membership. Starting in the nineteenth century, long before implementation of the Beveridge Plan, early occupational pension schemes were created as a way of providing employees with retirement benefits. The Bank of England granted an early form of pension to its staff from 1735 onwards, and early private occupational pension schemes also included the Chartered Gas Light and Coke Company Superannuation Fund, which was founded in 1841.[11] Early public sector pensions developed in the Civil Service, with the practice growing up of an employee retiring from ill health being recompensed through a right to receive part of his successor's salary.[12] After several reforms, the Civil Service scheme was made available to all employees by 1810, for several reasons, including the need to provide employees with adequate recompense, following an initiative to stop customs officials from taking 'fees and gratuities' to supplement their income.[13] Pension schemes were also developed in the private sector, notably through the creation of pension schemes by railway companies from the 1860s onwards, and by employers such as Cadbury and Rowntree, motivated to some degree by altruistic concerns.[14]

Aside from providing pensions as a benefit to encourage the best potential employees to join a sponsoring employer's business, pensions also performed a vital role in supporting the families of workers with low incomes and low life expectancies. Arguably, therefore, occupational pensions have always fulfilled two functions: on the one hand, to supply a private benefit, a supplement to salary in exchange for work; and on the other, to implement necessary saving, supported by an employer and the state working in tandem, as a means of protecting retired workers and their families. However, the private or individual rights and obligations generated by occupational

[10] ibid.

[11] Pensions Archive Trust, 'Early Occupational Pension Schemes', available at: www.pensionsarchive.org.uk/77/. Further examples are discussed in Sinéad Agnew's chapter in the present volume.

[12] P Thane, *Old Age in English History: Past Experiences, Present Issues* (Oxford, Oxford University Press, 2000) 236.

[13] ibid 240–41.

[14] ibid 245.

pension schemes are usually easier to identify than the public or social element of such schemes. The former can be defined by the application of legal rules to disputes between scheme members and the sponsoring employer which are brought before the courts or the Pensions Ombudsman; but the latter must be inferred not only from a scheme's content but also from current government policy relating to the state pension system. In other words, the relative social importance of occupational pension schemes can vary with the changing social policy agendas of successive governments.

Historically, the framework of the UK pensions system has been based upon a low state pension which has encouraged citizens to work and save privately for their retirement in order to provide for themselves and their families. However, the legislative environment in which the UK pensions system developed was heavily influenced by post-war political influences. According to Glennerster, these 'set British pensions down a maze rather than a path'.[15] The UK system relies on occupational pensions to provide an adequate level of financial support above the 'subsistence' level which was first planned for by Beveridge. However, this original goal was not achieved, as the final implementation of the state pension in 1946 was set at a lower level than anticipated, and the increases that were planned to occur during a transitional period were never introduced. The resulting system has been criticised for creating an inadequate state pension. As Harris observes, what was seen at the time as a 'progressive implementation of the Beveridge Plan … eventually shifted the pattern of British old-age pensions provision in a direction quite different from, and opposite to, the one that Beveridge himself had originally envisaged'.[16]

Pemberton argues that the 'short term political horizons' of the Labour government after the Second World War resulted in a state pensions system that was begun too early, before it could be afforded, and that it was designed to placate key groups of voters with the result that benefits were provided at a level that was high for some but inadequate for others.[17] Rather than introducing 'full subsistence' over a 20-year period, the resulting system meant that what was intended to be a 'golden staircase' to an adequate pension that would be implemented over a period of time, became the start of a state system in which the flat rate contribution tied 'the level of that contribution to what the lowest-paid worker could afford'. Pemberton notes that this effectively created a 'pay-as-you-go' system, rather than an insurance-based system, with a level of 'subsistence' that was not actuarially calculated and was unlikely to meet the needs of an increasing and ageing population. The Beveridge 'straitjacket' thereby produced long-term inequities in the UK state pensions system.[18]

To identify the public roles which might be performed by occupational pension schemes today, it is also instructive to consider the roles which the state pension system has been designed to play. The promoters of the Beveridge Plan faced essentially the

[15] H Glennerster, 'Why So Different? Why So Bad a Future?' in H Pemberton, P Thane and N Whiteside (eds), *Britain's Pension Crisis* (Oxford, Oxford University Press, 2006).

[16] J Harris, 'The Roots of Public Pensions Provision: Social Insurance and the Beveridge Plan' in H Pemberton, P Thane and N Whiteside (eds), *Britain's Pension Crisis* (Oxford, Oxford University Press, 2006).

[17] Pemberton et al (n 4) 49–53.

[18] In Helen Fawcett's words: H Fawcett, 'The Beveridge Straight-Jacket: Policy Formation and the Problem of Poverty in Old Age' (1996) 10 *Contemporary British History* 20.

same problems as have been faced by governments in more recent times: financial difficulties and political disagreements about the best ways to provide for those in need. In his report, Beveridge acknowledged three guiding principles.[19] The first was that change should be revolutionary and not 'restricted by the consideration of sectional interests'. The second was that social security was only part of a wider scheme of social progress that addresses the problem of 'want', alongside four other 'giant' social problems: 'disease, ignorance, squalor and idleness'. The third was that security should be achieved by cooperation between the state and the individual. The state should offer security for service and contribution, and in organising security it should not stifle incentive, opportunity, or responsibility. In establishing a national minimum, it should therefore leave room and encouragement for voluntary action by each individual to provide more than that minimum for himself and his family. Later in the Beveridge Plan, the philosophy behind Beveridge's work is described as follows:

> The plan is not one for giving to everybody something for nothing and without trouble, or something that will free the recipients forever thereafter from their personal responsibilities. The plan is one to secure income and keep men fit for service. It cannot be got without thought and effort. It can be carried through only by a concentrated determination of the British democracy to free itself once and for all of the scandal of physical want for which there is no economic or moral justification. When that effort has been made, the plan leaves room and encouragement to all individuals to win for themselves something above the national minimum, to find and to satisfy and to produce the means of satisfying new and higher needs than bare physical needs.[20]

The decision to establish such a system was intended to create an affordable pensions system with fewer obligations placed on the state than in many other European countries, such as Germany, for example, which historically had an insurance-based system that provided higher levels of state benefit. First introduced by the German Chancellor, Count Otto von Bismarck, in 1889, and thus known as 'Bismarckian' systems, such systems of state welfare provision depend upon contributions from employees, employers and the government.[21] They have a more overtly public role and essentially provide earnings related benefits. In the case of Germany, the state provides a pension on a points-based system in relation to earnings; those with low pensions may also receive support from additional means-tested social assistance. In contrast, the UK Beveridge system provides a universal level of pension to everyone who meets the required amount of contributions through National Insurance payments. Following the introduction of the Beveridge Plan, the growth of occupational pension schemes was then encouraged by successive UK governments through the provision of tax reliefs which enabled capital to be increased inside such schemes in a tax efficient manner.

Historically, many central European state pension systems have been more generously funded by the state than the UK state pension system, and have provided a higher

[19] Beveridge (n 2) paras 7–9.

[20] ibid para 455.

[21] For an economic comparison of Bismarckian systems with the UK state pension system, see M Kolmar, 'Beveridge Versus Bismarck: Public-Pension Systems in Integrated Markets' (2002) 37 *Regional Science and Urban Economics* 649.

level of benefits than 'pay-as-you-go' systems, under which individuals pay into a pension pot to provide for themselves in later life. Increasingly, however, such generosity has come to be seen as unaffordable, as financial circumstances have changed and life expectancies have increased. In 1994, the World Bank published a report on 'Averting the Old Age Crisis',[22] which recommended three types of pension provision – mandatory public pensions, mandatory private pensions including occupational schemes and voluntary pensions – and promoted the idea that state pension provision would have to decrease and private pension provision increase. Since then, many state-funded systems have been reformed with such ends in mind. The global financial crisis in 2008, and the sovereign debt crisis in the European Union (EU) in 2010, have also spurred the reform of expensive public pension provision and the privatisation of pension systems. These trends are as observable in the UK as elsewhere: the state's role in pension provision has been reduced and private pension schemes have been encouraged by legislation starting in the 1980s,[23] the state pension age has been increased, and automatic enrolment in private pension schemes has been introduced to encourage individuals to take on private, defined contribution pensions to supplement their low state pension.

The reduction of state pension benefits has increased the social importance of additional pension provision through other means, and particularly through occupational pension systems. By implementing policies such as automatic enrolment, governments have signalled that they regard occupational pension provision (and other forms of private supplementary pension) as an increasingly important part of their public welfare planning, despite their private nature. Such changes are particularly evident in countries of the EU other than Britain, such as Portugal, Greece and Ireland, where economic adjustment measures have been imposed by the EU as conditions of the financial 'bail out' packages created to address a series of economic, social and political crises.[24] As Casey has observed, the financial crisis developed through several 'mutations' originating in a credit crisis, evolving to a crisis of government finance and a crisis of European cohesion that has increased the pace of pension reform.[25] Barnard has additionally noted the detrimental impact of EU measures on labour standards through the limits imposed as a condition of receiving EU financial aid, including a reduction in the levels of state pension provision.[26]

Faced with the increasing costs of state support, the British government has repeatedly looked to the private sector to provide occupational pensions as a key social function of saving for old age. An example is the introduction of automatic enrolment

[22] World Bank, 'Averting the Old Age Crisis: Policies to Protect the Old and Promote Growth' (World Bank Policy Research Report, New York, Oxford University Press, 1994).

[23] Key reforms in the Thatcher era saw the removal of the correlation between earnings and rises in the state pension under the Social Security Act 1980 and the encouragement for private pensions through the Financial Services Act 1986: P Ireland, 'Law and the Neoliberal Vision: Financial Property, Pension Privatisation and the Ownership Society' (2011) 62 *Northern Ireland Legal Quarterly* 1.

[24] D Ashiagbor, 'The Global Financial Crisis: Impact on Labour and Employment Law' in P Maynard and N Gold (eds), *Poverty Justice and the Rule of Law: The Report on the Second Phase of the IBA Presidential Taskforce on the Global Financial Crisis* (London, International Bar Association, 2013).

[25] B Casey, 'The Implications of the Economic Crisis for Pensions and Pensions Policy in Europe' (2012) 12 *Global Social Policy* 246.

[26] C Barnard, 'The Financial Crisis and the Euro Plus Pact: A Labour Lawyer's Perspective' (2012) 41 *Industrial Law Journal* 98.

by the Pensions Act 2008. This requires employers to enrol all eligible employees into an occupational pension scheme (although employees are permitted to opt out if they wish) and to contribute 3 per cent of an eligible employee's earnings into the scheme each year. According to the Department for Work and Pensions (DWP) this legislation will result in an estimated increase in annual pension contribution of approximately £20 billion from the year 2019/2020.[27] The DWP stated that it wished to consolidate this success, and that to achieve this, three strategic issues needed to be addressed, one of which was the lack of individual engagement in pension savings.[28] According to the DWP, 'whilst more individuals than ever before are saving, they are not necessarily engaged with saving nor looking to take greater responsibility to plan'.[29] To encourage individuals to think more about their savings, the DWP therefore proposed to focus on the communication methods used by sponsoring employers and pension scheme providers. Initiatives of this kind illustrate the enthusiasm felt by government policy-makers to give occupational pension schemes a more prominent place on the social welfare map.

A similar observation can be made about the decision to allow private employers to fulfil a function of the state by enabling occupational pension schemes to provide part of the earnings-related element of the state pension, known as the State Second Pension, or 'SERPS', until it was replaced by the new state pension from 6 April 2016. This was achieved by reducing the obligations on employers and employees to pay National Insurance and relieved the state of part of its pensions burden, essentially by contracting out responsibility for the provision of this part of the state pension package to employers and employees.

B. Occupational Pension Schemes and Social Contract Theory

On a private level, it can be said that the benefits provided by occupational pension schemes form an important part of an individual employee's salary: they are deferred remuneration for the employee's work. However, occupational pension schemes also have a social purpose, which should be kept in view when theorising about their 'purpose' or 'function'. The point has been made above that schemes provide benefits to a range of stakeholders beyond the employer and employee. From a theoretical standpoint, moreover, one can conceive the social role of occupational pension schemes in terms of the 'Social Contract', a concept developed by political philosophers to offer an ideological explanation for the role of the state in society which has at its core the idea that the state must abide by fair principles to protect the property of individual citizens.[30]

[27] Department for Work & Pensions, *Automatic Enrolment Review 2017: Maintaining the Momentum* (Cm 9546, 2017) 20.

[28] The other two strategic aims look at improving coverage over an individual's working life and addressing issues with self-employed savers: ibid 8–15.

[29] ibid 13.

[30] These arguments develop points made about the 'social role' of occupational pension schemes in J Kolaczkowski, 'What is the Proper Role for the European Union in Occupational Pensions in the United Kingdom?' (University of Bristol, PhD Thesis, 2017) ch 2.

Early proponents of Social Contract theory include Thomas Hobbes, John Locke and Jean-Jacques Rousseau. For Hobbes, the Social Contract existed to explain why humans, who are essentially self-interested yet rational beings, are pre-disposed to cede authority to the sovereign and the state rather than live in an unregulated and immoral 'state of nature'.[31] In contrast, Locke applied the moral Law of Nature and the concept that humans living together would create and seek to abide by moral laws.[32] However, for Locke, the right to personal property and the right to enjoy the fruits of your labour should be regulated by a higher authority such as the state. Rousseau, meanwhile, developed an idealised version of the Social Contract to challenge the inequalities which are essentially present in a complex society.[33] He focused on the concept of ownership of private property and developed a theory for a successful democracy according to which the individual earns freedom through making sacrifices for the collective good. Locke and Rousseau, in particular, envisage situations where the governing powers have a duty to fulfil their side of the bargain.

A more modern take on Social Contract theory can be found in the work of John Rawls, who uses the concept to put forward an abstract theory of justice under which the rationale for an individual conceding autonomy to live in a legal community is justified by the actions of a rational, self-interested person, in an 'original position' where a person has no identifying characteristics.[34] Rawls made the argument that a Social Contract should operate around two central principles of maximising civil liberty and the Difference Principle that seeks to justify inequalities, provided that all benefits are initially available to all on an equal basis, and the least prosperous individual is no poorer than they would have been under different circumstances.

A common theme in the work of Social Contract theorists is that the state must perform certain overarching promises to the individual: it must facilitate an environment in which the individual can retain some level of freedom, as well as benefit from the state's protection. From an ideological standpoint, therefore, state legislation to regulate an individual's private income through pension benefits may be justifiable if a wider social purpose will be achieved by such a measure. For example, the state might legitimately change the taxation laws in ways which affected an individual's pension savings, or which compelled an individual to pay money into a pension scheme, if this were necessary to improve the living conditions of society as a whole. In such cases, the state's intervention in what would otherwise be a private arrangement by employer and employee, and the extent of this intervention, can be explained in the terms of Social Contract theory. Concessions are given by the state to create a legislative and regulatory environment which allows pension funds to exist and accumulate, subject to significant legislative restrictions upon how such funds operate. The justification from the perspective of an employee looking to save his earnings, his 'personal property', could be that there is a social contract between the individual and the state

[31] T Hobbes, *Leviathan* (CB Macpherson ed, London, Penguin Books, 1985).

[32] J Locke, *Two Treatises of Government and A Letter Concerning Toleration* (New Haven, CT, Yale University Press, 2003).

[33] J Rousseau, *The Basic Political Writings* (DA Cress tr, Indianapolis, IA, Hackett Publishing Company, 1987).

[34] J Rawls, *A Theory of Justice* (Cambridge, MA, Harvard University Press, 1971); J Rawls, *Political Liberalism* (New York, Columbia University Press, 1993).

whereby state intervention in an employee's private savings is desirable, so long as it promotes the development of pensions as a wider social good.

McDaniel suggests that valuable insights can be gained from applying Social Contract theory in a pensions context, viewing this as a call for a 'transcendent collective good', seen as a progressive force, based upon rational and reasonable will.[35] However, Clark considers that a key difference exists between pensions policy in continental European jurisdictions, which view the concept of the Social Contract as a statement of fact rather than an aspirational ideal, and the pensions policy of Anglo-American jurisdictions, for which 'the ideal has given way to claims of individual autonomy and separate benefit'.[36] To like effect, Reynaud has described pension systems as being 'the product of the societies concerned' and has added that they 'inevitably reflect a series of specific characteristics, especially concerning the relationship between the State, society, political traditions, industrial relations, structure of the economy, and perceptions of justice and equality'.[37]

As observed by both Clark and Reynaud, the social welfare systems of states do not always deliver on the promises to the performance of which Social Contract theory would say their citizens are entitled. The theory holds that a state must fulfil its proper role and provide something to its citizens in exchange for their loyalty. Yet the varying models of social welfare provision across Europe supply different levels of benefit, some of which arguably fall below the standard that is expected from the state. Many central European countries have historically provided higher state welfare benefits than the UK and they do not have the same industrial relations history which has affected the British perception of occupational pensions provision as being an essentially private matter. This might lead one to suppose that these other countries would have a stronger perception of their pensions systems being essentially public in nature. However, state pension provision across EU countries generally has significantly declined as a result of demographic trends and financial pressures which have forced many countries to reform their state pension systems.[38] Although its state pension system is comparatively small, the UK has enacted a good deal of interventionist legislation affecting the management of occupational pension schemes, following the Maxwell affair in 1991 (which heightened fears of fraudulent misappropriation of funds) and as a result of an increased awareness of the financial problems faced by large schemes.

III. THREE CASES

The point having been made that scholars have characterised pension benefits as a key element of the interaction between the individual and the state, the discussion

[35] S McDaniel, 'Pensions, Privilege and Poverty: Another "Take" on Intergenerational Equity' in J Véron, S Pennec and J Légaré (eds), *Ages, Generations and the Social Contract* (Dordrecht, Springer, 2007) 314.

[36] G Clark, *EU Pension Funds and Global Finance* (Oxford, Oxford University Press, 2003) 1.

[37] E Reynaud, 'Introduction in Summary' in E Raynaud (ed), *Social Dialogue and Pension Reform* (Geneva, International Labour Office, 2000).

[38] C Daykin, *The Challenge of Ageing: Pension Reforms, International Trends and Future Imperatives* (London, Politeia, 2006).

now turns to three cases where disputes relating to occupational schemes have been decided. In cases of this sort, the judiciary is typically asked to consider the application of contract and trust law rules in the light of arguments focused on the parties' legal powers, rights and duties. However, such cases can also have a wider public resonance, as the following studies demonstrate.

A. *Re Courage Group's Pension Schemes*[39]

This case concerned the powers of amendment vested in a company which was the sponsoring employer of three pension schemes but which was taken over by another company following a (hostile) takeover bid. Among other issues, Millett J had to decide whether these powers could be used to substitute a second company as the sponsoring employer. The purpose of this was to enable the second company to access surplus funds in the schemes, while the first company was sold off. This would be achieved by amending the schemes to close them to new entrants and replace the sponsoring employer; the schemes would then be reopened at a later date and the surplus stripped out. The question was whether there were any legal restrictions on the exercise of the powers of amendment which prevented this plan from being implemented.

Re Courage is a fundamental and far-reaching case, which predated the Maxwell affair in 1991 and subsequent investigation by the Pension Law Review Committee and enactment of legislation designed to create a tighter framework within which occupational pension schemes would have to operate.[40] The case shows that the wording of a power of amendment can be crucial to a court's decision whether particular amendments can be made, and that the courts are likely to give effect to specific wording that requires amendments to retain a link to a scheme member's final salary. In *Re Courage* the powers of amendment in two of the three schemes stated that the employer could not 'reduce … the accrued pension of any employed member', with 'accrued pension' being defined in the rules to mean a pension based upon final salary at the relevant date of retirement. The court's decision means that in a pension scheme which contains such a power of amendment and which provides a defined benefit calculated in relation to a final salary, any amendment must retain a final salary link, so that a member's benefit is calculated in reference to their accrued rights at date of closure with reference to their true final salary when they are eligible to take their pension.[41]

An additional issue that Millett J had to decide was whether, on a proper construction of the wording of the powers of amendment in two of the trust deeds, the trustees were obliged to execute certain amending deeds on the employer's say-so in all circumstances, or whether the trustees' consent was required before any

[39] *Re Courage Group's Pension Schemes* [1987] 1 WLR 495 (Ch).

[40] See the Pension Law Review Committee, *Pension Law Reform Volume 1: Report* (Cm 2342, 1993). This Committee was chaired by Professor Roy Goode and its recommendations led to the enactment of the Pensions Act 1995 and the Pensions Act 2004.

[41] *Re Courage* (n 39) 512–13.

such amendment could be validly executed.[42] The wording of the relevant clause was as follows:

> The company may at any time by deed supplemental hereto add to or delete or vary all or any of the provisions of this deed or of the rules and the committee of management shall concur in executing any such supplemental deed provided that no such addition or deletion shall be made which would
>
> (a) have the effect of altering the main purpose of the fund namely the provision of pensions on retirement at a specified age for members.[43]

Millett J did not accept that the trustees had to do what they were told by the employer and held that they retained a discretion whether or not to agree to changes. He declined to hold that the proposed exercise of the power of amendment would be for a proper purpose, as he considered that this could not be said of any exercise that would have the effect of 'altering the main purpose of the scheme'. In Millett J's words, the purpose of the proposed exercise of power was 'foreign to the purpose for which the power to amend the trust deeds and rules is conferred, and invalidates any exercise of that power'.[44] In relation to the substitution of the sponsoring employer, Millett J held on the facts that replacing the sponsoring employer would have been ultra vires and that the power to replace the sponsoring employer could have been validly exercised only if this had been necessary to preserve the scheme for the benefit of those people for whom the scheme was established. This had not been the purpose of substituting the sponsoring employer, which had been to strip out the surplus funds rather than to help the scheme members. In this connection, it was a relevant consideration that the company which was to be made the new sponsoring employer had not employed any of the scheme members and would not have retained any connection with the existing employer after it had been sold.

Millett J's analysis was tightly focused on the interpretation of the scheme documents and the law governing the construction of such documents. It is notable, however, that Millett J showed some awareness of the purpose for which the occupational pension scheme had originally been established. He considered the motivation behind the proposed changes, being to access the surplus funds after sale of the business, rather than to facilitate a restructuring which would continue to provide for the employees. Regarding the proposed substitution, he stated that 'The circumstances must be such that substitution is necessary or at least expedient in order to preserve the scheme for those whose benefit it was established'.[45] One could regard such language as pointing to the social purpose of the scheme, namely the purpose for which it was created, being to provide benefits for the members, along with the additional benefits which that entailed. It is true that Millett J did not explicitly refer to any wider social purpose of the scheme, but still such considerations may have been present in his thinking.

[42] ibid 504.
[43] ibid 503.
[44] ibid 512.
[45] ibid 511.

Regarding the interpretation of pension schemes, Millett J also said that

> [a] pension scheme is established, not for the benefit of a particular company, but for the benefit of those employed in a commercial undertaking; and provision can properly be made for the scheme to continue for their benefit if, on a reconstruction of the group, the undertaking is transferred from one company to another within the group, and remains identifiably the same.[46]

Millett J referred here to cases involving reconstruction where there was an intention to keep a pension scheme on foot; these differed from cases involving a sale, such as the one before him, where there was an intention to wind a pension scheme down and strip out a surplus. However, his reference to a scheme being established for the benefit of the members rather than the company can be read alongside another part of his judgment where he observed that

> there are no special rules of construction applicable to a pension scheme; nevertheless, its provisions should wherever possible be construed to give reasonable and practical effect to the scheme, bearing in mind that it has to be operated against a constantly changing commercial background.[47]

The judgment thus acknowledged the complex business context within which pensions are typically provided. The emphasis placed by Millett J on the practical realities of pensions provision, and on the need to give effect to a scheme's purpose, suggests that there is scope for courts to take wider social objectives into account in addition to the individual economic goals of schemes, when they decide similar issues in the future.

B. *South West Trains Ltd v Wightman*[48]

In this case, Neuberger J had to decide several issues raised by members of the British Rail Pension Scheme. Their complaint concerned the revised calculation of pensionable salary as part of the establishment of a new, industry-wide Railways Pension Scheme following the privatisation of British Rail. During the privatisation, negotiations had taken place between representatives of the employer, SWT, and the railway workers' union, ASLEF. It was agreed that contributions to pensions would be made from a lower amount of salary, and this was recorded in several documents including a letter of information and a ballot paper on which the train drivers could indicate acceptance of the proposals. However, it was not possible to change the rules for the whole scheme to implement these proposals as one of the other employers refused to execute the deed. It was then sought to amend the scheme for the section relating to SWT employees only, but this was met with resistance as a change in the rules would have worsened the position of members, irrespective of what had been agreed during the negotiation phase. The case is well known for the judge's decisions regarding the

[46] ibid 509.
[47] ibid 505.
[48] *South West Trains Ltd v Wightman* [1998] Pens LR 113.

protection of accrued members' rights under the Pensions Act 1995, section 67, and also in relation to the strength of contractual rights which may be claimed following the supply of documentation to members, for example, following a restructuring negotiation process.

Among other things, SWT argued that there was a binding contract between the drivers and SWT, which prevented alternative interpretations of what pensionable salary should be. The drivers had indicated agreement through their responses to a package of documentation sent to them following the negotiations between SWT and ASLEF. In the course of deciding this point, Neuberger J referred to Lord Reid's observation in *Parry v Cleaver* that the 'products of the sums paid into the pension fund are in fact delayed remuneration for [an employee's] current work' and that this is 'why pensions are regarded as earned income'.[49] The judge also referred to Nicholls LJ's comment in *Mihlenstedt v Barclays Bank International Ltd* that the pension scheme in that case was held out by the employer to its staff 'as a valuable part of the staff's overall remuneration package'.[50] From these dicta it followed that questions about pension entitlements were questions about the content of private legal rights which should be decided 'upon the basis of the law, and not on the basis of financial implications'.[51] Nevertheless, the judge also paid regard to the moral and financial realities of the case when reaching his decision, stating that 'the conclusion I have reached accords with the broad merits of the matter as well as with the wider financial realities … [for otherwise] there would have been conferred on the drivers a wholly unintentional windfall'.[52]

While Neuberger J's reasoning was focused on the legal arguments in the case, principles of fairness also formed part of his analysis, and he took account of the broader context of the relationship between employer and employee, in a way that would not have been appropriate had he been concerned with a dispute arising out of a purely private transaction with no broader social relevance. His approach would have been different if, for example, the employee had entered into a prize draw that had been managed incorrectly.

C. *IBM United Kingdom Holdings Ltd v Dalgleish*[53]

The *Dalgleish* case concerned a complex plan to restructure an occupational pension scheme, to achieve which the employer had purported to exercise an unfettered personal discretionary power. A key issue in the case was the application of the rule established by *Imperial Group Pension Trust Ltd v Imperial Tobacco Ltd*,[54] which

[49] *Parry v Cleaver* [1970] AC 1, 16.
[50] *Mihlenstedt v Barclays Bank International Ltd* [1989] Pens LR 91 [78].
[51] *Wightman* (n 48) 133.
[52] ibid 131.
[53] *IBM United Kingdom Holdings Ltd v Dalgleish* [2014] EWHC 980 (Ch), [2014] Pens LR 335; reversed [2017] EWCA Civ 1212, [2018] ICR 1681.
[54] *Imperial Group Pension Trust Ltd v Imperial Tobacco Ltd* [1991] 1 WLR 589, 569 (Ch).

requires the holders of such powers to act in good faith, meaning that the powers must be exercised for a proper purpose and must not be exercised perversely or irrationally. In *Dalgleish*, Warren J held that when determining whether an employer has acted irrationally for the purposes of this rule, the correct test to be applied is the *Wednesbury* test of reasonableness familiar from public law.[55]

Prior to initiating the project which formed the main subject matter of the litigation, IBM had undertaken two earlier projects designed to reduce their pension scheme liabilities. These were Project Ocean in 2004 (which concerned an increase to employee contribution rates) and Project Soto in 2005/2006 (which introduced the option to remain in the defined benefit scheme with benefits calculated at a different, less favourable rate or transfer to a defined contribution scheme). The implementation of both projects had been disputed by scheme members and had only been carried through after protracted negotiations. The main subject of the litigation was a third project, Project Waltz. Among other things, this sought to effectively close the pension scheme to future accrual by excluding members from membership of the defined benefit scheme from a certain date and to alter the early retirement policy. At first instance, Warren J held that IBM's exercise of powers in the course of implementing Project Waltz had entailed a breach of their *Imperial* duty towards the scheme members, because the members had had 'reasonable expectations' regarding IBM's behaviour resulting from the negotiations associated with the first two projects.

On appeal, the Court of Appeal held that Warren J had given too much weight to the 'reasonable expectations' argument and that this had resulted in a misapplication of the *Wednesbury* test to determine whether IBM had acted rationally. The correct approach would rather have been to ask whether the employer's decision was

> so outrageous in its defiance of logic or accepted moral standards that no sensible person who had applied his mind to the question to be decided could have arrived at it, or is it completely lacking in any logical connection between the relevant circumstances and the ostensible reasons for the decision.[56]

The *IBM* decision is complex and contains detailed analysis of many legal arguments. The Court of Appeal's judgment does not include consideration of the nature of pension schemes and is tightly focused on the legal issues raised by Warren J's decision and in particular his interpretation of the *Imperial* duty. Importantly, the Court of Appeal did not accept that the 'reasonable expectations' of the scheme members had as central a role to play when deciding whether this duty had been breached as Warren J considered. Nonetheless, there is scope for future courts to develop this idea, possibly to include within it not only expectations that deferred remuneration for the employee's work will be paid but also expectations that an employer will provide and maintain a pension scheme as part of its social responsibility to contribute to the welfare of its employees and society more generally.

[55] *Named for Associated Provincial Picture Houses Ltd v Wednesbury Corp* [1948] 1 KB 223 (CA).
[56] *Dalgleish* (CA) (n 53) [228].

IV. CONCLUSIONS

A. A Statutory Obligation

A functional definition of an 'occupational pension scheme' appears in the Pension Schemes Act 1993, section 1. This section provides that the expression means

> any scheme or arrangement which is comprised in one or more instruments or agreements and which has, or is capable of having, effect in relation to one or more descriptions or categories of employments so as to provide benefits, in the form of pensions or otherwise, payable on termination of service, or on death or retirement, to or in respect of earners with qualifying service in an employment of any such description or category.

This definition does not say why such schemes are established or why it is socially desirable for them to be supported. If occupational pension schemes have a social purpose, however, then it is worth considering what a statutory definition which addressed these points might look like and whether the enactment of such a definition might make a practical difference.

One approach could be to enact a statutory definition which stated that an employer which establishes a scheme assumes a duty to provide for its employees and a wider range of stakeholders associated with the scheme. Stating the social role of occupational schemes in this way might be accompanied by the imposition of similar duties on employers in other legislative provisions and regulatory guidance which affects the management of pension schemes. If this were thought desirable, then one way forward might be to amend the Companies Act 2006. Like all company directors, the directors of companies which are the sponsoring employers of pension schemes have a duty to act in a way that they consider, in good faith, would promote the success of the company. The legislation contains a list of six non-exhaustive criteria to which directors must pay regard when taking managerial decisions, and these include the interests of employees.[57] Directors were placed under this obligation as part of a statutory move to codify the principle of 'enlightened shareholder value' and to promote corporate social responsibility within directorial decision-making. The legislation makes clear that it is up to directors, and not a matter for the courts, to decide on strategic decision-making in a business, although the directors must act within the limits of their authority and in accordance with the reasons why their powers have been given to them (which is the essence of their duty of good faith).[58] Following from their general duty to act with reasonable skill, care and diligence,[59] however, directors are expected to pay more than 'lip service' to the six factors.[60] And it is suggested that section 172 could be amended to introduce a seventh factor to which directors should be required to pay attention, namely the interests of stakeholders in any occupational pension scheme established by the company, to include not only employees who are active scheme members, but also pensioner and deferred

[57] Companies Act 2006, s 172(1)(a)–(f).
[58] Explanatory Notes to the Companies Act 2006, 325–27.
[59] Companies Act 2006, s 174.
[60] Explanatory Notes (n 58) 328.

members and families of those direct beneficiaries of the scheme who all benefit from its existence.

An amendment to this effect could also be complemented in the guidance issued by the Pensions Regulator. This could take the form of amending the Code of Practice on Funding Defined Benefits,[61] by requiring employers to take note of the social role of their pension scheme. This would require consideration to be paid by employers to the position of scheme members and stakeholders, including but not limited to members who are current employees. Employers should be required to take this into account in consultation with the trustees. Consideration of the social role of a scheme could act as an early warning, to complement the existing Notifiable Events regime, which requires an employer to notify the trustees of any significant activity that may have a detrimental effect on the scheme, such as a change in the employer's credit rating or where a company with control over the employer relinquishes that control, as could happen as part of restructuring of the business, for example.[62]

The introduction of a statutory definition which required consideration by an employer of the social role played by its pension scheme, supported by amendments to the Codes of Practice and associated guidance issued by the Pensions Regulator, would not in itself create enforceable far-reaching binding obligations that could be relied upon in the courts. However, a requirement to consider the social implications that come with managing a pension scheme could improve scheme governance, and enhance the dialogue between employers and trustees. The extent to which it improved the behaviour of employers towards their schemes would depend upon the governance structures of the schemes and the levels of communication which exist between employers, trustees and members.

B. Employee Engagement

Statutory recognition of the social role of pensions and the imposition of duties on an employer to pay due regard to the interests of all the stakeholders of a scheme would align with recent initiatives in the wider field of corporate social responsibility. As Djelic and Etchanchu have described in their review of corporate governance approaches, current thinking about this has been inherited from nineteenth-century concepts of paternalism and twentieth-century ideas about managerial trusteeship.[63] They argue, however, that a more radical adjustment is needed than can be found in the proposals which have so far been made to improve stakeholder representation in corporate decision-making.[64]

[61] The Pensions Regulator, '*Code of Practice No 3: Funding Defined Benefits*' (July 2014), available at: www.tpr.gov.uk/code3.

[62] The Pensions Regulator (Notifiable Events) Regulations 2005 (SI 2005/900) reg 2(2)(e) and (f); see also Pensions Act 2004, s 69; The Pensions Regulator, '*Code of Practice No 2: Notifiable Events*' (April 2005), available at: www.tpr.gov.uk/code2.

[63] M Djelic and H Etchanchu, 'Contextualizing Corporate Political Responsibilities: Neoliberal CSR in Historical Perspective' (2017) 142 *Journal of Business Ethics* 641.

[64] See, eg, D Metten and A Crane, 'What is Stakeholder Democracy? Perspectives and Issues' (2005) 14 *Business Ethics* 6; G Pallazzo and A Sherer, 'Corporate Social Responsibility, Democracy, and the Politicization of the Corporation' (2008) 33 *Academy of Management Review* 733.

When taking decisions that have the potential to affect the stakeholders in occupational pension schemes, trustees and employers must strike a delicate balance between the individual and the communal, between the private and the public elements of the scheme. Obviously, this is hard to get right, but it is suggested that employee engagement with schemes, as well as employer attitudes towards the stewardship of schemes, would be improved if employers were incentivised to see their schemes as fulfilling an essential role in society, and not just another liability on their books in need of ongoing management.

More formal recognition of the social role played by schemes could also help employees understand and engage with amendments to scheme benefit structures as well as encouraging employers to take a more responsible approach to supporting their schemes. Novitz has suggested that there may be scope for a different approach to how pensions issues are considered in the UK courts,[65] arguing for an understanding of labour rights as property rights, which leads her to propose that employees should be able to challenge proposed changes to their pension rights if these breach their human rights to peaceful enjoyment of possessions. One might go further than Novitz, however, and argue that pension benefits are not simply deferred pay supplied in exchange for work done as a matter of private agreement between employers and employees. They are mechanisms for the supply of retirement benefits to very large numbers of people, responsibility for whose support in old age would otherwise fall upon the state. For this reason, occupational pension schemes are afforded special tax treatment and are overseen by regulatory bodies; and for this reason, also, there are strong arguments for the proposition that pension rights, like employment rights, have a public flavour to them.[66]

C. Investment

The consideration of economic, social and corporate governance factors (ESG) in pension fund investment strategy is on the legislative agenda following a report from the Law Commission in 2017,[67] which resulted in the government declaring its intention to amend existing legislation to encourage the consideration of ESG factors by trustees when making pension scheme investment decisions.[68] The government stated that it wished to 'focus on ensuring that current work is capitalised on [and] on identifying, and where appropriate, proposing the removal of longer-term behavioural and legislative barriers'.[69] Established case law emphasises the need for trustees to act

[65] T Novitz, 'Labour Rights and Property Rights: Implications for (and Beyond) Redundancy Payments and Pensions' (2012) 41 *Industrial Law Journal* 136.

[66] As contended in the chapter by Alan Bogg and Mark Freedland in the present volume.

[67] Law Commission, *Pension Funds and Social Investment* (Law Com No 374, 2017).

[68] Occupational Pension Schemes (Investment) Regulations 2005 (SI 2005/3378).

[69] Department for Work & Pensions and the Department for Digital, Culture, Media and Sport, *Pension Funds and Social Investment: The Government's Final Response* (Joint Report in response to Law Comm No 374, June 2018) 11.

in the best financial interests of their beneficiaries,[70] but permits investment decisions to be made by trustees which consider the social impact of their decisions provided that they have 'good reason' to believe that the beneficiaries would share their concern and that the decision would not risk 'significant financial detriment' to the fund.[71] Social investment by pension fund trustees would benefit not only from legislative amendments of the kind which are now being contemplated but would also require a cultural shift in decision-making, requiring the engagement of scheme members and those who are responsible for scheme management. If it were understood by these groups that schemes have a social role that is of equal if not greater importance than their private role, then this could improve long-term decision-making in trustee governance, including decision-making about investment.

D. Final Remarks

It has been argued in this chapter that occupational pension schemes have both a private function of supplying deferred pay to employees and a wider public function of improving the welfare of pensioners and indirectly supporting society as a whole. Occupational pensions have evolved within a legal and political context which has itself developed in a piecemeal way, responding in different ways at different times to changing government policies, which themselves have often been formed as a result of short-term decisions taken in response to political pressures.

It has been suggested that decision-making in pensions cases often focuses on the private relationship between an employer and employee, but could benefit from a formal accepted understanding of the role played by occupational pension schemes in modern society. This role is more public and outward facing than is currently recognised when pensions issues are debated in Parliament and pensions disputes are analysed in the courts. In addition to its economic role, a pension scheme not only supports the worker who has been an active scheme member, but also supports the families of the worker, either directly through spouses' pensions, or indirectly through improving the financial wellbeing of the family through employer contributions. The social element of occupational pensions is becoming increasingly important as a result of automatic enrolment which has caused the number of scheme members to grow – as Brigden and Meyer have argued, one consequence of this has been that UK pensions have entered a more social democratic phase.[72]

The questions of what any formal acknowledgement of the social role of occupational pensions would look like, and the extent to which this could improve the functioning of occupational pension schemes, turn on the extent to which government is prepared to intervene in the private relationship between employers and

[70] *Cowan v Scargill* [1985] Ch 270 (Ch); *Harries v Church Commissioners* [1982] 1 WLR 1241.

[71] As summarised in Law Com No 374 (n 67) para 5.15.

[72] P Brigden and T Meyer, 'Britain: Exhausted Voluntarism – The Evolution of a Hybrid Pension Regime' in B Ebbinghaus (ed), *The Varieties of Pension Governance* (Oxford, Oxford University Press, 2011) 286.

employees. However, it has been suggested that recognising and formalising the social role of a pension scheme would benefit the dialogue between these groups and could help to preserve the wider social benefits of pension scheme membership for future generations. The enhancement of the social side of pensions need not be detrimental to the private interests of scheme members, who would benefit along with other stakeholders in pension schemes if their interdependence were properly recognised. Amending existing legislation and regulatory guidance to acknowledge the social role of occupational pensions therefore has the potential to improve employer and employee relations and to enhance the function of pension schemes in society.

11

Public Law Perspectives on the IBM *Case*

PHILIP SALES*

I. INTRODUCTION

THE *IBM* CASE[1] concerned the reorganisation of the main UK pension schemes for IBM businesses. A simplified account of the facts is as follows. The decision is referred to in order to set the scene for a discussion of the appropriateness and utility of public law analogies in relation to the control of the exercise of discretion in relation to powers to modify pension terms under a relevant contract or trust deed.

Up until 2009 those schemes provided either final salary (defined benefit) or defined contribution benefits. The defined benefit part of the schemes had been closed to new members for years, but they still had about 4,000 employee members. There had been discretionary changes to the schemes to reduce benefits in 2005 (Project Ocean) and 2006 (Project Soto), in relation to which certain assurances had been given to members that there would be no further changes. However, in 2009, under pressure from IBM group, which was seeking to reassure or attract investors by increasing earnings per share (and had given a commitment at group level to achieve this), and from the impact of the 2008 financial crash on asset prices, IBM[2] decided in Project Waltz to close the defined benefit parts of the schemes altogether, except for some employees who were contractually entitled to such benefits. The trustee of the schemes brought proceedings to test the lawfulness of the new proposed changes. In a series of lengthy judgments, Warren J held that the changes were not lawful. The Court of Appeal allowed the appeal by the relevant IBM companies.

* Lord Sales JSC.

[1] *IBM United Kingdom Holdings Ltd v Dalgleish* [2017] EWCA Civ 1212, [2018] ICR 1681.

[2] This is convenient shorthand. Two UK companies in the IBM group were defendants: IBM United Kingdom Holdings Ltd, which had no relevant employees but had duties to fund the schemes, and IBM United Kingdom Ltd, which was the employing company. The latter company owed a contractual duty of trust and confidence to the claimant employees, and both companies owed a similar duty pursuant to the *Imperial Group* case: *Imperial Group Pension Trust Ltd v Imperial Tobacco Ltd* [1991] 1 WLR 589 (Ch).

The principal relevant duty of IBM which was in issue was the implied obligation identified in the *Imperial Group* case,[3] namely that the pension trust deed and rules are taken to be impliedly subject to the limitation that the rights and powers of the sponsoring companies could not be exercised in a manner calculated or likely to destroy or seriously damage the relationship of trust and confidence between employer and employee (in shorthand, the 'duty of good faith').[4] The judge also restated this as a test of irrationality or perversity, in the sense that no reasonable employer could act in the way IBM did.[5] This limited the discretionary power of IBM under the relevant pension scheme instruments to exclude members from benefits in future and its power to consent (or not) to early retirement.

The judge found[6] that assurances had been given in the context of Project Soto which generated what he called 'Reasonable Expectations' on the part of employees in the scheme in relation to future service that benefit accrual according to the Project Soto changes would continue until at least 6 April 2011, subject only to an understanding that a significant change in financial and economic circumstances might permit IBM to make further changes. He also found that assurances had been given in the context of Project Ocean in relation to past service up to the implementation of that project which generated Reasonable Expectations that a member would be able to take advantage of IBM's then current early retirement policy (ie, on generous early retirement terms) until 2014 unless there was a relevant justification for a change in policy.

According to the Court of Appeal's reading of his judgment, Warren J held that these Reasonable Expectations fed into the *Imperial Group* duty such that it was only if IBM could not achieve its commercial objectives and meet its commitment to investors by any means other than by overriding those expectations that it would avoid breach of that duty.[7] IBM was required to act, so far as reasonably possible, consistently with the Reasonable Expectations.[8] By contrast, absent the Reasonable Expectations, there was a sufficient commercial justification for the changes that their adoption would not have breached the duty,[9] save that the changes to the early retirement policy had been introduced with insufficient notice to employees to allow them to have a fair chance to consider how to react to them.[10] He found that the Project Waltz changes in the pension schemes conflicted with the Reasonable Expectations.[11]

The Court of Appeal held that in adopting the approach he did Warren J applied the *Imperial Group* duty incorrectly. The *Imperial Group* duty involved application of the same approach as applies in public law under the *Wednesbury* test,[12] and requires no more than that the discretion will be rationally exercised having regard to all

[3] ibid 596–99.
[4] *IBM v Dalgleish* (n 1) [27]–[29].
[5] ibid [202].
[6] See ibid [64].
[7] ibid [195]–[202].
[8] ibid [224].
[9] ibid [209].
[10] ibid [214].
[11] ibid [206] and [241].
[12] *Associated Provincial Picture Houses Ltd v Wednesbury Corp* [1948] 1 KB 223 (CA).

the circumstances relevant at the time of the decision.[13] That indeed was common ground.[14] The test identified by the Court of Appeal was the conventional public law rationality test:

> [W]as the decision by IBM so outrageous in its defiance of logic or accepted moral standards that no sensible person who had applied his mind to the question to be decided could have arrived at it, or is it completely lacking in any logical connection between the relevant circumstances and the ostensible reasons for the decision?[15]

Relevant factors had to be taken into account and irrelevant factors had to be left out of account; but it was not argued that any relevant factors had been ignored nor that any irrelevant factors had been taken into account.[16] The reasonable expectations said to have been generated by IBM in the course of Project Ocean and Project Soto were relevant considerations to be taken into account, but were not to be treated as having overriding significance as compared with other relevant factors.[17] Since the judge had erred in his approach, his judgment was set aside.

The Court of Appeal then itself applied the *Wednesbury* test. It held that IBM had not acted irrationally. IBM had had legitimate commercial reasons for wishing to implement the Project Waltz changes to the pension scheme. At a later point in the judgment, the Court said that IBM was entitled to have regard to adverse trading conditions in which it found itself after the financial crash in 2008[18] and emphasised that the Court should not assess the wisdom of IBM's decision to implement Project Waltz, in the exercise of IBM's commercial judgment, with the benefit of hindsight.[19]

The Court of Appeal identified a further error by the judge. He had found that the Reasonable Expectations were subject to the qualification that they could be departed from in the event of 'a significant change in financial and economic circumstances';[20] but he failed to consider whether the impact of the financial crash in 2008 constituted such a change;[21] and for reasons to do with the burden of proof on the claimants, the judge should have found that they had failed to establish the absence of a relevant significant change.[22]

The judge found that, based on the practice of IBM, employees had a Reasonable Expectation as to the availability of early retirement under the pension scheme in 2004, and that it could well give rise to a breach of the *Imperial Group* duty to

[13] *IBM v Dalgleish* (n 1) [226]–[229].

[14] ibid [218]–[219].

[15] ibid [228]; also [232].

[16] ibid [232]. If the *Wednesbury* approach is the correct one, it may not be so easy to avoid argument about which factors are relevant or irrelevant in other cases. In public law, what counts as a relevant factor depends on interpretation of the applicable statute. A factor may be a mandatory relevant factor, to which the decision-maker must have regard; a mandatory irrelevant factor, to which it must not have regard; or an optional relevant factor, to which the decision-maker may or may not have regard, according to its choice: *R (Corner House Research) v Director of the Serious Fraud Office* [2008] UKHL 60, [2009] 1 AC 756 [40] (Lord Bingham).

[17] *IBM v Dalgleish* (n 1) [229].

[18] ibid [336].

[19] ibid [339].

[20] ibid [235].

[21] ibid [246].

[22] ibid [247].

change that practice with only a month's warning in relation to a 58-year-old man with 20 years' pensionable service, though not in relation to a 35-year-old man with only 4 years' service.[23] However, the Court of Appeal held that this expectation was simply the result of adoption of a policy by IBM, which could be changed at any time.[24] If an expectation generated by things said by IBM was to be treated as having a determinate effect, the Court of Appeal considered that 'there is much to be said for IBM's proposition that the standards ought to be equivalent to what is required for a contract or an estoppel', in terms of standards of clarity and certainty.[25]

II. ANALYSIS

The *IBM* case proceeded on the basis of an assumption by the parties and the courts that the relevant legal framework for assessment of the lawfulness of the exercise of discretion by IBM was akin to what would be expected in public law, if IBM had been a public authority, and in particular according to the test of *Wednesbury* rationality. No doubt this reflected a trend in modern cases to say that the exercise of discretionary contractual powers must not be arbitrary, irrational or capricious.[26] However, the assumption seems questionable.[27]

The claimant scheme members also seem to have adopted an approach redolent of the public law doctrine of legitimate expectations (although under the rubric of 'Reasonable Expectations'). Warren J's analysis at first instance seems to have followed such an approach, in that he treated the Reasonable Expectations generated by IBM in its statements in connection with Project Soto and Project Ocean as having determinative effect, unless IBM was able to show that it had no practical means available to it to allow it to meet its commercial objectives in terms of securing returns to shareholders without defeating those expectations. The Court of Appeal was less impressed with this. Its observation that assurances sufficient to generate contractual obligations or an estoppel in private law would be required if IBM was to be bound in this way is significant.

I will address the application of the public law rationality test and the relevance of a public law legitimate expectations analogy in turn below. Although the relevant discretion in the *IBM* case arose in part under a pension trust instrument, it was in the context of a reciprocal relationship between employer and employees, corresponding to that between scheme trustee and scheme members. It is therefore appropriate to analyse it as a contractual discretionary power.

[23] ibid [250]–[251].

[24] ibid [258]–[259].

[25] ibid [269].

[26] See, eg, *Socimer International Bank Ltd v Standard Charters Bank Ltd* [2008] EWCA Civ 116, [2008] Bus LR 1304; *Braganza v BP Shipping Ltd* [2015] UKSC 17, [2015] 1 WLR 1661. C Himsworth, 'Transplanting Irrationality from Public to Private law: *Braganza v BP Shipping Ltd*' (2019) 23 *Edinburgh Law Review* 1.

[27] Compare J Morgan, 'Against Judicial Review of Discretionary Contractual Powers' [2008] *LMCLQ* 230; M Bridge, 'The Exercise of Contractual Discretion' (2019) 135 *LQR* 227.

A. Public Law Rationality

There is a superficial similarity between contractual discretions and discretions in public law (which are typically conferred by statute). Where a discretion is conferred by statute, it is because Parliament wishes to ensure that the decision-maker should have flexibility to modify the way in which its power is exercised in the light of changing circumstances and as more information comes to hand. Conferring a discretion is a legal technique to make law in the present which is capable of allowing adaptation for an uncertain future. The same is true where a contract or trust instrument confers a discretion on a decision-maker. This is particularly the case in the context of a pension scheme, in which a fund has to be administered over a long period of time in order to deliver benefits far into the future. The application of the *Imperial Group* duty and the employer's duty of trust and confidence in conjunction with such a discretion is a way of giving content to limitations on the way in which the discretion can lawfully be exercised, as examined further below.

However, there is a fundamental difference of context between contractual discretionary powers and public law discretionary powers. To speak of a standard of rationality governing the exercise of discretion presupposes that a relevant context can be specified. Rationality does not exist in a vacuum, but in relation to purposes which are being pursued in the context of a particular relationship. The context for the assessment of rationality in the exercise of public law powers is materially different from the context for the exercise of discretionary powers in contract.

Public law powers are conferred in particular statutory contexts for the purpose of promoting the public good. Although that is a flexible and vague concept, open to a good deal of argument, it does provide a basic orientation for the purposes of analysis whether a public authority has acted rationally or not; in particular, it does at least indicate that a public authority may not pursue its own self-interest (in any simple sense of that concept) when exercising discretion.

But that outward directed orientation is precisely what is missing in the context of most contractual relationships. Where the power in question is not fiduciary in nature (in the sense that the donee of the power is not entitled to have any regard at all to its own self-interest when deciding what to do), it is implicit that the donee *may* have regard to its self-interest.[28] IBM was entitled to do so in this case. The core difficulty in articulating rules to constrain the exercise of a contractual discretion is that typically the party exercising that discretion is entitled to have regard to its own self-interest; and, what is more, in the context of what may often be a zero-sum situation vis-a-vis the other party. In such a context, it cannot be said that the party exercising the discretion acts irrationally when it decides to act for self-interested reasons.

[28] It should be noted that the *Braganza* case (n 26) was not about a contractual discretion in the pure sense, but about the circumstances in which an employer was entitled to make a particular finding of fact (whether the employee had committed suicide or not) which was relevant to provision of death in service benefits to his dependants. Given the specific object to which the contractual power was directed, it was relatively easy to derive a rationality standard from the contract itself. In light of the fact-finding task to be performed by the employer, it was not entitled to have regard to and act on the basis of its self-interest.

Further, according to the so-called principle of legality the interpretation of statutory powers is informed by long-standing constitutional principles with a life of their own, which reflect values which exist outside any particular statute and inform its interpretation, and hence inform the context in which any assessment of the rationality of action must be made.[29] By contrast, in a trust or contract situation, by reason of the basic principles of freedom of contract and freedom in the disposition of property there are few significant external background norms or values to inform the interpretation of the contract or the context in which assessment of the lawfulness of the exercise of discretion takes place. Business common sense plays a limited role.[30]

More important in the context of the *IBM* case is the *Imperial Group* duty and the employer's duty of good faith and confidence; but these beg the question of what IBM was entitled to do when acting having regard to its own self-interest, without going so far as to be taken to breach those duties. Unlike in the public law context, the parties themselves generate the values which are to apply, as something inherent in the contract they have made.

For these reasons, I think there is something unsatisfactory and unsatisfying about the reasoning of the courts in the *IBM* case in relation to the rationality test. When the courts say that contractual discretions may not be exercised arbitrarily or irrationally, it makes more sense to take them to be driving at the basic point that such discretions are not intended by the parties to create a situation in which one party is utterly at the mercy of the other in any zero-sum situation which may arise between them in the future. Rather, the parties stipulate for such powers with the intention that they should be a mechanism to adjust for uncertain future events within the framework of the ongoing legal relationship which the parties have created for themselves.[31] In place of a non-contextualised, free-floating idea of rationality, this suggests two legal techniques for assessing the lawfulness of exercise of a contractual discretionary power: (i) whether the exercise is for a proper purpose, the range of proper purposes being derived from interpreting the agreement itself in its business context;[32] and (ii) whether it is of a character likely to undermine the relationship of trust and confidence between employer and employees (the *Imperial Group* duty).

The *Imperial Group* duty is a term implied in law. It can be seen as a somewhat more intensive extension of technique (i), in recognition of the fact that the more a rule creating a discretion is supposed to extend into the future, the less the parties are able to contemplate clearly the precise situations in which it will be applied; and

[29] P Sales, 'A Comparison of the Principle of Legality and Section 3 of the Human Rights Act 1998' (2009) 125 *LQR* 598.

[30] eg, business common sense or common expectations in the context of particular relationships may play a role, but in a much weaker way than under the principle of legality: *L Schuler AG v Wickman Machine Tool Sales Ltd* [1974] AC 235 (HL).

[31] See *Re Courage Group's Pension Schemes* [1987] 1 WLR 495 (Ch) 505 (Millett J): '[the scheme's] provisions should wherever possible be construed so as to give reasonable and practical effect to the scheme, bearing in mind that it has to be operated against a constantly changing commercial background. It is important to avoid unduly fettering the power to amend the provisions of the scheme, thereby preventing the parties from making those changes which may be required by the exigencies of commercial life'.

[32] See *Bank of New Zealand v Bank of New Zealand Officers Provident Association Management Board* [2003] UKPC 58, [2003] OPLR 281 [19]–[22].

the more it is obvious they are conscious of that position, the more readily can it be inferred that they intended (and policy justifications exist to support) a standard of equity or fairness to govern the discretion at the time it is exercised. In a pensions context, the time over which the legal regime is intended to last may be very long indeed. A term like this operates much like Equity does in relation to hard rules of the common law, to smooth out what might otherwise be scope for one party to take opportunistic advantage in relation to the other by strict enforcement of what appear to be its rights, but in a context not within the contemplation of the parties when the contract/trust relationship was created.[33] But again, it is necessary to have some method to identify the standard of fair treatment which is to be applied.

It is submitted that a better conception for technique (i) is that a discretionary power is created for a particular purpose or purposes and must be used within the scope of such purpose.[34] This conception is in fact widely used: see the notion of so-called 'fraud on a power' in equity;[35] limits on use of a power to change the articles of association of a company[36] or similar organisation;[37] limits on the use of a power to modify rights under the articles of an insurance society;[38] limits on the use of a power to modify rights under loan notes;[39] and other parallels in contract law, such as the limits identified on exercise of discretionary powers in relation to a 10-year agreement to base and operate aircraft at a particular airport.[40]

As Dixon J put it in the *Peters' American Delicacy* case:

> The chief reason for denying an unlimited effect to widely expressed powers such as that of altering a company's articles is the fear or knowledge that an apparently regular exercise of the power may in truth be but a means of securing some personal or particular gain,

[33] Thus the duty can, like equity, be viewed as a form of the Aristotelian concept of *epieikeia* (usually translated as equity), based on the idea that it is intrinsically difficult to predict when a rule is made all the situations in which it will fall to be applied, so that some supervening rule of fair application going beyond the strict terms of the rule itself is required, to ensure its actual application conforms to the underlying rationale for the rule and a concept of fairness between the parties.

[34] One could, I suppose, say that identification of the relevant purpose of a contractual or trust power supplies a sufficiently determinate context in which a rationality standard might then be applied. But it seems unnecessary to treat rationality as a super-added element in the analysis in this way: it is easier and clearer simply to analyse the position by reference to the purposes for which the power may legitimately be used, as derived from the interpretation of the contract or trust instrument.

[35] In particular, as explained in *Vatcher v Paull* [1915] AC 372 (PC) 378; *Howard Smith v Ampol Petroleum* [1974] AC 821 (PC); *Eclairs Group Ltd v JKX Oil & Gas Plc* [2015] UKSC 71, [2016] 3 All ER 641; P Sales, 'Use of Powers for Proper Purposes in Private Law' (2020) 136 *LQR* (forthcoming): I argue there that this doctrine is better seen as an aspect of interpretation of contracts and trusts, rather than as a distinct legal principle.

[36] *Allen v Gold Reefs of West Africa Ltd* [1900] 1 Ch 656 (CA); *Greenhalgh v Arderne Cinemas Ltd* [1951] Ch 286 (CA): the majority must exercise the power bona fide in the interests of the company as a whole. Also see *Peters' American Delicacy Co Ltd v Heath* [1939] HCA 2, (1939) 61 CLR 457, 511–13 (Dixon J).

[37] *Hole v Garnsey* [1930] AC 472 (HL).

[38] *Equitable Life Assurance Society v Hyman* [2002] 1 AC 408 (HL). The House of Lords in that case was prepared to use a different public law analogy: *Padfield v Ministry of Agriculture, Fisheries and Food* [1968] AC 997 (HL), which was concerned with the use of public law discretionary power for proper purposes.

[39] *Redwood Master Fund Ltd v TD Bank Europe Ltd* [2002] EWHC 2703 (Ch), [2006] 1 BCLC 149, [99]–[104].

[40] *Durham Tees Valley Airport v BMIBaby Ltd* [2010] EWCA Civ 485, [2011] 1 All ER (Comm) 731.

> whether pecuniary or otherwise, which does not fairly arise out of the subjects dealt with by the power and is outside and even inconsistent with the contemplated objects of the power.[41]

The identification of the relevant purpose can take account of the legitimacy of the donee of the discretion having regard to its own self-interest in exercising the discretion. Unless the instrument specifies that the discretionary power is to be exercised reasonably, the ambit within which the donee may lawfully use it should be within wider parameters given by what is in the contemplation of the parties at the time they enter into the agreement or relevant relationship (for instance, when individuals join the pension scheme). In a reciprocal relationship, this reflects a basic conception of loyalty to the joint endeavour on which the parties have embarked.[42] A certain level of uncertainty in applying this standard merely reflects that it is impossible accurately to predict the future in a long-term relationship – which is the very reason the parties have chosen to provide for a discretion, to allow for adjustment to future events within the framework of a continuing relationship between them; while at the same time, it cannot be supposed that they intended that the counterparty should be completely at the mercy of the donee of the discretionary power, with the donee having complete freedom to act purely in its own interests without any regard to the interests of the counterparty.

In the *BMI Baby* case, for example, the Court of Appeal cited Lord Wright's dictum in *Hillas & Co Ltd v Arcos Ltd*[43] that 'in contracts for future performance over a period the parties may neither be able nor desire to specify many matters of detail, but leave them to be adjusted in the working out of the contract', and held that the absence of a minimum performance obligation in the contract for use of the airport was not fatal to its enforceability, since although the number of flights and destinations would be within the airline's commercial discretion, that would be subject to clear instances of non-performance such as token flights or a complete absence of flights, and damages could be worked out by reference to proof of how the airline would have been likely to operate the contract in order to generate profits for itself.[44]

Similarly, whether particular action is likely to be in breach of the *Imperial Group* duty should reflect whether it is within the contemplation of the parties as a legitimate thing for the donee of the power under the pension scheme to do. If it was within the contemplation of the parties that the donee of the power would be entitled to have regard to its own commercial interests in deciding what to do, there will not be a breach of duty when it does that.[45] That is effectively what the Court of Appeal

[41] *Peters'* (n 36) 511. Also see *Bank of New Zealand* (n 32) [19]–[22].

[42] *cf Mackay v Dick* (1880–81) LR 6 App Cas 251.

[43] *Hillas & Co Ltd v Arcos Ltd* (1932) 147 LT 503.

[44] *BMIBaby* (n 40) [60]; see also [69] and [79].

[45] *cf F & C Alternative Investments (Holdings) Ltd v Barthelemy* [2011] EWHC 1731 (Ch), [2012] Ch 613 [221]–[254] (discussion of modified fiduciary duties in relation to the management of a joint venture vehicle specifically set up to allow each manager to have regard to his own self-interest as co-owner as well as requiring due consideration for the interests of other co-owners); and see the discussion in Lord Sales, 'The Interface between Contract and Equity' (Lehane Memorial Lecture, Sydney, 28 August 2019), available at: www.supremecourt.uk/docs/speech-190828.pdf.

decided in the *IBM* case, but using the opaque concept of what constituted rational or irrational behaviour on the part of IBM. On the other hand, if IBM had used its discretionary power to curtail benefits out of spite, or to punish employees for lawful behaviour which the company did not like, that would be outside the scope of what the parties would have contemplated would be a legitimate purpose for which the power could be used.

In the context of the IBM scheme, it seems fair to say that it must have been in the contemplation of IBM and scheme members that IBM could make decisions regarding its contributions (and hence regarding pay-outs and benefits under the scheme) with reference to IBM's own financial position and current market circumstances. The changes it introduced by Project Waltz did not remove any already vested (or 'earned') rights, but only the possibility of acquiring more rights under the scheme in the future. Accordingly, the decision of the Court of Appeal seems right, though for different reasons from those it gave. If, on the other hand, Project Waltz had purported to remove vested rights, it seems likely that this would have been beyond the scope of what the parties contemplated IBM should be able to do and would have been an unlawful use of the discretionary power.[46]

What the *Imperial Group* duty may add in terms of affecting the way in which the discretionary power might be used by the pension provider is a requirement that before exercising the power within its proper parameters, it should take into account as a relevant factor any Reasonable Expectation which the provider may have created on the part of scheme members by assurances or representations it has made in the past. Arguably, it would undermine the duty of trust and confidence to ignore expectations of scheme members generated in that manner.[47] But expressed in that way, the obligation would provide a relatively low level of protection for scheme members. At the time of exercising the power, there would be compliance with the duty if due consideration was given to the position of scheme members, without IBM being obliged to honour previous assurances or indications as to how it would behave, provided it had some legitimate commercial reason of its own for departing from them. If IBM has a legitimate commercial interest, the existence of the discretionary power is intended to allow IBM to act to protect that interest (see above); and, assuming there is no estoppel or contract, it retains that power and it is not for the court to substitute its view as to how it should be exercised.

It may be, however, that the *Imperial Group* duty would extend to an obligation to give scheme members information promptly about the changes in benefits under the scheme[48] and possibly also an opportunity to make representations before any decision is made to defeat their Reasonable Expectations. The *Imperial Group* duty has been imported into occupational pension schemes by analogy with the duty of trust and confidence in the employment contract. The practical implications of the

[46] The point I am making here is a contractual one. Now, of course, there is a statutory provision to the same effect: s 67 of the Pensions Act 1995.

[47] *cf* again *F & C Alternative Investments (Holdings) Ltd v Barthelemy* (n 45).

[48] *cf Scally v Southern Health and Social Services Board* [1992] 1 AC 294 (HL).

latter duty have been explored more fully in the case law. It has various dimensions which may serve to inform the practical content to be given to the *Imperial Group* duty.[49] In fact, this may offer a better way for employee claimants to frame their claim in pensions cases than by trying to use public law analogies based on the concepts of rationality and legitimate expectations. Owing to the doctrinal limitations to which the public law concepts are subject, it may often be easier for an employer to say it has complied with a duty framed by reference to such concepts than if the *Imperial Group* duty is framed more directly by reference to the various dimensions of the employer's duty of trust and confidence. The *IBM* decision by the Court of Appeal tends to illustrate the danger. There is thus a risk that recourse to public law analogies could actually undermine employee/pensioner protection.

A more problematic case would arise if, by mistake[50] or oversight, IBM failed to appreciate that scheme members had Reasonable Expectations to which IBM should have had regard when it acted. Breach of the obligation might only be identified some years after it occurred, rather than being a point of current controversy (capable of being resolved by court proceedings) at the time of exercise of the discretionary power. However, it seems that a suitable remedy for such a breach of duty would be to assess how IBM would in fact have acted if it had fulfilled its duty and to award damages for any loss so identified.[51]

Where the *Imperial Group* duty may also have a significant additional role to play is in importing some limited substantive protection for scheme members in employment. If detrimental changes are to be introduced in terms of scheme benefits, should a reasonable period of notice be given to allow scheme members to adjust their position? That might be said to be an obligation analogous to the requirement for a notice period to end employment, so that the employee has an opportunity to find alternative employment should they wish to do so, now that the benefits to be accrued from working for IBM are no longer so attractive. The Court of Appeal's brief discussion of the possible obligation of IBM to give fair notice to long-term scheme members before the changes took effect, so they could take advice and decide what to do, seems to be a gesture in this sort of direction.

[49] In his review in A Bogg, 'Good Faith in the Contract of Employment: A Case of the English Reserve' (2011) 32 *Comparative Labor Law & Policy Journal* 729, Alan Bogg identifies five strands in the case law: (i) control of employer's discretionary powers, eg, *Gogay v Hertfordshire CC* [2000] IRLR 703 (CA), *TFS Derivatives Ltd v Morgan* [2004] EWHC 3181 (QB), [2005] IRLR 246, *Land Securities Trillium Ltd v Thornley* [2005] UKEAT 0603_04_2006, [2005] IRLR 765 – exercise of suspension, garden leave and flexibility clauses; (ii) concern to ensure consistent treatment of workers – *Transco Plc v O'Brien* [2002] EWCA Civ 379, [2002] ICR 721; (iii) disclosure to workers or prior consultation in advance of decisions which directly affect them – *Visa International v Paul* [2003] UKEAT 0097_02_2005, [2004] IRLR 42, *McBride v Falkirk Football & Athletic Club* [2011] UKEAT 0058_10_1706, [2012] IRLR 22; (iv) protection of certain reasonable expectations – *French v Barclays Bank plc* [1998] IRLR 646 (CA); (v) reasonable notice in certain contexts, eg, when an employer invokes a mobility clause to require relocation – *United Bank v Akhtar* [1989] IRLR 507 (EAT).

[50] eg, IBM thinks that what it said gave rise to no Reasonable Expectations on the facts, but the court concludes otherwise.

[51] *cf Lion Nathan Ltd v CC Bottlers Ltd* [1996] 1 WLR 1438 (PC).

B. Reasonable Expectations/Legitimate Expectations in Public Law

A brief sketch of the public law doctrine of legitimate expectations follows. To found an enforceable legitimate expectation, usually a promise or assurance by the decision-maker is required which is 'clear, unambiguous and devoid of relevant qualification'.[52] The expectation is derived from whatever is the policy or assurance in place at the time a relevant decision is taken.[53] A legitimate expectation may be overridden if there is a competing public interest at the time of decision and it is proportionate to defeat the expectation.[54]

There is also scope for a decision-maker to decline to apply a policy which covers an individual case. This arises by reason of the rule that a public authority is not entitled to fetter its discretion: it is obliged to keep open the possibility of not applying that policy in any particular case if the specific circumstances of that case warrant the disapplication of the policy in relation to it.[55] Thus, an individual who would suffer from the application of the policy in his case is entitled to contend that the policy should not be applied to him, and the public authority has to consider that contention on its merits. Conversely, since the public authority may not fetter its public law obligation to consider how it should exercise its discretion in the public interest, it may disapply a policy which favours an individual by having regard to the particular circumstances of that individual's case, even though the policy itself remains unchanged, provided the authority acts fairly (by giving the individual an opportunity to make representations) and rationally in doing so.[56]

There is a distinction between substantive legitimate expectations (a promise that a discretion will be exercised in a particular way)[57] and procedural legitimate expectations (a promise that a particular procedure will be followed before a decision is made as to how to exercise a discretion).[58] The existence and enforcement of a substantive legitimate expectation involves the court, in effect, stepping in as decision-maker to dictate a particular result in a field which, *ex hypothesi*, is covered by discretion, and in circumstances where the designated decision-maker on further reflection (after initially giving an assurance) thinks the best solution is to depart from the assurance. Strong reasons are required to justify this encroachment on the decision-maker's function.

By contrast, where all that is to be enforced is a legitimate expectation as to the procedure to be followed before a substantive decision is made, there is much less

[52] *R v Inland Revenue Comrs, ex p MFK Underwriting Agents Ltd* [1990] 1 WLR 1545, 1569 (Bingham LJ) (CA); *R (Gaines-Cooper) v Inland Revenue Comrs* [2011] UKSC 47, [2011] 1 WLR 2625 [28]–[29].

[53] *Re Findlay* [1985] AC 381 (HL).

[54] *Nadarajah v Secretary of State for the Home Department* [2005] EWCA Civ 1363.

[55] See, eg, *British Oxygen Co Ltd v Board of Trade* [1971] AC 610 (HL).

[56] See, eg, *R (Mullen) v Secretary of State for the Home Department* [2004] UKHL 18, [2005] 1 AC 1 [58]–[62].

[57] *R v North and East Devon Health Authority, ex p Coughlan* [2001] QB 213 (CA). It is sometimes said that a substantive legitimate expectation only arises in relation to assurances given to a small group of people, but it is doubtful whether it is easy so to limit the principle.

[58] *AG of Hong Kong v Ng Yuen Shiu* [1983] 2 AC 629 (PC).

intrusion into the sphere of substantive judgement for which the public authority has been designated as decision-maker; moreover, the court is much closer to its proper constitutional role to ensure that decisions are taken fairly, where it is the judge of fairness. If the public authority has itself stated that, say, it will consult before deciding, then it is relatively easy for the court to say that this can be regarded as fair and that this represents a reasonable (and not excessively burdensome) standard of procedural justice, since the public authority had itself selected it. Also, it can be said that there is positive value in holding a public authority to its promise regarding such a procedure (which does not intrude substantially on its ultimate substantive decision), so as to foster public confidence in the administration, unless some good overriding reason can be shown to depart from it.

Mindful of the tension between an assurance which has been given and its impact on the use of limited resources in the overall public interest, the courts sometimes seek to give a substantive legitimate expectation only a procedural effect: ie, where there has been a promise of a substantive advantage, the expectation may be satisfied if the authority is made to consider whether to honour it, but is allowed to weigh it against other public interest factors.[59]

There are two distinct strands in the law that have until recently been gathered under the rubric of legitimate expectations: (i) clear assurances given to a group on which they can be expected to rely and on which they have relied to their detriment; and (ii) clear policy statements (whether known to the claimant or not, and including policies which are internal to a public authority) which, on grounds of consistency and non-capricious decision-making, a public authority can be expected to adhere to, absent good reason not to do so.

As to (i), as observed by Peter Gibson LJ in *R v Secretary of State for Education, ex p Begbie*:[60]

> [I]t would be wrong to understate the significance of reliance in this area of the law. It is very much the exception, rather than the rule, that detrimental reliance will not be present when the court finds unfairness in the defeating of a legitimate expectation.[61]

There is an effort under way to disaggregate (i) and (ii), which is helpful, because the issues which arise and the balance of fairness are rather different in the two cases: see now, in particular, *Mandalia v Secretary of State for the Home Department*,[62] where (ii) is described as not really being a case of legitimate expectations at all. This is really more of a semantic point. It is true that case (ii) is not the same as case (i), but it still seems that one could fairly describe case (ii) as involving legitimate expectations, in the sense that, as a member of the public, anyone might legitimately expect that a public authority will comply with its stated policy commitments (which may be known to that person at the time, or only learned about later on). What could be said

[59] *R (Bibi) v Newham BC* [2001] EWCA Civ 607, [2002] 1 WLR 237 is a good example of this.

[60] *R v Secretary of State for Education, ex p Begbie* [2000] 1 WLR 1115, 1124B–C.

[61] For the significance of detrimental reliance, see also 1126H–1127D (Peter Gibson LJ), 1131F–G (Laws LJ) and 1133F–H (Sedley LJ); *ex p MFK Underwriting Agents Ltd* (n 52) 1569H (Bingham LJ); and *R (Bamber) v HMRC* [2005] EWHC 3221 (Admin), [2006] STC 1035 [56], [59] and [72]–[73] (Lindsay J).

[62] *Mandalia v Secretary of State for the Home Department* [2015] UKSC 59, [2015] 1 WLR 4546 [29]–[31].

to unite (i) and (ii) is an underlying consideration that ordinarily public authorities should abide by what they have promised to do, unless there is good reason why not. However, what is a sufficient good reason to depart from an assurance will be affected by the nature of the legitimate expectation in issue (ie, is it procedural or substantive?) and the extent to which by doing so the authority will in fact inflict harm on an individual if there has been detrimental reliance.

Warren J in the *IBM* case identified from things said by IBM in relation to Project Ocean and Project Soto a set of Reasonable Expectations on the part of scheme members as regards the rate at which in future they would accrue rights under the pension scheme and what future benefits (in particular, in relation to early retirement) would be available under the scheme. Where the implementation of Project Waltz involved departing from these assurances, the judge treated IBM as being under a special, heightened form of obligation to justify that departure. He reversed the sort of *Imperial Group* analysis proposed above: IBM had to show that its commercial options were so limited that it was forced to defeat the expectations. In the judge's formulation, the assurances were subject to an implicit qualification that a significant change in financial and economic circumstances would allow IBM to depart from them.

This seems to have been an analysis similar to that for legitimate expectations in public law. The implicit qualification resembles the way in which legitimate expectations in public law are capable of being overridden where the public interest justifies that.[63]

I suggest that the Court of Appeal was right to reject this public law infused approach. There is a mismatch between the operation of the *Imperial Group* duty in this sort of case and the law governing the doctrine of legitimate expectations in public law. There are three basic differences between the two contexts, all deriving from the orientation of public law duties to promote the public interest. That orientation is missing in private law.

First, one justification for the public law on legitimate expectations is that it is right to hold government and other public bodies to (non-contractual) promises they have made, all other things being equal, in the interests of good government and securing public confidence therein.[64] This consideration does not apply in the private context. Private rights should be governed by relevant concepts of private law: in particular, contract and estoppel.

Second, the doctrine of legitimate expectations has significant flexibility built into it. Even where there has been detrimental reliance by a person who learned of the assurance in question, their interests can be overridden if there is a sufficient public interest in doing so. For this reason, the House of Lords has emphasised that the doctrine of legitimate expectations and the private law of estoppel should be

[63] Although treating the qualification as implicit in the assurance itself would, in public law analysis, bring into question whether the assurance given was sufficiently clear and unambiguous.

[64] See *Mandalia* (n 62). See also T. Endicott, "The Public Trust", in E. Griddle et al. (eds.) Fiduciary Government (Cambridge; Cambridge University Press, 2018), 306–330.

kept distinct.[65] Similarly, in the context of unfair prejudice petitions in company law, it has been emphasised that it is not appropriate to try to transplant the public law concept of legitimate expectations in place of private law equitable standards traditionally found to be applicable to govern the relationship between the parties.[66]

Third, there are important differences in the remedies available in public law and in private law. The typical remedy for breach of public law, including breach of legitimate expectation, is to make the public authority reconsider the matter on a proper basis and decide again. Absent the application of human rights provisions, compensation is not available. By contrast, if there is a breach of obligation in private law the remedial response is not to quash the decision and require it to be reconsidered, but to treat it as a completed act in respect of which compensation may be payable. Given the powerful substantive effect of a breach of duty in private law, there appears to be no sound basis for weakening the criteria according to which a relevant private law duty can be identified in respect of substantive outcomes such as promised by IBM, namely by finding a binding contract to provide such outcomes or a relevant estoppel.

In public law, the doctrine of legitimate expectations is a way of combining a degree of stability and predictability for citizens with continuing discretion for public authorities which allows them to react to future events with reference to the public interest as it appears then. In the pensions context, the *Imperial Group* duty achieves a balance between a degree of stability and predictability for employees/pensioners and a continuing discretion for the employer to have regard to its own interests according to developing circumstances. At a high level of abstraction, there is a certain similarity between what legal doctrine seeks to achieve (ie, a balance between predictability and continuing discretion), but the practical reality is that the contexts are very different, as are the relevant elements being introduced into the balance. As outlined above, the employer's duty to maintain trust and confidence provides the better analogy for occupational pensions, not public law.

[65] *R v East Sussex CC, ex p Reprotech (Pebsham) Ltd* [2002] UKHL 8, [2003] 1 WLR 348 [34]–[35] (Lord Hoffmann).

[66] *O'Neill v Phillips* [1999] 1 WLR 1092, 1102 (Lord Hoffmann) ('The concept of a legitimate expectation should not be allowed to lead a life of its own, capable of giving rise to equitable restraints in circumstances to which the traditional equitable principles have no application').

12

Pensions Law, IBM v Dalgleish *and the Public/Private Divide*

ALAN BOGG AND MARK FREEDLAND*

I. INTRODUCTION

IN 2003 GORDON L Clark and Noel Whiteside published a volume entitled *Pension Security in the 21st Century*.[1] At the end of the second decade of this century, the main themes identified in that work have become more troubling and urgent. The authors frame their analysis around the shifting balance between the 'private' and 'public' in delivering 'security' in pension provision. A range of institutional, fiscal and demographic pressures have precipitated important shifts in the balance between 'private' and 'public' provision of pension security for workers. This has been reflected in a greater recourse to privatised provision through market mechanisms, based on 'rational choice' models of individualised decision-making.[2] As the authors astutely recognise, the basic binary distinction between 'public' and 'private' is a misleading dichotomy. Instead,

> underpinning prevailing notions of private pension provision lie a myriad of different systems encompassing individual and collective provision and public and private administration and management. Such variations on the theme of public–private partnership demonstrate the panoply of arrangements that are possible.[3]

From time to time, a judicial decision is handed down that encapsulates the general anxieties of the time in a specific dispute. We suggest that the themes of 'security' and the 'public/private divide' are central to the leading case of *IBM v Dalgleish*.[4]

* We are grateful to Michael Ford QC and Dan Schaffer for comments on an earlier draft. We acknowledge Lord Sales' vigorous but generous engagement with our arguments in the panel discussion at which they were presented. Professor Bogg records his gratitude to the Leverhulme Trust for its generous support of his work.

[1] GL Clark and N Whiteside, *Pension Security in the 21st Century* (Oxford, Oxford University Press, 2003).

[2] ibid 9.

[3] ibid 19.

[4] *IBM United Kingdom Holdings Ltd v Dalgleish* [2017] EWCA Civ 1212, [2018] Pens LR 1.

That controversy has tended to become identified with the question of where judicial review sits in relation to the perceived dichotomy between public law and private law. It is that question, centred upon the *Dalgleish* case but regarded as having very widespread ramifications, which is considered in this chapter.

Perhaps the best path into the understanding of the controversy which surrounds *Dalgleish* consists of examining, in broad terms, the nature and extent of employers' powers or discretions under or in relation to occupational pension scheme trusts. It is easy to form an artificially restricted view of those powers or discretions. We might be misled into imagining that the formal separation between employing enterprises and their occupational pension schemes is also a substantive one. On this approach, occupational pension schemes are set up as trusts managed by their own boards of trustees which are, as such, genuinely independent of the employing enterprises which sponsor and finance them. This stands apart from some specific contractual discretions which are reserved to those employing enterprises under the terms of the trust deed which forms the constitution of the scheme in question.

Such a vision of the role of the employing enterprise in the management of its occupational pension schemes would greatly understate the real extent of its imbrication in the working of those schemes. Apart from various regulatory efforts to ensure that occupational pension funds are not vulnerable to predatory raiding by their parent employing enterprises, the management of those funds has been allowed – perhaps necessarily, it must be said – to remain intricately bound up with the management of the employing enterprise itself. This is particularly so with its handling of its contractual relations with its current workers.[5] Thus, the *Dalgleish* case concerned various steps taken or proposed by various corporate entities within the IBM Group in pursuit of a general strategy of moving from defined benefits to defined contributions pension schemes for its workers. Those steps consisted partly in effecting modifications to the contracts of employment of its current workers (by making offers of pay increases conditional upon their being non-pensionable) and partly in proposing to bring about changes to its occupational pension schemes (by closing the defined benefits parts of the schemes except to workers already contractually entitled to participate in them), and it was both of those kinds of measures that were under judicial scrutiny in that case.

It is important for us at this point in our argument to identify the basis for that judicial scrutiny, and to make the point that this basis for judicial scrutiny has evolved so as to apply in parallel to both those two aspects of the employer's conduct in relation to its occupational pension scheme arrangements. In the course of the 1980s and 1990s, the common law courts developed a *mutual obligation of trust and confidence* as between employers and employees, which primarily applied as an implied term of their contracts of employment. In the landmark decision of the House of Lords in the *Imperial Tobacco* case,[6] the obligation was extended to cover employers' conduct under and in relation to their occupational pension schemes.

[5] An extremely valuable analysis of the employer's involvement in the management of occupational pensions schemes is to be found in R Nobles, *Pensions, Employment, and the Law* (Oxford, Clarendon, 1993) esp ch 4, 'The Duties of the Employer under a Pension Scheme'.

[6] *Imperial Group Pension Trust Ltd v Imperial Tobacco Ltd* [1991] 1 WLR 589 (Ch).

This straddling of the implied obligation of trust and confidence across both domains has been a hugely significant development. It assumed a real importance as a potential control upon the whole gathering dynamic of employers' retrenchment from the final salary pension schemes which had become an archetypal feature of the 'standard contract of employment' in its post-Second World War heyday. The supersession of the final salary pension scheme by the essentially less worker-protective model of the defined contribution but speculative benefit pension scheme has become an inexorably rising tide. Resistance to it may have become somewhat Canute-like. Yet the evolution of the employer's implied obligation of trust and confidence in the occupational pensions scheme context has nevertheless become an important part of the strategy of resistance to this development. Its importance has also grown with the decline of collective bargaining and trade union strength.

The implied obligation in the employment law context, first decisively articulated by Browne-Wilkinson J as he then was, as President of the Employment Appeal Tribunal, in *Woods v WM Car Services*[7] in 1989, attained its zenith in the decision of the House of Lords in *Malik v BCCI* in 1997.[8] Its sphere of operation was considerably restricted by the decision of the House of Lords in *Johnson v Unisys Ltd* in 1991,[9] and its importance was thereby diminished. However, it received a significant boost and was in a sense re-energised by the decision of the Supreme Court in the *Braganza* case in 2015.[10] Contrastingly, the implied obligation in the pensions law context, memorably articulated by Browne-Wilkinson VC as he by then was in the *Imperial Tobacco* case in 1991[11] did not develop very vigorously until it seemed to acquire a new velocity from the decision of Warren J in the High Court in *Dalgleish* in 2015.[12] This development came abruptly to a standstill when that decision was reversed by the Court of Appeal in 2017.[13] The Court of Appeal rejected the development of a doctrine of substantive legitimate expectations, and reasserted a much thinner rationality standard of review. In broad terms, recent developments suggest a divergence in the relevant normative standards as between these two contexts.

This brings us to the central point of our narrative: the implied obligation of mutual trust and confidence authorises and requires a judicial review of the exercise by the employer of its powers and discretions in these two linked but distinct legal contexts. The *Braganza* case stands for a relatively high intensity of review or scrutiny in the employment law context. By contrast, *Dalgleish* in the Court of Appeal represents relatively low-intensity review in the pensions law context. High-intensity review of course favours the employees and/or pension scheme members who are challenging the employer's actions or decisions; low-intensity review is conducive to employers' resistance to such challenges. Admittedly, this divergence should not be overplayed. In both cases, the court was purporting to apply the standards associated with *Wednesbury* review drawn from the public law context. In terms of outcome,

[7] *Woods v WM Car Services (Peterborough) Ltd* [1982] ICR 693 (CA).
[8] *Malik and Mahmud v Bank of Credit and Commerce International SA* [1997] UKHL 23, [1998] AC 20.
[9] *Johnson v Unisys Ltd* [1991] UKHL 13, [2003] 1 AC 518.
[10] *Braganza v BP Shipping Ltd & Anor* [2015] UKSC 17, [2015] 1 WLR 1661.
[11] *Imperial Group Pension Trust* (n 6).
[12] *IBM United Kingdom Holdings Ltd v Dalgleish* [2015] EWHC 389 (Ch), [2015] Pens LR 99.
[13] *IBM v Dalgleish* (CA) (n 4).

however, the effect of this in *Dalgleish* was to insulate the employer's discretion from legal challenge, whereas in *Braganza* the judges engaged in very detailed scrutiny of the employer's investigative processes. How should we account for this divergence, and should it be viewed as a necessary legal trajectory?

That view of the implied obligation as involving judicial scrutiny of employers' exercise of their powers and discretions has, ever since the implied obligation was first articulated in the late 1980s, provoked reflection upon the similarity of the implied obligation to public law's doctrinal apparatus of judicial review. Opinions have differed as to the basis for this similarity: some theorists have viewed the implied obligation as having been shaped by analogy with the public law of judicial review, others regard the implied obligation as a conscious importation or transplant from public law into the employment and pensions sphere, while yet others think of the implied obligation as an example of the fusion of public and private law. We could think of these as, respectively, the analogy view, the transplant view and the fusion view of this doctrinal relationship.

Those different opinions, about the nature of the relationship between the implied obligation and the public law of judicial review, tend to coincide with normative perceptions as to what the nature of that relationship *ought to be*. There has been a general tendency for the protagonists of the interests of workers and pension scheme members to favour the fusion view, or at least to regard the influence of public law doctrine upon the implied obligation as beneficial and supportive. The contrasting tendency has been for proponents of employers' interests to resist what they see as an illegitimate importing or transplanting of public law doctrines into the implied obligation of mutual trust and confidence. Hence, the contestation about the scope and application of the implied obligation becomes identified with rival normative approaches to the so-called 'public/private divide' between public law and private law. It represents, we might say, a deeply politicised choice.

Moreover, and this is an absolutely crucial point, there is also a more specific and fine-grained debate, between the proponents of those basic rival positions, as to *the terms on which* public law judicial review doctrines are aligned with the implied obligation. The public law of judicial review contains a wide range and variety of approaches to judicial scrutiny which lie along a broad spectrum from low-intensity review to high-intensity review. The main debate between proponents of the rival positions with regard to the development of the implied obligation has not so much been about the legitimacy of *any* influence of public law judicial review doctrines. Rather, it has been about *which particular elements or approaches* of the public law of judicial review may legitimately be carried across to the implied obligation.

All that said, we have to recognise that there are those who take up extreme positions at the two ends of this spectrum of doctrinal positions, that is to say those who argue on the one hand for *complete fusion* and, on the other, for *complete separation* between the public and private law. We regard those extreme positions as unhelpful, and indeed contradicted by Clark and Whiteside's exploration of the complexities and nuances in the 'public' and 'private' interactions in pensions. We prefer to approach this set of problems as involving more fine-grained and contextual enquiries that must be sensitive to specific contractual powers.

In the fine-grained debate, two contrasting positions can be identified in the *Braganza* case on the one hand and the *Dalgleish* case on the other. We might wish to think that this represents a divergence in approaches to the development of the implied obligation in, on the one hand, the employment law context in *Braganza* and in the pensions law context in the *Dalgleish* case on the other. That might represent a slight over-simplification, in that the *Dalgleish* case is partly concerned with the employer's discretions under its contracts of employment as well as with its discretions under the pension scheme deed and rules. Nevertheless, the proposition broadly stands, since the contractual discretions in issue are those concerned with pension scheme provision.

The two decisions manifest different ways of thinking about the implied obligation of mutual trust and confidence in those two contexts. In the *Braganza* case, the implied obligation was not centrally in issue, the question being whether the employer had acted 'reasonably' in a contractual sense in withholding death in service benefits from the widow of an employee who had disappeared overboard from a ship on which he had been working. The investigation had concluded that the employee must have committed suicide, thus triggering the application of a 'wilful default' exception to the widow's contractual entitlement to those benefits. In deciding that the employer had not acted reasonably, the judges in the Supreme Court did not directly invoke the implied obligation but clearly regarded themselves as engaged in a scrutiny of the employer's decision for irrationality which was exactly of the kind required by the implied obligation.[14]

The judgments in *Braganza* are conspicuous for their positive engagement with the public law of judicial review. Admittedly, their focus on the *Wednesbury* standard of review does not reflect the most modern of approaches to judicial review, since it fails to incorporate the more state-of-the-art review conceptions such as the requirement of proportionate responses to human rights infringements. However, one can understand why the *Wednesbury* reasonableness test was in the whole context of the case regarded as the appropriate standard to apply. It appears from the judgment of Lady Hale that it was common ground between the parties that the question was whether the opinion formed by the employer had been 'reasonable', and this had been regarded as referring to the *Wednesbury* standard in various cases concerning the exercise of contractual discretions.[15] Within that compass, the judgments in the Supreme Court pursue a relatively high-intensity approach to the scrutiny in question. In particular, they insist that both the two limbs of the *Wednesbury* test must be regarded as applicable, that is to say both the requirement to take into account relevant considerations and to ignore irrelevant ones and the further requirement to avoid a conclusion so unreasonable that no reasonable decision-maker could have come to it.[16] The pursuit of this dual approach led the Supreme Court to decide the

[14] Compare, eg, Lord Hodge's reference in *Braganza* (n 10) [52] to the application of the irrationality test by Burton J in *Clark v Nomura International Plc* [2000] IRLR 766 (QBD), a case which is regarded as being concerned with the application of the implied obligation to the awarding of discretionary bonuses.

[15] See *Braganza* (n 10) [52] referring in particular to *The Vanqueur Jose* [1979] 1 Lloyd's Rep 557 (QBD) [91].

[16] See *Braganza* (n 10) [30] (Lady Hale), [103] (Lord Neuberger).

appeal in favour of the employee's widow. This was on the basis of a failure to take account of a relevant consideration, namely the inherent improbability of suicide and the need for cogent evidence to support a finding that it had occurred.

The story of the engagement between the public law of judicial review and the implied obligation of mutual trust and confidence took a subtly but decisively different turn in the pensions law context in the decision and judgment of the Court of Appeal in *Dalgleish*, diverting it into a track which we might describe as that of 'public law minimalism'. The Court of Appeal concluded that there were no 'reasonable expectations' on the facts. Nevertheless, it also seems to have been unwilling to treat regard for the reasonable or legitimate expectations of the employees and/or pension scheme members (that their pensions entitlements would not undergo further negative modifications) as a distinct ground of scrutiny. It was folded into the general *Wednesbury* scrutiny of the employer's exercise of its powers and discretions in the pension scheme context, thus significantly reducing the intensity of the overall review.

This line of reasoning consisted of an acceptance of the proposition that *Wednesbury* scrutiny, although generally regarded as a particular sort of test of reasonableness, was actually nothing of the kind; it was merely a test of *rationality* conceived of as an essentially less exacting requirement. This distinction had been developed by Lord Sumption in *Hayes v Willoughby*, where he said that:

> Rationality is not the same as reasonableness. Reasonableness is an external, objective standard applied to the outcome of a person's thoughts or intentions … A test of rationality, by comparison, applies a minimum objective standard to the relevant person's mental processes. It imports a requirement of good faith, a requirement that there should be some logical connection between the evidence and the ostensible reasons for the decision, and (which will usually amount to the same thing) an absence of arbitrariness, of capriciousness or of reasoning so outrageous in its defiance of logic as to be perverse.[17]

This analysis was proffered by Lord Sumption in a case concerning the standard of criminal liability, and in particular the mens rea requirement, imposed by the Protection from Harassment Act 1997. This distinction between reasonableness and rationality was invoked in the very different context of the *Dalgleish* case to sustain a very low-intensity approach to the *Wednesbury* test as the guiding principle for the application of the '*Imperial* duty' (ie, the implied obligation as recognised in the *Imperial Tobacco* case) to the exercise of the employer's powers and discretions in the pension scheme context.[18] These subtle diminutions in the stringency of scrutiny – that is to say firstly, the folding of legitimate or reasonable expectations into the *Wednesbury* test, and secondly, the downgrading of that test to one of rationality rather narrowly conceived – were sufficient to sustain the upholding of the employer's challenge to the decision of the High Court in the *Dalgleish* case itself.

In his contribution to this book, Lord Sales argues for the fundamental non-applicability of 'public law rationality' in the context of private-law contractual relationships. Somewhat controversially, he would include the relationships between employers and employees/pension scheme members in the domain of private law.

[17] *Hayes v Willoughby* [2013] UKSC 17, [2013] 1 WLR 935 [14].
[18] *IBM v Dalgleish* (CA) (n 4) esp [227]–[228].

In his view, the employer's exercise of powers and discretions in the pension scheme context ought to be governed by a different rationality, in effect a private law rationality, according to which it is fully legitimate for the employer to consult and to be guided by its own commercial self-interest where that was 'within the contemplation of the parties'.

This involves the assertion of a particularly sharp form of the public/private divide, and the assignment of employment relationships to the strictly private legal realm. In this chapter, we challenge Lord Sales' arguments and we put forward our own defence of a doctrine of legitimate expectations in labour and pensions law. First, we address Lord Sales' argument that *Braganza* represents a misstep in translating public law doctrines into the employment law context. We argue that labour law should be viewed as an autonomous legal discipline, which diverges in important ways from the general private law of contract and trusts. This divergence reflects the distinctiveness of employment contracts. Employment contracts involve an inequality of power, in circumstances where there is a conflict of interest between the stronger party and the weaker party. These features mean that the public law principles of judicial review, concerned with restraining 'abuse of power', are particularly apposite in employment contracts. Any judicial move against *Braganza* would be an attack on labour law itself, and we regard this as a deeply regressive development.

Second, having defended the relevance of public law to employment contracts in *Braganza*, we argue that this should extend to the full range of public law doctrines. This could include reasonableness, proportionality and legitimate expectations. In this respect, it is far too reductive to fixate on *Wednesbury* as *the* public law approach. There is no such thing as *the* public law approach. In *Dalgleish*, we suggest that a legitimate expectations doctrine could be justified (though we emphasise that the use of public law analogies must be undertaken cautiously and contextually). This represents a more nuanced view of the public/private divide, and it gives pension security its appropriate due. These arguments are developed in the succeeding parts of this chapter.

II. THE BACKLASH AGAINST *BRAGANZA:* PRIVATE LAW RETRENCHMENT?

There has been a significant critical reaction to the use of public law reasoning in *Braganza*, some of which is relied on by Lord Sales in his own critique of that decision. From a private law perspective, Jonathan Morgan[19] and Michael Bridge[20] have each provided powerful critiques of the decision and its wider ramification for the private law of contract. From a public law perspective, Chris Himsworth has for his own part offered a salutary perspective on the risks of transplantation of public law doctrines into private law.[21] The arguments are powerful, and it is important to address them.

[19] J Morgan, 'Against Judicial Review of Discretionary Contractual Powers' [2008] *LMCLQ* 230.

[20] M Bridge, 'The Exercise of Contractual Discretion' (2019) 135 *LQR* 227.

[21] C Himsworth, 'Transplanting Irrationality from Public to Private Law: *Braganza v BP Shipping Ltd*' (2019) 23 *Edinburgh Law Review* 1.

We can distinguish two types of argument against *Braganza*. The first criticises the disruption of party autonomy and freedom of contract where public law doctrines are used to regulate discretionary powers in contracts. Let us call this the 'contractual autonomy' objection. The second criticises the transplantation of public law categories into private law. This transplantation is inappropriate because it presupposes a unity of public law and private law which disregards the important differences between each context. Let us call this the 'transplantation' objection. We think that both objections can be countered. It is important to do so because, as we shall make clear, we believe that the countermove against *Braganza* is associated with a philosophy of strong judicial restraint and non-intervention. Such a development would be highly regressive in the law of the personal employment contract. It would undermine the incremental development of a discrete body of worker-protective common law norms, which constitute a distinctive common law of the personal employment contract. In its most extreme forms, it would seem to correspond with a denial of the very idea of worker-protective labour law as an autonomous discipline. In an era of trade union decline, the simultaneous contraction of judicial protection would be very regrettable.

Starting with the 'contractual autonomy' objection, we note that Morgan has been a prominent critic of the judicial review of discretionary contractual powers. The main shape of this argument was set out in his critique of *Lymington Marina v Macnamara*,[22] 'Against judicial review of discretionary contractual powers'.[23] In *Lymington*, the judge at first instance had used the *Wednesbury* formulation to support his conclusion that a discretionary refusal to approve a sub-licensee under a contractual licence arrangement was a contractual breach. This use of *Wednesbury* was criticised by the Court of Appeal as unnecessary and undesirable.[24] The construction of the contractual power ought to have been addressed using orthodox contractual principles, which would require the discretion not to be exercised in an arbitrary or capricious fashion.[25] This stands apart from the approach in *Braganza*.

Despite the Court of Appeal's repudiation of the *Wednesbury* analogy, a step that is welcomed by Morgan, his analysis is nevertheless critical of the Court of Appeal judgment in countenancing *any* review of discretionary contractual powers based on caprice or arbitrariness. It must be acknowledged that Morgan is no fan of capriciousness in commercial relations. Reassuringly, he regards it as a very bad thing. His argument is that judicially developed tools are too blunt to respond effectively to the mischief, and indeed give rise to further risks of opportunism in the governance of the contract. It would be better 'to leave it to the market, or more specifically contractors, to design their own protection mechanisms, if indeed they desire them, without the "help" of judicially implied terms'.[26] The risks of opportunism are better addressed through social sanctions, such as damage to commercial reputation in the marketplace:

> In commercial cases, where parties are perfectly able to police wayward behaviour, by placing appropriate terms in their contracts where judicial supervision is required and relying

[22] *Lymington Marina v Macnamara* [2007] EWCA Civ 151, [2007] 2 All ER (Comm) 825.
[23] Morgan, 'Against Judicial Review of Discretionary Contractual Powers' (n 19).
[24] ibid 232.
[25] ibid 235.
[26] ibid 238.

upon extra-legal sanctions where it is not, the courts should go further and disclaim any jurisdiction to review the exercise of contractual discretions.[27]

In this way, 'non-intervention' should be the default rule in commercial contracts.[28]

This 'contractual autonomy' objection should, we suggest, be viewed as highly attenuated in relation to employment contracts. In Morgan's 2008 paper, there is some equivocation on this point. He recognises that 'there may be areas where extra-legal sanctions are for some reason ineffective, and the risk of opportunism high, and where therefore judicial review of contractual discretions may on balance be desirable'.[29] In the accompanying footnote, he refers to employment as one such contractual context, although in that same footnote he also refers approvingly to Richard Epstein's 'powerful defences' of an unlimited power to dismiss workers.[30]

The reference to Epstein's work on the contract at will would be regarded as highly provocative by many labour lawyers. The burden of Epstein's argument is that the special regulation of employment contracts is inefficient and unjust, and that a laissez-faire regime of freedom of contract should apply. It is a manifesto for the abolition of labour law, in fact. While we regard Epstein's arguments as riddled with flaws, and widely discredited, we confine ourselves to the narrower doctrinal point that the 'contract-at-will' position is incompatible with the English common law authorities.[31] The special nature of the employment contract has been given judicial recognition at the highest level in cases such as *Malik*, *Johnson*, and *R (on the application of UNISON) v Lord Chancellor*.[32] In *Autoclenz v Belcher*, Lord Clarke referred to 'the relative bargaining power of the parties' as a relevant consideration in developing the common law governing employment contracts.[33] For this reason, there is a 'critical difference' between commercial contracts and personal employment contracts, and this 'critical difference' rests upon the contractual inequality between employers and the employed.[34] The common law principles governing the personal employment contract are different from those applicable to 'ordinary contracts and, in particular, to commercial contracts'.[35]

It is also relevant that the issue in *Autoclenz* was the use of standard-form written contracts, drafted by employers and presented to workers on a take-it-or-leave-it basis, and designed to negate a finding of employment status. The realities of contracting practices in the labour market make it untenable to assume that the parties will be in

[27] ibid 242.

[28] ibid 240. In his recent critique of *Braganza*, Bridge (n 20) is also critical of *Braganza* because 'private contract law is above all concerned with obligations that the contracting parties have voluntarily assumed' (227). He further suggests that 'a preoccupation with administrative law threatens to undermine the consensual character of private contract law' (248).

[29] ibid 239.

[30] ibid 239, fn 56, referring to RA Epstein, 'In Defence of the Contract at Will' (1984) 51 *University of Chicago Law Review* 947.

[31] We leave to one side the extensive structure of protective legislation regulating, among other things, the employer's dismissal powers.

[32] *Malik* (n 8); *Johnson* (n 9); and *R (on the application of UNISON) v Lord Chancellor* [2017] UKSC 51, [2017] 3 WLR 409.

[33] *Autoclenz v Belcher* [2011] UKSC 41, [2011] 4 All ER 745 [35].

[34] ibid [34].

[35] ibid [21].

the business of drafting their own bespoke 'protection mechanisms'.[36] In this respect, it is also significant that the implied term of trust and confidence has been conceptualised by Lord Steyn as 'an overarching obligation implied by law as an incident of the contract of employment. It can also be described as a legal duty imposed by law'.[37] Neither its existence nor its normative content is rooted in the intentions of the contracting parties. Its content has been judicially elaborated as being, 'apt to cover the great diversity of situations in which a balance has to be struck between an employer's interest in managing his business as he sees fit and the employee's interest in not being unfairly and improperly exploited'.[38] This marks another important contrast with the commercial contract context, where the focus is on terms implied in fact.[39]

In a later intervention following *Braganza*, where Morgan is now in rearguard action, his position on employment contracts appears to have shifted.[40] This later critique is focused on confining *Braganza* to the specific domain of employment contracts and limiting any spillover into commercial contracts. In commercial contracts, 'sophisticated commercial parties' can be trusted to negotiate their own arrangements.[41] Employment contracts are different because of 'the structural power imbalance between employers and employees'.[42] The divisibility of employment and commercial contracts 'hardly needs to be vouchsafed by reference to authority'.[43] We readily concede the value in tailoring the arguments against *Braganza* to commercial contexts, where considerations of private autonomy, commercial certainty, and freedom of contract are stronger. We reject entirely the extension of these considerations to employment contracts. The common law of the personal employment contract is now something other than 'commercialist or mercantilist, essentially committed to the values and techniques of private law in a narrow sense'.[44] It would require an act of judicial power of great magnitude to repudiate these common law principles, which have now culminated in Lord Reed's powerful rejection of 'freedom of contract' in the *UNISON* case:

> Relationships between employers and employees are generally characterised by an imbalance of economic power. Recognising the vulnerability of employees to exploitation, discrimination, and other undesirable practices, and the social problems which can result, Parliament has long intervened in those relationships so as to confer statutory rights on employees, rather than leaving their rights to be determined by freedom of contract.[45]

[36] H Collins, 'Legal Responses to the Standard Form Contract of Employment' (2007) 36 *Industrial Law Journal* 2.
[37] *Johnson* (n 9) [24].
[38] *Malik* (n 8) 46.
[39] Bridge (n 20) 228.
[40] J Morgan, 'Resisting Judicial Review of Discretionary Contractual Powers' [2015] *LMCLQ* 483.
[41] ibid 483.
[42] ibid 485.
[43] ibid.
[44] M Freedland, *The Personal Employment Contract* (Oxford, Oxford University Press, 2005) 521. See also A Bogg, 'Sham Self-Employment in the Supreme Court' (2012) 41 *Industrial Law Journal* 328.
[45] *UNISON* (n 32) [6].

Accordingly, we regard the 'contractual autonomy' objection as a non-starter in the employment context. The 'transplantation' objection must be taken more seriously, and it has been developed very persuasively by Himsworth.[46] Himsworth argues that there are numerous difficulties with transplantation of public law concepts into the private law of contract. For example, Himsworth wonders whether such transplantation can occur where a given concept is

> shorn of its conceptual underpinning in public law. In particular, the question has to be asked whether that language can survive its transplant without the accompanying core/foundational device of 'jurisdiction' or vires, within which the decision-maker, in the public context, must, in most judicial presentations of the field, operate.[47]

Where the scrutiny of powers is detached from a discrete statutory context, it might be difficult to predict how courts will determine which purposes are proper or improper, which considerations relevant and irrelevant, and so forth. This could undermine the legitimacy of the judicial role by enlarging the discretionary judgement of the courts in 'private' judicial review cases. On such grounds, Himsworth concludes that 'the differences between the public law functions of the courts in judicial review and their private law functions in the interpretation of commercial contracts are too large to accommodate a transplant of the review of discretion'.[48]

While this objection must be taken seriously, we think that the language of 'transplantation' is apt to mislead in understanding the relevant phenomena in decisions like *Braganza*. It represents a kind of 'fusion fallacy' in relation to the public/private law distinction. The use of public law analogies in the contractual sphere need not involve 'transplantation' or 'fusion' of public and private values. It is possible to view the interaction in a far looser way than the language of 'transplantation' implies. We suggest that an exemplar of this looser approach is represented in ACL Davies' work on the interaction between public law and labour law.[49] We regard this looser approach as far less vulnerable to the transplantation objection. Davies is careful to identify the similarities and differences between the contexts of labour law and public law, while tracing the influence of public law on labour law. In so doing, she is scrupulous in maintaining the distinctiveness and 'autonomy' of the fields of labour law and public law. This allows for a productive engagement between them, without any suggestion that the fields are fused. In particular, judicial concern with the 'intensity' of review, and the appropriate limits of adjudication has been central in the modern development of public law doctrines. The relevant principles have been developed in an explicit and transparent fashion. By contrast, this discourse is still underdeveloped in labour law. A principled approach to 'intensity' of review in labour law would be greatly supported by considering the public law principles. This is not through some process of mechanistic application of public law norms, but by understanding how those principles might operate in the specific context of employment adjudication.

[46] Himsworth (n 21).

[47] ibid 18.

[48] ibid 20. Like Morgan, Himsworth appears to be more content with an approach that would confine *Braganza* to employment contracts and restrict its applicability to commercial contracts. Yet the transplantation objection would seem to apply to employment contracts too.

[49] ACL Davies, 'Judicial Self-Restraint in Labour Law' (2009) 38 *Industrial Law Journal* 278.

To this end, Davies discusses 'deference' or, as she prefers, 'judicial self-restraint', in the public law sphere. These concerns about the appropriate limits of the judicial role inform the development and application of public law doctrines. The factors that inform the appropriate degree of judicial self-restraint include sensitivity to the democratic position of legislatures, the relative expertise of the court vis-a-vis the primary decision-maker, the general 'institutional competence' of courts compared with other types of public institution, and the nature of the claimant's interest.[50] These considerations are sensitive to the context of specific judicial review claims. This is reflected in the variability of intensity of review. Generally speaking, the high level of judicial self-restraint in *Wednesbury* has given way to review based on 'reasonableness' or a more structured proportionality analysis, particularly in human rights cases.[51] What is clear is that it is no longer appropriate to talk in terms of *the* public law approach, as if this were a unitary phenomenon reducible to the *Wednesbury* test. Reasonableness 'works alongside a raft of other requirements (proper purposes, relevant considerations, respect for legitimate expectations and so on), and therefore, in public law, it is never the only standard against which the decision must be evaluated'.[52] In public law, the courts have tended to adopt a more interventionist approach where it is constitutionally appropriate to do so, particularly in fundamental rights and legitimate expectations cases.

As Davies notes, these 'deference factors' are also operative in labour law. However, they have often been obscured by more political concerns about the regressive role of the judiciary in employment cases, with the common law viewed as structurally biased in favour of employer interests.[53] Furthermore, the context to employment cases means that the weight and significance of these factors is often different: 'In public law … the courts' aim in developing deference has been to keep within their own constitutional limits in the light of their understanding of the separation of powers. In labour law, these issues do not apply'.[54] Although the constitutional context to employment law is somewhat different, other deference factors remain relevant. In particular, Davies identifies institutional competence, expertise and democratic accountability as particularly relevant.[55] These considerations invite the courts to reflect upon their own limits in scrutinising employer decision-making. Institutional competence highlights the limitations of bipolar litigation between two parties where certain issues are 'polycentric', engaging a multiplicity of interests.[56] Expertise directs the court to assess whether it is well placed to evaluate certain matters, compared with an employer. Where the decisions involve commercial judgements or balancing

[50] ibid 284–87, discussing the leading public law cases on deference.

[51] ibid 281.

[52] ACL Davies, 'Labour Law as Public Law' in A Bogg et al (eds), *The Autonomy of Labour Law* (Oxford, Hart Publishing, 2015) 239.

[53] This is the leitmotif of Bill Wedderburn's work on the 'autonomy' of labour law. See A Bogg, 'The Hero's Journey: Lord Wedderburn and the 'Political Constitution' of Labour Law' (2015) 44 *Industrial Law Journal* 299.

[54] Davies, 'Judicial Self-Restraint in Labour Law' (n 49) 289.

[55] ibid 291.

[56] ibid 290. Davies gives the example of equal pay litigation, where an equal pay determination may have a wide range of effects on different parties in the employment nexus who may be unrepresented in the litigation.

competing economic interests, the court may be reluctant to interfere. By contrast, where the decisions concern the appropriate process to be adopted in a disciplinary suspension, or the weighing of relevant evidence as in *Braganza*, the court would have a greater claim to expertise. Finally, democratic accountability would justify restraint where decisions have been preceded by a consultative or negotiation process of democratic approval by the workforce. These democratic considerations would be attenuated where a disadvantaged minority's rights were overridden by the majority,[57] or where the consultative process was procedurally flawed.

Davies identifies the implied term of trust and confidence as a key site where these values play out.[58] Indeed, she regards Lord Steyn's formulation in *Malik* as resembling a proportionality approach to the application of the relevant normative standard.[59] Once we interpret trust and confidence jurisprudence through the lens of judicial self-restraint, we can detect a similar variation in the intensity of review. For example, in *Clark v Nomura International*,[60] the employee was dismissed following a breakdown in the relationship between the employer and the employee. During the notice period, the employer declined to award the employee a discretionary bonus corresponding to the previous year's performance. In reviewing the employer's exercise of discretion, Burton J observed that

> the right test is one of irrationality or perversity (of which caprice or capriciousness would be a good example) ie that no reasonable employer would have exercised his discretion in this way …. In reaching its conclusion, what the court does is thus not to substitute its own view, but to ask the question whether any reasonable employer could have come to such a conclusion.[61]

This can be contrasted with *Gogay v Hertfordshire County Council*[62] where the Court of Appeal engaged in very intensive scrutiny of the employer's exercise of a disciplinary power of suspension following an allegation of sexual abuse against an employee. This variation of intensity is precisely what should be expected. In *Clark*, the determination of reward following an assessment of employee performance is a matter squarely within the expertise of the employer rather than the reviewing court. In *Gogay*, however, the procedural and evidential proprieties surrounding a disciplinary suspension are more apt for intensive review since these are concepts more familiar to courts and the judicial role. Moreover, the importance of the employee's interest in *Gogay* also suggests that more intensive review is appropriate, given the catastrophic consequences of unfounded allegations of child sexual abuse for the employee's reputation and psychological wellbeing.

So the appropriate standard of judicial review of the employer's contractual powers depends upon the interplay of 'deference factors': the expertise of the

[57] ACL Davies, 'Exploitative Compromises' (2012) 65 *Current Legal Problems* 269.

[58] Davies, 'Judicial Self-Restraint in Labour Law' (n 49) 294–98.

[59] ibid 295. On the public law influences on the normative content of trust and confidence, see Freedland (n 44); D Brodie, 'Mutual Trust and Confidence: Catalysts, Constraints and Commonality' (2008) 37 *Industrial Law Journal* 329; A Bogg, '*Bournemouth University Higher Education Corporation v Buckland*: Re-establishing Orthodoxy at the Expense of Coherence' (2010) 39 *Industrial Law Journal* 408.

[60] *Clark* (n 14).

[61] ibid [40].

[62] *Gogay v Hertfordshire CC* [2000] IRLR 703 (CA).

reviewing court, aspects of institutional competence, democratic legitimacy of the primary decision-maker's decision, and the nature of the interest affected by the decision. The latitude of reasonableness will reflect the balance of these factors. At one extreme on the spectrum of judicial self-restraint, it will correspond to a test of perversity. At the other extreme of the spectrum, it may correspond to the intensive application of a proportionality standard. This modulating feature of review under trust and confidence means that there is no single labour law standard, just as there is no single public law standard. Engagement with public law reasoning has great value in providing a more critical perspective on the ingrained deference of courts in the labour field to the employer's economic freedoms.[63] Davies has described labour law's mode of engagement with public law as a 'magpie' discipline, 'borrowing strategies and concepts from other disciplines such as public law' while adjusting those concepts to its own functional imperatives.[64] This is quite different from a process of fusion or transplantation. It is more in the style of dialogue between fields that each retain their autonomy.

The real concern with *Braganza*, particularly in private law quarters, is the expansion beyond *Wednesbury* to encompass other public law doctrines such as proportionality and legitimate expectations. Indeed, both Morgan and Bridge are quite explicit in their expansionist fears in their critical reactions to public law influence. We hope we have said enough at this stage to dismiss the 'contractual autonomy' and 'transplantation' objections to such expansion, at least in relation to employment contracts. We have not yet provided a positive argument *in favour* of a legitimate expectations/proportionality approach in *Dalgleish*. We shall make this positive case in the next section. Before we do so, we should remind ourselves of Lady Hale's formulation in *Braganza* itself:

> [T]he party who is charged with making decisions which affect the rights of both parties to the contract has a clear conflict of interest. That conflict is heightened where there is a significant imbalance of power between the contracting parties as there often will be in an employment contract. The courts have therefore sought to ensure that such contractual powers are not abused. They have done so by implying a term as to the manner in which such powers may be exercised, *a term which may vary according to the terms of the contract and the context in which the decision-making power is given*.[65]

The italicised part of that statement rejects the idea that *Braganza* stands for a single review test based on *Wednesbury*. The standard of review varies in accordance with the context. It is likely to shift depending upon the precise nature of the contractual power, its subject matter and the nature of the employees' interest. Judicial scrutiny will be particularly strict where fundamental rights are engaged. This modulating feature of trust and confidence is exactly to be expected, once the role of deference factors is understood. In appropriate circumstances, the courts should be prepared to apply a legitimate expectations/proportionality analysis. We shall argue next that the situation in *Dalgleish* warranted a legitimate expectations approach to judicial review.

[63] Davies, 'Labour Law as Public Law' (n 52) 254.
[64] ibid.
[65] *Braganza* (n 10) [18].

III. DEFENDING LEGITIMATE EXPECTATIONS IN THE EMPLOYMENT CONTEXT

A. Introduction

The doctrine of legitimate expectations represents one of the areas in which Dawn Oliver identifies 'common values' across the public/private divide.[66] The values of trust and security provide a normative underpinning to legitimate expectations in public law. Where an individual has relied upon undertakings given by a public authority in how it will exercise its discretion, especially in matters related to the livelihood of the citizen, it promotes trust and good administration to give judicial protection to those legitimate expectations.[67] These values recur across private law, in domains such as contract and trusts. Oliver argues that legitimate expectations are protected through a range of different private law techniques in ways that parallel the public law doctrine. Given that the contractual powers in *Dalgleish* sit at the intersection of labour law and trusts law, we begin by identifying the current position on legitimate expectations in these two domains. It is significant that Oliver identifies pensions as a key area where the values of trust and security are engaged in the employment context, reflected in the 'increased acknowledgement in … areas of law such as insurance and pensions of the importance of security to those with whom providers of these benefits deal'.[68] We might expect, therefore, a role for legitimate expectations to regulate the discretionary powers of the providers. At the very least, the context suggests that it is a question worth pursuing.

Starting with employment contracts, *French v Barclays Bank* is an important example of a case where the implied term of trust and confidence provided a doctrinal underpinning to legitimate expectations.[69] In *French*, the employee was required to relocate by his employer, and as part of this arrangement the employer extended an interest-free bridging loan to the employee. In the meantime, there was a collapse in the housing market and the employer sought to readjust the loan arrangement. The upshot of this readjustment would have led to Mr French suffering a financial loss of £40,000. The Court of Appeal concluded that this readjustment was a breach of trust and confidence because it had defeated the legitimate expectation of Mr French. This expectation had been induced by his reasonable reliance upon the contractual terms and settled practices of his employer.[70] Thus, the Court of Appeal concluded that

> to seek to invoke a change of a policy or a change in the terms in which loans were made to employees requested to relocate which (a) has been applied to other employees over many years and (b) appeared in terms in the manual at the time when the loan was made,

[66] D Oliver, *Common Values and the Public Private Divide* (Oxford, Butterworths, 1999).

[67] ibid 100. That does not mean that the legitimate expectation should be protected at all costs. There may be good reasons in the particular case to depart from the legitimate expectation. The point is that the legitimate expectation should count for *something* in the balancing exercise.

[68] ibid 145.

[69] *French v Barclays Bank plc* [1998] IRLR 646 (CA).

[70] ibid [18].

> is conduct which would be likely to destroy the confidence and trust between the bank and its employees.[71]

The facts in *French* disclosed an especially strong argument for protecting the employee's legitimate expectation. His reliance was reasonable, he had suffered extreme detriment and hardship as a result of that reliance and there were no weighty identifiable countervailing reasons justifying the (retrospective) change of policy in his case.

Another employment case that may be understood through the lens of legitimate expectations is *Transco v O'Brien*.[72] The litigation arose in the context of a restructuring exercise where all permanent employees were offered a new contract with enhanced redundancy terms. The employer took the view, erroneously but honestly, that Mr O'Brien was not a permanent employee. As a result, he was not offered the new contractual package. The Court of Appeal concluded that this inconsistency in application of the policy breached the implied term of trust and confidence. Since Mr O'Brien was in fact a permanent employee, his singling out and exclusion was arbitrary and capricious. According to Pill LJ, 'there are few things which would be more likely to damage seriously' the relationship of trust between employer and employee than this.[73] The significance of *Transco* lies in its engagement with the issue 'whether the employing enterprise was giving effect to the reasonable expectations of the employee arising out of the contractual relationship as it had actually evolved and been conducted'.[74] The treatment of Mr O'Brien involved a departure from an existing policy that should have been applied to his situation. It therefore violated the fundamental requirement of equality as consistency. This has been identified as an important value in some categories of public law legitimate expectation cases where there have been departures from an existing policy in individual cases.[75]

In the trusts context, there have also been incipient stirrings of a doctrine of legitimate expectations. This is recognised in the judgment of Robert Walker J in *Scott v National Trust*:

> [I]f (for instance) trustees (whether of a charity, or a pension fund or a private family trust) have for the last ten years paid £1000 per quarter to an elderly, impoverished beneficiary of the trust it seems at least arguable that no reasonable body of trustees would discontinue the payment, without any warning, and without giving the beneficiary the opportunity of trying to persuade the trustees to continue the payment, at least temporarily. The beneficiary has no legal or equitable right to continued payment, but she or he has an expectation. So I am inclined to think that legitimate expectation may have some part to play in trust law as well as in judicial review cases.[76]

It is interesting that these observations are not limited to charitable trusts, but also include discretionary powers in pension funds. It is also interesting that Robert Walker J chooses the specific example of an impoverished pensioner to

[71] ibid [50].
[72] *Transco Plc v O'Brien* [2002] EWCA Civ 379, [2002] ICR 721.
[73] ibid [17].
[74] Freedland (n 44) 279. See further A Bogg, 'Good Faith: A Case of the English Reserve' (2011) 32 *Comparative Labor Law & Policy Journal* 761.
[75] P Craig, *Administrative Law*, 8th edn (London, Sweet & Maxwell, 2016) [22-008].
[76] *Scott v National Trust* [1998] 2 All ER 705, 718 (Ch).

support his legitimate expectation argument. Robert Walker J recognises that a *substantive* legitimate expectation (to the continuation of the payment) might generate a *procedural* right to make representations on the part of the beneficiary.[77] Guy Newey suggests that *Scott* should extend to a matters of substance too, as an element of the general duty on trustees to take relevant matters into account.[78] This would correspond to the rationality limb in Lady Hale's *Wednesbury*-style approach in *Braganza*. We would be inclined to press the point even further, and to explore the possibilities for a proportionality-style enquiry where an employer seeks to depart from a legitimate expectation. This would be in line with the public law approach to substantive legitimate expectations, which no doubt reflected the concern that on a *Wednesbury* approach it would 'be almost impossible for the individual to succeed' in judicial review.[79]

So far, our remarks are no more than suggestive. We have identified a potential doctrinal basis for legitimate expectations in relation to the powers at issue in *Dalgleish*. In the remaining sections, we will make a positive argument that there should have been more exacting scrutiny in *Dalgleish*. First, we set out the current position on legitimate expectations in public law, and the ascendancy of a proportionality test for substantive legitimate expectations. We note the fact that in his earlier published work, Lord Sales has defended a conservative approach to legitimate expectations, where he is critical of Laws LJ's application of a proportionality standard in *Nadarajah*.[80] We suggest that Lord Sales' approach to *Dalgleish* fits with his conservative view of the judicial role in public law.[81] It is a view that is now at odds with the general thrust of the authorities on substantive legitimate expectations. Second, we offer a normative account of why legitimate expectations in a *Dalgleish*-type case should attract strong judicial protection, based in the human capabilities approach. Finally, we return to the discussion of 'deference factors' in judicial review. While some of those 'deference factors' would counsel judicial self-restraint in the pensions field, we suggest that the overall effect of *Dalgleish* is to leave employees' fundamental human capabilities without adequate judicial protection. The development of a proportionality standard offers a more principled approach than the mechanistic application of the thin *Wednesbury* standard.

B. The Doctrine of Substantive Legitimate Expectations in Public Law

There is now an extensive body of case law in English administrative law recognising the doctrine of substantive legitimate expectations. In general terms, where a

[77] Compare *R (on the application of Bibi) v Newham LBC (No 1)* [2001] EWCA Civ 607, [2002] 1 WLR 237.

[78] G Newey, 'Constraints on the Exercise of Trustees' Powers' in PG Turner (ed), *Equity and Administration* (Cambridge, Cambridge University Press, 2016) 52.

[79] Craig (n 75) [22-018], discussing *R v North and East Devon Health Authority, ex p Coughlan* [2001] QB 213 (CA).

[80] *Nadarajah v Secretary of State for the Home Department* [2005] EWCA Civ 1363; P Sales, 'Legitimate Expectations' (2006) 11 *Judicial Review* 186.

[81] See, eg, P Sales and R Ekins, 'Rights-Consistent Interpretation and the Human Rights Act 1998' (2011) 11 *LQR* 217.

public body has issued a general policy or made representations that have been relied upon by an individual citizen, the unjustified departure from that stated position may undermine a range of public goods. Such a departure could undermine public trust and damage the principle of fairness in public administration.[82] It also undermines legal certainty and the ability of citizens to plan their lives.[83] It is important to recognise that there may be *justified* departures from such policies or representations. In the public law context, there is a constitutional dimension to substantive legitimate expectations. Where Parliament has accorded decision-making powers to certain bodies, it is important that the body has sufficient discretion to exercise its judgement in the light of new information. The court must be wary of trespassing beyond the appropriate constitutional limits of its role. Nevertheless, it is now well settled that there should be some protection in certain circumstances for substantive legitimate expectations in administrative law. The disagreements have rather focused on the standard of review in the judicial assessment of whether a departure from existing policy is justified in the claimant's situation.

In its origins, the doctrine of substantive legitimate expectations touched a neuralgic point in wider debates around judicial power. In *Hamble Fisheries*, Sedley J supported the recognition of substantive legitimate expectations.[84] In *Hargreaves*, the Court of Appeal described Sedley J's approach as 'heresy'.[85] The recognition of substantive legitimate expectations came in *Coughlan*, where a local authority sought to resile from representations that an individual could live in a residential care facility for as long as required.[86] In this case, the local authority needed to do more than simply demonstrate that it had considered the claimant's expectation in its deliberations. This would be tantamount to bare rationality review of the kind countenanced in *Dalgleish* itself. As Craig has argued, where the decision-maker is free to determine how much weight to attach to this consideration in its own deliberations, it would be 'almost impossible for the individual to succeed on this criterion'.[87] In *Nadarajah*, Laws LJ articulated this in terms of a proportionality standard, such that the departure must be 'objectively justified as a proportionate measure in the circumstances'.[88]

In his published work, Lord Sales has been critical of the proportionality standard in *Nadarajah*.[89] As he acknowledges, 'argument about the relevant standard shades into the arguments about whether proportionality should be adopted as a general test of lawfulness under domestic administrative law'.[90] We think that the background concern for Lord Sales is that proportionality leads to an undue encroachment on the decisional autonomy of the primary decision-maker. Where Parliament has allocated decision-making power to a public body, in circumstances where that body

[82] Craig (n 75) [22-005]–[22-008].

[83] ibid [22-008].

[84] *R v Ministry of Agriculture, Fisheries and Food, ex p Hamble (Offshore) Fisheries Ltd* [1995] 2 All ER 714 (QBD).

[85] *R v Secretary of State for the Home Department, ex p Hargreaves* [1997] 1 WLR 906 (CA) 921.

[86] *Coughlan* (n 79).

[87] Craig (n 75) [22-018].

[88] *Nadarajah* (n 80) [68].

[89] Sales (n 80) 190.

[90] ibid.

has expertise and sensitivity to particular factual circumstances, the adoption of a proportionality standard could lead the court beyond the proper limits of its review function. He is also concerned about the 'extremely diffuse' nature of 'legitimate aim' in the proportionality enquiry, which may lead the court into disrupting political judgements about the distribution of public resources.[91] In these circumstances, it is less intrusive to afford procedural rights to the claimant, and the opportunity to make representations to the public body.[92] For these reasons, Lord Sales is sceptical about the proportionality standard in substantive legitimate expectation cases.

Given this general scepticism about the proportionality standard in administrative law, Lord Sales' approach to *Dalgleish* is unsurprising. While we recognise the validity of Lord Sales' concern that courts should respect appropriate constitutional limits, this can be accommodated within the existing doctrinal parameters of substantive legitimate expectations. First, we note that the approach in *Nadarajah* has been affirmed by the Supreme Court and must now be regarded as authoritative.[93] We also note that *Wednesbury* has been treated as relevant to employment contracts by the Supreme Court in *Braganza*. In light of this, there must be a reasoned justification as to why other public law concepts, such as substantive legitimate expectations, are not also relevant to employment contracts in appropriate cases. Second, we agree with Craig that the proportionality standard provides a structured and transparent method of review, with the flexibility to be applied with varying intensity depending upon the facts.[94] There is nothing in proportionality that leads the court ineluctably into substitution of judgement. Third, the practical effect of an irrationality standard is to insulate the exercise of the power from legal challenge in all but the most extreme cases. The primary decision-maker can decide what weight to attach to the expectation. Provided that it can demonstrate it has considered the expectation and exercised its discretion within the wide boundary set by perversity, the court cannot intervene. We think that substantive legitimate expectations should be given stronger weight than this, and the court should be able to scrutinise the weight attached to those expectations in the decision-maker's deliberations. Fourth, the proportionality standard is flexible enough to discriminate between the different factual scenarios that may arise under the broad umbrella of substantive legitimate expectations. For example, the courts should be particularly cautious where a decision-maker is seeking to change a general policy, rather than to depart from a narrowly targeted representation to an individual or identifiable group in a specific case. Where there are far-reaching consequences in holding the decision-maker to its policy, drawing the court into complex political questions about the appropriate allocation of resources, there should be less intensive application of the proportionality standard.

We acknowledge that the doctrine of substantive legitimate expectations cannot simply be transplanted into the very different constitutional context of employment contracts. In *Dalgleish*, the employer is not acting as a public body. Its powers are rooted in a private contractual arrangement, albeit within the context of general

[91] ibid.

[92] ibid 191.

[93] *Re Finucane's Application for Judicial Review* [2019] UKSC 7, [2019] 3 All ER 191.

[94] Craig (n 75) [22-020].

statutory regulation and oversight of pension powers. The concept of public interest does not operate in the same way where private contractual powers are subjected to judicial review. At the level of normative justification, the rationales for substantive legitimate expectations, such as fairness in public administration or trust in government, do not translate easily into the context of private contractual powers. Furthermore, the identification of reasons that could justify a departure from the general policy is less amenable to judicial determination where there is no statutory context to inform the content of 'public interest'. We are nevertheless confident that it is possible to translate doctrines such as substantive legitimate expectations in ways that are sensitive to the particularities of the employment contract. We turn to this in the following two sub-sections.

C. Substantive Legitimate Expectations, Pensions and Human Capabilities

Why should we protect substantive legitimate expectations in a case like *Dalgleish*? The normative justifications for a doctrine of substantive legitimate expectations in public law are tailored to the distinctive context of public power. Even if we were to appeal to some general unifying idea such as 'abuse of power',[95] this invites a series of further questions about its meaning in the distinctive context of employment. Is there an 'abuse of power' where a private entity changes its policies using its discretionary powers under the employment contract? We are somewhat sympathetic to the view that 'abuse of power' operates more as a conclusory label, with the normative work being done by other more particular principles.[96]

We suggest, however, that the capabilities approach could provide a normative justification for the judicial protection of substantive legitimate expectations in the pensions field. The capabilities approach has been very prominent as a framework in labour law.[97] While there are some important differences between the leading protagonists, Amartya Sen and Martha Nussbaum, the core idea is that of substantive human freedom: which rights, resources and supports do human beings need in order to lead the kinds of lives that they have reason to value? In this vein, Nussbaum has developed an account of the 'central capabilities'. These 'central capabilities' identify the basic conditions of human flourishing by setting a minimum threshold for a life that is worthy of human dignity. As fundamental entitlements, the 'central capabilities' provide 'the core of an account of minimal social justice and constitutional law'.[98] These capabilities are listed as: life; bodily health; bodily integrity; senses, imagination, and thought; emotions; practical reason; affiliation; relations with other species; play; and control over one's environment (political and material).[99]

[95] J Laws, 'Public Law and Employment Law: Abuse of Power' [1997] *Public Law* 455.
[96] Craig (n 75) [22-018].
[97] See generally B Langille (ed), *The Capability Approach to Labour Law* (Oxford, Oxford University Press, 2019).
[98] MC Nussbaum, *Creating Capabilities: The Human Development Approach* (Cambridge, MA, Harvard University Press, 2011) 71.
[99] MC Nussbaum, 'Capabilities and Human Rights' (1997) 66 *Fordham Law Review* 273, 287–88.

Nussbaum has described this project as a form of 'Aristotelian Social Democracy'. It is reflected in a broad understanding of what counts as 'constitutional'. On Nussbaum's approach, the institutions and rules that regulate labour 'are absolutely basic, at least as basic, and perhaps more so, than the scheme of offices and concrete judicial and deliberative institutions'.[100] This necessitates 'a searching examination of the forms of labour and the relations of production, and for the construction of fully human and sociable forms of labour for all citizens, with an eye to all the forms of human functioning'.[101]

Many contractual powers do not engage the 'central capabilities' in an obvious way. For example, the failure to be awarded a financial bonus in a given year is unlikely to damage the employee's prospects to such a degree that it interferes with the threshold of a dignified life. We contend that matters are somewhat different with pensions powers. We think that the capabilities of 'practical reason' and 'control over one's material environment' are engaged in the circumstances of the *Dalgleish* case, and this makes the case law on bankers' bonuses an unreliable normative benchmark. The capability of practical reason requires that the citizen has the rights and resources to formulate and live in accordance with a life plan. The capability of material control requires that the citizen has a measure of control over their material circumstances, including the ability to exercise democratic influence over the major decisions that impact upon working life. Both capabilities were undermined very considerably in *Dalgleish*. The employer effectively pulled the rug from beneath the employees' feet, at a point in their lives where many life decisions of long-term consequence had already been taken. For many of them, it was far too late to encourage 'exit' as a credible remedial response to the employer's actions. We regard this as a reheated version of the Epstein 'contract-at-will' argument, far removed from the realities of lived experience for employees whose lives are rooted in family and social commitments, and long-term and committed employment based upon a specific vocation. Furthermore, the employer's decisions in *Dalgleish* had been taken without appropriate consultation or negotiation, thereby undermining the democratic accountability of the decision-makers. It was, in short, a decision that had highly disruptive consequences for the long-term plans of employees. Moreover, these employees appear to have been treated as components in an economistic calculation about boosting share prices, rather than human agents pursuing important long-range goals.

There are three further reasons why this specific undermining of capabilities in *Dalgleish* should be treated as having moral urgency. First, 'practical reason' has been described by Nussbaum as 'architectonic', which emphasises its overarching importance as a human capability.[102] Practical reason gives human shape to a life, and it supports and underpins the other central capabilities. Where the capability of practical reason is damaged, for example where public or private authorities disrupt fundamental planning decisions that propagate across an entire life course, the public responsibility to intervene and uphold the capability may be regarded as

[100] MC Nussbaum, 'Aristotelian Social Democracy' in RB Douglass et al (eds), *Liberalism and the Good* (Abingdon, Routledge, 1990) 229.
[101] ibid 231.
[102] ibid.

especially strong. Second, the kinds of decision at issue in *Dalgleish* may give rise to what has been described as 'corrosive disadvantage'.[103] This occurs where certain capability failures propagate across a range of capabilities, setting off a chain reaction of cascading disadvantages. It is not fanciful to suppose that unexpected economic deprivation for ageing workers might lead to these 'corrosive disadvantage' effects in later life.[104] Finally, Nussbaum has emphasised the value of 'capability security' in her work.[105] Jonathan Wolff and Avner de-Shalit have also drawn attention to the disadvantage that results from capabilities being exposed to the arbitrary will of the powerful.[106] A doctrine of substantive legitimate expectations may be understood as a form of 'capability security' for workers, and this has a particular moral urgency where the relevant capability is 'architectonic' and a potential source of 'corrosive disadvantage'. *Dalgleish* is an exemplar of this kind of situation. It provides a strong moral argument as to why expectations in the pensions field should be treated as having much greater weight than expectations in the field of discretionary bonuses.

D. Substantive Legitimate Expectations and the Standard of Review

The capabilities approach thus provides a strong normative rationale for protecting substantive legitimate expectations in the pensions field. However, even acknowledging the force of the normative justification, there are still important questions about the application of a *Nadarajah*-style proportionality standard in the very different context of employers' powers under the employment contract. This raises questions about the appropriate degree of 'judicial self-restraint' in the employment context. The relevant 'deference factors' might operate differently given the context, and this has implications for the judicial formulation of the standard of review. Thus, ACL Davies points out, as we have previously noted, that the constitutional context to public law and labour law cases is often very different, since in public law 'the courts' aim in developing deference has been to keep within their own constitutional limits in the light of their understanding of the separation of powers'.[107]

Davies has identified a range of 'deference factors'. These are: 'institutional expertise', which is concerned with the capacities of courts and bipolar litigation in addressing the challenges of polycentricity, particularly in situations involving complex trade-offs and resource allocation decisions; 'expertise' in relation to the specific subject matter of the decision-making power; and the existence of mechanisms of democratic accountability in the decision-making process, evaluating whether the decision was preceded by an appropriate consultative or negotiation process.[108]

In her examination of different areas of judicial review in labour law, Davies has identified a highly deferential pattern in the context of implied terms and

[103] J Wolff and A de-Shalit, *Disadvantage* (Oxford, Oxford University Press, 2007) 120–28.

[104] P Alon-Shenker, 'Capabilities and Age Discrimination' in B Langille (ed), *The Capability Approach to Labour Law* (Oxford, Oxford University Press, 2019).

[105] Nussbaum, *Creating Capabilities* (n 98) 73.

[106] Wolff and de-Shalit (n 103) 3.

[107] Davies, 'Judicial Self-Restraint in Labour Law' (n 49) 289.

[108] ibid 289–91.

reasonableness review.[109] She offers two explanations for this pattern. First, many of the cases involve discretionary bonuses, and this is an area of employer decision-making where the courts feel ill-equipped to adopt an interventionist role. Courts do not have the expertise to assess the employee's performance or the financial situation of the firm, and the distribution of resources in the firm raises polycentric issues that bipolar litigation cannot adequately address. We would add to this that there are rarely fundamental rights issues at stake in these cases. Second, since this is a common law jurisdiction, rather than one underpinned by statute, the courts may be conscious of legitimacy concerns with adopting a more interventionist approach.

To what extent are these considerations relevant to the situation in *Dalgeish*? We think that the 'expertise' and 'institutional expertise' considerations will weigh heavily with courts in the pensions context. The decisions will involve complex trade-offs between different stakeholders, in circumstances where there is a high degree of polycentricity. We also recognise that there are significant ramifications for large numbers of individuals in *Dalgleish*, and in this respect it is quite unlike the limited impact of upholding legitimate expectations in cases like *French* and *Transco*. Courts are also not well placed to engage in scrutiny of the economic basis to employer decision-making. These 'expertise' considerations would seem to point towards a *Wednesbury*-style review test and away from more intensive proportionality review.

However, the *Dalgleish* case is dissimilar to the bankers' bonuses cases in two critical respects. First, the exercise of the power in *Dalgleish* undermined fundamental capabilities of workers, positioning this in the same normative space as 'fundamental rights' cases. This would warrant more intensive judicial review. Second, this was a case where there had been a demonstrable failure of consultation procedures in the decision-making process. In these circumstances, employer decision-making occurred without the necessary democratic accountability. This must also be understood within the wider context of declining collective bargaining and trade union strength. The intervention of the court was necessary as a corrective to the serious democratic deficit in decision-making. For these reasons, we would suggest that the *Nadarajah* approach should have been adopted in *Dalgleish*.

IV. CONCLUDING THOUGHTS: THE LAW ON PENSIONS AS A JUDICIAL POWER PROJECT

'[Labour law] … is a place where law, politics and social assumptions meet in a person'.[110]

Labour law will always be a key site of the political. It is striking how configurations of the judicial role in labour law often reflect a wider set of commitments about constitutional structure, the role of parliamentary sovereignty, the scope for legal protection of fundamental rights, and the legitimacy of judicial power. A judge's public law orientation will usually be a reliable guide to her orientation in other legal

[109] ibid 294–98.

[110] Lord Wedderburn, *The Worker and the Law* (London, Penguin, 1986) 835.

fields such as labour law. At one level, *Dalgleish* is a dispute arising out of a highly technical body of legal rules at the intersections of pensions law, labour law, contract law and public law. Beneath the surface of these legal technicalities, it is a deeply political judgment. That is not a criticism. Judgments of this kind are inescapably political. Criticism is only warranted where the politics of judging is concealed rather than the cards being placed face up on the table, and the disputes are asserted to be merely technical or doctrinal.

The critics and defenders of judicial power usually line up in two broad political camps. On the one side, progressive judges like Sedley LJ and Laws LJ have been associated with a developing common law that operates as a corrective to abuses of public and private power. There is an alignment with their respective positions in public law and labour law, and it is an alignment that we do not regard as coincidental. It is no surprise that both Sedley LJ and Laws LJ were architects of the modern law on substantive legitimate expectations, which is widely regarded as an administrative law success story. They are also associated with a progressive worker-protective approach in labour law. On the other side, judges such as Lord Sumption have asserted a strong distinction between 'law' and 'politics', as a part of a broader project to restrain the judicial role.[111] That is not to say that these judges treat abuse of power as ethically legitimate. That is not so. It does reflect a strong preference for political over judicial mechanisms, 'politics' over 'law', to address those social and economic problems. We would read Lord Sales' arguments on *Dalgleish* as fairly closely aligned with Lord Sumption's juridical world-view.

For much of the twentieth century, the labour lawyer's encounter with the common law was a Sisyphean task. Each occasion marked the beginning of a new homily on the distinctiveness of the employment contract, the common law myth of bargaining equality, the subordination inherent in the employment relation, and the fundamental fact that to sell one's labour power is in fact to sell *oneself* to a purchaser of labour power for an allotted period of time. It was a homily that almost always fell on deaf judicial ears.

For now, we live in better times. The distinctiveness of the employment contract, and its public dimensions, have now been affirmed by the highest courts on many occasions. Labour law as an autonomous worker-protective field now has a firm foothold in common law precedent. However, we should not be complacent about that. Changes to the compositions and dispositions of the highest courts may have significant doctrinal implications. Labour lawyers will certainly be watching closely following the retirement of Lady Hale. In our view, *Dalgleish* represents a missed opportunity to give that public dimension its appropriate due, through a doctrine of proportionality and legitimate expectations. Judicial power is a potent tool. It must be wielded wisely and in accordance with constitutional constraints. Fundamentally, it should be guided by respect for the minimum threshold conditions of a dignified life, which is based upon respect for human capabilities. For the time being, we are left wondering at how pension security will be underwritten for workers in the twenty-first century, and which public institutions should bear that responsibility.

[111] As, eg, in J Sumption, *Trials of the State* (London, Profile Books, 2019).

Those reflections, and that last question, lead us to a final assertion. A grand and existential question has hovered almost silently in the air above this chapter, perhaps even above all the chapters in this book. The stated enquiry of this chapter has been as to where pensions law stands in relation to the perceived dichotomy between public law and private law. But our attempts to resolve that problem have largely turned upon a different and more specific juridical issue, namely that of the relationship between pensions law and labour law. In the course of discussing and writing this chapter, we have become more than ever convinced of the nature and importance of that relationship: but we have allowed that certainty to sit in the background as an unstated assumption. We now place it in the foreground, openly identifying it as both an analytical and a normative proposition.

The law of occupational pensions could always have been regarded as functionally part of or continuous with labour law in the UK. In many legal systems, this would be regarded as obvious and uncontroversial, in the sense that occupational social security provision has been bracketed together with labour law under the general umbrella of 'social law'. In the UK, pensions law has tended to develop as a distinct discipline, not least because of the extent of its technical dependence upon the law of trusts. But we are of the view that its functional integration into labour law should be re-emphasised. We think that the extension of labour law's key obligation of mutual trust and confidence into the sphere of pensions law in the *Imperial Tobacco* case was entirely appropriate in the analytical sense. Its maintenance in a vigorous condition in that context is quite crucial to the preservation of the general normative fabric of labour law. In this chapter, we have debated the place of public law in pensions law, and we are content to regard that as a complex and ongoing controversy, albeit one in which we have taken up a strong position especially with regard to public law's doctrine of legitimate expectations. Yet as to the place of pensions law as falling squarely within the broad province of worker-protective labour law, we hope that we have been fully clear and unequivocal with our readership.

13

The Improper Purpose Rule: An Employer's Tool to Control Pension Trustees in Need of Reappraisal

DAN SCHAFFER

I. INTRODUCTION

THE IMPROPER PURPOSE rule, used as a tool by employers to control pension scheme trustees, needs serious reappraisal. This chapter is concerned with an employer's ability to challenge its pension scheme trustee on its exercise of discretions.[1] The employer's motivation for challenge is the considerable economic impact that trustee decisions can now have on corporate cash flow, balance sheets and corporate activity against a backdrop of deficits in pension schemes.[2] Viewed from the membership's perspective, where these challenges to the trustee are made by the employer, they can impact members' reasonable expectations and the security and value of their benefits and pensions in payment.

There is a range of ways in which trustees' decision-making can be challenged by an employer. This chapter is specifically concerned with examining when it is legitimate to challenge on the ground that the trustees would be exercising the power in question – while within its scope – for an improper purpose[3] or in classical terminology, in a way that constitutes a 'fraud on a power'. The chapter argues that

[1] Some trustee discretions are conferred by statute, eg, in the Pensions Acts 1995 and 2004. However, this chapter is focused on discretions vested in trustees by trust deeds drafted by the companies which set up the schemes. The first trustees are not typically involved in the design and drafting of the first trust deed and rules. Exceptionally they can be, eg, the industry-wide Railways Pension Scheme established on railway privatisation, where the British Rail Pension Trustee Company Limited was heavily involved in scheme constitutional design.

[2] See the annual Scheme Funding Analysis published by the Pensions Regulator. The UK's defined benefit pension schemes deficit stood at £180 billion at the end of April 2019 according to PWC's Skyval Index: www.pwc.co.uk/press-room/press-releases/PwC-Skyval-Index-shows-80bn-drop-in-UK-pension-deficit-during-April.html.

[3] For the consequences of acting outside the purpose see J Hudson, 'One Thicket in Fraud on a Power' (2019) 39 *OJLS* 577.

the latest appellate development in this area[4] highlights a need for serious reappraisal of the principle in an occupational pension scheme context.

In the words of Lord Westbury in the leading decision, *Duke of Portland v Topham*, a power must only be exercised for the 'entire and single view to the *real purpose* and object of the power',[5] ie, the power cannot be used 'for the purpose of accomplishing or carrying into effect any … object … beyond the purpose and intent of the power'.

The trustee's obligation to act in accordance with the purpose of the power is a general principle of Equity. It is not a duty that is dependent upon being found in the particular trust deed through implication. As Lord Sumption put it, in a company law context, in *Eclairs Group Ltd v JKX Oil & Gas plc*:

> I do not doubt that a term limiting the exercise of powers conferred on the directors to their proper purpose may sometimes be implied on the ordinary principles of the law of contract governing the implication of terms. But that is not the basis of the proper purpose rule. The rule is not a term of the contract and does not necessarily depend on any limitation on the scope of the power as a matter of construction. *The proper purpose rule is a principle by which equity controls the exercise of a fiduciary's powers in respects which are not, or not necessarily, determined by the instrument.*[6]

This chapter focuses on three issues with the improper purpose rule that have not been satisfactorily addressed. First, the problem with the concept of 'the real purpose'. Second, what is and should be the ambit of judicial discretion (in the Dworkian sense)[7] to rule that, while the purported exercise complies with its letter, it does not comply with its 'intended' 'real purpose'?[8] Third, is and should the position be different if the purpose[9] is expressly addressed on the face of a power – is and should there be any room for judicial discretion to 'search' further for the 'real purpose'?

II. THE PROBLEM WITH THE CONCEPT OF THE 'REAL PURPOSE' OF A POWER

Lord Sumption remarked in *Eclairs*:

> The purpose of a power … is rarely expressed in the instrument itself. It was not expressed in the instrument in any of the leading cases about the application of the proper purpose rule to the powers of directors which I have summarised. But it is usually obvious from its context and effect why a power has been conferred.[10]

[4] *British Airways plc v Airways Pension Scheme Trustee Ltd* [2018] EWCA Civ 1533, [2018] Pens LR 19.

[5] *Duke of Portland v Topham* (1864) 11 HL Cas 32, 54, 11 ER 1242 (emphasis added).

[6] *Eclairs Group Ltd v JKX Oil & Gas plc* [2015] UKSC 71, [2016] 3 All ER 641 [30] (emphasis added).

[7] R Dworkin, *Taking Rights Seriously* (Cambridge, MA, Harvard University Press, 1977) 31: 'Discretion is like the hole in a doughnut it does not exist except as an area left open by a surrounding belt of restriction'.

[8] The improper purpose rule focuses on whether the action would be outside the purpose. For the history of the rule, see Lord Sumption's judgment in *Eclairs* (n 6) [14]–[29].

[9] It is a different question from the effect and relevance of an objects clause which is not determinative: see Lord Walker in *Bank of New Zealand v Bank of New Zealand Officers Provident Association Management Board* [2003] UKPC 58, [2003] OPLR 281 [20]–[21].

[10] *Eclairs* (n 6) [31].

However, as Professor Worthington quite rightly observes: 'But however "obvious", reasonable minds are likely to differ, and it is this that makes the proper purposes jurisdiction so fraught'.[11]

The word 'real' has a psychological impact that creates the instant false impression that there must be a quasi-scientific forensic process to determine what the donor of the power intended the limits of the power's usage to be, even though he had not written them down in the provision. The impression 'real' gives is that there must be a process, with the focus on objective and possibly subjective contemporaneous intention of the party or parties who created the power. The appeal to what the donor of the power must have *intended* is what gives 'the real purpose' concept its legitimacy.

However, the process the courts actually follow to reach a judgment on 'intention of the donor' does not have the rigour of either the rules of contractual interpretation of words to determine the scope of a power, or the forensic process to deduce intention in rectification[12] or even equitable rescission proceedings.[13]

Thomas on Powers calls purpose a 'slippery concept'.[14] Rather than try to pin down an inherently imprecise concept, it is suggested that it would be more productive to focus – not on a supposed objective concept – but rather on the ambit of judicial discretion to rule on what the limits of the power's usage in a particular context should be.

III. THE AMBIT OF JUDICIAL DISCRETION

There is unsurprisingly no clear answer in any of the leading practitioner trusts law texts on what the ambit is. *Lewin on Trusts* classifies the case law under the broad headings of exercising a power: (i) for a 'corrupt purpose'; (ii) where there is a bargain to benefit a non-object; (iii) other foreign purpose.[15] *Thomas on Powers* concludes that the application of the improper purpose rule in the pensions area is difficult because it is 'difficult to distinguish the boundaries between fraudulent and excessive exercise of powers'.[16] Dr Michael Ashdown concludes 'there remains a high degree of uncertainty as to the doctrinal basis of the fraud on a power doctrine'.[17]

It is, therefore, helpful to begin by asking what is a judge, when faced with only the highest level of guidance, likely to start with as first principles (shorn of all the obfuscating mantra language) for the legitimating basis for intervention.

[11] S Worthington, 'Directors' Duties and Improper Purposes' (2016) 75 *CLJ* 213.

[12] *FSHC Group Holdings Ltd v GLAS Trust Corporation Ltd* [2019] EWCA Civ 1361, [2019] 7 WLUK 545.

[13] *Pitt v HMRC* [2013] UKSC 26, [2013] 2 AC 108.

[14] G Thomas, *Thomas on Powers*, 2nd edn (Oxford, Oxford University Press, 2012) ch 9.

[15] *Lewin on Trusts*, 19th edn (London, Sweet & Maxwell, 2014) [29-289]–[29-303]. See also *Thomas* (n 14) paras [9.13]–[9.26]. There is an interesting discussion on the doctrinal basis for fraud on a power in: M Ashdown, *Trustee Decision Making: The Rule in Re Hastings-Bass* (Oxford, Oxford University Press, 2015) ch 9. See also D Pollard, 'Application of the Proper Purpose Test to Pension Schemes' (2016) 30 *Trust Law International* 159; and D Pollard, 'Exercising Powers: Proper Purposes Rather than Best Interests: Fiduciaries and Eclairs' (2016) 30 *Trust Law International* 71.

[16] *Thomas* (n 14) para [9.35].

[17] *Ashdown* (n 15) para [9.13].

Lord Sales, speaking extra-judicially, describes the most probable answer.[18] He describes how he sees the justification for the improper purpose rule being founded on the law responding to humans in long-term business relationships being unable prophetically to foresee all future circumstances and, aware of this, providing flexibility to meet changes the world may present. They do this by conferring a power to make decisions and in doing so turn their minds to 'contemplate' the limits of what the power should be used for.

If this is right – and it sits with the language of the case law[19] – the judge's legitimating basis to intervene and prevent one party acting on the express words of a power to exercise it to the disadvantage of another is likely to be the following. Intervention prevents inequitable exploitation of lack of prophetic foresight. It prevents a party inequitably resiling from a shared, but unspoken, understanding of the principles that created: (i) the mutual trust that allowed them to commit to that long-term relationship; and (ii) the predictability that facilitates economically Pareto efficient outcomes.

Lord Sales put it this way in the Chancery Bar Association 2019 and the 2019 Lehane Memorial lectures:[20]

> On this approach to analysing how to construe the ambit of a contractual power, one has to stand back from the mere language of the power-conferring provision, which may be entirely general. *It is necessary instead to form a broad view of the purposes of the venture to which the contract gives effect*, and of what loyalty to that venture might involve for a party to it, and to take those broad purposes as providing the inherent limits for the exercise of the power. Those limits will constrain the due exercise of the power whether the illegitimate purpose for which it is exercised is patent at the time of the exercise or is latent.
>
> It might be said that this seems a rather vague test for the limits of a discretionary power. But the vagueness does not mean that the limits are contentless; nor that there is an absence of a methodology for working out in a particular case where the limits lie. That can be done having regard to the nature of the venture, the other contractual terms and what is sought to be achieved by the exercise of the power.
>
> In fact, the vagueness is just a reflection of the situation the parties find themselves in when they contract, in which they cannot predict future circumstances but wish to make provision for their relationship to be capable of continuance into the future, including by adjustment to future events via the exercise of discretionary powers created for that very purpose. If the court can discern the broad outlines of what the parties contemplated such powers could or should be used for, and can tell when a purported exercise lies outside such

[18] Lord Sales, 'The Interface between Contract and Equity' (Lehane Memorial Lecture, Sydney, 28 August 2019), available at: www.supremecourt.uk/docs/speech-190828.pdf; Lord Sales, 'Fraud on a Power: the interface between contract and equity' (Lecture for the Chancery Bar Association, 2 April 2019), available at: www.supremecourt.uk/docs/speech-190828.pdf. See also Lord Sales' chapter in this volume.

[19] See: *Snell's Equity*, 33rd edn (London, Sweet & Maxwell, 2015) para [10–22] 'expectations of the settlor(s) of the trust'. *Thomas* (n 14) para [9.03], fn 26: 'ascertaining the true purpose of a power as at the date of its creation may well be problematic if the question arises many years later, particularly in commercial contexts'. There is a powerful case being argued for here for focus on the evidential practicability and consistency in pension cases where the powers in issue were created perhaps 50 years ago or more in the trust deed. This is very different from a private trust focused on the more recent intention of one settlor, a natural person.

[20] Lord Sales (n 18) (emphasis added).

> contemplation, it is difficult to see why as a matter of contractual interpretation the court cannot say that the use of the power exceeds those contractual powers.

This confirms the suggestion of Professor Grantham that the donor of the power

> *cannot foresee every eventuality* and cannot, therefore enumerate every use of the power [he] must confer a power that is in its terms literally wider than he intends [but the law must] devise means to ensure that quite apart from the literal terms of the power it is used only for the purposes for which *it was intended*.[21]

This 'imperfect foresight and contemplation/intention' thesis for the legitimating basis for judicial intervention and the emphasis on 'interpretation' (rather than on extrinsic evidence) to divine that 'intention' may well be apposite to a commercial contract. However, it is not appropriate in the context of unilateral trustee discretions in occupational pension scheme trusts.[22] The Court of Appeal decision in *British Airways plc v Airways Pension Scheme Trustee Limited*[23] is an object lesson as to why. It highlights why the improper purpose rule demands fundamental reconsideration of its juristic basis. This was denied in that litigation because the parties settled and the appeal hearing in the Supreme Court was vacated.[24]

The majority in the Court of Appeal in the *British Airways* case takes the Lord Sales approach on both the parties' intention and on divining that intention through 'interpretation' of the scheme's trust deed. However, as explained below, what the 'imperfect foresight and contemplation/intention' justification thesis hands judges is a licence to do exactly what Professor Paul Davies eloquently addressed in his UCL inaugural lecture.[25] It allows judges to rewrite bad bargains or – more accurately in a pensions trust context – to remedy the obvious oversight of the employer who established (or subsequently allowed to be amended) the trust deed many decades ago and conferred a unilateral power on the trustees.

It is suggested that neither 'imperfect foresight' nor loyalty to the 'intent' of the original employer as settlor by the parties can convincingly be described as the basis that should lead to judicial intervention (if judicial intervention is appropriate at all) to allow the letter of the power to be overridden.

A. Oversight in Drafting the Power is not a Convincing Basis for Holding that it would be Improper to Allow Exercise in Accordance with the Letter of the Power

It has always been open to employers to vest powers in a pension trust jointly in the employer and trustee. Most powers of consequence in a trust deed are vested in the trustee and employer or in the employer alone. The compendium of precedents

[21] R Grantham, 'The Powers of Company Directors and the Proper Purposes Doctrine' (1994–95) 5 *King's College Law Journal* 16, 44 (emphasis added).

[22] Compare Lord Sales' Lehane Memorial Lecture (n 18), where he put forward the opposing view.

[23] *British Airways* (n 4).

[24] *Airways Pension Scheme Trustee Ltd v Fielder* [2019] EWHC 3027 (Ch).

[25] P Davies, 'Bad Bargains' (Inaugural Lecture, 31 January 2019), (2019) 72(1) *Current Legal Problems* 253–286.

for the drafting of pension schemes published in 1957, Phillips' *Pension Scheme Precedents*, testifies to this.[26] Only the investment power, as a result of statutory override introduced in the 1990s,[27] must be a unilateral trustee discretion, but even then the scope of investment powers can be circumscribed.[28]

Nevertheless, it is the case that some trust deeds of UK occupational pension schemes were established or amended such that a key discretionary power was unilaterally vested in the trustees, and now, decades later, that same unilateral power causes serious concern to the corporate sponsor.[29] These crucial powers include: the contribution power that allows the trustees to set the employer funding obligation;[30] the power to wind up the scheme which brings with it a section 75 debt to be paid into the scheme;[31] a trustee power to change the balance of power in favour of members following a change of control of the principal employer;[32] a power to alter the index used for revaluation of benefits accrued by a former active member of the scheme; a power to alter the index used to increase pensions in payment; and finally the power of amendment itself.

Why, one must ask, would these employers ever vest these crucial powers unilaterally in their trustees? The answer is that the twenty-first-century scenarios where trustees' decisions come into conflict with the employer's financial interests would more than likely have not been addressed when the scheme was set up or when the unilateral power was conferred. Most UK defined benefit pension schemes that exist today were set up between the 1920s and the 1980s. In that period there is unlikely to have been any conscious consideration by a company setting up or amending a scheme that conferring a power unilaterally on trustees would eventually come to have serious financial implications.[33] While the precedents in the leading work, Phillips' *Pension Scheme Precedents*,[34] are drafted to vest the above key powers in the employer and trustee jointly, there is nothing in the commentary that warns[35] the draftsman of potential reasons for not conferring powers unilaterally in the trustee. However, rather presciently, the author states:

> It is the author's view that the amending of an existing scheme presents more pitfalls than the drafting of a new scheme. Certainly when inconsistencies or contradictions are found in the constitution of an existing scheme, they are more often than not the results of amendments, those amendments having been made without regard to their effect on other provisions.[36]

[26] W Phillips, *Pension Scheme Precedents* (London, Sweet & Maxwell, 1957).

[27] Pensions Act 1995, s 35(5); Pensions Act 2004, s 244.

[28] Pensions Act 1995, s 36; Pensions Act 2004, s 245.

[29] Writing in 1993 before the Goode Report, see R Nobles, *Pensions, Employment, and the Law* (Oxford, Clarendon Press, 1993) 28 for an excellent description of the balance of powers in schemes.

[30] Thereby controlling the Pensions Act 2004 funding regime and imposing potentially more onerous funding obligations than those which are statutorily required.

[31] Bringing a significant debt payable as a single lump sum under the Pensions Act 1995, s 75.

[32] Typically inserted in the 1980s and 1990s to deter a corporate raider seeking to access a pension fund surplus. It can include the power to increase benefits, control funding and even wind up the scheme.

[33] By 1990 the position had begun to change with, eg, the Electricity Supply Pension Scheme where the balance of powers is extremely employer-centric with minimal trustee power.

[34] Phillips (n 26).

[35] Including in the express warnings about drafting in the Preface.

[36] Phillips (n 26) ch 42, 4203.

Therefore, to attribute to the employer at the time when the unilateral power was conferred on the trustees an *implicit* assumption that the trustees would only use the unilateral power *in certain types of circumstances* and not in others, must be called into question and at the very least would need to be seriously investigated where it is contended in an individual case. Lord Sales' emphasis in his 2019 lectures on using interpretation of the terms of the instrument as the means to derive this intention underplays the importance that extrinsic evidence plays and should play in the area of fraud on a power.[37] This underplaying was also evident in the approach of the majority in the Court of Appeal in *British Airways*.[38]

Finding extrinsic evidence should be regarded as critical to support a contention that the donor of the power actually gave thought to how the unilateral power would or might be used. And this will, in a pensions domain, be very challenging where the power conferral may have taken place over half a century before. Witnesses may all be dead and there will be no company records. Without such contemporaneous evidence, however, the law is taking an inconsistent approach to addressing failure in the drafting (for eventualities). The law takes a strict evidential approach to rectifying pension deeds and to equitable rescission. If the employer who conferred a unilateral power were to contend that, in the course of conferral, he had mistakenly assumed that the trustee's exercise of the power would be restricted (even though the employer did not take the simple step of drafting the power to qualify it by retaining an employer veto), a court should be asking itself why it is justified to recharacterise oversight (ignorance) as an assumption. Lord Walker addressed this issue in *Pitt v HMRC* with the answer that the court had witness evidence to be able to draw this assumption:

> For present purposes a mistake must be distinguished from mere ignorance or inadvertence, and also from what scholars in the field of unjust enrichment refer to as misprediction (see Seah, 'Mispredictions, Mistakes and the Law of Unjust Enrichment' [2007] RLR 93; the expression may have first received judicial currency in *Dextra Bank & Trust Co Ltd v Bank of Jamaica* [2002] 1 All ER (Comm) 193). These distinctions are reasonably clear in a general sort of way, but they tend to get blurred when it comes to facts of particular cases. The editors of *Goff and Jones, The Law of Unjust Enrichment*, 8th ed (2011) para 9–11 comment that the distinction between mistake and misprediction can lead to 'some uncomfortably fine distinctions', and the same is true of the distinction between mistake and ignorance

[37] See *Snell's Equity* (n 19) para [10–22]. However, see *Thomas* (n 14) 9.03, which questions extrinsic evidence. This further underlines why the improper purpose rule cries out for Supreme Court consideration in a pensions context. The problem with over-reliance on interpretation is that it has been exhausted in determining the scope of the power. The process then becomes what American jurisprudence terms construction (implication), see LB Solum, 'The Interpretation-Construction Distinction' (2010) *Georgetown Law Faculty Publications and Other Works* 676, available at: www.scholarship.law.georgetown.edu/facpub/676; AL Corbin, 'Conditions in the Law of Contract' (1918–19) 28 *Yale Law Journal* 739; EW Patterson, 'The Interpretation and Construction of Contracts' (1964) 64 *Columbia Law Review* 833; EA Farnsworth, '"Meaning" in the Law of Contracts' (1967) 76 *Yale Law Journal* 939; A Schwartz and RE Scott, 'Contract Theory and the Limits of Contract Law' (2003) 113 *Yale Law Journal* 541; A Schwartz and RE Scott, 'Contract Interpretation Redux' (2010) 119 *Yale Law Journal* 926; RJ Gilson, CF Sabel and RE Scott, 'Text and Context: Contract Interpretation as Contract Design' (2014) 100 *Cornell Law Review* 23; G Klass, 'Interpretation and Construction in Contract Law' (2018) *Georgetown Law Faculty Publications and Other Works* 1947.

[38] *British Airways* (n 4).

> …
>
> The fullest academic treatment of this topic is in *Goff & Jones* at paras 9–32 to 9–42. The editors distinguish between incorrect conscious beliefs, incorrect tacit assumptions, and true cases of mere causative ignorance ('causative' in the sense that but for his ignorance the person in question would not have acted as he did). The deputy judge's first-instance decision in *Pitt* [2010] 1 WLR 1190, para 50 is suggested as an example of mere causative ignorance: 'If someone does not apply his mind to a point at all, it is difficult to say that there has been some real mistake about it'. The Court of Appeal adopted a different view of the facts, treating the case (para 216) as one of an incorrect conscious belief on the part of Mrs Pitt that the SNT had no adverse tax consequences. The editors of *Goff & Jones* are, on balance, in favour of treating mere causative ignorance as sufficient. They comment (at para 9–41, in answering a 'floodgates' objection):
>
> …
>
> 'denying relief for mere causative ignorance produces a boundary line which may be difficult to draw in practice, and which is susceptible to judicial manipulation, according to whether it is felt that relief should be afforded – with the court's finding or declining to find incorrect conscious beliefs or tacit assumptions according to the court's perception of the merits of the claim'.
>
> It may indeed be difficult to draw the line between mere causative ignorance and a mistaken conscious belief or a mistaken tacit assumption. I would hold that mere ignorance, even if causative, is insufficient, but that the court, in carrying out its task of finding the facts, should not shrink from drawing the inference of conscious belief or tacit assumption when there is evidence to support such an inference. I shall return (paras 131 and 132 below) to the suggestion that this may involve 'judicial manipulation'.
>
> I add a postscript as to the criticism made by the editors of *Goff & Jones* (para 9–41), already quoted at para 108 above, of 'a boundary line which may be difficult to draw in practice, and which is susceptible to judicial manipulation, according to whether it is felt that relief should be afforded – with the court's finding or declining to find incorrect conscious beliefs or tacit assumptions according to the court's perception of the merits of the claim'. There is some force in this, although the term 'manipulation' is a bit harsh. The fact that a unilateral mistake is sufficient means that the court may have to make findings as to the state of mind, at some time in the past, of a claimant with a lively personal interest in establishing that there was a serious causative mistake. This will often be a difficult task. But as a criticism of the Court of Appeal in *Pitt* I would reject it. The case was heard on affidavit evidence, without cross-examination, and the Court of Appeal was in as good a position as the deputy judge to draw inferences and make findings of fact.[39]

It is suggested that if limits on the exercise of the power by reference to the cost that the trustees could cause the employer had actually received *any* critical attention, the outcome would have been as follows. A prudent, rational employer would have reacted by vesting that power jointly in itself and the trustee. It is no answer to say there is no such risk because the law implies constitutional limitations on the role of the pension trustees. This is because there needs to be a basis for that implication, and if that basis is to be the parties' intention, then we are back to the search for evidence of that intention.

[39] *Pitt v HMRC* (n 13) [104], [108] and [127].

If positive extrinsic evidence cannot be found for such intention then the starting point should be that the 1920s–1980s employer in practice did not contemplate limits on how the power vested unilaterally in the trustee would be used. This starting point is justified by the following observations:

1. The economic, demographic, actuarial, accounting and regulatory factors that now lead to the focus on the exercise of unilateral powers did not exist when most UK defined benefit pension schemes were set up. At the time the unilateral power was created, there was none of the tension between trustees and the corporate sponsoring employer that exists today. Tension only started to arise in the 1980s and 1990s and that tension revolved around the use of an actuarial surplus and whether a 'refund' to the employer or a 'contributions holiday' could be effected. And even then some employers would have been sanguine about the boundaries of powers because as Richard Nobles remarked in 1993: '[I]ndirect control is maintained by the employer's power to appoint and/or dismiss the trustees, and thereby choose persons likely to be sympathetic to the company'.[40]
2. Specialist pensions legal advice[41] focusing on the balance of power only really started in the mid-1980s and when the focus began it was on the use of an actuarial surplus.
3. Between the 1920s and 1980s there was no need for an employer[42] to think about the trustee board as being anything other than an extension of the company. Trustee boards were, until the mid-1990s and the Pensions Act 1995, dominated by senior management. There was no scrupulous management of conflicts of duty as exists today in a Pensions Regulator, post-Maxwell world. The prospects of a trustee board acting in a way the company would regard as detrimental to it would simply not have occurred. The Goode Report in 1993[43] appraised trustee governance, following Robert Maxwell's behaviour as chair of the Mirror Newspapers pension fund, noting:

   > 2.1.24 – Many schemes had trustee boards consisting entirely of trustees appointed by the employer, a practice which did not pass without criticism.
   >
   > 4.5.37 – There appears to be much cynicism about the ability of the majority of trustees to act in a 'textbook' fashion, paying regard to the interests of all beneficiaries at all times. It appears that many people do not perceive trustees to be independent and are concerned that employer-dominated trustee boards do not act in the best interests of the members. Indeed, the general feeling of ordinary members from whom we heard seemed to be one of isolation from their own scheme, with no say in any aspect of the administration or management of that scheme.

[40] Nobles (n 29) 29.

[41] The Association of Pension Lawyers was established with 20 members in 1984. In 2019 it has over 1,000 members.

[42] Or Minister of Government. Counsel in his submissions in *British Airways plc v Airways Pension Scheme Trustee Ltd* [2017] EWHC 1191 (Ch), [2017] Pens LR 16 [372] asserts that it 'cannot have been intended' to have conferred additional power on the trustees. It is submitted that the obverse is equally true, ie, there was no intention not to so confer. It would appear to the author that it is quite possible that the potential consequences were not addressed in 1971 and the point was possibly not revisited when the Minister's power to reverse usage of the trustee's unilateral power was removed on privatisation of BA in 1987. See Morgan J [423].

[43] Department for Social Security, *Pension Law Reform* (Cm 2342, 1993).

A court today must resist the urge to address unilateral power conferral in the 1920s–1980s through twenty-first-century spectacles. Today, employers would not confer unilateral powers on trustees and indeed are seeking to manage down defined benefit scheme liability on their balance sheets. The world has changed and corporate sponsors[44] will now robustly challenge unilateral power exercises and seek to persuade trustees to exercise *jointly* vested powers of amendment to reduce liability, for example, to agree to cease future service accrual of benefits. An interesting and important question arises of whether the doctrine of not exercising a power for an improper purpose will ever be applied by a court to a trustee's decision *not* to exercise a joint power. It may well do so by characterising that decision as itself an exercise of a power.[45]

B. If Lord Sales's 'Imperfect Foresight and Contemplation/Intention' Justification for Judicial Intervention is not Convincing in a Pensions Context, what would be a Legitimate Basis for Intervention under the Doctrine of 'Improper Purpose'?[46]

One possible basis would build upon Lord Sumption's remark in *Eclairs* that 'it is usually obvious from its context and effect why a power has been conferred'.[47] The basis would legitimise intervention where there is extrinsic contemporaneous evidence that the purpose was widely well known and that there is now no good, uncontroversial reason to extend the power to another circumstance and this makes sense for all parties. A concrete example where this basis would apply in practice – from the list of unilateral powers set out above – is the following. Trust deeds do sometimes contain a provision which provides that, where there is a change of control of the scheme's principal employer, then the trustee has the unilateral power to trigger a fundamental change in the balance of power under the trust deed, such that the trustee thereafter controls funding, pension increases and scheme wind-up. This type of provision would usually have been inserted in the late 1980s as a poison pill to deter corporate raiders intent on stripping surplus from the pension fund. This is very well known. The power could however have been drafted so that it would be triggered by a benign corporate reorganisation of shareholding, perhaps

[44] The company may not actually be a current employer. See, eg, *IBM United Kingdom Holdings Ltd v Dalgleish* [2017] EWCA Civ 1212, [2018] Pens LR 1 where the principal employer, IBM Holdings Limited, was not an employer. This may not make a difference in terms of how its own powers should be exercised. However, it was important to the outcome of that litigation (see [436], [446] and [453]).

[45] This is perfectly plausible. No distinction was made in *IBM v Dalgleish* by the High Court or Court of Appeal, in the application of the employer's *Imperial* duty to exercise powers in good faith, between the two employer powers in issue: the positive power in the rules to cease future service accrual; and the negative power IBM exercised not to continue to grant enhanced early retirement factors.

[46] There will be occasions where it will be easy for the court to reject intervention. An example would be an argument to restrain usage of a particular power that completely overlooks the objectives of the trust deed. In *IBM v Dalgleish* it was argued that exercise of the cessation of accrual power to impose defined contribution benefits in the scheme must be using that power for an improper purpose. This overlooked the fact that the employer had a separate power to readmit employees into the defined contribution section.

[47] *Eclairs* (n 6) [31].

motivated by tax efficiency, or by other reasons which have nothing to do with the well-known (but unstated in the rules) original rationale for the rule. It is helpful to both the employer and trustee[48] to know in advance before any reorganisation that, were the trustee to exercise the power, a court would strike it down as an exercise for an improper purpose. This suggested basis would require extrinsic evidence of the factual matrix when the power was inserted to support the contention that the purpose was sufficiently obvious and uncontroversial. It is recognised that allowing the factual matrix to delimit the meaning of the words is resisted by appellate courts' approach to interpretation of pension scheme trust deeds.[49] However, it is suggested that there is a justifiable distinction to be drawn between: (i) seeking to interpret and then delimit the meaning of express words where the purpose of the power has already been defined by the donor of the power; and (ii) where the donor of the power has not defined the purpose, and the court effectively reads in a limitation which is obvious and – importantly – uncontroversial from the context at the time. If there is any controversy whatsoever, this basis for legitimate intervention should not apply as it would amount to the court correcting the donor's oversight to the detriment of the members, which ought properly to be the domain of rectification or rescission proceedings with their more exacting evidential requirements. This approach sits with Lord Hoffmann in the House of Lords[50] and Walker J at first instance[51] in *National Grid Company plc v Mayes and Others*.

A second possible basis for legitimate intervention where the purpose of the power has not been specified would be where the use of that power would be wholly inconsistent with another separate provision in the trust deed which, if 'overridden', would prejudice beneficiaries' interests. This appears to be the basis upon which Knox J decided *Hillsdown Holdings plc v The Pensions Ombudsman*.[52] Knox J held that the use of the transfer power by the transferor trustee, with the result that surplus would be transferred to another scheme from which it could then be paid to the employer, was an improper exercise of that power. Knox J said: 'What [the transferor trustee] did was intrinsically in breach of trust and damaging to the interests of the members'.[53]

A third possible basis for legitimate intervention where the purpose of the power has not been specified would be where there is an arrangement to pay lip service to compliance with the scope of the power, but the true objective is to achieve a substantive outcome that the power explicitly or implicitly prohibits. The paradigm cases concern private family settlements where the trustee makes a distribution to a

[48] Trustees will be concerned about criticism from members for missing the opportunity to change the balance of power or use it as leverage in ongoing funding negotiations.

[49] As explained in more detail below: see *Safeway Limited v Andrew Newton, Safeway Pension Trustees Limited* [2017] EWCA Civ 1482, [2018] Pens LR 2; *Barnardo's v Buckinghamshire and Ors* [2018] UKSC 55, [2019] 2 All ER 175; *Arnold v Britton* [2015] UKSC 36, [2015] AC 1619.

[50] *National Grid Co plc v Mayes* [2001] UKHL 20, [2001] 1 WLR 864 [18]: 'In my opinion the most relevant background is the fiscal origin of clause 41(2)(b)'.

[51] *The National Grid Company plc v Laws* [1997] Pens LR 157 [66]: 'Major legislative or economic changes … are often the reason (or "mischief") behind amendments to occupational pension schemes and a purposive construction requires them to be taken into account'.

[52] *Hillsdown Holdings plc v Pensions Ombudsman* [1997] 1 All ER 862, [1996] Pens LR 427 [72].

[53] ibid [76].

beneficiary in the defined class and so acts within the scope of the power but, pursuant to an arrangement, the disponee later transfers the distributed property on to an object outside the class. Equity reads into the power the inference that the objective of that power was not limited to requiring an interim meaningless disposition within the class as a prelude to the ultimate goal of making a disposition outside the permitted class of objects.[54] This paradigm has application for death benefit lump sum discretionary benefits in a pension scheme trust.

It is not suggested that these three bases constitute an exhaustive list. However, it is hoped that when the principle of 'proper purpose' eventually comes before the Supreme Court, they will be a contribution towards the intellectual heavy lifting that should be undertaken in a fundamental reassessment of the basis for Equity's intervention in a pensions context.

IV. WHERE THE PURPOSE IS EXPRESSLY ADDRESSED ON THE FACE OF A POWER

Is and should the position be different if the purpose[55] of the power is expressly addressed on the face of a power? Should there be any room for judicial discretion to 'search' further for the so-said 'real purpose'? The majority of the Court of Appeal in *British Airways* consider there is room.[56]

The majority appear to reason in two stages. First, the reference to purpose in the power in issue was not to be *interpreted* as *exhaustive* of the employer's intention as to the 'real purpose' of the power. Second, the employer did not 'intend' – despite the width of the words of the power – that the power should confer the ability to do what the trustees were seeking to use it for: increase pensions in payment.

The power primarily in issue was an amendment power unilaterally vested in the trustees. The trustees purported to exercise that power to confer a unilateral power on themselves to award increases in pensions above the level the rules conferred. Both the creation of the increase power and its subsequent exercise were challenged by British Airways.

It is not unusual in pension scheme trust deeds to find a number of restrictions on an otherwise wide amendment. One such typical restriction is a prohibition against the power being used contrary to the stated purposes of the scheme. The Airways Pension Scheme states:

> The provisions of the Trust Deed may be amended or added to in any way by means of a supplemental deed … PROVIDED THAT no amendment or addition shall be made which
>
> (i) would have the **effect of changing the purposes of the scheme** (emphasis added).

[54] *Lee v Fernie* [1839] 1 Beav 483, 48 ER 1027.

[55] This is a different question from the effect and relevance of an objects clause which is not determinative. See Lord Walker in *Bank of New Zealand* (n 9) [20]–[21].

[56] *British Airways* (n 4).

The purposes of the scheme are stated in another clause:

> The main object of the scheme is to provide pension benefits on retirement and a subsidiary object is to provide benefits in cases of injury or death for the staff of the Employers in accordance with the Rules.

Three Reasons to Question the Majority's Reasoning

i. Where Parties have Defined their Own Terms the Court should Give Effect to those Defined Terms and not the Judge's Defined Terms

As a matter of conventional interpretation it is not at all easy to see how the defined purpose, which circumscribes the amendment power's usage, can be legitimately supplemented by the court's own view of what the parties contemplated as to the usage of the power. As Lewison LJ said in *Honda Motor Europe Ltd v Powell*, when considering how a judge should approach interpretation of provisions in a pension trust deed:

> The task is to determine what the words of the instrument, read against the relevant background, would have meant to a reasonable reader. It is an iterative process in which possible meanings are checked against their likely consequences and the background facts. If the language is reasonably susceptible of two or more meanings, the court should choose that which best serves the object or purpose of the transaction, objectively ascertained. Any interpretation must, so far as possible, be one that is not impractical or over-restrictive or technical in practice. But three further points are of importance in this case. First, *the question is not what the parties meant to say; but what is the meaning of what they did say. Second, the language that they used is likely to be the most important factor*, unless the court can conclude that something has gone wrong with the language. Third, *where the parties have themselves defined their own terms, the court must give effect to those definitions*.[57]

It is not clear how Lewison LJ in *British Airways* then held that '[i]t is, of course, necessary to try to delimit the proper purpose for which the power has been conferred'.[58] The Airways Pension Scheme amendment power expressly addressed its limits by reference to purpose – the defined main purpose of the scheme. Contrary to his analysis in *Honda Motor Europe Ltd*, Lewison LJ in the Court of Appeal in *British Airways* did not 'give effect' to the parties' own defined terms. Instead, he used another provision (an express obligation on the trustee to administer the scheme) to infer a narrower purpose for the amendment power than the express language of the amendment power conferred. In order to make this inference, he relied on his view of the factual matrix: that employers are the paymasters and would not confer unlimited power on trustees to increase benefits.

[57] *Honda Motor Europe Ltd v Powell* [2014] EWCA Civ 437, [2014] Pens LR 255 [24] (emphasis added).
[58] ibid [99].

Lewison LJ's approach is inconsistent with the Court of Appeal's decision in *Safeway Limited v Andrew Newton, Safeway Pension Trustees Limited*[59] and with two Supreme Court decisions: *Barnardo's v Buckinghamshire*[60] and *Arnold v Britton.*[61]

In *Safeway Limited v Andrew Newton, Safeway Pension Trustees Limited*, Briggs LJ (as he then was) said:

> [T]he Deed exists primarily for the benefit of non-parties, that is the employees upon whom pension rights are conferred whether as members or potential members of the Scheme, and upon members of their families (for example in the event of their death). It is therefore a context which is inherently antipathetic to the recognition, by way of departure from plain language, of some common understanding between the principal employer and the Trustee, or common dictionary which they may have employed, or even some widespread practice within the pension industry which might illuminate, or give some strained meaning to, the words used.[62]

In *Barnardo's v Buckinghamshire*, Lord Hodge emphasised the primacy of language used:

> A pension scheme, such as the one in issue on this appeal, has several distinctive characteristics which are relevant to the court's selection of the appropriate interpretative tools. First, it is a formal legal document which has been prepared by skilled and specialist legal draftsmen.
>
> Judges have recognised that these characteristics make it appropriate for the court to give weight to textual analysis, by *concentrating on the words which the draftsman has chosen to use and by attaching less weight to the background factual matrix* than might be appropriate in certain commercial contracts
>
> …
>
> Instead, the focus on textual analysis operates as a constraint on the contribution which background factual circumstances, which existed at the time when the scheme was entered into but which would not readily be accessible to its members as time passed, can make to the construction of the scheme.[63]

In *Arnold v Britton*, Lord Neuberger said:

> First, the reliance placed in some cases on commercial common sense and surrounding circumstances (eg in *Chartbrook* [2009] AC 1101, paras 16–26) should not be invoked to undervalue the importance of the language of the provision which is to be construed. The exercise of interpreting a provision involves identifying what the parties meant through the eyes of a reasonable reader, and, save perhaps in a very unusual case, that meaning is most obviously to be gleaned from the language of the provision. Unlike commercial common sense and the surrounding circumstances, the parties have control over the language they use in a contract.[64]

[59] *Safeway* (n 49).
[60] *Barnardo's* (n 49).
[61] *Arnold v Britton* (n 49).
[62] *Safeway* (n 58) [22].
[63] *Barnardo's* (n 59) [14]–[16] (emphasis added).
[64] *Arnold v Britton* (n 49) [17].

Patten LJ in a powerful dissent in *British Airways* adopted the orthodox and correct approach. He said:[65]

> The equitable overlay embodied in the proper purposes rule can have no application in my view unless it is clear that the Trustees intend to use the powers they were granted to achieve something which can be characterised as improper. Even if one puts aside Lord Sumption's suggestion in *Eclairs* that this involves a subjective test of intention,[66] it clearly requires regard to be had to the terms of the trust instrument and any other relevant background material in order to construct the limits of the discretion. This means that the starting point in this case must be clause 18 itself and, in particular, clause 18(i) which expressly forbids an amendment that would change the purposes of the scheme. *It must be highly debateable whether, in the light of this provision, there is any or very much room for the operation of the proper purposes rule in relation to clause 18. But even if it is not excluded, its content must equally depend on what the Trust Deed itself identifies as the purpose of the scheme.*

Patten LJ referred to *Equitable Life Assurance Society v Hyman* and the speech of Lord Steyn, who said:

> Their policies must be read subject to the powers and decisions of the directors in respect of the declaration and payment of final bonuses. If properly construed the powers of the directors under article 65 are wide enough to override the terms of the guaranteed annuity rates, the GAR policyholders can have no valid complaint. On the other hand, if article 65 expressly or impliedly contains a prohibition on directors exercising their discretion to override or undermine guaranteed annuity rates, the Society's practice is invalid. Beyond that there can be no liability on the Society. It follows that there are not two separate principal issues but only one. In the circumstances of the present case *one never reaches the question whether the power was exercised for an improper or collateral purpose*: see *Howard Smith Ltd v Ampol Petroleum Ltd* [1974] AC 821. *Everything hinges on the meaning of article 65.*[67]

This approach to interpretation of the trust deed respects the primacy of the words used by the draftsman as evidence of the objective intention of the employer, and leaves no further room for a judge to impute a narrower and different intention to the employer (to engage Equity's improper purpose rule). This was the approach taken in the leading pensions case *Re Courage Group's Pension Schemes*.[68] Millett J reasoned:

> In each case, clause 15 of the trust deed as amended [of the Courage Staff Pensions Scheme and the Courage Employees' Pension Scheme] is in the following terms:
>
> 'The company may at any time by deed supplemental hereto add to delete or vary all or any of the provisions of this deed or of the rules and the committee of management shall

[65] *British Airways* (n 4) [70] (emphasis added).

[66] The extent to which a court should be taking account of the subjective intention of a donor of a power is questionable and not settled. In any event, this chapter argues that the intention of the donor is not a convincing basis for judicial intervention on purpose grounds, in a pensions context. However, to the extent that intention is to be found by a court, there should be more than mere implication. There should be compelling extrinsic evidence. It is noted that subjective intention now plays a part in rectification: see *FSHC Group Holdings Ltd* (n 12). When the proper purpose rule eventually receives Supreme Court reappraisal in a pensions context, the relevance of the subjective intention of the donor should form part of that reconsideration.

[67] *Equitable Life Assurance Society v Hyman* [2002] 1 AC 408, [2000] 3 WLR 529 (emphasis added).

[68] *Re Courage Group's Pension Schemes* [1987] 1 WLR 495 (Ch).

> concur in executing any such supplemental deed provided that no addition deletion or alteration shall be made which would (a) have the *effect of altering the main purpose of the fund* namely the provision of pensions on retirement at a specified age for members'
>
> …
>
> 'The simple fact is that Hanson does not employ, and never has employed, any of the employees for whose benefit the schemes were established; and now that the sale to Elders has been completed, Hanson has no remaining connection with IBL, its associated companies, or their employees at all. If the trust deeds and rules can be amended now to permit the substitution of Hanson for IBL, then they can be amended to permit the substitution of ICL or British Gas or the company which carries on the business of the local Chinese take-away. In my judgment, any such substitution would manifestly alter the main purpose of the schemes and be ultra vires'.[69]

ii. In No Meaningful Sense does an Employer 'Intend' that a Power should be Delimited by the 'Constitutional Limits of the Role' of the Trustee

Peter Jackson LJ justified intervention on the ground that the employer could only have ever 'intended' that the trustee would use the amendment power to administer the scheme and not to 'redesign'[70] it by increasing benefits:

> But there is nothing to suggest that the power of amendment was intended to give the trustees the right to remodel the balance of powers between themselves and the employer
>
> …
>
> The amending power granted to these trustees was never intended to permit them to impose discretionary increases upon BA and the amendment of Rule 15 in 2011 and the exercise of the purported power in 2013 were 'for purposes contrary to those of the instrument'.[71]

Two points should be made in response to this. First, Peter Jackson LJ relied on Lord Sumption in *Eclairs* to explain how intention of purpose should be deduced, and Lewison LJ cited the same judgment when considering how the boundaries of 'purpose' should be identified. In doing so, both overlooked Lord Sumption's critical qualification as to when Equity's deductive process can legitimately be deployed.

Lewison LJ cited[72] Lord Sumption's judgment in *Eclairs*:

> Ascertaining the purpose of a power where the instrument is silent depends on an inference from the mischief of the provision conferring it, which is itself deduced from its express terms, from an analysis of their effect and from the court's understanding of the business context.[73]

Peter Jackson LJ cited the same passage from *Eclairs*, and then stated: '[T]he purpose of a scheme is to be ascertained from the contents of the instrument, an analysis

[69] ibid 503 and 510 (emphasis added).

[70] This language is loaded. 'Redesign' suggests more than reinstituting the RPI level increase which would stop in 2010 because of the incorporation by reference of the legislation which determines the level of increase given in public sector schemes. The Trustee did not use a new power it created for itself in 2011 or 2012 to decide in 2013 to award a 0.2% additional increase on top of CPI.

[71] *British Airways* (n 4) [121] and [126].

[72] ibid [100].

[73] *Eclairs* (n 6) [30].

of their effect and an understanding of the business context'.[74] The majority in the Court of Appeal were not entitled to rely on *Eclairs*, however, because the amendment power was not silent – it delimited its usage by reference to purpose.

Second, and even more fundamentally, the Court of Appeal did not apply a forensic approach to the evidence of intention at the relevant moment of conferral of the power. Pension scheme trust deeds are technical, detailed and complex. They are the product of long hours of careful drafting followed by approval at board level, often of the parent company who will be the principal employer. One must question the extent to which the twentieth-century employer before the 1980s will have given any consideration to the risk of the trustees imposing costs on the employer through the exercise of a discretion conferred under the trust deed. If an employer did actually contemplate such risk it is reasonable to expect that the employer would have addressed that risk expressly and clearly. The most obvious and usual way is to ensure that the trust deed does not confer a power unilaterally on the trustee. Another way is to qualify the wording of the power, for example, by requiring that the scheme actuary confirms that the cost impact on the employer is not material. It is not credible that an employer addressing his mind to a risk would then have addressed that risk in an oblique manner.

In the world of pensions drafting, where the drafting of the parties has gone wrong through oversight, there needs to be compelling evidence of the common intention of the parties to correct the document. In *British Airways*,[75] no such evidence was placed before the court to support the contention that, in the language of Lord Sales' lectures, the donor in 1971 of the unilateral power to the trustee '*contemplated*' the outer limits of the amendment power that a court in 2018 went on to 'discern' as having been contemplated.[76] In fact, paragraph [2] of Patten LJ's judgment is illuminating. From 1948 until 1971 the power of amendment was jointly vested in the trustees and the Minister (as the employer was state owned). In 1971 the Minister conferred a unilateral power of amendment on the trustees in all but one respect where the Minister's consent would still be required. This specific exception related to the admission of new joiners. The requirement for ministerial consent was not similarly explicitly retained in respect of any change to benefits. The Minister could have required that any increases in benefits be made subject to actuarial confirmation that the cost would be met entirely from actuarial surplus. However, the Minister did not choose to do so. Patten LJ explained:

> The APS is a balance of cost defined benefit scheme which was established in 1948 as the pension scheme for the employees of BA and its predecessors including British Overseas Airways Corporation, British European Airways Corporation and British South American Airways Corporation (together 'the Corporations') all of which were established as state owned corporations under the provisions of the Civil Aviation Act 1946 (CAA 1946). The Minister was required by s 20 CAA 1946 to make regulations setting up one or more pension schemes to provide 'pensions and similar benefits' in respect of the service of

[74] *British Airways* (n 4) [125].
[75] *British Airways* (n 4).
[76] Lord Sales (n 18).

> employees of the Corporations including benefits in the case of injury or death and the public ownership of the Corporations was reflected in the requirement in clause 18 of the Trust Deed as originally executed that the power of the Management Trustees to amend the provisions of the Trust Deed should take effect subject to regulations made by the Minister under s 20 CAA 1946. Regulation 7 of the Airways Corporations (General Staff Pensions) Regulations 1948 ('the 1948 Regulations') provided that no amendment of or addition to the Trust Deed should have effect unless confirmed by Regulations made under s 20. The consent of the Minister (by regulation) to any rule change was therefore mandatory.[77]

There is no focused discussion in the High Court or Court of Appeal judgments of the intention underlying this change in 1971 to the power of amendment, even though, as Henderson J said in *Independent Trustee Services Ltd v Hope*: '[T]he proper purposes of any power must be ascertained as at the date when the power was conferred'.[78] The judgment of the High Court in *British Airways* does not record what, if any, extrinsic evidence was put forward of the intention underlying the change in 1971 through the Air Corporations (General Staff, Pilots and Officers Pensions) (Amendment) (No 2) Regulations 1971.[79] The majority of the Court of Appeal also did not appear to consider the intention existing in 1971 to be relevant.[80] In Peter Jackson LJ's judgment, he seems to address intention during the period from 1948 to 1971, namely, that the trustee should not have powers beyond management and administration of the scheme.[81] However, the key moment for consideration of intention was 1971, when the change to the power of amendment was made. Therefore, it is suggested that Peter Jackson LJ was wrong to dismiss the conferral of a wider power in 1971 without examining the counter-argument and most natural reading of the power, which is that it was intended to confer an unlimited power except for admission of employees, for which the Minister's consent was required.

The decision in *British Airways* therefore provides no coherent basis at all for concluding that an employer could be said to intend that a trustee power be delimited by the 'constitutional limits of role' of the trustee.

[77] *British Airways* (n 4) [2].

[78] *Independent Trustee Services Ltd v Hope* [2009] EWHC 2810 (Ch), [2009] Pens LR 379 [78].

[79] *British Airways* (n 42). In the High Court proceedings, Counsel for British Airways plc made submissions summarised by Morgan J as follows at para [372]: 'In relation to the history of the APS, Mr Tennet referred to the original requirement in clause 18 that a proposed amendment be confirmed by the Minister. He asserted that the Minister in 1971 would be unlikely to approve a proposed increase in benefits contrary to the wishes of the employer. Even after the requirement of confirmation by the Minister was removed in 1971, the Minister initially retained the power to make new regulations providing for the operation of the APS. These powers were removed when BA was being prepared for privatisation. Before these powers were removed the purposes of the scheme would have prevented the trustees increasing benefits against the wishes of the employer. The removal of these powers cannot have been intended to change the purposes of the scheme. In particular, a power for the trustees to increase benefits against the wishes of BA would have been wholly unsuitable for a private sector pension scheme'. Morgan J did not accept this submission: see para [423]. This focus on the position before privatisation in 1987 fails to address the key moment for consideration of intention: 1971. Instead, it only considers what intention might hypothetically have been while BA was being 'prepared for privatisation'.

[80] *British Airways* (n 4) [123].

[81] ibid [103].

iii. 'Improper Purpose' is not the Appropriate Tool to Stop Trustees doing 'Whatever they Like'

Lewison LJ sought to fortify his reasoning by articulating his concern that it cannot be right that 'the trustees can do whatever they like so long as their ultimate purpose is to provide pensions'.[82] However, in no meaningful sense are trustees ever allowed to do 'whatever they like'.

There are established rules of Equity to constrain the behaviour of trustees. They do not involve the analysis of each provision of a trust deed which the majority of the Court of Appeal advocated in order to derive the 'real purpose'. Such an approach is unworkable because most schemes have 100-page-plus trust deeds built up in a patchwork manner with amendments over years, so it will be very uncertain which clause might possibly be regarded as determinative of the overall 'constitutional role of the trustee'. The majority relied on this as their route to imply intention. Patten LJ in his dissent was correct to say that 'the formulation of the purpose of clause 18 suggested at [126] would in my view place the Trustees in a position of complete uncertainty about the scope of their powers'.[83]

In contrast, established rules of Equity are more than capable of being deployed by a court in an exacting manner to control trustees in appropriate circumstances. These are: control of the decision-making process; irrationality; and perversity.

a. Control of the Decision-Making Process

The rule in *Mettoy Pension Trustees Ltd v Evans*[84] requires trustees to consider all relevant factors[85] and no irrelevant factors. As part of this, trustees must consider whether the exercise of the power is consistent with the main purpose of the scheme, and they must also consider the effect of their decision on the employer. In *Edge v Pensions Ombudsman*, Chadwick LJ said:

> They must, for example, always have in mind the main purpose of the scheme – to provide retirement and other benefits for employees of the participating employers. *They must consider the effect that any course which they are minded to take will have on the financial ability of the employers to make the contributions which that course will entail. They must be careful not to impose burdens* which *imperil the continuity and proper development of the employers' business* or the employment of the members who work in that business. The main purpose of the scheme is not served by putting an employer out of business. They must also consider the level of benefits under their scheme relative to the benefits under comparable schemes; or in the pensions market generally. They should ask themselves whether the scheme is attractive to the members whose willingness to continue paying contributions is essential to its future funding. Are the benefits seen by the members

[82] ibid [110].

[83] ibid [74].

[84] *Mettoy Pension Trustees Ltd v Evans* [1991] 2 All ER 513.

[85] There is no paramount duty to act in the best interests of members: J Nugee, 'The Duties of Pension Scheme Trustees to the Employer – Revisited' (2015) 29 *Trust Law International* 59; Asplin J in *Re Merchant Navy Rating Pension Fund; Merchant Navy Ratings Pension Trustees Ltd v Stena Line Ltd* [2015] EWHC 448 (Ch), [2015] Pens LR 239.

> to be good value in relation to the contributions; would the members find it more attractive to pay higher contributions for higher benefits; or to pay lower contributions and accept lower benefits? The main purpose of the scheme is not served by setting contributions and benefits at levels which deter employees from joining; or which causes resentment. And they must ask themselves whether the benefits enjoyed by members in pension have kept up with increases in the cost of living; so that the expectations of those members during their service – that they were making adequate provision for their retirement through contributions to an occupational pension scheme – are not defeated by inflation.[86]

b. Policing Irrational Decisions

Second, the court is able to intervene if the decision actually reached does not appear to be logically connected to the consideration process, ie, *Wednesbury* unreasonable.

In *Wellington City Council v Local Govt Mutual Funds Trustee Ltd* the New Zealand High Court, dealing with a trust to allow local authorities to pool risk, explained:

> In *Equitable Life Assurance Society v Hyman*, Lord Cooke explained 'the principle that no legal discretion, however widely worded … can be exercised for purposes contrary to those of the instrument by which it is conferred'. His Lordship observed that this principle is 'common to administrative law … and sundry fields of private law'. Similar observations were made by members of the Supreme Court of the United Kingdom in *Braganza v BP Shipping Ltd*, in which it was explained that the exercise of a contractual discretion is subject to an implied term that the decision-making process will: 'exclude extraneous considerations, [and as] … part of a rational decision-making process … take into account those considerations which are obviously relevant to the decision in question … [and be] lawful and rational in the public law sense, [and] that the decision [will be] made rationally (as well as in good faith) and consistently with its contract purpose.[87]

The principles in these authorities lead to the conclusion that when a request from a member to cover a claim is received by Riskpool, the Board is required to exercise its discretion in a way that gives effect to the terms of the governing documents as well as the purpose of the Scheme. The purpose of the Scheme includes the mutual nature of Riskpool and the fact that it was established to assist local authorities manage their public liability risks. In order to exercise its discretion consistently with the terms of the governing documents and the purpose of the Scheme, the Board must not exercise its discretion arbitrarily, capriciously or irrationally.

Irrationality (or arbitrariness or capriciousness) is an objective concept and does not allow a judge to use it as a label to impugn a decision because (s)he considers the decision to be unacceptable. This was the error made by Warren J at first instance in *IBM v Dalgleish*.[88] The Court of Appeal in *IBM v Dalgleish* held:

> Baroness Hale in *Braganza* [identified the risk that] … 'concentrating on the outcome runs the risk that the court will substitute its own decision for that of the primary decision-maker'. In particular, reference to the reasonable employer may lead to the application,

[86] *Edge v Pensions Ombudsman* [1999] Pens LR 215 [48] (emphasis added).
[87] *Wellington City Council v Local Govt Mutual Funds Trust Ltd* [2017] NZHC 2901 [167]–[168].
[88] *IBM UK Holdings Ltd v Dalgleish* [2015] EWHC 389, 1385, and 1439 (Ch), [2015] Pens LR 99 and 477.

> even if unconsciously, of a test diluted and distorted from the true test of irrationality, as enunciated, for example, by Lord Diplock in *Council of Civil Service Unions v Minister for the Civil Service* [1985] AC 374, 410:
>
> By 'irrationality' I mean what can by now be succinctly referred to as 'Wednesbury unreasonableness'... It applies to a decision which is so outrageous in its defiance of logic or of accepted moral standards that no sensible person who had applied his mind to the question to be decided could have arrived at it.[89]

In what Baroness Hale (quoting both passages at paragraph 23 of *Braganza*) described as an obvious echo of this, Lord Sumption said this, in *Hayes v Willoughby*:

> Rationality is not the same as reasonableness. Reasonableness is an external, objective standard applied to the outcome of a person's thoughts or intentions ... A test of rationality, by comparison, applies a minimum objective standard to the relevant person's mental processes. It imports a requirement of good faith, a requirement that there should be some logical connection between the evidence and the ostensible reasons for the decision, and (which will usually amount to the same thing) an absence of arbitrariness, of capriciousness or of reasoning so outrageous in its defiance of logic as to be perverse.[90]

c. Holding Perverse or Wholly Unreasonable Trustees to Account

Even if the decision is logically connected to the consideration process, the court is able to intervene if it is persuaded that no reasonable trustee (in the judge's view) in that context would have come to that conclusion. In *Bramston v Haut*, Kitchin LJ said:

> In reaching these conclusions I believe Arnold J fell into error in each of the following respects. First, he adopted the Wednesbury unreasonableness test and stated, at para 42, that this was a flexible standard that could be moulded to the exigencies of the case when, in the circumstances of this case, he ought to have asked himself whether the trustee had acted perversely.[91]

V. CONCLUSION

Use of the proper purpose rule needs reappraisal in an occupational pension trust context.

Basing deployment of the rule on an implication of what the donor of the power intended is impractical, as the extrinsic evidence to support it is unlikely to exist decades later. Implying intention from an exercise in interpreting the whole trust deed is both uncertain and unreal – when the obvious step the donor could and should have taken is simply to have made the power joint, so retaining a veto power.

Courts should either not intervene on grounds of 'proper purpose', or only intervene on bases other than implied (constructed) intention (which is a recharacterisation

[89] *IBM v Dalgleish* (n 44) [226]–[227].
[90] *Hayes v Willoughby*: [2013] UKSC 17, [2013] 1 WLR 935.
[91] *Bramston v Haut* [2012] EWCA Civ 1637, [2013] 1 WLR 1720 [71].

of oversight). Three alternative bases have been suggested in this chapter. The first is where the reason for including a power was well known and uncontroversial at the time. The second is where use of a power would be wholly inconsistent with another separate provision in the trust deed which, if 'overridden', would prejudice beneficiaries' interests. The third possible basis is where there is an arrangement to pay lip service to compliance with the scope of the power but the true objective is to achieve a substantive outcome that the power explicitly or implicitly prohibits.

If the donor's intention as to the purpose of a power is, however, express on the face of the power itself (as it is qualified by reference to a definition of purpose), that intention should be determinative. Established principle dictates that it is not for a court to seek to find a way of bringing in an implicit different and narrower purpose.

Employer oversight[92] in conferring the unilateral power on the trustee can and should be remedied through equitable rescission or rectification. If the employer's oversight cannot be so remedied, the trustees' exercise of the discretion can still be challenged where the trustees have not followed due process or would be acting irrationally or perversely.

[92] Provided that the 'oversight' is in consequence of a mistaken assumption (for rescission) or oversight in the drafting that does not reflect true intention for rectification.

14

Pensions and the Modern Workforce

ALYSIA BLACKHAM*

I. INTRODUCTION

OLD AGE PENSIONS play a fundamental role in ensuring adequacy of income for the elderly into old age. While pensions fulfil a key social and economic role, there is increasing concern that pension systems in developed countries are not sustainable in the face of demographic ageing and following poor investment returns during the financial crisis. The UK, for example, is facing a recurrent 'pensions crisis':[1] the number of people over the state pension age (SPA) is projected to increase by 28 per cent, from 12.2 million people in 2011 to 15.6 million people in 2035.[2] People are living longer, and are therefore also likely to draw on pensions for a longer period; some will spend nearly a third of their life in retirement.[3] National Insurance Fund expenditure on pensions is therefore expected to increase from around 5 per cent of GDP in 2008–09 to 8 per cent in 2070–71.[4]

In the face of these ongoing challenges to pension sustainability, there is an increasing move towards restructuring pension systems to ensure their long-term viability and to reduce exposure to demographic ageing. Pension reform is occurring

* This research was funded by the Australian government through the Australian Research Council's *Discovery Projects* funding scheme (project DE170100228). The views expressed herein are those of the author and are not necessarily those of the Australian Government or Australian Research Council.

[1] J Harris, 'The Roots of Public Pensions Provision: Social Insurance and the Beveridge Plan' in H Pemberton et al (eds), *Britain's Pensions Crisis: History and Policy* (Oxford, Oxford University Press, 2006) 34.

[2] ONS, 'UK Population Projected to Reach 70 Million by Mid-2027' (2011): www.ons.gov.uk/ons/rel/npp/national-population-projections/2010-based-projections/sum-2010-based-national-population-projections.html.

[3] MW Riley and JW Riley Jr, 'Age Integration and the Lives of Older People' (1994) 34 *The Gerontologist* 110, 110.

[4] Government Actuary's Department, 'Government Actuary's Quinquennial Review of the National Insurance Fund as at April 2005' (London, The Stationery Office 2010) 16. To put this in perspective, in 2009 public healthcare spending accounted for 8.2% of UK GDP (dropping slightly to 8.0% in 2010): U Qaiser, 'Expenditure on Healthcare in the UK' (London, The Stationery Office 2011) 4. This is projected to rise to 8.8% of GDP in 2062–63, with an additional 2.4% being spent on long-term care: Office for Budget Responsibility, 'Fiscal Sustainability Report' (London, The Stationery Office 2013) 80.

or being contemplated at both governmental and pension fund level across OECD countries. This reform, however, is often undertaken in abstract and with limited consideration of broader employment trends, which themselves pose fundamental challenges to the future of pension systems. Reconciling labour law scholarship with scholarship on pensions is itself a major challenge for academic scholars.

This chapter takes up this challenge. Drawing on trends in pension law and policy in the UK and Australia, it commences with a discussion of how we might conceive of pensions from a theoretical perspective (part II), and considers the emerging challenges to established pension systems from the changing nature of work and social and demographic shifts (part III). The chapter argues that existing pension systems are not yet able to accommodate the changing nature of work, and puts forward normative criteria for evaluating and developing more appropriate pension systems for the modern workforce (part IV). It then maps emerging trends in pension reform (part V), and considers the tensions that are playing out in trying to navigate these normative criteria. Part VI concludes.

II. THEORETICAL UNDERSTANDINGS OF PENSIONS AND PENSION PROVISION

How we normatively understand pensions is nationally and temporally dependent. Following the advocacy of the World Bank, national pension systems are increasingly moving towards 'three-tier' mixed pension systems, which combine basic state-based pay-as-you-go pensions (the first pillar) with funded occupational and individual supplements (the second and third pillars).[5] The move towards a three-pillar structure decentres the role of governments to provide for pensions, and shifts responsibility towards private, funded pension solutions.[6] The UK has embraced this approach wholeheartedly, adopting a clear three-tier model with a very low state basic pension as the first tier, and supplementary state, occupational and individual pension provision as the second and third tiers. In 2008–09, UK government pension benefits[7] for a median earner constituted only 37 per cent of average UK earnings, representing one of the lowest replacement rates in the OECD.[8] The UK is now significantly more reliant on private pension provision than other countries in Europe and the OECD.[9]

This shift towards private pension provision will also influence how we conceive of pensions from a normative perspective. Within this policy framework, old age pensions could be perceived in three key ways, depending on their structure and the form of pension provision.

[5] M Leimgruber, 'The Historical Roots of a Diffusion Process: The Three-Pillar Doctrine and European Pension Debates (1972–1994)' (2012) 12 *Global Social Policy* 24, 25.

[6] ibid 26.

[7] Including the flat-rate basic pension plus any earnings-related additional pension and pension credit. However, the figure does not include mandatory or voluntary private pensions.

[8] OECD, 'Pensions at a Glance 2011: Retirement-Income Systems in OECD and G20 Countries' (2011) 118–19.

[9] S Diepeveen, 'Impact of the Recession on Age Management Policies: United Kingdom' (Dublin, Eurofound, 2012) 10.

First, we could conceive of (government) pensions as a form of *social right* delivered by the government, to which individuals are entitled due to their citizenship and residency in a country. This view of pensions is most likely to be relevant to government provided basic pensions – that is, the first pillar – particularly where the scheme is unfunded and/or non-contributory.

Second, we could see pensions as a form of *deferred wage*, where individuals set aside their earnings to facilitate a later income in retirement. In this conception, individuals might be regarded as having proprietary or contractual rights and entitlements to a pension pay-out, at least to the extent to which that would be based on their earlier contributions and any related investment returns.[10] This view is most likely to apply to the second and third pillars of pension provision, namely occupational and individual supplements.

Third, we can see pensions as a form of paternalistic *gratuity*, given either from the state or from employers. This sees pensions as essentially a gift, binding only in individual expectations and, perhaps, the potential for detrimental reliance based on the promise of the pension 'gift'. Thus, pension reform might be limited via a form of estoppel, either legally or at least in the public imagination.

The second view, of pensions as individual property rights, has been given substantial support by decisions relating to the European Convention on Human Rights. Article 1 of Protocol 1 to the Convention says:

> Every natural or legal person is entitled to the peaceful enjoyment of his possessions. No one shall be deprived of his possessions except in the public interest and subject to the conditions provided for by law and by the general principles of international law.
>
> The preceding provisions shall not, however, in any way impair the right of a State to enforce such laws as it deems necessary to control the use of property in accordance with the general interest or to secure the payment of taxes or other contributions or penalties.

This has been held to apply to old age pensions, even if they are non-contributory. For example, in *Carson v United Kingdom*,[11] the European Court of Human Rights held that

> while there is no obligation on a State under Article 1 of Protocol No 1 to create a welfare or pension scheme, if a State did decide to enact legislation providing for the payment as of right of a welfare benefit or pension – whether conditional or not on the prior payment of contributions – that legislation had to be regarded as generating a proprietary interest falling within the ambit of Article 1 of Protocol No 1 for persons satisfying its requirements.[12]

Thus, individuals can have a proprietary interest in both contributory and non-contributory pension schemes, so long as they satisfy the legislative requirements.

[10] Supiot explicitly rejects the idea that pension systems are a 'contract between the generations': A Supiot, *The Spirit of Philadelphia: Social Justice vs the Total Market* (London, Verso, 2012) 131. According to Supiot, pension systems are 'incomprehensible' to contract law, given both the time frame and vertical axis on which obligations are based: ibid. Instead, pensions should be regarded as non-contractual obligations in response to the 'debt of life': ibid.

[11] *Carson v United Kingdom* 42184/05 (2010) 51 EHRR 13.

[12] ibid [64]–[65].

This broad reading of Article 1 is not without its critics: in *R (on the application of Carson) v Secretary of State for Work and Pensions*[13] Lord Hoffmann opined that:

> I must confess that my first instinct would not be to regard a social security benefit like a state pension as a possession until it had actually fallen due. But the European Court has developed a somewhat artificial jurisprudence on this question. It has clearly felt frustrated by the need to find a Convention pigeon hole into which to fit every objectionable form of discrimination. Social security benefits are a good example. In principle it does not seem at all unreasonable that in distributing public money in the form of social security benefits, the state should be obliged to treat like cases alike … But the virtual absence of economic rights in the Convention has made it difficult to relate this principle to the enjoyment of any specified right.
>
> The preferred choice of the Strasbourg court in locating a Convention right in cases of economic discrimination by the state has been [Article 1 of Protocol 1]. In *Müller v Austria* (1975) 3 DR 25 the Commission said that a claim to contributory benefits was a 'possession' by analogy with the proprietary right of a contributor to a private pension fund … But the analogy is weak because (at any rate in the United Kingdom) contributions are hardly distinguishable from general taxation, the 'fund' exists purely as a matter of public accounting and no one is entitled to anything beyond that which the legislation may from time to time prescribe. The Strasbourg court has been obliged to accommodate this state of affairs by saying that although a claim to a social security benefit is a possession … it does not entitle one to anything in particular.[14]

In this case, then, Lord Hoffmann assumed that the pension rights in question were a 'possession' for the purposes of Article 1.[15] Thus, while the Convention may mean that individuals have a right to an old age pension as a 'possession', this does not equate to any particular quantum of money.[16] This 'right' therefore stands in stark contrast to traditional ideas of property rights at common law.

III. CHALLENGES TO PENSION SYSTEMS FROM THE CHANGING NATURE OF WORK

Regardless as to how pensions are conceived, they are under substantial and sustained challenge from the changing nature of work and the decline of the traditional male breadwinner norm. These challenges are originating from growing job mobility and international mobility, work precarity, women's workforce participation and the gender pension gap, and demographic ageing. Each of these challenges is mapped in turn.

A. Job Mobility

Job mobility is increasing in the modern workforce. This reflects a growth in work precarity, the decline of the 'job for life', and increasing job-to-job transitions.

[13] *R (on the application of Carson) v Secretary of State for Work and Pensions* [2005] UKHL 37, [2005] 2 WLR 1369.

[14] ibid [11]–[12] (Lord Hoffmann).

[15] See also ibid [84] (Lord Walker), [95] (Lord Carswell).

[16] See the detailed discussion in *Carson v Secretary of State for Work and Pensions* [2003] EWCA Civ 797, [2003] 3 All ER 577, [17]–[23] (Laws LJ).

For example, Gregg and Wadsworth argue that job stability declined in Britain for the majority of the workforce between 1975 and 2000, and for those without dependent children in particular.[17] Around a quarter of this trend was attributable to the changing nature of work, such as a shift to part-time work, temporary jobs and self-employment.[18] The decline in long-term jobs (that is, those that last over 10 years) was particularly concentrated among men over the age of 50.[19] However, the authors concluded that the most likely explanation for the decline in job tenure was a growth in job-to-job mobility across the workforce.[20]

Growing job mobility makes pensions tied to one particular employer increasingly unsuitable for the modern workforce, and poses a particular challenge to occupational pensions. Indeed, requiring an extended period of service at one employer to receive an old age pension, and prohibiting workers from transferring their benefits to a new scheme, can seriously affect job mobility.[21] While this may actually have been one of the intentions of those establishing occupational pensions for particular employers, as a means of increasing job tenure and loyalty, it is likely to be inappropriate for a global and mobile workforce.[22] The move to personal – and portable – pension arrangements may address these issues to some extent. However, it means that employees may have to decline more generous occupational pension schemes – which reduce mobility – if they wish to move jobs later on. This is likely to reduce individual pension savings overall.[23]

B. International Mobility

At a broader level, pension mobility across national borders is an emerging issue for the modern workforce. The International Labour Organization (ILO) estimates that there are 150.3 million migrant workers worldwide, comprising 4.4 per cent of all workers.[24] Nearly 80 per cent of migrant workers are located in high-income countries such as Australia and the UK.[25] While high-income countries often have well-developed social protection systems, encompassing areas such as healthcare, pensions and other forms of social security, there is growing concern regarding the extent to which migrant workers have entitlements to these social benefits.

[17] P Gregg and J Wadsworth, 'Job Tenure in Britain, 1975–2000. Is a Job for Life or Just for Christmas?' (2002) 64 *Oxford Bulletin of Economics & Statistics* 111, 132.

[18] ibid.

[19] ibid.

[20] ibid.

[21] *cf* Disney and Emmerson, who argue that workers take subsequent job mobility into account when choosing their pension arrangements, if the occupational pension offered does not facilitate mobility: R Disney and C Emmerson, 'Choice of Pension Plan and Job Mobility in Britain' (Discussion Paper, Sydney, 23 July 2004). This implies that individuals will take a less generous pension arrangement that offers mobility, if they intend to leave their job in the future.

[22] JA Turner et al, *Pension Policy for a Mobile Labor Force* (Kalamazoo, MI, Upjohn Press, 1993).

[23] Of course, this is something of a moot point, given the closure of many occupational pension schemes to new entrants. See below.

[24] ILO, 'ILO Global Estimates on Migrant Workers: Results and Methodology' (2015) xi, 8–10.

[25] ibid xiv, 8–10.

Pensions – and old age pensions in particular – pose particular challenges for migration. First, old age pension entitlements are highly nation-specific, meaning it is difficult to simply transfer entitlements between countries. Indeed, while high-income countries often have generous and well-developed social security systems, low-income countries often make no provision for old age pensions. Thus, it is difficult (if not impossible) to simply transfer entitlements between jurisdictions, particularly where migrants are moving between high- and low-income countries.

Second, in high-income countries, pensions can constitute a significant proportion of governmental expenditure, meaning there is limited appetite to extend pension coverage to new entrants,[26] and migrants in particular. This is particularly challenging in an era where there is a backlash generally against migration, including in Europe.

Third, pension entitlements are often built up over a significant period of time, and may be subject to citizenship and residency requirements. Temporary labour migration may prevent individuals from satisfying these requirements, undermining social protection.[27] Thus, migration challenges the very founding principles of some social security regimes.

Fourth, ensuring effective pension portability for migrant workers as they move between countries raises the need for extensive intergovernmental cooperation and agreement between the countries of origin and destination, as well as needing supportive domestic legislation. This adds a substantial additional hurdle for securing pension portability, as it is largely dependent on political appetite for cooperation and reform.

In practice, Holzmann and Koettl have identified four different pension portability regimes:

1. *Portability*, where all migrants have access to pensions benefits. This is often secured via bilateral or multilateral agreements with other countries, and is most often seen in the European Union (EU), and between high income countries. This situation applies to approximately 23 per cent of migrant workers, who are mostly EU-27 migrants.
2. *Exportability*, where migrants are entitled to benefits in their host countries, but there is no agreement between the host country and the country of origin. Thus, migrants cannot have a totalisation or consolidation of their contribution periods to the social security system, meaning there may be issues when a migrant leaves the host country. This affects around 55 per cent of migrants.
3. *Access exclusion*, where migrants do not have access to social benefits in their host country, either because they are not allowed to join the system, or because there is no system at all. This affects approximately 5 per cent of migrants globally.[28]

[26] See, eg, ILO, 'Towards a Fair Deal for Migrant Workers in the Global Economy' (2004) 35.

[27] ibid 77.

[28] Or, perhaps, migrants might be excluded from social security systems even when they are entitled to join them, such as where migrants are employed as 'contractors' to avoid employment obligations: B Xiang, 'Structuration of Indian Information Technology Professionals' Migration to Australia: An Ethnographic Study' (2001) 39 *International Migration* 73.

4. *Informality*, for undocumented migrants, which affects around 18 per cent of migrants globally.[29] Informal migrants are likely excluded from any social security provision, and experience a host of other employment issues.

This demonstrates that regimes for pension portability are highly context- and country-specific, and change frequently as government priorities shift. For migrants outside the EU, pension portability is generally unattainable, and labour migration has a significant deleterious effect on pension provision. Given the global absence of portability, there is a growing concern in the literature for how social benefits might limit or deter labour mobility,[30] both within and between countries. Unsurprisingly, difficulties in the transfer of social security benefits appear to deter mobility in the European context.[31]

Beyond this impact on individual mobility, pension portability also has significant implications for social risk management and the structural sustainability of pension systems. While work on pension mobility between EU countries, as part of the literature on the free movement of persons, has started to consider the possible impacts of mobility on pension systems themselves,[32] this discussion has not extended beyond the EU. It is clear, however, that labour migration raises pension risks for both individuals and nation states. If migrants lack pension benefits, or cannot port their benefits upon moving, this puts them at risk of poverty in old age, particularly if they are in low-paid work. Where pensions are dependent on workers' own contributions to the scheme ('contributory'), worker migration can lead to underinsurance in old age, particularly when migrant workers change country[33] or have unstable labour market biographies.[34] Relatedly, pension mobility or immobility is a key factor in the passing of social risks between national governments. If pensions are not portable, this will likely lead to a financial windfall to the country the migrant worker is leaving, which will no longer be responsible for the workers' welfare in retirement, but which benefited from their skills and contribution during their working life, and create an additional financial burden to the migrant's new country, which may become liable to support the migrant worker into old age.[35] Thus, if there is no redistribution or portability of pension rights, this will increase social risks,[36] both for individuals and for their destination country. This is particularly problematic if temporary

[29] R Holzmann and J Koettl, 'Portability of Pension, Health, and Other Social Benefits: Facts, Concepts, and Issues' (2015) 61 *CESifo Economic Studies* 377, 382 (Table 1).

[30] AC d'Addio and MC Cavalleri, 'Labour Mobility and the Portability of Social Rights in the EU' (2015) 61 *CESifo Economic Studies* 346; R Holzmann and M Werding, 'Portability of Social Benefits: Research on a Critical Topic in Globalization' (2015) 61 *CESifo Economic Studies* 335.

[31] d'Addio and Cavalleri (n 30).

[32] A Jousten and P Pestieau, 'Labor Mobility, Redistribution, and Pension Reform in Europe' in M Feldstein and H Siebert (eds), *Social Security Pension Reform in Europe* (Chicago, IL, University of Chicago Press, 2002).

[33] P Frericks, 'Funded Pensions and Their Implications for Women and Migrant Workers' (2012) 12 *Global Social Policy* 342, 343.

[34] ibid.

[35] R Holzmann and J Koettl, 'Portability of Pension, Health, and Other Social Benefits: Facts, Concepts, Issues' (IZA DP, Bonn, May 2011) 11; Holzmann and Koettl (n 29) 8.

[36] Frericks (n 33) 343.

migrant workers are spending time in high-income countries during their working lives, but returning to low-income countries in their later years, as this will likely lead to a transfer of wealth *away* from the low-income countries where it is most needed. Further, if migrant workers are returning to low-income countries which do not have adequate social security provision, they will be at an increased risk of poverty in old age. Thus, adequacy of pensions in old age fundamentally depends on transferability between countries.[37]

C. Work Precarity

Precarious work is of growing concern in the modern workplace.[38] 'Precarious' work is that which 'departs from the normative model of the standard employment relationship … and is poorly paid and incapable of sustaining a household'.[39] The GMB union estimates that up to 10 million workers in Britain – nearly a third of the UK workforce – are in precarious employment, including those in the gig economy, on zero- or short-hours contracts, temporary workers, underemployed or at risk of false self-employment.[40] Thus, precarious work is a growing feature of the modern workforce.

Precarious work challenges established pension systems in a number of compelling ways. First, precarious work is often associated with lows level of income; indeed, level of income is one of Rodgers's dimensions of work precarity,[41] and Vosco defines 'precarious employment' as that characterised by low income. Workers with low income are unlikely to be able to consider saving for their future retirement or, indeed, may never be in a financial position to 'choose' to retire. Those on very low incomes may fall below the minimum income for making contributions to statutory pension schemes, reducing their ultimate pension entitlements. For example, pension 'automatic enrolment' under the Pensions Act 2008 (UK) only requires employers to enrol workers into a workplace pension scheme if they earn more than £10,000 per annum in 2018–19 *from that employer*. This will not capture those who are in very low paid positions, or those working for multiple employers at once. Workers with periods in and out of employment and with broken work histories will also have substantially reduced pension savings.

[37] ibid.

[38] S McKay et al, 'Study on Precarious Work and Social Rights' (London, Working Lives Research Institute, 2012) 14.

[39] J Fudge and RJ Owens, 'Precarious Work, Women and the New Economy: The Challenge to Legal Norms' in J Fudge and RJ Owens (eds), *Precarious Work, Women and the New Economy: The Challenge to Legal Norms* (Oxford, Hart Publishing 2006) 3; see also LF Vosko, *Managing the Margins: Gender, Citizenship, and the International Regulation of Precarious Employment* (Oxford, Oxford University Press, 2010) 2; G Rodgers, 'Precarious Work in Western Europe: The State of the Debate' in G Rodgers and J Rodgers (eds), *Precarious Jobs in Labour Market Regulation: The Growth of Atypical Employment in Western Europe* (Brussels, International Institute for Labour Studies, 1989) 3.

[40] S Butler, 'Nearly 10 Million Britons Are in Insecure Work, Says Union' *The Guardian* (5 June 2017), available at: www.theguardian.com/business/2017/jun/05/nearly-10-million-britons-are-in-insecure-work-says-union.

[41] Rodgers (n 39) 3.

Second, precarious workers on zero- or short-hours contracts, undertaking temporary and casual work or who are 'self'-employed may not fall within the scope of existing pension schemes and rules, which typically capture 'employees'.[42] Pension provision for the 'self-employed' in particular is haphazard in many EU countries, and often relies on workers self-declaring their earnings and apportioning their own pension savings, posing a risk that workers may have insufficient funds in retirement.[43] Further, precarious workers are unlikely to have access to most occupational pension funds, even if they had sufficient earnings to make contributions.

Third, precarious work is increasingly concentrated among young workers.[44] The Resolution Foundation estimates that 37 per cent of those on zero-hours contracts are between 16 and 24 years of age.[45] Over 40 per cent of employees under 30 are employed in low-wage jobs, compared with 14.68 per cent of those aged 30 to 49;[46] and only 68 per cent of those aged under 35 are employed on an indefinite contract, compared with 85.7 per cent for those aged 36 to 49.[47] This poses a challenge to the sustainability of unfunded pension systems that have traditionally relied on contributions from younger workers to fund the pensions of the elderly. If younger workers are not occupying well-paid jobs, or making contributions to pension schemes, they are unlikely to be able to finance the pensions of a sizable cohort of older workers.

Fourth, employers' growing reliance on a pool of precarious workers has gone hand-in-hand with the closure of occupational pension schemes to new entrants. If employers are increasingly relying on a precarious and transitory pool of workers, there is less need to offer incentives for employee retention and loyalty. Kilpatrick has described the 'truly spectacular flight away' from defined benefit (DB) pension schemes[48] in the UK private sector:[49] at 31 March 2011, only 16 per cent of DB occupational schemes were open to new members.[50] Some employers instead offer their employees DC pension schemes, shifting the risks of longevity and investment returns to the individual.[51] Other employers ceased to make any provision for employees'

[42] Though the Pensions Act 2008 applies to the broader category of 'workers': s 1(1).

[43] C Barnard and A Blackham, 'Self-Employed: The Implementation of Directive 2010/41 on the Application of the Principle of Equal Treatment between Men and Women Engaged in an Activity in a Self-Employed Capacity' (Luxembourg, Publications Office of the European Union, 2015).

[44] See RM Carmo et al, 'Time Projections: Youth and Precarious Employment' (2014) 23 *Time & Society* 337.

[45] M Pennycook et al, 'A Matter of Time: The Rise of Zero-Hours Contracts' (Resolution Foundation, 2013) 10.

[46] Eurostat Structure of Earnings Survey, 2010.

[47] Fifth European Working Conditions survey, 2010.

[48] Defined benefit or salary-related pension schemes pay pensions based on individuals' pensionable earnings and years of service. The schemes pay a guaranteed pension upon retirement, irrespective of investment returns. In contrast, in defined contribution (DC) schemes individuals build up a pension 'pot' which may be used to purchase an annuity upon retirement. The level of pension is not guaranteed and is linked to investment returns.

[49] C Kilpatrick, 'The New UK Retirement Regime, Employment Law and Pensions' (2008) 37 *Industrial Law Journal* 1, 21.

[50] The Pensions Regulator, 'Annual Report and Accounts 2010–2011' (London, The Stationery Office, 2011) 15.

[51] D Hirsch, 'Crossroads after 50: Improving Choices in Work and Retirement' (York, Joseph Rowntree Foundation, 2003) 7; P Thornton, 'A Note on the Investment Management of Defined Contribution Schemes' in P Thornton and D Fleming (eds), *Good Governance for Pension Schemes* (Cambridge, Cambridge University Press, 2011).

pensions: the 2009 Employers' Pension Provision Survey of 2,519 UK organisations found only 28 per cent were making any provision for pensions (down from 41 per cent in 2007), and occupational pensions were being offered by only 2 per cent of private sector employers (down from 5 per cent in 2007).[52] This decline may be addressed, in part, by auto-enrolment under the Pensions Act 2008. However, the level of saving required by auto-enrolment is unlikely to address chronic issues of 'under-saving' for retirement.[53]

Precarious work is therefore a serious challenge to pension adequacy, particularly given how widespread precarity has become in the modern workforce. Precarious work can undermine reliance on individual saving, occupational pensions and government contributory pension schemes. Thus, it is a substantial risk facing established pension arrangements. If not addressed via pension reform, precarious work could lead to a substantial increase in the number of pensioners in poverty in years to come, and increasing demand for other government services and support. Thus, precarious work will have substantially deleterious effects on both individual and societal financial wellbeing, now and in the future.

This is particularly problematic given pension adequacy was already a major concern. The move towards privatising and individualising pension risk through reliance on DC pension schemes has seen a significant decline in pension assets with the financial crisis and shocks to the stock market. This has generated concerns in relation to both the adequacy and sustainability of individual pension schemes,[54] and has flagged the need to better regulate private pensions, both to address declining pension values, and to better protect individuals against the risks of the market.[55] As it stands, however, private pension provision in the UK is well below that required to avoid individual poverty and ensure adequacy of income for retirees: according to 2012 figures, 10.7 million individuals in Great Britain are likely to have inadequate income in retirement.[56] Thus, the growth in precarious work is building on a system where pension adequacy was already doubtful.

D. Women's Workforce Participation

Older women are less likely to participate in the workforce than older men, though participation rates are slowly increasing.[57] Further, women (especially those with

[52] J Forth and L Stokes, *Employers' Pension Provision Survey 2009* (London, The Stationery Office, 2010) 15–16.

[53] Select Committee on Public Service and Demographic Change, *Ready for Ageing?* (HL 2012–13, 140) 10. Individuals may also 'opt out' from the scheme, which may reduce its effectiveness.

[54] A Zaidi, 'Sustainability and Adequacy of Pensions in EU Countries: A Cross-National Perspective' (European Centre for Social Welfare Policy and Research, September 2010); J Draxler and J Mortensen, 'Towards Sustainable But Still Adequate Pensions in the EU: Theory, Trends and Simulations' (ENEPRI Research Report, April 2009).

[55] B Ebbinghaus and T Wiß, 'Taming Pension Fund Capitalism in Europe: Collective and State Regulation in Times of Crisis' (2011) 17 *Transfer: European Review of Labour and Research* 15.

[56] Select Committee on Public Service and Demographic Change (n 53) 7.

[57] See, eg, Australian Institute of Health and Welfare, 'Older Australia at a Glance, Employment & Economic Participation' (September 2018), available at: www.aihw.gov.au/reports/older-people/older-australia-at-a-glance/contents/social-economic-engagement/employment-economic-participation.

caring responsibilities) are more likely to have disjointed careers than men, with periods in and out of the workforce. In addition to the gender pay gap, this has also led to a substantial gender pension gap.

In Australia, for example, according to the Association of Superannuation Funds of Australia, average superannuation balances for women at retirement (that is, for those aged 60–64) are 42 per cent lower than those for men. The median superannuation balance is three times higher for men than women (see Table 1).[58] The fact that median superannuation account balances are so much lower than average account balances reflects the substantial number of Australians with no or very little superannuation. In 2015–16, around 32.7 per cent of women reported having no superannuation, compared with 27 per cent of men.[59] The dramatic difference between the mean and median figures for women aged 60–64 indicates that some women have excellent superannuation provision; however, the vast majority have none, or very little.

Table 1 Superannuation account balances by age and gender, 2015–16, Australia

Age	Male		Female	
	Mean	Median	Mean	Median
30–34	\$43,583	\$30,000	\$33,748	\$23,396
60–64	\$270,710	\$110,000	\$157,049	\$36,003

The Association of Superannuation Funds of Australia estimates that to achieve a 'modest' standard of living in retirement, individuals need superannuation savings of \$70,000.[60] Few women in Australia will achieve even this modest standard of living in retirement. Thus, concerns about pension adequacy are particularly acute for women.

These concerns are compounded by two social trends. First, women tend to retire earlier than men – for example, in Australia, the average age at retirement from the labour force for persons aged 45 years and over in 2016–17 was 55.3 years, being 58.8 years for men and 52.3 years for women.[61] For women retirees, 46 per cent had retired at an age earlier than 55; 39 per cent between the ages of 55 and 64; and only 15 per cent aged 65 and over. However, the average age at retirement for recent retirees (who had retired in the last five years) was 62.9 years. For this group, retirement ages were similar for women and men, with average retirement ages of 63.6 years for men and 62.1 years for women. Thus, women may be retiring later over time.[62]

Second, exacerbating the gender pension gap, women on average live longer than men, meaning their pensions also need to stretch for a longer period of time. In 2017 in Australia, women constituted 51 per cent of those aged 65–74, 54 per cent

[58] R Clare, 'Superannuation Account Balances by Age and Gender' (Association of Superannuation Funds of Australia, October 2017), available at: www.superannuation.asn.au/ArticleDocuments/359/1710_Superannuation_account_balances_by_age_and_gender.pdf.aspx?Embed=Y.

[59] ibid.

[60] Association of Superannuation Funds of Australia, 'ASFA Retirement Standard Summary 2018' (2018) 4.

[61] ABS 2017. 6238.0 – Retirement and Retirement Intentions, Australia, July 2016 to June 2017.

[62] ibid.

of those aged 75–84, and 63 per cent of those aged 85 and over.[63] Thus, inadequate pension entitlements will be even more problematic for women than for men, over a longer time period. Current contributory pension arrangements do not recognise or accommodate women's disrupted career paths and unequal caring responsibilities.

E. Demographic Ageing

Demographic ageing is another obvious challenge facing established pension systems in all developed countries. In Australia, for example, in 2017 there were 3.8 million people aged 65 years and over, amounting to 15 per cent of the country's total population.[64] By 2057, it is projected that this will rise to 8.8 million people, or 22 per cent of the population, and, by 2097, 12.8 million people or 25 per cent of the population.[65] Thus, older people represent a growing proportion of the national population.

Further, those in this cohort are living longer lives, meaning 'older people' are, on average, getting older. In 2017, the majority (57 per cent, or 2.2 million) of older people in Australia were aged 65–74, one-third (30 per cent, or 1.2 million) were aged 75–84, and 13 per cent (497,000) were aged 85 and over.[66] By 2047, this is projected to shift substantially towards the older demographic, with those over 75 (those aged 75–84: 35 per cent or 2.6 million; those aged 85 and over: 20 per cent, or 1.5 million) outnumbering those aged between 65 and 74 (3.4 million people, or 45 per cent).

These shifts represent a triumph of modern medicine, with people, on average, living longer and healthier lives. However, they pose fundamental challenges to the sustainability of existing pension systems and the labour force more generally. If retirement ages remain static, there will be a growing cohort of retirees drawing on a pension, who are living for many more years than was originally envisaged. The success story of demographic ageing, then, comes with a financial cost.

Demographic ageing may challenge the fundamental assumptions of existing pension arrangements. Pension systems in Europe have traditionally been grounded in norms of intergenerational solidarity. This has served to justify and rationalise intergenerational transfers and redistribution where required to support adequacy of income, including through the pension system. Supiot defines solidarity as a way of conceiving a collective obligation not based on individual consent, family ties or community allegiance.[67] More specifically, intergenerational solidarity involves 'each generation recognis[ing] its responsibilities towards the others'[68] and a degree of

[63] Australian Institute of Health and Welfare, 'Older Australia at a Glance, Australia's Changing Age & Gender Profile' (September 2018), available at: www.aihw.gov.au/reports/older-people/older-australia-at-a-glance/contents/demographics-of-older-australians/australia-s-changing-age-gender-profile.

[64] ibid.

[65] ibid.

[66] ibid.

[67] A Supiot, *Homo Juridicus: On the Anthropological Function of the Law* (London, Verso, 2007) 208.

[68] Eurofound, 'Foundation Findings: Intergenerational Solidarity' (Luxembourg, Eurofound, 2012) 3.

bonding between individuals of different age groups.[69] Intergenerational solidarity is a form of 'contract across generations',[70] with shared expectations and obligations around ageing and the 'succession of generations',[71] grounded in the idea of reciprocity[72] and intergenerational transfers.[73] Intergenerational solidarity is therefore a form of social cohesion between generations.[74]

While intergenerational solidarity might have previously supported redistributional pension structures, this social cohesion is increasingly being challenged with demographic ageing and increasing youth unemployment and underemployment during the crisis. Supiot argues that solidarity in Western states is undergoing 'a major crisis',[75] and there are calls for the UK to reconceive the nature of its 'intergenerational contract'.[76] According to Bengtson and Oyama, intergenerational norms and the sense of reciprocity between age groups are changing as younger generations receive fewer financial succession benefits from older generations and there is increased geriatric dependency.[77] As individuals live for longer and the population ages, a greater proportion of social goods will be consumed by older generations. In this context, Bengston and Oyama question whether norms of reciprocity between generations are still intact at the macro level, and flag the possibility that perceptions of 'generational inequity' may increase with time.[78] This may reduce the acceptability of intergenerational transfers occurring within pension systems. Indeed, intergenerational solidarity may be disrupted by dissimilar interests between generations and conflicts around the distribution of social assets and equity.[79] Intergenerational solidarity may now require the 'acceptance of changed expectations among workers about when and how they leave the labour market' to extend working lives[80] and reduce demand on pension systems. Intergenerational solidarity may therefore now require and justify pension reform, to reflect changing social expectations about retirement and levels of social support.

[69] MA Cruz-Saco, 'Intergenerational Solidarity' in MA Cruz-Saco and S Zelenev (eds), *Intergenerational Solidarity: Strengthening Economic and Social Ties* (New York, Palgrave Macmillan, 2010) 9.

[70] As noted above, Supiot explicitly rejects this idea: *The Spirit of Philadelphia* (n 10) 131.

[71] VL Bengtson and PS Oyama, 'Intergenerational Solidarity and Conflict' in MA Cruz-Saco and S Zelenev (eds), *Intergenerational Solidarity: Strengthening Economic and Social Ties* (New York, Palgrave Macmillan, 2010) 38.

[72] M Izuhara, 'Introduction' in M Izuhara (ed), *Ageing and Intergenerational Relations: Family Reciprocity from a Global Perspective* (Bristol, Policy Press 2010) 5.

[73] Bengtson and Oyama (n 71) 36; A Lowenstein, 'Determinants of the Complex Interchange among Generations: Collaboration and Conflict' in MA Cruz-Saco and S Zelenev (eds), *Intergenerational Solidarity: Strengthening Economic and Social Ties* (New York, Palgrave Macmillan, 2010) 58. At the same time, it is clear that individuals will have differing opinions on how the intergenerational contract should operate: Izuhara (n 72) 5.

[74] Bengtson and Oyama (n 71) 35.

[75] Supiot, *Homo Juridicus* (n 67) 209.

[76] DM Butts, 'Key Issues Uniting Generations' in MA Cruz-Saco and S Zelenev (eds), *Intergenerational Solidarity: Strengthening Economic and Social Ties* (New York, Palgrave Macmillan, 2010) 94.

[77] Bengtson and Oyama (n 71) 38–39.

[78] ibid 46–47.

[79] Cruz-Saco (n 69) 11.

[80] Eurofound (n 68) 3; see also Butts (n 76) 94.

IV. NORMATIVE CRITERIA FOR DEVELOPING MORE APPROPRIATE PENSION SYSTEMS FOR THE MODERN WORKFORCE

Old age pensions therefore raise a number of legal and normative tensions, and need to be considered from a number of angles. More particularly, normative evaluation of pension systems – and consideration of their future development – needs to take into account:

1. The viability of government, occupational and individual pension systems.
2. Adequacy of income for retirees.
3. Respect for individual property rights.
4. Fairness between generations, both in terms of contributions (whether via taxation or direct payments) and pay-outs.
5. Fairness within generations, including on the basis of class or socio-economic status and gender.
6. Portability within and across national borders.

These normative principles and ideals create a complex web of interlinked rights, responsibilities and expectations, which need to be carefully managed throughout the process of reform. To make this even more complex, pensions are situated in the public imagination, and seen by some as an entitlement and 'right'. Thus, any change or deviation from the status quo may be seen as an attack on individuals and a certain vision of society.

More generally, these normative principles also flag fundamental tensions in how we conceive of the role of pensions, and their fundamental rationale. For example, what counts as 'fair' in an intergenerational and intragenerational context? Should pension systems advance redistributional aims (either between or within generations) and, relatedly, to what extent should we expect individuals to support each other via the pension system? At what level of funding will a pension system become 'viable' and, conversely, what level of underfunding is 'unviable'? What quantum of pension income is required for an 'adequate' level of income?[81] Our answers to these questions will be socially and culturally contingent, and are likely to vary across the political spectrum: there are no clear-cut or true-false answers to these issues. While recognising the complexity of all of these issues, two criteria require further exploration here: intergenerational fairness, and portability.

A. Intergenerational Fairness

At a base level, we need to think about how we can best conceptualise 'intergenerational fairness', and what this means in relation to pension contributions and pension pay-outs. Intergenerational fairness could be seen in a variety of ways:

- ensuring pension benefits are commensurate or proportional to the level of contributions (either from taxation or directly from salary) made by individuals over the life course (consistent with a contractual or deferred salary model);

[81] See, eg, AG Grech, 'How Best to Measure Pension Adequacy' (Centre for Analysis of Social Exclusion, 2013).

- securing adequacy of income for all generations in retirement (a social right or paternalistic gratuity model);
- ensuring a similar level of pension payments for individuals of all ages (again, consistent with a social right or paternalistic gratuity model); and/or
- matching individual expectations of the level of pension provision they will obtain in retirement (either derived from past behaviour and contractual entitlements, or from the social or employment contract).

These forms of fairness are likely consistent with the various ways of conceiving of pensions (see part II above). However, achieving most of these conceptions of 'fairness' is likely to seriously jeopardise the sustainability of pension systems. Further, some forms of fairness are easier to achieve than others – for example, the first idea of commensurability or proportionality is best achieved via individual funded pension accounts, where it is clear what individuals have contributed over the life course and the present-day value of those contributions. However, commensurability or proportionality does not necessarily secure adequacy of income, as the discussion of the gender pension gap shows, and is difficult to determine in unfunded, non-contributory or communal pension schemes.

It is clear that this balance between intergenerational and intragenerational fairness, sustainability and adequacy of income in governmental pension reform is an area of significant concern in the UK. In practice, young workers are often disadvantaged in pension provision. Under Article 6(2) of the Framework Directive:

> Member States may provide that the fixing for occupational social security schemes of ages for admission or entitlement to retirement or invalidity benefits, including the fixing under those schemes of different ages for employees or groups or categories of employees, and the use, in the context of such schemes, of age criteria in actuarial calculations, does not constitute discrimination on the grounds of age, provided this does not result in discrimination on the grounds of sex.

The UK has made use of this exception, and many forms of age discrimination in relation to pensions are excluded from the Equality Act 2010 (UK) under section 61(8).[82]

In addition to this direct discrimination, young people are also indirectly discriminated against in relation to pension provision. For example, with the move away from DB pension schemes in the private sector,[83] many DB pension schemes are now closed to new entrants. Instead, some employers are now offering their employees DC pension schemes, where pension entitlements are dependent on contributions paid and investment returns, rather than final salary.[84] Younger workers are disproportionately likely to be new entrants to pension schemes, meaning they are disproportionately affected by these changes.[85] Even where younger workers are entitled to join a pension scheme, there has been a progressive re-evaluation of pension benefits, which again is likely to disproportionately affect younger workers.[86] At the national level, too, a

[82] See Equality Act (Age Exceptions for Pension Schemes) Order 2010 (UK) SI 2010/2133.

[83] Kilpatrick (n 49) 21.

[84] Thornton (n 51) 265.

[85] See, eg, *Dumbreck v OFCOM* [2012] EqLR 1164 (ET).

[86] For occupational pensions see, eg, Universities Superannuation Scheme, 'Employer Consultation 2015' (2015), available at: www.ussconsultation.co.uk/members/abouts.

series of changes to government pensions (see part V) all operate prospectively, meaning that younger workers are likely to have lower pension entitlements than their older colleagues, and will only be able to claim a pension at a later age. There is no sign that the changes will end here: young people's pension entitlements may continue to be eroded in the years to come.

Despite this disparate impact on different age groups, there have been few claims of age discrimination in relation to pension schemes, likely because the broad exceptions to the Equality Act 2010 under the Equality Act (Age Exceptions for Pension Schemes) Order 2010 (UK) SI 2010/2133 preclude such claims in most cases. At the EU level, increases in the amount of contributions to an occupational pension scheme on the basis of age were challenged in *HK Danmark v Experian A/S*.[87] In that case, the employee's contract provided for occupational pension contributions that varied by age, as follows:

- Under 35 years of age: employee contribution 3 per cent and Experian contribution 6 per cent.
- From 35 to 44 years of age: employee contribution 4 per cent and Experian contribution 8 per cent.
- Over 45 years of age: employee contribution 5 per cent and Experian contribution 10 per cent.

The employee claimed that this was a form of age discrimination.

The Court of Justice of the European Union (CJEU) held that the Framework Directive applied to the dispute between two private parties 'on the basis of the principle of non-discrimination on grounds of age, enshrined in Article 21 of the Charter and given specific expression by Directive 2000/78'.[88] The employer's contributions to the pension scheme constituted 'pay' within the meaning of Article 157(2) of the Treaty on the Functioning of the European Union, and therefore fell within the scope of the Framework Directive.[89] When the pension contributions were added to an employee's base salary as a form of pay, 'The fact that the overall monthly pay of younger workers is lower and, accordingly, the fact that the treatment they are afforded is less favourable, are, therefore, directly linked to age'.[90] The scheme therefore constituted a difference in treatment on the basis of age.

The exception in Article 6(2) of the Framework Directive for occupational pension schemes was to be interpreted restrictively, to only cover: (1) occupational social security schemes that cover the risks of old age and invalidity;[91] and (2) 'fixing … of ages for admission or entitlement to retirement or invalidity benefits', including the 'use … of age criteria in actuarial calculations'.[92] With this restrictive interpretation,

[87] Case C-476/11 *HK Danmark v Experian A/S* [2013] CJEU 590.

[88] ibid [31].

[89] ibid [24]–[30].

[90] ibid [35].

[91] See similarly, Case C-546/11 *Dansk Jurist-og Økonomforbund v Indenrigs-og Sundhedsministeriet* [2014] ICR 1 [43].

[92] *HK Danmark v Experian A/S* (n 87) [44]–[49].

the CJEU held that age-related increases in pension contributions did not fall within the scope of Article 6(2) of the Framework Directive.[93] Therefore, the difference in treatment needed to be justified.

The employer argued that the difference in treatment was justified by two legitimate aims: (1) providing a means for all employees to build up reasonable retirement savings, by enabling older workers to build their savings over a relatively short contribution period, while allowing younger workers to have a larger proportion of their wages at their disposal; and (2) covering the risks of death, incapacity and serious illness, the cost of which increases with age.[94] The CJEU held that these were capable of being legitimate aims.[95] While the CJEU noted that 'it does not appear unreasonable to regard the age-related increases in contributions as enabling the aims',[96] this was ultimately a matter for determination by the national court.[97] This case suggests that employers will need to justify any age-based differences in contributions to social security schemes. However, it also appears that this will not be a difficult hurdle in most cases.[98]

Disparate treatment on the basis of age in relation to pension provision does not appear to often be the subject of legal claims,[99] perhaps reflecting young workers' low levels of engagement with pension entitlements.[100] The exception is in relation to judicial pensions, where the transitional provisions in the New Judicial Pension Scheme 2015 were successfully challenged as a form of age discrimination against younger judges.[101] It was ultimately held that the transitional provisions were not justified as a proportionate means of achieving a legitimate aim.[102] However, the broader changes wrought by the scheme – which impose higher individual contributions on judges, and revert to a career-average defined benefit pension, rather than a final salary pension – were not challenged. Thus, the intergenerational fairness of pension reforms remains a live and challenging issue.

[93] ibid [54].
[94] ibid [58]–[59].
[95] ibid [62].
[96] ibid [66].
[97] ibid [68].
[98] Though see *Patterson v Merseyside Police Authority* (2009) ET 2106251/08, where it was held that there was no legitimate aim to support the pension policy other than cost saving.
[99] Though see *R (on the application of Harvey) v Haringey LBC* [2018] EWHC 2871 (Admin), [2019] Pens LR 3; *British Gurkha Welfare Society v Ministry of Defence* [2010] EWCA Civ 1098; *R (on the application of Smith) v Secretary of State for Defence* [2004] EWHC 1797 (Admin), [2005] 1 FLR 86. In relation to welfare payments, see *R (on the application of Reynolds) v Secretary of State for Work and Pensions* [2002] EWHC 426 (Admin).
[100] See National Association of Pension Funds, 'Workplace Pensions Survey' (2013); H Osborne, 'Young Workers "Face Grind to 70s"' *The Guardian* (14 June 2005), available at: www.theguardian.com/money/2005/jun/14/business.pensions.
[101] See Ministry of Justice, 'New Judicial Pension Scheme: Scheme Guide' (2014).
[102] *McCloud v Lord Chancellor* (2017) ET 2201483/2015; *Lord Chancellor v McCloud* [2018] EWCA Civ 2844, [2019] Pens LR 12. In the Employment Tribunal, the provisions were held to be both not pursuing a legitimate aim, and not proportionate. In the Employment Appeal Tribunal, it was held that there was a legitimate aim, but that the provisions were not proportionate. In the Court of Appeal, the decision of the Employment Tribunal was upheld. Permission to appeal to the Supreme Court was refused. A similar challenge to the transitional provisions of the New Firefighters' Pension Scheme was also upheld.

B. National and International Portability

For Andrietti, 'pension mobility' is defined as the 'capacity of workers covered by an occupational pension plan to preserve the actuarially fair value of their accrued rights while moving to a different employer and possibility to a different pension scheme'.[103] However, in a globalised labour context, pension mobility could be defined more broadly, to extend to pensions other than occupational pensions, and to encompass moving to a different country. For d'Addio and Cavalleri, then, *portability* is the possibility of acquiring and keeping social benefit entitlements and/or social rights when workers are mobile for work reasons.[104] This might encompass a change of employer within a country (job-to-job mobility) or a change of employer and a change of country (country-to-country mobility).[105] Thus, portability might be defined as the ability to preserve, maintain and transfer benefits from one country to another and between localities in a country (spatial portability); between jobs; and between members in a household (social portability).[106] Given the growth of migrant work, we must be concerned with both 'cross-border' portability,[107] and 'within-border' portability.[108]

We can posit three key criteria to evaluate the fairness and efficiency of pension portability provisions between countries. First, there should be no benefit disadvantage for the pensions of migrants: that is, migrants should not be disadvantaged when they move between countries. Second, there should be fairness for both countries, particularly in relation to their financial responsibilities for departing and arriving migrants. Third, there should be bureaucratic effectiveness, so that there is a limited administrative or bureaucratic burden for institutions or migrants themselves.[109]

While straightforward in theory, these criteria are fiendishly difficult to achieve in practice. Pension portability can be secured through a variety of measures. First, governments can enact unilateral measures (that is, national policies or laws) that facilitate portability.[110] Second, governments can enter into bilateral agreements between different countries, to facilitate movement.[111] Traditionally, these intergovernmental agreements are the key means of securing portability, though the agreements vary significantly in their scope and terms.[112] Often, however, the agreements will remove or modify residency or nationality requirements for claiming social benefits, or facilitate cooperation between countries.[113] Third, governments could enter into

[103] V Andrietti, 'Portability of Supplementary Pension Rights in the European Union' (2001) 54 *International Social Security Review* 59, 60.
[104] d'Addio and Cavalleri (n 30) 346.
[105] ibid.
[106] N Taha et al, 'How Portable is Social Security for Migrant Workers?' (2013) 573 ISS Working Paper Series/General Series 1, 7–8.
[107] Andrietti (n 103) 62.
[108] *cf* B Lu and J Piggott, 'Meeting the Migrant Pension Challenge in China' (Portability of Social Benefits: The Economics of a Critical Topic in Globalisation, Venice, August 2012), available at: www.cesifo-group.de/link/vsi12-psb_lu.pdf.
[109] Holzmann and Koettl (n 29) 9.
[110] Taha et al (n 106) 10.
[111] ibid. On bilateral agreements and migration generally, see P Wickramasekara, *Bilateral Agreements and Memoranda of Understanding on Migration of Low Skilled Workers: A Review* (Geneva, ILO, 2015).
[112] d'Addio and Cavalleri (n 30) 347.
[113] Taha et al (n 106) 10.

multilateral agreements, to facilitate mobility within a region or group of countries, as has occurred in the EU. Thus, while governments have options to secure pension portability, this will require intergovernmental and international cooperation, within a common framework of normative goals. Understandably, this is hard to achieve in practice.

V. TRENDS IN PENSION REFORM

With these normative criteria in mind, it is illuminating to consider how pension reform is actually occurring in practice. Pension reform can shift provision in two broad directions: first, by moving towards stronger solidarity, using regulation to secure welfare; or, second, by moving towards privatisation and individualisation of pension provision. In reality, most pension reforms incorporate a mix of these trends.[114] For example, according to Ebbinghaus and Whiteside, there has been a general push to privatise pensions in Europe, both to secure the sustainability of pension systems, and to reduce national debt. However, lacklustre investment performance in pension funds has also led to a renewed push for regulation:

> The uneven performance of funded pensions, particularly since 2001, has fostered political pressure for more state intervention: to contain costs, remove discrepancies, promote transparency and offer guarantees. The objective can appear less pension privatization than a regulation-based 'colonization' of private providers for policy purposes.[115]

Thus, the pendulum continues to swing between privatisation and (re)regulation of pensions, as public sentiment and political factors drive reform in both directions.

Where pension reform is undertaken, it generally manifests in four key ways. First, we can increase the age at which pension benefits can be drawn, reflecting increased life expectancy and the growing number of 'good years' in old age for many older workers. In the UK, the SPA will increase to 67 years of age by 2028,[116] saving the government around £60 billion between 2026–27 and 2035–36.[117] This is likely to disproportionately affect blue-collar workers and those in physically intensive work, as it pushes individuals to remain in employment for a longer period. Remaining in work is most likely to be viable for middle-class, white-collar workers in physically undemanding positions. Thus, increasing pension ages may not ensure intragenerational fairness, though it may secure intergenerational fairness consistent with a new understanding of the intergenerational contract.

Second, we can decrease the quantum of pension benefits that are payable, including by changing the formula by which pensions benefits are calculated. In the UK, for example, the move to a single-tier, flat-rate 'new State Pension' for those retiring

[114] P Frericks et al, 'Toward a Neoliberal Europe? Pension Reforms and Transformed Citizenship' (2009) 41 *Administration & Society* 135.

[115] B Ebbinghaus and N Whiteside, 'Shifting Responsibilities in Western European Pension Systems: What Future for Social Models?' (2012) 12 *Global Social Policy* 266, 268.

[116] HM Treasury and HM Parliament, *Autumn Statement 2011* (London, The Stationery Office, 2011) 23.

[117] ibid 6.

from April 2016 (rather than the former basic State Pension and earnings-based Additional State Pension) may provide a lower level of pension entitlement for many workers, though the government denied that anyone would be worse off.[118] Further, since April 2017, entitlement to a full state pension in the UK requires 35 years of National Insurance contributions, rather than the previous 30 years.[119] Depending on how a reduction of the quantum of pension benefits is implemented in practice, this approach could jeopardise the adequacy of income for individuals in retirement, particularly for those with few other savings to complement their pension payments. It may lead to an increase in the number of pensioners in poverty, and increasing demand for other government services and support. Thus, this reform may jeopardise adequacy of income for the elderly, and may increase government expenditure in other areas. It is also likely to disproportionately affect those with lower pension entitlements, where any reduction will constitute a larger proportion of their overall income. Thus, it may not secure intragenerational fairness, and may indirectly affect the sustainability of government expenditure.

Third, it is possible to increase government, individual and/or employer contributions to the pension system, for current and/or future members, to increase the level of funding in the pension system. Depending on the extent to which a pension system is underfunded, this may or may not address the fundamental disparity between pension benefits and contributions: the scale of underfunding may mean increased contributions make little difference to overall viability. Thus, it may not be effective to ensure the sustainability of the pension system. Further, if later generations are making larger contributions, only to receive smaller pension payments in later life, this may jeopardise intergenerational fairness. The extent to which it is seen as 'fair' that one generation subsidises the retirement of another is likely to be historically and culturally contingent. However, in the context of growing youth unemployment, stagnating wages and precarious work among younger generations, imposing higher contributions on younger workers is unlikely to be seen as fair or appropriate, particularly if this is accompanied by a reduction in future benefits.

Relatedly, we could encourage greater individual saving for retirement, reducing the burden on government and organisational pension systems. This has been modelled in the UK to some extent through the introduction of pension auto-enrolment; and in Australia through the introduction of compulsory superannuation. However, those who are most likely to be able to make provision for their own retirement (middle- and upper-income earners) likely already have plans in place to finance their retirement, including through other investment structures and/or personal pension plans. Those who would benefit from additional savings in retirement (particularly lower-income earners) may not have sufficient resources to invest in other saving vehicles. Indeed, the increase in individual debt, including credit card debt, indicates that many individuals are unable to maintain their current obligations, let alone save for the future. This is exacerbated by the trend towards precarious work, particularly for younger workers.

[118] 'State Pension: "Only 45%" to Get Full New Payout' *BBC News* (12 January 2015), available at: www.bbc.co.uk/news/business-30777166.

[119] ibid.

Fourth, for government pensions, we could increase levels of taxation and/or redirect taxation income towards the payment of pension benefits. This will likely redirect income away from other important services, particularly in an era of austerity where government services have already been significantly cut back. This may again disproportionately affect younger generations, who may be more likely to use other government services (such as schools).

Thus, while a range of potential pension reforms could be pursued, they are all attended by risks and challenges, particularly in securing intergenerational and intragenerational fairness, sustainability and adequacy of income. Preferred models of reform are likely to be nationally and temporally contingent. For example, Jaime-Castillo has found that individuals' preferred models of pension reform are largely dependent on their approach to solidarity:

> [I]ndividuals who adhere to universalistic [conceiving of pensions as a universal social right] or conservative principles [seeing pensions as for maintaining status] are more in favour of increasing contributions in order to maintain the level of pensions, whereas they oppose a postponement of retirement age. In contrast, those who adhere to liberal [believing that pensions should match contributions] or familistic principles [seeking the family as obligated to support retirement] are against increasing contributions and prefer extending retirement age.[120]

Despite this diversity, attitudes to pension reform are surprisingly similar across the EU Member States, particularly in the general level of pessimism in relation to the impact of ageing on the sustainability of pension systems.[121] There is a general preference in both Eastern and Western Europe to raise taxes and extend working life, rather than to reduce pension benefits.[122]

Overall, though, these reforms do not help to address the more fundamental challenges to pension systems from the changing nature of work: a new approach is required, that balances these tensions and normative criteria.

VI. CONCLUSION

As the world of work changes and evolves, the link between (stable, long-term) employment and old age pensions is becoming increasingly precarious. Challenges to established pension systems – particularly those from job mobility, international mobility, work precarity, gender pension disparities and demographic ageing – reveal that established models of accruing pension rights are not sustainable into the future.

We need a new approach, which disentangles pension rights from work status. This may, then, support calls for a universal citizens payment or form of basic income,

[120] AM Jaime-Castillo, 'Public Opinion and the Reform of the Pension Systems in Europe: The Influence of Solidarity Principles' (2013) 23 *Journal of European Social Policy* 390, 393–94.

[121] K Velladics et al, 'Do Different Welfare States Engender Different Policy Preferences? Opinions on Pension Reforms in Eastern and Western Europe' (2006) 26 *Ageing and Society* 475.

[122] ibid.

which is not contributory or dependent on work status.[123] This would help to ensure adequacy of income into old age, address job precarity, ensure intergenerational and intragenerational fairness, and collectivise the risks of old age and demographic change.

That said, providing everyone with the same payment will not achieve substantive equality.[124] While recognising that pensions have never been substantively fair,[125] moving towards a system that values fairness is still a normatively desirable goal. Going further, though, it is unclear how this sort of model might be adapted for an internationally mobile workforce, particularly given the potential political and economic costs of a universal basic income.[126] While these questions have no easy answers, the difficulties facing pension systems mean they must be grappled with.

[123] D Arthur, 'Basic Income: A Radical Idea Enters the Mainstream' (Parliament Library Research Paper, November 2016), available at: www.aph.gov.au/About_Parliament/Parliamentary_Departments/Parliamentary_Library/pubs/rp/rp1617/BasicIncome#_Toc467232178.

[124] See ibid.

[125] eg, the UK state pension was originally introduced in 1908 for only the 'very old, the very poor, and the very respectable': L Hannah, *Inventing Retirement: The Development of Occupational Pensions in Britain* (Cambridge, Cambridge University Press, 1986) 15–16; P Thane, *Old Age in English History: Past Experiences, Present Issues* (Oxford, Oxford University Press, 2000) 225, which would have excluded most members of the working class who would not live to be 'very old'.

[126] Arthur (n 123).

15

The Courts, Non-Discrimination and Systemic Change in UK Public Sector Pension Schemes

LYDIA SEYMOUR

I. INTRODUCTION

IN 2012 THE coalition government introduced sweeping changes to pension provision across the public sector in order to reduce costs. The mechanism was the Public Services Pensions Act 2013, which provided that all existing public sector schemes would close on 31 March 2015, with new schemes being introduced for all service thereafter.[1]

Unsurprisingly, given that the motivation for the changes was cost reduction, the new schemes were in broad terms less generous than the schemes which they replaced. Existing members were to be transferred from the old to the new schemes in April 2015, but following discussions between the government and trade unions, it was decided that there would be 'transitional protection' for members who were within 10 years of retirement age in April 2012. This group would be allowed to remain in the old, more generous, schemes until such time as they retired. The effect was to divide existing members of the schemes into: (i) people who were within 10 years of retirement age in April 2012, who were protected from the effect of the reforms; and (ii) people who were more than 10 years from retirement age in April 2012, who were simply moved into the less generous schemes for all service from 1 April 2015.[2]

The decision to provide transitional protection only to those within 10 years of retirement was challenged in the Employment Tribunal by members of five different schemes (judges, firefighters, police officers, prison officers and Ministry of

[1] Other than the Local Government Pension Scheme, which was to close a year earlier.

[2] In fact the position was slightly more complex than this suggests, as members who were between 10 and 14 years away from retirement age were allowed to remain in their old scheme for a defined further period, the length of which was determined by their age, before being put into the new schemes. This group – known as the 'taper protection group' do not raise any different issue of principle for the purpose of this chapter, and hence for simplicity it will refer simply to the protected and unprotected groups.

Defence police officers).[3] The primary claims in all cases were for direct age discrimination. Pension payments are deferred pay, and younger scheme members complained that allowing their older colleagues to remain in more generous schemes meant that they were being paid less than those older colleagues on the grounds of age. In addition, because women and BME people have traditionally been under-represented in the judiciary and uniformed services, the decision to focus protection on older workers was alleged also to be indirect race discrimination and a breach of the principle of equal pay.

In November 2018 the claims reached the Court of Appeal, and in a judgment dated 20 December 2018 the claims of both the judges and the firefighters were upheld.[4] The government sought permission to appeal from the Supreme Court but was refused, and the cases have now been sent back to the Employment Tribunal to determine remedy.

This chapter will look at the following:

- How the decision to provide transitional protection for older public sector workers was made.
- The litigation and what we have learnt in terms of legal principle from the decision of the Court of Appeal.
- The policy implications of the decision, and how it may influence future cases challenging decisions to reduce pension entitlements. In particular what it tells us about:
  a. The role of the Courts in considering social policy decisions made by the executive.
  b. The limits of the ambit of the Age Exemptions for Pension Schemes Order.
  c. Justification defences in the context of progressive reductions of pension benefits. intergenerational fairness and limited horizons.
  d. The importance of agreements with social partners/trade unions.

II. HOW THE DECISION TO PROTECT OLDER MEMBERS WAS MADE

In addition to being legally interesting, the disclosure provided in the judges' and firefighters' litigation has provided an insight into the way in which governmental decisions relating to pension entitlements are taken, and the role (and influence) of civil service advice in social policy changes.

A. The Hutton Report and the Rejection of Transitional Protection

The factual background to the claims starts with the Hutton Report on 10 March 2011, which set out a variety of recommendations for the reform of public sector pensions,

[3] *McCloud v Lord Chancellor* (2017) ET 2201483/2015. This was later appealed to the Employment Appeal Tribunal: *Lord Chancellor v McCloud* [2018] 3 All ER 208 (EAT). The claims by police officers, prison officers and Ministry of Defence police officers have been stayed awaiting the outcome of the judges' and firefighters' claims.

[4] *Lord Chancellor v McCloud* [2018] EWCA Civ 2844, [2019] Pens LR 12.

focusing on the creation of new, less generous, defined benefit pension schemes across the sector.[5]

The report specifically considered whether it would be appropriate to provide any form of transitional protection in relation to the changes, but rejected such an approach, saying:

> The Commission's expectation is that existing members who are currently in their 50s should, by and large, experience fairly limited change to the benefit which they would otherwise have expected to accrue by the time they reach their current scheme NPA. This would particularly be the case if the final salary link is protected for past service, as the Commission recommends. This limitation of impact will also extend to people below age 50, proportionate to the length of time before they reach their NPA. Therefore special protections for members over a certain age should not be necessary. Age discrimination legislation also means that it is not possible in practice to provide protection from change for members who are already above a certain age.[6]

In essence, the Commission's view was that the impact on those close to retirement was likely to be limited, both because there was to be a three-year lead-in, and because the final salary link was being retained for all service up to the date of the changes. There was therefore no need for transitional protection to 'cushion the blow' and recommendation 5 of the Hutton report said simply, 'As soon as practical, members of the current defined benefit pension schemes should be moved to the new schemes for future service'.[7]

B. The Government's Initial Position

Initially the government agreed. A discussion paper from the Chief Secretary to the Treasury, undated but apparently written in the period following the Hutton Report, said:

> The Government recognises that people close to retirement will not want to face a sudden change in their retirement age. However, the Commission's proposals would not lead to a sudden change for those close to retirement [because protection of accrued rights means that they will see little change].[8]

And the May 2011 Treasury paper: 'Workforce, Pay and Pensions' set out the following analysis:

> Could we agree to offer further protection of (sic) for those nearing retirement?
>
> Unions are likely to ask for further transitional protection for those nearing retirement (for example, on pension age, or leaving members over a certain age in their existing schemes) … There is no policy reason to do this. It is very likely that this sort of approach

[5] Independent Public Service Pensions Commission, *Independent Public Service Pensions Commission: Final Report* (2011) (Hutton Report).

[6] ibid [7.34].

[7] ibid 9.

[8] Employment Tribunal Hearing Bundle, File 6, 4774, [37] from the firefighters' claim before the Employment Tribunal (*Sargent v London Fire and Emergency Planning Authority* (2017) ET 2201483/2015).

> would face legal challenge on the grounds of age discrimination ... [redacted section]. Hutton's final report is explicit that there should not be protection of this type.[9]

i. Transitional Protection to 'Sweeten' the Deal with the Unions

This position appears to have changed after the government began discussing the pension reforms with trade union representatives. In June 2011, a Treasury paper which set out the overall shape of the reform package said, at paragraph 16:

> The unions are particularly concerned about:
>
> Transitional arrangements. Unions represent existing workers so transition is disproportionately important to them. In practice, someone close to retirement has already accrued most of their pension and we have committed that they will be able to take their already accrued rights at the pension age they accrued it for. But those in their late 50s may mistakenly fear suddenly being asked to work till 65 or 68. As an additional concession, we are exploring options for delay to implementation for existing members, although due to age discrimination legislation these are limited.[10]

There followed a period of negotiation between the UK government and the TUC, and a Treasury paper dated 16 September 2011 suggests that by this point the Chief Secretary to the Treasury's view had changed to being in favour of transitional protection for older members:

> Transitional arrangements for pension reform are disproportionately important to unions because their incentives are to get the best deal for current members, even if this [is] at the expense of future members. We understand that you are minded to make a future concession on transitional arrangements if it could help secure a deal.[11]

A Treasury paper dated 13 October 2011 said, 'To secure a deal with the unions you [that is the Chief Secretary to the Treasury] asked us to assess the options for offering enhanced transitional protection in the move to new public service schemes' and went on to set out three possible options for transitional protection. These were:

(i) Option 1 – Wholesale delay of introduction of the Schemes;
(ii) Option 2 – Staggered introduction (existing members moving later than new members); and
(iii) Option 3 – Age protection (those over a certain age staying in their current scheme).[12]

ii. Concerns about Age Discrimination and Targeting the Better Off in Relation to Age Protection

The legal advice relating to this Option was redacted in the copies provided to the Employment Tribunal. However, under the heading 'Policy Considerations' the document said, 'Honouring acquired rights and the final salary link means that those who

[9] ibid File 2, 836.
[10] ibid File 2 [16].
[11] ibid File 2, 693.
[12] ibid File 3, 1056.

have been in the scheme the longest will be least affected by changes, so the savings foregone will be targeted on those who would see the least change'.[13]

In a paper of the same date, in response to a request from the Chief Secretary to the Treasury, officials considered two different forms of age protection. The paper notes that 'both [forms of age protection] target protection at those already most protected (as they are likely to have spent longer in existing schemes)'.[14]

Thus, it is clear from the outset that civil servants (and the Chief Secretary to the Treasury) were aware both that providing transitional protection to older scheme members was targeting financial support on those who had already received the greatest financial benefit, and that there was a risk that such protection would constitute unlawful discrimination.

C. The Decision to Proceed with Age-Based Protection for those 10 Years from Retirement

Despite having received repeated advice that any form of age-based protection would be likely to face an age discrimination challenge, and the policy advice that the effect of this choice would be to target savings on those who would see the least change, the Chief Secretary to the Treasury chose Option 3 – age based protection.[15]

The only evidence that the Tribunal had as to why he took the decision to proceed with Option 3 was set out in an email from his Private Secretary dated 14 October 2011 which says (where not redacted):

> [The Chief Secretary to the Treasury's] preference is for the age protection option (option 3) … considers this the simplest and easiest to communicate. The [Chief Secretary to the Treasury] also thinks that this option can be justified on the grounds that it is closest to the years of notice agreed for the [State Pension Age] change.[16]

As to the type of age protection, the Chief Secretary to the Treasury's view (on 19 October 2011) was that it should be 'within 10 years of retirement' for consistency with the likely approach on State Pension Age changes.[17]

D. The Changes and their Impact on Members

This decision was applied across the whole public sector. However, the impact of the changes on scheme members differed significantly between different groups, because whilst the new schemes were broadly similar across different public sector employees, the benefit structures of the pre-existing schemes had varied significantly. For example, the pre-existing schemes that related to uniformed services (such as firefighters

[13] ibid File 3, 1060.
[14] ibid File 3, 1102.
[15] ibid File 3, 1054.
[16] ibid File 3, 1054.
[17] ibid File 3, 1098.

and the police) were particularly generous in respect of some members, to reflect the arduous nature of the roles and the difficulty of continuing in active service into old age. The impact on these members of placing them into the new, less generous, schemes which would apply across the public sector was therefore particularly significant. Similarly, the judicial pension scheme had traditionally been a generous one, to reflect the fact that judges tended to commence pensionable service relatively late (the judiciary generally being a second career in the UK) and the fact that many judges would be taking a pay cut on appointment. There was therefore a larger difference between the benefit entitlements of the old and new schemes in the case of judges than in most other public sector jobs. This difference was exacerbated by the fact that the new judicial pension scheme was a tax registered scheme (the old judicial pension scheme having been an unregistered scheme, which was something of an anomaly in the public sector).

The extent of the impact on public sector scheme members also varied according to when they had begun pensionable service. Before the 2012 reforms there had been a number of previous rounds of changes to public sector schemes, generally providing progressively less generous entitlements for new joiners but allowing existing members to continue to be entitled to more generous benefits. This meant that the members who were worst affected were those who had joined their schemes when they remained at their most generous, but who were not old enough to receive transitional protection and were now being placed into significantly less generous schemes.

To give a flavour of the impact on individual members of being excluded from transitional protection, the agreed expert evidence before the Employment Tribunal showed that in the case of judges, the annual capital investment required (from taxed income) to provide an annuity giving approximately the same benefits on retirement as those earned each year by their older comparators was at least £30,000 (on a gross salary of £110,000) rising to at least £46,000 (on a gross salary of £132,000).

In the case of firefighters, the agreed expert evidence showed that a full-time firefighter would need to make an annual capital investment of between about £16,000 and £19,000 to receive the same level of pension entitlement as their comparators. To put these figures in context, the basic gross pay of a trained firefighter is £29,638 per annum.

III. THE LITIGATION

A. The Claimants

Given the variation in impact across the public sector, it is perhaps not surprising that despite the changes being applied across all public sector schemes, discrimination claims have thus far been brought only in respect of a relatively small group of schemes. This reflects the fact that the claims have been brought only by those who were worst affected – that is, members of the uniformed services who joined their schemes before benefits were made less generous, and judges. The numbers of claimants are significant. There were 230 judges; over 6,000 firefighters; approximately 9,000 police officers; approximately 3,500 prison officers; and approximately 1,000 Ministry of Defence police officers.[18]

B. The Key Legal Dispute

From the outset the government accepted that the transitional protection provided to older judges and firefighters constituted less favourable treatment on the grounds of age. The focus of the age discrimination claims was, therefore, whether the government could show that the less favourable treatment was justified.

The availability of a justification defence to direct discrimination is unique to age discrimination. In respect of all other forms of discrimination direct discrimination cannot be justified. However, age is different, and a justification defence to direct discrimination exists by virtue of Article 6(1) of the Equality Directive, which says:

> (1) Notwithstanding article 2(2), Member States may provide that differences of treatment on grounds of age shall not constitute discrimination, if, within the context of national law, they are objectively and reasonably justified by a legitimate aim, including legitimate employment policy, labour market and vocational training objectives, and if the means of achieving that aim are appropriate and necessary.
>
> Such differences of treatment may include, among others:
>
> a. The setting of special conditions on access to employment and vocational training, employment and occupation, including dismissal and remuneration conditions, for young people, older workers and persons with caring responsibilities in order to promote their vocational integration or ensure their protection.
> b. The fixing of minimum conditions of age, professional experience or seniority in service for access to employment or to certain advantages linked to employment.
> c. The fixing of a maximum age for recruitment which is based on the training requirements of the post in question or the need for a reasonable period of employment before retirement.

This prohibition on direct discrimination, and the justification defence, are set out in domestic law in section 13 of the Equality Act 2010 (EA 2010):

> **13 Direct discrimination**
>
> A person (A) discriminates against another (B) if, because of a protected characteristic, A treats B less favourably than A treats or would treat others.
>
> If the protected characteristic is age, A does not discriminate against B if A can show A's treatment of B to be a proportionate means of achieving a legitimate aim.

Once less favourable treatment under section 13(1) has been made out (or, as in this case, conceded) there are two stages for a court or tribunal to consider when

[18] Thus far only the judges' and firefighters' claims have been heard, with the police, prison officer and Ministry of Defence police cases having been stayed awaiting the outcome of those proceedings (n 3).

determining whether or not a justification defence to direct age discrimination is made out under section 13(2):

> (1) The respondent must show that the impugned provision is consistent with a legitimate social policy aim of the UK as a member state. This requires that there be a legitimate social policy aim in the sense set out in Article 6(1), and a margin of appreciation is to be applied in determining whether an aim is potentially a legitimate social policy aim consistent within the meaning of that article. This first requirement can be referred to as a 'gateway' requirement, in that it is a necessary step in establishing the justification defence – if the respondent cannot show that the treatment is consistent with the legitimate social policy aim, then the treatment cannot be justified; and
>
> (2) if the respondent gets through the 'gateway' of establishing a legitimate social policy aim, then it must also establish that the treatment in question is in fact justified in the circumstances of the particular case.

The legitimate aim relied upon by the government in both the judges' and firefighters' cases was 'to protect those closest to retirement from the financial effects of pension reform'.

As to why the transitional protection constituted a proportionate means of achieving this legitimate aim, a variety of arguments were put forward, including: that those who are closer to retirement would have a greater legitimate expectation that their pension entitlements would not change significantly; that the transitional protection arrangements enabled a clear and simple message to be communicated; and that they provided for consistency across the public sector.

The key area of dispute between the parties was the appropriate test to be applied by the Tribunal to the second part of the justification defence, given that the legislation that was being challenged related to a large-scale, systemic change which was being applied across the public sector.

The Claimants' position was that the Tribunal should apply the ordinary principles that would be applied to any other justification defence in a discrimination claim, including private claims. These have been set out in various cases, most notably in the judgment of the Court of Appeal in *Hardy & Hansons plc v Lax*:

> [It] is for the tribunal to determine whether the employer has shown that the proposal is justifiable irrespective of the sex of the person to whom it is applied. As it is the tribunal which must decide on justification without according any margin of appreciation to the employer, the tribunal must therefore set out a critical and thorough evaluation following the tests set out in *Bilka-Kaufhaus GmbH v Weber von Hartz* (Case 170/84) [1987] ICR 110 when making its determination of the merits of the justification advanced.[19]

Thus, the Claimants argued, in this case it was for the Tribunal to make its own decision as to whether the transitional protection for older judges and firefighters was justified, on the basis of a critical and thorough evaluation, and without according a margin of appreciation to the employer. Any alternative approach, on the Claimants' case, would mean a two-tier system of discrimination rights – with public sector workers having lesser protection against discrimination than private sector

[19] *Hardy & Hansons plc v Lax* [2005] EWCA Civ 846, [2005] ICR 1565 [54].

workers, because it would be easier for a government employer to justify less favourable treatment.

The Respondents disagreed that the *Hardy & Hansons* approach was correct. They contended that the factual background to this case, and in particular the fact that the impugned legislation had been decided upon at a high governmental level, and formed part of a political decision as to the appropriate level of occupational pensions across the public sector, required a different approach. In essence, they argued that this was a social policy decision made by the government; that the Tribunal should be wary of straying into matters beyond its remit, and should adopt a light-touch approach to its consideration of the discrimination claims. The 'ordinary' *Hardy v Hansons* level of scrutiny, by which the Tribunal decides for itself whether the justification defence is made out, should not be followed. Rather, they relied upon a strand of European decisions which, they argued, limited the role of the courts in considering government decisions in the social and employment field. An example of this approach was set out in the decision of the Court of Justice of the European Union in *Unland v Land Berlin* in which the Court said:

> It should be noted, that under EU law as it currently stands, the member states and, where appropriate, the social partners at national level enjoy broad discretion in their choice, not only to pursue a particular aim in the field of social and employment policy, but also in the definition of measures capable of achieving it.[20]

This, the government argued, required a broad margin of appreciation to be applied when a government was acting as legislator even when it was doing so as an employer itself. It was an important aspect of the Respondents' case that the decision to offer transitional protection to older workers was a moral decision, made by the elected government, and that it was not for the Tribunal to interfere in such decisions.

The crux of the dispute, therefore, was the level of scrutiny to be applied to the government's justification defence given that this was a social policy decision made in respect of the whole public sector. In such circumstances should the Tribunal apply a margin of appreciation to every aspect of the justification test, such that its role was limited to a review of the decision similar to a judicial review function or the application of a band of reasonable responses test? Or, was this at heart simply a claim by employees against their employer about less favourable treatment in the form of lower pay, to which the ordinary principles of discrimination law should apply?

C. The Evidence

It is worth noting that the reason why this legal dispute as to the level of scrutiny to be applied by the Tribunal was so crucial to the claims, was that the evidence as to why the government's decision to provide protection for older workers was limited. The only witnesses called by the Respondents at the Tribunal hearings were civil servants, who were not themselves the relevant decision-makers, and were thus only able to

[20] Case C-20/13 *Unland v Land Berlin* [2015] ICR 1225.

provide indirect evidence as to the reason why the transitional protection provisions were adopted.

Further, a number of the reasons which were put forward at the time for the granting of transitional protection to those within 10 years of normal retirement age fell away under scrutiny during the Employment Tribunal process. For example, at the time the changes were introduced it was suggested by the government that younger workers would be better able to make lifestyle changes to ameliorate the impact of the pension reforms than their older colleagues. This was part of the reasoning relied upon by the government in deciding that older workers would be protected from the effects of reform. Upon analysis, however, this reasoning is difficult to sustain. The impact on any individual of the pension reforms was dependent upon the number of years that they had remaining before retirement. Thus, whilst it is true that a younger worker had longer to make adjustments before retirement, they equally had greater adjustments to make. In fact, the amount of adjustment required was directly proportionate to the length of time the individual had to adjust, and it is therefore difficult to see that the mere fact that younger people are further from retirement can justify a decision that they would not be protected from the effects of pension reform.

Further, as can be seen from the figures set out above, it was wholly unrealistic that any younger firefighter or judge would be able to make lifestyle changes that could enable them to make up the difference between their pension entitlement and those of protected colleagues. This laid bare an essential difficulty in the justification defence – that the transitional protection was a financial benefit to older members in circumstances in which they were the group who would suffer the least financial impact from the changes.

As the litigation proceeded, the focus of the government's defence moved away from putting forward specific reasons for the decision, and towards more general assertions that the provision of transitional protection to older workers was morally right, and 'felt fair'. In addition, as it became clear that the reasons initially put forward as justifying the transitional protection for older workers did not withstand analysis, the importance of the level of scrutiny issue increased. Realistically, the government's reasons for its decision to grant transitional protection to older workers were only likely to withstand light-touch scrutiny.

D. The Litigation

The judges' and firefighters' claims were brought separately, and were heard at first instance by two separate employment tribunals.[21] The judges' claims were heard first, and the decision in that case was promulgated shortly before the conclusion of the firefighters' hearing. Despite this, the two employment tribunals reached wholly different decisions: the judges' claim was upheld and the firefighters' dismissed. The decisions contained a number of points of distinction, but the key reason for

[21] *McCloud v Lord Chancellor* (Employment Tribunal) (n 3) (judges' claim) and *Sargent* (n 8) (firefighters' claim).

the different outcomes was the Employment Judge's finding on the 'level of scrutiny' issue discussed above.

The Employment Judge in the judges' claim accepted the Claimants' argument as to the appropriate test to be applied, and undertook his own scrutiny of the government's justification defence.[22] On that basis, he did not accept either that the government had shown that the transitional protection was introduced in pursuit of a legitimate aim,[23] or that it was proportionate.[24] The Employment Judge who heard the firefighters' claims, in contrast, accepted the government's contention that a 'light-touch' approach was necessary to the Tribunal's consideration of justification because the decision which was being challenged was of a political nature and taken at a high level of government.[25] On this basis, she found both that the government was pursuing a legitimate aim and that the transitional protection was a proportionate means of achieving that legitimate aim.[26]

All parties appealed to the Employment Appeal Tribunal, and the appeals in the two sets of claims were heard together by Sir Alan Wilkie. He dismissed the government's appeal in the judges' case and allowed the firefighters' appeal on proportionality, but not legitimate aim.

E. The Court of Appeal Decision

Again, all parties appealed, and in a decision dated 20 December 2018, the claims of both the judges and firefighters were upheld by the Court of Appeal.[27] On the central question of the degree of scrutiny, having considered the domestic and European Court of Justice authorities, the Court said:

> [We] see no difference between the domestic authorities and the European authorities … as Lady Hale said in para 59 of *Seldon*, establishing that an aim is capable of being a legitimate aim is only the beginning of the story. It is for the tribunal then, according an appropriate margin of discretion, to decide whether it is legitimate in the circumstances of the case. For this purpose, an aim must at least be rational and, if it is not, the employment tribunal is entitled to say so. Margin of discretion cannot rescue an aim that is irrational.[28]

This reference to irrationality reflects the central problem with the government's case on justification: the lack of evidence to explain why the government thought it appropriate to provide more generous benefits to those least affected by the pension changes. As to the relevance of the fact that this was a high-level government decision which related to changes that would apply across the public sector, the Court of Appeal said:

> [W]here government has a legitimate interest in any issue which arises in a discrimination claim, it is to be afforded a margin of discretion but it is for the fact-finding tribunal to

[22] *McCloud v Lord Chancellor* (EAT) (n 3) [81]–[121].
[23] ibid [94].
[24] ibid [118].
[25] *Sargent* (n 8) [47] (summary of the government's submissions).
[26] ibid [117].
[27] *Lord Chancellor v McCloud* (CA) (n 4).
[28] ibid [84]–[87]. See also [143]–[144].

> assess both whether the government has such a legitimate interest and the amount of discretion it should be afforded and then the tribunal should decide the case itself in accordance with ordinary principles.[29]

Thus, the central question of the appropriate 'level of scrutiny' was resolved in favour of the Claimants. The Court of Appeal's view was that even in a case such as this, where the Tribunal is considering a social policy decision by government which has a political element and which is to be applied across the whole public sector, the Tribunal should decide the justification issue itself in accordance with ordinary principles.

Applying these principles to the Employment Tribunal decision in the firefighters' claims, the Court of Appeal was critical of the Employment Judge's approach, and specifically the failure adequately to scrutinise the justification defence put forward by the government:

> By inference, [the Employment Judge in the firefighters' claim] found that the aims asserted were legitimate. But whether or not they were legitimate required an objective analysis by her of the nature we have described. Instead, however, of carrying out such an analysis, she proceeded from a finding that the claimed aims were social policy aims straight to the conclusion that they were also legitimate ones. She at no point engaged in any objective assessment as to their legitimacy. That was an exercise that required her to ask herself why the oldest members of the FPS were being so generously preferred over younger members.[30]

In essence, they found that the Employment Judge had been inappropriately deferential to the government's arguments. The Court of Appeal judgment said that:[31]

> [T]he primary reason [the Employment Judge in the firefighters' claim] did not engage in an objective assessment of the legitimacy of the aims was because she considered she did not have to. She regarded the chosen aims as a decision of the Governments, perhaps of a moral nature and/or as one that had a political element, and that it was not for her to substitute her view for that of the Governments'.[32]

The Employment Tribunal judgment was therefore overturned.

This left the question of whether it was appropriate for the matter to be remitted for rehearing or whether the Court of Appeal could effectively substitute its own judgment. In a key passage of the judgment their Lordships said:

> We have considered whether we should remit the age discrimination claims to the employment tribunal for a re-consideration of the issue of legitimacy of aims but have concluded that there is no point in doing so. The only conclusion to which the tribunal could properly come is that, in the absence of evidence supporting the claimed legitimacy of the aims, the respondents' case as to justification must fail. In those circumstances, we consider that

[29] ibid [87].

[30] ibid [152].

[31] ibid [154].

[32] The Court of Appeal judgment makes reference to 'Governments' in the plural because the claims were brought against both the relevant departments of state and the Welsh Ministers. As precisely the same defence was advanced by all government respondents this chapter uses the term 'government' in the singular for simplicity.

> this court should deal finally with the issue of liability in the age discrimination claims by upholding the firefighters' claims that they have been the victims of unlawful age discrimination and substituting an order to that effect.[33]

This was an unusually direct approach for an appellate court, perhaps particularly in a case with such significant financial implications. It reflects the paucity of the evidence put forward by the governments for their decision to provide transitional protection to older workers and the Court of Appeal's view that it would effectively be impossible for the government to justify that decision were the claims to return to the Employment Tribunal.

As to the judges' claims, the position was simpler. The Court of Appeal's judgment meant that the government's appeal failed, and the original Employment Tribunal judgment in the judges' favour was upheld.

The government applied for permission to appeal from the Court of Appeal, but this was denied. They therefore sought permission to appeal directly from the Supreme Court, but in June 2019 permission was refused on the grounds that the applications did not raise an arguable point of law.

IV. POLICY IMPLICATIONS

The current Chief Secretary to the Treasury has announced that the potential financial impact of the judges' and firefighters' cases could be over £4 billion. However, the significance of these cases in policy terms will go beyond the financial implications. In this chapter I would like to consider four aspects of the judges' and firefighters' cases which are of particular significance to pensions policy issues.

A. The Role of the Courts in Considering Social Policy Decisions by the Executive

The first point to note about the decision is the rejection by the Court of Appeal of the government's submissions that the courts and tribunals should afford a margin of appreciation when considering justification defences put forward by the government in social policy cases. This central plank of the government's case would have had wide-ranging implications if accepted. Given that the government employs large numbers of people it will frequently be the case that decisions which relate to individuals' employment rights in the public sector will be taken at a high level of government and affect large groups of people. Had the government's arguments in the judges' and firefighters' cases been accepted, then the result would have been a lesser degree of protection for members of public sector schemes (and by analogy public sector employment rights generally) than applies to the private sector.

[33] *Lord Chancellor v McCloud* (CA) (n 4) [164].

Of course, the question of the appropriate extent of judicial intervention into government decisions has been considered in numerous previous judgments, and by many academics. The judgment of Mr Justice Blake in *R (on the application of Age UK) v Secretary of State for Business and Skills* contains a useful summary of many of the key authorities and texts on the point and concludes:

> I must give full effect to Lord Nicholls's observation in Seymour-Smith (No 2) [2000] ICR 244, para 29: governments must be free to govern, and businesses must be free to conduct business, but I would add that judges must also judge, which they can do in this field by applying well established principles of proportionality and in so doing apply an appropriate intensity of inquiry whilst ensuring that they do not stray beyond their proper constitutional competence and usurp the prerogatives of the executive on sensitive social issues for which it is ultimately accountable to the electorate.[34]

The decision in the Court of Appeal in the judges' and firefighters' claims represents a robust rejection of the government's argument that careful scrutiny by the Employment Tribunal of its justification defence would have been, in the language of *Age UK*, usurping the prerogative of the executive on a sensitive social issue. Rather, they found, that it was the Employment Judge's role to scrutinise the reasons put forward by the government. By doing so, the Employment Judge in the judges' claim did not stray beyond his proper constitutional competence, and in refusing to do so the Employment Judge in the firefighters' claim failed to apply the correct test.

B. The Limits of the Age Exemptions for Pension Schemes Order

The second significant aspect of the Court of Appeal's judgment is its significance in marking the limits of the exemptions for age discrimination claims in pensions cases. Until these cases were brought, the impact of age discrimination legislation in the field of occupational pensions muted by the wide-ranging exemptions in the Equality Act (Age Exemptions for Pension Schemes) Order 2010 (Age Exemption Regulations). In broad terms, these prevent discrimination claims in circumstances in which people are treated differently on the basis of different joining dates.

These exclusions are hugely significant, as they effectively prevent the vast majority of 'intergenerational fairness' claims in occupational pensions. For example, it has been very common over the past two or three decades for defined benefit schemes to provide progressively less generous benefits over time, with changes initially being made only in respect of members who joined after a particular date, and then the scheme closing entirely to new members. Clearly, the effect of such changes is that new joiners (who will in general be younger) receive less generous pension entitlements than colleagues who joined earlier (who would in general be older). However, the Age Exemption Regulations provide that occupational pension schemes are entitled to discriminate on the grounds of joining date in a number of different ways,

[34] *R (on the application of Age UK) v Secretary of State for Business and Skills* [2009] EWHC 2336 (Admin), [2009] Pens LR 333 [41].

and there is therefore frequently no legal basis to challenge the gradual diminution of pension entitlements for members with different joining dates, despite the fact that this has led to significant differences between generations.

Previous amendments to public sector pensions had generally followed the same approach: existing members would retain more generous pension entitlements, and new schemes were created for new joiners with less generous benefits. The changes made in 2015 marked a new approach, in which the distinction as to who would retain more generous benefits was drawn purely in terms of date of birth, rather than date of joining. This meant that younger judges and firefighters who had joined on the same day or even earlier than older colleagues were being paid less per day solely on the grounds of their age. Importantly, in legal terms, it meant that the exemptions in the Age Exemption Regulations did not apply, and that the decision to allow older members to retain more generous benefits whilst their younger colleagues were moved into less generous schemes was therefore open to legal challenge.

C. Progressive Reductions of Pension Benefits, Intergenerational Fairness and Limited Horizons

This in turn led to a third important aspect of the Court of Appeal's judgment. Because previous cases have been prevented by the Age Exemption Regulations this is the first comprehensive judicial analysis of age discrimination in the context of reduction in pension entitlements over time. In the course of that analysis it became clear that a number of the arguments relied upon by the government to support the protection of older workers from the effects of reform were without substance and relied upon little more than stereotypical assumptions. These included the argument that it was appropriate to protect only older people because younger people had longer to adjust to the changes and set aside savings. As noted above, whilst it is true that younger people had longer to adjust, this did not in truth provide a justification for the protection of older people, because younger people also had to adjust to a greater degree of change. The justification arguments also included the assertion that younger people had more time to alter their lifestyle and spending expectations. Again, this is correct as a matter of fact, but it is hard to see that it constitutes a justification defence – in essence, it is simply saying that younger people have the option to suffer financial disadvantage over a different period; that cannot of itself justify imposing a financial disadvantage upon them in preference to their older colleagues.

It was this lack of substance which drove the governments towards an argument that this was a political or moral choice on the part of the government which was not provable by evidence nor reliant upon concrete factors. The governments argued that there are many examples of transitional protection arrangements in occupational pension schemes, and that it is generally recognised that protection against change will be provided to those who are close to retirement. They submitted that there were no cases at all in which transitional protection had been provided only to younger members of the pension scheme. That was because, they contended, it is 'intuitive common sense' that people close to retirement care more about their pension, and are more invested in it.

This latter point is of particular interest in policy terms. It may well be correct that older people generally care more about their pension, and would therefore be likely to protest more vociferously about reductions in their entitlements. It is human nature to assign greater importance to events that are closer in time. However, in most areas of occupational pensions policy, the government's interest is in battling a tendency to short-termism, by incentivising (and in some instances forcing) people to save for retirement from the earliest age possible. The introduction of auto-enrolment is an obvious example.

The decision to provide transitional protection only to those close to retirement, expressly on the basis that pensions are more important to older people, therefore appears to stand in stark contrast to the government's approach elsewhere. Further, insofar as the government was correct to assert that transitional protection against pension changes is never provided only to younger workers, that is at least in part likely to be a reflection of the limitations imposed by the Age Exemption Regulations, which effectively allow age discrimination in relation to pension entitlements provided that the differently treated groups have different joining dates.

All that said, whilst the judgment can be seen as rebalancing interests between generations, in that younger judges and firefighters will receive the same benefits as their older colleagues, from a policy perspective it is important to bear in mind that the younger judges and firefighters who brought these claims were themselves only a subset of the affected members. Taking the case of firefighters, for example, a new scheme had been introduced in 2006 for all firefighters who joined after that date. That scheme was itself significantly less generous than the 1992 Firefighters' Pension Scheme which had gone before it. All of the Claimants in the firefighters' pension challenge were members of the more generous 1992 Firefighters' Pension Scheme. That was no coincidence. It reflected the enormous gulf between the benefits provided by the 1992 Scheme and the new scheme which was introduced in 2015 as part of the pension changes across the public sector. The position for firefighters who joined from 2006 was different. They were already receiving significantly less generous benefits than their colleagues who were members of the 1992 Scheme, and thus the introduction of the new scheme in 2015 had less impact. In fact, in some respects, the new scheme was more generous for 2006 Scheme members.

So, taking the example of the firefighters who were successful in the Court of Appeal, they were in generational terms a 'slice' of pension scheme members – people who joined the fire service before 2006, but who were not within 10 years of retirement in 2012. Very roughly, they were therefore firefighters who were born between 1971 and 1988. It follows that whilst the effect of the judgment will to some extent address and imbalance of pension entitlements between generations, in that some younger firefighters will now receive benefits at the same level as their older colleagues, its effect will be limited in this respect because the only younger firefighters who will benefit will be those who were members of the old, pre-2006 scheme. Those who joined the fire service after 2006, and who will therefore of course in general terms be younger than those who joined before that date, will never have had the more generous benefits to lose.

D. The Relevance of Agreement from Social Partners/Trade Unions

The fourth aspect of the judges' and firefighters' claims which is interesting from a policy perspective relates to the influence of the trade unions in the government's decisions as to the public sector pension changes. As I set out above, the documents disclosed by the government during the course of the Employment Tribunal proceedings showed that the decision to adopt the transitional protection for older workers was influenced by their desire to 'sweeten' the deal with the trade unions. This in turn was influenced by the Treasury's belief that trade unions cared disproportionately about transitional arrangements, because their primary concern was their existing membership.

If the Treasury was correct about that, it suggests that there could be a structural bias in trade union objectives, by which the interests of older members are likely to be preferred to those of younger members. In relation to judges and firefighters specifically, this point was of only limited relevance, as the judges were not represented by a trade union and the Fire Brigades Union did not at any point agree to the government's proposals. However, in terms of legal principle this potential structural bias is important, because the existence of an agreement with social partners can be used as part of a justification for a policy which would otherwise be discriminatory.[35]

V. CONCLUSION

Bringing these policy strands together, the Court of Appeal judgment in the judges' and firefighters' cases raises a number of interesting social policy issues, as well as important points of legal principle. Perhaps most importantly, the claims required the Court to address head-on the question of whether a Tribunal is required to accord the government a 'margin of appreciation' when considering whether social policy decisions which result in less favourable treatment are justified. This required an analysis of the tensions between the roles of the executive and judiciary more commonly explored in public law than in pensions claims. These tensions were exemplified by the contrasting first-instance judgments – one essentially deferential to the government and the other asserting the primary role of the Tribunal in determining justification. The Court of Appeal's judgment has resolved that central issue against the government and the Supreme Court has refused permission to appeal.

The cases have therefore now returned to the Employment Tribunal to determine the appropriate remedy in the discrimination claims. The issues that arise on remedy are themselves potentially complex, particularly those relating to retrospectively unravelling members' pension entitlements. We may therefore see further important issues of legal principle addressed (and further appellate decisions) before this litigation is concluded.

[35] See, eg, in the context of equal pay C-427/11 *Kenny and others v Minister for Justice, Equality and Law Reform, Minister for Finance, Commissioner of An Garda Síochána* [2013] 2 CMLR 50, in which the fact that pay rates had been determined by collective bargaining was taken into account as 'one factor among others' when assessing justification.

16

Cutting Pension Rights for Public Workers in the United States: Don't Look to the Courts for Help

RONALD H ROSENBERG*

I. INTRODUCTION

THROUGHOUT AMERICAN HISTORY, all levels of government have employed people to serve the public in a myriad of ways: teachers, police, fire and other workers. At the creation of America, private citizens were asked to support the new country by joining as soldiers in the army of the rebellious colonies during the Revolutionary War. In exchange for this dangerous loyalty these courageous people were to be compensated by their colonies and later, by the Continental Congress. As in modern times, these military 'public employees' were offered current wages and, sometimes, future income with pensions or land in order to induce their service and to discourage desertion during the lengthy and dangerous war.[1] Pension incentives were thought to be crucial for the colonies to attract soldiers willing to risk their lives for this dangerous and uncertain cause. The need for this support was apparent, since injured soldiers could spend their elderly years impoverished and disabled by their war injuries. Even then, this policy of attempting to mitigate economic dependence of elderly workers recognised a public goal of shifting the main responsibility of supporting older, injured soldiers to the general public and away from the soldiers themselves and their families.[2] Such a policy was thought to be necessary for the public welfare and humane at the same time.

*This chapter is an excerpt from my longer article, 'Cutting Pension Rights for Public Workers: Don't Look to the Courts for Help' (2019) 62 *Howard Law Journal* 541.

[1] Revolutionary War Pension and Bounty, Land-Warrant Application Files, National Archives and Records Service, pamphlet describing M804 (1974). The practice of offering pensions for soldiers and their widows had been a long-standing public policy.

[2] See US Social Security Administration, *Historical Background and the Development of Social Security*, available at: www.ssa.gov/history/briefhistory3.html.

However, then as now, such public promises were easy to make but, occasionally, difficult to honour. Foreshadowing today, these promised Revolutionary War benefits were either not paid in a timely way or, occasionally, they were not paid at all.[3] Not surprisingly, this resulted in tremendous dissatisfaction among soldiers. Over 200 years ago, reneging on military pensions nearly triggered a mutiny of colonial officers threatening the impending colonial military victory.[4] In this stark example, denying pensions could have affected the course of American history. These eighteenth-century conflicts pitting soldiers against their government employer anticipated a serious twenty-first-century problem that is growing in significance – whether, and to what degree, public employers may reduce or change earlier retirement promises made to their workers.

This chapter considers current legal and policy changes that have been mandated at the state level of government and have affected nearly 20 million American workers and millions of current retirees. New state policies have far-reaching consequences affecting a surprisingly large component of the American workforce, representing almost 1-in-8 American employees.[5] These are the teachers, police officers, firefighters, emergency technicians and other state and local government workers with whom we are familiar and upon whom we rely every day. Having been promised benefits by politicians of earlier times, whose successors would now determine those promises to have been too generous, these workers find themselves facing a less financially secure retirement future than they expected.

Honouring these retirement promises has become a serious problem across the nation, becoming a hotly contested political issue in many states.[6] Since the financial crisis of 2007–09, policy changes have been adopted in the face of some extremely alarming financial predictions about the long-term financial solvency of retirement systems.[7] Accurate actuarial projections have given more precision to the extent of this problem, with recent estimates of the current unfunded liabilities of most state and local government pension ranging from nearly $4 trillion[8] to more

[3] RL Clark, LA Craig and JW Wilson, *A History of Public Sector Pensions in the United States* (Pension Research Council, Wharton School of the University of Pennsylvania, 2003).

[4] Even then, promises of current wages and future pensions presented fiscal demands on the newly created government that could not be met. Colonial wage defaults enraged the Revolutionary officers and caused them to threaten the Continental Congress with a virtual mutiny in 1783. The timely intervention of George Washington quelled this revolt after an emotional speech known as the Newburgh Address on 15 March 1783, where he promised to use his best efforts to have the soldiers' claims met. See generally EJ Teipe, *America's First Veterans and the Revolutionary War Pensions* (Lewiston, NY, Edwin Mellen Press, 2002).

[5] In 2017, the civilian, non-institutional workforce was 155.5 million workers with state and local government employees comprising 19.54 million or 12.6% of the total. Teachers and other workers counted for 53% of the state/local governmental workers or nearly 7% of the workforce. See US Dept of Labor, Bureau of Labor Statistics, *Labor Force Statistics from the Current Population Survey* (19 January 2018) Table 18b, available at: www.bls.gov/cps/cpsaat18b.htm.

[6] See, eg, J Fox, 'Is a Battle Brewing Over Prop 13?' *Los Angeles Times* (17 November 2016); T Loftus, 'Bevin: Tax Reform Tough' *Courier-Journal* (Louisville, Kentucky, 9 February 2017) A2.

[7] The issue of state retirement cutbacks has arisen at the same time when the solvency of the major federal social benefit programmes of Social Security and Medicare has also been questioned.

[8] JD Rauh, 'Hidden Debt, Hidden Deficits: 2017 Edition: How Pension Promises Are Consuming State and Local Government Budgets', Hoover Institution Essay (2017) 1, available at: www.hoover.org/sites/default/files/research/docs/rauh_hiddendebt2017_final_webreadypdf1.pdf.

than \$6 trillion.[9] These staggering sums have grown from year to year and they currently represent twice the general revenues collected by these state and local governments.[10] Put into another perspective, this unfunded pension liability dwarfs all the outstanding bonds issued by these jurisdictions and forms an 'off-the-books' debt that they have refused to recognise.[11]

The realisation that state pension plans have offered retirees benefits that may be financially impossible to honour has led numerous state legislatures to make policy changes and enact new laws that alter the existing array of public retirement benefits for public workers and retirees. Justified by limited state and local revenues, by more compelling public spending priorities, and by an aversion to increasing taxes, state after state has attempted to rein in these benefits. These new policies have been highly controversial and have been intensely resisted by employee groups and retirees.[12] The cutbacks on employee pensions have been the subject of numerous court challenges in at least 70 per cent of the states, reflecting the deep dissatisfaction which is felt with these new policies.

This chapter analyses pension reform challenges occurring over the past decade in both the state and federal courts. It categorises the patterns of legal attack employed to challenge these new policies and evaluates the legal and constitutional constraints faced by policy-makers in reforming their state's policies. The central questions presented here are 'what are the legal boundaries for public policy-making in this area' and 'how does law limit public policy choices?' The chapter also assesses the litigation outcomes to determine the relative success of workers resisting lawfully adopted pension policy changes. The general conclusion reached is that although the law in this area follows no uniform pattern, governments have been overwhelmingly successful in defending the changes even when they have had negative effects on workers. Such a conclusion runs counter to the commonly held beliefs of public employees, who think they have stable and secure pension rights that are free from subsequent legislative clawback. Such beliefs are incorrect and unfounded and government pension policy may be adjusted to reduce benefits when the popular will supports the cutbacks. Employee and retiree 'rights' are truly subject to the changing winds of public opinion and political support.

II. MODERN STATE AND LOCAL RETIREMENT PENSION SYSTEMS: STATE AUTONOMY IN PENSION POLICY-MAKING

States are largely free to fashion the terms and conditions of employment for their workers. Labour market conditions and long-standing payment practices guide the

[9] American Legislative Exchange Council (ALEC), 'Unaccountable and Unaffordable: Unfunded Pension Liabilities Exceed \$6 Trillion' (2017), available at: www.alec.org/app/uploads/2017/12/2017-Unaccountable-and-Unaffordable-FINAL_DEC_WEB.pdf.

[10] Rauh (n 8) 3.

[11] R Novy-Marx and JD Rauh, 'Public Pension Promises: How Big Are They and What Are They Worth?' (2010) 66 *Journal of Finance* 1207, 1207.

[12] C Butera, 'Kentucky Judge Deems Governor's Pension Law Unconstitutional' *Chief Investment Officer News* (22 June 2018), available at: www.ai-cio.com/news/kentucky-judge-deems-governors-pension-law-unconstitutional/.

government employers in formulating their compensation policies. Each state determines the legal structure and the funding mechanism of its own employee pension plan and they maintain near total autonomy in devising their state policy. Not surprisingly, there is no uniform national law driving the policy discussion forward and, importantly, there is no mandate requiring any state-level retirement benefits or any kind of benefit protection.[13] When Congress enacted the Employment Retirement Security Act 1974 (ERISA),[14] it was responding to failures of private sector pension plans rather than public sector plans. The law required private sector retirement plans to satisfy minimum coverage, participation, vesting, funding and fiduciary requirements as a means of improving retirement income security for employees. However, the law intentionally excluded government pension plans from important sections of the statute.[15] Concerns about federalism values and the limits of federal legislative authority persuaded Congress to do this.[16] As a result, even after ERISA was enacted there emerged no nationally consistent rule structure for sub-federal governmental retirement plans.[17] Without the discipline of uniform federal pension programme rules imposing uniform standards, state and local pension plans have been structured and administered under state law following state and local political direction.[18] This autonomy has had highly varied results: some state and local government workers have benefited from well-run and sufficiently funded plans, but employees in other jurisdictions have faced substantial uncertainty about their post-retirement future owing to poor plan design and funding. Some commentators have even recommended the extension of ERISA or ERISA-like rules to apply to these governmental retirement systems,[19] but as of now, none of these recommendations has been implemented.

This decentralised state control over pension design and funding has had widely disparate effects on the sustainability of state pension plans and their ability to meet future pension payments. Some states have consistently funded their retirement systems adequately to provide a high degree of coverage for future pension costs,[20]

[13] In fact, the main federal law governing retirement policy – the Employee Retirement Income Security Act 1974 (ERISA) – does not apply to state and local government retirement benefits. Section 4(b)(1) of ERISA provides that Title I of ERISA does not apply to an employee benefit plan that is a 'governmental plan' as defined in ERISA §3(32).

[14] 29 USC §1001 ff.

[15] 29 USC §1003(b)(1): 'The provisions of this [title] shall not apply to any employee benefit plan if such plan is a governmental plan (as defined in §1002(32)'.

[16] In *Rose v Long Island Railroad Pension Plan* 828 F 2d 910 (2nd Circuit, 1987) 914, the court noted three other reasons.

[17] PM Secunda, 'Litigating for the Future of Public Pensions' [2014] *Michigan State Law Review* 1353, 1363–64: 'Federalism concerns also played a dispositive role as far as Congress not trying to assume power over public plans'.

[18] AB Monahan and RK Thukral, 'Federal Regulation of State Pension Plans: The Governmental Plan Exemption Revisited' (2013) 28 *ABA Journal of Labor & Employment Law* 291, 292: a pension plan subject to ERISA 'must design, structure, and fund its plan in accordance with federal rules', whereas public pension plans 'are largely free to structure their pension plans as they see fit and are not subject to any funding requirements other than what state law might impose'. See also AB Monahan, 'State Fiscal Constitutions and the Law and Politics of Public Pensions' [2015] *University of Illinois Law Review* 117, 127.

[19] Secunda (n 17) 1402–04.

[20] Six states have reported exemplary pension funding ratios >90%, namely South Dakota (100%), Wisconsin (100%), Tennessee (99%), New York (95%), North Carolina (94%) and Nebraska (91%): ALEC (n 9) Table 4.

while others have made inadequate annual payments or have even completely skipped making yearly contributions.[21] This autonomy has provided each state with the independence to fashion its own response to the financial aspects of operating their retirement systems and this freedom has led to a range of responses, running from the courageous and well designed through to the ill-informed and, in some cases, to the truly dishonest. All have been highly controversial.[22]

The recent state legal and policy changes have been adopted in the face of some alarming financial predictions. In 2017, state and local government retirement systems controlled $3.96 trillion in financial assets in trust funds for workers' pensions.[23] Sizeable as these funds appear, however, the Federal Reserve calculated in 2017 that these pension entitlements were underfunded by 32 per cent.[24] Analysts fear that some existing retirement trust funds may be so seriously underfunded that they may be unable to pay promised pensions.[25] Although the health of these plans is unevenly distributed across the nation, the overall shortfall is truly astounding, reaching trillions of dollars.[26] So large are these shortfalls, in some states, that the financial health of the entire state has been called into question.[27] With pension expenses growing so quickly, legislators view pension costs as crowding out other budget priorities.[28] This realisation has motivated the recent policy changes.

States and local governments have sorted themselves into three broad categories. *Group One* jurisdictions are those that have invested in expert assessments of their pension funds' current condition and future glide path. These jurisdictions are well informed and have taken financially responsible action. They have attempted to shore up the financial underpinnings of their existing retirement systems with increased employer and employee contributions to their pension fund,[29] and they have made

[21] Five states demonstrated weak pension fund coverage ratios <55%, namely Kentucky (44%), Connecticut (47%), Illinois (47%), Mississippi (54%) and Hawaii (55%): ALEC (n 9) Table 4.

[22] See KC Becker, 'Putting PERA on a Path to Prosperity' *Denver Post* (17 June 2018) 4D; B Brickman, 'Beshear Suit Threatens Future Pensions' *Courier-Journal* (Louisville, Kentucky, 18 June 2018) A12.

[23] Board of Governors of the Federal Reserve System, *Financial Accounts of the United States, First Quarter* (8 June 2017) Table L, 120.

[24] ibid. The Society of Actuaries analysed 130 state and large city public pension plans covering 27 million workers and retirees and concluded that the unfunded liability in this sample was 27% in 2014: Society of Actuaries, 'US Public Pension Plan Contribution Indices, 2006–2014' (June 2017), available at: www.soa.org/research-reports/2017/public-pension-indices.

[25] State and local government pensions represent a huge future liability. Recent estimates have estimated the future unfunded liability of state and local government pensions to be $4 trillion and some think that these liabilities have been greatly underestimated: eg, Novy-Marx and Rauh (n 11) 1207–08. Viewing these governmental pension promises as deferred compensation and a debt of governmental employers, this number dwarfs all existing state and local bond liability by a 4:1 ratio.

[26] Pew Charitable Trust, *States Pensions Funding Gap: Challenges Persist* (2015) Figure 3, available at: www.pewtrusts.org/en/research-and-analysis/issue-briefs/2015/07/the-state-pensions-funding-gap-challenges-persist. See too ALEC (n 9).

[27] Illinois presents the most vivid current conflict between a state's governor and legislature with its employee unions and its Supreme Court. See BJ McNeil and JE Karns, 'Illinois Supreme Court Deal Says to the Government: The Price is Right for the Pension Prize' [2015] *Journal of Pension Planning & Compliance* 35; DR Godofsky and E Hootkins, 'Illinois Supreme Court Affirms Constitutional Protection of State Pensions' (2015) 28 *Benefits Law Journal* 79.

[28] eg, J Nation, 'Pension Math: Public Pension Spending and Service Crowd Out in California, 2003–2030' (2017) Stanford Institute for Economic Policy Research Working Paper No 17-023.

[29] For a recent comprehensive list of state pension plan condition, see C Eyermann, 'How Well Funded Are Government Employee Pension Plans in Your State?' *The Beacon* (11 October 2019), available at: blog.independent.org/2019/10/11/how-well-funded-are-government-employee-pension-plans-in-your-state/.

necessary administrative changes to their fund management that will probably keep them well positioned.[30] Some have even issued long-term pension bonds to shore up their pension funds.[31]

Group Two jurisdictions are well informed but they are not financially responsible. These places have received clear actuarial information about necessary financial steps that they should take to provide for timely pension payments, but they have not taken the hard steps required to add to pension reserves. Unfortunately, in these states policy autonomy has permitted short-term political judgements to ignore the clear path dictated by actuarial projections requiring increased current contributions to return to the proper financial path.[32]

Group Three jurisdictions have received the same actuarial predictions of needed change to their employee retirement benefit problems. However, these places have taken another approach to the problem: they have taken legislative steps to reduce the state's future retirement benefit liability by making significant pension benefit changes. It is the litigation challenging these recent legal and policy changes that constitutes the main focus of this chapter.

III. RECENT STATE POLICY RESPONSES TO PENSION FUND INADEQUACY

States and local governments have begun to recognise the serious deficiencies in their retirement systems. Over the last few years, a large number of states and localities have begun to address these difficult questions through the adoption of a range of measures under the general heading of 'pension reform'.[33] Other nations have done the same.[34] These changes are widespread: a recent study of nearly 260 state and local government pension plans found that between 2009 and 2014, 74 per cent of state plans and 57 per cent of large local plans reduced retirement benefits and/or raised

[30] In New Jersey, the 2018 budget contained a $2.5 billion contribution to the state's pension fund representing a 35% increase from the prior year and adding the New Jersey State Lottery as a pension system asset going forward. The state's treasurer estimated that the lottery would add $37 billion to the pension system over the next 30 years and improve the pension fund's funding ratio by 14% See: www.Pionline.com/article/201770705/ONLINE/170709972/new-jersey-approves-budget-shifting-state-lottery-to-pension-fund.

[31] See, eg, R Williamson, 'Houston Speeds $1 Billion Pension Bond Deal After Voter Approval' *The Bond Buyer* (9 November 2017), available at: www.bondbuyer.com/news/houston-to-price-1b-of-pobs-quickly-after-voters-approve.

[32] The most common tactic employed by retirement fund managers to understate the degree of their plan's underfunding is to calculate the present value of future benefits while using a discount rate that is higher than private plans and higher than might be reasonably obtainable with investments in the future. See JR Brown and DW Wilcox, 'Discounting State and Local Pension Liabilities' (2009) 99 *American Economics Review* 538, 539–42; DJ Boyd and PJ Kiernan, 'Strengthening the Security of Public Sector Defined Benefit Plans' (Nelson Rockefeller Institute of Government, State University of New York, Blinken Report, 2014), available at: rockinst.org/wp-content/uploads/2018/02/2014-01-Blinken_Report_One.pdf.

[33] JR Brown, 'Reforming Public Pensions Subject to Political and Legal Constraints: The Illinois Experience' (2014) 67 *National Tax Review* 941; MO Hylton, 'The Case for Public Pension Reform: Early Evidence from Kentucky' (2014) 47 *Creighton Law Review* 585.

[34] eg, L Bovenberg and R Gradus, 'Reforming Occupational Pension Schemes: The Case of the Netherlands' (2015) 18 *Journal of Economic Policy Reform* 244; R Disney, 'Pension Reform in the United Kingdom: An Economic Perspective' (2016) 237 *National Institute Economic Review* R6.

employee contributions.[35] Most frequently, new employees have been affected most by these changes, although in some places current workers have also been affected.

Different reform policies have been adopted across the United States. These run from making technical retirement calculation adjustments through to the imposition of wholescale revisions to existing systems. The most common reforms have fallen into the following categories:

1. Requiring current employees to make higher rates of employee pension contributions and applying higher rates to new hires.
2. Requiring increased age and service requirements before pension eligibility for new hires and existing workers.
3. Reducing pension benefits by reducing the defined benefit pension multiplier 'factor'.
4. Increasing the number of years to determine the employees 'average final salary'.
5. Disallowing employees from using accrued sick leave, vacation leave or overtime pay to augment their number of years of work or final average income.
6. Reducing or eliminating pension cost of living adjustments (COLA adjustments).[36]

The stakes in this public policy conflict could not be higher: the outcome will have serious consequences for both government employees and for taxpayers. How will governments deal with their long-term employees who have served them well and who have relied on earlier promises regarding their pensions and other benefits?[37] Will state legislators honour these earlier promises by diverting scarce financial resources from other much needed public expenditures? Without supporting tax increases, how will basic governmental services be provided if employee pension costs greatly increase? With these current assessments of pension funds, each state has been confronted with a series of policy and legal choices. How would this ever-expanding future financial obligation be met? Would future employee retirement income and other benefits be reduced? These important, and highly controversial, questions have surfaced in many state-level political conflicts and they have been examined in academic policy analysis.[38] Unfortunately, however, there appears to be no 'perfect' answer about

[35] J-P Aubry and CV Crawford, *State and Local Pension Reform Since the Financial Crisis* (Center for State and Local Government Excellence, 2016). The major plan changes were increased employee contributions, reduced COLA adjustments to received pensions, calculations for the final average salary, reduction in the benefit factor used to calculate pension benefits, increasing the retirement age or pension vesting time, and the shift to a defined contribution or hybrid system of pensions.

[36] In Kentucky, public school teachers threatened to strike if the Kentucky legislature reduced the retiree cost of living adjustment from 1.5% to 1% annually: T Loftus, 'State Pension Fight Nears End; Fate of Big School Cuts Also Hangs in Balance' *Courier-Journal* (Louisville, Kentucky, 27 March 2018) A2.

[37] This chapter will focus its discussion on retirement income provided by pensions. State and local governments have made similar post-employment promises with regard to retiree health insurance and other benefits. Rapid healthcare cost hikes may also make these benefits underfunded and be the next target for cost-cutting employers. See ME Fitch, 'Connecticut Has $36 Billion in Unfunded OPED Liabilities' (Yankee Institute for Public Policy, 29 March 2018), available at: www.yankeeinstitute.org/2018/03/connecticut-has-36-billion-in-unfunded-opeb-liabilities/.

[38] J Perez Jr, 'CPS Slates 4 Furlough Days to Aid Budget Gap: District Says Move Will Save $35M, Won't Cut Class Time' *Chicago Tribune* (14 January 2017) C1 (Governor's veto of bill granting $215 million to teacher pension fund since it did not broadly reform the pension system).

how to proceed. Finding ways to meet existing pension obligations will undoubtedly impose serious financial demands on state and local government budgets, potentially crowding out other important government programmes when no politician wants to raise taxes.[39] In this political environment, policy-makers have been left with only one alternative: cutting back on current employee costs and making public retirement benefits less generous.

Finding a way to reduce pension costs has been a primary concern of state and local governments. With this cost-saving goal, these new policies have also been associated with providing reduced benefits to public workers or with making it more difficult for them to qualify.[40] The overall goal of these varied changes has been to lower present and future benefit costs to government employers, making these future obligations sufficiently funded and more likely to be honoured.[41] As a result, state and local employees have been presented with pension policy changes that work to reduce expected retirement benefits or to increase employee costs.[42] Not surprisingly, widespread court challenges have resulted. The outcome of this litigation has varied and these case decisions are the main subject of the next section of this chapter.

IV. SEEKING JUDICIAL PROTECTION FOR PUBLIC EMPLOYEE PENSION 'RIGHTS'

A. Litigation by Employees and Retirees?

As the prior discussion indicates, pension reforms have taken a range of forms as state and local governments have attempted to shore up the financial foundations for their employee retirement benefits. With these changes being considered adverse to collective employee and retiree financial interests, it is not surprising that litigation has ensued. Seeking court review of pension reforms also represents a response to the changing political fortunes of public employees. As such, these lawsuits represent political statements of protest as much as attempts to use legal principles to invalidate or limit the benefit changes that have been enacted. This litigation history is important to understand for both its symbolic significance as well as its practical importance.

[39] In its 2017 ranking of the state by fiscal condition, a George Mason University study evaluated state fiscal solvency and it found that the unfunded pension liabilities drive them into fiscal peril: E Norcross and O Gonzalez, 'Ranking States by Fiscal Condition' (Mercatus Centre, George Mason University, 9 October 2019), available at: www.mercatus.org/statefiscalrankings.

[40] 45 states had reduced public pension benefits: M Corkery, 'Pension Crisis Looms Despite Cuts' *Wall Street Journal* (21 September 2012), available at: www.online.wsj.com/articles/ SB1000087239639044 38903045780107528289356 88.

[41] A secondary benefit of implementing pension reform has been to improve the credit worthiness of the state or city as reflected in maintaining or raising the quality of their debt and lowering their borrowing costs: see A Albright, 'Memphis No Longer Sings Pension Blues Ahead of Biggest Bond Sale' *Benefits & Executive Compensation News, Bloomberg Law* (17 April 2018) (the Memphis, Tennessee experience).

[42] Similar warning alarms have recently sounded with regard to retiree healthcare benefits which nearly 77% of all local governments pay for their retirees and whose unfunded liability has recently been estimated at $1 trillion or about one-third of all state and local government annual revenue. See B Lutz and L Sheiner, 'The Fiscal Stress Arising from State and Local Health Obligations' (2014) 38 *Journal of Health Economics* 130 (constituting half of the unfunded liability of retirement pensions).

Disappointed with changes made to their benefits, workers have elected to litigate their claims in an effort to vindicate their 'rights' which the current political system has failed to respect. They have also accused state pension officials of mismanagement and poor judgement.[43] Unfortunately, much of this recent litigation has been unsuccessful for employees and retirees.[44] These case results often reflect workers' misperceptions about the true nature of their employment 'rights' – often believing that these are permanent and unchangeable. This has been a mistake as courts have been unwilling to strike down many of the recent reform measures. The cases ultimately illustrate the futility of using courts to rectify these kinds of political decisions.

This review of selected state and federal litigation from 2008 to 2018 has comprised a total of 100 reported case decisions from 35 states reflecting a wide national distribution.[45] Twenty-seven of these decisions were from the federal courts while 72 of them were rendered in state courts. Each year saw some decisions although the peak frequency was between 2014 and 2016.[46] This distribution probably reflects the time lag between the adoption of the pension reform, litigation and the issuance of a reported decision. The analysis revealed patterns in the nature of the retirement policy changes that led workers to seek judicial review and their potential invalidation.[47] Obviously, this litigation was triggered by the government adopting the challenged pension reforms. The challengers were seeking to have the popularly supported reform measures invalidated as being contrary to specific statutory standards or constitutional principles. Viewed in this light, the court challenges attempted to use legal concepts to block democratically adopted policy choices that disadvantaged workers.

B. How does the Law Characterise Employee Retirement Benefits?

Citizens often believe that they have 'rights' in many things: free speech, voting and fair treatment under the law. They consider these rights in the abstract, assuming

[43] T Loftus, 'Workers Sue Retirement System: Allege State Officials Bungled Portfolio, Concealed Situation' *Courier-Journal* (Louisville, Kentucky, 28 December 2017) A8 (accusing retirement officials, consultants, hedge funds of entering a 'civil conspiracy' on poor investment choices that were concealed from employees).

[44] This concentrates on litigation challenging systematic changes in state and local government retirement benefit plans. Other cases, which are not the main focus of this chapter, consider individual claims based on complaints based on the administration of existing pension systems. See, eg, *Kendall v Government of the Virgin Islands* No 13-1919 (3rd Circuit, 2015) (affirming district court judgment against retired judge's challenge to pension calculation).

[45] In selecting the cases for review there was a conscious effort to avoid merely procedural decisions related to pension reform challenges. See, eg, *Wood v Unified Government of Athens-Clarke County* 818 F 3d 1244 (11th Circuit, 2016) (reversing district court on statute of limitations issue to retiree benefits change).

[46] The pension reform litigation analysed in this review had the following distribution. Total number of cases reviewed: 100. Total number of states involved: 35. Level of courts: State Supreme Court – 36 cases; State Appellate Court – 33 cases; US Circuit Court of Appeals – 17 cases; US District Court – 10 cases; US Bankruptcy Court – 1 case.

[47] The group of cases chosen for review in this analysis is a representative sample of reported litigation of pension reform policies in the eight-year period from 2010 to early 2018 does not constitute an exhaustive survey but rather it seeks to provide a general description of the most common forms of pension reform challenges.

that they have some form of legal protection grounded in a general conception of 'the law'. Most public employees consider their compensation and other employee benefits to be earned and, once earned, to be their property or something that they 'own'. Workers look to their representatives and to their employers to explain these complicated future rights and often they have been given concrete verbal or written predictions of their retirement benefits. Consequently, when state and local officials act to change the expected terms of these pension 'rights', many of these workers feel that trust has been betrayed and that they must take legal action to challenge the change.

When these challenges move from the arena of public opinion and employee belief to the courts, the legal characterisation of employee retirement benefits becomes a central focus strongly affecting the resolution of the legal challenge. What exactly does the employee own and what rights are actually associated with these pensions? In the absence of federal pre-emption, the states have been free to fashion their own policy to answer these questions. A state's legal characterisation of pensions provides a framework that can determine the ultimate lawfulness of pension reforms.[48] While fitting into a group of patterns, each state has made its own jurisprudence.[49] The states have been broken down into five theoretical pension rights categories:

1. Pensions are the employer's gratuity or gift to the employee when made.
2. Pension rights are governed by promissory estoppel principles focusing on justifiable reliance.
3. Pension benefits are property rights when earned and are protected under Due Process and Takings principles.
4. Pensions are employee contract rights when earned and protected by general contract law principles as well as constitutional 'impairment of contract' prohibitions.
5. Pensions are employee contract rights when earned and have additional protection under specialised state constitutional provisions.[50]

i. The Gratuity Approach

Perhaps the most unrealistic view of public employee pension rights is the view taken in the states of Texas and Indiana which view the pension as a gratuity or gratuitous allowance.[51] The gratuity approach believes that the employer should have unfettered

[48] Some cases review administrative decisions about the operation of a pension plan. See, eg, *Public Employee Retirement Administration Commission v Contributory Retirement Appeal Board* 2018 WL 830563 (Supreme Judicial Court Massachusetts, 2018) (upholding decision that sick pay and vacation pay are not regular compensation); and *Worcester Regional Retirement Board v Contributory Retirement Appeal Board* 88 NE 3d 1169 (Appeals Court Massachusetts, 2017) (upholding decision to allow purchase of additional work credit).

[49] See generally, AB Monahan, 'Public Pension Plan Reform: The Legal Framework' (2010) 5 *Education, Finance and Policy* 617.

[50] See WT Payne, JR Hunt and R McDonnell, 'The Constitutional Limitations on Public Employee Pension Reform Legislation' (2017) 25 *Public Law* 10, 12–13.

[51] Indiana Constitution, art X, § 5 and art XI, § 12. *See Board of Trustees of the Public Employees' Retirement Fund v Hill* 472 NE 2d 204 (Indiana, 1985); and *Ballard v Board of Trustees of Police Pension*

discretion to determine the amount and availability of pensions.[52] In the nineteenth and early twentieth centuries, employers considered this form of deferred compensation to be truly discretionary and dependent on the continuing goodwill and financial solvency of the employer.[53] The main legal theory supporting this view was that the employer's current promise of future retirement income was a gratuitous promise to make a future gift of money.[54] Viewed from the Texas perspective, the existence and character of pension rights would be a subject of legislative supremacy that is

> made subject to the reserved power of the Legislature to amend, modify, or repeal the law upon which the pension system is erected, and this necessarily constitutes a qualification upon the anticipated pension and a reserved right to terminate or diminish it.[55]

This position has been taken in an array of cases including one holding that retiree pensions actually being received could legally be reduced or terminated because the retirees had 'no vested rights in future instalments'.[56] Curiously, the theory of 'gratuity' pensions has not been attacked as being unconstitutional under state laws making gifts of government funds to private persons. Pensions would seemingly violate the prohibition on these gratuities.[57] The legislatures of Texas and Indiana are seemingly empowered to make restrictive pension policy changes with great freedom, and are primarily constrained only by the limits of public opinion.

ii. The Promissory Estoppel View

Taking a unique legal view grounded in a sense of fundamental fairness towards employees, Minnesota has established a legal framework for assessing public employee pension rights under the theory of promissory estoppel. In a 1983 case,[58]

Fund of Evansville 324 NE 2d 813, 815 (Indiana, 1975): the Court of Appeals correctly held that in Indiana pensions under a state compulsory contribution plan like the Police Pension Fund have traditionally been considered gratuities from the sovereign involving no agreement of the parties and, therefore, creating no contractual rights.

[52] Annotation, 'Vested Right of Pensioner to Pension' (1928) 54 ALR 943. See also *Pennie v Reis* 132 US 464, 470–72, 10 Sup Ct 149, 151 (1889) (employee had no property interest in public pension benefits because state retained the contribution in its retirement fund).

[53] See, eg, *Eddy v Morgan* 216 Ill 437, 449, 75 NE 174, 178 (1905): public pensions are 'a bounty springing from the graciousness and appreciation of sovereignty'.

[54] N Stein, 'An Article of Faith: The Gratuity Theory of Pensions and Faux Church Plans' *American Bar Association Employee Benefits Committee Newsletter*, Summer 2014, available at: www.web.archive.org/web/20180109033327/www.americanbar.org/content/newsletter/groups/labor_law/ebc_newsletter/14_sum_ebc_news/faith.html.

[55] This view was expressed by the Texas Supreme Court in *City of Dallas v Trammell* 101 SW 2d 1009, 1014 (1937) and recently affirmed in *Klumb v Houston Municipal Employees Pension System* 458 SW 3d 1, 16 (Texas, 2015). The Fifth Circuit has consistently followed this view. See also *Van Houten v City of Fort Worth* 827 F 3d 530 (5th Circuit, 2016).

[56] *Trammell* (n 55) 1012–13. See also *Klumb* (n 55) 17.

[57] Texas Constitution, art 3, §51: 'The Legislature shall have no power to make any grant or authorize the making of any grant of public moneys to any individual, association of individuals, municipal or other corporations whatsoever'. When a governmental entity is not liable on a claim, the payment of that claim constitutes 'a pure gift or donation' and violates the Constitution. See *Tompkins v Williams* 62 SW 2d 70, 71 (Texas Comm App, 1933); and *State v City of Austin* 331 SW 2d 737, 742 (Texas, 1960).

[58] *Christensen v Minneapolis Municipal Employees' Retirement Board* 331 NW 2d 740 (Minnesota, 1983).

the Minnesota Supreme Court established the doctrine when a municipal employee had existing pension benefits suspended under a new state law requiring a minimum age for retirement pensions and applying it retroactively.[59] The Minnesota Court announced a new approach, which continues to be identified with the state to this day.[60] It holds that a reviewing court must examine two questions in considering the lawfulness of a benefit change: (1) what has been promised by the state; and (2) to what degree and to what aspects of the promise has there been reasonable reliance on the part of the employee?[61] As this framework reveals, the promissory estoppel view eschews a formalistic contractual approach to existence of employee benefits. The *Christensen* view has been followed since it was announced and it appears to be tied to the equity principles mentioned in the Restatement (Second) of Contracts.[62] Occasionally Minnesota's idiosyncratic promissory estoppel analysis has been argued in cases arising in other jurisdictions but usually without success.[63]

iii. The Property Approach

There are six states that are believed to have taken a property law approach to characterising retirement benefits.[64] Since state law defines the existence and the features of individual ownership of things of value, it is hardly surprising that these states have used this conceptual framework to analyse employee pension rights. Most often this property characterisation must be discerned from court opinions that use terms such as 'vested rights' or 'statutorily created property interest(s)' to describe the pension rights under review.[65] This analysis is frequently undertaken as a second-tier alternative discussion in court opinions concluding that employees do not have contract rights to pension benefits, replacing the contract characterisation. It is not difficult to apply this property view to retirees currently receiving pension income, since they are enjoying the financial transfer from an annuity 'paid for' by a working career. The situation presented by non-retired, currently employed workers creates a more nuanced situation where the property is 'earned' in increments over time. The concept of property is not bound to the limited list of conventional forms including land, buildings, financial assets and personal property, since property is a flexible legal

[59] Anonymous, 'Public Employee Pension Benefits – A Promissory Estoppel Approach – *Christensen v Minneapolis Municipal Employees' Retirement Board* 331 NW 2d 740 (Minn 1983)' (1984) *William Mitchell Law Review* 287, 288–89.

[60] The Minnesota promissory estoppel approach has been adopted in a small number of decisions outside Minnesota. See, eg, *City of Long Beach v Mansell* 3 Cal 3d 462, 91 Cal Rptr 23, 476 P 2d 423 (1970); *Shafer v State* 83 Wash 2d 618, 521 P 2d 736 (1974).

[61] *Christensen* (n 58) 749.

[62] American Law Institute, *Restatement (Second) Contracts* (1981) §90.

[63] See, eg, *Weaver v Town of New Castle* 153 AD 3d 531 (NY App Div, 2017) (no reliance and no promise for retiree health insurance); *Vallejo Police Officers Assoc v City of Vallejo* 2017 Cal App LEXIS 811 (California Ct App, 2017) (promissory estoppel theory derivative to failed contract theory regarding retiree health insurance coverage); *Christiansen v County of Douglas* 849 NW 2d 493 (Nebraska, 2014) (equitable estoppel did not prevent increased in health insurance premiums).

[64] These states are Maine, Wyoming, Connecticut, New Mexico, Ohio and Wisconsin. However, careful examination of opinions reveals some confusion over the accuracy of this summary. See *Pierce v State* 121 NM 212, 910 P 2d 288, 298 (New Mexico, 1995) (finding that Connecticut, Maine, Minnesota, New Jersey and Rhode Island had recognised pensions as 'important property interest(s) or rights').

[65] *Pierce* (n 64) 299–300, 302 (property rights that could later be made taxable).

concept dealing with the relationship between owners and the assets they own, which is capable of expanding to meet new situations.[66] Due to this flexibility, making the property concept applicable to protect employee and retiree pension rights is clearly within the prerogative of the courts.

States adopting the property view of pensions adopted this idea in a small number of court decisions the 1980s and 1990s.[67] This classification has often been done in a muddled fashion with minimal analytical rigour. Finding the existence of property right is the predicate for the analysis under federal and state constitutional law theory,[68] although many cases end at the start through dismissal, with the courts declining to hold that a property right exists.[69] These property-based challenges usually arise under the authority of the Fifth and Fourteenth amendments to the Federal Constitution as well as their state analogues.[70] While state law is the source of property rights through their statutes, common law rules, constitutions and judicial opinions, the Federal Constitution imposes a floor that limits how states and localities can affect these property rights. These federal protections have applied to the states for over a century and there is no modern precedent for finding any state immunity from these federal constitutional norms.[71]

When considering a retirement policy change under substantive due process, the first element is the establishment of the existence of an individual's property right that has been adversely affected by some government action. While some state courts have explicitly found pensions and other retirement benefits to constitute property,[72]

[66] Concerning the breadth of the property concept in American law, Justice Stanley Mosk wrote a notable dissent in *Moore v Regents of the University of California* 51 Cal 3d 125, 165 (California, 1990), saying that 'The concepts of property and ownership in our law are extremely broad … A leading decision of this court approved the following definition: "The term 'property' is sufficiently comprehensive to include every species of estate, real and personal, and everything which one person can own and transfer to another. It extends to every species of right and interest capable of being enjoyed as such upon which it is practicable to place a money value"'.

[67] See *Pineman v Oechslin* 488 A 2d 803, 810 (Connecticut, 1985) (property interest in the existing state retirement fund which is protected from arbitrary state treatment by the Due Process clause); *Association of State Prosecutors v Milwaukee County* 544 NW 2d 888, 889 (Wisconsin, 1996); *Peterson v Sweetwater County School District No One* 929 P 2d 525, 530 (Wyoming, 1996); *Pierce* (n 64) (the right to receive benefits confers a property right upon vesting but may be subject to later taxation).

[68] See *Van Houten* (n 55) (all aspects of the pension system were made subject to the reserve power of the legislature to amend, there was no vested property right).

[69] *Clifford v Raimondo* Supreme Court of Rhode Island, 25 May 2018 (upholding a judgment approving a class action settlement affecting retirement age and COLAs); *Puckett v Lexington–Fayette Urban County Government* 60 F Supp 3d 772, 778 (ED Kentucky, 2014); *Frazier v City of Chattanooga* 151 F Supp 3d 830, 839 (ED Tennessee, 2015) (no property right exists in cost of living or COLA pension adjustments); *Dodd v City of Chattanooga* 846 F 3d 180, 187 (6th Circuit, 2017) (if the state has total discretion to award or remove a benefit, a person cannot claim entitlement to the benefit). Both district court cases mentioned were later affirmed by the 6th Circuit: *Puckett v Lexington–Fayette Urban County Government* 833 F 3d 590, 602–03 (6th Circuit, 2016); *Frazier v City of Chattanooga* 841 F 3d 433, 439 (6th Circuit, 2016) (abandoning property arguments, the COLA is not a vested financial benefit that is a contract right).

[70] US Constitutional Amendment V: 'nor be deprived of life, liberty, or property, without due process of law; nor shall private property be taken for public use, without just compensation'; and US Constitutional Amendment XIV, §1: 'nor shall any state deprive any person of life, liberty, or property, without due process of law'.

[71] *See Chicago, Burlington & Quincy Railroad Co v City of Chicago* 166 US 226, 239 (1897) (incorporation of the Fifth Amendment through the Fourteenth Amendment).

[72] See, eg, *Peterson* (n 67) (legitimate retirement expectations may constitute property rights that cannot be deprived without due process of law); *Madison Teachers Inc v Walker* 11CV3774*26–27 (Dane County

in many cases the due process enquiry ends at this initial stage with a decision that no vested property right existed in the employees.[73] As crucial as this issue is to the property-based constitutional analysis, many courts have struggled in their reasoning and have often failed to provide a coherent explanation of why the right does or does not exist.[74] Judges must look to state law to answer questions about its existence, aware that the US Supreme Court ruled in *Board of Regents v Roth* that property interests were 'defined by existing rules or understandings that stem from … state law rules or understandings that secure certain benefits and that support claims of entitlement to those benefits'.[75]

Identifying these 'understandings' in specific cases appears to be extremely difficult when governments act to change the rules. Some courts have been clearer than others in setting forth when property interests exist although the analysis is often conclusory.[76] As straightforward as this enquiry might appear in states with a tradition of property characterisation for pensions, some courts do not extend the 'property' label to policies which are considered to be peripheral to core pension benefits. This is true with COLAs, health insurance and tax exemptions for pension income. Narrowly construing the definition of a vested property right, only the base retiree pension has been found to be such a right.[77] Some court opinions have restricted the recognition of property rights created by statute in the same way that they have limited the finding of contractual pension rights: by setting a high presumption against finding the existence of these rights.[78] Without showing an 'unmistakable' legislative intention to create a binding right, no cognisable property interest might be found, thereby terminating the due process and takings analysis.[79] Without finding a vested property right, courts effectively conclude that the governmental employer may change the retirement benefit to the employee's disadvantage and these Fifth and Fourteenth Amendment challenges largely have failed.[80]

Circuit Court, 2012) (challenge to state law shifting pension contributions to workers a 'legitimate claim' but no due process arbitrariness or irrationality shown).

[73] *Duncan v Muzyn* 833 F 567 (6th Circuit, 2016) (reducing COLA found not unconstitutionally taken since they are not a 'cognizable property interest' because COLAs are not 'vested'); *Frazier* 151 F Supp 3d 830 (n 69) 838–39 (no legally cognisable contract or property right in a higher COLA found).

[74] For examples of a more thoughtful consideration of the property issues, see *Puckett* 833 F 3d 590 (n 69); *Hussey v Milwaukee County* 740 F 3d 1139, 1142–43 (7th Circuit, 2014).

[75] *Board of Regents of State Colleges v Roth* 408 US 564, 577 (1972).

[76] See, eg, *Pierce* (n 64) (statutes 'create vested property rights' that do not 'mature' until the final statutory condition is met).

[77] *Bartlett v Cameron* 316 P 3d 889, 896 (New Mexico, 2013) (retirement benefits protected by the state constitution are property rights but COLAs or tax exemptions for pensions are not).

[78] *Berg v Christie* 225 NJ 245, 279–80, 137 A 3d 1143, 1163 (New Jersey, 2016) (vested rights created by statute requires a 'clear indication' to meet the 'heightened standard'); *Borders v City of Atlanta* 298 Ga 188, 194, 779 SE 2d 279, 284 (Georgia, 2015) (no legislative statement recognising vested pension rights nor a reduction or termination of existing pension rights); *Dodd* (n 69) (no property right in a death benefit because there was no entitlement due to the fact that the city had the discretion to remove the benefit).

[79] *Duncan* (n 73) 583. But see *Degan v Board of Trustees of the Dallas Police and Fire Pension System, Degan v Board of Trustees of the Dallas Police and Fire Pension System* Civil Action No 3:17-CV-01596-N (US Dist Ct ND Texas, 14 March 2018) (retirement plan balance considered to be a vested property right).

[80] *Degan* (n 79) (no procedural or substantive due process or takings claim shown in retirement fund change).

a. Pension Reforms as Denials of Property Rights without Due Process of Law

Once courts have found a property right in a pension, they use two forms of constitutional analysis to evaluate the lawfulness of the government restrictions. These are: (1) due process; and (2) the taking of property principles derived from the US Constitution's Fourteenth and Fifth Amendments and their state constitutions.[81] Due process arguments have been the most common form of 'property-based' constitutional review, with courts using both substantive and procedural branches of due process analysis,[82] often blending federal and state constitutional provisions.[83] While the substantive due process approach has employed a variety of 'rational basis' approaches with each testing the sufficiency of the justifications provided for pension reductions.[84] With economic and social values at stake, low-level due process scrutiny usually has been applied by the courts[85] and this has been a relatively easy standard for state policy changes to satisfy. As the Michigan Supreme Court noted, substantive due process claims face 'an exceedingly high hurdle of demonstrating that the law is unreasonable' and that the government policy is 'not reasonably related to a legitimate government interest'.[86] Justifications offered by the government based on the state's or locality's need to maintain its pension fund solvency and to resolve financial deficiencies, not surprisingly, have provided courts with an adequate 'rational basis'.[87] Courts have been unwilling to question policy judgements shifting financial resources away from worker benefits and towards other priorities.[88]

[81] This argument has also been used in private sector pension cases reaching the US Supreme Court. See, eg, *Pension Benefit Guaranty Corp v RA Gray & Co* 467 US 717, 720 (1984) (applying due process rational basis review on changes to private sector pension benefits).

[82] For examples of a procedural due process claim, see *Hipsher v Los Angeles County Employees Retirement Assoc* 24 Cal App 5th 740 (California Ct App, 2018) (retirement benefit forfeiture of vested pension denied procedural due process); *Puckett* 833 F 3d 590 (n 69) 606–08) (rejected a claim that legislation was improperly adopted by the state).

[83] In *Klumb* (n 55) 15, the Texas Due Course of Law provision found in the Texas Constitution art I, §19 was argued while the Texas Supreme Court equated the federal due process norms with the Texas Due Course of Law concept.

[84] A few courts have also used an equal protection critique when programmes have distinguished between different categories of employee in pension benefits and while others have added §1983 claims seeking damages and attorneys' fees. See *Teamsters Local 97 v State* 84 A 3d 989 (New Jersey Super App, 2014) (law requiring employees to makes contributions for health benefits did not violate equal protection); *Awdziewicz v City of Meriden* 317 Conn 122, 127, 115 A 3d 1084, 1088 (Connecticut, 2015) (suit includes constitutional claims enforced by 42 USC §1983).

[85] Under the Fifth and Fourteenth Amendments to the US Constitution, government action may not deny an individual liberty or property interests without providing the equal protection and due process of law. Laws impacting fundamental freedoms or making suspect classifications may be reviewed under a tightened strict scrutiny review. Under rational basis review, a law or policy having adverse social or economic effects may be challenged requiring the government to justify its action by showing that the law advances a legitimate government purpose. See generally E Chemerinsky, *Constitutional Law: Principles and Policies*, 5th edn (New York, Wolters Kluwer, 2015) §9.2.1–§9.2.3.

[86] *AFT Michigan v State* 866 NW 2d 782, 808 and 810 (Michigan, 2015) (requiring mandatory employee salary contribution for retiree health care benefit).

[87] See *Puckett* 833 F 3d 590 (n 69) 608–09.

[88] *AFT Michigan* (n 86) 810.

b. Pension Reforms as an Unconstitutional Taking of Private Property

Arguments have also been made that state pension reforms reducing benefits have unconstitutionally taken employee property rights.[89] Borrowing from the late twentieth century, US Supreme Court case precedent principally applying the Fifth Amendment taking doctrine to land use and environmental regulation, this argument has claimed that recent pension reform policies have 'taken' the property rights of employees and retirees.[90] These Fifth Amendment cases have usually focused on regulatory takings or regulatory condition issues and any use of them in pension benefit cases would require careful analysis and argument by analogy to be effective.

As with the substantive due process claims, the taking arguments against pension reform must begin with the identification of a private property interest owned by the plaintiffs that has been 'taken' by the employer. Plaintiffs often fail at this stage in establishing a property interest. Since the Fifth Amendment only applies to governmental action, the pension reform policy must be shown to destroy an existing private property right in order to be held an unconstitutional taking of property for which 'just compensation' must be paid.[91] In comparison to the due process attacks which consider the adequacy of the 'rational basis' for the government's action and weigh the sufficiency of the policy basis, the takings argument focuses on the destructive effect of the governmental action on a property right owned by the employee. In the few recent cases considering this property-based claim, very few courts do a careful analysis under the prevailing takings law precedent.[92] None of this property rights-oriented litigation has been successful in invalidating new pension reform policies with both federal and state courts usually rejecting both procedural and substantive due process as well as takings arguments. In conclusion, recent case holdings indicate that a property characterisation of retirement benefits provides workers and employees with very little legal protection from policy changes that reduce employee benefits.[93] This legal categorisation is relatively uncommon and litigation rarely applies the usual constitutional law protections that have been accorded to conventional forms of property, like land and buildings.

iv. The Contract Approach

The most natural and the most common interpretation of a public employee's pension rights is that they represent an element of deferred compensation that has been paid to the worker as an implied or express benefit included in the employment contract. The majority of states categorise public employee pensions as a form of contract right. However, there is great variation in the legal theory serving as the basis

[89] *Cherry v Mayor and City Council* 762 F 3d 366 (4th Circuit, 2014); *Van Houten* (n 55); *Dodd* (n 69).

[90] *Penn Central Transport Co v City of New York* 438 US 104 (1978) (setting forth a three-factor test for finding a governmental taking of real property).

[91] US Constitutional Amendment V: 'nor shall private property be taken for public use, without just compensation'.

[92] But see *Degan* (n 79) (reasoned analysis finding no per se or regulatory taking of property).

[93] AB Monahan, 'Public Pension Plan Reform: The Legal Framework' (2010) University of Minnesota Law School Legal Studies Research Paper 10-13, 30, available at: www.ssrn.com/abstract=1573864.

for these important rights. Three explanatory categories have emerged in state law defining the existence of retirement benefits as contract rights: (1) a state constitutional recognition of public employee retirement benefits as contract rights;[94] (2) state statutes identifying them as contracts;[95] and (3) court decisions finding contracts to exist employing a 'facts and circumstances' type of analysis.[96] A court's conclusion that retirement benefits are contractual in nature only begins the analysis.[97] Once that conclusion has been made, complex interpretive questions follow often requiring courts to analyse litigated issues in terms of an interwoven pattern of state constitutions, statutes, regulations and prior case decisions.

Litigation in these 'contract' jurisdictions usually focuses on two important questions: (1) what is the scope or content of the contract related to pension rights and (2) are the modifications of pre-existing benefits providing less generous worker entitlements lawful and enforceable? The first of these questions addresses a myriad of practical issues affecting all aspects of public employee retirement pensions. What are the elements of the employment contract and what is its term? Several recent cases provide examples of these content questions and they have considered a range of issues including what working income is includible when calculating pension amounts,[98] which retirement system applies when there has been a change,[99] does a new collective bargaining agreement increase retiree health insurance premiums,[100] and what terms of pension calculations apply to certain employees?[101] Questions related to the employment contract's period of coverage also presents courts with a range of challenging issues. Is the agreement permanent providing for continuous and long-lasting employee benefits or does it represent a segmented series of contracts each possessing different terms?[102] These cases raise complicated interpretive issues of contractual composition and often require courts to undertake a wide-ranging analysis.[103]

[94] See, eg, Alaska Constitution, art XII, §7: 'membership in employee retirement systems of the State or its political subdivisions shall constitute a contractual relationship. Accrued benefits of these systems shall not be diminished or impaired'.

[95] See, eg, Ky Stat §61.692 (benefits pre-2014 hired employees constitute an inviolable contract of the Commonwealth, and the benefits provided therein shall, except as provided in KRS §6.696, not be subject to reduction or impairment by alteration, amendment, or repeal).

[96] *Ambrose v City of White Plains* 2018 US Dist LEXIS 56309 *29–40 (SDNY, 2018) (no contract found to exist).

[97] A number of decisions find that no contract right exists and no analysis of the legality of the benefit change is needed. See *Dodd* (n 69) 185.

[98] *Pennsylviana State Police v State Employees' Retirement Board* 2018 WL 1356052 (Pennsylvania Sup Ct, 2018).

[99] *Lynch v City of New York* 2018 NY App Div LEXIS 4758 (New York Superior Court Appellate Division, 2018) (no service credit is given for correction officer's childcare leave).

[100] *Re New Brunswick Municipal Employees Association* 2018 WL 1122157 (New Jersey Superior Court Appellate Division, 2018).

[101] *New Orleans Fire Fighters Pension & Relief Fund v City of New Orleans* 2018 La App LEXIS 515; 2017-0320 (4th Circuit, Louisiana App, 21 March 2018) (upholding trustee's decision to apply a higher compensation percentage to the calculation).

[102] *Wood v Unified Government of Athens-Clarke County* 818 F 3d 1244 (11th Circuit, 2016).

[103] Sometimes courts simply treat the matter as a breach of contract action and award damages if they find a breach. See *Board of Trustees v City of Harvey* 96 NE 3d 1 (Illinois App Ct, 2017) (city failed to adequately fund pension fund and damages were awarded).

The second question that courts have considered in these 'contract' states deals with the legality of government action reducing worker retirement benefits. Lawsuits challenging the lawfulness of these reductions have been common and have occurred widely since 2008. This legal issue assumes clarity in the meaning of the terms of the revised employment contracts. Rather than directly suing the government employer for breach of contract,[104] the overwhelming majority of these 'legality' cases present a state or federal constitutional claim that the pension policy change 'impairs' an existing contract right of workers and, therefore, violates the Contracts Clause.[105] The remedial result sought by the employees challenging the state pension policy change is a decision that the modification is unconstitutional and void. Using the federal Contracts Clause also seeks to use federal supremacy principles to invalidate state policy decisions, although state Contracts Clause cases generally follow a similar analysis but sometimes employ a state constitutional rationale.[106]

Contracts Clause analysis requires that a valid contract providing worker benefits exists and that the contract has been unconstitutionally 'impaired' by state action. Recent case holdings have demonstrated that a very large number of courts wish to avoid the entire Contracts Clause enquiry holding that workers do not have an enforceable contract right to pension benefits.[107] Courts reach this conclusion in a wide variety of ways including: by finding a lack of clarity in legislation creating the contract right;[108] a temporary nature or unenforceability of the benefit;[109] the prospective nature of the right;[110] the employee's ability to opt out of the impaired system;[111] and an unsatisfied contractual vesting requirement.[112] It is striking just how many recent court decisions employ this tactic to deny employees recovery and to completely avoid Contracts Clause analysis.

If a contract right is found to exist, the Contracts Clause claim will be analysed focusing on two principal questions: (1) is there proof that a state policy or law

[104] The availability of a state law breach of contract damage remedy would presumably bar a Contracts Clause claim and several federal courts have so held. See, eg, *Cherry* (n 89) 371; *TM Park Avenue Associates v Pataki* 214 F 3d 344, 349 (2nd Circuit, 2000); *Crosby v Gastonia* 682 F Supp 2d 537, 543–44 (WDNC, 2010).

[105] US Constitution, art I, §10, clause 1: 'No State shall … pass any … Law impairing the Obligation of Contracts'. State constitutions also contain versions of the federal constitutional clause. See, eg, Texas Constitution, art 16, §66(d).

[106] See, eg, *Dannenberg v State* 383 P 3d 1177 (Hawaii, 2016) (under state Contracts Clause); *Moro v State* 351 P 3d 1 (Oregon, 2015) (state Contracts Clause analysis of COLA change).

[107] *Justus v State* 336 P 3d 202 (Colorado, 2014) (no contract right to COLA); *Underwood v City of Chicago* 779 F 3d 461 (7th Circuit, 2015) (no contract right to enduring health care benefits); *Puckett* 833 F 3d 590 (n 69) (no vested contract right to COLA); *Maine Association of Retirees v Board of Trustees* 758 F 3d 23 (1st Circuit, 2014) (no contract right to COLA).

[108] See, eg, *Cranston Firefighters v Raimondo* 880 F 3d 44, 49–50 (1st Circuit, 2018) (unmistakability doctrine not satisfied); *Leff v Clark County School District* 210 F Supp 3d 1242 (Nevada, 2016) (no statutory text offered to prove contract); *Frazier* 841 F 3d 433 (n 69) 436 (no unmistakable contract right to COLA); *Maine* (n 107) (no unmistakable intent to create a contract right).

[109] *Aquirre v State* 891 NW 2d 516, 526–27 (Michigan Ct App, 2016).

[110] *City of Hollywood v Bien* 209 So 3d 1 (Florida Ct App, 4th District, 2016).

[111] *AFT Michigan* (n 86) 803.

[112] *Borders v City of Atlanta* 779 SE 2d 279, 286 (Georgia, 2015) (increased employee contribution to pension plan was not unconstitutional since it worked prospectively); *Rieder v Milwaukee County* 868 NW 2d 198 (Wisconsin Ct App, 2015) (contract right to healthcare benefit does not vest until retirement).

change has affected a 'substantial impairment of a contractual relationship';[113] and (2) is the state law 'appropriate … and reasonable' and designed to advance a 'significant and legitimate public purpose'?[114] Recent US Supreme Court Contracts Clause decisions have reinforced the analytical approach using these twin enquiries.[115] The first hurdle is successfully proving that the pension reform measure constitutes a 'substantial impairment of a contractual relationship'. There could be many kinds of contract changes – both large and small – that could constitute an impairment of the contract. The critical point would be a court's finding that the contract modification was 'substantial' in nature since a 'non-substantial' impairment would not be barred by the Contracts Clause. As Justice Elena Kagan wrote in *Sveen v Melin*, the substantiality of the impairment should be evaluated by 'the extent to which the law undermines the contractual bargain, interferes with a party's reasonable expectations, and prevents the party from safeguarding … his rights'.[116] In one case a federal court granted a preliminary injunction after finding a substantial impairment when an employer imposed large increases in deductibles and co-payments for retiree healthcare benefits under an agreement.[117]

Many other decisions fail to find substantial impairment with little discussion or confusing analysis unrelated to the Contracts Clause.[118] Although sounding as though it requires a careful judicial appraisal of the impact of a change in benefits, this test actually has presented the courts with a great deal of discretion in making their judgement call about 'substantiality'. Relying on the Supreme Court's statements that contractual impairment occurs when legislation 'alters the contractual relationship between the parties'[119] and 'deprives one of the benefit of a contract, or adds new duties or obligations thereto',[120] decisions from the 1980s and 1990s appeared to make this element relatively easy to satisfy, with state changes to public pension systems triggering this factor.[121] Case decisions during the last decade have been highly variable in their results but the clear trend has been away from finding 'substantial impairment' when public employee retirement rights are narrowed,[122] making this first prong of the Contracts Clause argument very difficult to prove.

Ruling that a pension benefit change does constitute a 'substantial impairment' of worker contract rights is merely the first step in the Contracts Clause analysis. A court's determination that such an adverse change occurred does not on its own

[113] *Allied Structural Steel Co v Spannaus* 438 US 234, 244 (1978).

[114] *Energy Reserves Group, Inc v Kansas P&L Co* 459 US 400, 411–12 (1983).

[115] See *Sveen v Melin* 584 US 2018 WL 2767640*5 (upholding a Minnesota statute automatically revoking a life insurance beneficiary designation upon divorce).

[116] ibid. Some state courts also apply a gloss to the 'substantial impairment' element by negating that conclusion if the pension benefit reduction is offset by a corresponding benefit. See *Cloutier v State* 42 A 3d 816, 826 (New Hampshire, 2012).

[117] *Welch v Brown* 935 F Supp 2d 875, 882 (ED Michigan, 2013).

[118] *Ambrose* (n 96).

[119] *Allied Structural Steel* (n 113).

[120] *Northern Pacific Railway Co v State* 208 US 583, 591 (1908).

[121] See *Valdes v Cory* 139 Ca App 3d 773 (Cal App, 1983); *Deonier v State* 760 P 2d 1137, 1143 (Idaho, 1988).

[122] *Washington Education Assoc v Washington Department of Retirement Systems* 332 P 3d 428 (Washington, 2014).

force a finding of a constitutional violation. Assuming that a 'substantial impairment' has been found, the second factor places the burden on the employer to demonstrate that the policy change is 'reasonable and necessary to serve an important public purpose'.[123] Such an open-ended standard is obviously subject to a wide range of judicial interpretation with some courts simply ruling that adverse changes were reasonable[124] and others scrutinising legislative policy alternatives much more rigorously.[125] Earlier analysis of the Contracts Clause litigation challenging pension reform measures suggested that this approach of constitutional theory might impose serious limits to state and local government policy flexibility in dealing with pension reform.[126] Some cases even repeated the *US Trust Co v New Jersey* dicta indicating that the Contracts Clause should be more rigorously enforced against a state when it seeks to impair its own contracts with its workers.[127] However, this has not been the case over the last decade. Advocates for workers have continued using this 'impairment of contract' Contracts Clause approach in their challenges in more than 60 reported cases since 2009. Unfortunately, employing this most common and previously successful litigation theory has been a largely futile effort achieving very few court victories with 85–90 per cent of the reported decisions upholding the states' policies against these constitutional challenges and rejecting worker claims.

v. State Constitutional Protections

Several states have adopted constitutional provisions specifically giving security to public employee pension benefits.[128] These provisions are focused upon the specific worker retirement rights and they do not rely upon the more general constitutional prohibitions against the impairment of contracts.[129] The language employed in these state constitutional provisions is often surprisingly direct and unambiguous. For example, Hawaii's Constitution provides that 'membership in any employees' retirement system of the State or any political subdivision thereof shall be a contractual relationship, the accrued benefits of which shall not be diminished or impaired'.[130]

[123] *US Trust Co v New Jersey* 431 US 1, 25 (1977). This decision is frequently cited for the analytical framework for pension policy changes reducing benefits.

[124] *Marin Association of Public Employees v Marin County Employees' Retirement Assoc* 2 Cal App 5th 674 (California App, 2016).

[125] *Moro* (n 106) 41 (Oregon, 2015); *Roberts v New York* 911 F Supp 2d 149, 1880–82 (NDNY, 2012); and *Stone v North Carolina* 664 SE 2d 32 (North Carolina App, 2008).

[126] A Monahan, 'Understanding the Legal Limits on Public Pension Reform' (American Enterprise Institute, May 2013) 2.

[127] See also *US Trust Co* (n 123) 30–31, noting that 'a State is not completely free to consider impairing the obligations of its own contracts on a par with other policy alternatives'; and 25–26: 'complete deference to a legislative assessment of reasonableness and necessity is not appropriate because the State's self-interest is at stake'.

[128] See, eg, Alaska Constitution, art XII, §7: 'membership in employee retirement systems of the State or its political subdivisions shall constitute a contractual relationship; accrued benefits of these systems shall not be diminished or impaired'.

[129] See, eg, Colorado Constitution, art II, §11; Florida Constitution, art I, §10; Georgia Constitution, art I, §1; Mississippi Constitution, art 3, §16.

[130] Michigan Constitution, art IX, §24 (the accrued financial benefits of each pension plan and retirement system of the state and its political subdivisions shall be a contractual obligation thereof which shall not be diminished or impaired thereby).

The power of this constitutional provision obviously lies in the meaning of the words 'diminished or impaired'. In this example, the Hawaiian provision has been interpreted as only protecting past accruals of pension rights as they are earned while reserving the right of state employers to change, and possibly reduce, future benefits.[131] Texas has a similar provision.[132] Although these provisions are constitutional in nature, they find specific meaning through court decisions interpreting them. Interpretation of state constitutional protections and parsing of the state's jurisprudence has enormous social and economic impact making dry pension rights decisions infused with powerful political implications.[133]

Not all constitutions are similar in coverage. Several other states' constitutional provisions have even broader reach asserting protections for both accrued and future benefits having the effect of 'freezing' benefits at the level expected on the first day of employment. This sweeping policy means that a retirement system could not be altered in a manner that would reduce or lessen employee retirement benefits from the level that would have been received in the plan in place on the first day of employment. Such a provision would have tremendous benefit to employees when later state legislation reduces retirement benefits and several recent cases have so held.[134] The states of Illinois and New York have constitutional provisions specifically setting forth this policy.[135] Alaska and Arizona have constitutional sections that have been interpreted in the same fashion.[136] In these states with strong pension-protecting constitutions, until these strong constitutional sections are amended or repealed, the policy choices available to state legislatures will be restricted by the language and interpretation of the state's constitution.[137]

V. CONCLUSION: HAVE THE COURTS PROTECTED PENSION RIGHTS THAT LEGISLATURES HAVE ATTEMPTED TO CUT?

The subject of this chapter is a difficult one: how to reconcile the competing interests of public employees against the larger interest of state and local governments and their taxpaying citizens. On the purely economic level, this conflict could be characterised as an ordinary struggle between two competing constituencies attempting to

[131] See *Association of Professional & Technical Employees v City of Detroit* 398 NW 2d 436 (Michigan Ct App, 1986); and *Smith v Board of Trustees of Louisiana State Employees Retirement System* 851 So 2d 1100, 1105 (Loiusiana, 2003).

[132] Texas Constitution, art XVI, §66 (service retirement benefits may not be reduced or impaired except on a prospective basis).

[133] Not all court decisions under these constitutional provisions favour the employees. See *Eddington v Tomasovic* 2016 Tex App LEXIS 13204 (Texas constitutional pension protection does not extend to future interest rate applied to benefits).

[134] See *Fields v Elected Officials' Retirement Plan* 320 P 3d 1160 (Arizona, 2014) (Pension Clause confers additional, independent protection beyond the Contracts Clause).

[135] A number of other states have reached the same policy position by statute. See Ky Rev St §61.692(1); Wis Stat §40.19.

[136] *Municipality of Anchorage v Gallion* 944 P 2d 436 (Alaska, 1997); *Yeazell v Copins* 98 Ariz 109, 402 P 2d 541 (Arizona, 1965).

[137] See *Re Pension Reform Litigation* 32 NE 3d 1 (Illinois, 2015) (statute lowering pension benefits declared unconstitutional under state pension protection clause).

determine who should bear the deferred cost of service. But this is more than a tussle between employers and their workers, since these employees are people who serve us as our teachers, police, fire, first responders and others providing critical services for long periods, sometimes for their entire working lives. While public worker salaries do vary, in general they support a modest, middle-class existence for people who work every day.[138] The recently adopted pension reforms have created great anxiety about the future in these workers striking a visceral chord. Will I have stable retirement income? How will I live when I can no longer work? These are critically important issues for all people, but they are even more significant for modestly paid public workers.

This is also a tale about competing misunderstandings, both on the part of workers and of employers. Employees frequently believed that they had earned stable retirement income through their work and they strongly felt that once earned, these 'rights' were permanent and not subject to later reduction. This was a hopeful belief that drove workers' groups to court to defend their perceived rights. It is also a tale about government leaders' misunderstandings of the implications of employee work agreements and pension promises. Over many years, retirement benefits have been offered with little serious consideration of their long-term costs. Granting benefits without providing for their actual payment also reveals a wilful ignorance of the economic consequences of prior promises. As history shows us, it is easy for politicians to make current promises that will have to be honoured by others in the future.

Both of these misunderstandings have led to the introduction of pension 'reforms'. In every instance, government policy changed employee benefits in a way that was adverse to workers' interests, usually at times of fiscal stress and after the precise costs of providing existing benefits had become better understood. These episodes also demonstrate another theme of the eroding public support for funding the true costs of state and local government services.[139] The reform of pension systems for fiscal reasons has succeeded following the usual democratic process with the citizens giving tacit approval. It is not clear that these cut backs are the result of any deep animus towards government workers, but rather reflect an increased resistance to higher taxation to fund the existing pension system.[140]

[138] In May 2017, the US Bureau of Labor Statistics set the average annual salary for all local government employees at $52,980 and the average state worker salary at $55,820. See Occupational Employment Statistics, Local Government, NAICS 999300 and State Government, NAICS 999200 (May 2017). Some teacher annual teacher salaries for 2016–17 were far less than these averages: South Dakota ($42,668), Mississippi ($42,925), Oklahoma ($45,245) and West Virginia ($45,701): National Center for Education Statistics, 2017 Tables and Figures, Table 211.60.

[139] Media portrayals of abusive and unreasonable public employee pension practices in some parts of the country have harmed public perceptions of worker entitlement to their retirement benefits even though these episodes distort average public worker's conduct. See, eg, Star-Ledger Editorial Board, 'Audit Port Authority for Pension Scams – And, While We're at It' (27 June 2016), available at: www.nj.com/opinion/2016/06/audit_port_authority_for_pension_scams_and_while_w.html; MW Walsh and A Schoenfeld, 'Padded Pensions Add to New York Fiscal Woes' *New York Times* (21 May 2010) A1.

[140] Although public attitudes towards the federal government have declined, state and local governments score consistently higher on surveys of favourability. See generally 'State Governments Viewed Favorably as Federal Rating Hits New Low' (Pew Research Center, 15 April 2013).

As a reaction to their failure in the legislative arena, employees have asked courts to moderate the impacts of these reform policies through judicial review. In order to do this, employee groups have had to prove that their 'rights' to the affected pension system benefits have been unlawfully damaged. In cases where states have had strong constitutional protections for pension benefits, or where state statutes undeniably limited government retrenchment of existing rights, the courts have been willing to rebuff the policy changes. However, when asked to 'stretch' the meaning of statutes or prior interpretive precedent to block these reforms, most often courts have said 'no'.[141] Interestingly, this has been especially true with regard to claims based upon constitutional rights theory where the exercise of discretion has rarely been exercised in favour of workers.[142]

Perhaps all this reveals is that pension claims have been considered economic in nature and not protected by stronger constitutional or statutory norms. Judges have been extremely reluctant to intervene in what they perceive as a socio-economic conflict between employees and their employer. Such non-interventionist judicial attitudes have been consistent with the majoritarian decisions made by elected officials. Courts have also been very careful not to challenge the authority of the legislature, and with their narrow rulings they have protected themselves from 'judicial activism' criticism.[143] The clear import of this analysis has been that public workers must look to the political process for protection of their work-related rights – and not to the courts.[144] These employees must build public understanding, appreciation and support for the important work they do. Litigating to overcome legislative defeats is ultimately a losing game.

[141] Some exceptions do exist and some state supreme courts have made expansive readings of state pension rights statutes. See, eg, *Milwaukee Police Assoc v Milwaukee* 2018 Wisc LEXIS 314 (6 July 2018).

[142] Compare demanding judicial review of state legislative restrictions on the exercise of public employee First Amendment constitutional rights.

[143] Perhaps state courts are less inclined to challenge legislative choices perceiving legislatures to be more willing to cut back on the judicial role. See, eg, 'Legislative Assaults on State Courts – 2018' (Brennan Center for Justice, 6 February 2018), available at: www.brennancenter.org/analysis/legislative-assaults-state-courts-2018 (legislatures in at least 16 states considering legislation that would diminish the role or independence of state courts); Editorial, 'Courts Shouldn't Be Partisan Punching Bags' *New York Times* (9 April 2018) A18.

[144] There was no completely uniform pattern in all case decisions and a small number of state courts, like Arizona and Illinois, clearly demonstrated a pro-worker/retiree emphasis.

17

Till Pensions Do Us Part: The Pension Advisory Group and the Search for Consensus on Divorce

HILARY WOODWARD AND RHYS TAYLOR

I. INTRODUCTION

ONLY AROUND ONE third of divorces with final decrees include a final financial remedy order, and of those, a relatively small (albeit increasing) proportion include an order dealing with the parties' pensions. The rest are either dealt with by offsetting the pension against another asset such as the family home, or quite often not properly considered at all. Empirical and anecdotal evidence indicates that the quality of pension disclosure on divorce is poor, that practice in this complex field has been operating inconsistently and has led to a large proportion of potentially unfair outcomes, particularly for divorcing wives, and an increasing number of negligence claims.

It is against this background that in mid-2017 the Pension Advisory Group (PAG) was convened. PAG is a multidisciplinary group of professionals with a range of experience in the field of pensions on divorce. Its common purpose has been to produce a good practice guide to pensions on divorce. The project was supported by the President of the Family Division and the Family Justice Council and partially funded by the Nuffield Foundation. PAG consulted widely on the issues to be addressed, published two draft reports, held focus groups with family lawyers and pension experts, conducted an online survey, and invited feedback via various blogs and at numerous presentations around the country. Achieving a consensus within PAG on key issues such as when an expert report might be needed and whether methods and assumptions could be standardised was challenging. The main guide was published on 1 July 2019.[1]

[1] The Pensions Advisory Group, 'A Guide to the Treatment of Pensions on Divorce' (July 2019), available at: www.nuffieldfoundation.org/pensions-divorce-interdisciplinary-working-group.

Here, as two of the individuals most intensely caught up in the creation and execution of the project, we reflect on the context for this work and some of the themes which have particularly struck us during the project. We start with a brief summary of the legal and statistical background.

II. THE BACKGROUND TO PENSIONS ON DIVORCE

A. The Legal Background

There are four main ways in which pensions can be dealt with on divorce: by the making of a pension attachment order or a pension sharing order; through a process known as offsetting; or by doing nothing at all. The power to make a pension attachment order (previously known as earmarking) was introduced in 1996.[2] Such an order directs the pension provider to pay part or all of the member's pension benefits to the ex-spouse on retirement or death, but the pension remains owned by the original member. Pension sharing orders were introduced in 2000[3] and provide for part or all of the member's benefits to be legally transferred on divorce, as a pension debit from the member spouse to the other as a credit. The pension credit can then be used by the non-member spouse to invest in a new pension arrangement with the existing provider or a new one.[4] Offsetting is nowhere legally defined or referred to in statute but is statistically more popular than the two pension orders put together. PAG describes it as the process by which the right to receive a present or future pension benefit is traded for present capital or 'money now'. The most common example is the wife keeping the family home in return for the husband retaining his pension. The final approach, which is worryingly popular, is to ignore the pensions or do little or nothing about them at all.

Orders for both pension attachment and pension sharing are made by reference to the 'cash equivalent value'(CE) of the pension in question.[5] The CE is the value which a pension provider places on an individual member's pension rights in their scheme. It is the figure which the provider would pay to another pension fund in order to be relieved of their liability to the scheme member, and this is usually less than the costs of purchasing equivalent benefits. While the CE will usually be an accurate reflection of the value of a *defined contribution* pension which has no in-built guarantees, there are a number of actuarial factors which come into play when calculating the CE of a *defined benefit* pension. Due to a combination of these factors, differences in trustee assumptions, economies of scale and the costs of investing in a personal

[2] Pensions Act 1995, s 166.

[3] Welfare Reform and Pensions Act 1999.

[4] Some pension providers, eg, public sector schemes, will only allow an internal transfer of the new arrangement; others may insist on it being transferred externally to a different provider; yet others give the non-member spouse the choice between an internal or external transfer.

[5] Matrimonial Causes Act 1973, s 21A(1)(b). See also *H v H (Financial Relief: Pensions)* [2009] EWHC 3739 (Fam), [2010] 2 FLR 173, which put this practice beyond doubt.

pension, a CE figure, of, say, £100,000 in a defined benefit (salary-related) pension, will usually provide greater benefits than the same figure invested in a defined contribution (personal) pension. Quite often the only option open to a spouse seeking to share the member spouse's defined benefit pension is to transfer it to a defined contribution pension scheme.

Almost all types of pension in England and Wales (apart from the New State Pension)[6] may be the subject of a pension sharing or attachment order, including pensions in payment. The same powers exist in proceedings for nullity and dissolution of civil partnership, but only pension attachment is available in judicial separation proceedings. There are no equivalent powers for separating cohabitants. Section 25 of the Matrimonial Causes Act 1973 gives the court wide discretion when adjudicating financial remedy orders or approving draft consent orders. The overall aim is to achieve fairness between the parties while giving priority to the needs of any children of the family. The way that fairness is achieved in divorce financial remedy cases may vary depending on the overall value of the parties' assets. The vast majority of cases, including some with a value in the low millions of pounds, will be ones where, broadly speaking, the parties' assets do not exceed their needs. In such cases, described as 'needs' cases, the court can have resort to any assets, whenever acquired, in order to ensure that the parties' needs are appropriately met. In contrast, in the much rarer 'big money' cases where, broadly speaking, the assets exceed the parties' needs, the court may treat assets acquired before, from outside (for example, by way of inheritance) or after the marriage as 'non-matrimonial' and distribute them accordingly. These are known as 'sharing' cases.[7] An important point to bear in mind is that pension assets can only be shared or attached if they are the subject of an order of the court. In this respect they are very different from non-pension assets such as the family home, with which the parties can deal however they wish without a court order, for example, by sale, transfer and/or the sharing of proceeds.

B. Family Court Statistics

In 2018 there were just over 118,000 petitions for divorce and just under 92,000 decrees absolute.[8] In the same period, there were fewer than 35,000 final financial remedy

[6] Even with a New State Pension, transitional arrangements are in place for those who had Additional State Pension alongside their Basic State Pension in the old state pension system, which subsisted for individuals who retired before 6 April 2016. For those with full Basic State Rights and Additional State Pensions who have transitioned into the New State Pension, the portion of Additional State Pension over the maximum New State Payment is known as the Protected Payment and this may be the subject of a pension sharing order.

[7] See *White v White* [2001] 1 AC 596 (HL) 610; *Miller v Miller, McFarlane v McFarlane* [2006] UKHL 24, [2006] 2 AC 618.

[8] Ministry of Justice, 'Family Court Statistics Quarterly: January to March 2019' (27 June 2019) Table 12. The decrees absolute do not necessarily relate to the same marriages for which divorce petitions were filed – they may relate to petitions from previous years. The number of petitions filed in 2018 is not dissimilar to previous years but the number of decrees absolute was lower than average.

orders ('total cases disposed'), representing just under 38 per cent of final decrees,[9] meaning that over 60 per cent of the divorcing population had no final financial remedy order. Of those who did have such an order, more than 80 per cent of those orders were uncontested,[10] supported, at best, by basic financial information and subject to (usually) modest scrutiny by the court.

The total number of pension orders (ie, both pension attachment and sharing orders) recorded in this period was just over 16,000,[11] amounting to under 18 per cent (or one in six) of divorces with final decrees. Thus, five out of six divorces did not include a formal pension order, although in some of those the pensions will have been offset against non-pension assets.

III. THE 2014 PENSIONS ON DIVORCE STUDY

The 2014 Pensions on Divorce study[12] included a mix of quantitative and qualitative data: a detailed survey of 369 randomly selected divorce court files with a final financial remedy order made on or before 31 December 2011 in three courts in England and Wales; one-to-one interviews with 32 purposively selected family solicitors lasting one to one and a half hours each; meetings of similar length with a total of seven district judges from the three courts from which the files had been surveyed; and an assessment by a pensions on divorce expert[13] of 130 (44 per cent) representative cases of the 293 which disclosed any pension other than the Basic State pension. Of the court cases sampled, 14 per cent included a pension order. This was a slightly higher percentage than the 12 per cent revealed by the family court statistics at that time.

The report made several key findings as follows. First, the quality of pension disclosure on the court files was poor compared with that for non-pension assets and income. The pension expert assessed over two-thirds of the cases which he examined as providing inadequate or unclear pension information, which we suggest reflected a lack of understanding of pension complexities in general as well as the low priority placed on them in the context of divorce in particular. Pension disclosure tended to be better in cases where there was a pension order but such cases were, of course, very much in the minority.[14] Second, the expert assessed over half the orders which he examined as economically irrational, that is to say, the approach to pensions did not make economic sense even allowing for the wide discretion of the court. Further, looking at the quantum of the awards, only about one third were assessed as clearly fair; approximately 15 per cent were deemed clearly unfair; and the remainder unclear or potentially unfair.[15]

[9] ibid Table 15. The number of total cases disposed in 2018 is similar to previous years but the percentage is higher because of the lower number of decrees absolute.

[10] ibid Table 15. See (n 8): the same point applies here.

[11] ibid Table 16. See also (n 8).

[12] H Woodward and M Sefton, *Pensions on Divorce: An Empirical Study* (funded by the Nuffield Foundation, Cardiff Law School, 2014) (*Pensions on Divorce Study*).

[13] George Mathieson, Mathieson Consulting.

[14] *Pensions on Divorce Study* (n 12) 52.

[15] ibid 147, 149.

Third, discussions with the solicitors revealed big variations of experience and confidence in dealing with pensions. A good working relationship with a pensions expert had a positive impact on this, but most solicitors admitted to a lack of confidence in key aspects.[16] As will become apparent below, they were not, and are still not, helped by the fact that case law provides little and/or inconsistent guidance on pensions on divorce and most of it relates to bigger money cases which are not the mainstream of family work. Finally, from the judicial perspective, financial remedy cases made up a tiny proportion of their total caseloads (even including their 'box' work, ie, draft consent orders). Judicial training on pensions and financial remedy cases was at that time minimal and/or not compulsory.[17]

IV. THE BIRTH OF THE PENSION ADVISORY GROUP (PAG)

In 2015 the present writers were invited to deliver a paper to the annual conference of the Family Law Bar Association. This platform provided the pretext to invite 15 of the leading pension experts in the field to answer three simple problems involving small, medium and bigger money cases. In our small money case, there was a stakeholder pension with a CE of £100,000; the medium money case involved a defined benefit pension with a CE of £500,000; the bigger money case included a Self-Invested Personal Pension with a CE of £1,500,000 and non-pension assets of over £3,000,000. In all three problems the trade between pension rights and current capital, ie, offsetting, was the heart of the conundrum. The experts were invited to provide reports as if delivering them as a single joint expert in court proceedings. Fourteen experts engaged in the project and provided high-quality reports. As we had anticipated, the results were significantly divergent. In order to try and explain the differences the experts were invited to attend a joint meeting chaired by David Salter, a highly respected family solicitor specialising in pensions. Most were able to attend.

A fascinating discussion took place. While the express reason for the meeting was to discuss differences in expert approaches, the experts also quickly turned the tables on the writers, venting their frustrations at how poorly family lawyers grasped issues relating to pensions on divorce. Most brutally, it was suggested to us that had we put our questions better, we may have elicited better and more consistent answers. Rather than descending into acrimony, the meeting proved a fascinating interdisciplinary discussion in which each side of the room (experts versus lawyers) had, for the first time, a context in which to discuss issues of common interest and misunderstanding away from the more unforgiving environment and formal arena of litigation. We delivered our paper in November 2015.[18]

The project opened up an important seam of discussion which deserved wider attention, and so it was that we set about convening PAG, which held its first meeting

[16] ibid 157.

[17] ibid 164. The piloting of financial remedy courts in England and Wales marks a significant and welcome step forward in addressing the potential deficiencies highlighted by the study.

[18] R Taylor and H Woodward, 'Apples or Pears? Pension Offsetting on Divorce' [2015] *Family Law Journal* 1485.

in June 2017. PAG consisted of representatives from all key stakeholders: judges, lawyers in practice (solicitors and barristers), academics, actuaries, financial advisers and a mediator. Francis J and HHJ Hess co-chaired the group, which worked largely on a pro bono basis, save that the Nuffield Foundation kindly provided funding for two of the academics who would not have been able to take part without it. The project was supported from the outset by the President of the Family Division, then Sir James Munby, and later Sir Andrew McFarlane. The report was also endorsed by the Family Justice Council. Professional associations such as Resolution, The Law Society, Family Law Bar Association, Association of District Judges, and Institute and Faculty of Actuaries were all represented in the constitution of PAG.

The whole group split into three smaller working groups. Legal issues were tackled in one, valuation issues in another and expert competence and regulation in the third. Members of each working group sat on a second working group, and sometimes even a third, so that the left hand was always aware of what the right hand was doing. This work resulted in two interim reports being published in the spring of 2018, for consultation with a wide range of interested parties. In addition, formal focus groups with family lawyers and pension experts were conducted, and an extensive online survey for professionals. There was a good response to the consultation. Most of the responses were supportive of PAG's aims and interim conclusions. There were also some constructively critical responses upon which PAG reflected carefully, and which caused it to adjust its provisional recommendations and conclusions in some material respects.

Armed with the most exhaustive review of pensions on divorce to date, PAG set out to execute its final report. It might be observed here that the sheer complexity of pension issues sometimes appears to require more than one judicial mind to determine them. When it came to writing up the final report, PAG faced the inverse of this problem: with so many minds contributing and debating the issues, it was a significant task to draw the threads together and then perfect a final draft upon which all could agree and which spoke with one authoritative voice. PAG's final report was published online on 1 July 2019[19] as a free-to-access guide, primarily (but not exclusively) for practitioners in 'everyday' family cases.

V. THEMES SEEN IN PLAY

Readers are directed to the main PAG report for an exhaustive guide as to how pensions should be treated on divorce. Here we take a 'sideways glance' at the forces which drive the arguments in this area of the law and describe some of the themes which have been particularly striking to us. We consider the themes of (1) complexity versus expediency, (2) the character of pensions, (3) differing approaches towards the valuation of pensions on divorce, and (4) where pensions sit in the psychology of a financial remedy case.

[19] See Pensions Advisory Group (n 1).

A. Complexity Versus Expediency

The first point is to note the complexity of the issues which pensions on divorce can throw up and set that in the context of an almost overwhelmed family justice system. Care work, where the subject child may be suffering significant harm, rightly gets the first slice of judicial time. Such time as remains in an overstretched judicial system must include private children disputes and money disputes, in the latter of which pensions on divorce will feature. It is not at all uncommon to find eight complex cases in one judicial list for a day at the Central London Family Court. Each case will no doubt have its own labyrinthine complexities to be mastered, before pensions are even looked at.

It will be apparent to anyone who reads the PAG report how fiendishly complicated pensions on divorce can be and how many issues are potentially in play. The outcomes, in contrast, can appear deceptively simple, with the denouement being either a percentage figure dropped into a pro-forma pension sharing template, or, even more opaquely, with more capital being awarded to one spouse in return for a reduction in her claim to a share of the other spouse's pension.

The current highly discretionary system of property distribution on divorce governed by section 25 of the Matrimonial Causes Act 1973 means that one judge may arrive at a different conclusion from his brother or sister judge and still have made an unappealable decision. Parties negotiate and strike deals in the shadow of the law and of this very wide discretion. The parish of the fair outcome is a wide one, whether by agreement or adjudication.

The combination of fiendish complexity, an overburdened court system and the pressure from parties to get everything over and done with as quickly and cheaply as possible makes for a context where it is simply too easy to hide poor quality decision-making behind the fig leaf of discretion. Provided *an* answer is rendered it seems that many in the family justice system have simply tolerated a situation where issues of expediency have taken ascendancy over the need to subject pensions on divorce to the detailed consideration they deserve. This has significant implications for negligence claims against family lawyers, with claims companies seeing pension on divorce as a fertile area of business.[20]

B. The Chimerical Character of Pensions on Divorce

Family law has had to wrestle with the developing character and accessibility of pensions in order to find a home for them in the narrative and analysis of a financial remedies application. Over the last 20 years, judges' attitudes towards whether a pension on divorce is treated as an income or capital asset have varied, the case law has not always been consistent, and developments in underlying pension legislation have rendered some of the older pronouncements now redundant. From a

[20] See G Lazarus, 'You Need the House, Love, Let Him Keep His Pension' [2019] *Family Law Journal* 373.

practitioner's point of view, this makes it hard to confidently advise on how a pension will be treated, in any given case, by the court.

In a duo of cases decided in the early 2000s, Thorpe LJ treated pension benefits as an income asset. In *Maskell v Maskell*,[21] he stated that the first instance judge had made 'the seemingly elementary mistake of confusing present capital with the right to financial benefits on retirement'.[22] A few years later, in *Martin-Dye v Martin-Dye*[23] his Lordship held that there were good reasons for treating pensions in payment as different from other assets and apportioning them by means of a pension sharing order. In his view, 'A pension in payment is no more than a whole life income stream akin to an annuity. It cannot be sold, commuted for cash or offered as security for borrowings. It has no capacity for capital appreciation'.[24] However, Dyson LJ took a more nuanced approach. He stated that he did not read Thorpe LJ as saying that 'as a matter of law, it is never open to the court to aggregate the value of pensions with that of other assets and distribute the resultant total between the parties'.[25] And he remarked that such an approach might well be appropriate, for example, where 'the parties have pensions in payment that are approximately equal in value and/or where the value of the pension is small in comparison with other assets'.[26]

As pension legislation has developed in the last 10–15 years, the views of Thorpe LJ have appeared increasingly simplistic and antiquated, and the courts seem to be more prepared to treat pensions as capital assets. For example in *Vaughan v Vaughan*[27] Wilson LJ (as he then was) indicated that a convenient method of presenting pensions to the court was to include their capital value as a balance sheet item under the heading, 'other capital'.[28] In a later case of the same name[29] his Lordship acknowledged that people approaching retirement age tend to 'treat the distinction between income and capital as fluid'[30] and he suggested that 'the court will recognise this reality'.[31]

Mostyn J's approach to pensions in two recently reported cases has also been to treat them as being akin to capital which can be drawn down, rather than an income stream. In *BJ v MJ (Financial Order: Overseas Trusts)*,[32] he was invited to assume that the wife would purchase an annuity award. He opined: 'I decline to make that assumption. No-one nowadays seriously would think of buying an annuity. Rather, they would likely draw down on the pension within prescribed GAD limits'.[33]

[21] *Maskell v Maskell* [2001] EWCA Civ 858, [2003] 1 FLR 1138.

[22] ibid [6].

[23] *Martin-Dye v Martin-Dye* [2006] EWCA Civ 681, [2006] 1 WLR 3448.

[24] ibid [48].

[25] ibid [85]. See also *Norris v Norris* [2002] EWHC 2996 (Fam), [2003] 1 FLR 1142; and *GW v RW (Financial Provision: Departure from Equality)* [2003] EWHC 611 (Fam), [2003] 2 FLR 108 as examples of cases where current and pension capital were aggregated together.

[26] ibid.

[27] *Vaughan v Vaughan* [2007] EWCA Civ 1085, [2008] 1 FLR 1108.

[28] ibid [25].

[29] *Vaughan v Vaughan* [2010] EWCA Civ 349, [2010] 3 WLR 1209.

[30] ibid [42].

[31] ibid.

[32] *BJ v MJ (Financial Order: Overseas Trusts)* [2011] EWHC 2708 (Fam), [2012] 1 FLR 667.

[33] ibid [75]. Prior to the introduction of the 2015 pension freedoms, The Government Actuary Department had a formula which prescribed the maximum amount of pension income which could be taken in a pension year.

Subsequently, in *JL v SL (No 3)(Post-Judgment Amplification)*,[34] Mostyn J used capital to be drawn from a pension share to fund a *Duxbury* calculation. A *Duxbury* calculation is a series of assumptions conventionally applied by the Family Court to capitalise a wife's right to a future income stream. Inherent in Mostyn J's approach was the assumption that the wife would draw down pension capital deploying 'pension freedoms' legislation, rather than purchase an annuity with her fund. In his view:

> That was a perfectly reasonable assumption to make given the increased flexibility afforded to the holders of pension funds by the Taxation of Pensions Act 2014, which received royal assent on the 17 December 2014. It probably would have been a reasonable assumption even had the reform not been enacted. I heard no argument to the contrary. It would have been unreal to take some annuity figure calculated by a pension expert for the trial before [the district judge] in October 2013 well before the pension reforms were announced in July 2014.[35]

In *SJ v RA*[36] (a big money case worth £28 million) a husband and wife each had pension investments. The CE of the husband's pension was worth more than twice that of the wife's pension. The wife argued that the court should make a pension sharing order to provide her and the husband with an equal income. Mr Nicholas Francis QC, sitting as a deputy high court judge, (as he then was) declined to make the order on the basis that it would be discriminatory and unacceptable. His reasons were expressly limited to big money cases and accord with the view of Mostyn J that the pension could be characterised as a capital asset value rather than income:

> The wife says that there should be a pension sharing order to provide her and the husband with an equal income. Given that the wife is younger and female, this would provide her with a greater share of the combined fund values. I would regard such an approach as unfair and anachronistic in a case where assets exceed the parties' needs. The recent well publicised changes to pension regulations will mean that pension investments are virtually to be treated as bank accounts to people over 55, as these people are. Why should someone receive more just on the basis of gender? There may have been an explanation when the rules required the purchase of an annuity. However, to give the wife more than the husband, on account of either age or gender would seem to me to be unacceptable discrimination unless it is a case which is governed solely by needs. If a person should receive more of a pension fund under the modern rules simply because she (or he in the case of a marriage where the husband is much younger) is likely to live longer, then such an approach would logically extend to all capital assets.[37]

The inconsistency in judicial approaches to the characterisation of pensions over the last 20 years may partly be explained by the fact that it is difficult to draw a bright line between capital and income. This conundrum has been highlighted by Max Lewis in an article which considers the difference between income and capital in financial remedy claims.[38] He refers[39] to *Heather v P-E Consulting Group*[40] in which

[34] *JL v SL (No 3)(Post-Judgment Amplification)* [2015] EWHC 555 (Fam), [2015] 2 FLR 1220.
[35] ibid [6].
[36] *SJ v RA* [2014] EWHC 4054 (Fam), [2015] All ER (D) 60 (Jan).
[37] ibid [83].
[38] M Lewis, 'What is the Difference between Income and Capital?' [2009] *Family Law* 1146.
[39] ibid 1146.
[40] *Heather v P-E Consulting Group* [1973] 1 Ch 189 (CA).

Lord Denning MR made some remarks (relating to expenditure, but nonetheless highly pertinent here):

> The question – revenue expenditure or capital expenditure – is a question which is being repeatedly asked by men of business, by accountants and by lawyers. In many cases the answer is easy but in others it is difficult. The difficulty arises because of the nature of the question. It assumes that all expenditure can be put correctly into one category or the other. But this is simply not possible. Some cases lie on the border between the two, and this border is not a line clearly marked out. It is a blurred and undefined area in which anyone can get lost. Different minds may come to different conclusions with equal propriety. It is like the border between day and night, or between red and orange. Everyone can tell the difference except in the marginal cases, and then everyone is in doubt. Each can come down either way.[41]

Lewis also cites an interesting historical analysis by Thorpe LJ in *McFarlane v McFarlane*,[42] wherein the learned Lord Justice reviews the breaking down of the 'hallowed distinction' between capital and income from Victorian times to the present. Lewis concludes:

> Purists may decry an approach which, in the words of Thorpe LJ in *McFarlane*, fails to respect the hallowed distinction between income and capital. However, on close examination, that distinction has always been chimerical, changing with the context and impossible to precisely pin down for all circumstances.[43]

And so it is with pensions on divorce. In one context a pension asset may at first appear as capital, but looked at though another lens it all of a sudden appears more akin to a deferred income. Sometimes there is no easy, 'obviously correct' way in which to categorise and characterise a pension for the purposes of a schedule of finances on divorce. This lack of certainty on the character of pensions, for the purposes of a divorce, has made advising on the likely outcome of a financial remedy claim harder to predict when pensions are a key consideration.

PAG has recommended that annuity purchase should be assumed for the purposes of calculating pension sharing orders. This reflects PAG's majority view that many 'women of middle years' who have been through a divorce simply do not have the resources or appetite for the risks of investing that are involved with holding capital for draw down. Many simply yearn for a secure income that will meet their needs for life, without the risk of funds expiring through overspend, unfortunate investment strategies, or the dubious advantage of rude longevity.

For these reasons, while the approach in *SJ v RA* is undoubtedly correct in those cases where assets really outstrip needs (in the south east of England, such cases will run to several million pounds before being considered to be 'big money' when they will be determined by reference to sharing rather than need), in the 'everyday' money cases PAG, and the reality on the ground, often favour treating pension money as deferred income rather than as a capital asset.

[41] ibid 216.
[42] *McFarlane v McFarlane* [2004] EWCA Civ 872, [2004] 3 WLR 1480.
[43] Lewis (n 38) 1149.

C. Different Approaches to Valuing Pensions on Divorce

There is a heady range of opinion when it comes to valuing pensions for a divorce. PAG had around its table a variety of these views. Readers of the PAG report will have to determine how successful it has been in encouraging more consistent practice between different experts. PAG is proud to have narrowed the differences in approach as described below, but there remains space for individual professional/actuarial judgement on the facts of any particular case.

In the previous section we highlighted differing judicial approaches to the characterisation of pensions. The flip side of the coin is that, when considering pension sharing as a remedy, a fault line exists between those who favour calculating the pension *income* on divorce and those who favour alighting upon a true/fair/consistent (the terms are used interchangeably and essentially mean the same thing) *capital* valuation by which a division is made without reference to the income enjoyed by the parties upon their ultimate deployment of their respective funds in retirement. The capital valuation is based on the cost of purchasing equivalent pension benefits. The balance of opinion of the experts who contributed to the PAG report favoured the calculation of income in retirement, but there is a forceful minority view contending otherwise.

One practical problem with the 'true' capital valuation approach is that pension sharing orders must, by regulation, be expressed as a percentage of the CE. As we have already noted,[44] the CE does not always accurately reflect the benefits enjoyed in a defined benefit scheme for the purposes of divorce, and is usually lower than the capital value of the pension. This can lead to situations where the 'true' value of a pension can (and, in our experience, does) turn into a stumbling block to settlement.

Take the not atypical example of a defined benefit pension which has a CE of £400,000 but has been calculated to have a 'true' value of £600,000. The claimant wife may say she wants 'her £300,000 share' of this asset, but if the parties' aim is for a pension sharing order, the order awarding the wife such a share can only be expressed as a percentage of the CE, which in this instance would be 75 per cent. The husband holding the pension rights is unlikely to agree to a pension share on that basis and the wife then feels short-changed. Of course, running through all of this is a misunderstanding of the difference between the CE and the true capital value of a pension, but such disputes would not arise if the parties concentrated instead on what the pension would render in income terms on their retirement.

The situation is different if the parties are considering offsetting – then the true capital value of a defined benefit pension does need to be known. If, for example, the house is worth £300,000 and the CE is £400,000, and the wife is to keep the home in exchange for the husband keeping his pension, it is clearly very material to know that the cost of purchasing equivalent pension benefits would actually be £600,000. Such valuations can not only reveal the appropriate quantum but also affect the direction of settlement payment.

[44] See part II.A above.

If it is accepted that the better basis for approaching pension sharing is *income in retirement*, the question arises as to what retirement date should be used? In practice, usually as a result of poorly drafted letters of instruction, expert reports are frequently overburdened with too many dates on a 'splatter-gun' approach. This often reflects a lack of any prior financial planning for the parties, whether formal or otherwise. PAG concluded that the most appropriate date to aim for is the normal retirement age of the 'dominant private pension' in the matrimonial basket and/or the State Pension age of the parties.

If there is a material age disparity between the parties, the 'income in retirement' approach may be of limited utility and then it may be appropriate for a 'balancing' lump sum to be paid to the party who is later to attain retirement age. However, in some circumstances the difference in age is not particularly material and it will be enough to say that the younger party will 'make up' for the other's earlier receipt of their pension by their (the younger party's) (notional) longer life expectancy.

D. The Psychology of Pensions in Financial Remedy Proceedings

A profound question arose during PAG's deliberations. As discussed above, the debate about pensions on divorce often centres around whether the pensions should be valued according to their capital or their income value. In both cases, however, the default goal of the exercise appears to be equalisation between the parties. However, when considering the division of *current* capital (ie, non-pension assets) it is readily accepted that the 'yardstick of equality' is no more than a yardstick and that more often than not the outcome is an unequal division, based upon needs-driven considerations.

PAG is unable to identify a reported case where it has been said that a wife should have an unequal (greater) share of pension in her favour, upon the basis that her husband is more capable of making up the consequent shortfall in his own pension provision in due course. To date, the conventional approaches to pensions on divorce have typically looked no further than equality, irrespective of what the wife's needs or fairness may actually demand.

Waggott v Waggott[45] has settled conclusively (unless or until the Supreme Court gives leave in a like case to reconsider the question) that a wife does not have an entitlement to share in future income post-divorce. The lodestar for the quantification of maintenance via periodical payments is a wife's needs (perhaps 'generously assessed'). This approach accords with a process which has been under way for some years,[46] with courts taking a more parsimonious approach to periodical payments in favour of a clean break, the making of which should only be delayed if the wife is caused 'undue' hardship (some hardship is permitted by the statute).[47]

[45] *Waggott v Waggott* [2018] EWCA Civ 727, [2019] 2 WLR 297.

[46] In *Flavell v Flavell* [1997] 1 FLR 353 and *C v C (Financial Relief: Short Marriage)* [1997] 2 FLR 26 the Court of Appeal took a reasonably generous approach to periodical payments, but these cases are cited and relied on less often than the more frugal approach of Mostyn J in *SS v NS (Spousal Maintenance)* [2014] EWHC 4183 (Fam), [2015] 2 FLR 1124.

[47] Matrimonial Causes Act 1973, s 25A(2).

These developments are apt to muddy the waters when it comes to pensions on divorce. As already noted, the pension often has a chimerical character in proceedings, with rival arguments as to whether it is capital or income. If it is a capital asset, then it may be cut in two. The conventional approach by a court appointed pension single joint expert is to calculate pension sharing orders upon the assumption that the recipient will purchase an annuity to equalise the income that can be enjoyed by the pension holder. However, it can seem illogical for the equalisation of income to be the conventional starting point for a pension sharing order, when the starting point for any award of maintenance via periodical payments is the lodestar of needs. The competing approaches appear almost schizophrenic side by side.

The traditional justification for limiting periodical maintenance payments by reference to a wife's needs is that an income must be earned and why should a wife, once her needs are met, have any share in the husband's post-separation endeavour? This approach, however, fails to acknowledge the significant direct and indirect financial, domestic and emotional contributions a wife may have made to assisting her husband acquire his earning capacity at the cost of her own. What is more, a different approach to pensions can be justified on the basis that, as Wilson LJ (as he then was) remarked in *Vaughan v Vaughan*,[48] pension capital, 'unlike any attempted capitalisation of earning capacity … does not depend on the application of future effort but, subject to market and other vagaries, is in the bag'.[49] Therefore, despite the differing conceptual provenance of an earned income and a pension income, we suggest that care should be taken to ensure that the tighter approach to maintenance does not unduly infect a fair approach to the division of pensions on divorce. As a matter of principle, we can see no reason why there could not be an unequal division of a pension in favour of a wife.

Too often it seems as if the court is encouraged by the modern maintenance approach to think only about the immediate short term (often the question is, is it a three- or a five-year term?) when a mature consideration of pensions requires a far longer vista. For example, we are aware of an unreported case at district judge level where a court ordered a clean break for a wife in two years' time on the basis that by then she would have attained the age of 55 and would be able to draw upon her pension, and as a result would not be suffering 'undue hardship'. This approach fatally ignored the fact that if the wife had to draw her pension at 55 while the husband could defer accessing his pension for many years (as his income needs were being met by his earned income), their standard of living in retirement would be markedly different. It is hard to view this outcome as fair.

One of the most striking features of the current approach towards pensions, and a partial explanation for it, is the vehemence with which husbands fight for their pensions in comparison with other assets. There often appears to be an attitude that the pension is a 'breed apart', that 'he has worked for it', it is 'his pension' and it is morally unfair for the wife to make a claim against it. In comparison wives are often desperate to keep the family home, even if it is beyond their needs and likely to cost more than they can realistically afford. The desire to 'hang on to the nest' is most

[48] *Vaughan v Vaughan* [2007] (n 27).
[49] ibid [25].

often driven by the practicalities of caring for children, but even after their children have left home many women are prepared to strike a very poor deal on pensions in return for keeping the house, a deal which can be akin to trading the inheritance for a bowl of broth. Offsetting pension against non-pension assets in this way is often seen by the parties, especially by those with limited resources, as a quick and cheap way of achieving a settlement, and, even better, a 'clean break' settlement, ie, one in which they sever all the financial ties between them. Not only do they avoid the time and expense involved with securing a pension order, they also avoid, for example, a situation in which the husband has to wait for his interest in the family home until the children reach independence and the wife has to wait for a share of his pension until she is at least 55. This sort of outcome is seen as messy and is increasingly unpopular. The apparent simplicity of offsetting, however, too often belies the value of the pension.

Pensions are also often considered last in divorce cases, with the sound and fury of the divorce vented in arguments about the quantification and presentation of the matrimonial pot, capital division and maintenance. By the time everyone gets to the question of pensions, many appear to have lost the energy to remain focused, despite the fact that pensions are often one of the most valuable assets and the most technically demanding of the case and have significant implications for the long-term future of both parties.

VI. THE SPECTRE OF NEGLIGENCE

The themes which we have described above have all, in their own way, played a part in the increase in negligence claims arising from pensions on divorce cases. One of the responses to our consultation was a paper by Grant Lazarus,[50] in which he summarised his experience of 163 negligence claims relating to pensions on divorce over a period of five years. The main sources of the claims were: family solicitors relying on the CE when it was not appropriate to do so; solicitors not understanding the difference between defined benefit and defined contribution schemes or the fact that £1 in a defined contribution CE may have much less value than £1 in a defined benefit CE; and the parties' and solicitors' failure to take, follow or understand expert advice. The two most striking points were, first, that all but two of the 163 claimants were wives, and second, almost all of the negligence claims related to offsetting settlements. This highlights the need for professional advisers to improve their understanding of the importance of pensions and how they are to be valued and dealt with on divorce. It is hoped that the PAG report will assist in this regard.

VII. CONCLUSION

The practice regarding pensions until now could, perhaps, be seen as the last bastion of unintended discrimination against women on divorce. PAG's work over the

[50] This paper subsequently formed the basis of his article referred to in (n 20).

past two years has opened up the channels of communication between the various professionals working in the field of pensions on divorce. Its aim has been to provide advisory guidance to judges and practitioners, to help to level the playing field and improve the consistency and fairness of the outcomes. We hope that practitioners will use the guide and that as a result the parties will appreciate the value of any pensions they might be giving up, retaining or acquiring and make better informed decisions. Of continuing concern is the loss of public funding for the vast majority of divorce cases since 31 March 2013,[51] and the consequent increase in the number of litigants in person. To expect those going through divorce to have enough understanding of the nature of pensions and how to deal fairly with them on divorce without professional advice is a tall order indeed. There is a clear need for a companion guide for use by litigants in person and non-specialist advisers, but this is another major project which may take a little longer to bring to fruition.

[51] The scope of eligible funding was drastically reduced by the coming into force of the Legal Aid, Sentencing & Punishment of Offenders Act 2012.

18

'Pension Freedoms', Social Care and Inheritance

BRIAN SLOAN

I. INTRODUCTION

Unlike healthcare, generally provided free at the point of delivery in England, social care for elderly and disabled people who need help with everyday tasks is the subject of a significant means test. Local authorities responsible for a person's care will undertake a detailed financial assessment of a person's capital and income in order to determine her liability to pay for her own care, using an extremely complex set of regulations made under the Care Act 2014. The system is very controversial because it can prejudice family members' ability to inherit a care recipient's property, including the family home. This is true notwithstanding the controversy that exists in contemporary social conditions about the extent to which family members, and particularly adult children of the deceased, might reasonably expect an inheritance.[1]

Pension income from a traditional annuity is generally treated as relevant income for the purposes of a local authority's social care financial assessment. 'Pension freedoms', however, whereby people were given greater freedom to withdraw money from their pension pots and decide for themselves how to fund later life under the Taxation of Pensions Act 2014, complicate this position. Exercising such freedoms could cause property derived from a pension scheme to be treated as capital instead (for example), and gifting such capital could even trigger anti-avoidance action by a local authority. The aim of this chapter is to explore the potential implications of pension freedoms for liability to fund social care, including the knock-on effect on survivors' inheritance rights and expectations. It begins by outlining the social care system and its funding, including the general financial assessment process undertaken by local authorities. In part III, it then considers the particular treatment of pensions within

[1] See, eg, B Sloan, '*Ilott v The Blue Cross* (2017): Testing the Limits of Testamentary Freedom' in B Sloan (ed), *Landmark Cases in Succession Law* (Oxford, Hart Publishing, 2019).

that system, both in the context of traditional annuities and pension freedoms. It will evaluate the particular risks and potentially unexpected consequences of exercising pension freedoms for the increasing numbers of people likely to require social care. The chapter will argue that while social care is unlikely to be the primary consideration for a person contemplating the exercise of pension freedoms, proper advice is still essential in order to avoid unexpected complications to funding assessments, prejudice to inheritance rights and even litigation between local authorities and the family members of social care recipients.

II. SOCIAL CARE, PROPERTY AND INHERITANCE

A. The Social Care System

Adult social care is the responsibility of local authorities in England. While it lacks a statutory definition, it has been said that it 'supports people of all ages with certain physical, cognitive or age-related conditions in carrying out personal care or domestic routines'.[2] It is distinct from healthcare provided by the National Health Service (NHS), which is designed to 'secure improvement'[3] 'in the physical and mental health of the people of England'[4] and 'in the prevention, diagnosis and treatment of physical and mental illness'.[5] This distinction assumes particular importance as regards the funding of care, but is frequently criticised.[6]

The charging regimes for healthcare and social care have been separate since the beginnings of the NHS.[7] The National Health Service Act 2006 mandates that '[t]he services provided as part of the health service in England must be free of charge' except where legislation expressly provides otherwise.[8] By contrast, however, the Dilnot Commission on the Funding of Care and Support explained that '[v]ery broadly, under [the social care] system, people with assets over £23,250 receive no financial state support and need to fund their own care' and '[t]he level and type of state support for people with assets below this threshold depends on their needs and income'.[9] A study by Baxter estimated that in the recent past between 20 and 25 per cent of those receiving care in their own homes, and between 43 and 45 per cent of those doing so in a care home, paid for their own care, as well as predicting future increases in those figures.[10]

[2] Commission on Funding of Care and Support, *Fairer Care Funding* (2011) 4.
[3] National Health Service Act 2006, s 1(1).
[4] ibid s 1(1)(a).
[5] ibid s 1(1)(b).
[6] See, eg, J Herring, *Medical Law and Ethics*, 7th edn (Oxford, Oxford University Press, 2018) 57.
[7] J Bilton, 'Care Arrangements: Who Cares? Who Pays?' (2014) 1 *Bulletin of the Social Work History Network* 14, 14.
[8] National Health Service Act 2006, s 1(4).
[9] Commission on Funding of Care and Support (n 2) 11.
[10] K Baxter, 'Self-funders and Social Care: Findings from a Scoping Review' (2016) 31 *Research, Policy and Planning* 179.

The starkness of the funding differences is not, however, reflected in the distinction between the types of care.[11] There is also controversy over NHS Continuing Healthcare,

> a package of ongoing care … arranged and funded solely by the [NHS] for individuals outside a hospital setting who have complex ongoing healthcare needs, of a type or quantity such that they … have a 'primary health need' … as a result of disability, accident or illness.[12]

The King's Fund describe NHS Continuing Healthcare (with its very stringent criteria) as involving an 'all or nothing' assessment, whereby those who pass it receive free care and accommodation.[13]

Mayhew and Smith emphasise that '[a] … system for funding social care … along similar lines to the NHS … would involve a combination of higher taxes, more borrowing and/or redirecting public finances from other priority areas',[14] at a time of a perceived need for austerity and in which local authorities are already struggling to meet demands[15] and the dignity of those who require care is far from guaranteed.[16] Even so, the King's Fund assert that pressures in health and social care and the needs of an ageing population 'call for a response that goes well beyond patching up existing services and making the changes set out in the Dilnot report [involving the capping of liability]'.[17] They make the bold claim that 'higher public spending on health and social care is affordable if it is phased in over a decade' and recommend that it be funded 'through tax and national insurance increases, reallocating funds from other areas of spending, and changes to prescription charges'.[18] For the time being, however, the marked distinction between the funding arrangements for health and social care looks set to stay.

The charging and funding regime in the Care Act 2014 was nevertheless 'intended to make charging fairer and more clearly understood by everyone'.[19] Hopkins and Laurie describe it as 'a significant rebalancing of the individual–state relationship in terms of responsibility for funding … social care, whilst maintaining the underlying model of funding through both individual and state contributions'.[20]

Under the regime originally planned to be introduced via the Care Act, based somewhat on the Dilnot Commission's proposals but then delayed by the government

[11] See, eg, T Spencer-Lane, *Care Act Manual*, 2nd edn (London, Sweet & Maxwell, 2015) [1–268].

[12] Department of Health, 'Care and Support Statutory Guidance' (2019), available at: www.gov.uk/guidance/care-and-support-statutory-guidance [15.33]. See National Health Service Commissioning Board and Clinical Commissioning Groups (Responsibilities and Standing Rules) Regulations SI 2012/2996, Part 6.

[13] King's Fund, *A New Settlement for Health and Social Care: Final Report* (2014) 3.

[14] L Mayhew and D Smith, 'Personal Care Savings Bonds: A New Way of Saving Towards Social Care in Later Life' (2014) 39 *Geneva Papers* 668, 670–71.

[15] See, eg, Age UK, '1.2m Older People Don't Get the Social Care They Need' (2016), available at: www.ageuk.org.uk/latest-news/archive/12m-older-people-dont-get-the-social-care-they-need/.

[16] See, generally, B Sloan, 'Adult Social Care and Property Rights' (2016) 36 *OJLS* 428.

[17] King's Fund (n 13) vi.

[18] ibid.

[19] Department of Health, 'Care and Support Statutory Guidance' (n 12) [8.2].

[20] N Hopkins and E Laurie, 'Social Citizenship, Housing Wealth and the Cost of Social Care: Is the Care Act 2014 "Fair"?' (2015) 78 *MLR* 112.

until 2020 before being scrapped,[21] people with assets of £118,000 (where the person's home is included in the financial assessment, the figure being £27,000 otherwise)[22] would start to receive help with care costs;[23] and £17,000 would have been the new lower limit of the means test below which no contribution will be expected from the individual on the basis of capital,[24] increased from £14,250.[25]

The cap was a central aspect of the Dilnot proposals and the Act.[26] It was expected to be £72,000 for those developing eligible care needs after the age of 25 if it was first introduced in April 2016,[27] and it would be adjusted annually to account for inflation.[28] The effect of the cap would have been limited, however. Even before its implementation was delayed, the King's Fund emphasised that only the cost of meeting *eligible* needs would count towards the cap, which are likely to be critical or substantial and not low or moderate.[29] There is also concern that progress towards the cap could be set below what it costs *an individual* to pay for care[30] because the local authority could secure cheaper provision itself.[31] It should also be emphasised that the cap would exclude so-called 'general' or 'daily' 'living costs' within a care home, and these were expected to be set at around £12,000 per year.[32] These limitations on the cap would have left many people paying a considerable sum towards their care even if the cap were brought into effect.[33] For example, the Institute and Faculty of Actuaries has estimated that those who reached the £72,000 cap would have spent an average of £140,000 before doing so because of the cap's exclusion of living costs and 'top-up' fees designed to secure a higher standard of care,[34] and that only around 10 per cent of those who pay for care would ever reach it.[35] As a consequence, they recommend an inclusive £100,000 cap that includes the local authority rate, daily living costs and 'excess' top-up fees based on average care costs.

Aside from the cap, a major area of funding reform within the Care Act relates to the offering of deferred payment agreements (DPAs), allowing the payment of social

[21] *BBC News*, '£72,500 Social Care Cap to be Scrapped, MPs Told' (7 December 2017), available at: www.bbc.co.uk/news/uk-politics-42266076.

[22] Department of Health, *The Care Act 2014: Consultation on Draft Regulations and Guidance to Implement the Cap on Care Costs and Policy Proposals for a New Appeals System for Care and Support* (2015) [9.7].

[23] ibid.

[24] ibid [9.8].

[25] National Assistance (Assessment of Resources) Regulations, SI 1992/2977, r 28(1).

[26] Care Act 2014, s 15.

[27] Department of Health, *The Care Act 2014* (n 22) [10.2].

[28] Care Act 2014, s 16.

[29] King's Fund (n 13) 3.

[30] Department of Health, *The Care Act 2014* (n 22) ch 4.

[31] Spencer-Lane (n 11) [1–317].

[32] Department of Health, *The Care Act 2014* (n 22) [7.3]. See also J-L Fernández and P Nadash, 'The Long-term Care Financing Problem' in C Gori et al (eds), *Long-term Care Reforms in OECD Countries: Successes and Failures* (Policy Press, 2016) 32.

[33] Institute and Faculty of Actuaries, *How Financial Products Can Work Alongside the Care Act 2014 to Help People Pay for Care: An Overview* (2015) 30.

[34] Institute and Faculty of Actuaries, *How Pensions Can Help Meet Consumer Needs under the New Social Care Regime* (2014) 6.

[35] Independent Age and Institute and Faculty of Actuaries, *Will The Cap Fit?* (2017).

care costs to be deferred (via a secured loan) until a point such as the death of the care recipient or the sale of her home.[36]

The government hoped that a market in insurance products would develop once the cap came into effect, to help people pay for care.[37] The King's Fund, however, claimed that there were 'no signs' that such a market would develop.[38] Mayhew and Smith express concern that '[i]f spending by the state and by the individual does not keep pace with need … the quality and availability of care will suffer unless there are better mechanisms to help people support themselves'.[39] Pledges for increased spending have been made, but there are concerns that these remain insufficient to improve the level of care appropriately and cope with increased demand.[40]

The future of the funding of social care remains in doubt following the 2017 general election. In fact, the Conservative Manifesto proposed to remove the 'disregard' preventing a person's home being included in the assessment where she is to receive care in her own home.[41] The objective was said to be to increase fairness in the system while also assisting it to cope with increased demands as a result of the ageing population. This would have meant some people currently receiving free care being expected to pay for it in future, but would have been offset by an increase in the current £23,250 threshold to £100,000 (which local authorities have indicated they are unable to afford).[42] The aim was expressed to be to ensure that self-funders would have £100,000 to pass on via inheritance. The cap was not mentioned in the manifesto at all, although the then Prime Minister Theresa May later indignantly asserted that there would be such a cap without specifying what it would be.[43] The expected Green Paper following the scrapping of the original cap[44] was delayed several times (no doubt exacerbated by seemingly interminable wrangling over Brexit).[45] The 2019 Queen's Speech then said, somewhat ambiguously, that the government would 'bring

[36] The DPA prima facie falls due for repayment 90 days after the person's death or on disposal of property on which the local authority has a charge: Department of Health, *The Care Act 2014* (n 22) [9.104]; Care and Support (Deferred Payment) Regulations, SI 2014/2671, r 7. See, generally, B Sloan, 'Charges for Charges: Home Sales under the Care Act 2014' in H Conway and R Hickey (eds), *Modern Studies in Property Law: Volume 9* (Oxford, Hart Publishing, 2017).

[37] Department of Health, *Review of Care Products – Key Messages* (2014).

[38] King's Fund (n 13) vi.

[39] Mayhew and Smith (n 14) 670. They therefore propose Personal Care Savings Bonds.

[40] D Campbell, 'Hammond's budget bows to demands for social care cash injection' *The Guardian* (8 March 2017), available at: www.theguardian.com/uk-news/2017/mar/08/hammonds-budget-bows-to-demands-for-social-care-cash-injection.

[41] Conservatives, 'Our Manifesto' (2017), available at: www.conservatives.com/manifesto 60.

[42] J Elgot, 'We Cannot Afford to Fund "Dementia Tax" Proposals, Councils Warn' *The Guardian* (17 October 2017), available at: www.theguardian.com/society/2017/oct/17/we-cannot-afford-to-fund-dementia-tax-proposals-councils-warn.

[43] A Asthana, 'Theresa May Will Not Reveal Social Care Cap Before General Election' *The Guardian* (28 May 2017), available at: www.theguardian.com/society/2017/may/28/theresa-may-will-not-reveal-social-care-cap-before-general-election.

[44] HM Government, 'The Queen's Speech and Associated Background Briefing, on the Occasion of the Opening of Parliament on Wednesday 21 June 2017' (Crown, 2017) 58.

[45] A Matthews-King, 'Fury as Government Delays Promised Social Care Reform for Sixth Time Amid Brexit Gridlock' *The Independent* (29 March 2019), available at: www.independent.co.uk/news/health/social-care-conservative-green-paper-brexit-elderly-disabilities-austerity-matt-hancock-a8846171.html.

forward proposals to reform adult social care in England to ensure dignity in old age',[46] but substantive progress before the further general election anticipated at the time of writing seems extremely unlikely.

The reality is that, pending any further reform, a significant portion of the population in England will have to pay a considerable sum towards their care, not least since the average annual cost of a care home in 2017–18 exceeded £44,000 if nursing care was necessary.[47] This could have significant implications for the inheritance prospects of the relatives of social care recipients, which is true even if Hopkins and Laurie argue, with reference to theories of social citizenship and the social contract, that 'the Care Act 2014 operates to reinforce the expectation of leaving housing wealth as an inheritance which perpetuates inequalities across generations', such that 'the funding model provided by the Act is neither fair nor sustainable'.[48] More broadly, the current situation perpetuates a form of discrimination between people with different types of care need by providing healthcare free at the point of delivery but means-testing social care. Even if that the discrimination is not actionable, the prevailing approach can produce situations where the system fails fully to meet the needs of a social care recipient in a manner consistent with her dignity and charges her catastrophically for the privilege of enduring that failure.[49] The potential undesirability of the extent of the current 'user pays' principle must, however, be seen in the context of the fact that any reduction in the amount going into the system might prejudice its ability to meet the needs of those who genuinely cannot afford to pay for their care,[50] particularly since a considerable care funding shortfall for the future has already been predicted.[51]

The next subsection of this chapter explains how the broad social care funding principles considered above are manifested in the detailed rules of the financial assessment, before part III analyses the implications of the system for pension entitlements.

B. The Financial Assessment

A care recipient's liability to pay is assessed by a local authority (separately from a needs assessment)[52] using an extremely complex set of regulations to determine the existence of relevant capital and income.[53] The local authority's obligation to

[46] HM Government, 'The Queen's Speech and Associated Background Briefing, on the Occasion of the Opening of Parliament on Monday 4 October 2019' (Crown, 2019) 8. *cf BBC News*, 'Labour pledges free personal care for over-65s in England' (23 September 2019), available at www.bbc.com/news/uk-politics-49787468 (accessed 31 October 2019).

[47] Paying for Care, 'Care home fees', available at: www.payingforcare.org/care-home-fees.

[48] Hopkins and Laurie (n 20) 113.

[49] See, eg, Sloan, 'Adult Social Care and Property Rights' (n 16); B Sloan, 'Formal and Informal Care in the Public and Private Spheres in England and Australia' in L Gelsthorpe, P Mody and B Sloan (eds), *Spaces of Care* (Oxford, Hart Publishing, 2020).

[50] See, eg, ibid.

[51] See, eg, Full Fact, 'The Adult Social Care Spending Gap' (2017), available at: fullfact.org/health/adult-social-care-spending-gap/.

[52] Care Act 2014, ss 9–13.

[53] Care and Support (Charging and Assessment of Resources) Regulations, SI 2014/2672, made under Care Act 2014, ss 14 and 17, inter alia.

assess needs applies irrespective of the adult's resources, and the outcome of the needs assessment will begin progress towards any new cap on lifetime care costs that an individual will have to bear. There is a current statutory obligation to carry out a full financial assessment where a local authority identifies needs meeting the eligibility criteria and thinks that it would charge for meeting them,[54] except where a light-touch assessment is appropriate or the adult is not cooperating.[55] There must be regular reassessment of an adult's ability to pay.[56] It should be noted that each person must be assessed individually.[57] Capital and income can be taken into account[58] (except where disregarded), although the thresholds are based on capital.[59] There is an obligation to charge only when capital limits are exceeded in the context of care homes,[60] although the Impact Assessment suggests that this will be removed and replaced with a discretion if the funding reforms come fully into effect.[61] Local authorities will have quite some discretion concerning disregards, maximum charges etc, but the guidance urges them to exercise it consistently with reference to a developed policy.[62] The Regulations appear similar to the old National Assistance (Assessment of Resources) Regulations;[63] however, it is significant and arguably beneficial to the rule of law and accessibility that non-residential care is also now subject to regulations rather than mere guidance. Statutory guidance is clearly key to the operation of the system. The Care Act expressly imposes an obligation on local authorities to 'act under the general guidance of the Secretary of State in the exercise of functions given to it by [the relevant] Part [of the Act] or … regulations under [it]'.[64] According to the Act's Explanatory Notes, that provision was intended to have the 'same legal effect' as section 7 of the Local Authority Social Services Act 1970.[65] The courts have interpreted section 7 as requiring local authorities 'to follow the path charted by the … guidance, with liberty to deviate from it where the local authority judges on admissible grounds that there is good reason to do so, but without freedom to take a substantially different course'.[66] It has been said that 'the guidance does not have

[54] Care Act 2014, s 17(1)–(2).

[55] Care and Support (Charging and Assessment of Resources) Regulations 2014, r 10; Department of Health, 'Care and Support Statutory Guidance' (n 12) [8.22]–[8.26].

[56] This will usually be annual, but should also occur upon a change in circumstances or if the adult so requests: Department of Health, 'Care and Support Statutory Guidance' (n 12) [8.16]–[8.17].

[57] ibid [8.8].

[58] Care Act 2014, s 17(11).

[59] Department of Health, 'Care and Support Statutory Guidance' (n 12) Annex B [55]–[57].

[60] Care and Support (Charging and Assessment of Resources) Regulations 2014, r 12(2).

[61] Department of Health, *Impact Assessment: The Care Act 2014* (2014) [1.116].

[62] Department of Health, 'Care and Support Statutory Guidance' (n 12) [8.43]–[8.48].

[63] Department of Health, 'Charging for Care and Support', available at: careandsupportregs.dh.gov.uk/category/charging/. See generally D Coldrick, L Bradley and A Thornton, *Coldrick on Care Home Fees*, 2nd edn (London, Ark Group, 2012). The Care Act's Impact Assessment notes that the government took the 'opportunity to make some minor adjustments' even if those changes 'are designed to be cost neutral': Department of Health, *Impact Assessment: The Care Act 2014* (n 61) [1.113]; see also *Walford v Worcestershire County Council* [2015] EWCA Civ 22, [2016] 1 All ER 801 [17] (Underhill LJ).

[64] Care Act 2014, s 78(1).

[65] Explanatory Notes to the Care Act 2014 [472].

[66] *R v Islington LBC ex parte Rixon* [1997] ELR 66 (QB) 71 (Sedley J).

the binding effect of secondary legislation and a local authority is free to depart from it, even "substantially"', albeit that 'it is difficult to envisage circumstances in which mere disagreement with the guidance could amount to a cogent reason for departing from it'.[67]

The Regulations and guidance do not define 'capital' exhaustively, but the term generally 'refers to financial resources available for use and tends to be from sources … more durable than money in the sense that they can generate a return'.[68] The value of capital is reduced to account for selling expenses, and by the amount of outstanding debts secured on the asset.[69] Capital that is not immediately realisable is still included.[70] A person is assessed on the basis of her actual and notional capital, which includes capital that would be available to the person if she applied for it, is paid to a third party in respect of a person, or the person has deliberately deprived herself of it to reduce liability.[71] The value of notional capital is reduced by the difference between the weekly amount the person pays and the amount she would pay if the notional capital did not apply.

A number of assets are disregarded for the purposes of assessing capital.[72] Outside a care home context, assessment must exclude the adult's main or only home.[73] Even if the person *is* in a care home, there is a disregard if the person is there temporarily and intends to return to the main home or is taking reasonable steps to dispose of it, or the main home is occupied by a non-estranged partner, a single parent who is an estranged partner, a relative aged 60 or over or who is under 18 and is also a child of the recipient, or who is incapacitated.[74] It should nevertheless be noted that several categories of relative (who may be informal carers and/or would-be heirs not legally *obliged* to care for elderly parents) are put at risk of losing the family home by the social care system.[75]

[67] *R (on the application of X) v Tower Hamlets LBC* [2013] EWHC 480 (Admin), [2013] 3 All ER 157 [35] (Males J), affirmed on appeal by Maurice Kay LJ: [2013] EWCA Civ 904, [2013] 4 All ER 237 [28].

[68] Department of Health, 'Care and Support Statutory Guidance' (n 12) Annex B [5].

[69] Care and Support (Charging and Assessment of Resources) Regulations 2014, r 20; Department of Health, 'Care and Support Statutory Guidance' (n 12) Annex B para 14.

[70] Department of Health, 'Care and Support Statutory Guidance' (n 12) Annex B [23].

[71] Care and Support (Charging and Assessment of Resources) Regulations 2014, r 22. See further B Sloan, 'Trusts and Anti-Avoidance under the Care Act 2014' [2015] *Conveyancer and Property Lawyer* 489 and part III.B below.

[72] Care and Support (Charging and Assessment of Resources) Regulations 2014, r 18(2); sch 2. Department of Health, 'Care and Support Statutory Guidance' (n 12) Annex B, [33].

[73] Care and Support (Charging and Assessment of Resources) Regulations 2014, sch 2, para 4; Department of Health, 'Care and Support Statutory Guidance' (n 12) para 8.43.

[74] Care and Support (Charging and Assessment of Resources) Regulations 2014, sch 2, paras 1–8; Department of Health, 'Care and Support Statutory Guidance' (n 12) Annex B, [34]. There is a discretion to disregard the home in other circumstances, and temporary disregards, inter alia, where the adult first enters a care home: Care and Support (Charging and Assessment of Resources) Regulations 2014, sch 2; Department of Health, 'Care and Support Statutory Guidance' (n 12) Annex B, [42]–[47].

[75] See, eg, B Sloan, 'Solidarity Across Generations in England and Wales' in E Kasagi (ed), *Solidarity Across Generations* (Dordecht, Springer, forthcoming 2020).

Where a person has relevant assets between the lower and upper limit, the local authority assumes that for every £250 of capital (or part thereof) the person can contribute £1 per week towards care costs. This is known as 'tariff income'.[76]

As regards income, it is significant that income from current employment[77] and self-employment is disregarded, and that these are widely interpreted.[78] Most benefits are included, but direct payments, armed forces compensation payments and the mobility component of a Disability Living Allowance or Person Independence Payment are fully disregarded.[79] Most *income* from annuities is taken into account (considered in more detail in the next part of this chapter),[80] although there can be a disregard if, inter alia, half of it is being paid to a spouse or civil partner occupying the main home. Income from insurance policies is usually taken into account, but there is an exception relating to mortgage protection insurance.[81] Income from a range of state benefits, and discretionary trusts, for example, is fully disregarded.[82] The same applies to charitable and voluntary payments.

There are partial disregards for the first £10 per week of certain war-related payments, and there is also a savings disregard.[83] Notional income is treated in the same way as notional capital,[84] although there are some exceptions including payments under discretionary trusts.[85]

There is also a binding 'personal expenses allowance' (currently £24.90 per week) for someone in a care home that is disregarded.[86] Outside a care home, a similar function is performed by the 'minimum income guarantee', which is set at the level of income support plus 25 per cent.[87] Where a person receives disability-related benefits, local authorities are also advised to ensure that charging arrangements enable people to meet their needs that are not eligible needs.[88] The consideration of income begun in this subsection continues in part III.A of this chapter, with a detailed analysis of the treatment of *pension* income. First, however, a brief general discussion of the relationship between pensions and social care is undertaken.

[76] Care and Support (Charging and Assessment of Resources) Regulations 2014, r 25; Department of Health, 'Care and Support Statutory Guidance' (n 12) Annex B [27].

[77] Department of Health, 'Care and Support Statutory Guidance' (n 12) [8.21].

[78] Care and Support (Charging and Assessment of Resources) Regulations 2014, r 14; Department of Health, 'Care and Support Statutory Guidance' (n 12) Annex C [8]–[9]. See, generally, Care and Support (Charging and Assessment of Resources) Regulations 2014, sch 1. Oddly, it seems that earnings do not include expenses payments, meaning that these can be assessed: Department of Health, 'Care and Support Statutory Guidance' (n 12) Annex C [10].

[79] Department of Health, 'Care and Support Statutory Guidance' (n 12) Annex C [15].

[80] ibid Annex C [19]–[20].

[81] ibid Annex C [26].

[82] ibid Annex C [28].

[83] ibid Annex C [31].

[84] Care and Support (Charging and Assessment of Resources) Regulations 2014, r 17; Department of Health, 'Care and Support Statutory Guidance' (n 12) (n 12) [32]–[35].

[85] Department of Health, 'Care and Support Statutory Guidance' (n 12) (n 12) Annex C [36].

[86] Care and Support (Charging and Assessment of Resources) Regulations 2014, r 6; Department of Health, 'Care and Support Statutory Guidance' (n 12) [8.35].

[87] Care and Support (Charging and Assessment of Resources) Regulations 2014, r 7; Department of Health, 'Care and Support Statutory Guidance' (n 12) [8.42].

[88] Department of Health, 'Care and Support Statutory Guidance' (n 12) [8.42].

III. PENSIONS AND SOCIAL CARE

The Institute and Faculty of Actuaries has claimed that, 'after an individual's [real] property, his or her pension is likely to be the most substantial asset available to meet the personal contribution to [long-term care] costs', and that,

> [g]iven the general lack of any other material savings by the general public and the continuing resistance to releasing value from the 'family home' the use of pension assets [to contribute to care costs] may become more of a necessity than an option.[89]

Conversely, and significantly, Braun has written that '[a]lthough the primary purpose of [occupational and personal pension] schemes is to provide for the retirement of the scheme member, they can also benefit someone on the death of the member', even if '[t]he type of death benefit payable varies considerably, depending on the nature of the scheme and on whether or not the member dies before or after retirement'.[90]

A particular purpose of this part of the chapter is to consider the relationship between the expectation that pension entitlements be used to fund social care, the assessment of such entitlements by local authorities, and inheritance. The following subsections consider, first, the treatment of income from traditional annuities within the social care system; and second, the implications for it of exercising 'pension freedoms'.

A. Treatment of Traditional Pension Arrangements

According to a House of Commons Briefing Paper, '[t]he pension tax legislation in force until 6 April 2015 strongly encouraged the purchase of an annuity, allowing flexible or lump sum payments only in limited circumstances'.[91] An annuity is a contract with an insurer to provide a series of payments, whether for the lifetime of the holder, a survivor or a guaranteed period.[92] As Braun summarises the position:

> There are two main types of annuities: guaranteed term annuities and joint-life annuities. In the case of the former, the insurance company will make the payments for a guaranteed period, even if the member dies, while in the latter case, the payment is made for the life of the survivor.[93]

Most *income* from annuities is taken into account (as income rather than capital)[94] in a local authority's social care financial assessment of a care recipient during her life.[95] Income from the state pension and pension credit is specifically included in what *must* be taken into account in the assessment.[96]

[89] Institute and Faculty of Actuaries, *How Pensions Can Help Meet Consumer Needs* (n 34) 11.
[90] A Braun, 'Pension Death Benefits: Opportunities and Pitfalls' in B Häcker and C Mitchell (eds), *Current Issues in Succession Law* (Oxford, Hart Publishing, 2016) 233.
[91] D Thurley, 'Pensions: Annuities' (Briefing Paper SN06552, House of Commons Library, 2015) 3.
[92] ibid 4.
[93] Braun (n 90) 233.
[94] Care and Support (Charging and Assessment of Resources) Regulations 2014, r 16(2); Department of Health, 'Care and Support Statutory Guidance' (n 12) Annex B [33]; see also Annex C [15].
[95] Department of Health, 'Care and Support Statutory Guidance' (n 12) Annex C [19]–[20].
[96] ibid Annex C [15].

Importantly, there is specific protection for pension annuities including a payment directly to a spouse or civil partner of the holder. The guidance provides that:

> [w]here a person is in a care home and has a spouse or civil partner who is not living in the same care home and is paying half of the value of their occupational pension, personal pension or retirement annuity to their spouse or civil partner, the local authority must disregard this payment.[97]

While '[t]his does not automatically apply to unmarried couples', 'the local authority may wish to exercise its discretion in individual cases'.[98]

There is also an exception if the annuity is purchased with a loan secured on the person's main or only home or a 'gallantry award such as the Victoria Cross Annuity or George Cross Annuity'.[99] In addition, 'payments to veterans under the War Pension Scheme, with the exception of Constant Attendance Allowance which is specifically intended to pay for care, must be disregarded in the assessment of what a veteran can pay for care from 10 April 2017'.[100] There are additional partial disregards concerning certain war-related pension arrangements.[101]

The guidance specifically addresses pensions in the context of deprivation of assets, in that a person 'could give away or sell the right to an income from an occupational pension'.[102] A consequence of treating this right as notional income means that a care recipient can be treated as possessing it for the purposes of the assessment even though she does not. There is also the possibility that a local authority could bring proceedings against the third-party recipient of such an asset. These processes are considered further in the next subsection. There are limitations on pension income that must be treated as notional income, however. Notional income does not include income that is unpaid because a pension scheme's trustees/managers have suspended or ceased payments due to insufficient resources, and because they have insufficient resources to meet the scheme's liabilities in full.[103]

In a sense the system is 'prejudiced' against pensioners, since earnings from employment etc are broadly *excluded* but pension income is broadly *included*. This might be thought justifiable in light of the claim that '[p]ensioners now have higher incomes on average than the rest of the population, once housing costs and family composition are taken into account'.[104] The important point for present purposes, however, is that where pension benefits are intended for someone other than the care recipient, there is some protection for that person, whether by virtue of the benefit never truly forming part of the care recipient's property, or not being treated as if it did. Even if the benefit forms part of the care recipient's estate and falls to be distributed according

[97] ibid Annex C [20]; Care and Support (Charging and Assessment of Resources) Regulations 2014, sch 1, para 16.
[98] ibid Annex C [45b)].
[99] ibid Annex C [19].
[100] ibid [8.21a].
[101] ibid Annex C [33].
[102] ibid Annex E [13].
[103] ibid Annex C [38d)].
[104] Institute for Fiscal Studies, 'Press Release: High Levels of Income for Current Retirees Shouldn't Blind Us to Future Challenges' (20 October 2015), available at: www.ifs.org.uk/publications/8026.

to the will and/or intestacy rules,[105] the beneficiaries will receive it unless the care recipient is in debt to the local authority (by virtue of an assessment that has already taken place) at the date of death.[106] The next subsection highlights that this situation may not prevail if a care recipient exercises pension freedoms to buy and possibly gift other assets *inter vivos*.

B. Implications of 'Pension Freedoms'

'Pension freedoms' were introduced by the Taxation of Pensions Act 2014, and took effect in April 2015. As Braun put it,

> [t]he primary rationale behind the reforms was to provide greater flexibility, [so that s]ince April 2015, [defined contribution scheme] members can draw down their entire pension once they reach the age of 55, and are no longer forced to invest their pensions in annuities or drawdown pensions.[107]

It has been claimed that 'for most people, annuitizing at retirement is *not* the best option and … income draw-down is preferable, especially where there is a bequest motive and/or the individual has other valuable assets such as [real] property', inter alia, because '[p]eople are living longer and annuity rates are at a historic low and are expected to remain so'.[108] Somewhat consistently, *The Times* reported in September 2018 that '[m]any have taken advantage of the rule change, with the amount withdrawn from final-salary schemes rising from £7.9 billion in 2016 to £20.8 billion last year',[109] but by March 2019, the same newspaper noted that despite fears of 'irresponsible spending', 'those with defined contribution pensions withdrew only 28% of their savings on average, which is only slightly above the 25% they were entitled to withdraw, tax-free, before the freedoms were introduced', and '[o]f the funds withdrawn, a quarter of the money has typically been put into savings accounts and another quarter into investments'.[110] It has also been observed that 'a significant number of contract-based and trust-based pension schemes are not making the new flexibilities available within the scheme'.[111]

As regards social care, it is interesting that, in the letter announcing the (original) delay of the implementation of the Care Act's cap, the then Minister of State for Community and Social Care specifically asserted that 'the new pension flexibilities … create a real opportunity for us to work with the financial sector to look at what new products may be developed, thereby creating even more choice, and this is

[105] Braun (n 90) 233.

[106] See, generally, Sloan, 'Charges for Charges' (n 36) 168–72.

[107] Braun (n 90) 235.

[108] L Mayhew, D Smith and D Wright, *Pension Pots and How to Survive Them* (International Longevity Centre – UK, 2015) 5.

[109] D Byers, 'Take a Pause Before Raiding Your Company Pension Pot' *The Times* (1 September 2018), available at: www.thetimes.co.uk/article/take-a-pause-before-raiding-your-company-pension-pot-w2l5zndls.

[110] A Hussain, 'New Pensioners Shun Spending Splurge' *The Times* (10 March 2019), available at: www.thetimes.co.uk/article/new-pensioners-shun-spending-splurge-gf0ssvq2q.

[111] T Kenny et al, 'The Future of Social Care Funding: Who Pays?' (2017) 22 *British Actuarial Journal* 10, 13.

something I am keen to explore'.[112] It has been said that there are 'a number of products that might complement the new flexibilities and help people make provision for care costs', some of which are currently available in the UK, some of which have had success elsewhere, and some of which would be new.[113]

The Institute and Faculty of Actuaries has identified some positive consequences of the pension changes for individual care funding. These include that '[i]f more money is attracted into pension savings at earlier ages this should increase the overall wealth of people reaching retirement[, giving] greater opportunity for retirees to invest in products aimed at meeting their potential [long-term care] costs',[114] even if they concede that 'the incentive for retaining funds in a pension product committed to meeting [long-term care] costs may need to be increased'.[115] Moreover, '[t]he flexibility provided by Income Drawdown lends itself to meeting care costs and the new relaxation of restrictions in the current Income Drawdown regime will increase how Income Drawdown could be used to fund care costs'.[116] There is also the fact that '[t]he provision of free, impartial, face-to-face guidance at retirement', under the Pension Schemes Act 2015,[117] 'should ideally allow the potential costs of [long-term care] to be identified and the products available to help meet such costs to be fully explained',[118] albeit that effectiveness will depend on the level of knowledge of the social care funding system and amongst advisers and the reforms 'will strengthen the need for improved clarity and communication in many areas including the expected costs of [long-term care]'.[119] The care and support statutory guidance states that the service provided by 'Pension Wise'[120] 'will include information and advice on later life, including the risk that they may need care and support in the future, and will have to pay for it'.[121]

There is also reason for caution, however. 'Pension freedoms' inevitably 'put more onus on individuals to ensure they manage their resources appropriately and plan ahead'[122] and, despite the complex picture on take-up considered above, the Institute and Faculty of Actuaries recognised the risk that '[t]here will be some, and possibly many, who will withdraw and spend all their pension savings and thus find themselves in a position of being unable to meet their share of their [long-term care] costs'.[123] While they then claim that '[i]n the event of these individuals needing care the State would then need to fund their care needs',[124] in fact there is the prospect that (as explained further below) local authorities will use anti-avoidance powers to access

[112] Department of Health, 'Letter from Rt Hon Alistair Burt MP: Delay in the Implementation of the Cap on Care Costs' (17 July 2015), available at: www.gov.uk/government/publications/delay-in-the-implementation-of-the-cap-on-care-costs.
[113] Kenny et al (n 111) 14.
[114] Institute and Faculty of Actuaries, *How Pensions Can Help Meet Consumer Needs* (n 34) 9–10.
[115] ibid.
[116] ibid 27.
[117] Pension Schemes Act 2015, s 47.
[118] Institute and Faculty of Actuaries, *How Pensions Can Help Meet Consumer Needs* (n 34) 11.
[119] ibid.
[120] See: www.pensionwise.gov.uk (accessed 31 October 2019).
[121] Department of Health, 'Care and Support Statutory Guidance' (n 12) [8.66].
[122] Mayhew, Smith and Wright (n 108) 5.
[123] Institute and Faculty of Actuaries, *How Pensions Can Help Meet Consumer Needs* (n 34) 9–10.
[124] ibid.

property that would otherwise be the subject of a disregard, or to recover it from third parties.

For its part, the guidance states that

> [t]he government expects there to be a range of new products that people will use to manage and access money from their pensions as and when they need it, and where possible, these should be treated similarly to existing drawdown products for charging purposes.[125]

Moreover, '[w]here a person has chosen to withdraw funds from their pension pot and manage it directly, for example combining it with other assets rather than through a pensions product, this may be treated as capital' rather than income.[126] There are some other specific principles in the guidance, to the effect that 'if a person is only drawing a minimal income, or choosing not to draw income, then a local authority can apply notional income, [namely] the maximum income that could be drawn under an annuity product'.[127] Similar considerations apply 'where a person who has reached pension credit qualifying age and has a personal pension plan but has not purchased an annuity or arranged to draw down the equivalent maximum annuity income that would be available from the plan'.[128] Conversely, 'if a person is drawing down an income that is higher than the maximum available under an annuity product, the actual income that is being drawn down should be taken into account'.[129]

The fact that 'because of their small value a typical annuity will only make a modest contribution to care home fees'[130] complicates the matter under discussion. On the one hand, investment in a more valuable product could in some instances facilitate a care recipient's ability to secure a higher standard of care by paying top-up fees or self-funding. On the other, some such investments might simply increase a person's liability to fund her own care and correspondingly reduce the local authority's obligation to fund it, particularly since the *capital* value of the right to receive income under an annuity is the subject of a disregard. In particular, it is significant that whether the recipient receives no support, full support or something in between is significantly determined with reference to capital rather than the income associated with traditional annuities. The effect of this is similar to the 'reduced incentive to save specifically to meet eventual [long-term care] costs' that has been identified.[131]

Some examples of the implications of purchasing particular assets using pension freedoms may help to illustrate the concern of this chapter. A non-annuity investment product purchased by exercising pension freedoms,[132] and income derived from it,[133] could be treated as capital rather than income. If the would-be care recipient decides to buy a holiday home instead of buying an annuity with present enjoyment but also inheritance in mind, she will be assessed on the value of that asset rather than merely

[125] Department of Health, 'Care and Support Statutory Guidance' (n 12) [8.65].
[126] ibid [8.67].
[127] ibid Annex C [26].
[128] ibid Annex C [35].
[129] ibid Annex C [26].
[130] Mayhew, Smith and Wright (n 108) 5.
[131] Kenny et al (n 111) 29.
[132] Department of Health, 'Care and Support Statutory Guidance' (n 12) Annex B [6].
[133] ibid [57].

the income that would have been generated by the annuity. She will be liable to fund the full cost of her care unless and until her relevant capital assets are whittled down to £23,250, and will be expected to make a contribution via tariff income while they remain above £14,250,[134] and any rental income may also be taken into account.[135] Her converted pension entitlement would also be treated as capital if she moved the money to a savings account.[136] If she decides to give away the holiday home or savings during her lifetime, there are potentially significant consequences. The local authority has the ability to assess a care recipient as still possessing 'notional' property of which she has in fact deprived herself.[137] Under the Care Act 2014 and its Care and Support (Charging and Assessment of Resources) Regulations 2014, a person 'is to be'[138] assessed on the basis of her actual and notional capital, including 'capital of which the adult has deprived themselves for the purpose of decreasing the amount that they may be liable to pay towards the cost of meeting their needs for care and support'. The guidance states that if a person uses savings to buy a painting, which she then gives away with the intention of avoiding care fees, the value of the painting could be assessed as notional capital even though a painting previously owned and retained by the care recipient herself or given away would be a personal possession subject to a disregard.[139] Notional capital could also be invoked where the would-be care recipient sells the painting or the holiday home and uses the proceeds, or spends savings, on a period of 'substantial expenditure … incurred suddenly [that] is out of character with previous spending'[140] or simply 'living extravagantly'.[141]

The consequence of being assessed as having relevant notional property could be that (for example) a person has to use property that formally should be subject to a disregard to fund care in order to make up for the property that she is regarded as beneficially owning but in fact does not. Similarly, she may have to continue paying for care due to notional capital even if her actual capital alone places her below the lower capital limit, and she might be denied the 'personal expenses allowance'[142] or the 'minimum income guarantee'[143] to which she would otherwise be entitled. In principle, a person who deprives herself of property in order (and not necessarily *solely* in order) to avoid care fees but long before the care is actually required or provided is within the scope of the notional property rules.[144] It is particularly significant that, unlike a claim against a third party, a local authority's decision to include a particular

[134] ibid Annex B [6a)–b)].

[135] ibid Annex B [33i)–(vii)].

[136] ibid Annex B [5b)].

[137] Care and Support (Charging and Assessment of Resources) Regulations 2014, rr 22 and 17; Department of Health, 'Care and Support Statutory Guidance' (n 12) Annex E, paras [19]–[20]. For more detailed discussion, see Sloan, 'Trusts and Anti-Avoidance under the Care Act 2014' (n 71).

[138] Care and Support (Charging and Assessment of Resources) Regulations 2014, r 22(1).

[139] Department of Health, 'Care and Support Statutory Guidance' (n 12) Annex E [10].

[140] ibid Annex E [9b)].

[141] ibid Annex E [9f)].

[142] Care and Support (Charging and Assessment of Resources) Regulations 2014, r 6; Department of Health, *Response to the Consultation on Draft Regulations and Guidance for Implementation of Part 1 of the Care Act 2014* (Cm 895536, 2014) [8.35].

[143] Department of Health, Response to the Consultation on Draft Regulations (n 142) [8.42].

[144] See, eg, *Yule v South Lanarkshire Council (No 1)* 1998 SLT 490, 493 (Lord Philip), considering the similar pre-Care Act provisions.

piece of notional property would usually be scrutinised by a court only if proceedings are brought by the care recipient herself. It must be noted, however, that the guidance is generally quite nuanced, and emphasises the importance of whether the asset in question would have been included in a financial assessment in the first place.[145] Relevant considerations specified are: '[w]hether avoiding the care and support charge was a significant motivation'; '[t]he timing of the disposal of the asset'; and in particular whether 'the person ha[d] a reasonable expectation of needing to contribute to the cost of their eligible care needs'.[146] Many such needs may be optimistically unanticipated, although greater public awareness to ensure proper financial planning might be something of a double-edged sword for a particular individual in this respect. In any case, in the guidance, it is specifically reiterated to be

> unreasonable to decide that a person had disposed of an asset in order to reduce the level of charges for their care and support … if at the time … they were fit and healthy and could not have foreseen the need for care and support.[147]

There are therefore respects in which the guidance appears more sensitive to the difficulties faced by a care recipient than the primary and secondary legislation itself, and this is welcome. It is interesting that while the guidance (like the regulations) implies an obligation as to consideration of notional property in the context of asset deprivation,[148] the decision-making process outlined by the guidance might produce something of a discretionary approach. But it has been seen that local authorities are not absolutely obliged to follow the guidance, and I have elsewhere criticised its ambivalent approach.[149]

In addition to the ability to treat a care recipient as if she still had property of which she has deprived herself, a local authority can alternatively claim the value of the asset, such as the cash, the holiday home or the painting considered above, from a disponee. Under section 70 of the Care Act, certain below-market-value 'transfers' intended to avoid liability for social care charges can give rise to a debt between the third-party transferee and the relevant local authority, which can be recovered under section 69. Section 70 is expressed to apply where 'an adult's needs have been or are being met by a local authority under sections 18 to 20'.[150] In such circumstances, the local authority's recovery powers are exercisable where 'the adult has transferred an asset to another person' (the 'transferee');[151] 'the transfer was undertaken with the intention of avoiding charges for having the adult's needs met';[152] and either there was no consideration for the transfer or 'the consideration for the transfer was less than the value of the asset'.[153] An 'asset' is 'anything which may be taken into account for

[145] Department of Health, 'Care and Support Statutory Guidance' (n 12) [10]; Care and Support (Charging and Assessment of Resources) Regulations 2014, sch 2, para 13.
[146] Department of Health, 'Care and Support Statutory Guidance' (n 12) Annex E [11].
[147] ibid [12].
[148] ibid Annex E [8]; *cf* Department of Health, *Charging for Residential Accommodation Guidance* (2014) [6.062].
[149] Sloan, 'Trusts and Anti-Avoidance under the Care Act 2014' (n 71).
[150] Care Act 2014, s 70(1).
[151] ibid s 70(1)(a).
[152] ibid s 70(1)(b).
[153] ibid s 70(1)(c).

the purposes of a financial assessment',[154] and its 'value' (where it is not cash) is 'the amount which would have been realised if it had been sold on the open market by a willing seller at the time of the transfer',[155] with a deduction for any encumbrance on it[156] and 'a reasonable amount' to represent sale expenses.[157]

Where the above requirements are met, section 70(2) makes the transferee 'liable to pay to the local authority an amount equal to the difference' between what it would have charged the adult (had it not been for the transfer) and what it did charge the adult,[158] and the local authority can enforce the debt against the third party using its recovery powers.[159] The liability is expressed not to include 'an amount which exceeds the benefit accruing to the transferee from the transfer',[160] and is 'in proportion to the benefit accruing to [each] transferee' where there is more than one.[161] These powers are potentially very wide, particularly in light of doubts about whether the transfer is subject to any substantive time limit.[162]

The ability to bring litigation against a family member donee may come as a particular shock to a care recipient who exercised 'pension freedoms' *inter vivos* to 'advance' an inheritance. While such litigation may be rare, and the guidance makes clear that the use of the notional property provisions (instead) is a 'first step' and adopts a generally nuanced approach,[163] the use of powers against third parties may become more frequent as under-resourced local authorities struggle to cope with demand.

There may be all sorts of other reasons that such purchases and transactions consequent on pension freedoms as considered in this chapter would be ill-advised, but social care liability is an important consideration. Similar principles of deliberate deprivation apply in relation to means-tested benefits.[164] It is not necessarily unjustifiable that the system treats alternative transactions to annuity purchases in this way, but it is important that, so far as possible, a would-be social care recipient is aware of the risks, particularly since the protection within some pension products for benefits deliberately designed for survivors may be unavailable.

IV. CONCLUSION

Social care is far from the most important consideration for most individuals when they consider exercising 'pension freedoms'. Other matters, such as tax implications and fees, are likely to be what constrains a properly advised person from exercising

[154] ibid s 70(5).
[155] ibid s 70(6).
[156] ibid s 70(6)(a).
[157] ibid s 70(6)(b).
[158] ibid s 70(2).
[159] ibid s 69; see further Sloan, 'Trusts and Anti-Avoidance under the Care Act 2014' (n 71) 496–97.
[160] Care Act 2014, s 70(3).
[161] ibid s 70(4).
[162] Sloan, 'Trusts and Anti-Avoidance under the Care Act 2014' (n 71) 494–97.
[163] Department of Health, 'Care and Support Statutory Guidance' (n 12) Annex E [19].
[164] Kenny et al (n 111) 14.

pension freedoms to buy a particular sort of asset rather than a traditional annuity, whether with a desire for present enjoyment or with inheritance in mind. This chapter has nevertheless shown that pension freedoms in the context of social care have the potential to complicate funding assessments, prejudice inheritance and even generate litigation between local authorities and the family members of social care recipients. As is often the case with pension arrangements, proper advice is essential.

A broader question, of course, is whether it is reasonable to expect people to use their pension entitlements to fund social care costs. This goes to the heart of the appropriate balance of welfare spending between older and younger generations.[165] But since the 'user pays' principle is unlikely to disappear from the English social care system (in favour of a free at the point of delivery system funded by taxation) any time soon, it seems inevitable that pension entitlements will be a key part of local authority assessments, despite the claim that only around half of social care expenditure occurs in respect of those over 65.[166] The important point is that pension entitlements must be assessed in a fair, predictable and *predicted* manner.

[165] See, eg, Sloan, 'Solidarity Across Generations in England and Wales' (n 75).
[166] King's Fund (n 13) 4.

Index

www.ingramcontent.com/pod-product-compliance
Ingram Content Group UK Ltd.
Pitfield, Milton Keynes, MK11 3LW, UK
UKHW020230290926
15470UKWH00002B/461